FUNDAMENTALS OF MUSICAL ACOUSTICS

Second, Revised Edition

ARTHUR H. BENADE

DOVER PUBLICATIONS, INC.
New York

This Dover edition, first published in 1990, is an unabridged,
extensively corrected republication of the edition originally published by Oxford University Press in 1976. A Note to the Dover
Edition has been added.

Manufactured in the United States of America
Dover Publications, Inc., 31 East 2nd Street, Mineola, N.Y.
11501

Library of Congress Cataloging-in-Publication Data

Benade, Arthur H.
   Fundamentals of musical acoustics / Arthur H. Benade.
       p.   cm.
   Reprint. Originally published: New York : Oxford University
Press, 1976.
   Includes index.
   ISBN 0-486-26484-X
   1. Music—Acoustics and physics.   I. Title.
ML3805.B328 1990
781.2—dc20   90-40159
                                                          CIP
                                                          MN

Acknowledgments

I owe a heavy debt to a large number of scientists, craftsmen, and musicians, both students and professionals, who have provided me with information, peppered me with well-thought-out questions, lent or given instruments, aided in doing experiments, and helped me to recognize and correct errors or inconsistencies in what I have said or done in musical acoustics. There is space here to single out by name only those contributors to my understanding whose influence has been of long duration and of particular intensity.

My indebtedness to Walter Worman, Erik Jansson, James Gebler, and Michel Chotteau arises chiefly through my having enjoyed with each of them a period of close collaboration in the laboratory and in the theoretical analysis of musical air columns. I owe a different debt to Earle Kent, Bruce Schantz, George Jameson, John Stavash, George McCracken, Carleen Hutchins, Philip Bate, and Paul Hailperin, who have freely shared their expert knowledge of current practice (often including its scientific aspects) in the making and adjusting of musical instruments both ancient and modern. Performing musicians whose interest, aid, and deep knowledge have been of inestimable value are Jürg Schaeftlein, Frederic Cohen, William Waterhouse, Charles Schlueter, Alexander Murray, Gerald Corey, and Edward Tarr. I am also grateful for the opportunity to have had long (and sometimes heated) discussion of matters concerning our perception of musical sounds with Paul Boomsliter, Warren Creel, and Johan Sundberg. C. G. Conn Ltd., King Musical Instruments, G. Leblanc Corp., Fox Products Corporation, Gebr. Alexander, and H. & A. Selmer have been particularly generous with gifts of instruments or parts, occasional financial support, and frequent willingness to share some of their confidential information.

The wisdom, experience, and scientific insight of my colleague Robert Shankland and also (on too few occasions) of John Schelleng have been of immense value to me, even beyond the contributions of their considerable expertise in acoustics.

Beyond the debt I owe to people named here is the debt to my wife Virginia. Her interest, patience, musical knowledge, stylistic taste, and intellectual curiosity have always provided me with a stimulus and an opportunity to try out a half-born idea.

Her sensitive musical ear and familiarity with the structure and practice of both Western and Indian music have been particularly helpful in elucidating the relation between musical custom and the way musical sounds are produced and heard. Beyond this she has struggled along with me through several drafts of each chapter to make this book accurate and understandable for its intended readers.

Cleveland, Ohio A. H. B.
August 1975

Note to the Dover Edition

This book is a reprinting of a major monograph on musical acoustics by a distinguished scientist. In nearly three decades of research in musical acoustics, Arthur H. Benade (1925–1987) built a body of scientific work that remains as readily appreciated by the musician as by the physicist. This book provides the framework in which Benade's contributions to musical acoustics can be understood, and it is highly readable because the subject matter is addressed from the viewpoints of the scientist, musician, and instrument-maker. Significant emphasis is placed on the interaction of the physics of musical instruments and concert halls with the perceptual skills of listeners and the musical skills of performers. Perhaps the most welcome aspect of this new edition is that Benade's unique insights will continue to be available to students.

Subsequent to the book's original publication in 1976, Benade maintained a detailed set of corrections and minor revisions, which are reflected in this new Dover edition. Technical questions regarding these revisions were resolved by Carleen Hutchins, Ian Lindevald, Walter Worman, and me. All revisions were coordinated by Virginia Benade.

Douglas H. Keefe
University of Washington

Contents

Contents

x

Contents

xi

FUNDAMENTALS OF
MUSICAL ACOUSTICS

1
Preliminaries to a Study of Musical Acoustics

Starting an extensive book on a closely knit subject is akin to beginning a journey, since it carries a certain feeling of anticipation and perhaps trepidation as the author and the reader search for ways in which to work together. For the author the journey will be through territory he has visited before, most of which he has explored thoroughly. For some readers, almost everything will be new; a few may feel at times overwhelmed by the new things crowding about them that seem familiar and even trivial to those who have been there before. The author must hark back to his own first visits to the territory of his subject as he tries not to introduce too many new words and ideas all at once. His ultimate aim must be to give enough guidance on a limited number of carefully chosen subjects that the interested reader will eventually be able to explore new territory on his own. As you read on in this book, constant attention to two things can add much to the success of our travels together through the subject of musical acoustics: (1) your active participation is needed to make the joint exploration meaningful, and (2) retrospection will be encouraged as we return several times to things seen or heard earlier for closer examination from a more mature viewpoint.

1.1. Musical Acoustics: *The Meeting Place of Music, Vibration Physics, Auditory Science, and Craftsmanship*

This book is addressed most directly (though not exclusively) to people having a reasonable playing knowledge of music who would like to learn something of the ways in which music as an art form intertwines itself with our understanding of vibrating objects, with the study of auditory perception, and with the craft of the instrument maker. The focus of the book is on the vibrations of objects and of the air which surrounds them, but the particular manifestations of vibration physics that are chosen for discussion are those which play a significant role in actual music-making. Because music is intended to be heard, we must give considerable attention to the way in which our auditory nervous system functions as it picks out musical patterns from the complex acoustical signals that reach our ears. In the parts of this book dealing with vibration physics and practical music, I shall be quite explicit in telling how and why various phenomena take place. The perception aspects of our subject will be dealt with somewhat differently. I will tell *what* it is we hear when various kinds of sound are presented to our ears, but will not describe *how* the vibrations of an eardrum are led through the middle and inner ear to produce a myriad of nerve impulses that travel by many pathways to the central nervous system. Nor will I detail how these impulses come to act upon one another in several ways simultaneously, in a continuous process that can span a number of successive sounds to provide us with recognizable patterns of sensation. In other words, in this part of the subject we will confine ourselves to a description of phenomena, without much concern for the ways in which they come about.

The manner in which each topic is introduced, the order of presentation, and the choice of the topics themselves have all been predominantly influenced by my experience with musicians and instrument makers as we have worked together over the past two decades. Much of the material in this book is of recent origin, a considerable fraction of it being the result of my own observations and calculations, or of my analysis of the recent work of others. While I have tried everywhere to make clear the reasoning behind each assertion and to present examples of the data which support it, it must be understood that the reasons and examples shown here are merely illustrative and constitute only a small part of the basis for my conclusions. Almost everything in this book has had the benefit of extensive rehearsal in both spoken and written form. Over the years I have been blessed with a number of extremely capable students and laboratory guests. The opportunity to sharpen up the various ideas by talking with these people and with interested colleagues in physics and engineering has been immensely valuable. More recently I have had to deal with the ex-

pository problems connected with teaching various methods of adjustment to craftsmen or explaining the reasoning behind my activities as I trimmed up someone's trumpet, flute, clarinet, oboe, or bassoon. These experiences have added a certain intensity to the more relaxed classroom atmosphere of the courses and lecture series in musical acoustics I have given.

One question that immediately arises in the mind of a prospective reader of a book on acoustics written by a physicist concerns the amount of mathematical knowledge that will be required of him. If you will leaf quickly through the book you will notice that I have rigorously confined myself in the text to the simplest of arithmetic—addition, subtraction, multiplication, and division; a number may occasionally be squared or carry a square root sign. Numerical illustrations of the various calculations are supplied in almost every case, partly as a way to show what is going on and partly as a convenient way to supply ourselves with numbers for later use.

While the level of overt mathematics has been kept to the lowest possible, I do not at all wish to leave the impression that the book makes similarly low demands on your ability to follow a line of reasoning or on your ability to do a little courageous speculating. It will perhaps reassure many of you to learn that reasonably diligent efforts on the part of musician-students in my musical acoustics course have always rewarded them with a good understanding of the subject. Their greater familiarity with musical instruments seems to offset certain slight advantages possessed by their scientifically trained classmates who (except for those who are in the life sciences) are likely to be a little ill at ease with logical reasoning carried on without the help of mathematics.

Those of you who come to this book already supplied with a good knowledge of engineering acoustics or of physics and mathematics will sometimes find my presentation a little strange or at least unfamiliar. At times the strangeness comes from the fact that musical vibrations can have somewhat different properties from the vibrations with which you are familiar, or that different aspects of these vibrations come to the fore as dominant. Sometimes the feeling of unfamiliarity may come from my going quickly over something that you considered difficult because you learned it late in graduate school, and other times I will labor mightily over points that you found obvious in high school. Remember that all of this is new to my major audience, and enjoy with me the fact that what an intelligent musician finds straightforward in vibration physics is conditioned greatly by his intensive experience with things that oscillate. Remember also with me that perhaps one of the reasons he chose music as a profession is that his high-school mathematics was taught in such a way as to frighten him, whereas yours attracted you! Another reason for the unfamiliarity you may feel in this book comes from the fact that you may not be used to taking as careful account of the properties of ears as we are forced to do in a musical context.

There is one other group of prospective readers to whom I should address a note of comment and explanation—those of you who have some knowledge of modern psychoacoustics. Perhaps the main thing that will attract your attention (and maybe your concern) is the fact that I

seem to attribute to the ears of musicians and musical listeners a far greater ability and achievement than might seem justified by the careful laboratory experiments in hearing that have been carried on during the past forty-five years. There are a number of reasons for this apparent discrepancy, reasons which are themselves of considerable importance to all of us as we begin our exploration of musical acoustics. In the first place, skilled experimenters measuring the properties of ears have almost always taken great pains to supply their auditory signals to their subjects' ears in the most sanitary fashion possible. This calls for the use of carefully calibrated earphones constructed in such a way as to exclude all outside sounds. This exclusion not only of noise but also of the distracting and hard-to-control reverberations of sound in the room is necessary in certain circumstances. In musical surroundings the human auditory apparatus exploits the possibility of hearing and re-hearing the echoing sounds of the instrument. Musical sounds are by their very nature highly organized collections of acoustical components which are grouped into patterns by the composer and the player. The emission of sound by musical instruments is of such a nature (especially in a room) that a few missing or out-of-place pieces of sensory input have little effect on our ability to detect or recognize their relationships. A further difference between the capabilities shown by subjects of a psychoacoustical laboratory experiment and by musicians practicing their profession arises from the fact that we are comparing the performance of a heterogeneous group in unfamiliar surroundings with the accomplishments of a group of people who by talent, training, and experience have become quite expert at what they are doing. However, this is an expertise which we should not expect them to bring into the laboratory unless great care is taken to test them in musically relevant ways. Perhaps you will be stimulated to extend and clarify the nature of some of the musical-perception phenomena I describe and thus join the growing number of people who see this as an area of enquiry that promises many rewards to our understanding.

1.2. The Organization of This Book

Now that I have completed a fairly extended discussion of how various groups of my readers may find themselves reacting to this book, it is time for me to outline its general structure. It will then be possible for me to suggest some ways in which you can use the book to extract the fullest measure of understanding from it.

The general principles that governed the writing of this book may be summarized compactly in a set of numbered statements of a sort which will be used for similar purposes throughout this work.

1. Use is made of a carefully chosen minimum of technical terms beyond those commonly used in music. Most technical terms are italicized on their first appearance and defined there either in a formal way or by means of an illustrative example of their usage.

2. This technical terminology is normally identical with that used in other branches of physics or engineering. Occasionally there will be small differences, these being identified and the reasons for them explained. It has been necessary to define a very limited number of terms that are not used elsewhere; special attention is called to these and an explanation is given of why they are needed.

3. Fundamental ideas are introduced whenever possible in the setting of everyday experience (at least that of musicians), or else new concepts are developed by making use of ideas that have already been dealt with thoroughly in earlier parts of the book. Many of the fundamental ideas are initially presented in simplified form, their fuller development taking place as we go on through the book. I have tried to prevent the initial simplification from having possible misinterpretations.

4. Great care has been taken to keep a clearly marked distinction between mechanical phenomena in an instrument or in the room (which are the special province of a physicist or engineer) and the human auditory response to these phenomena (which is the primary concern of a perception psychologist). For example, the word *loud* is never used to denote a vigorous oscillation; the word is reserved as a description of the perceived nature of this oscillation. In similar fashion care has been taken to keep specifically musical terminology from confusing itself with terminology used for other purposes.

Let us now turn our attention to a description of the various chapters and of their relationships. While musical instruments and musical sounds are dealt with constantly in chapters 2 through 6, the main effort here is to give the reader an introduction to the way one goes about studying things acoustical and an understanding of some of the basic ideas of vibration physics and their perceptual correlates.

Chapters 7, 8, and 9 are concerned with the behavior of some explicitly musical objects (e.g., plucked and struck strings, kettledrum heads, and glockenspiels). Here we are getting ready to think about guitars, pianos, etc., by providing ourselves with some of the applications of ideas developed earlier. In chapters 2 through 9 we confine our attention to vibrations that are set in motion by impulsive excitations such as striking or plucking.

In chapters 10, 11, and 12 we begin the study of the behavior of systems that are set into motion by repetitive forces, such as when one pushes a child on a swing. This part of the book widens its concerns to include the acoustical phenomena that manifest themselves as sound in a room. These chapters deal in part with the production of sound in a room, its spread, and its detection from the point of view of physics. They also provide us with a solid foundation of knowledge about what our hearing mechanism can do as it copes with such sounds. As in earlier chapters, most of the illustrations of the various ideas are chosen from musical practice, along with a certain amount borrowed from the audio industry, with its concern with microphones and loudspeakers.

Chapters 13, 14, and 15 are devoted primarily to a description of the manner in which our ears "put together" various sounds in the comparison of pitch and of loudness. Also discussed are the ways in which the properties of certain classes of sounds allow the ear to combine them into relationships that are recognized in music. We will find that a great deal of what shapes formal music (e.g., harmonic and scale relations) is strongly influenced by the fact that we commonly listen to music in a room rather than outdoors, where as a matter of fact a musician may feel quite uncomfortable and insecure.

The rest of the book applies the principles developed earlier to an explanation of the nature and behavior of the major types of musical instruments. Chapters 16, 17, and 18 take up the keyboard instruments, which are constrained to produce tones having rigidly fixed pitch. The pipe organ is touched upon only as the simplest example of such instruments and as a means for showing the existence of certain tuning problems and how they may be dealt with. Pianos, harpsichords, and clavichords, on the other hand, are discussed in more detail; the impulsively excited vibration of their strings is described and account is taken of the way the string reacts back on the exciting hammer or plectrum, as well as of the way in which the strings "talk" with the soundboard and so also with the room. The practices of instrument makers in proportioning strings, hammers or plectra, and soundboards to one another are described and explained, with examples ranging from the latest in pianos back to harpsichords of the seventeenth century. Notice that the choice of keyboard stringed instruments as our starting point for the systematic study of instruments is a repetition of our earlier choice of impulsively excited systems as the first type to be dealt with on an introductory level.

Chapter 19, on the human voice as a musical instrument, introduces us to the family of sustained-tone instruments having adjustable pitch. The voice makes a good introduction because it has a virtually autonomous sound source (the larynx) whose output is shaped by the vocal passages to produce the various vowel sounds, etc., before being transmitted into the room. Studying the larynx by itself enables us to learn the general principles governing the maintenance of self-sustained oscillations, undistracted by the subsequent modification of the resulting sound by the vocal tract, whose operations are also susceptible to study in isolation. Once these physical systems are adequately described it becomes possible to consider how their properties can be exploited for musical purposes, an exploitation which is of course strongly influenced by the way we perceive sounds in various contexts.

The brass and woodwind families of instruments are taken up next, in chapters 20, 21, and 22. The nature of these chapters is quite similar to that of the previous ones dealing with musical instruments. The sound source is examined, this time along with the air column by which it is controlled, if not enslaved. The nature of the internally generated sound at various dynamic levels of playing is discussed, along with modifications to this sound that occur as it leaves the instrument for the listening room. Once again we find that the interplay of source, room, and ear has a great deal to do with the way in which an instrument is used for music. One additional subject is touched on in these three chapters: the scientifically guided means that have been developed for the diagnosis and correction of discrepancies in the construction of the wind instruments. Some of these techniques are available to the player himself, while some of them stay within the province of the instrument maker or repairman. These adjustment techniques are interesting not only because of their direct usefulness to the musician, but because they provide us with examples of the way in which one can learn to exploit his musical, auditory, scientific, and tool-using skills to unravel and apply information about the acoustical events that take place within an instrument.

Chapters 23 and 24 are devoted to an analogous description of the structure and behavior of the violin and of its immediate relatives.

The final chapter serves almost as a coda in which we examine some musically peculiar sounds such as the "multiphonics" which have excited the recent interest of composers and woodwind players, the wolf tones that sometimes bother string players, and certain sounds produced by the brasses. In all of these examples the sound production processes are very similar to one another, being an elaboration and offshoot of the processes that generate the more ordinary sounds of these instruments. In a similar vein, the perception processes that take place when we listen to these sounds turn out to be an elaboration of those we have studied throughout the rest of the book.

1. 3. A Brief Operating Manual

This book is written in a very close-knit fashion, with each part depending very much on what comes before and also preparing the way for what is to follow. The efficacy of your reading will, as a result, be considerably enhanced if you try to keep some awareness of what you have already covered and what is coming.

At many places in this book references are made back to earlier sections or to earlier diagrams. Your choice of whether or not to interrupt your reading to go back will obviously be governed by several things. If you have no idea of what the reference is about, you may be missing an important piece to the puzzle. You should also be aware that a great deal more is hiding in the earlier material than was apparent on your first reading. You will come to understand why things were said in a certain way, and why certain things were *not* said. As to references forward, it would be a source of unending frustration if at every turn I were to include a description of every future use of an idea or fact under discussion. For this reason you will find almost no allusion to later parts of the book, even where a set of summarizing statements is manifestly incomplete.

At the end of every chapter you will find a section labeled "Examples, Experiments, and Questions." This section is a little free-wheeling and allows you to exercise your ingenuity and imagination upon the ideas which have been presented in the chapter. Some of the suggested experiments are extremely easy to do, some quite difficult. There are puzzles and problems of all degrees of challenge, and there are also simple descriptions of various phenomena that serve to cast light on the text material, but which would fit nowhere else in the formal structure of the chapter. Even if you do not wish to try to do the experiments or to solve the problems, you should read them and the examples, considering them to be an integral part of the text. Go after this book in somewhat the way you should treat everything else to be learned in the world—grab hold anywhere, strive for understanding by any means at your disposal, look for successive unfoldings of the truth, and constantly test your understanding by trying to go back and forth between application and implication.

The problem of providing up-to-date, accurate, and intelligible reference material suitable for readers of a book of this sort proves to be severe, though the situation gives promise of improving in the near future. The problem is particularly acute when one is trying to meet the needs of nontechnical readers who have studied only the first few chapters; this is one of the reasons why the number of notes grows rapidly as we approach the end of the book. You will find the references collected in a group at the end of each chapter. Notes referring to books and journal articles usually include a few words of explanation and comment, which serve to tie the references to the text and to each other. The articles and books are generally chosen not only for their direct contribution to something in the text, but also as an entryway (via their own sets of references) to the current literature on the subject and to the names of its leading contributors. For this reason, no separate bibliography is provided.

2

Impulsive Sounds, Alone and in Sequence

If one strikes the top of a table with his fist, knocks on a door with his knuckles, or taps on a cup with a teaspoon, easily recognized sounds are produced. Our everyday language is full of nouns referring to what we will term *impulsive sounds*. Let us list a few such words before we begin to think about them acoustically: snap, crack, tap, rap, knock, bump, and thump. Perhaps you have noticed that this list forms a sequence; noises whose names appear early in the sequence sound more abrupt and are generated by harder objects striking one another than are the sounds named later in the list. Our language also has a vast number of adjectives that describe such sounds. Interestingly enough, many of these come from the names of particular sound sources, sources that typically produce sounds with these special characteristics. Thus mankind has noticed that there is a strong common element in the sounds made by hitting metallic objects, or by striking a block of wood, whence such adjectives as "tinny" and "woody." Vivid aural sense impressions are suggested by words like "glassy," "tinkling," "hollow," and even "soggy."

The correlation between impulsive sounds and their sources is quite durable in the sense that additional, distracting noises do not spoil the sense impression; their recognizability survives transmission over the crudest telephone connections and most ill-favored of loudspeakers, nor does it change when one experiments in rooms of different size and shape. It is this dependability and undistractability of human response to impulsive sounds that brings us to the fundamental questions of chief concern to us in this book. What is the physical nature of any given recognizable sound as it comes through the air to our ears? How does the mechanical motion of its source give rise to the sound in the air? In what way was the source set in motion? What is the nature of perception, or, to say it another way, how do our ears and our nervous system process the sounds that come to them? In what way does the human mind produce a distillation and synthesis of those properties of the sound that are in some way interesting or important to it?

We could begin our exploration of musical acoustics in many ways, each of which suggests some interesting facet of the subject. We could, for example, seek the common elements (physical and perceptual) that are found in sources having the same verbal description. We could on the other hand make changes in the production, transmission, or perception of some particular sound, to see what effect these have. Another approach would be to alter the context in which a given sound is produced or detected. These alterations might be either musical or mechanical. For example, a sound that is heard as a pitchless buzz when listened to as part of a laboratory experiment may be perceived as an integral part of a chord when it is sounded as one voice in a musical performance. A physicist's example of the effect of a change in mechanical context is found in experiments dealing with the set of three strings that belong to a given note on the piano. Each of these strings vibrates differently when all three of them are struck together from how it behaves when the other two strings of the set are removed or blocked.

There are also many possible tools that we can use in our investigations. In addition to the full panoply of laboratory equipment used to measure various physical quantities, we have also the powerful help of computers which can be used to aid both the synthesis and the analysis of sounds. Whatever tools we employ, however, the human ear must remain our constant guide and most reliable witness. On the one hand, it is as sensitive as any laboratory mechanism; on the other, it is attached to the best of devices for the sorting and correlating of information— the nervous system and the mind. For musical acoustics, the ear is the final arbiter for yet another reason: music is meant to be heard, and so our researches must be built around sounds as we hear them.

At the beginning of our study of acoustics we will depend heavily on our knowledge of familiar sounds as an introduction to new concepts. Later on we will find that a cultivated pair of ears can be often used in conjunction with our technical knowledge of music and of acoustics to provide us with precise numerical information about the physical properties of musical instruments. There are many occasions when the skilled researcher is able to obtain otherwise unavailable numerical information by listening to the changes produced in an instrument's sound when small changes are made in the manner of playing it. Similarly instructive are experiments in which small changes are made in the instrument itself, as by the use of lumps of wax or pieces of masking tape attached to it at some critical point. The researcher often finds out a great deal by noticing also how such changes affect the feel of the instrument in relation to the player—e.g., warm, edgy, muffled, bright, friendly, harsh, etc. In many cases these observations are made with the help of a musician who is playing the instrument under investigation. This points up the necessity for people doing research in musical acoustics to cultivate good communication with members of the musical profession; practicing musicians offer a prime source of information about where the questions lie and where the answers may be sought. Ideally, a researcher should be able to play any instrument he is investigating. The more actual playing experience he has, the more efficient and accurate he is likely to be in tracking down his instrument's nature and habits.

A musical acoustician must of course have a fairly good understanding of the neurophysiological processes that take place when he uses his hearing. This understanding is necessary if he is to make proper use of his sensory information. In exactly similar fashion, he must understand his electronic and mechanical research apparatus. The student of musical acoustics needs at least a smattering of the same understanding. It helps all of us to have some idea of both the usefulness and the limitations of our equipment, natural and man-made. Our ears and our machines are not waiting for a chance to lie to us, but they are perfectly capable in their own blind fashion of misleading their naïve users.

One cannot expect to acquire a thorough understanding of musical acoustics (or of anything else) by a single-minded attempt to learn all by a single route. Success cannot be achieved through the use of only a single type of equipment, or of only one kind of experiment, or through the exclusive pursuit of sounds in the concert hall or in the laboratory. The skillful and productive researcher (or student, if there is really a difference) is one who knows when to stick to a given approach and when to change it. He also knows how to put together ideas coming to him at many levels of abstraction. He learns to enjoy the contradictions that such synthesis exposes, as well as the agreements. In one case he has been handed the challenge of a new question to resolve, in the other he is told of his success in answering the most recent one.

2.1. Sequences of Impulsive Sounds

Suppose one takes a stick and taps slowly and regularly on a table top. Each tap has its own characteristic sound in the sense of being an impulsive sound having fairly short duration. Let us now focus our attention on the new things that take place when such taps become members of a reg-ular sequence. First we need to know how to describe such a sequence in terms of how fast the tapping is repeated. If the time interval between successive taps is 1/5 of a second, in the time of one second we would have 5 sets of tap-plus-time-interval. In this case, then, what we will call the *tapping rate,* or *repetition rate,* or *tapping frequency* of the sounds is found to be 5 per second. Similarly, if the inter-tap time is 1/3 of a second, simple arithmetic shows that the repetition rate is 3 per second. In every case the number that gives the tapping rate is the reciprocal of the inter-tap time interval. We can of course go the reverse direction in our calculations; for example, given that a certain sequence of taps occurs at the rate of 23 per second, we deduce that the inter-tap time interval is $1/23 = 0.0435$ seconds.

Digression on Terminology: Rate.
We have arrived at our first piece of technical terminology: rate. The word "rate" in physics almost always answers questions such as, "How many items are there per unit time?" Suppose for example that we count 45 taps in a period of 15 seconds. The number of taps taking place in 1 second is then found as follows:

$$\frac{45 \text{ taps}}{15 \text{ seconds}} = \frac{3 \text{ taps}}{1 \text{ second}} = 3 \text{ taps/second}$$

In similar fashion one chooses a water pump for a summer cottage on the basis of the rate at which it can raise water from the well; a common size for a small cottage is 10 gallons/minute. We might imagine a nineteenth-century Englishman who finds it convenient to describe the progress of turtles in their cross-country migration by saying that they travel at the rate of so many furlongs/fortnight. The metronome markings familiar to most musicians are also rate indications. The metronome number tells the number of ticks per minute.

If we have a set of evenly spaced noises, what happens if we vary the time interval between successive sounds, so that they repeat many times a second or only occasionally? A simple experiment which anyone can do will give us an easily variable set of impulsive sounds to help us answer this question. Take the corner of a small plastic card (or use your thumbnail) and pull it along the teeth of a comb where they emerge from the solid part of the comb. If desired, the corner can be made to jump slowly from tooth to tooth so that the individual ticks can be heard one by one. If one traverses the length of the comb somewhat more quickly with the point, the separate ticks can still be heard, but the listener is increasingly likely to describe the sound as a buzz. In other words, we tend to perceive a moderately rapid sequence of ticks as being a new sound in its own right to which we give a new name—buzz. When the point is pulled along the comb still faster, we notice that the buzz becomes a slightly harsh tone with definite musical pitch. We also notice that as we draw the point along the comb's teeth faster and faster, the pitch of the resulting noise becomes higher and higher.

A physicist speaking within the narrowest and most naïve confines of his subject would say that we have provided ourselves with a means for generating a sequence of identical ticks having an adjustable repetition rate. He might want to suggest various elaborations on the experiments. Some years ago he might have suggested using a toothed wheel instead of the comb, the wheel being turned by a crank or by a motor of adjustable speed. Today he might propose the use of an electronic pulse generator having adjustable repetition rate, attached to the input

of a hi-fi amplifier and its loudspeaker (sec. 2.4 of this chapter deals briefly with electronically controlled repetition rates). The experimenter's teenage son might point out that a piece of insulated wire draped over the center wire of an automobile engine distributor and led into the neighborhood of the car radio antenna or a pocket transistor radio will cause the radio to emit a sequence of pops whose repetition rate depends on engine speed. All of these more sophisticated mechanisms generate a variable sequence of impulsive sounds, but for our purposes the device of comb plus edge of card or fingernail is every bit as useful, and it has the advantage of simplicity and availability.

If we experiment with some sort of generator that produces ticks at an adjustable rate, we will find that as human beings we perceive the sequence of ticks in different ways, *depending on the repetition rate,* as summarized in table 2.1. A warning is in order here concerning tables such as this and, in general, the relation between descriptions drawn from different disciplines. While many physicists' descriptions have their counterparts in the realm of perception, we must not demand or even expect any sort of simple parallelism between such descriptions. The parallelism between the physicist's words when he says, "I am increasing the repetition rate," and the musician's when he says, "I hear a tone of increasingly high pitch," should be taken as an interesting observation rather than as an obvious consequence of common logic. Similarly, the change when one's perception of the separate ticks at low repetition rates becomes an entirely different kind of perception when the ticks combine into a buzz, and again when the buzz smoothes out into a

Table 2.1

| Relation between Repetition Rate and Perceived Sound | |
Impulse Repetition Rate	Perceived Sound
Less than about 20/sec	Separate impulses having slow to fast *tempo*
Roughly 20/sec to 150/sec	*Buzz* (this shades into the other two categories
Above about 100/sec	Tone of progressively higher *pitch*

tone, should be taken as an observation of fact and as a stimulus to deeper investigation.

Digression on Terminology: Pitch.

I have used the word pitch *several times in the preceding paragraphs without really telling what its precise meaning is. As a matter of fact, it is an exceedingly difficult word to define properly, although we can settle upon an unambiguous way of using it for present purposes. If we experiment with sequences of continuously repeating impulsive sounds, we find that the pitch we assign to a sufficiently rapid succession of impulses depends almost completely on the repetition rate and hardly at all on the nature of the special sound belonging to each individual impulse that makes up a given repetition series. Let me put this another way. If we conduct an experiment in which the ear is presented first with a tone from one source of repeated impulses and then with a tone from another source, we find that the source having the faster repetition rate of the two will be perceived as having the higher pitch. Furthermore, we normally hear the two pitches as being very nearly equal when the repetition rates are equal.*

2.2. A Scale of Reference Pitches

Everywhere in the course of our further work in this book we will need to be able to specify the pitch of the sounds that concern us. We find that perceived sounds need a pitch specification in addition to the repetition rate specification for two reasons. One reason is that equal alterations of pitch are not directly associated with equal alterations in the repetition rate. The second reason is that some sounds have definite pitch even though they may lack a repetition rate at all, or they might possess several interlaced repetition rates.

We are in no position at this early stage in our investigations to weigh various alternative ways in which pitch can be specified. We can, however, provide ourselves with a set of reference sounds having definite repetition frequencies, with the idea of using the set as a system of pitch standards in very much the way we use a tape measure with carefully spaced marks along it as a scale for the measurement of lengths.

The world of music provides us with the particular sequence of repetition rates that we will use for reference purposes (at this point in the book we do not necessarily know the reason for this particular choice of rates). Let us make a preliminary set of definitions in the following way. The various tones of what is called the equally tempered chromatic musical scale have definite pitches. These tones also have definite names. One system for naming these tones is based on the tone whose pitch nominally matches the low-

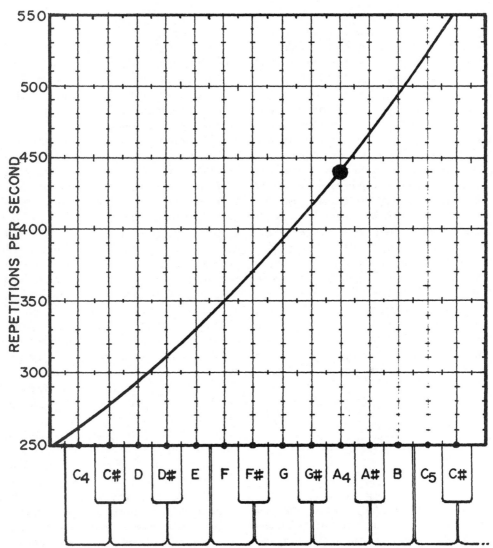

Fig. 2.1. A Reference Scale Relating Pitch, Repetition Rate, and Musical Note Name

est C of the piano. This C is named C_1 and the sequence runs up the scale thus: C_1, $C_1\#$, D_1, $D_1\#$, . . . , B_1. The tones of the next higher octave are labeled with the subscript 2; that is, C_2, $C_2\#$, etc. The tones of the next octave higher yet will have the subscript 3, and so forth.

We can use the note names from our reference scale to label the matching pitches produced by our sequences of impulsive sounds. Figure 2.1 shows in diagrammatic form the repetition rates (frequencies) that give rise to the pitches associated with the musical notes extending from C_4 to C_5 in the middle of the piano scale. This figure will continue to be useful to us throughout this book since it can serve as a ready reference from which the frequencies associated with all the notes of the scale may be obtained.

It is necessary to give the numbers only for a single òctave of our reference scale, because it turns out (for reasons we will eventually discover) that the frequency associated with any given named note may be found with the help of the diagram by use of the following prescription: *for every octave one goes up the scale, the frequency doubles, and for every octave one goes down, the frequency becomes half of its former value.* Since the frequency associated with A_4 in the middle of our diagram is 440 repetitions/second, the next A up the scale, A_5, has a frequency of 880 repetitions/second, and A_6 is found to be associated with an impulse rate of 1760/second. Going down an octave from A-440, a pulse train whose pitch matches A_3 repeats at 220/second.

2.3. Repetition Rates of Rhythmic Patterns

So far we have been dealing with sequences of uniformly spaced identical impulses. In our quest of further understanding let us now add some complexity. Suppose that we give a percussionist a tin can to strike with his left drumstick, and a block of wood as the target of his right-hand stick. If we ask that both hands strike in synchronism at the rate of 3 taps/second (metronome marking 180), our ears are supplied with a new, composite, impulsive sound. Perhaps one could make up a name for this sound, but more likely the remarkable abilities of the human nervous system would permit the listener to "analyze" the sound into its components: a tap on a block of wood and a simultaneous one on a tin can. Aside from the new sound of each impulse, nothing is changed. Slow tapping rates are perceived in terms of individual impulses; more rapid tappings advertize the fact that the individual sounds are part of a sequence which would convert to a buzz and then to a tone of some characteristic color and pitch if the rate could be increased sufficiently.

If our drummer is instructed to strike at the same tempo, but to have his left hand anticipate the right by a tiny interval, we would have what he calls a close flam, which he would write in the manner shown in figure 2.2. A physicist or engineer might consider writing out the same pattern diagrammatically along a time axis in some way such as the one shown in figure 2.3. Here the o's stand for impulses of the left-hand sort and the x's represent impulses generated by the right hand. The musician, the physicist, and the casual listener will have no trouble agreeing that the repetition rate is exactly the same now as it was when the two kinds of impulse were precisely superimposed. Furthermore, the repetition

Fig. 2.2.

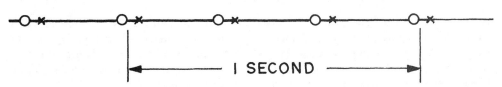

Fig. 2.3.

rate for both these cases is exactly what would be deduced if the drummer simply stopped using his left hand at all! In other words, we all agree that the word "repetition" is to be taken literally. When the player uses both hands he must go through his *entire* ritual (left and then right) if we are to count his activity as a repetition. Notice that it would really have made no difference to this result if we had asked our drummer to reverse his usual habits, and to play his flam "right before left." The resulting sense impressions would be recognizably different, of course, but we would still consider the repetition rate to be unchanged.

We are now in a position to think about a somewhat more subtle version of the same situation. Suppose our percussionist is told once more to keep the same 180 metronome tempo, but we ask that his right hand strike slightly earlier than midway between the left-hand strokes, as

indicated in the upper part of figure 2.4, or slightly later than the midpoint, as shown in the lower part. This makes little significant change. The repetition rate is still the same and our ears are still able to associate the left- and right-hand impulses into pairs, either left-before-right or right-before-left.

If now the right-hand taps are moved so that they fall exactly midway between the left-hand taps, we *still* consider the repetition rate to be unchanged whether we approach the question as musicians, listeners, or practitioners of some kind of physico-mathematical logic. This is because the two kinds of taps have different sounds. We are still able to tell them apart, and to recognize the sound pattern in the way the taps are arranged, even though the symmetry in time of the pattern has caused us partially to lose the ability to associate a given right-hand tap with its immediate left-hand predecessor

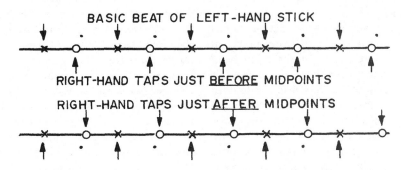

Fig. 2.4.

or with its successor. As before, the repetition rate is found from the number of times per second the complete pattern is repeated, not from the total number of separate taps taking place in each second.

Our experiment has one more variation that must be investigated before we go on to other things. This time we will provide our percussionist with two identical targets for his drumsticks, so that the left-hand and right-hand taps have exactly the same sound. We will also assume that both hands are equally strong so that the taps are of the same loudness. Under these conditions, a repetition of all our earlier experiments gives us results that are exactly the same as before, except for one special case. As long as the right-hand taps come somewhat before or somewhat after the midpoints in time between the left-hand taps, the repetition rate is clearly perceived as being 3/second. However, if the right-hand taps fall *exactly* halfway between the left-hand ones, we suddenly perceive the repetition as taking place at the rate of 6/second! Ordinary logic also requires this, since we count the rate of repetition of a given pattern. When two identical sequences of taps are perfectly interlaced, we have a pattern in which everything repeats at twice the rate at which each sequence separately generates sounds.

With normal ears in normal surroundings there will be a narrow range of "almost-centeredness" (of the right-hand taps relative to the left-hand ones) for which the doubled repetition rate will still be heard, especially if the two sequences have slight random irregularities in their timing. When the two sequences are slightly farther off from being perfectly interleaved, our perceptions are ambiguous: we seem to have the choice of hearing the sound as being associated with paired taps at the old repetition rate or as being due to a uniform series of equally spaced taps at double the original rate.

2.4. Electronically Controlled Repetition Rates

If one has a pair of electrical pulse generators at one's disposal, it is possible to repeat all of the drummer's experiments we have investigated in the previous section. Whether the rates are set at a few per second, or at several tens of pulses per second (in the "buzz" range of frequencies), or at higher frequencies yet where we hear tones of definite pitch, the phenomena persist in the forms that we have already discussed. However, in the high-frequency experiments, a musician will find himself describing his perception of evenly interlaced pairs of identical impulses in a way different from his reaction to the drummer's experiments.

In the previous section, the repetition rates beaten out by the drummer were heard in terms of tempo. When the pulse generator is set to give us sufficiently high repetition rates, we may expect similar phenomena to be expressed in terms of pitch. At the point where the impulses from one generator are interleaved so that they fall exactly halfway between the impulses from the other generator, we perceive the pitch of the sound to be unchanged as long as the two generators produce distinctly different-sounding impulses. If on the other hand we arrange the two generators so that they produce *identical* pulses and again have the impulses from one generator fall exactly halfway between the impulses from the other generator, a musician will find himself describing his perception of the interlaced pairs as an upward pitch jump of an octave, and this signals the doubled repetition rate belonging to this special case.

Let us now run through the entire set of experiments that were done by the drummer, this time using an electronic source as the basis for our thinking. We will examine the phenomena from a slightly different point of view, partly to clarify certain of the fundamental ideas and partly as a first introduction to the use of what are known as block diagrams.

In a block diagram of the sort we are going to use, one draws a labeled box to represent each of the various functions, and then draws lines to show how signals, after being processed in accordance with the label of the box, are passed on to the next part of the system. Figure 2.5 shows the block diagram for the problem at hand. To begin with, at the left of the diagram there is a box representing the electronic pulse generator that puts out the impulses which ultimately determine what we might call a tempo for our experiment. This pulse generator can be set to provide any desired repetition rate. It makes short, sharp, electrical impulses which are then sent to two impulse shapers, one of whose output signals

eventually produce the sounds corresponding to the beats of the drummer's left hand. The other shaper gives rise to impulses which are converted by a loudspeaker to give sounds corresponding to those made by the drummer's right hand. The right-hand, or number 2, shaper is not, however, supplied with pulses directly from the repetition rate generator. On the contrary, the signal to it comes from the repetition rate generator via an adjustable delay circuit which can be set to produce any desired amount of lag between the output of shaper number 2 and that of shaper number 1. The signals from these two shapers are then combined in the summing circuit and fed through an audio amplifier to a loudspeaker.

In figure 2.6 we have a set of horizontal parallel lines, each of which stands for the passage of time. The top line has a series of equally spaced points marked on it which stand for the times of occurrence of the individual pulses from the repetition rate generator. The inter-pulse time T shown on the diagram can be used to calculate the repetition rate.

The second line shows the timing of the impulses coming out of shaper 1. As one can see from this diagram, the timing of the impulses from shaper 1 coincides exactly with that of the initiating pulses. In other words, whenever there is a pulse

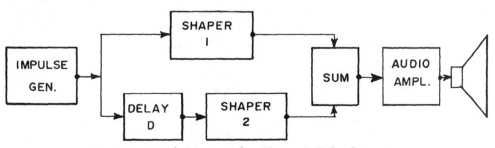

Fig. 2.5.   Block Diagram of an Electronic Pulse Generator

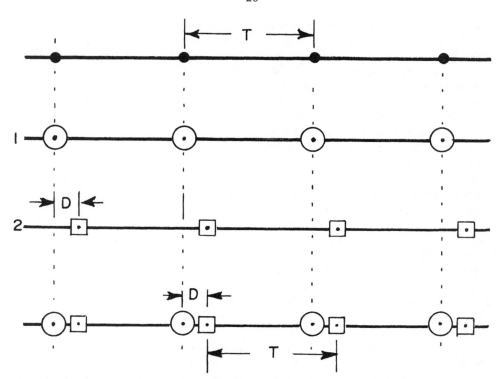

Fig. 2.6. T = inter-pulse time; D = delay time. *Line 1,* impulses from repetition rate generator; *line 2,* impulses from shaper 1; *line 3,* delayed impulses from shaper 2; *line 4,* combined signals from shapers 1 and 2.

from the repetition rate generator, a suitably shaped impulse is generated by shaper 1.

The third line of figure 2.6 shows the timing of the pulses coming from impulse shaper 2. The diagram also shows that each of these impulses arrives later than the impulses produced by shaper 1 by an amount labeled D, the delay.

The combined signals from both of these impulse shapers are fed to the loudspeaker to produce a sequence of signals of the sort indicated on the fourth line of figure 2.6. The basic repetition time T and the left-right pulse delay time D are

also shown on this line (fig. 2.4 is an earlier example of a diagram of this sort).

When we use the apparatus shown diagrammatically in figure 2.5, it gives us a chance to vary the delay D that controls the time of arrival of pulses from shaper 2 in relation to the pulses from shaper 1. When the delay control is set at zero we have a situation that is analogous to the case in which the left and right drum signals happened simultaneously. Turning the delay dial slowly can give us the entire range that our drummer had at his command: exact coincidence, left-before-right in varying amounts, the middle point where the beats are all equidistant from each other, and right-before-left in varying amounts. As one might expect, when the delay time D is exactly equal to half the inter-pulse interval determined by the repetition rate generator (when $D = T/2$), we will hear a doubling of the rate, *if the two pulse shapers produce identical signals*. If the repetition rate is fast enough to give a sense of pitch, our ears will perceive this doubling as a jump upward of one octave.

This octave jump (the perceived correlate of the doubled repetition rate) takes place over an extremely narrow range of mis-centering of one pulse train relative to the other. On each side of the narrow range in which a pure upper octave is heard is a region in which the listener hears two sounds simultaneously, one an octave above the other. As exact interleaving of the pulse trains is approached, the lower of these tones weakens and disappears. (In these experiments using identical pulses it is important for the two generators to be fed into the *same* loudspeaker for the experiments to work properly, for reasons having to do with room acoustics and the way in which we perceive sounds produced in a closed space.)

In this chapter we have devoted our efforts to an exploration of some of the more elementary phenomena that are associated with one's hearing of sequences of impulses. We have come across some rather curious effects, some of which are familiar and some not so commonly known. We have found that the physicist's notion of a "rate" is a useful concept to use in organizing our thinking about the various phenomena we have encountered. Everything so far is based on the

everyday notion of an impulsive sound, which we have taken as a starting point without inquiring exactly what it is like either from the point of view of the physicist or of the psychologist. In the next few chapters we will be able to meet impulsive sounds of greater musical interest, such as those produced by glockenspiels, bells, guitars, and pianos. A study of these instruments will lead us toward an understanding of the producers of sustained sounds such as the woodwinds, brasses, strings, and the human voice.

2.5. Examples, Experiments, and Questions

1. It is often helpful for one to be able to go back and forth in one's mind between the description of an impulse sequence expressed in terms of its repetition rate and the description of the same impulse sequence expressed in terms of its pulse time.

(a) Calculate the pulse repetition rates corresponding to an interpulse time $T = 2.0$, 0.2, 0.02, and 0.002 seconds.

(b) Use the results of your calculations to permit classification of the way in which each pulse sequence is perceived; i.e., is it heard as a buzz, as a tone, or as a sequence of pulses?

(c) Use figure 2.1 to verify that the name of the note corresponding to the pulse sequence that has the highest pitch is a little higher than B_4.

2. A musically trained person is asked to tap out the two rhythmic patterns shown in figure 2.7. Remember that if he does this properly, a listener in the next room will be able to recognize the time signature and to pick out the primary and secondary accented beats in the bar. Why

Fig. 2.7.

is the repetition rate (as actually played) 30/minute (equal to 0.5/second) in the first example and 40/minute (equal to 0.66/second) in the second? There are several implied connections here among the time signature, the location of the bar lines, and the metronome markings. Do they appear to be universally applicable or are they part of our particularly simple special case?

3. Two musicians are asked to tap out the rhythmic duet shown in figure 2.8. A casual listener should have no difficulty in recognizing it as being in waltz time. Each musician is now supplied with his own portable electronic sound source whose loudspeaker generates a single popping sound whenever he presses a button. The two sources are identical in their construction, and each player can only control the instant at which his instrument emits its impulse. Once again the listener will recognize the rhythmic pattern.

Let us replace the two musicians by an electronic repetition rate generator set to produce signals *exactly* 1/3 of a second apart. This generator is connected through some sort of distribution device which is programmed to send one out of every three impulses to the first source so that it is stimulated to emit a pop. The distribution circuit sends the remaining two impulses to the second source. In short, we have arranged the impulse generator to be a sort of conductor who calls forth a pop from one source on the down beat, and pops from the other source for the other two beats of the bar. The two-part "music" is therefore being played with the utmost of electronic exactitude.

It is instructive to seek reasons from your everyday experience (since we have provided no explicit information on the subject so far) as to why the listener might be expected still to recognize the waltz-like nature of the rhythm when it is played by our electronic system. In a similar vein you might seek an explanation for the fact that the 3/4 rhythm pattern

Fig. 2.8.

will disappear if the repetition rate generator is arranged to send all of its impulses to a *single* sound source, or loudspeaker.

4. The buzz of an ordinary electric alarm clock has a repetition rate of exactly 120/second over most of North America, and exactly 100/second in Europe. One does not ordinarily perceive this sort of a buzz as having a very clearly defined pitch, at least in the context of an early morning awakening. However, it does provide an accurate and easily obtainable pitch reference. Figure 2.1 can be used to find the note names most closely associated with these two buzzing frequencies, as well as to find qualitative descriptions of how much the pitches of these buzzes differ from the reference values. That is, it is possible to devise statements like "a 100/second buzz has a pitch about 1/4 semitone above X_2." While you are at it, work out the pitch interval in semitones (a number and a fraction) separating the two alarm clock buzzes.

5. The clapper of a telephone bell itself is driven by an electrical signal that has a repetition rate of 20/second. Normally there are two bells that are struck alternately during each repetition of the clapper's motion. As a preparation for our future work, attempt to make a clear description of what (at present) you suspect is going on when a listener assigns a pitch to the sound coming from the telephone bells. Recall that one can learn to recognize the sound of his own telephone, even though the ringing current is of the same sort everywhere.

6. A clarinetist playing the note written D_5 can lower the pitch to C_5 by pressing a lever with either his left or his right little finger. The first part of figure 2.9 shows one of the normal ways in which a C-to-D trill is played (using the right little finger for the C). The second part of the figure shows another way in which the trill can be done. Work out the repetition rates for the two ways to trill, and comment on some of the reasons why the second version presents a rather astonishing appearance to the casual onlooker. If you are a woodwind player you might also think about the relative practicality of the two patterns in various musical contexts.

7. Make use of figure 2.1 to find the *change in repetition rate* that is associated with the following semitone changes in pitch: C_4 to $C_4\#$, G_4 to $G_4\#$, B_4 to C_5. Notice that the *frequency* changes associated with these nominally equal (semitone) changes in musical pitch are not equal. Although we are not yet in a position to discuss the reasons why the musical scale referred to in this diagram is called equally tempered, it is not difficult to do piano keyboard experiments that tend to verify the fact that the *perceived* pitch changes associated with striking adjacent keys are (at least in the middle of the piano) roughly equal. The point of this problem is to underline once again the distinction between the mechanical attribute (frequency) and its perceived correlate (pitch). Equal increments, or changes, in what we perceive to

Fig. 2.9.   A Clarinet Trill with Peculiar Fingering

be the pitch of successive sounds do not come from producing equal increments in the physical frequency of the repetitions.

Return now to figure 2.1, using it as a help to determine the frequency change associated with the C_5 to $C_5\sharp$ interval. Compare this with the change belonging to the C_4 to $C_4\sharp$ interval. Attempt to deduce some sort of generalization about the relation of the frequency changes required to produce the same musical interval (a semitone in this case) in different octaves.

3
Simple Relations of Sounds and Motions

In chapter 2 we noticed that the impulsive sounds that result from striking various objects tend to be recognizably different from each other. We noted further that something surprising happens when we strike an object repeatedly in a steadily accelerating rhythm: we first perceive the string of impulses as a sequence of isolated events; as the blows arrive more rapidly the sound becomes more like a buzz; eventually, as the tempo gets even faster, the sound transforms itself into a tone of definite pitch. We may ask whether the buzz or tone perceived in response to a rapid succession of impulses from a source will somehow be recognizably different from that arising from a different source even when the repetition rates are the same. It is a matter of experimental fact that we usually can distinguish between the acoustic impulses produced by striking different objects, whether the repetition rate is fast or slow.

Another thing to consider in seeking the physical basis for our ability to distinguish between the sounds from different sources is simply the strength of the impulse. We find it intuitively obvious (i.e., it is unconsciously assumed) that striking an object vigorously produces a loud version of that object's characteristic sound, while a soft blow produces a

weaker but otherwise very similar sound. While the relative loudness of sounds gives us one way to distinguish between them, there must be yet other features of these sounds that permit us to tell them apart. Since our ears deal with changes in repetition rate and loudness in a manner that is essentially the same for all impulsive sounds, we will need to look further into the details of the impulse itself if we are to answer the question posed in chapter 2: how do we distinguish between different categories (tinny, woody, etc.) of impulsive sound?

3.1. Mechanical Motion of Sound Source and Eardrum

If an empty coffee can is held by the fingertips while one beats it with a spoon, the can will be felt to vibrate at the same time that the tapping sound is heard. This impulsive vibration is stronger the closer the fingers are to the struck bottom. It is also easy to notice that the metal of the can's bottom can be made to bend slightly under the pressure of the fingers. A physicist might play around with several informal observations of this sort and then try to summarize the situation to himself:

1. Pressing on the can with my thumbs bends it.

2. Striking something exerts forces on it of limited duration.

3. These two remarks are consistent with my fingers' sense impression of momentary deflections when the coffee can is struck.

4. Whenever I sense a momentary deflection of the can with my fingers, my ears hear an impulsive sound.

5. I suspect that the production of sound is associated with the motion of its source.

Digression on Developing a Theory.

The foregoing numbered sentences are intended to illustrate typical early steps of a physical theory as it learns to walk in the real world. Notice that it leans on real things some of the time and sometimes it staggers ahead to a rather bold generalization based upon nothing more than its creator's hunch. This is the hard part of theory-making. All of the high-powered formal machinery of physics can only work on a new idea after it has gotten past this early stage.

The point of our example of the physicist and the coffee can is to emphasize the fact that sounds are produced by the mechanical motion of some object. Let us continue our informal exploration of the physical nature of sound. Most of us have noticed the rattling of windows when an airplane flies overhead. Many have similarly felt the vibrations of a guitar body in response to the sounds produced by a singer or by musicians playing nearby. With the help of a second empty coffee can, we can confirm these observations in a form most directly useful to our present purposes. Lay a finger lightly on the bottom of one can and notice the impulsive vibrations of this metal can that take place whenever a friend strikes the bottom of the other can. It may be necessary for the two cans to be quite close to one another for this experiment to work, but care must be taken to assure that the two cans are not in direct mechanical contact with one another or with some solid object that could transmit a vibration directly from one can to the other. This simple experiment shows that an impulse can somehow be transferred promptly from one object to another that is not in direct contact with it.

The fact that a mechanical object is set into momentary vibration whenever we hear an impulsive sound suggests (correctly) that our eardrums move when sound impulses impinge upon them. We will not concern ourselves in this chapter with the mechanisms whereby the air in a room is able to transmit a disturbance from a struck object to our eardrums, but we will devote considerable care to the ways in which these transmitted disturbances may be described and analyzed. We will also have to save till the later chapters of this book any consideration of the fact that once the eardrum is set in motion, there is a complex chain of transmitted vibrations extending beyond the eardrum back into the inner ear. Here it turns out that the mechanical vibrations stimulate nerve endings which give rise to coded trains of electrical impulses that are used to carry information deeper yet, into the central nervous system for processing and for recognition as sounds of various kinds.

3.2. The Representation of Motion

Let us see how we can go about making a diagram to represent the motion of some object observed over a period of time. Not only will this permit us to use compact yet accurate diagrammatic descriptions of various kinds of acoustical motion, we will also find it possible to adapt such procedures to the representation of many other ideas besides the motion of bodies.

Consider the following simple motion of someone's hand: the hand is first raised vertically from its original position and held there briefly; then it is brought straight down smoothly but quickly to a point slightly below the starting point; finally, the hand is returned slowly to the place of departure. It has required a lengthy, compound sentence to describe

this motion, and it may take the reader one or two readings plus a hand-waving rehearsal before he can be confident that he has understood it. But a diagram can present the identical actions in a manner that is much more easily and directly understandable.

Let us now see how the up-and-down hand motion described above can be represented graphically in a diagram. Hold a piece of chalk in your hand and press it against a blackboard; now walk along parallel to the blackboard while your

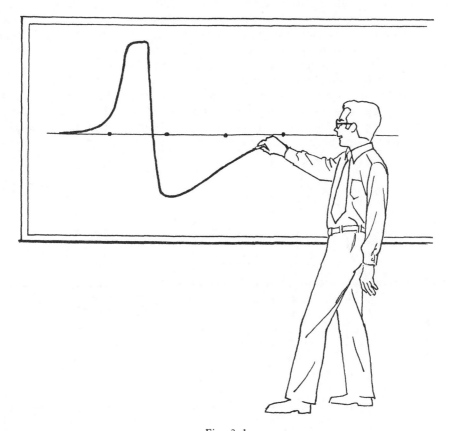

Fig. 3.1.

hand moves up and down in the prescribed motion. The chalk line in figure 3.1 represents the resulting diagram traced out in such a walk. If you walk at a steady pace while drawing the line, horizontal distances from the starting point measured along the blackboard can be used to represent the passage of time during the up-and-down motion of your hand. For reference purposes a horizontal dotted line has been drawn in to indicate the initial (and final) height of the moving hand. In chapter 2 we have already used horizontal lines of this sort to indicate the passage of time, with various circles and crosses drawn along them to show the instants at which various events have taken place. In very much the same way we can think of any particular point along the chalk line as representing the event corresponding to a given time, with the distance of that point from the reference line indicating how far above or below the starting position the hand was at that instant.

In figure 3.2 we see our chalk line redrawn, now provided with vertical and horizontal scales from which measurements can be made. We see that the person who traced this line walked for slightly more than 3/4 of a second before his hand began to rise, and that 1.25 seconds after starting, the hand had very nearly reached its maximum height of 2 feet. We notice that the hand did not move vertically at all from the point at about 1.3 seconds until about 1.6 seconds (a time interval of 0.3 seconds), at which time it began a rapid fall to a position 1.3 feet *below* the reference line, reaching this point at a time $t = 1.75$ seconds. Following this rapid fall came a slow rise which hardly reached the reference height even 4 seconds after the start of the walk.

After a little practice in using graphs of the sort shown in figure 3.2, you should be able to extract a great deal of information from them at a glance. For example, we see that the hand initially moved upward and then moved below its

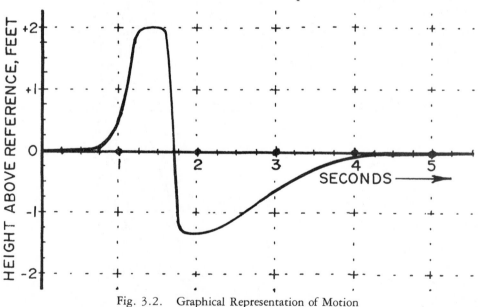

Fig. 3.2. Graphical Representation of Motion

initial position. The above-reference portion of the motion lasted about 3/4 of a second. We notice that whenever the graph *slopes* upward, the hand was *moving* upward. There are two parts of the diagram that show this, from 0.75 to 1.25 seconds, and for all times later than t = 1.9 seconds. Similarly, whenever the hand was moving downward, the graph slopes downward. The more rapid the physical motion in either direction, the steeper is the corresponding slope. The fact that the graph takes a sharp drop from + 2.0 feet to − 1.3 feet in about 1/10 of a second implies that the hand was moving downward with extreme rapidity during this part of the motion.

We can quite easily find the speed of the downward hand motion shown in figure 3.2 by using the concept of *rate* discussed in chapter 2. One might measure the rate of motion (the speed) of a hand in some units such as feet/second (seeking to answer the question, "How many feet does the hand move in one second?"). From the graph we find numbers for the following arithmetic:

$$\frac{\text{distance traveled}}{\text{time elapsed}} = \frac{(2 + 1.3 \text{ feet})}{1/10 \text{ sec}} =$$

$$\frac{10 \times 3.3 \text{ ft}}{1 \text{ sec}} = 33 \text{ ft/sec}$$

I might remark in passing that this speed could be restated as being equal to 22.5 miles/hour, a vigorous but by no means unobtainable speed for a downward chop of the human hand.

3.3. Displaying Motion: *The Strip Chart Recorder and the Oscilloscope*

One is not always restricted to the plotting of graphs by means of chalk on a

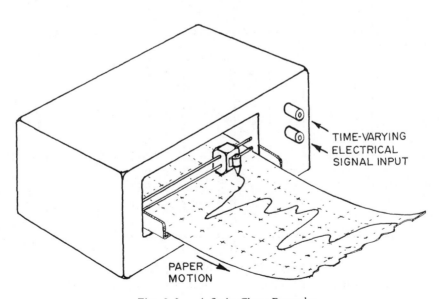

TIME-VARYING
ELECTRICAL
SIGNAL INPUT

PAPER
MOTION

Fig. 3.3.   A Strip Chart Recorder

blackboard. The laboratory strip chart recorder (see fig. 3.3) has close kinship to
our elementary method and also provides
us with an easy entryway into an understanding of many other devices. The chart
recorder has a pen whose position along a
track is determined by an externally provided electrical signal. This pen is the
exact analog of the chalk, the leftward
and rightward displacements of the pen
position corresponding exactly to the upward and downward displacements of our
hand. A motor drive pulls a long paper
chart off a storage roll and past the pen
point at a steady rate. This motion of the
paper chart past the pen as time goes on
serves the same purpose as walking past

the blackboard. In both cases the recording medium (blackboard, chart paper)
and the recording device (chalk, pen) are
moving steadily relative to each other so
that a wavy line is traced out which is a
record *along the medium* of the motion of
the recording device *in time.*

Many chart recorders are provided with
adjustable speed drive, so that a given
impulsive pattern can be displayed more
or less stretched out along the chart
paper. This gives a chance to display
more clearly the short-time or the long-
time character of the disturbance under
study. The recordings described in the
next section will give us a good illustration of the usefulness of this option.

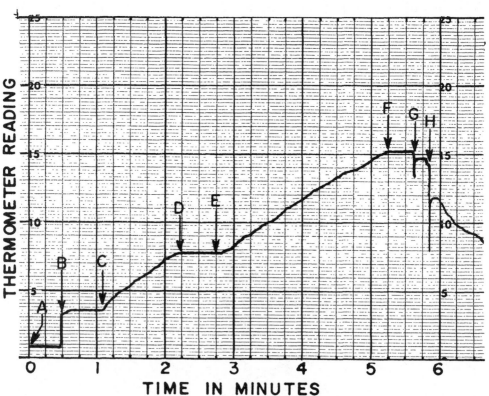

Fig. 3.4.   Strip Chart Recording of Temperature Changes in a Pan of Water

Figure 3.4 shows an easily understood example of the use of a strip chart recorder, in which the changing readings of a kind of thermometer probe are recorded over a period of several minutes. Reading from left to right, the trace shows the following changes. During the half-minute interval from A to B the probe was immersed in a mixture of cracked ice and water. The levelness of the trace during this time shows that the temperature did not change. At the time B we see an upward jump in the trace, signalizing the transfer of the probe out of the ice water into a pan of ordinary tap water. Once again the temperature reading remained constant for a while, until a fire was lit under the pan. From C to D (a time of about 65 seconds) the temperature rose fairly steadily, causing the trace to follow an upward-slanting line. The fire was removed for the half-minute between D and E, leaving a horizontal trace that indicates an unchanging temperature. Between E and F the heat was once again applied and the water came to a boil. It is a property of freely boiling water that its temperature cannot change, and we see evidence for this in the flatness of the curve between F and G. At the time marked G (5 minutes and 35 seconds after the beginning of the trace at A) the fire was removed and a small piece of ice dropped into the hot water next to the thermometer, brushing it momentarily. This cooled the thermometer strongly for an instant before the ice floated away to begin melting rapidly. The abrupt downward spike on the trace at G and its subsequent recovery to a somewhat lower height is the visible record of these happenings. A second and much larger piece of ice was then dropped in, producing once more a sharp downward spike

(shown at H) followed by partial recovery and then progressive cooling as the two pieces of ice melted and so reduced the water temperature.

The electrocardiograph is a particular example of a strip chart recorder which many people have seen, even if they have never been in a physics laboratory. In this device the stylus traces out the pattern of electrical signals associated with the action of one's heart. This pattern repeats in step with the repeated beating of the heart and the details of each repeated pattern give the doctor information about the workings of the heart muscles and nerves.

The modern oscilloscope is another, purely electronic cousin to the strip chart recorder. If required, the oscilloscope is able to display disturbances that take place millions of times more rapidly than those that can be fed to a mechanical device. We will make use in this book of oscilloscope displays whenever they are convenient.

3.4. Oscilloscope Display of a Particular Clang

The clangs produced when one strikes the bottom of an ordinary aluminum skillet with various objects provide us with an ideal set of examples on which we can practice the understanding that has been gained so far. The clangs will also bring to light a number of new things that will prove to be of use to us, not only when we study percussion musical instruments such as the glockenspiel and the piano, but also when we consider the bowed string and wind instruments. Furthermore, the rough clang of a skillet is a sound which conveniently brings to our attention certain things about the way we hear that ultimately provide the common elements that shape organized music all over the world.

The top part of figure 3.5 shows an oscilloscope picture of the vibratory motion set up in the diaphragm of a microphone held near the skillet when it is struck once. We get an overall view of the impulsive nature of the disturbance. On the left half of the picture we see a complicated up-and-down pattern of the trace that dies away toward the right. The left-hand edge of the picture corresponds to the instant the skillet was struck. Even though we are unable in this photograph to make out any detail of the motion, it is possible to get a clear idea of the overall trend of the vibration. The initially large disturbance becomes progressively weaker as time goes on, as shown by the decreasing height of the pattern at

later times. By mid-scale, the whole vertical disturbance has dwindled almost to nothing and the trace of the moving spot of light (the "pen") runs smoothly along the reference axis, making a horizontal line. In this photograph the vertical lines of the grid represent successive time intervals of 50/1000 seconds (or, more conveniently said, 50 *milliseconds*). Using this information permits us to observe that the particular impulsive sound we are studying decays to almost nothing in about 250 (5 times 50) milliseconds. Horizontal lines of the grid have no particular meaning here for us beyond serving as references against which we can compare the magnitude of the disturbance during the time it decays to nothingness.

The middle part of figure 3.5 shows the same decaying impulse; this time, however, the time axis has been chosen to give an interval of 10 milliseconds be-

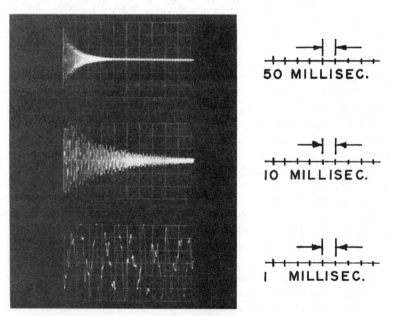

50 MILLISEC.

10 MILLISEC.

1 MILLISEC.

Fig. 3.5.   Oscilloscope Traces of a Skillet Clang

tween the vertical grid lines instead of 50 milliseconds. A moment's thought will show that this change is equivalent to stretching out the upper picture in the horizontal direction to a fivefold extent and then only showing the earliest one-fifth of it. Having arranged a fivefold increase in our ability to see fine temporal details, we are able to discover that the microphone diaphragm is moving rapidly back and forth in an irregular manner. However, even with the speeded-up time scale, we are still unable to make out the detailed nature of the motion.

The lowest part of figure 3.5 shows the initial part of the microphone diaphragm's motion on an expanded time scale such that each division of the reference grid corresponds to an elapsed time of 1 millisecond (1/1000 second). Now at last it is possible to make out details of the motion and to see that the diaphragm is moving back and forth in an extremely irregular and complicated manner.

At first sight it would seem that the behavior of our struck skillet is hopelessly complex and beyond the ability of a rational being to comprehend. As a matter of fact, we already have available a considerable amount of useful information (once we realize how to extract it), and a further study of this skillet clang in the next chapter will allow us to understand the essentials of the motion.

Returning to the top line of figure 3.5, we find that careful inspection of it will yield further information. Not only can we see that the entire motion has died away in a time interval of the order of 250 milliseconds (as pointed out before), we can also notice a further detail in the nature of the decay process. Notice that at the beginning of the vibration the up-and-down excursion of the oscilloscope

trace covers the region extending from almost two divisions above to nearly two divisions below the reference axis. Similarly, we notice that 50 milliseconds later on in the decay, the trace is confined to a region reaching from just short of one division above to almost one division below the axis. That is, the extent of the motion has fallen by very nearly one-half during the course of the first 50 milliseconds. In like manner, the scale of the motion seems to have fallen by a half once again in the time interval from 50 to 100 milliseconds.

Digression: A Guess at the Nature of the Decay Process.
In order for a practicing scientist to have something to guide his thinking when he is ready to become more formal, he must train himself to be quick at noticing details of the sort we have been describing. His mathematical mills can do nothing if they lack grist for the grinding. At the present stage of our observing and thinking we might surmise *that the decay process is one in which the magnitude of the back-and-forth excursions (complex as they may be) dies away perhaps by equal fractional amounts in equal intervals of time. If an experimentalist has observed the simpler though very similar oscilloscope trace that records the sound produced by an empty bottle from which the cork is suddenly withdrawn, he will be tempted (if he is even marginally competent as a scientist) to make a further and recognizably more speculative surmise: that all decays of the motion associated with impulsive sounds have the property of decaying by equal factors in equal times. If he has something definite in mind, our scientist is in a position to devise experiments to test the basic correctness of his surmises.*

So far, we can say that our skillet clang decays away in a time of the order of 250 milliseconds and that *perhaps* the decay follows a fairly regular trend, in that it appears to die away by equal *factors* in equal times. The lower and middle parts of figure 3.5 can now be examined for what they can tell us. It is at once apparent that whatever the nature of the vibration, the microphone diaphragm moves back and forth many times during the decay time. Our observations of this impulsive sound can be summarized in two brief statements at this stage of our investigation:

1. In this disturbance, which is of impulsive character, there is clear evidence for a great deal of irregular back-and-forth motion of the microphone diaphragm, and therefore of the listener's eardrums. This is true despite the fact that we perceive the clang of a skillet as a *single* impulsive sound.

2. The overall duration of the complex motion is of the order of 250 milliseconds (1/4 second). The motion is violent at first and dies down rapidly. There is also reason to surmise that the decay takes place in such a way that the extent of the motion falls by equal fractions in equal intervals of time.

Inspection of the lowest segment of figure 3.5 shows that the finer *changes* in the diaphragm's motion (as evidenced by kinks, offsets, and bends in the trace) take place at intervals whose durations are typically of the magnitude of two or three tenths of the 1-millisecond distance between successive reference lines. We also notice that the gross reversals of the motion take place in times of the order of 1/2 to 1 millisecond. That is, these kinks and reversals take place at a rate of 1000 to 2000 per second. We find confirmation for this observation in the middle photograph. Here the finest details of the motion are obscured and what have just been referred to as the gross features of the back-and-forth motion have become compressed into what look like ir-

regularly spaced vertical lines. We can count 10 to 20 such lines within the space between successive time reference lines and we recall that the latter are spaced 10 milliseconds apart. The reversal rate may then be estimated by our usual method:

$$\frac{(10\,to\,20\,reversals)}{(10\,milliseconds)} = \frac{(1\,to\,2\,reversals)}{(1\,millisecond)} =$$

$$\frac{(1\,to\,2\,reversals)}{(1/1000\,second)} = (1000\,to\,2000)\frac{reversals}{second}$$

We can complete our summary description now by adding the following two statements to the pair made earlier:

3. The gross behavior of the vibrational motion involves reversals that take place at a rate of the order of 1000 to 2000/second.

4. The finest details visible in the motion take place in such a way as to imply alterations in the motion that take place at a rate that is in the range of 3000 to 5000/second.

This carries the analysis of a skillet clang as far as is possible on the basis of what has been outlined so far in this book. We have also provided ourselves with some surmises upon which we can hang our future investigations. As remarked earlier, chapter 4 will carry us deeper into the study of mechanical vibrations and the audible sounds that may arise from them. We will continue to use the information contained in figure 3.5 (the oscilloscope tracing of a skillet clang), together with information gained from further experiments on the skillet, as the background material from which we will develop our understanding of struck and plucked musical instruments such as the guitar, the piano, and the harpsichord. At this point you may find it helpful and interesting to look ahead at the diagrams associated with section 2 of chapter 10, to see simpler examples of traces that can be unraveled by the method sketched out here.

3.5. Examples, Experiments, and Questions

1. In order to get your ear accustomed to listening to various kinds of sounds, and in order to demonstrate the wide variety of sounds that can be elicited even from a skillet, it is worthwhile to strike the skillet at a variety of spots over its surface with a fairly hard object. It is convenient to use the more-or-less rounded plastic butt end of a ball-point pen as a hammer. A good technique is to strike the skillet with the pen using a hand motion similar to the one used in dotting an *i* or making a period at the end of a sentence, holding it lightly so as to let the pen bounce away freely from the skillet at each blow. Verify that the sounds are different depending on the place on the skillet the striking point may lie.

2. To continue the experiment, tap the skillet with a rubber eraser tip slipped over the end of the pen. Investigate in similar fashion the sounds produced by bouncing your knuckle off the skillet, and then try the same thing using your fingertip. At this stage of your observations it is an interesting (though perhaps difficult) undertaking to devise preliminary surmises about the gross nature of the oscilloscope patterns to be expected for sounds generated by hammers of varying hardness. (For example, how would the number of fine-grained reversals of the trace be expected to change as the hardness of the hammer is changed?)

3. Listen once again to the impulsive clang from a struck skillet or other simi-lar object, this time with your ear quite close to it. Notice that after the main clang has died out, there often remains a low-pitched humming sound which may persist for a while. Having observed this, you may wish to go back and revise the hypothesizing in section 3.4 about the nature of the decay process characteristic of vibrations of a struck object.

4. Now that we have gained somewhat more insight into the nature of clanging sounds, it is useful to go back to question 5 of chapter 2 concerning the nature of the sounds emitted when a telephone bell is ringing. Compare the surmises you made earlier about this sound with the ones you would make having worked this far through chapter 3.

5. Obtain a cheap loudspeaker (uncased) and observe the motion of its cone (diaphragm) when a flashlight battery is connected across its terminals. The cone moves forward abruptly and comes to rest in its displaced position as long as the battery is left connected if the battery polarity is arranged one way. A similar abrupt displacement takes place in the opposite direction if the battery polarity is reversed. Notice that one hears a click or pop only while the cone is in motion. Notice also that the click sounds very much the same at the moment the battery is connected as it does when the connection is broken. Notice in addition that one gets unsteady scraping and popping sounds when poorly made electrical connections produce unsteady deflections of the cone.

6. Connect the two terminals of the loudspeaker via a shielded cable to the "mike" or "mag phono" input jack of an ordinary record player. Under these conditions, instead of having its cone displaced by an electrical current sent

through its windings, the loudspeaker is functioning as a microphone: displacements imposed on the cone give rise to electrical signals which can be amplified and themselves used to drive another loudspeaker. When you tap or scrape on the cone of the "microphone" with a fingernail, the record player's own loudspeaker will emit tapping and scraping sounds. Follow the logical chain of phenomena for this case, proceeding from the small motions imposed on the first (microphone) loudspeaker by your finger to the motions of the second (record player) loudspeaker, and thence to the audible motions of your own eardrum. If the volume control of the amplifier is turned up high enough, the system may howl or scream. What is the probable causal chain giving rise to this self-sustained acoustical disturbance?

7. The wavy line marked on a strip of chart paper by the pen of an electrocardiograph makes a good example of the representation by means of a graph of signals that vary with time. The tracing shown in figure 3.6 was made from the electrical signals from a human heart. Mark a suitable time scale on the chart to make the repetition rate of the graph match the rate at which your heart is beating. Attempt then to categorize the variations taking place during each heartbeat into major and minor alteration rates in a way similar to our analysis of the waveform recorded from a microphone that was "listening" to the clang from a struck skillet.

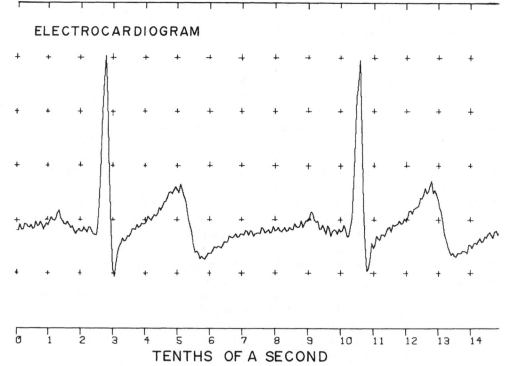

ELECTROCARDIOGRAM

TENTHS OF A SECOND

Fig. 3.6. An Electrocardiogram

4

Characteristic Frequencies and the Decay of Composite Sounds

In chapter 3 we examined the microphone signals arising from the clanging of a skillet, thereby meeting a first example of the complex way in which a struck object can vibrate. In the course of experimenting with hitting the skillet at different points with hard and soft objects you may have noticed that it is sometimes quite difficult to assign a pitch to the sound produced when something hard strikes the skillet. On the other hand, the pitch is generally easy to settle upon when the pan is struck by something soft, such as a fingertip. We will have to wait until chapter 5 for a proper discussion of the question of pitches resulting from complex sounds. It is nevertheless worthwhile here to organize our thoughts on the subject by doing a little speculation on the implications of what we have learned so far.

4.1. A Preliminary Speculation on the Pitch Behavior of Skillet Clangs

In chapter 2 we met the notion that definiteness of pitch is normally to be associated with the definiteness of some sort of repetition rate. We are therefore led to speculate as follows about the sound of a skillet struck by soft and hard objects:

perhaps when the skillet is struck by a soft object it is set into a fairly repetitive motion, giving us a good pitch cue of the sort we first noticed in connection with the ringing of a telephone bell, whereas blows on the skillet from a hard object may give conflicting suggestions to the repetition-rate machinery of our ears by somehow exciting *several* repeating motions that manage to take place simultaneously.

The idea of several simultaneous repetition rates being imposed on the motion of a microphone diaphragm or on an eardrum may at first seem strange or even inconsistent. We are forced, however, to accept it on the simple evidence of our ears. For instance, if two widely spaced notes are struck on the piano or if a singer and a pianist each produce a tone, our ears have no difficulty in perceiving the two superimposed sounds as separate entities. Presumably, then, our eardrums can in fact move in some way that involves two separate repetition rates.

4.2. Repetitive Properties of an Impulsive Motion

We return now to the question of whether it is conceivable that an impulsive sound is repetitive in its own right: the answer is yes. Invoking our knowledge that the production of sound involves mechanical motion, we must seek an example of impulsive mechanical motion of such large scale that we can see it, and moving slowly enough that we can follow its repetitive motions. Such a motion is the repetitive rocking of the water surface in a filled drinking glass that has been bumped. The surface tilts back and forth in a smoothly oscillating motion that dies away in the course of time. We notice also that the repetition rate of this motion appears to be reasonably constant.

Similar repeated motion can be observed directly by experimenting with a tuning fork. If the tuning fork is struck with a knuckle at a point lying between 1/2 and 1/4 of the way down from the end of the tines, it will give a beautifully clear sound of definite pitch. We can also feel the vibrations in the fingers that are holding the fork by its stem. Hold a vibrating tuning fork so that the part of one of its tines that is near its root is in the gentlest possible contact with the surface of a table (see fig. 4.1). A harsh buzz-

ing sound is produced which is quickly quenched. This buzzing sound is due to rapidly repeated blows struck on the table top by the vibrating tine. The pitch of this manifestly repetitive sequence of tiny blows is exactly the same as the pitch of the normal smooth tone of the tuning fork. The impulsive blow from our knuckles on the fork has in fact set up a repetitive swinging motion of the fork tines, just as a blow on the water glass set up a much slower swinging motion in the water.

4.3. Several Simultaneous Repetition Rates

Use the tuning fork once more, and this time strike it near the tip of one tine instead of part way down. As we are led to expect from experiments with the skillet, the sound is different now: instead of a single, smooth sound of well-defined pitch (the tuning reference sound that is the sole purpose of the design of the tuning fork), we seem to hear two (or more) pitches simultaneously. One of these pitches is the one perceived earlier, while the other one is very much higher and is clearly heard as a separate entity. For example, the tuning fork I use at home (designed to sound A_4, which has a repetition rate of 440/second) is found to have its higher pitch lying between the notes F_7 and G_7 of a piano. In other words, if there is indeed a repetition rate associated with this upper pitch, it lies in the neighborhood of 3000/second, as we can calculate with the help of figure 2.1.

Digression on the Higher Sounds from Tuning Forks.
Experiments with a number of tuning forks made by different manufacturers and having different

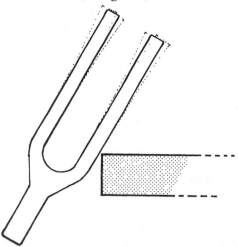

Fig. 4.1.

physical shapes show that the higher sounds produced by the different forks have no recognizable pitch relations one to another even though the lower (main) sounds are accurately alike in pitch. We have here another example (albeit a subtle one) of the fact that objects of different shape produce different sounds when they are struck. It is also sometimes possible to adjust some one attribute of the sound without regard to the others.

There have been strong hints so far that a mechanical object can in fact be driven in such a way that one can identify several repetition rates in the motion. Examples of objects that are driven at several rates are actually very easy to find. For example, we notice that if one taps on the side of a glass full of water with a fingernail or spoon, a soft tinkling sound is heard and small ripples are seen on the water surface. If the tapping impulse is strong enough to jar the glass sideways on the table, we see that ripples will again appear on the water surface, but the surface will also be rocking back and forth in the way we described earlier. Furthermore, the tinkling sound we hear (associated no doubt with the rapid repetition rate of some motion of the glass and the water) is not altered by the presence of the slower rocking motion. We have therefore observed at least one special case in which two repetition rates are simultaneously visible as a consequence of an impulsive excitation, and we are entitled to suspect that the tuning fork is a second example.

4.4. Experimental Search for Vibrations Having Several Repetition Rates

The observations and speculations that have been described in the earlier parts of this chapter should suggest that we might see a fair amount in oscilloscope traces obtained from a microphone placed near a tuning fork. For one thing, the normal function of a tuning fork is to serve as a pitch reference, and we have come to associate this pitch with a definite single repetition rate. Simply by altering the manner in which the fork is struck, we will be able to choose between the simple (normal) sound of the fork and one that appears to have two widely separated by clearly marked pitches. With luck we will obtain a picture of greater complexity in the latter case than in the former, which may well provide clues to what is going on.

The top line of figure 4.2 shows the oscilloscope pattern associated with the motion of a particular A-440 tuning fork when it has been struck by a soft hammer at a point lying between 1/4 and 1/2 of the way from the end of one tine. The horizontal axis covers a time duration of many seconds, and the distance between successive reference lines on the grid corresponds to one second of elapsed time. Aside from the greatly increased time scale, this pattern looks like a particularly smooth version of the decay pattern shown for a struck skillet in the upper part of figure 3.5. Close examination of the decay pattern for the tuning fork shows that the extent of the vibratory motion (as measured by the vertical height of the oscilloscope pattern) dies away *precisely* in accordance with the guess made in section 3.4 of chapter 3. We find that the motion falls away by a factor of 1/2 for each 3.5 seconds of elapsed time.

The middle part of figure 4.2 shows the same tuning-fork decay pattern displayed now with reference lines whose spacing represents a time interval of only

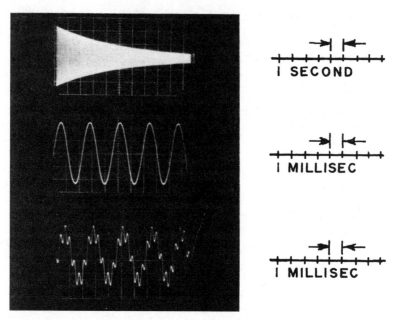

Fig. 4.2. Oscilloscope Traces of Sound from a Tuning Fork

1/1000 second (1 millisecond). Here we can see the nature of the microphone's diaphragm motion in all its simplicity. The oscilloscope trace is a smooth, sinuous line, with an exact and well-defined repetition time. Curves of this sort, which are very important in acoustics, are known as *sinusoids*. There are no irregular details in the pattern; it is not possible to make catalogs, as we did for the skillet clang, of the approximate range of rates at which the dominant motion reverses direction or of the approximate frequency with which small irregularities occur. We see only a single, simple, repeating pattern whose dying away is so slight as to be almost invisible. Close inspection of the pattern shows that 4 repetitions of the back-and-forth motion take place in the time corresponding to 9.1 reference divisions. The repetition rate (as determined by our admittedly rough measurement) is therefore:

$$\frac{4 \text{ repetitions}}{0.0091 \text{ seconds}} = 439.6/\text{second}$$

The lowest part of figure 4.2 shows the trace (on the same time scale as before) of the sound produced when the same fork is struck at the end of a tine by something fairly hard. Once more we observe a basic pattern of repetitive motion that takes place 440 times per second, except that the recorded trace is made to appear wavy, as though it had been drawn by someone with a severe but extremely regular palsy. Examination of the repetition rate of the tremor itself shows that it matches the repetition rate (approximately 2660/second) belonging to the higher pitch sound produced by this particular fork. Here is a clear indication that the microphone is responding to disturbances that take place at two different repetition rates.

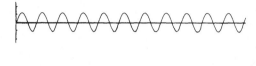

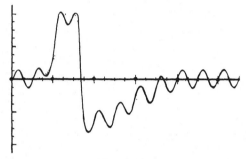

Fig. 4.3.

4.5. Patterns Made by Adding Two Different Repeating Motions

Let us make sure we know how to interpret displays of the sort shown at the bottom of figure 4.2. That is, let us find the relation between two traces that separately represent two distinct types of motion and a third trace that is produced when the pen moves under the influence of both disturbances acting at the same time. Suppose that the blackboard pattern shown in figure 3.2 (in chap. 3) is to be retraced by a person having a palsied hand. The top part of figure 4.3 shows the sort of wavy line he would draw if he attempted to walk along beside the blackboard with the intention of drawing a straight horizontal line. The lower part of the figure shows what would be the result of his attempt to reproduce the trace shown in figure 3.2. We see that the actual trace made on the blackboard is drawn alternately above and below the desired smooth curve, the extent and direction of the discrepancies being exactly equal to the extent and direction of the

motions due to the palsy. In general, then, we realize that it is possible to "add" the graph of one sort of disturbance to the graph of a different disturbance in order to work out a representation of the composite motion arising from the two disturbances when they take place simultaneously.

Figure 4.4 shows how one can make use of a draftsman's divider to carry out the addition of two graphs to produce their composite or sum. The top part of the figure shows the pattern traced out in time by one of the disturbances (call it disturbance A). The trace belonging to the second disturbance (B) is shown in the lower part of the figure, along with a curve marked C which gives the combined motion. The diagrams also show how a pair of dividers is used to transfer the magnitude of disturbance A (at each given instant of time) down onto the curve B in a way that adds disturbance A to disturbance B. One simply moves along the diagram marking out sufficient points to permit a careful sketching of the resultant curve C.

We can see that a pattern similar to the trace for the doubly ringing tuning fork shown in the bottom of figure 4.2 might also be accomplished by a palsied man drawing a sinusoid, or by using dividers to add together a sinusoid with a repetition rate of 440/second and another sinusoid whose rate is around 3000/second.

4.6. Composite Motions of a Skillet

Our experimental study of microphone signals produced by a struck tuning fork has strengthened the plausibility of the various surmises made earlier in the chapter and leads us to suspect that the

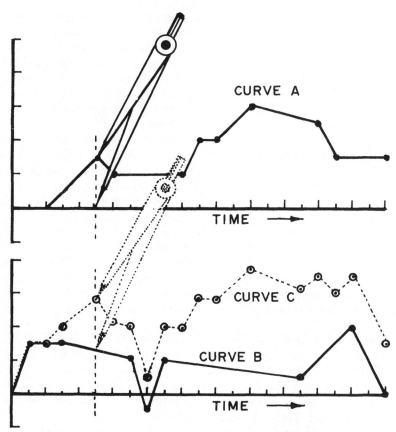

Fig. 4.4.   Addition of Two Graphs Using a Pair of Dividers

oscilloscope traces shown in figure 3.5 are in fact the resultant of several oscillations of a simpler type, all of which begin at the instant when the skillet is struck. In today's world it is relatively easy to test this hypothesis, making use of electronic equipment which is able to transmit selectively signals of specified repetition rate from microphone to oscilloscope while it ignores electrical disturbances of any other repetition rate. Such an electronic device, called a band-pass filter, is usually provided with control knobs. One of these is used to set the "center

frequency," which is the repetition rate that is transmitted through the filter with least attenuation. Another determines the "bandwidth," or the *range* of frequencies above and below the center frequency that are transmitted almost equally well. For present purposes we will imagine that signals having repetition rates that are close enough to the filter's center frequency to lie within its bandwidth will be transmitted without alteration. Signals having repetition rates lying outside this "pass band," or range of perfect transmission, are similarly presumed to have been

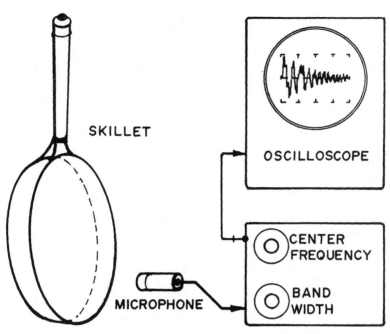

SKILLET

OSCILLOSCOPE

CENTER
FREQUENCY

BAND
WIDTH

MICROPHONE

Fig. 4.5.   Band-Pass Filter Setup for Studying Skillet Clang

eliminated completely from the filter's output.

Figure 4.5 shows how a band-pass filter may be connected between the microphone and the oscilloscope in order that we can search among the sounds from a skillet for characteristic frequencies of a sort found earlier in the sound produced by a tuning fork. A convenient way to proceed is to set the filter bandwidth control to 50/second, so that the filter will pass signals whose repetition rates lie in the range 25/second above and below the value set on the center frequency knob. One then varies the center-frequency setting slowly, while striking the skillet over and over. Whenever the filter has its center frequency set so that some vibrational component of the microphone signal has a repetition rate lying within the filter bandwidth, the oscilloscope trace takes on an appearance of the sort shown for a tuning fork in the upper two parts of figure 4.2.

When the band-pass filter is used to study the microphone signals from the skillet that we used in discussing figure 3.5, oscillations are found that take place at rates of about 260, 1055, 1630, 1750, 2505, etc., repetitions/second. In every case the oscilloscope patterns associated with these repetition rates are of the smooth, sinuous type of the sort observed from a tuning fork. Each of these patterns has its own decay time, but in the special case of our skillet all but the first of the listed signals are audible over their halving time of 25 milliseconds. It is easy to understand now why the simple observation of the unfiltered clang from the skillet showed a similar decay time.

Digression on Some Irregular Components of the Skillet Clang.

In addition to the group of frequencies listed above for the skillet clang, there are certain other center-frequency settings of the filter that give oscilloscope displays of appreciable magnitude, but the patterns are rough and irregular looking. We cannot ignore these irregular patterns mixed in among the expected ones, but it is reasonable to postpone consideration of them, particularly since they are not produced invariably on every blow. That is, they seem to appear or disappear at random, from tap to tap of the skillet. Meanwhile we can stay alert to any clues concerning what is going on. Possible hints may be expected from our observation that blows from a soft hammer tend not to produce these "extra" irregular signals and that with a hard hammer they appear at fairly well-defined settings of the filter center frequency.

4.7. The Characteristic Oscillations of a Struck Object

Sounds produced by striking or plucking a wide variety of different objects can be analyzed to show in every case that the microphone signal is made up of a collection of sinuous oscillations of exactly the sort we have met in our study of the tuning fork and the skillet. *Each object has its own characteristic collection of these oscillations,* with each oscillation having its own frequency. Regardless of the source, all the oscilloscope patterns have exactly the same shape when we look at them swing by swing. Furthermore, all of these characteristic oscillations die away in a similar manner. Suppose for example that the magnitude of one of these oscillations is observed to decay to half its original value by the end of the first 1/10 second of its motion; we find then that during the second 1/10 second the motion decreases once again by half. This means that at the end of the first 2/10 second of the oscilla-

tion the motion has decayed until its magnitude is reduced by $1/2 \times 1/2 = 1/4$ of its original size. Similarly, by the time 3/10 second has elapsed the pattern has shrunk to $1/2 \times 1/2 \times 1/2 = 1/8$ of its original size, and so on. We can therefore characterize the whole dying-down process in our example by saying that the oscillation has a *halving time* of 1/10 second. Some other oscillation of the same object might (in the same sense) be said to decay with a halving time of 1/100 second, and yet another with a halving time of 10 seconds. In every case, each of our smoothly decaying oscillatory patterns is found to have a definite halving time, regardless of how the object is struck (provided of course that the hammer is not left jammed against it in such a way as to kill off the oscillation).

4.8. The Formal Description of a Decaying Sound

The sinuous oscillatory patterns produced by striking or otherwise impulsively exciting an object always have a well-defined repetition rate, a particular manner of decay, and a certain shape when looked at swing by swing. These patterns represent motions which we will refer to as being *damped sinusoidal oscillations,* that is, oscillations of a certain sinuous shape which die away (are damped) eventually. A given damped sinusoid is completely specified when one gives a) its repetition rate (usually called the *frequency* of oscillation), b) the *initial amplitude* (the initial distance of excursion each side of the reference line), and c) the *halving time* ($T_{1/2}$), which gives us a way to state the amplitude of the motion at any later time in terms of the initial amplitude.

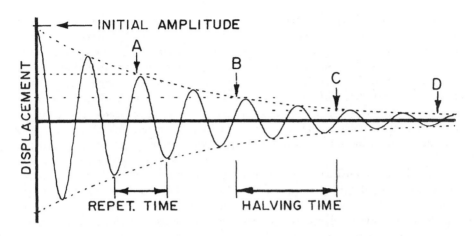

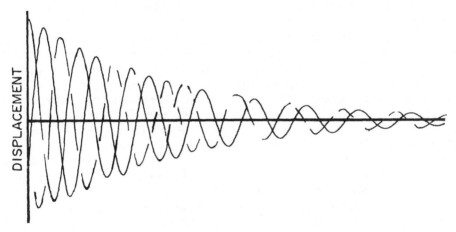

Fig. 4.6. Amplitude Halving Time of a Damped Sinusoid

The top part of figure 4.6 is a drawing of one of our newly defined damped sinusoidal patterns. The letters A, B, C, . . . show the instants at which the magnitude of the oscillation has fallen by successive factors of 2. The time interval between any adjacent pairs of these in- stants is what we will formally call the halving time. The diagram also shows one example of the repetition time, after which the oscillatory motion repeats itself exactly (except for its inevitable decaying away). The lower part of figure 4.6 shows an example of several damped sinusoidal oscillations, all having the same frequency, initial amplitude, and halving time as the sinusoid in the upper diagram. For present purposes we will not need to distinguish between them. However, we note that they differ only in the way they are started out at $t = 0$. Once a sinusoid is started, its course later is completely determined by our three specifications.

We will have a continual need to deal with decaying oscillatory patterns of the sort we have been studying. They are found in the sounds produced by guitars and harpsichords as well as in those from pianos and from bells. We also find them (albeit more deeply buried) in the reverberations of a concert hall. It is because of their continual presence in what we hear that we have taken the trouble to provide ourselves with a terminology to describe various features of these patterns. All of these matters will be taken up again in considerable detail in chapter 10.

4.9. Examples, Experiments, and Questions

1. A hacksaw blade clamped firmly at one end in a vise makes a good vibrator on which to practice many of the ideas contained in this chapter and the earlier ones. Plucking the blade at the free end with a fingertip will start it vibrating back and forth at a frequency easily followed by the eye at the rate of about 5 repetitions/second. After an initial twanging sound has died out, the blade moves back and forth almost silently, with an amplitude that gradually decreases.

As a first experiment, hold a board or a screwdriver where it can be lightly struck in a series of taps by the end of the blade as it oscillates. Listen to this tapping as though it were in unaccented 4/4 time, and beat time on the table with a pencil in step with every fourth blade tap. These two sets of synchronized tapping rates can be used together with a metronome (or stop watch) as a means for measuring the actual frequency at which the hacksaw blade is swinging. Once you have acquired the knack of beating time in synchronization with the blade's own taps, it is possible to shorten the projecting length of the blade and repeat the frequency measurement for the more rapidly oscillating blade. Keep shortening the free length of the blade until it is no longer possible to keep step with it by pencil tapping at the one-for-four rate. It may then be possible to shift the rhythmic relationship to one in which the pencil taps once for every 6 or 8 swings of the hacksaw blade. This will permit accurate measurements of the blade's vibration rate to somewhat higher frequencies. Notice how usefully the rhythmic abilities of the human nervous system can be exploited as a means for extending the range of physical measurements done with the simplest of apparatus. With a little practice one can learn to measure vibration rates thus to an accuracy of 1 percent or better. Whatever the level of sophistication attained in our laboratory equipment, its usefulness can be extended or its accuracy improved if its workings can be tied in with our perceptual machinery.

2. The next experiments on our clamped hacksaw blade call for it to be struck with a screwdriver blade or other hard object at various points along one of its flat sides. As in the experiments with skillet clangs, you should attempt to single out the pitches of the various twang-

ing sounds that may be produced. Work out, with the help of figure 2.1, the note names and repetition frequencies associated with these pitches. You may well find this easier to do than was the case with a skillet. Compare now the arrangement of vibrational frequencies given in this chapter for a particular tuning fork with those given for the skillet and those you have deduced for the hacksaw blade. Try to construct an orderly speculation about the relative ease of identifying clang pitches for objects having widely or closely spaced frequencies for their sets of damped sinusoids.

3. Clamp the hacksaw blade to leave a progressively shorter free length, and pluck the free end. Notice that as the blade is shortened the vibration rate goes up. When the length is sufficiently short, the back-and-forth vibration begins to be-

come audible and to have a definite pitch. Notice also that the pitch rises rapidly as the blade's free length is shortened. You might find it interesting to construct an analogue to figure 2.1 in which the frequency values are replaced by numbers giving the free lengths of hacksaw blade whose twanging frequencies are associated with the various note names. Be sure to clamp the blade tightly, at right angles to the vise jaws. It will be necessary to measure very carefully, since small length changes produce large pitch changes.

4. Because the effects of combining one motion with another will be important to us all through the book, you may wish to practice on one or two examples. Thus curve B of figure 4.7 may be added to curve A in the way that was discussed in section 4.5 and illustrated in figure 4.4. Just to get you started, part of the

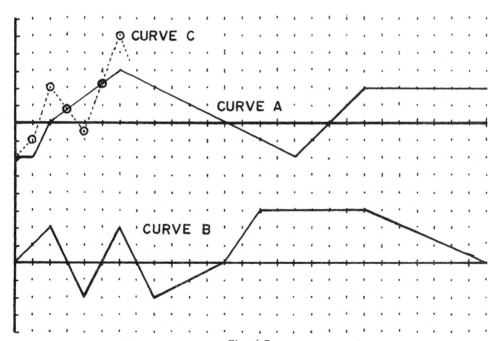

Fig. 4.7.

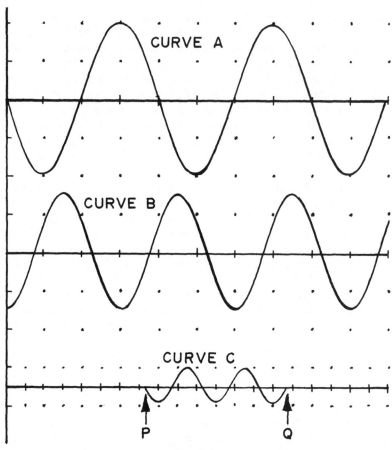

Fig. 4.8.

resultant curve C is also shown at the left end of the diagram.

5. In figure 4.8, segments of three sinusoidal curves are shown, each with its own amplitude and frequency. These curves are labeled A, B, and C. They may be used to provide additional practice in sketching out the sum of two curves as well as an introduction to some of the ways in which the resultant may be interpreted. To begin with, sketch out carefully the resultant curve produced by adding curves A and B. Label this new composite curve with the letter D. Now find the result of graphically adding curves C and D. This will have the same general appearance as curve D except in its middle portion (marked by the letters P and Q on the time axis). Now compare this middle segment of your curve with the bottom photographic trace of figure 3.5. If you reread the description of the reversal rates of this curve, keeping the appearance of your latest computations clearly in mind, it will help to put a number of ideas in a new perspective.

6. You may have available some electrical facilities which can be used for conveniently exploring some of the ideas we have met so far. Connect a variable frequency electronic oscillator that produces an electrical output of continuous sinusoidal form (that is, one in which the halving time is indefinitely long) to the input of an audio amplifier and its associated loudspeaker. If possible, connect the oscillator to the input terminals of an oscilloscope so as to display the pattern characteristic of an undamped sinusoidal disturbance. Vary the oscillator frequency setting over the range of 200 to about 1000 repetitions/second, keeping the loudness at a very low level. Listen to the sound produced by the loudspeaker. Notice first of all that the tone is almost exactly like that produced by a tuning fork. Observe that as the numerical frequency setting on the oscillator dial is raised, the pitch rises. Notice also that when the amplitude of the oscillator signal is made larger, the sound becomes louder. Do not, however, permit the amplitude of the sinusoidal oscillator signal to become so large as to "overload" the amplifier, since there is some risk of damaging the amplifier, the loudspeaker, or your ears. Later in the book we will be able to deal with the changed sound that results from overloading.

5

Pitch: The Simplest Musical Implication of Characteristic Oscillations

In chapter 4 we learned that essentially any object can be impulsively set into motion. When this motion is analyzed, it is always found to consist of a collection of damped sinusoidal oscillations; each of these oscillations has its own frequency and its own halving time. We can observe the details of the motion of an impulsively excited object by placing a microphone near it. The microphone diaphragm moves in response to the motion of the struck object, giving us an electrical signal that can be easily studied. The frequencies and decay times of the microphone signals are directly related to the frequencies and decay times of the oscillations of the struck object. Using an oscilloscope and a band-pass filter, we can determine that the motion of our struck object is made up of a characteristic set of oscillations of sinusoids. However, it takes only the briefest of additional experimentation to discover that the relative strengths (the initial amplitudes) of the various sinusoids making up this motion *are not characteristic of the object*. Not only do these amplitudes depend on the nature of the hammer and the striking place, but they depend also on the position of the microphone relative to the object.

Our studies with microphone and oscilloscope show that when a tuning fork is struck in a suitable spot by a suitably soft hammer, only a single sinusoidal oscillation is excited, and its perceived pitch can be related directly to the oscillation frequency by using the musical convention described in figure 2.1. Striking the tuning fork with a harder hammer excites two or more of the characteristic vibrations of the fork. Our hearing mechanism in this case finds it possible to distinguish these two or more vibrations from each other and to assign separate pitches to them. The higher oscillations are so weakly excited in normal use and their pitches are so much higher than that of the lowest vibration that we have no trouble labeling the fork with the musical note name that is conventionally associated with its lowest characteristic oscillation frequency.

5.1. Perceived Pitch of a Composite Sound I: *Rectangular Bars*

The rectangular steel bars of the glockenspiel provide us with a further example for our study of the pitches associated with sounds from impulsively excited objects. We will begin with an examination of the sounds from the bar that gives the instrument's lowest note, C_6. Here, just as in the case of the tuning fork, the pitch name agrees exactly with the frequency of the lowest characteristic sinusoidal vibration, 1046.5 oscillations/second. The hardwood mallets used to strike the bar also excite the second, third, and fourth characteristic vibrations which (in my particular glockenspiel) have frequencies of 2810, 3906, and 5494 oscillations/second.

Inspection of a glockenspiel or its close cousins, the xylophone and the marimba, shows at a glance that the longer bars give lower pitched notes than do the shorter bars. We notice, however, that the "kind" of sound from one bar is very much the same as that from the next one. One is led to ask what is the common element among the sounds produced by bars tuned to different pitches. Many people will automatically say that there is something characteristic of the sound of a *bar*, whether it is made of wood, brass, or steel, or perhaps even of plastic. This suggests that the *shape* of an object somehow determines the tone, so that we should measure the characteristic frequencies of a shorter bar and see how they are related to those belonging to the longer bar. When this is done, we find that many of the *ratios* of the characteristic frequencies of one bar are somewhat similar to those of any other bar of the set. Let us assign the alphabetical letter names P, Q, R, S, . . . in order to the first, second, third, etc., characteristic frequencies of our bar. This sort of labeling helps us keep track of the various frequencies without risk of confusion with the letter names A through G which are given to notes of the musical scale. For the partic-

ular bar that concerns us here, the ratios may be written out as follows:

$$\frac{\text{first frequency}}{\text{first frequency}} = \frac{P}{P} = \frac{1046}{1046} = 1.00$$

$$\frac{\text{second frequency}}{\text{first frequency}} = \frac{Q}{P} = \frac{2810}{1046} = 2.68$$

$$\frac{\text{third frequency}}{\text{first frequency}} = \frac{R}{P} = \frac{3906}{1046} = 3.73$$

$$\frac{\text{fourth frequency}}{\text{first frequency}} = \frac{S}{P} = \frac{5494}{1046} = 5.25$$

Conventionally one summarizes frequency ratios of the sort shown above by a statement such as: "The characteristic frequencies for this particular bar are related to the lowest one by the numbers (ratios) 1.00, 2.68, 3.73, 5.25, . . ."

Digression: The Discrepancy between Measured and Textbook Frequency Ratios.
The frequency ratios characteristic of a precisely rectangular bar made of uniform material and floating freely in space may be calculated in a straightforward way by mathematical methods which have been known since the first half of the nineteenth century, although the operation is beyon.[1] the scope of this book. Using that somewhat simplified calculation would give us ratio numbers which are reported in most textbooks as 1.000, 2.756, and 5.404. Much of the difference between the textbook ratios and those shown above is explained when proper account is taken of a mounting hole that is drilled in the actual bar and the grinding away of the underside of the center of the bar which is done for tuning purposes. The very severe discrepancy between our measured ratio for R/P and the textbook value has a different explanation. The traditional calculation has neglected to include one of the characteristic vibrations of the bar, so that the third textbook ratio actually refers to the fourth member (S/P) of our set of measured ratios. Once the frequencies are properly assigned, the discrepancy has only the usual small value associated

with the holes and the tuning process. We will continue our study of bars in chapter 9 and at that time will learn the nature of the missing oscillation and the reason for its mathematical disappearance (see sec. 9.1).

There seems to be little added complication when we go from the sound produced by a tuning fork to that produced by a metal bar. The lowest characteristic frequency for the bar (which is incidentally the one that is most strongly excited in normal playing) determines the playing pitch, and the weakly sounding and far-distant higher components merely add pungency and brightness to the sound. The hardwood bars of the xylophone give us, at the level of our present investigation, very little that is different from what is found from a study of metal bars. The chief differences are found in the greatly shortened characteristic halving times belonging to the damped oscillations of a wooden bar and in the possible addition of one or two extra frequencies arising as a consequence of the nonuniform character of wood (the presence of grain makes the transverse and longitudinal properties of the wood quite different from one another).

5.2. Perceived Pitch II: *Small Clock Chimes*

We turn our attention now to a different sort of "musical instrument" in which the relations between the frequencies supplied to our ears and the pitch we assign to the sound are less easily interpreted. A favorite way for makers of grandfather clocks to simulate the huge bells of a tower clock is to make use of slender steel rods which are thinned down near one end where they are anchored in a massive block. There is one such rod supplied for each note of the chime tune, and each rod is struck by a leather-faced hammer driven by small gears and levers. The lengths of these rods are graduated. The length and the amount of thinning of each rod are adjusted to give the needed notes (usually a conventional musical scale) and a tone suggestive of bells.

Let us consider what goes on when we strike one of the rods in a particular set which I had occasion to examine. First we will set down the lower few members of the list of characteristic frequencies belonging to this rod:

$$P = 5 \text{ to } 10 \text{ oscillations/second (inaudible)}$$
$$Q = 180 \text{ oscillations/second}$$
$$R_a = 525 \text{ oscillations/second}$$
$$R_b = 530 \text{ oscillations/second}$$
$$S = 1063 \text{ oscillations/second}$$
$$T = 1772 \text{ oscillations/second}$$

If one plays a tape recording of the sound of this rod struck in isolation from its brothers and asks a group of musically inclined listeners to find the corresponding note on the piano, one gets two sets of responses. Some listeners say that the sound has a pitch lying somewhat above F_3 (or somewhat below $F_3\sharp$), and some assign the pitch at a little above C_5. In either case the listener tends to be aware of the other pitch that is identified by some members of the group, and he is also aware of the very high-pitched sound belonging to what is labeled T (near A_6), but despite these distractions he feels quite comfortable that his own assignment is the most reasonable one. Neither group of listeners has any hesitation in saying that the set of rods of which this is a member will sound a well-tuned musical scale.

At first glance either one of the two pitches assigned to the rod's sound seems plausible. If you consult figure 2.1, it seems quite clear that Q lies about halfway between the frequencies conventionally associated with F_3 and $F_3\#$. Similarly, both of the closely spaced frequencies that we have called R_a and R_b imply a pitch slightly above that assigned the name C_5. We are now faced with some difficulties. First of all, why does no one assign the pitch name in accordance with the frequency of the fourth vibrational type (the sound labeled S)? Secondly, why does no one assert that the pitch is truly to be given as being a trifle above A_6, as is implied by T standing by itself?

Our first reaction to the questions posed above is to ask whether it is not true that the initial amplitudes (and hence the loudnesses) of the vibrations that are attracting our attention are not extremely large compared with those belonging to the other vibrations. If this were to prove correct, then we would find an easy way to understand the responses of our listeners. One group would fasten its attention on the lower one of the predominant sounds, and the other group would express a preference for the paired upper one. Actual measurement of the amplitudes of the various characteristic sinusoids recorded on the tape shows that our projected explanation is totally unusable. If we compare the strengths of the various sinusoids in my particular recording to those belonging to Q, taking the latter to be of unit size, the list is as follows: 1.0, (10.0 and 6.3), 22.0, 44.7. That is, the vibration labeled R_a has 10 times the initial amplitude of the Q os-

cillation, while R_b has an initial amplitude 6.3 times larger, and so on. These measured amplitude relations show that some of our listeners assign the pitch in agreement with the lowest frequency audible component in our sound despite the fact that higher frequency components of the tone are many times stronger. Other listeners assign the pitch to agree with the next two paired (closely matching) characteristic oscillations even though the fourth and fifth members of the collection are again very much stronger. In no case does anyone assign the pitch on the basis of the very strong fourth vibration (S) or the even stronger fifth one (T).

At this stage the thoughtful reader may be led to ask whether the halving times of the various vibrations are not able to give a clue as to what is going on, the idea being that perhaps one's ear assigns pitch to agree with that implied by long-persisting characteristic oscillations, whether or not they are loudly produced. The answer to this question is easily found. Measurement shows that the halving times of all the oscillations are roughly alike. Furthermore, one finds that our two sets of pitch assignments are not changed when the halving times are drastically altered by holding one's finger, or, better, a wad of cotton, lightly against the rod near its anchorage while it is being struck.

Our investigation of people's pitch assignments for the sound of rods in a clock chime has shown us that their relation to the physical nature of the sounds is not explained at the present point in our study. However, we have had the opportunity to become familiar with the way in which one investigates an acoustical phenomenon by means of physicists' experiments intertwined with listeners' experiments, under the guidance of temporary hypotheses and speculations that are based on our understanding so far. At the end of this chapter we will be in a position to summarize the behavior of our hearing mechanism when it is supplied with composite sounds. We will find that pitch assignments are made in part with the help of information concerning the *relations* between the frequency components and not simply on the basis of the frequencies themselves. Meanwhile let us look at some more examples of the behavior of ears confronted by clangorous sounds.

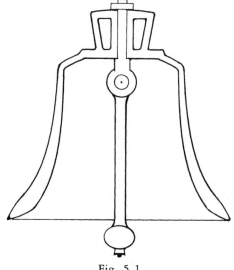

Fig. 5.1.

5.3. Perceived Pitch III: *Bells*

For centuries music has been made by striking church bells of different pitches, and it will serve our acoustical purposes to inquire into the arrangement of the characteristic vibration frequencies they produce. Not only are these sounds interesting in their own right, they will also help us in our thinking about the sounds produced by the rods of a clock chime which we examined in the previous section. This is especially worthwhile because the clock chimes were invented as a simple way to get sounds that roughly imitate those from real bells.

Musical bells are made in all sizes from small hand bells to large church bells weighing as much as fifteen tons. It is significant that regardless of their size, musical bells have a shape very similar to that shown in figure 5.1. This is a shape that has developed over several centuries to give what is considered an appropriate sound.

In the latter part of the nineteenth century, Lord Rayleigh, a distinguished British physicist who contributed enormously to our understanding of acoustics, made a study of eight tuned church bells which were used together in his own parish church at Terling.[1] It is interesting that the bells of the Terling Peal were used as a set even though they were cast in various years between 1623 and 1888. Bells of this sort give the listener a well-defined sense of pitch, and the members of this set are acceptably similar in the nature of the sounds they produce. An inter-comparison of the characteristic oscillations of some of these bells will teach us a great deal about how they vibrate and how we hear them.

Because each of these bells was intended to sound a definite note of the musical scale, we expect that the characteristic frequencies of one bell will be quite different from those of another bell in the set. Since each of the five bells we will consider possesses a half dozen characteristic frequencies that are of interest to us, we could easily become lost in a welter of numbers if no way can be found to simplify our handling of this mass of data. Let us devise an artifice that puts them all upon a common basis. Many people have noticed that a phonograph record which was recorded so as to give proper reproduction at a turntable speed of 33 ⅓ r.p.m. will, when played at 45 r.p.m., produce its music transposed up by an amount which a musician would say is a trifle more than a perfect fourth. That is, every note in the music is transferred in pitch to a spot that is slightly more than five semitones farther up the musical scale. Similarly, playing this same record at 78 r.p.m. is found to transpose the music by about 2⅔ semitones more than an octave. This suggests that we imagine our bells to be recorded and then played back on an adjustable-speed phonograph or tape machine, using carefully chosen speeds which make all the bells sound at the same perceived pitch. Let us choose the playback speed to be such that all bells sound at a pitch that listeners agree on calling C, and it will be the one termed C_4, found at the middle of the piano. You may recall that this pitch is conventionally associated with a repetition rate of 261.6/second. A band-pass filter can be used to measure the characteristic frequencies present in the played-back sounds. The five rows of table 5.1 give Rayleigh's measurements converted to a common basis of perceived pitch by making use of my own electrical synthesis of these sounds plus a record-and-playback procedure similar to the one described above. The correctness of my pitch adjustments was confirmed by a group of about twenty musically experienced listeners.

A glance at the column giving the first (lowest) characteristic frequency (P) for each bell shows that none of these frequencies seem to match the expected 261.6/second oscillation rate. The pitches implied by the first oscillation frequencies of the bells are scattered over a range of about a semitone and a half *above* the expected frequency. In a similar fashion we notice that the pitches we would assign to the second characteristic frequencies (Q) of these bells randomly cover a range of almost two-and-a-half semitones.

It is a common experience among musicians to make an error of an exact octave either way in comparing the pitches of unfamiliar sounds with the notes of a piano. We are therefore led to ask

Table 5.1

Frequencies of a Set of Church Bells

| Bell Number | Characteristic Frequencies: | | | | |
	Lowest (P)	2nd (Q)	3rd (R)	4th (S)	5th (T)
1	278	467	620	786	1046
2	286	458	590	832	982
3	267	532	641	764	1071
4	275	512	620	796	1026
5	272	544	622	819	1033

Note: To aid comparison, the sound of each bell has been transposed by variable-speed tape recorder so that its pitch matches the piano middle C (C_4) when the two sounds are presented alternately.

whether the second characteristic frequency (Q) is not close to the frequency associated with C_5. Again we find that none of the bells have frequencies that lie close to the 523/second oscillation frequency that is normally associated with C_5.

Continuing our examination of the table, we find that the third characteristic frequencies (R) of these bells agree only crudely with one another. Their pitches would agree within about a semitone if they could be excited independently of the other bell sounds. We do not, however, find any obvious relation between the R sounds from our bells and the frequencies belonging to the various musical Cs, nor do we find any for the more scattered frequencies for S, so we turn our attention to the column listing the fifth characteristic frequency for each bell. Here again we find a random spread of a little more than a semitone.

The first conclusion we can draw from our examination of the sounds of church bells is that accurate tuning of their pitch does not require exactitude in the adjustment of each one of the various characteristic frequencies. Further experiment shows also that the amplitudes of the various components in the sound may be drastically varied with only small alterations in the perceived pitch. Students of musical perception have not, unfortunately, given much attention to bell-like sounds. They have however made extensive studies of simpler sounds which have the same curious properties. We will return at the end of the chapter to describe the general habits followed by our ears in assigning pitch to composite sounds. At the moment, however, we must satisfy ourselves with simply noticing that the bells have called our attention to the *possi-*

bility of sounds whose pitches are not connected in some obvious manner to the frequencies of their components. Our experience with the clock chimes has also illustrated the general fact that the pitch assignments made by our ears are quite insensitive to the relative amplitudes of the various components. By the way, comparison of Rayleigh's measurements with those made on over one hundred bells manufactured recently in Germany shows that our observations are a fair representation of the basic properties of bells as they exist today.[2]

Let us turn our attention now to the sounds which arise from musical strings such as those of a piano or a guitar. For these sounds we find that there are indeed easily detected numerical relationships between the characteristic frequencies and the repetition rates by means of which we have agreed to measure pitch. These numerical relationships turn out to give us clues to an understanding of what is going on when we listen to the more mysterious sounds of chimes and bells.

5.4. Frequency Components of the Sounds from a Plucked or Struck String: *Guitars and Pianos*

The piano is a very familiar musical instrument whose sound is impulsively excited; a similar close cousin is the guitar. From our present preliminary point of view, the differences between struck piano strings and the plucked strings of a guitar or a harpsichord are only matters of detail. In all three instruments a tightly stretched string is abruptly set in motion and afterwards left free to oscillate in the ways that are characteristic of this particular kind of elongated vibrator.

We at once discover that the lowest characteristic frequency (P) of a string is almost exactly that corresponding to the conventional repetition rate that we assigned to a note of the same pitch. Because a guitar is particularly easy to experiment with, we will begin by using a band-pass filter to sort out the various damped sinusoidal oscillations characteristic of the strings of a guitar.

I have made several sets of measurements on my daughter's nylon-stringed guitar which will serve very well as the basis for our preliminary study of the vibrations of strings. In order to make it easier for us to discover the common features among the vibrations of the set of six strings, we will once again make use of the artifice of recording the sounds of all the strings at one speed and playing them back at another one, so as to transpose them all to the same pitch. For arithmetical convenience, we will record and play back in such a way that the first characteristic frequency (P) of every string is translated to the common value of 300 oscillations/second. The results of one set of measurements of the guitar are displayed in table 5.2. In the left-hand column we find the string number and note name for each string as it is found on the guitar. All of the frequencies under the heading P are given as 300/second, in accordance with our recording prescription. A glance at the column marked Q shows immediately that the second characteristic oscillation frequency of every string is very close to 600/second. Similarly we notice that R always lies very near to 900/second, while S and T are closely equal to 1200 and 1500 oscillations/second. If our table had been extended further we would observe the continuation of this simple-appearing behavior. In every case the characteristic frequencies of our guitar strings are found to be very nearly whole-number multiples of the lowest frequency that is characteristic of each string. For example, for the G string the ratios P/P, Q/P, R/P, . . . are 1.000, 2.007, 3.009, 4.015, 5.014. Notice how much more orderly these frequency ratios appear than do the ones listed in section 5.1 for the glockenspiel bar. Before we become too charmed by the simplicity inherent in this whole-number relationship, we should try to determine whether the discrepancies between the simple whole-number relation and the measured frequencies of the

Table 5.2
Measured Values of Components of a Set of Guitar Strings

String Number	Pitch Name	Characteristic Frequencies:				
		Lowest (P)	2nd (Q)	3rd (R)	4th (S)	5th (T)
1	E_4	300	600.9	900.2	1200.0	1500.9
2	B_3	300	599.2	900.0	1200.1	1500.0
3	G_3	300	602.0	902.8	1204.6	1504.1
4	D_3	300	600.6	900.0	1204.5	1508.2
5	A_2	300	595.4	897.0	1198.1	1500.0
6	E_2	300	603.7	900.0	1201.9	1500.0

Note: To aid comparison, the sounds of the strings have been transposed by variable-speed tape recorder to make the frequencies of their lowest component match.

strings are the result of experimental error in the measurement (so that they may be ignored here), or whether they are the manifestation of further complexities that we will perhaps need to study later. When the string frequencies are carefully re-measured by various techniques, we find that these discrepancies truly belong to the guitar and its strings. However, we do observe that re-tuning the instrument to a slightly higher pitch will *rearrange* the discrepancies.

In table 5.3 we see two examples of the effect of tuning the guitar up from its earlier pitch to one about half a semitone higher. We see here an alteration in every case of the discrepancy between the whole-number relation and the measured frequencies. One also finds that installation of a set of new strings or even a drastic change in the weather will cause a similar rearrangement of the measured discrepancies. When the frets are used in the usual way to get various pitches by altering the length of string which can vibrate, once again it turns out that the characteristic frequencies produced by the string display the same general pattern of whole-number regularity plus discrepancy.

Analogous measurements of the strings of a piano show that the frequency ratios are extremely close to being whole numbers (integers) through the middle part of the keyboard. The discrepancies observed for strings in the top and bottom two octaves of the piano range are found to be large.

What departure from the integer relations one observes can itself be resolved into two parts: (1) a smoothly varying progressive increase of the successive ratios above the integer values, and (2) small, randomly appearing but perfectly definite fluctuations above and below these smoothly modified numbers.

Let us distill the results of our preliminary investigations of impulsively excited strings into a few sentences. Careful measurements of the lowest, second, third, etc., characteristic frequencies (P, Q, R, . . .) for strings mounted on musical instruments show us that there are two major features to be recognized in the sounds:

1. The upper characteristic frequencies are found to be almost exactly whole-number multiples of the first one.
2. Small departures from the whole-number ratios are commonly observed.

We will find that both aspects of the behavior of strings are of musical importance. At the present moment we should

Table 5.3

Effect of Re-tuning on a String's Characteristic Frequency Relationships

| | Characteristic Frequencies: | | | | |
	Lowest (P)	2nd (Q)	3rd (R)	4th (S)	5th (T)
3rd string, old tuning	300	602.0	902.8	1204.6	1504.1
3rd string, new tuning	300	602.3	901.5	1202.3	1503.1
6th string, old tuning	300	603.7	900.0	1201.9	1500.0
6th string, new tuning	300	598.6	898.2	1198.7	1496.4

Note: Tunings have been transposed by tape to make the lowest characteristic frequencies match.

notice some of the remarkable implications of the first of these observations.

5.5. Sounds Having Whole-Number Frequency Ratios

Let us imagine that we have available to us a hypothetical string which, when plucked or struck, vibrates in a family of characteristic damped sinusoidal oscillations whose frequencies are arranged in an *exact* whole-number relation; that is, Q is exactly 2P, R = 3P, S = 4P, and so on.

Digression on the Numerical Labeling of Natural Frequencies.
We can express this whole-number relationship between oscillation frequencies very compactly as follows. If we use the letter n to stand for any one of the integers—that is, n = 1, or 2, or 3, etc.— and if the characteristic frequencies are given the serially numbered names f_1, f_2, f_3 instead of our alphabetical names, then the nth one of these frequencies can be referred to as f_n. The desired integer relation between the successive string frequencies can be written in a mathematically tidy fashion as follows:

$$f_n = nf_1$$

One reads this mathematical sentence thus: "f sub-n is equal to n times f sub-1," meaning that the nth frequency is n times as large as the first one in the set.

In the language of chapter 2, we can say that the repetition rate for any one of our idealized string's sinusoidal oscillations is a whole number times the repetition rate associated with its lowest frequency oscillation. Let us look into what happens when account is taken of the fact that the string is actually vibrating with a whole set of integrally related frequencies.

Suppose that for conceptual simplicity we assign an imaginary drummer to each characteristic oscillation of our string, giving him the job of tapping with a repetition rate equal to that measured for his "own" string oscillation. The whole-number relation between the string frequencies then requires that the drummer assigned to keep time with the second characteristic oscillation should beat twice as fast as drummer number 1. Similarly drummer 3 taps three times as fast

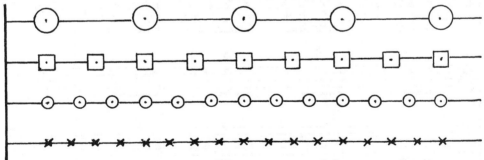

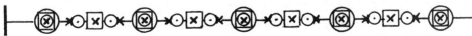

Fig. 5.2.   Pattern Made by Tapping Rates Having a Whole-Number Relation

as drummer 1, and so on. The upper four lines of figure 5.2 show the timing of the successive taps produced by the first four of our set of drummers. The bottom line of the diagram shows the resulting rhythmic pattern that one would hear. Every drummer strikes in unison with the blows of drummer 1, giving a strongly marked beat, and drummers 2, 4, . . . strike at the midpoints between these accented taps, giving a somewhat less accented tap. The important thing to notice is that the repetition rate of the *complete* rhythmic pattern produced by the composite set of tappings is exactly the same as that of the lowest frequency member (see sec. 2.3, "Repetition Rates of Rhythmic Patterns"). Musicians should not find this idea hard to understand if they compare my explanation above with what they would expect from a rhythmic pattern written out as in figure 5.3.

Let us look now at some examples using sinusoidal disturbances instead of drumbeats. The top two parts of figure 5.4 show sinusoids whose frequencies dif-

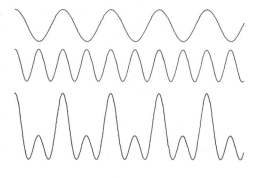

Fig. 5.4.   Combination of Sinusoids Having a Whole-Number Frequency Relation

fer by a factor of two. If our simplified string could be excited by some means that sets into motion only the first two of its characteristic oscillations, then the oscilloscope picture produced from a microphone in its neighborhood would look

Fig. 5.3.

something like the curve shown in the third part of the figure. This curve is produced by the addition of the two curves immediately above it. Notice that the repetition time of the somewhat spiky composite curve (and hence its repetition rate) is exactly that of the f_1 component at the top of the diagram. The bottom part of the figure shows the result of combining additional sinusoids, so that the curve is that belonging to the sum of the first six oscillations in our specially chosen set.

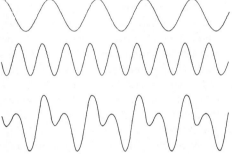

Fig. 5.5. This figure is identical with the upper three sections of figure 5.4 except that the second component has been displaced. Note that the repetition time is unaffected by this change.

Figure 5.5 shows a slightly modified version of the upper three sections of figure 5.4. This time the f_2 component is "slid over" in time so that it no longer has every second upward excursion coincident with every upward excursion of the f_1 component. We notice that the summation of these two oscillations gives a resultant pattern whose shape is different from the one obtained before, but once again we see that the repetition time is equal to that of the lowest frequency (f_1) oscillation.

Adding components whose frequencies are in whole-number relationships has

shown us something that will prove to be very important to our understanding not only of the physical basis of tone color but also of the special relationships between notes which underlie formal music all over the world. Let us set down some of the properties of the class of sounds that would be made by our hypothetical strings.

1. No matter what the strength of excitation of the various oscillations, the repetition rate for the whole signal as it reaches a microphone (or our ears) would be exactly that of the lowest frequency sinusoidal component that is characteristic of the string.

2. Because the net repetition rate of the vibration is independent of how or where the string is struck, one would always get the same perceived pitch sensation for the string sound. This means that *the pitch is unambiguous.*

Digression: Sounds with Only Even Harmonics.

In the strictest of logic, one might ask about a possible inadequacy of item 1 above. Imagine an ingenious excitation method that fails to excite the odd-numbered oscillations, so that only f_2, f_4, f_6, . . . are present. These may be written out as follows:

$$f_2 = 2f_1 = 1 \times (2f_1)$$
$$f_4 = 4f_1 = 2 \times (2f_1)$$
$$f_6 = 6f_1 = 3 \times (2f_1)$$
etc.

This shows that our new set of frequency components is itself constructed out of integer multiples of a new basic frequency whose value is $(2f_1)$. The repetition rate is therefore doubled, and the whole game begins again. We would perceive this altered sound as having a pitch one octave higher than the normally excited one.

As a practical matter, it is not particularly difficult to arrange peculiar excitations of the sort described in the preceding paragraph, and if one were to meet such a situation it could easily be recognized as such with the help of simple auxiliary experiments. One would need only to pluck or strike the string at random spots once or twice in order to find out the true nature of the string.

There is something intellectually very attractive about the apparent simplicity of sounds made up of components having integer frequency ratios, and it is easy to devise lengthy numerological games based on their presumed properties. Before we fall into this trap, however, it would be advisable to find out whether such sounds can in fact be generated. If such sounds can be generated, we then must ask whether our ears and nervous system deal with them in a way that corresponds at all with experiencing the sounds from real strings. The first question can be answered affirmatively in two ways:

1. A truly uniform slender string of suitable material, stretched tightly enough between sufficiently rigid supports, will produce sounds whose components have frequencies that are in very nearly perfect integer relation. The sounds from such a string differ only subtly from those produced by a string vibrating under less formalistic conditions. That is, nothing drastic happens to the perceived sound as long as the string has *nearly* integer frequency relations.

2. We find that there is a large class of familiar sound sources that normally produce sounds whose frequency components are found to be related in the *precisely* whole-number manner that we postulated for our hypothetical strings. Examples of sources of this kind are very common. The human voice is the most familiar one, while the woodwind and brass instruments join with the violin family to provide orchestral examples. These diverse sound sources have one common element in their nature that sets them apart from the bells, chimes, and strings we have considered

so far. Instead of simply ringing (and decaying away) in response to an impulsive stimulus, all of these instruments are capable of producing *sustained* sounds. They are devices that are capable of converting the steady flow of air from a man's lungs, or the steady motion of the bow in his hand, into the oscillatory vibrations which give rise to the sound we hear. We shall see in a later chapter that only under very special circumstances can such devices be persuaded to maintain steady oscillations whose frequency components are *not* in an exact whole-number relation to the basic repetition rate.

It turns out that the vast majority of our musical listening experiences are with sounds whose frequency components are in exact whole-number relation, or very nearly so. It is not surprising, then, that the formal structure of music (wherever it has developed over the world) is strongly influenced by the properties of sounds each of which has whole-number relations among its components. We also find that many subtleties in music arise through the slight *in*harmonicities which are present in the tones of some instruments.

This book has opened with an investigation of impulsive and heterogeneous sounds from struck objects, not only because of the simplicity of initial exposition but also as a means for underlining the special nature of the sound-producers that man has selected for his musical activities. It is time therefore to return to the sounds of bells and chimes in order to compare them with the sounds of plucked or struck strings.

5.6. The Pitch of Chimes and Bells:
Hints of Pattern Recognition

We have found that the characteristic frequencies that make up any one sound from any one of the commoner orchestral instruments are arranged as exact (or very nearly exact) integer multiples of a certain basic frequency. It is this basic frequency component that determines the repetition rate of the sound we hear and also, as we have learned, its musical pitch. Let us use this knowledge to help ourselves gain some understanding of the way in which we assign pitches to chimes and bells, whose characteristic frequencies do not arrange themselves in whole-number relationships.

Digression on Terminology:
Some Partials Are Harmonic.

It will save a great deal of circumlocution if we provide ourselves with some terminology carefully chosen for the description of the various components making up the sound we are dealing with. First of all, in any sound made up of sinusoidal components, we will continue to assign identifying letters from the latter part of the alphabet, or serial numbers, assigning them according to their order, beginning at the lowest one. That is, we will call these frequencies P, Q, R, . . . or f_1, f_2, f_3, . . . Sometimes it will be useful to refer to these components as the partials of the sound in question. When this word is used, we will understand that no particular relationship is to be assumed between the frequencies of these partials; their frequencies may or may not have a whole-number relationship. These components will still be referred to by their serial numbers as first partial (referring to the component labeled P or f_1), second partial (also known as Q or f_2), etc.

We turn now to the special case of sounds in which the frequencies of the various sinusoidal partials are whole-number multiples of some basic repetition rate. The sinusoidal component whose frequency matches that of the repetition rate will be referred to as the fundamental *component, and its frequency as the* fundamental frequency. *It is often referred to also as the* first harmonic. *The partial whose frequency is exactly double that of the fundamental will be said to have a frequency which is the* second harmonic *of the fundamental*

frequency. Similarly we will say that sinusoidal oscillations running at three times the fundamental frequency are vibrating at the third harmonic *of the fundamental frequency.*

We will have to be very strict in our terminology or endless confusion can result. The word harmonic *is to be used only when we mean to imply an exact whole-number frequency relationship. To help make things clear, we may notice that the partials of a guitar string have frequencies which are very nearly, but not exactly, harmonics of the frequency of the first (lowest) partial.*

We learned earlier in this chapter that musically experienced people won't necessarily agree on what pitch to assign to the sound of a grandfather clock chime. In the context of our present understanding of musical sounds, we may wonder whether the frequencies of the chimes' partials can be recognized by our nervous system as belonging to two differently organized sequences of harmonics. That is, can we find hints of a series of harmonics whose fundamental corresponds to the approximate F_3 that some listeners hear? Similarly, can we detect signs of a harmonic series whose fundamental implies the pitch just above the C_5 perceived by others? In our earlier investigation of this sound we recognized that the second partial has a frequency consistent with one of these pitch assignments while the two closely spaced partials (which were labeled R_a and R_b) are associated with the other one. Our earlier difficulty stemmed from our inability to dispose of all the other partials making up the tone; could these be members of harmonic series based on the assigned pitches?

Figure 5.6 shows the frequencies of all the partials up through f_4 (S) laid out as dots along a frequency scale. Above the frequency axis of this diagram we see a pair of arrows located at frequencies corre-

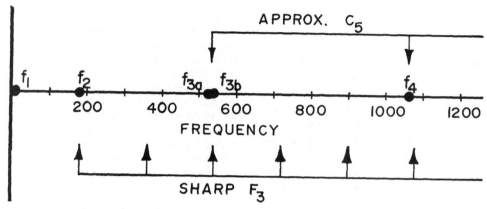

Fig. 5.6. Assignment of Pitches to Sound from a Clock Chime

sponding to a fundamental, belonging to the note C_5, and its second harmonic. The fundamental arrow is pointing at the pair of Rs, while the arrow for the second harmonic points almost exactly at the measured S. It seems possible, then, that our ears can seize on the relationship of these two strong components and accept them jointly as the two lowest members (fundamental and second harmonic) of a set of partials belonging to a sound whose pitch is near C_5.

Below the frequency axis we find in similar fashion a set of arrows indicating the frequencies making up the set (fundamental and its harmonics) belonging to the sharp-pitched F_3 which we associated with the measured f_2 (which was labeled Q earlier). This time we find that the arrows corresponding to the fundamental, the third, and the sixth harmonics point very nearly at the dots indicating the measured components Q, R, and S.

Our search for integer relations among the frequency components of a struck chime rod has been reasonably successful, in that it gives results that seem consistent with the *hypothesis* that our ears assign pitch (when possible) on the basis of

any whole-number sequences they can find.

We turn our attention next to the bell sounds, to see whether they give any support to our hypothesis that pitch is assigned on the basis of approximately whole-number frequency relationships. The individual lines of figure 5.7 show the frequencies of the first five partials for the first five bells in the Terling Peal, laid out by means of dots on a frequency axis in exactly the same way as was done for the chime rod. The dashed vertical lines appearing on the diagram indicate the fundamental repetition frequency and its harmonics belonging to a reference sound whose pitch matches that of the bells as made uniform by a variable-speed recording device.

Inspection of the line corresponding to bell 1 shows that the first partial (marked P) has a frequency quite close to that assumed for the fundamental. Furthermore, we see that partials 4 and 5 agree extremely well with harmonics 3 and 4 of the pitch reference tone. We note that partials 2 and 3 do not seem to agree with any member of the reference harmonic series.

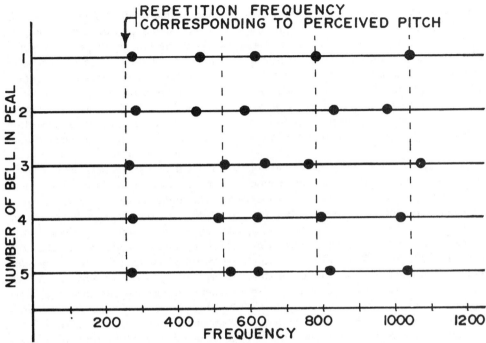

Fig. 5.7.   Frequency Components of Bells Adjusted to the Same Pitch

Skipping now to bells 3, 4, and 5, we find that partials 1, 2, 4, and 5 agree quite well with the fundamental and harmonics 2, 3, and 4 belonging to our pitch reference. Partial 3 never seems to fit in. Bell 2 does not show such a clear-cut relation, although the frequencies of partials 1 and 4 are roughly equal to those of the fundamental and third harmonic of our reference sound. Interestingly enough, most listeners feel quite uneasy about assigning pitch to this bell, even though they find no difficulty with the other ones.

Looking over the data we come to realize that for a bell to have a reasonably well-defined pitch (so that it can be matched with a normal sort of tone having harmonic partials), our ears do not demand any particular set of component frequencies from it. That is, our ears do not demand that the same (only approximately harmonic) partials serve identically as the "pointers" in the sounds for all the bells. All that is required is a sufficient number of sufficiently consistent clues. The frequencies of the skillet clang listed on p. 43 are similar to these bell sounds in that they are not harmonically related.

5.7. Another Pitch Assignment Phenomenon: *The Effect of Suppressing Upper or Lower Partials*

In the previous section of this chapter we found ourselves thinking about the ways in which our ears respond to sounds fed to them from bells and chimes. We noticed that the act of assigning pitch to sounds of this kind appeared to involve the detection of an *approximate* regularity in the frequency pattern of the partial components of the sound. Let us turn our attention now to a different kind of stimulus for our ears. This time we will experiment with the effect on pitch of removing one or more components from a collection of sinusoids whose frequencies are harmonically related.

We have already seen that a sound made up of sinusoidal components whose frequencies are whole-number multiples of some fundamental frequency (for example, the musical tone A_3 which is made up of components whose frequencies are 220, 440, 660, 880, . . . oscillations/second) forms a complex disturbance whose mathematical repetition rate is exactly equal to that of the fundamental component. It takes only a moment's thought to realize that since every one of the components "comes out even" at this repetition rate, one should be able to add or delete components from this collection without altering the repetition rate, at least as far as the physicist is concerned.

It is easy to verify in the laboratory that lopping off the higher frequency members of our collection of harmonics does not alter the perceived pitch of the sound. In a less rigorous fashion we can all verify the correctness of this observation by playing with the treble tone control knob on a high-fidelity amplifier as some music (or preferably a single note) is played. Changing this knob serves to strengthen or weaken the higher harmonics of the tone as it is projected to our ears by the loudspeaker. We certainly are aware of alterations in the sound, but pitch changes are not among them. We have already met a prime example of the fact that pitch can be independent of

changes in harmonic content. The single-frequency sound produced by a properly struck tuning fork serves perfectly well as a pitch reference for an oboist whose instrument generates a tone containing a dozen or more harmonics.

The stability of our pitch perceptions as the higher harmonics are removed from the tone is perhaps to be considered obvious on the face of it. The fundamental component by itself appears able to define the pitch. One might be tempted to say that the higher harmonics have no particular role, that they are merely present and do not provide conflicting cues. Let us check up on this apparent simplicity by performing new experiments in the laboratory, progressively removing not the higher components but the lower ones, beginning with the fundamental. Suppose that once again we start with a sound constructed of a 220/second fundamental sinusoid plus (for example) the next five partials whose frequencies are 440, 660, 880, 1100, and 1320/second. If we electronically remove the 220/second fundamental component from this collection, our ears will nevertheless assign the pitch in accordance with a 220/second repetition rate. If we eliminate the second harmonic component (440/second) as well as the fundamental from our tone, we still have no hesitation assigning the pitch exactly as before. As a matter of fact, removal of all the components except the highest two in our collection of six will still leave us with a sound to which we unhesitatingly assign the original pitch.

We have everyday experience which provides informal confirmation and generalization of this astonishing result. We are familiar with the fact that music remains perfectly recognizable when it is played on an inexpensive pocket transistor radio. The ordinary pitch relations of music remain exactly the same whether it is heard "live," or via a good high-fidelity system, or over a small radio. One can follow the various voices without difficulty on even the smallest radio. On such a radio, a downward running scale on the piano, for example, can be followed easily to its lowest note, which has a frequency of 27.5/second. This is true even though the small radio is hardly able to emit an audible sinusoid below a frequency of about 200/second (approximately G just below middle C on the piano)! As a result, the radio itself is operating on all of the bass instruments in exactly the same way as did our laboratory apparatus. In short, our experiments indicate that the ear is able to assign pitches and even recognize other musical relationships upon the basis of only a few harmonically related partials from each of the various instruments. Furthermore, we seem to have found that the pitch assignment made by our ears in this case is that which agrees with the pitch of whatever fundamental component is *implied* by the exact whole-number relationships between the frequencies of the sound components that are supplied to them.

5.8. Pitch Assignments and Frequency Patterns: *Summary and Conclusions*

In earlier sections of this chapter we found ourselves thinking about ways in which our ears respond to the signals fed to them from bells and chimes. We were led to suspect that the act of assigning pitch to a collection of component frequencies is one in which our nervous system copes with elaborate and irregular-seeming sets of signals, managing to sep-

arate traces of the "interesting" patterns from a welter of detail. Let us review the phenomena before giving a description of what the ear and the nervous system are doing in all these cases.

1. The tuning fork and the glockenspiel bar appear fairly simple to understand. There is no harmonic relation between the characteristic frequencies, these frequencies are far apart, and we simply hear two or more sounds having different pitches.

2. The sounds from plucked and struck musical strings give us an almost equally simple-appearing example since they provide us with a large number of partials that are arranged in an almost exact integer relationship. The frequency pattern of the partials so closely matches its exactly harmonic prototype that it is a little hard to imagine the complexity of the pitch assignment process that is actually going on.

Digression on the Repetition Rates of Almost-Harmonic Components.
Some people find it quite shocking to realize that because of the slight departures from integer relationships, a mathematician would calculate that the actual *repetition frequency for all the partials taken together for any one of the guitar strings of table 5.2 is of the order of 1 or 2/second, while we cheerfully assign it a pitch that matches a truly harmonic sound whose overall oscillation (fundamental plus harmonics) repeats at a rate close to 300/second.*

3. The clock chimes provide an example of a set of sounds among which several quasi-harmonic patterns co-exist. Figure 5.6 has led us to suspect that the musician who hears the pitch as being just above F_3 is responding to the fact that the frequencies of the partials Q, R_a and R_b, S, and T roughly approximate the fundamental, 3rd, 6th, and 10th harmonics of a whole-number series whose basis is near 180 oscillations/second. These partials are not

adjacent to one another, but there are enough of them to lay out a recognizable pattern. Similarly, listeners who hear the chime as being pitched at C_5 are responding to the fact that R_a and R_b taken together look like a slightly fuzzy fundamental component to go with an almost precise second harmonic provided by S. The fifth partial (T) does not fit the pattern and is clearly heard as a separate entity. The loudness of the various components has little influence on the way in which pitch is assigned here.

4. Observations made on the sounds of church bells add to our suspicion that the ear somehow picks out an approximately harmonic relationship between the various component frequencies, and assigns pitch accordingly. Deliberate experimental alteration of the amplitudes of the various components shows clearly that our pitch assignment is not sensitive to the relative strengths of the various partials. We pay attention (for pitch purposes) only to the frequencies.

5. Experiments involving the total suppression of all but two or three of the partial components of a sound having partials with harmonically related frequencies show in yet another way that pitch is assigned on the basis of an implied complete set of harmonic partials.

Everywhere in our experiments we have found indications that our nervous system processes complex sounds coming to it by seeking out whatever subsets of almost harmonically related components it can find. Each of these subsets then has a "best fitting" collection of true harmonics selected for it in the processor, and pitch is assigned on the basis of the repetition rate of these fitted components. Julius Goldstein and his co-workers have recently shown that the brain operates upon its sensory data in a manner closely analogous to the procedures followed by statisticians when they make estimations according to "the method of maximum likelihood." The better the heard components agree among themselves regarding the degree of harmonicity in their relationships, the quicker and more certain we are in our pitch decisions regarding them.[3]

Having met an apparently simple (i.e., mathematically expressible!) way in which the human nervous system operates while making pitch assignments, we should recognize the fact that we are constantly performing neurological tasks of a much more difficult sort on the stimuli coming to us from all of our senses. We have already noticed that the characteristic sounds of various struck objects can be recognized under the most unpromising conditions of recording and reproduction. We perform immensely more complicated tasks of the same sort when we recognize pieces of music when they are played on a cheap pocket radio, or when we carry on conversations in a noisy restaurant. We are able to perform equally well with our eyes. There is no difficulty in recognizing a friend from his distorted image in a fun-house mirror or a political figure from his caricature on the editorial page of a newspaper. No problem is posed by a five-year-old's simple line drawing of a house even though no house was ever built whose lines really follow those in his picture. We somehow relate the gross arrangement of lines in the drawing to the simplest aspects of the visual pattern that one can in fact receive when looking at a house.

The human nervous system displays a most remarkable ability to extract the essentials from a distorted or incomplete set of sensory data. In each case, we seem to be comparing signal patterns from the world around us with a collection of stored concepts from our earlier experience. Depending on how experienced we are and on what we plan to do once the relation of a new pattern to an old one is found, we demand more or less accuracy in the matching of details between the two patterns before we say that we have "recognized" the new one. Study of the neurological ways in which we accomplish these recognitions has been a very active business during the past few decades, and considerable progress has been made in understanding how it is done.[4] We will return to these perceptual matters in later chapters, when we take up a study of the instruments themselves and of the physical basis of music.

5.9. Examples, Experiments, and Questions

1. One can make a rather plausible imitation of the sound of a church bell by playing certain combinations of notes on

a piano. Let us consider the musical example given at the top of figure 5.8. For present purposes we will take the sound associated with the C_4 key to have exactly harmonic components whose fundamental has a frequency of 261.6/second. Similarly, the $D_5\#$ written note will be taken to mean a collection of sinusoids whose fundamental component oscillates at 622.25/second. The second part of figure 5.8 shows these frequency components by means of dots arranged in order along a line. Taking the first five of these components one by one, we see that they give a reasonably good match to the partials of the bells in the Terling Peal (see table 5.1 and fig. 5.7). Bell makers distinguish between two main kinds of bell. In one type the third partial (R) is found to lie among its neighbors in the place we have found it; in the other sort of bell, R lies higher, so that in the piano imitation one would replace $D_5\#$ by E_5.

It is interesting and worthwhile to speculate on why composers of piano

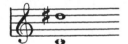

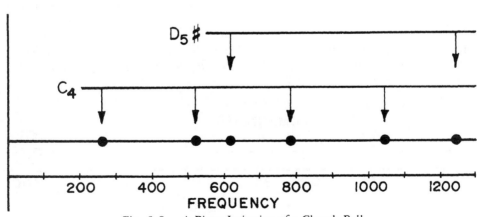

Fig. 5.8. A Piano Imitation of a Church Bell

music will often imitate bell sounds by writing combinations such as those indicated in figure 5.9.

Fig. 5.9.

2. The ways in which our ears operate to assign pitch on the basis of frequency patterns can be studied by asking a listener to identify various little tunes played with sound sources containing components that are carefully chosen to be in some sort of harmonic relationship implying a fundamental frequency. Let us play such a perception game on paper by searching for the familiar tune which is hidden in the following sequence of eight composite sounds (assume that the duration of each is one beat):

Frequency Components for
Notes of Hidden Tune

1st note	392	1176	1568
2nd note	1176	1568	1960
3rd note	880	1320	2200
4th note	1482	1976	none
5th note	392	784	1960
6th note	494	1482	2470
7th note	440	1760	2200
8th note	1172	1465	none

The rules of the game we are playing tell us that in every case the components set down for a given note are in fact exact harmonics of the fundamental frequency normally associated with the pitch of that note.

Most of us are not very good at recognizing patterns among numbers written out on a printed page. However, we are often able to recognize them when they are expressed in pictorial form. Suppose the components of each of these sounds are laid out along a frequency scale of the sort used in figure 5.6. It is usually not difficult then to figure out what fundamental frequency is implied by the components. Figure 5.10 shows an example of such a lay-out constructed for the first note in our little ditty. Heavy dots are drawn at positions corresponding to the frequencies of 392, 1176, and 1568 oscillations per second. If one squints a little at the diagram so that only the circles are easily seen, it is not hard to realize that they are evenly spaced members of a sequence having a missing component just below 800/second. In other words, we are dealing with a frequency pattern made up of the fundamental, plus its third and fourth harmonics; the second harmonic is missing. Once we have discovered that the component at 392/second defines the fundamental frequency, it is not difficult to look it up in figure 2.1 and discover that we are listening to a peculiar form of the note G_4

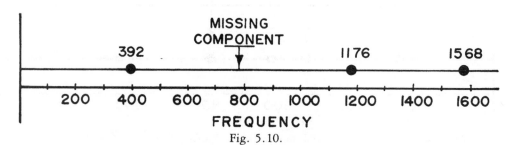

Fig. 5.10.

just above piano middle C. The rest of the notes can be worked out in an exactly similar fashion. Notice that in this exercise we are using our eyes to find a visual regularity, in a manner chosen to be the exact analog to what our ears would be doing to recognize the tune if it were to be played from the tabulated set of frequencies.

3. A flute player having a good instrument and a well-developed embouchure can smoothly vary the strengths of the odd-numbered sinusoidal components of his sustained tone relative to the strengths of the even-numbered components (while keeping the overall loudness of the sound roughly constant). This ability permits him to illustrate a number of features of our pitch perception process. For example, he can produce the note A_4 (just above piano middle C) whose fundamental component oscillates at 440/second, along with significant amounts of the first half dozen *exactly harmonic* components which lie at 880, 1320, and 1760/second (and so forth). The pitch of this tone is well-defined. As the player alters his manner of blowing and progressively weakens the odd partials relative to the even ones, the pitch continues where it was, even when only the slightest traces of the odd-numbered 440 and 1320/second components are left in the tone. Beyond a certain point, however, the listener comes to realize that he is listening to a flute that is no longer playing A_4, but rather the note A_5 an octave higher, having therefore a fundamental at 880/second, with second and third harmonics located at 1760 and 2640/second. If the player is sufficiently skillful, the listener is unsure exactly when the transition takes place, and if several listeners participate they are not likely to agree on

the time of transition. If the player continues his blowing in the manner that is heard as an A_5 and then gradually reverts to his original sound, our listeners will continue to hear A_5 even when considerable amounts of 440 and 1320/second components have been reintroduced. Eventually the pitch is re-assigned back to A_4, with the same indefiniteness in the listeners' choice of the transition time.

Here we have an example of a definite frequency pattern smoothly turning into a different one, with the possibility of traveling between the two patterns. Our ears will recognize one of them when it is clearcut, and will retain this recognition through a considerable region of overlap before they are forced to notice the other pattern. How one reacts to the overlap region depends on the context in which it is heard. In the present case the context is dominated by the previously heard definite sound. If the listener were, on the other hand, asked to listen to a regularly repeated sequence of alternating A_4 and A_5, the flute player could slip in a borderline tone and it would be cheerfully accepted as being the expected member of the alternating octave sequence.

4. When a flute player snaps closed the keys on his instrument, he can produce a series of hollow popping sounds whose pitches are approximately equal to those of his low register octave (C_4 to C_5). The sinusoidal frequency components of any one of these damped impulsive sounds are, curiously enough, *not* in an integer sequence, despite the fact that when blown, a flute produces a tone whose components are in *precisely* integer relationship. When one snaps keys to produce the note F_4, for example, the lowest component has a frequency f_1 near 349/second, as expected for this note,

while f_2 is about 705/second instead of being located at the second harmonic, which is at
$2f_1 = 2 \times 349/\text{second} = 698/\text{second}$. Similarly f_3 is at about 1058/second instead of matching the third harmonic of f_1.

Because the component frequencies in the popped sound of a flute are not harmonically related, our pitch assignment is made by recognitions of approximate pattern matches, and our sense of pitch is not strongly marked. If, on the other hand, one replaces the subtly tapered head joint of the flute (with its embouchure hole and the adjustable cavity beyond it) by an accurately fitted cylindrical tube whose inside diameter is the same as that of the main flute body, the popped frequency components take on an almost exact integer relationship. Snapping the keys on this modified flute gives clear ringing pops having extremely well-defined pitches. The decay times of the sounds from this modified flute are longer than they are on the regular instrument, which contributes somewhat to the ringing clarity of the sound. A tiny wisp of cotton tucked into the open tube end will, however, bring the decay times back to normal, but the strongly marked sense of pitch will persist, because the integer frequency relationship is preserved. Note: one should not leap to the conclusion that the non-integer relationship of the impulsively excited sinusoids of a flute is a sign of imperfection in the instrument. On the contrary, if a flute were built in such a way as to give an integer relationship to such popping sounds, it would play very badly.

Notes

1. Lord Rayleigh [John William Strutt], *The Theory of Sound*, 2 vols. bound as one, 2d ed. rev. and enlarged (1894; reprint ed., New York: Dover, 1945), I:393.

2. C.-R. Schad and H. Warlimont, "Akustische Untersuchungen zum Einfluss des Werkstoffs auf den Klang von Glocken," *Acustica* 29 (1973): 1–14.

3. Julius L. Goldstein, "An optimum processor for the central formation of the pitch of complex tones," *J. Acoust. Soc. Am.* 54 (1973): 1496–1517.

4. A good entryway into current knowledge of pitch perception is via Juan G. Roederer's paperback book, *Introduction to the Physics and Psychophysics of Music* (London: English Universities Press, New York: Springer-Verlag, 1973). Most research so far has been done under conditions that exclude the effects of the listening room on the hearing process; as a result, most theories postulate pitch assignment mechanisms that would fail to work on sounds heard in a room. Recent work is less subject to this criticism. See Frederic L. Wightman and David M. Green, "The Perception of Pitch," *Am. Scientist* 62 (1974): 208–15, and Frederic L. Wightman, "The pattern-transformation model of pitch," *J. Acoust. Soc. Am.* 54 (1973): 407–16.

6

The Modes of Oscillation of Simple and Composite Systems

In the earlier chapters of this book we studied the sounds that come from vibrating objects, but we have not yet given attention to the actual motions of these objects. We have learned that every object will, when impulsively disturbed, give rise to sounds which are found to be made up of damped sinusoidal components. We also found that the frequencies of these components are characteristic of the object producing them. That is, alterations in the manner of exciting the vibrations might well alter the initial amplitudes of the oscillations, but their frequencies depend only on the structure of the object. It is our task now to understand how the mechanical structure of the vibrating object correlates with the arrangement of its characteristic frequencies, and to learn something of the way in which these vibrations are set in motion.

It is important to keep in mind that there is a distinction between instruments giving a sustained tone (such as the human voice, the bowed string instruments, and the orchestral wind instruments) and those that ring and die away, such as bells and stringed instruments that are plucked or struck. In this chapter we will limit ourselves to instruments in the latter category. Figure 6.1 indicates their basic nature: in some of them the string is pulled to one side and released (harpsichord, guitar, harp) and in some the string is struck by some kind of hammer (piano, cymbalom, and also the clavichord). When one of these strings is excited the following chain of events takes place:

string vibrates→ drives bridge→ drives soundboard→ drives air in room→
drives our ears→ → →

It must be emphasized that a string alone cannot drive the air in a room directly in a manner that our ears find useful for musical purposes. Anyone who has plucked a solid-body electric guitar with the amplifier turned off knows that the instrument is almost inaudible. The string and also the sequence of things driven by it—the bridge, the soundboard, and the room—are all vibrational systems in their own right and they have many properties in common. Because of the importance of these shared properties, we will illustrate them one by one by means of simple examples, after which we will be in a position to learn how each system connects with its neighbors in the chain of excitations.

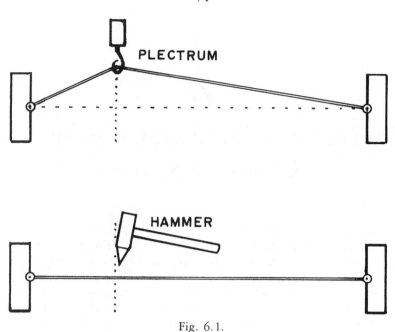

Fig. 6.1.

6.1. Properties of Simple Oscillators

In the preceding chapters we have talked about sinusoidal oscillations, but have not given much indication of the special properties that distinguish them from any other sort of sinuous back-and-forth motion which one might imagine. The following paragraphs describe an experimental arrangement (consisting of a pendulum and a phonograph turntable) which gives a definite description of sinusoidal motion in terms of its relation to circular motion.

The simple pendulum which we will use consists of a weight (commonly called a bob) hung on a string. When this bob is pulled to one side and released, it swings back and forth in a regular motion which eventually dies away. Hang such a pendulum over the center of a record

player turntable on which is placed a block of wood with a nail driven up through it. Place a lamp some distance from the pendulum and turntable so that their shadows are cast clearly upon a wall, as shown in figure 6.2. Adjust the length of the pendulum so that it makes a complete oscillation in the time of one revolution of the turntable. In other words, set the pendulum frequency to 33 1/3 or 45 oscillations/minute (0.555 or 0.750 oscillations/second), depending on the speed of the record player. If you should have trouble getting the frequency right, remember that a long pendulum oscillates at a lower frequency than does a short one. For use with a 33 1/3 rpm turntable, start out with a pendulum whose length is about 80 cm (somewhat less than a yard) and make *small* length modifications until the pendulum swings at

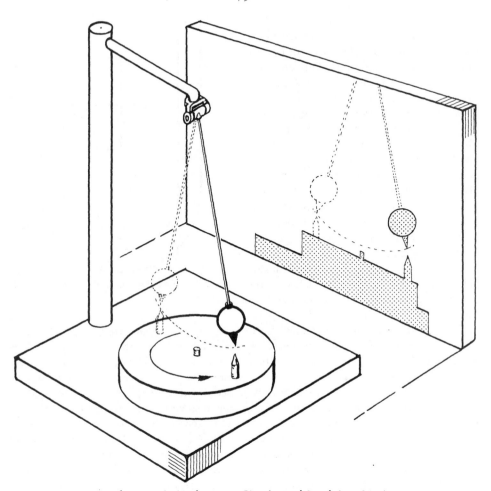

Fig. 6.2. Relation between Circular and Pendulum Motion

exactly the desired frequency. For the 45 rpm case, start with a string length somewhat less than 44 cm.

Once you have adjusted the pendulum to swing at the desired frequency, pull the bob aside and release it at the instant when the shadow of the bob is directly above the shadow of the revolving nail point. You will then find that the two shadows move back and forth exactly together on the wall. From this we can deduce that the shadow of a circularly moving nail executes a sinusoidal motion whose amplitude is equal to the radius of its path and whose frequency is equal to the number of revolutions the nail makes per unit time. We will find occasional use for the relation of sinusoidal motion to the revolution of a hypothetical point around a reference circle.

Our experiment shows us that sinusoidal motion is similar to that of the shadow of a circularly moving object. We are now in a position to seek the nature of the forces that must act on an object to produce sinusoidal motion. This question about the *causes* of the motion (as distinct from our earlier question about the *description* of the motion) is typical of the sort that has guided the development of physics since the pioneering studies of Galileo and Newton. (Galileo was a contemporary of Claudio Monteverdi and Giovanni Gabrieli. He died in 1642, the year that Newton was born. Purcell flourished during Newton's lifetime.)

Ever since the time of Newton, a concise answer has been available to our question about what forces cause sinusoidal motion: if a body feels a leftward *restoring force* proportional to its displacement when it is to the right of its central position and a similar rightward force when it is to the left, then it will execute a sinusoidal motion when it is pulled aside and released.

We can clarify our thoughts about the meaning of this "force" description of sinusoidal motion by experimenting with a U-tube partly filled with water, as shown in figure 6.3. Shaking the tube sets the mass of water into an oscillatory motion. Let us see whether the forces acting on it are of the sort prescribed for sinusoidal motion. At some instant when the water level in the left arm of the tube is a distance d below its equilibrium position, we find that there is an unbalanced slug of water of length 2d in the right arm of the tube. The weight of this unbalanced water is clearly acting in the direction that would restore the whole water column to its equilibrium configuration. If the water level is low on the right, then there will be an unbalanced slug of water in the left-hand part of the tube, so that

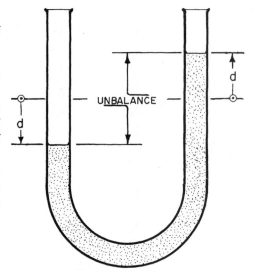

Fig. 6.3.　Oscillations of Water in a U-Tube

once again we find that a restoring force is present when the water is displaced from its equilibrium position. Furthermore, we notice that whatever the displacement d may be, the magnitude of the restoring force is proportional to d. This shows that the water in a U-tube will indeed move with a sinusoidal motion, since we have found that the whole mass of water is acted on at every instant by a restoring force supplied by the difference in level between the two arms.

The fact that oscillations generally die away in the course of time has been referred to several times so far in this book. As early as chapter 3 (see sec. 3.4) we described briefly this aspect of a motion in terms of the time required for the amplitude of oscillation to die away to half its value. We can use the liquid-filled U-tube to help us now gain an understanding of the additional forces that must be present if an indefinitely prolonged sinusoidal motion is to be converted into a *damped* motion, i.e., one that decays or dies away.

Whenever a fluid flows (at reasonably low speeds) past a stationary object (as for example when water oscillates inside the stationary walls of a glass U-tube), there is what is called a *viscous* drag force acting on the fluid which tends to retard the flow. That is, the viscous force acts on the fluid in a direction opposite to the direction of fluid *motion*, and we find that the magnitude of the retarding force is proportional to the velocity of flow. It is a viscous force of this sort which, when added to the springlike restoring force, converts undamped sinusoidal motion into a damped oscillation of the sort we have been studying.

Digression on the Viscosity of Fluids.

It is easy to acquire an intuitive feeling for the properties of viscous flow by means of simple experiments. One has merely to stir a cup of honey or thick syrup to discover that the spoon feels a much larger retarding force when it is moved rapidly than when it is slow-moving. As a matter of fact, one feels almost no retarding force at all at the slowest possible stirring speeds. The rocking back and forth of the free surface of a liquid in a half-filled saucepan or large jar is a simple cousin to the oscillation of fluid in a U-tube. A comparison of such rocking oscillations of honey, glycerine, salad oil, water, and acetone shows clearly the relation between the viscosity characteristic of each of these fluids and the rates at which these oscillations decay.

We have now completed our preliminary look at the nature of damped oscillations and have found them to have the following properties:

1. Sinusoidal oscillation is identical with the side-to-side motion of the shadow of a circularly moving object.

2. Such oscillations are produced when the object in motion is subjected to a (springlike) restoring force, that is, a force whose magnitude is proportional at any instant to the distance between the object and its position of equilibrium or center position.

3. The oscillation is damped if, in addition, it feels a (viscous) drag force, i.e., a force whose magnitude is proportional to the velocity of the object at every instant in time.

In any case of damped sinusoidal motion, some object (of mass M) moves under the influence of two forces, one which depends on what we shall call the *stiffness coefficient* S and one which depends on the *damping coefficient* D of some fluid-like viscous material. It is possible to write down quasi-mathematical formulas for the oscillation frequency and damping times that will help us recall these things throughout the rest of this book:

$$\text{frequency} = \sqrt{\left(\frac{\text{stiffness coefficient}}{\text{moving mass}}\right)}$$

or, $\quad f = \left(\sqrt{S/M}\right)$ times a numerical constant

$$\frac{\text{halving}}{\text{time}} = \left(\frac{\text{moving mass}}{\text{damping coefficient}}\right)$$

or, $\quad T_{1/2} = (M/D)$ times a numerical constant

These formulas tell us that in an oscillator the characteristic vibrational frequency is raised if one attaches a stiffer spring to a given mass, or the halving time is reduced if one provides a more viscous damper. Similarly we notice that increasing the amount of moving mass reduces the vibration frequency and lengthens its halving time if the stiffness and damping coefficients are left unchanged.

6.2. Possible Oscillations of a Mass Supported by Springs

On our way toward an understanding of guitar and piano strings, we will need to learn something about the vibrations of an elongated chain of alternating springs and masses. Let us begin by looking at a single link belonging to such a chain. Consider a lump of material suspended between a pair of springs. Figure 6.4 shows such a system in an easily made form: a large steel or brass nut (the 3/4-inch or 19-millimeter size is convenient) is attached to a pair of heavy rubber bands which are in turn anchored to rigid vertical posts. The figure indicates the possibility of a side-to-side (*transverse*) vibration. The solid lines in this diagram show the nut and its rubber bands at the right-hand extreme of the motion. The left-hand extreme of its motion is also indicated, whence it moves back towards its starting point. We could just as well imagine a similar transverse oscillation taking place at right angles to the one shown. Another oscillation which we can conceive of has a *longitudinal* motion back

and forth along the direction of the rubber bands. Yet another type of oscillation that this object can undergo involves the alternate clockwise and counterclockwise twisting of the rubber bands. This sort of vibrational motion is known as a *torsional* oscillation.

Figure 6.5 summarizes the above-mentioned oscillatory possibilities for a single compact mass anchored by means of elastic objects to a rigid external support. You may be able to discover two or three more types of oscillation that are possible for this system, but our present list is sufficiently complete to show that we can conceive of a variety of oscillations, and to show also how very much alike these vibrations are in several important respects. For example, we can make the following assertions about them all. If their amplitudes are not too large and if the rubber bands are stretched a reasonable amount, we find that they are all fairly accurate examples of damped sinusoidal oscillation. The frequency of each oscillation is determined jointly by the sum of the stiffness coefficients of the two rubber bands, which try to pull the mass to its resting position, and by the mass of the oscillating nut. If we write S for the stiffness coefficient associated with each of the two rubber bands (under the conditions of its present usage), and M for the mass of the nut, then,

$$f = \text{a constant times } \sqrt{2S/M}$$

As pointed out at the end of the last section, increasing the net stiffness coefficient (e.g., by using heavier rubber bands or adding one or more of them) increases the frequency; decreasing the mass will also increase the frequency. For example, if we were to reduce the inertia of our vibrating system by cutting the nut in half so that M is replaced by M/2, the

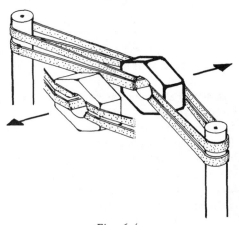

Fig. 6.4.

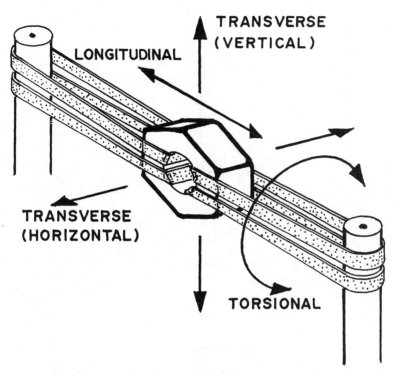

Fig. 6.5.   Various Oscillations of a Spring-Mounted Mass

frequency of any one of our oscillations would be increased by the factor $\sqrt{2} = 1.414$, as the following calculation shows:

$$f_{new} = \sqrt{\frac{2S}{(\frac{1}{2}M)}} = \sqrt{2 \times (2S/M)} =$$

$$1.414\sqrt{2S/M} = 1.414\ f_{original}$$

An exactly similar calculation shows that adding a single rubber band to one side of the system raises the frequency by a factor of $\sqrt{3/2} = 1.225$.

We are now in a position to recognize that the various ways in which our nut and its two rubber bands can oscillate will not in general have the same frequencies. The angles at which the strands of rubber pull on the displaced mass are

quite different in our four possibilities for linear and rotational oscillation. An exaggerated example is found in figure 6.6, in which the two loops of the left-hand rubber band are widely spaced where they go over the support rod. The stiffness coefficient associated with the restoring force for transverse oscillations parallel to the support rod is now clearly much larger than the coefficient belonging with transverse oscillations taking place at right angles to this direction.

Digression on the Utility of Simplified Models.

We have been a little cavalier in the foregoing calculations. For example, we have acted as though the rubber bands have no inertia. Such simplifica-

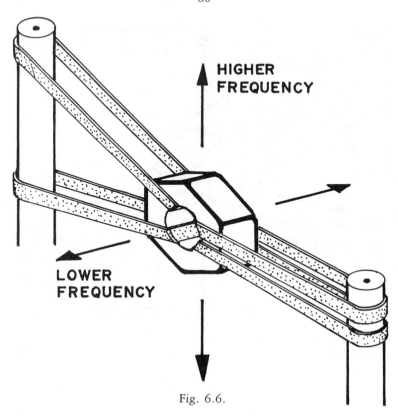

HIGHER FREQUENCY

LOWER FREQUENCY

Fig. 6.6.

tions are very useful and perfectly permissible for helping us to grasp the essentials of the situation. We should, however, always try to be clear about what simplifications we have made. In this way, we know how to react to the inevitable discrepancies that are found when we compare the results of our calculations with measurements of the real things. When the discrepancies are of the sort to be expected as a result of our simplifications, they confirm that we probably understand at least a part of what is going on. Sometimes, however, the discrepancies are not explainable in terms of our simplifications, which reminds us firmly to look more closely at the system under study.

A Simplified Mass-and-Spring Oscillator

Before going on to an examination of the vibrations characteristic of chains built up of two or more interlinked

built up of two or more interlinked masses and springs, we should pause a moment to translate our discoveries so far into terms that relate to what our ears can perceive. We cannot hear sounds whose frequency components are as low as those characteristic of our system of nut and rubber bands. However, we could presumably build an analogous system in which the nut is much smaller and the rubber springs are replaced by stiffer, steel ones. This would raise the characteristic frequencies sufficiently to make them audible, yet leave their interrelations essentially unchanged. This lets us imagine a system whose audible characteristic frequencies are directly related to its mechanical construction. It is easy to see that a glancing blow from a hammer on the mass will excite all of the types of oscillations and so produce a sound of maximum complexity. Similarly, we should find it comprehensible that a blow that is purely in the north-south direction will thereby fail to excite the east-west transverse oscillation, so that the characteristic frequency belonging to the east-west vibration will be missing from the sound. In short, here is our first clear illustration of how changes in the striking point can produce changes in the impulsive sound to which it gives rise.

6.3. Transverse Oscillations of Two Masses Connected by Springs

Let us turn our attention now to the behavior of a system made by connecting two massive objects in a row by means of springs.[1] In order to keep our ideas manageable we will restrict our attention temporarily to one of the two possible transverse oscillations, with the understanding that whatever we learn about these can later be adapted in a straightforward manner to apply to the other (e.g., longitudinal or torsional) kinds of vibration. Figure 6.7 shows that there are two distinctly different transverse *modes of vibration* that are possible for our two-mass system, in contrast to the single transverse mode that is available to the one-mass system.

In what is labeled as mode 1 for the two-mass system, the two masses move back and forth exactly in step with one another. If the amplitude of the motion is less than about 10 percent of the longitudinal spacing of the masses, the oscilla-

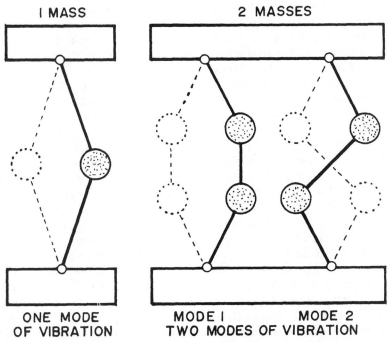

ONE MODE
OF VIBRATION

MODE 1
TWO MODES OF VIBRATION

MODE 2

Fig. 6.7. Transverse Modes of Vibration of One- and Two-Mass Systems

tion is once again quite accurately of the damped sinusoidal type. The other vibration, labeled mode 2, is one in which the two masses always move in opposite directions. They both oscillate in a sinusoidal motion, with precisely the same frequency.

Let us see if we can deduce any relationship between the two modes of oscillation that will allow us to say whether mode 1 or mode 2 oscillates at a higher frequency. Thoughtful examination of figure 6.7 suggests that the middle one of the three rubber bands is not stretched nearly as much at the extremes of the motion in mode 1 as it is in mode 2. This tells us that at any given instant during the oscillation, the total restoring force exerted by the two rubber springs attached to a single nut will be smaller when the motion is of the sort shown in mode 1 than in mode 2. In other words, the net stiffness coefficient (which relates the displacement of either mass to the restoring force acting on it) is less in mode 1 than in mode 2. The stiffness coefficient applicable to the motion of either mass taken by itself is of course what determines the motion of that mass, so that mode 1 is expected to oscillate at the lower frequency. A slightly oversimplified analysis shows that the net stiffness coefficient for each mass is threefold less for mode 1 than for mode 2, provided that all three rubber bands are alike and that the two nuts are identical. Each mass would therefore be expected to oscillate at a frequency $\sqrt{3} = 1.732$ times larger in mode 2 than in mode 1. A similar line of argument shows that the first mode frequency f_1 of our two-mass system is lower by a factor of $\sqrt{(1/2)} = 0.707$ than that belonging to the transverse oscillation of a single nut suspended between two rubber bands in

the manner shown in the left-hand part of figure 6.7. The geometrical symmetry in the motion of each of the two vibrational modes helps us understand how the two masses manage to cooperate in agreeing on a common frequency. As in figure 6.4, we have indicated one extreme position of the nuts by solid lines, while the other extreme position (that is reached a half-cycle later during the oscillation) is shown by dotted lines. It is to be understood that the masses move back and forth sinusoidally between these two extremes.

6.4. More Than Two Masses Connected by Springs

The observation that a chainlike two-mass system has two distinct modes of transverse oscillation, while a one-mass system has only a single such mode, suggests that a three-mass chain might be able to oscillate in three different ways, and that similarly one might expect a four-mass chain to have four distinct modes of sinusoidal oscillation. It turns out that this suggestion is correct, as illustrated in figure 6.8. The top part of this figure shows what we will call the *characteristic vibrational shapes* belonging to the three transverse modes of vibration possible for a three-mass chain. We may remark in passing that if all three masses are alike and if the springs are alike, then a simplified calculation of the characteristic frequencies shows them to be in the following ratios when they are compared with the frequency f_1 of mode 1: 1.000, 1.847, 2.415. The lower part of the figure shows the four vibrational shapes characteristic of the transverse modes of oscillation of a four-mass chain. Notice

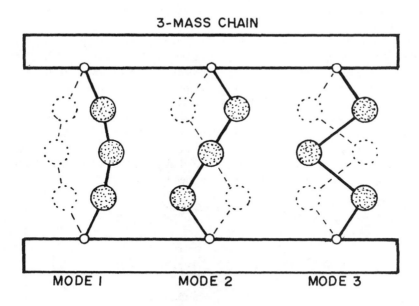

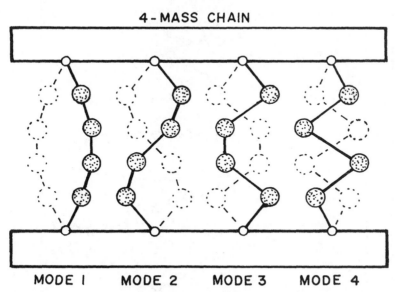

Fig. 6.8. Transverse Vibrational Modes of Three- and Four-Mass Chains

the great similarity of the first mode shapes in all four of our examples. In every case it could be said to have a single hump. In like manner we see that mode 2 has two humps, while modes 3 and 4 have three and four humps respectively.

We must be sure to understand that what we are calling humps are parts of the chain which undergo a relatively large back-and-forth displacement. That is, what would look like a rightward curving hump in a flash photograph taken at one instant will appear as a leftward hump a short time later, but regardless of the direction of the displacement, the hump keeps its general form. We will in due course find it useful to notice that adjacent humps along a chain are always found to be deflected in opposite directions. At present, however, it is the mere

existence of such humps which is of significance.

The top part of figure 6.9 shows the shapes characteristic of the first four modes of vibration of a sequence of a very large number of uniformly sized beadlike masses. This is of interest because it allows us to guess quite accurately about all of the characteristic mode shapes of a piano string (for example), since it may be thought of as a chain of thousands of molecules arranged in a row.[2] We have

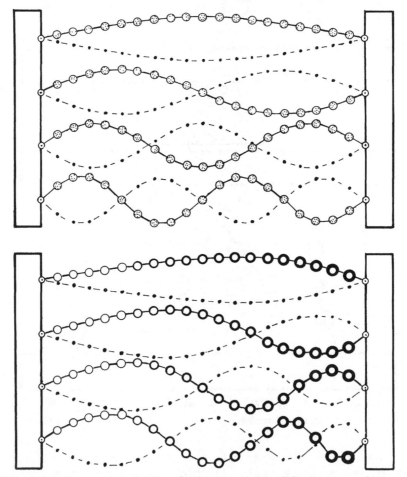

Fig. 6.9.   Characteristic Modes of Vibration of a Beadlike Sequence of Masses

seen in multiple systems that the first mode always has one hump in its characteristic shape, mode 2 has two humps, and so on. Thus a piano string can have many thousands of modes. Only the first two or three dozen have much relevance to music.

The lower part of figure 6.9 shows the first four vibrational shapes characteristic of the transverse modes of oscillation of a chain whose beads become progressively more massive as we go from left to right in the diagram. Notice that the relations are unchanged between mode number and the number of humps making up the vibrational shape. To be sure, the humps are no longer alike, and the relations between the characteristic frequencies are also changed in an amount which increases as the amount of nonuniformity is increased. For present purposes, however, we are interested chiefly in the common elements shared by all of our composite systems.

Digression on Terminology: Humps and Half Wavelengths.
Curiously enough, the technical vocabulary of acoustics seems to lack a formal, generic word for what we have called a hump. Acoustics books commonly refer to the length of what we have called a hump as a half *wavelength. Unfortunately, there are two main ways in which this term is used. In our dealings with wind instruments and with the wooden vibrators belonging to violins, guitars, and pianos we will meet cases where neither usage is appropriate. The word hump, though it has an informal sound, is very descriptive of the physical situation, and it keeps its meaning throughout our discussion of the subject.*

6.5. Characteristic Modes of Oscillation: *A Summary*

In general we find that a chainlike structure, made up of a sequence of springs and masses and anchored firmly at the two ends, finds itself able to oscillate transversely in as many distinct ways, or vibrational modes (to give them their technical name), as there are masses in the chain. Let us summarize the properties of these modes of oscillation as we have learned them and also extend our description in various small ways.

1. Each mode of vibration has its own characteristic frequency, determined by the nature and arrangement of the springs and masses.

2. When the system is oscillating in one of its modes, the chain oscillates at the frequency characteristic of that mode in a damped sinusoidal motion. The halving time for the oscillation is exactly the same for the decay of each mass's oscillation.

3. The various masses in the chain move either precisely in step with one another, or in precisely contrary motion. (We are ignoring here a minute effect which can arise if the damping is unequally distributed among the masses.)

4. All masses move in step in mode 1; adjacent masses move in contrary directions in the highest possible frequency mode belonging to any particular system.

5. Each mode of oscillation has its own characteristic vibrational shape. In other words, the amplitude of oscillation of each mass has a definite relation to the amplitude of motion of every other mass.

The foregoing statements apply to any chainlike system anchored at both ends, whether or not the masses are all alike or the springs are similar.

We have provided ourselves here with a set of generalizations introduced in connection with a study of the transverse (side-to-side) oscillations of a sequence of masses. This entire discussion can be adapted to the case of longitudinal oscillations, or of torsional oscillations, simply by making a few minor changes in the wording. The welter of characteristic frequencies which one might somehow discover can be separated into at least four interlaced sets, two sets being associated with the transverse modes of oscillation, one set with the longitudinal modes, and one more set having to do with the torsional modes of oscillation.

We should also be aware of the fact that today's mathematical physics is able to calculate the characteristic frequencies and modal shapes of any chain in terms of its specified springs and masses. Furthermore, it is possible to calculate one or more choices of a set of springs and masses that will oscillate at any specified set of characteristic frequencies. In other words, if we wish to do so, we are able to go either way in relating the system to its frequencies: given the chain, it is possible to find its frequencies; or, given the frequencies, it is possible to find a corresponding chain. The practical implications of this remark are enormous for the maker or adjuster of musical instruments.

Before we leave this chapter to look into the way in which a hammer or plectrum excites the characteristic modes of a piano or guitar string, we should look ahead briefly to notice that the sweeping generalizations that we have just made will also prove to be adaptable with only minor changes to the modes of vibration that are characteristic of elongated columns of air such as those found in wind instruments, to the characteristic modes of two-dimensional sheetlike objects such as drumheads and piano sound-

boards, and also to three-dimensional objects such as a bowl of jelly with cherries embedded in it or the air in a concert hall.

6.6. Examples, Experiments, and Questions

1. Long-persisting characteristic oscillations of a system of interconnected pendulums may be studied with the help of

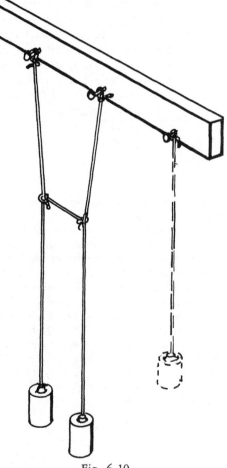

Fig. 6.10.

the arrangements shown in figure 6.10. Two or more long pendulums hung on a solid supporting beam (such as a door lintel) are joined by horizontal strings knotted so that they can be slid up and down the support strings. When two identical pendulums are coupled together in this way, we find that two modes of sinusoidal oscillation are possible when the bobs swing at right angles to the direction of the supporting beam. Similarly, there are two possible modes if we consider swinging motions that take place in a direction parallel to the support. In either type of oscillation we find both pendulums moving back and forth together in mode 1, while in mode 2 they move in opposition to one another. The difference between the two modal frequencies in this setup is fairly small, and it depends on the place where the coupling strings are attached. Once these frequencies are identified, it is interesting to watch the peculiar motion that takes place over a long period of time when only one of the two pendulums is initially pulled aside and released. The two pendulums appear to take turns in their swingings. In chapter 7 we will learn how to deal with complex motions of this sort, which turn out to involve both characteristic modes of oscillation at the same time. It is worthwhile to experiment with the two modes of oscillation of our two-pendulum system when the bobs are of different sizes,' or when their support strings have different lengths. Whether the pendulums are alike or not, in the mode having lower frequency the two masses move in step, while in the mode having higher frequency the two masses move in opposition. Notice that the amplitudes of motion of the two masses in either mode are alike only when the two

bobs and their support string lengths are exactly alike. The behavior of systems having three or more pendulums is also worth some attention, although their complexity may make things difficult to sort out.

2. Two versions of another chainlike structure may be put together from carts of the sort shown in figure 6.11. Three to five of these carts can be joined together in a row by means of compression springs screwed into coupling holes on the carts. Figure 6.12 shows two possible versions of the chainlike structure. The upper version consists of a sequence of five interconnected carts, the end ones being attached to fixed supports by means of springs (just as in the case of our rubber-band apparatus). The lower part of the diagram shows a three-cart system which is left free at its ends. Both of these systems are able to oscillate in various characteristic longitudinal modes of sinusoidal motion.

Mode 1 of the system fixed at both ends can be excited by rolling all five of the carts to the same side and releasing them. They will then move majestically back and forth together. Notice that the center cart moves the farthest, while the carts nearer the ends move less far. Mode 2 for our chain has carts a and b moving in a way that is the mirror image of the motion of d and e. Cart c is stationary in this mode. Mode 2 is very easily started by pulling carts a and b rightward toward the center while pulling d and e at the same time an equal distance leftward, and then releasing everything. In mode 3 the outermost two carts move one way while the center one moves in the opposite direction, etc.

Let us look now at the free-ended three-cart system. The lowest frequency

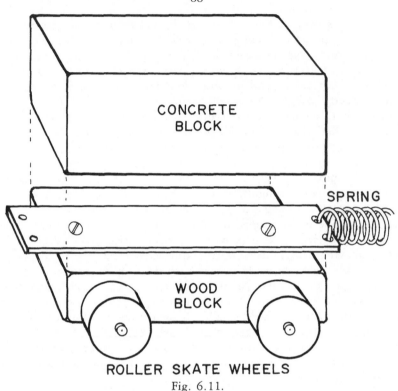

CONCRETE
BLOCK

SPRING

WOOD
BLOCK

ROLLER SKATE WHEELS
Fig. 6.11.

mode here is one in which the outer two carts alternately approach one another and recede, the center cart remaining stationary. In mode 2 the two outer blocks move in a direction contrary to the direction of the center block. There is no third mode of oscillation in this system. It is worthwhile to continue the exploration

by at least thinking about the behavior of a two-mass system attached at one end to a rigid anchorage by a spring, the other end being left free.

3. The sloshing of water in a pan, or better, in a length of rain gutter closed at both ends and about 2 meters (6 feet) long, provides further insight into the

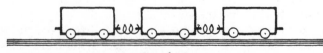

Fig. 6.12.

natural vibrations of extended objects. It also will demonstrate a kind of motion that is very similar to what takes place in the air columns of musical wind instruments. The first three sloshing modes of a water-filled horizontal trough are illustrated in figure 6.13. If one experiments with such a trough it is quickly apparent that the vertical motion of the water level at various points along the trough is very different in its nature from the water's back-and-forth horizontal flowing motion. Looking first at the vertical aspect of the fluid motion, we find that in mode 1 the level is falling in the left half of the trough when it is rising in the right half. There is no vertical motion at all at the trough's exact mid-point. In mode 2 the water level at the two ends rises and falls in step, while in the middle of the trough the level moves in the opposite direction. We find also that there are two places along the trough where the water level is unchanging. Customarily such points of zero disturbance are re-

ferred to as *nodes,* and what we have earlier called a hump extends from one node to the next. Notice that a half-hump is found at each closed end of the trough.

Sprinkling a little powder on the water surface will help us to see the horizontal motion of the water in the trough. In mode 1 there is a strong longitudinal flow of water to be seen in the center of the trough. There is of course no possibility of flow at the two closed ends (i.e., there are nodes for this horizontal motion at the two ends). In mode 2 we find that there is strong horizontal flow (in opposite directions) at two points along the trough, with a node between these points, in addition to the nodes forced on the system by the two end closures. Careful observation will help us realize that in every case the largest horizontal oscillation of the water takes place precisely at those points where the vertical motion is zero. Conversely we find that the nodes of the horizontal motion are located at the exact spots where the water's vertical os-

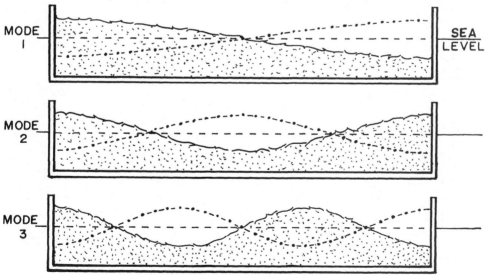

Fig. 6.13.   Sloshing Modes of Water in a Trough

cillation is the largest. We have discovered that every mode of watery oscillation in a trough has two interlaced aspects: a vertical motion and a horizontal motion. These two motions are inextricably coupled to one another by the simple fact that the only way to raise the water level at some point is to have water flowing toward it.

One can also experiment with a tilted gutter, so that the water is deeper at one end than at the other, making a nonuniform cross section below the quiescent waterline. The general nature of the water modes is little changed from before (see fig. 6.9 for the analogous comparison of vibrations of a uniform and a tapered string). The frequencies of oscillation are of course changed and we also find that the positions of maximum or zero vertical motion *no longer coincide* with those of their opposite numbers for the horizontal motion.

Up till now we have said nothing about how these various modes of oscillation may conveniently be excited. If we place an open hand paddle-fashion at a point of large flow, it is easy literally to stir up the desired oscillation. For example, our two hands placed 1/4 of the gutter length in from the ends, both being moved toward and then away from the center, will strongly excite mode 2.

Notes

1. Norman Feather, *An Introduction to the Physics of Vibrations and Waves* (Edinburgh: at the University Press, 1961; London: Penguin, 1964). Feather in chapter 3 gives a good introduction to the mathematics of this particular system and then presents many examples of other systems showing similar behavior.

2. John C. Slater and Nathaniel H. Frank, *Mechanics* (New York: McGraw-Hill, 1947), pp. 151–55. Figures 25a and 25b provide an interesting pictorial view of further relationships between the motion of a chain of masses and that of a flexible string.

7

Introduction to Vibration Recipes:
The Plucked String

In chapter 6 we learned that a chainlike collection of springs and masses can vibrate in certain characteristic modes, each with its own frequency. The frequencies and shapes of these vibrating modes can be calculated if one has the proper information about the strength of the springs and the sizes of the masses making up the chain.

The characteristic frequencies of the vibrational modes are often called the *natural frequencies* of the system, and the modes themselves are referred to as the *natural modes*. This terminology comes about from the fact that when a system is disturbed and left alone to pursue its natural tendencies, the free vibration is always composed of one or more of these characteristic modes.

At several points so far in the book (and especially in chap. 6) we have met the idea that different ways of striking or plucking an object produce different sounds, and that this is simply another way of saying that the initial amplitudes of oscillation of the various modes are influenced by the nature of the excitation. The guitarist becomes familiar with these ideas when he learns how to pluck the string at different distances from the bridge in order to vary the sounds he

produces. He also has various options concerning how he plucks; he may use a fingertip, a fingernail, or some one of several kinds of plectrum. In this chapter we will have our first look at what is going on when a musician makes changes of this sort. In other words, we will begin to learn how such variables as the plucking position or the breadth of a plectrum determine the initial amplitudes of the several vibrational modes of the string. First we will see how any possible transverse motion of a two-mass chain is actually a combination of its two characteristic modes of sinusoidal oscillation, and then we will progress to a beaded chain made up of a large number of masses, finally moving on to an examination of the behavior of a real musical string.

7.1. Combinations of Modes: *The Two-Mass Chain*

Assertion: *when a system is struck and left to its own devices, any possible motion it has is made up of a collection of the natural vibrational modes of the system. The initial amplitudes of these modes are determined by the manner of striking.*

In order to test and demonstrate the above assertion, let us make use of a fairly

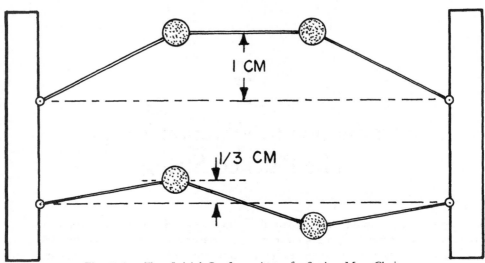

Fig. 7.1. Two Initial Configurations of a Spring-Mass Chain

simple system consisting of two balls connected by springs. Suppose for example that both balls are drawn upward a unit distance (for instance, 1 cm) so that their arrangement is of the sort shown in the top part of figure 7.1. If they are released from this initial position it is clear that the balls will vibrate back and forth sinusoidally with a frequency characteristic of what we have called mode 1 for a two-mass system (see fig. 6.7 in chap. 6). The balls initially are arranged so that their positions match the vibrational shape of mode 1, and upon their release the system oscillates at the mode 1 frequency, with (in our example) a 1 cm initial amplitude.

Suppose now that instead of pulling both balls upward 1 cm before releasing them to oscillate, we move the ball on the left upward a distance of 1/3 cm and hold it, and at the same time we move the ball on the right downward 1/3 cm, as shown in the lower part of figure 7.1. If we release the balls from this initial configuration (whose shape is exactly that

belonging to mode 2) we should not be startled to learn that the subsequent vibration is sinusoidal and that it takes place at the frequency of mode 2.

The experiments described in the preceding two paragraphs illustrate the fact that it is possible to start the vibration of a system purely in one or another of its characteristic modes. In order to do this, we must somehow arrange for the initial configuration of the system to agree exactly with the vibrational shape of the mode we wish to excite. Let us now look at a somewhat less specialized situation.

Suppose (step a) that we first pull both balls upward a distance of 1 cm to give a shape that matches that of mode 1, after which (step b) the ball on the left is pulled up 1/3 cm further and the ball on the right is depressed 1/3 cm, as shown in the top part of figure 7.2. This two-step procedure gives us an unsymmetrical, triangular arrangement for the balls, which shape could just as well have been achieved in the manner shown in the lower part of figure 7.2. Here the left and

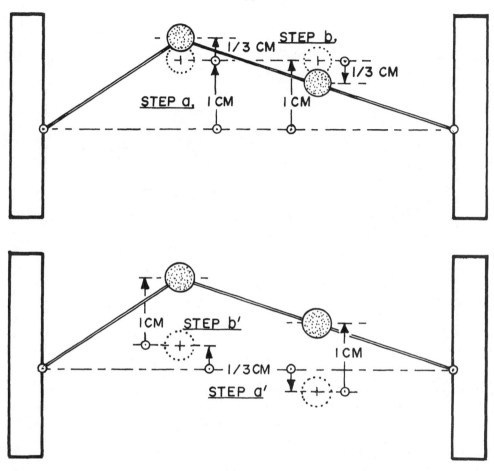

Fig. 7.2.

the right balls, respectively, are raised and lowered 1/3 cm (step a') and afterwards both are raised 1 cm (step b'). What we have done in both versions of our procedure is to achieve a certain shape by the process of combining the initial shapes of the two characteristic modes.

The particular configuration we have set up here by either one of our two-step procedures based on the characteristic mode shapes could have been obtained much more easily. All one would have to

do is pull the ball on the left upward a distance of 1 1/3 cm, the other ball being allowed to find its place, but this way of going at it does not display to us the initial presence of the two characteristic modes.

If we release the balls from the positions shown in figure 7.2, we find that the system vibrates in the fashion shown in figure 7.3. If these vibrations were to take place at audible frequencies, we would hear two components in the sound,

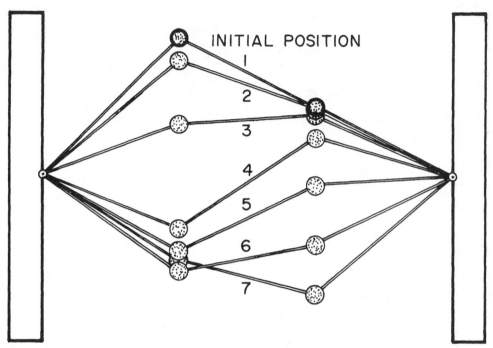

INITIAL POSITION

1
2
3
4
5
6
7

Fig. 7.3.   Complicated Motion of the System After Release

one having the mode 1 characteristic frequency and one having the frequency belonging to mode 2. The loudnesses of these two components would depend ultimately on the amplitudes of the two characteristic vibrations. In our particular example we have arranged to have the initial amplitude of mode 2 be exactly 1/3 of the initial amplitude of mode 1.

Figure 7.4 summarizes what we have done and suggests a way in which we can think about how an initial configuration may be constructed out of suitably chosen "amounts" of the characteristic modes. It is helpful here to borrow some language from the kitchen. A cake has a certain set of ingredients and its recipe must name not only the ingredients but also the

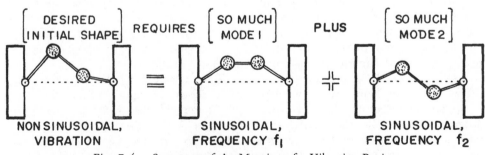

Fig. 7.4.   Summary of the Meaning of a Vibration Recipe

amounts needed. A one-egg cake, a four-egg cake, and a butter (or pound) cake all use the same ingredients in varying amounts, but each cake ends up with different flavor and texture. In an exactly similar manner we can cook up any conceivable initial shape of our vibrating system by combining suitably chosen amounts (initial amplitudes) of the complete set of characteristic mode shapes belonging to the system. One can thus write "recipes" for any desired vibration merely by listing the amounts (i.e., initial amplitudes) of the first, second, third, etc., characteristic modes that are present. We can call these initial amplitudes by the name a_1, a_2, a_3, etc.

Digression on Vibration Recipes.

A cook cannot usually deduce the recipe of a cake by tasting it. He may be able to guess the names of the ingredients, but not the exact amounts. It was a triumph of nineteenth-century physics that methods were, however, found for doing the analogous job for vibration recipes. To do this, the physicist must first figure out the shapes and frequencies of the various modes. After that it is only a little work to deduce the amounts of these modes that are present. That is, once he knows what the ingredients are, it is not difficult for him to discover the amounts. We will not have to study any of the formal methods for carrying out such analysis, but it often proves useful to know that procedures are available. The mere existence of vibration recipes allows us to make use of them in our thinking.

Before we apply our newly acquired knowledge of vibration recipes to musical strings, it is advisable to notice in figure 7.3 an important implication of the whole recipe idea. Here we see that as time runs on after the release of our two-bead system, the initial disturbance *does*

not keep its shape. What started out as a neat triangle at the instant of release becomes a very peculiarly shaped squiggle a few instants later. We can see the reason for this at once: the two natural vibrations that are going on will get out of step. For all intents and purposes, the initial shape will never recur. Suppose for example that the second mode frequency f_2 is exactly 1.732 times f_1 (as is approximately true if the masses are alike and the springs are alike). Then by the time that the mode 1 part of the recipe has repeated itself 1000 times, mode 2 will have gone through 1732 of its cycles of oscillation. At first glance one might think that then everything will be back where it started and that the whole performance will begin again. Something has been left out, however: the two oscillations decay at different rates (i.e., with different halving times), so that a vibration recipe that started out with $a_2 = 1/3$ a_1 will no longer have this same relationship after 1000 swings of mode 1. We are led, then, to the following generalizations:

1. A system released from an initial shape identical with any one of the natural (characteristic) modes of vibration keeps this shape as time goes on. Its amplitude dies away in a manner determined by its own halving time.

2. A system released from an initial shape that is constructed out of a *set* of characteristic mode shapes will *not* keep its initial shape as time goes on.

7.2. Vibration Recipe of a Stringlike Beaded Chain

Let us review briefly what we learned in chapter 6 about the characteristic shapes of the various vibrations of a chain made up of numerous small masses joined by springs. This sort of chain of many beads will of course quickly turn itself in our thinking into a simplified version of a real guitar or harpsichord string, so that we are coming very close to an examination of real musical instruments. Let us give the name *flexible string* to a closely beaded chain in which the connecting springs have stretchability, but because of the nature of their attachment to the beads they provide no resistance of their own to bending of the chain. When such a chain is pulled out tightly between two supports, it is the stretching (longitudinal) elasticity of the springs that provides the forces guiding any oscillation taking place. Such a flexible string is a direct de-

scendant of the sequences of nuts and rubber bands with which we experimented in chapter 6. The top part of figure 7.5 shows an example of a completely flexible chain made up of springs and masses, as just described. The lower part of the illustration is adapted from figure 6.9 to show the shapes of the first three vibrational modes of such a chain.

We are now in a position to inquire usefully about the vibrational recipes belonging to a plucked guitar string. More accurately, we may ask for the recipe belonging to a flexible beaded string under tension when it is pulled aside and released. Figure 7.6 shows diagrammatically what is involved in two cases. On

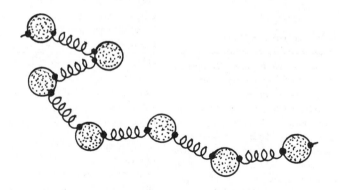

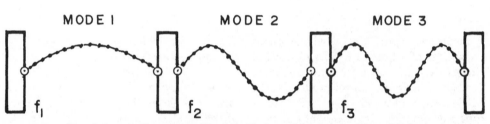

Fig. 7.5.   A Completely Flexible Chain and Its Lowest Three Modes

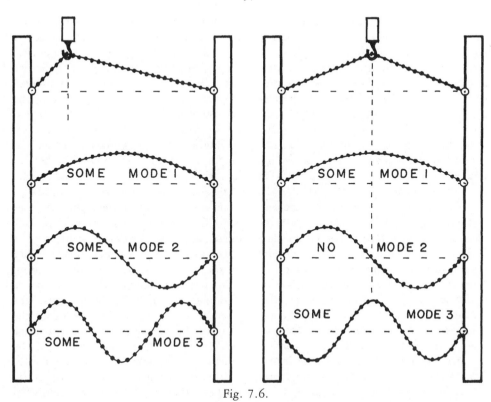

Fig. 7.6.

the right we see the string pulled aside by means of a hook located exactly halfway between the string's anchorages; on the left we find the hook displaced so that it is fairly close to one end of the string.

Our first glance at the left half of figure 7.6 reveals that the initial triangular-shaped deflection of the string has a recipe containing certain amounts of modes 1, 2, 3, etc. In a preliminary way we can observe that the addition of the unsymmetrical mode 2 shape to that of the symmetrical mode 1 will give a resultant whose lack of symmetry is of the same general sort as the desired triangular deflection. That is, adding these two modes together produces a shape in which the

left half of the string becomes more deflected than the right half. We cannot always succeed in attempts to extract in this manner much detailed information about a vibration recipe, attempts which are like a cook's attempts to work out a recipe by taste alone. It is possible however to go just a little farther in this particularly simple case, and this effort will help prepare us to understand certain general relations that have been found between plucking point and vibration recipe.

When the string is pulled aside at its exact center, as shown in the right half of figure 7.6, the string shape has enough symmetry to it that we can learn the basis for a number of useful things about vibration recipes in general. We have already noticed that the shape of mode 2 is not symmetrical about the string's center; clearly then it would be a most inappropriate candidate for inclusion in the recipe for a symmetrical initial shape. Another way of arriving at this same conclusion is based on the idea that one would hardly expect a mode to be excited if one tried to pluck it at a point that remains stationary, as is the case for the string's midpoint in mode 2. Looking further, we notice that mode 3 is symmetrical, so that it remains a candidate for inclusion in our recipe. Furthermore we notice that adding mode 3 to mode 1 gives a shape that is more peaked at the center and less arched on the sides than the mode 1 shape taken alone. These changes are of course exactly of the sort that are needed in our desire to convert the shape of mode 1 into a better imitation of the isosceles triangle that is produced by pulling the string aside at its center. So far, then, we have excluded mode 2 from membership in the recipe, and we have verified that it is at least plausible to include mode 3. Looking further down the list of modes, we realize that while mode 4 has more humps than mode 2, it has the same lack of symmetry. The left half of the pattern is upside down when compared with the right half. It takes only a few moments to make freehand sketches of the various higher-numbered mode shapes, all of which show that the even-numbered modes are like mode 2 in having this lack of symmetry (or more precisely, this flipped-over symmetry, which is referred to as *antisymmetry* by mathematicians, to distinguish it from *unsymmetrical* cases in which the two halves of the pattern bear no re-

semblance to one another). We also notice that all the odd-numbered modes of our uniform string have symmetrical shapes. Because of the similarities that we have noticed among the even-numbered modes, and other similarities among the odd-numbered ones, we are led to extend our conclusions about which modes are acceptable in our vibration recipe: if modes 1 and 3 are acceptable in the recipe, then all the odd-numbered modes could be part of the recipe; similarly, what makes mode 2 unacceptable rules out all even-numbered modes as candidates for this vibrational recipe.

Let us return to a remark made earlier to the effect that the central plucking point lies at a point on the string that is stationary for mode 2. We find that this point is stationary in the case of all the even-numbered modes, so that if it seems unlikely that one can excite mode 2 by plucking at its stationary point (or *node*, as it is properly named), then it is equally unlikely that the other even-numbered modes will be set in motion when plucked at the position of one of their nodes. It turns out that we can make very general statements about the degree of excitation of any given mode if the relation is known between the position of the plucking point and the position of the nearest node belonging to that particular mode of oscillation. The actual proof of the correctness of these statements requires a considerable grasp of mathematical physics. However, our investigations so far are sufficient to make them intelligible, and the commonsense insight into the nature of mechanical vibrations which we have striven to develop may well be sufficient to make them seem plausible.

The following numbered assertions

summarize the connections that exist between the location of the plucking point on a string and the amplitudes of the various vibrational shapes that form the ingredients of the initial string shape.[1]

1. One cannot excite a mode by plucking the string at a point where there is a stationary point (a node). That is, such modes will not be ingredients of the vibrational recipe.

Not only is it possible to say definitely where one must pluck if a mode is not to be excited, but also we can say how to give it the strongest possible excitation.

2. For a given plectrum force, a mode gets its strongest excitation if the string is plucked where this mode has its largest excursion.

Having told where one plucks to excite a mode most strongly and where plucking fails to excite the mode at all, it is now possible to say something about the excitation due to plucking at some intermediate point.

3. For a given force, the excitation of a mode is proportional to the size of the mode's excursion at the plucking point (this statement contains the implications of both the preceding statements).

Figure 7.7 shows everything we have said in pictorial form, using the characteristic shape for mode 3 as an example As one moves the plucking point along the string from its anchorage on the left toward the right-hand fixture, we find that this mode is excited weakly or

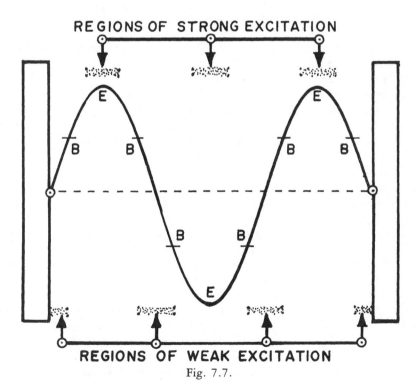

REGIONS OF STRONG EXCITATION

REGIONS OF WEAK EXCITATION

Fig. 7.7.

strongly depending on the region in which the plucking point finds itself. There are three regions along the string in which plucking produces strong excitation of mode 3. Between these regions and at the ends of the string, we find regions in which the excitation is small, or is even zero if one tries to pluck exactly at the position of a node. In between the regions that are identified with strong and weak excitation are parts of the string where plucking produces an intermediate excitation of mode 3. For example, at the points along the string that are marked by the letter B, the excitation is half as great as the maximum amount that is possible. Notice that at these points the excursion of the string away from the central straight line is half of the maximum excursion (which is found at the points marked E). It is sometimes useful to know that plucking anywhere in about the middle third of any string hump will produce an excitation that is more than 85% of the maximum possible excitation, so that we are justified in informally labeling it as being a region of strong excitation.

We now come to an additional assertion whose content cannot easily be discovered without the use of advanced mathematics, but which proves to be as simple in its application and as useful in its musical implications as the preceding three assertions. It turns out that the strength of excitation of the nth of our sequence of characteristic string modes depends in a simple way on the serial number n of the mode, over and above the relations described in assertions 1 through 3.

4. The strength of excitation (by plucking) of the nth vibrational mode of a string fixed at both ends is inversely proportional to the square of the mode number. That is, $a_n = (1/n)^2$ times the other proportionalities.

As a consequence of assertion 4, even if we pluck a string at one of the points that excite mode 3 with maximum efficacy, the initial amplitude a_3 of this mode will be only $1/3^2 = 1/9$ as large as the amplitude a_1 which mode 1 would have if the plucking point were such as to give maximum excitation for this mode.

We have struggled through a rather formidable list of closely interwoven assertions. It is therefore time to consolidate things by applying these ideas to a more or less practical example. In the next section we will use a slightly simplified guitar string for this purpose. (A similarly simplified piano string will turn up in the next chapter.)

7.3. The Basic Recipe of a Plucked or Struck String

In the preceding section of this chapter, some prescriptions were given that allow one to work out the actual vibration recipe for a plucked string. More precisely, the prescriptions tell how to find the initial amplitudes of the various vibrational modes that are characteristic of a slightly simplified (i.e., totally flexible) string excited by means of an extremely narrow, knife-edged plectrum which is used to pull the string aside before it is released. We will deal in due course with the small changes to our prescriptions that must be made when real strings are plucked by slightly extended or soft-tipped plectra, but at present we should see how very much information about string vibration is made available to us upon the basis of what we have learned so far.

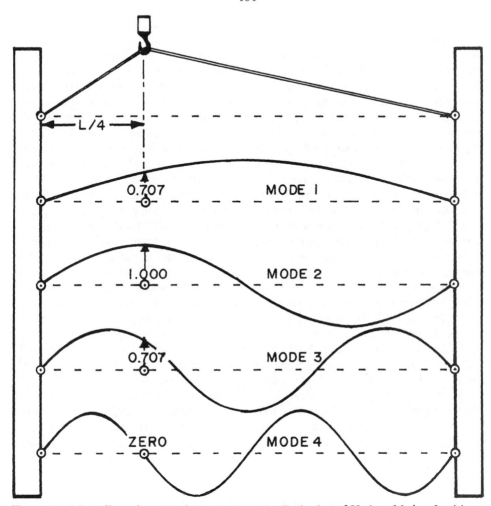

Fig. 7.8. The Effect of the Plucking Point on the Excitation of Various Modes. In this example the string is plucked one-quarter of the way from one end.

The top part of figure 7.8 shows the triangular shape produced when a flexible string (a chain of many tiny masses hooked together in a line by minute springs) under tension is pulled aside by something sharp which acts at a point one quarter of the way along the string from the left end. The lower parts of the diagram show the characteristic shapes of the first four vibrational modes of this string, all of them being drawn to have unit amplitude. A vertical dotted line is drawn through all five parts of the diagram showing the position of the plucking point relative to the humps of the various mode shapes. Let us first make use of our knowledge that the strength of excitation of a given mode is proportional to that mode's excursion at the plucking point. From the figure we see that mode 1 has an excursion at the plucking point that is very nearly 70% of the maximum excursion of this mode, which takes place at the string's center. Similarly we notice that mode 2 gets maximum excitation, since the particular plucking point we have chosen happens to fall at a point of maximum excursion. Continuing down the diagram we find that mode 3 gets 0.707 (70.7%) of its maximum possible excitation, while mode 4 is not excited at all because the plucking point happens to coincide with a node. The first line of table 7.1 gives a list of numbers showing how the plucking point affects the amount of excitation for the first eight modes, now that we have seen how four of them are determined.

The next step in finding the recipe is to divide each of these numbers by the square of the corresponding mode number. That is, we divide them by $1^2 = 1$, $2^2 = 4$, $3^2 = 9$, etc. These divisors are given in the second row of the table, while the third row presents the results of this arithmetic. It is this latter row that tells the initial amounts of the various ingredients in the vibration recipe. It is a little hard to interpret these numbers as they come to us from the arithmetic, because they are, so to speak, like a listing of the quantities of flour, sugar, etc., needed to make a 70-percent-sized cake. A very useful convention which we shall sometimes use is to *normalize* the recipe so as to give unit amplitude to mode 1. That is, we will convert the recipe given in row 3 of the table (in which the mode 1 ingredient has a magnitude of 0.707) to one in which mode 1 has unit amplitude. This is done simply by dividing every number in row 3 by 0.707, with a result shown in row 4. Here we can read off directly that the initial amplitude of mode 2 is 35.3 percent of the mode 1 amplitude, or that mode 3 has an initial amplitude that is 11.1 percent of the mode 1 excitation, and so on. Let us rewrite this one more time, using the symbol a_n for the initial amplitude of the nth mode: $a_1 = 1.000$, $a_2 = 0.353$ a_1, $a_3 = 0.111$ a_1, etc. If we were to draw the string aside more or less far before it is released, the amounts of all the ingredients would be changed in the same proportion, so that if we somehow find the amplitude a_1

Table 7.1

Amplitudes of First Eight Modes of a Plucked String

	Mode Number:							
	1	2	3	4	5	6	7	8
Effect of a plucking point located at one-fourth the string length	0.707	1.000	0.707	0.000	0.707	1.000	0.707	0.000
Mode number squared	1	4	9	16	25	36	49	64
Initial amplitude (plucking-point effect divided by squared mode number)	0.707	0.250	0.079	0.000	0.028	0.028	0.014	0.000
Normalized amplitudes (the amplitudes of the modes relative to the mode-1 amplitude	1.000	0.353	0.111	0.000	0.040	0.039	0.020	0.000

(say 0.5 cm maximum excursion) for a particular strength of plucking, then all the other amplitudes can be found by multiplying all of the normalized amplitudes by 0.5 cm, which is the mode 1 amplitude measured in a particular example.

Our numerical example can be used to illustrate a number of important properties of plucked strings, as we have studied them so far. For one thing we have confirmed that modes 4, 8, 12, etc., will not be present in the recipe belonging to a string plucked one-fourth of the way from one end. As a matter of fact, we can go further to realize that in exactly similar fashion, plucking 1/3 of the way along eliminates modes 3, 6, 9, 12, . . . from the recipe, or that plucking 1/7 of the way will prevent excitation of modes 7, 14, 21, 28, ... More generally, if we wish to remove the nth mode and its whole number multiples from the recipe, we have merely to pluck (1/n)th of the way from one end of the string. By the same token, and much more important for practical music, plucking *near* one of these spots rather than exactly on it gives the corresponding lists of modes a weak rather than a zero excitation. Another piece of information that can be gained from row 4 of table 7.1 is that because of the $1/n^2$ factor in the computations, the higher-numbered modes are very weakly excited in comparison with the lower-numbered ones, quite aside from any effect of the plucking position on the excitation.

The vibration recipe for a string that is *struck* by a hard, sharp-edged object at a given point along its length (rather than plucked) is almost exactly the same as the one given above. The only difference is that instead of dividing by n^2, as given in row 2 of table 7.1, one divides by n itself.[2] For example, the normalized amplitudes for a string that is struck 1/4 of the way from one end are found to be: 1.000, 0.707, 0.333, 0.000, 0.200, 0.236, 0.143, 0.000. These amplitudes fall away much less rapidly as we go up the series of mode numbers than is the case when the string is plucked. There is considerable similarity between the vibration recipes associated with the plucking and the striking of a string. In both cases higher modes are progressively less strongly excited than are the lower-numbered ones. One always finds, however, that the higher modes are more strongly excited by striking than by plucking a string. We will go into more detail about struck strings in the next chapter.

We are at a point where we are beginning to find some of the many implications for music that are hiding within what we have learned so far. However, we must take care not to jump too quickly from our ability to determine the vibration recipe for a string to any conclusions about the analogous recipe for the sounds that reach our ears. To be sure, it is the string vibrations of a harpsichord or piano that ultimately give rise to the sound we hear, but on the way to our ears the string vibrations must be passed to us via the soundboard and the air in the concert hall. As was pointed out in chapter 6, these intermediate objects are also endowed with characteristic modes of oscillation, each with its own natural frequency, vibrational shape, and decay (halving) time. It is only reasonable to expect that the overall behavior of the composite system made up of a string, a soundboard, and a room will show as marked a relation between excitation position and amplitude of response as we found for the string alone (the string itself being a composite of many tiny masses and springs). Fortunately, we will be able easily to extend our understanding of the excitation of strings to the excitation of soundboards and rooms in a way that is exactly analogous to the way in which the properties of a single spring and mass were used to explain the behavior of strings.

A simple description can be given of the first stage in the transformation of the string displacement's vibration recipe into the final recipe that reaches our ears. The first stage transforms the string displacement into the force exerted on the bridge, which then excites the body of the instrument and radiates acoustical waves to the listener. The amplitude of the nth vibrational mode of a *plucked* string is inversely proportional to the square of the mode number $(1/n)^2$ (see assertion 4), and the corresponding vibration recipe of the force on the bridge is inversely proportional to the mode number $(1/n)$. The amplitude of the nth vibrational mode of a *struck* string is inversely proportional to the mode number $(1/n)$, and the corresponding vibration recipe of the force on the bridge is independent of mode number. For both the plucked and struck strings, the force on the bridge emphasizes the higher frequency components of the string displacement vibration recipe.

In our quest for added realism in our descriptions of the vibrations of strings (and therefore also of more complex systems) we must consider one more item that is closely related to what we have learned in the present chapter. The strings of actual pianos, harpsichords, and guitars are not set into vibration by means of knife-edged hammers and plectra, nor are these real musical strings exactly like the simplified flexible strings that we have been imagining so far. In the next chapter, it will prove possible to make some very simple modifications in

what we have discovered so far, so that our results may be adapted to take into account the broader hammers and plectra and the stiffer strings one actually encounters in the non-idealized musical world.

7.4. Examples, Experiments, and Questions

1. In section 4.4 of chapter 4 it was pointed out that if a tuning fork is struck at a point lying between 1/4 and 1/2 of the way from the end of one tine, only mode 1 is excited. This observation allows us to pinpoint the location of nodes belonging to the fork's mode 2. By now we have enough general knowledge of the characteristic vibrations of various objects to be able to make good sketches of the vibrational shapes of the first two fork modes. Try to do this, making use of the fact that in all modes the free ends of the fork tines are in motion. In chapter 9 we will look at the analogous problem of deducing the vibrational shapes belonging to the glockenspiel bars discussed in section 5.1 of chapter 5.

2. The third modes-of-vibration example presented at the end of chapter 6 had to do with the sloshing of water in a long narrow channel. In this present chapter we have learned a good deal about the way in which a locally applied force excites a given mode of oscillation, and it is worthwhile to bring hindsight to bear on the suggestions made earlier on how to excite the various sloshing modes. Notice that even with a hand used as a paddle, we do not expect to excite a mode by disturbing it at a nodal point. How would one go about choosing excitation positions for one's hand if it were to be laid flat on the water surface and given a vertical motion rather than a horizontal motion prescribed earlier? Hint: one would

not expect to stir up mode 1 with vertical excitation applied half way along the trough.

3. The pickups of an electric guitar are small magnetized screws placed near the strings at some point between the bridge and the end of the finger board. Coils of wire wrapped around these screws are interconnected and provide electrical signals for the amplifier and loudspeaker whenever the strings vibrate. Let us confine our attention to a single one of these pickup screws, which is arranged relative to its own guitar string in the manner shown in figure 7.9. Leaving out extraneous electrical and mechanical details, we can see that if the electrical signal depends on string motion, then the pickup is blind (or better, deaf) to all those modes having a node at the screw position. Furthermore, some mode that has its maximum excursion at the screw position will contribute the maximum possible amount of its characteristic sinusoidal oscillation to the electrical signal from the pickup. In other words the recipe for the electrical signal depends on the location of the pickup screw, as well as upon the recipe of the complete vibration (see also example 5 below).

Assuming that the pickup is located 1/4 of the way along the string, try to deduce the electrical vibration recipe belonging to a vibration started by plucking the string at its exact center. First you should recall (with the help of assertions 3 and 4 of section 7.2) the recipe for the string vibration itself. There are no even-numbered modes excited, and the amplitudes of the odd-numbered ones are 1, 1/9, 1/25, 1/49, ... The second row of table 7.1 can now be used to get a numerical measure of the effectiveness of the pickup in responding to a given mode. Notice the exact parallelism between our ability to communicate an excitation to a string mode and our ability to extract a sample of this oscillation. In both cases the effectiveness of the transfer is proportional to the excursion of the string at the spot where the transfer is to take place.

Our glance at the relationship between the recipe of electrical signals produced by a guitar pickup and the vibration recipe of the string gives us our first clear example of the reason why vibration recipes of vibrating objects do not necessarily match the vibration recipes of the sounds we hear. The acoustic recipe depends not only on the vibration recipe but also on the details of the process which transforms the vibration into the sounds reaching our ears. What general deductions can be made about the relations between the electrical recipes as-

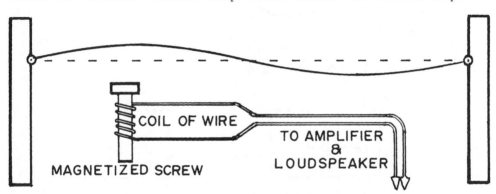

Fig. 7.9.   An Electric-Guitar String and Its Pickup

sociated with each of the two pickup assemblies that are often mounted on a guitar? Recall that one of these pickup sets is located near the bridge, while one is near the finger board. Comment also on the change in recipe that arises in going from note to note in a scale played on one string. The plucking point and the pickup position remain a fixed distance from the bridge, while the frets are used to shorten the string progressively. In other words, the plucking and pickup points progressively approach the center of the vibrating part of the string, and even pass it for the very highest notes.

4. Among the experiments described at the end of chapter 6 was an attempt to excite mode 1 of a chain formed by 5 carts coupled by springs, with additional springs connecting the ends of the chain to fixed anchorages (see fig. 6.12). It was suggested that if all five carts are pulled to one side and released, the system would oscillate in mode 1. From our present vantage point, we can recognize that the proposed initial configuration does not have exactly the shape of mode 1. In particular, the center cart is not pulled sufficiently far to one side. It is worthwhile to figure out why we can be sure that a small amount of mode 3 is in fact present in the initial shape, but none of mode 2. Is there any of mode 4 or mode 5 in the initial recipe?

5. Owners of steel-string guitars or similar instruments having metallic strings can repeat all of the experiments described for the electric guitar by using a trick which has been familiar to acousticians for about half a century (see fig. 7.10). If the two ends of the string are connected to the phono or microphone input terminals of a home music amplifier, bringing a magnet near the string will give rise to a signal whose recipe depends on the magnet position in a way

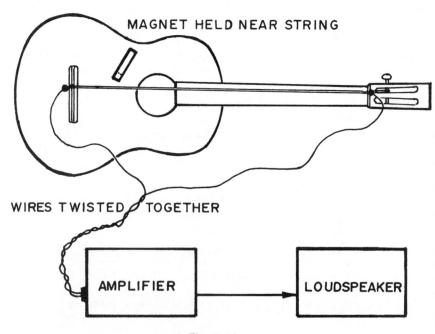

Fig. 7.10.

that is precisely the same as that described for a normal guitar pickup. (The metal-wound lower strings of a classical guitar can be used in the same way.)

Digression on Electric Guitar Pickups.

A physicist reading about electromagnetic pickups on vibrating strings takes it for granted that the electrical signal going to the amplifier is proportional at any instant to the velocity of the string's motion past the magnet. He may then be tempted to make some incorrect generalizations about the sound recipe produced by the loudspeaker, unless he takes into account the fact that phonograph and guitar amplifiers are both provided with equalizing or compensating circuits as well as with tone controls which drastically alter the sound recipe. Furthermore, the loudspeakers used with guitars are "voiced" differently from normal loudspeakers in order to make additional musically desirable adjustments to the sound recipe.

6. We have just learned that the amplitude with which a given mode is excited on a struck string depends jointly on the distance of the striking point from a node and on a factor $(1/n)$ which is determined by the serial number of the mode. Figure 7.8 in section 7.3 suggests that a string struck very near one end excites all the lower modes with *practically equal amplitude* (that is, all the modes whose interhump length is somewhat

more than twice the distance from hammer to fixed end). Verify this observation with the help of careful sketches. Notice that the modes having successively higher serial numbers than the ones described above are excited with rapidly decreasing amplitudes, because their first nodes lie ever closer to the hammer position. Note also that the analogous result for a plucked string leads to amplitudes for the lower modes that can be described simply as varying as $(1/n)$, rather than according to the formula (plectrum position) $\times (1/n^2)$, which is the description given in section 7.2.

Notes

1. Alexander Wood, *Acoustics*, 2d ed. (1960; reprint ed., New York: Dover, 1966), pp. 377–81, and Horace Lamb, *The Dynamical Theory of Sound*, 2d ed. (1925; reprint ed., New York: Dover, 1960), p. 73. We will examine further the behavior of plucked harpsichord strings in chapter 18.

2. Philip M. Morse, *Vibration and Sound*, 2d ed. (New York: McGraw-Hill, 1948), pp. 87–88; A. B. Wood, *A Textbook of Sound*, 3rd rev. ed. (1955; reprint ed., London: Bell, 1960), pp. 98–101; and Lamb, *Dynamical Theory of Sound*, pp. 73–74. We will return to a discussion of struck string behavior in chapter 17, which is concerned with sound production by the piano.

8

Broad Hammers and Plectra, Soft Hammers, and the Stiffness of Strings

What we have learned in chapter 7 about the vibration recipes associated with knife-edged exciters of strings will help us understand the vibrations produced when a broad plectrum or a wide hammer acts on a string. Once we have organized our thinking about somewhat more realistic plectra and hammers, it will not prove difficult to deal with the changes in vibration recipe that are associated with the stiffness of a real string or with the softness of a real piano hammer.

8.1. The Equivalence of Broad Plectra to Sets of Narrow Ones

The top part of figure 8.1 shows the initial shape of a string pulled aside by a broad hooklike plectrum. The middle diagram shows that identically the same shape may be produced by using two narrow plectra of the sort we have met with before. The bottom diagram of figure 8.1 suggests a way in which a more complicated initial shape may be obtained through the use of a suitable number of additional narrow plectra. In principle there is no limit to the number of plectra we could use; a sufficient number of them can be properly located and pulled aside the proper distances to produce any desired initial shape. In other words, a col-

lection of narrow plectra can take the place of whatever real-world combination of finger-tips, fingernails, and sharp-edged picks we wish to invent.

One may well ask what is the utility of the mental replacement of an actual string picker by a collection of narrow plectra. The answer is that the vibration recipe associated with any given initial shape may be deduced in a straightforward way simply by combining the recipes that would be produced by the narrow plectra acting one at a time. Let us see with the help of figure 8.2 how this comes about. The top part of figure 8.2 shows the characteristic vibrational shape of mode 1 for a flexible string, along with a possible arrangement of two plectra. Plectrum 1 is located at the string center, at a spot where (acting alone) it would produce maximum excitation of mode 1; plectrum 2 is located half way between the center and one end of the string. When it acts by itself, plectrum 2 would, as we learned in chapter 7, produce less than the maximum excitation of mode 1. If the two plectra acting one at a time are pulled aside equal distances, then plectrum 2 would in our example produce only 70.7% as strong an initial amplitude for mode 1 as would plectrum 1. We come now to the point of asking the result when both plectra are pulled aside in the same direction an

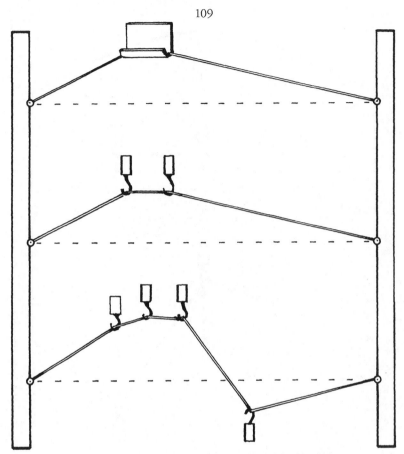

Fig. 8.1. Ways to Achieve Various Initial String Shapes

equal distance to produce an initial string shape of the sort shown in the middle part of figure 8.2. It is not hard to accept the plausibility of an assertion that the initial amplitude of mode 1 is now equal to the sum of the mode 1 amplitudes produced by the two plectra acting separately. In other words, let a_1 stand for the transverse deflection of plectrum 1 at the string midpoint. Let the corresponding mode 1 amplitude of the string be 1.0, under the condition when plectrum 1 acts by itself. Let b_1 stand for the transverse deflection of plectrum 2. The top plot of figure 8.2 shows that the corresponding mode 1 amplitude is 0.707 under the condition

when plectrum 2 acts by itself such that $b_1 = a_1$. When both plectra act together in the same direction (see middle plot of figure 8.2), the transverse displacement is constant and equal to $a_1 + (2/3)b_1$ between the two original plucking points. See figures 7.1 and 7.2 for the nature of the calculation of the factor 2/3. If the two plectra displacements are equal ($b_1 = a_1$), then the corresponding mode 1 amplitude of the string is

$$1a_1 + 0.707(2/3)a_1 = 1.47\ a_1$$

There is another way in which plectra at the same two plucking points could be used to excite the string. Suppose that

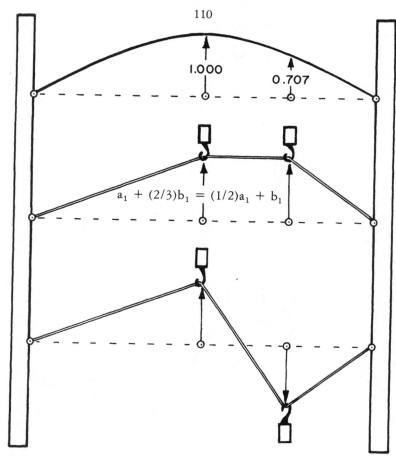

Fig. 8.2.

plectrum 1 is arranged to pull upward on the string exactly as before, while plectrum 2 acting separately pulls the string downward an equal distance. If both plectra act on the string, the initial string shape is now of the sort shown in the bottom part of figure 8.2. Plectrum 1 acting by itself produces a mode 1 hump which arches above the line made by the undisturbed string. Immediately after release, the string begins to move downward. Plectrum 2, acting by itself, on the other hand, gives rise to a downward arching of the mode 1 initial shape, and upon release the string will start to move in an upward direction. In other words, the effect of an upward pull of plectrum 1 in producing some mode 1 excitation is counteracted (at least in part) by the downward pull of plectrum 2. Because of the different efficacy with which the two plucking positions excite mode 1, there is not complete cancellation. Thus, as before, we use the symbol a_1 to stand for the transverse displacement of plectrum 1 acting alone, and the corresponding mode 1 amplitude is 1.0. We use the symbol b_1 to stand for the transverse displacement of plectrum 2 acting alone, and the corresponding mode 1 amplitude is -0.707, with the negative sign indicating a displacement downwards for the case $b_1 = -a_1$. For this same case (see bottom plot of figure 8.2), the corresponding mode 1 amplitude of the string for both plectra acting in opposition is

$$1a_1 - 0.707(2/3)a_1 = 0.53\,a_1$$

Let us further clarify the nature of our recipe addition process with the help of yet another example. The top line of figure 8.3 shows the vibrational shape characteristic of mode 7 of a flexible string. In the second line of the diagram we see the initial string shape produced by the ac-

tion of two plectra pulling upward at two of the positions of maximum excitation for mode 7. Arguments exactly similar to those in the preceding paragraph lead us to expect these plectra to result in an initial amplitude for mode 7 that is twice as big as that produced by either one of these plectra acting alone. We can realize further that mode 7 would be excited to exactly the same degree if the two plectra had been located at *any* pair of points marked p along the string. The third line

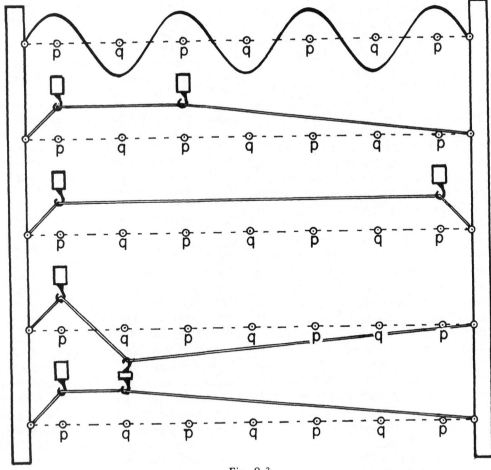

Fig. 8.3.

in the diagram presents one such example.

Suppose now that, instead of two plectra located at the two points marked p on the diagram, we have one located to pull upward at a p and one located to pull downward at a point marked q. A simple example of this case is illustrated in the 4th line of figure 8.3. Here again the two plectra are at points of maximum excitation for mode 7; since an upward pull at point p gives rise to exactly the same arrangement of upward and downward arching humps as does a downward pull at point q, we find again that mode 7 gets a joint excitation which is twice as large as the excitation produced by the two plectra acting separately.

The final arrangement of plectra which we need to consider is that shown in the bottom line of figure 8.3. Here the initial string shape is produced by a plectrum at p as before, while the second plectrum is still applied at q, but instead of pulling down it pulls up. In this case the two plectra are working against one another: the plectrum on the left is trying to produce an oscillation in which all parts of the string marked p have a downward initial motion after release (and all points marked q start to move upward). On the other hand, the plectrum on the right would, acting by itself, set up an oscillation in which all the points marked q will start to move downward upon release, with the p's moving upward. In other words the two plectra are acting in opposition, and because they produce equally strong excitations, the net result is that mode 7 is not excited at all in this case. Nor for that matter are modes 14, 21, 28, and 35 excited.

Once again we have undergone a long series of step-by-step investigations of the behavior of a plucked string, only this time we have dealt with two plectra instead of a single one. As before, we find it possible to summarize the results of our investigations in a very few words, and also to extend them in various ways whose interpretation is straightforward:

1. The vibration recipe produced by several plectra acting simultaneously is found by combining the recipes belonging to each plectrum acting alone.

2. In combining several recipes one must remember that they may have to be added or subtracted to take care of the fact that certain plectrum positions release a given mode so that it initially starts moving in the opposite direction to that produced by a plectrum located elsewhere.

3. Two plectra pulling in the same direction will act very much like a single plectrum pulled back twice as far, as long as we are considering modes for which the inter-plectrum distance is less than about one-third of the length of a hump.

4. Two plectra pulling in the same direction will produce zero excitation of any mode for which the hump length along the string is exactly equal to the distance between the plectra (or for which the inter-plectrum distance is exactly an odd number of hump lengths). This is true regardless of where along the string the pair of plectra may be placed.

5. Modes whose hump lengths are only a little larger or smaller than the inter-plectrum distance are weakly excited since they approximately meet the criterion for zero excitation given in assertion 4 above.

These five summarizing assertions will allow us to understand many things about plucked strings as they are used in musical instruments. The fact that all of these statements prove to be applicable, with only small changes, to the excitations of struck strings and of soundboards and rooms is another, very compelling reason why so much care and so many pages have been devoted to their exposition.

Let us focus our attention mainly on the last three of the assertions given above as we relate them to the real behavior of a guitar string. Reference back to the top two parts of figure 8.1 reminds us that a plectrum of width W acts on a string in very much the same way as a pair of narrow plectra separated by the distance W. This leads us to the realization that the width of a plectrum directly influences the total number of string modes that it is able to excite. For example, when one uses thumb and forefinger, the plectrum is something for which W is about 2 cm, implying that a string mode whose hump length is 2 cm will not be appreciably excited (assertion 4). (For present purposes the effect of the softness of the thumb and forefinger has been neglected.) Since a guitar string is about 60 cm long (call this length L) and since the mode number n itself is equal to the number of humps belonging to its own characteristic vibrational shape, we find that there is no excitation possible of the mode whose serial number n is found as follows:

$$n = \frac{L}{W} = \frac{60 \text{ cm}}{2 \text{ cm}} = 30$$

We can extend this result by using assertion 5 to show that there is very little excitation of the string modes near mode 30. Furthermore, the $1/n^2$ factor which we met for the displacement amplitude of plucked strings in chapter 7 assures us that modes above mode 30 are very weakly excited for this additional reason. Returning now to assertion 3, we find that the vibrational recipe for modes whose hump length is more than about three times the length of string covered by thumb and forefinger can be calculated with good accuracy by the simple narrow-plectrum substitutions outlined in the first part of this chapter. For the case at hand these modes, whose hump length is more than three times the 2 cm plectrum length, have serial numbers lower than 10:

$$n = \frac{L}{3W} = \frac{60 \text{ cm}}{3 \times 2 \text{ cm}} = 10$$

Let us now summarize the results of our computations. One can accurately describe the recipe for a string plucked by thumb and forefinger by telling the amplitudes of the first 10 or so modes as they are calculated by using narrow plectrum procedures. The simple calculations we are using will not give us the details for modes whose serial numbers lie between 10 and 30, but if we know something about the lower-numbered modes and also know the cutoff beyond which no modes are excited, then we have most of the essential information for a vibration recipe. As one might expect, the modes between numbers 10 and 30 progressively diminish.

If we pluck at the same guitar string using a pick for which W = 0.2 cm (only a tenth of the former width), exactly similar calculations show that the serial number of the highest modes to be excited is now tenfold larger (300), while the upper limit for applicability of simple theory is raised from mode 10 to mode 100.

As a matter of fact, our whole method of analysis breaks down for modes having serial numbers higher than about 40 (due to string stiffness effects with which we will deal shortly). Even so, this limitation on our ability to estimate recipes is useful, chiefly because modes having serial numbers above about 30 are weakly excited. Recall that there is a factor $1/n^2$ that governs the displacement of plucked strings and a factor n that governs the transformation to the force exerted by the string on the bridge (or string support). These reduce transmission of the initial string amplitudes by a factor more than $\frac{1}{30}$ below the amplitudes of lower frequency components so they make a nearly inaudible contribution to the sound. In any event, we have seen examples now of the ways in which plucking position and plectrum width can be used to control the vibration recipe of a string and therefore will ultimately influence the nature of the emitted sound from a musical instrument.

8.2. The Effect of Hammer Width on the Recipe for a Struck String

When one strikes a string with a hammer, the resulting vibrational recipe produced by a wide soft hammer differs from that resulting from a narrow hard hammer in ways that are very similar to those we found when the string is picked with a broad or a narrow plectrum. There are however two parts to what we might call the piano-designer's problem.

Typically the impulse transmitted to a string during the blow of a real hammer is not distributed uniformly along the part of the string touched by the hammer. The central part of the hammer is firmer than are the edges, since it is supported on both sides by the rest of the material, so that the momentary forces exerted on the string by the center of the hammer are larger than those exerted by the edges. Figure 8.4 illustrates what would happen if for example one were to strike a block of wax instead of a string by means of a piano hammer. The dent left in the wax would not necessarily be of the same shape as the undisturbed profile of the hammer felt; on the contrary, the depth of the depression would at any point across the region of hammer contact indicate the magnitude of the impulsive

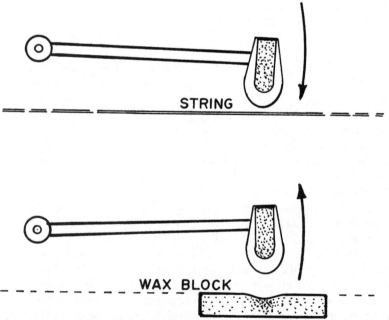

Fig. 8.4. Variation of Force Exerted by Different Parts of a Piano Hammer on a String

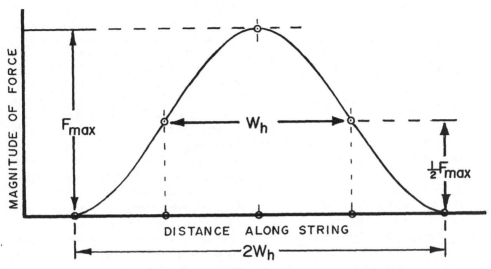

Fig. 8.5. Distribution of Hammer Force along the String

force that had been impressed on that post of the wax at the instant of the blow.

Figure 8.5 shows a slightly idealized version of the *force distribution* implied by our experiment with wax and a piano hammer. As a matter of fact such a force distribution is, in all its essential features, typical of the blows struck by all hammers in the real world, whether one is thinking of the felt piano hammer or of the rubber and wooden balls used by xylophonists, the metal clappers of church bells, or the pencil erasers and ballpoint pen butts we might use in the course of our informal experiments. For definiteness we will use the letter W_h to indicate the width of the hammer in the sense that *within the range W_h of position along the string,* the force rises to values that are at least half the magnitude of the maximum force (denoted by F_{max}) exerted at the central part of the struck region. We will further assume that the string has a limited region that is acted upon by any force at all, and this region is of width $2W_h$. While mathematicians find that

our desired conclusions are most easily obtained if we assume that the curve of figure 8.3 is of sinusoidal form, they also discover that almost any well-localized force distribution leads to essentially the same results, as long as W_h is defined as it is above, i.e., as the distance between points where the force is equal to $1/2$ F_{max}. The width W_h of the blow plays a role for struck strings that is almost exactly analogous to that of the inter-plectrum distance in the first half of this chapter. The nature of a struck-string vibration recipe produced by a broad-faced hammer whose width is identified by the letter W_h can be summarized by the following statements:

1. Vibrational modes for which the W_h is less than one-half the length of a hump are excited in almost exactly the same way as by a narrow hammer.

2. Modes for which the humps are approximately equal in length to the width W_h are excited about half as strongly as they would be by a narrow hammer.

3. If the width W_h extends over two or

more humps of a vibrational mode shape, the mode receives almost no excitation.

It is worth noticing how very similar these three statements are to the ones that deal with wide plectra. There are small numerical differences, but the overall qualitative behavior is exactly the same.

8.3. The Effect of Impact Duration on the Recipe for a Struck String

When any real hammer strikes a string, not only does the strength of its briefly exerted force vary from point to point along the region (of width W_h) in which it strikes the string, but also the force varies in time during the duration of the impact. The magnitude of the force varies during the blow in a straightforward manner, chiefly because of the progressive

compression of the hammer material during the first part of the collision and its subsequent relaxation during the latter part as the hammer rebounds. The top part of figure 8.6 shows (as in a multiple-flash photograph) the approach and rebound of a hypothetical hammer as it strikes the surface of a hard block. Clearly, there is no force exerted on the block by the hammer before the two come into contact. The force then rises smoothly as the hammer moves downward and compresses the material at its tip. The force reaches a maximum when the hammer reaches the end of its motion, at which moment the head is compressed the most. After this, the force becomes progressively weaker as the hammer recedes, in a manner that is very nearly a reversal in time of the behavior during approach. The lower part of figure

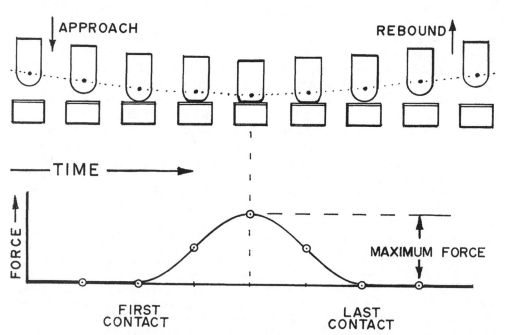

Fig. 8.6.   Time Variation of the Force Exerted by a Hammer as It Strikes and Rebounds

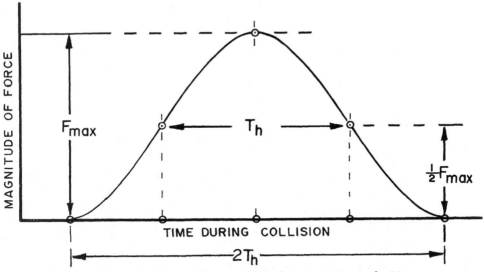

Fig. 8.7. Variation of Hammer Force during the Time of a Blow

8.6 shows in graphical form this variation of the force exerted on the block during the time of impact, the height of the curve at any time giving a visible measure of the magnitude of the force which acts at that time.

It turns out that figure 8.7 is a very good representation of the time variation of any impulsive force that we are likely to meet. This sort of time variation (which is well-known to communications engineers as a "hanning pulse") is drawn as a short segment of a sinusoid. The letter T_h indicates the time duration of the hammer blow. Strictly speaking T_h is the time interval over which the force is equal to or greater than half of the maximum force F_{max} that is exerted during the collision. Notice that the appearance of figure 8.7 is very similar to that of figure 8.5. In one case we have shown the variation *along the string* of the force exerted during a hammer blow, and in the other case it is the variation *in the course of time* of the same force. As we shall see in a moment, this similarity of temporal and spatial aspects of the behavior of hammer forces leads also to a similarity in the way in which they both affect the vibration recipe of a struck string.

As we know, every natural vibration of a string has its own characteristic frequency of (damped) sinusoidal oscillation, as well as its own characteristic vibrational shape. In dealing with the influence of plectrum width on the vibration recipes of plucked strings (or the influence of hammer width in the case of struck strings), we found that everything depended on the relation between the width W of the exciter and the length H of a hump belonging to a particular vibrational mode. When dealing with the duration T_h of a hammer blow we find an exactly similar sort of relationship between T_h and the repetition time required for one complete back-and-forth cycle of the oscillation for the mode in question. This repetition time, which is also called the *period* P of the oscillation, is of course equal to the reciprocal of the oscillation frequency f: $P = 1/f$. The close similarity between the relations between P and T_h to those found to connect W_h and H are very well displayed by the fact that the following assertions about the effect of a finite duration of the impact *time* on the vibration recipe of a struck string have been copied from those given earlier for the effect of hammer width, with only a few words changed:

1. Vibrational modes for which T_h is less than one-half of the time interval P/2 are excited in almost exactly the same way as by a hypothetical hammer that strikes and rebounds instantly.

2. Modes for which the time interval P/2 is approximately equal in length to the collision time T_h are excited about half as strongly

as they would be by a hammer that strikes and rebounds instantly.

3. If the duration T_h extends over a time of one or more oscillatory periods, the mode receives almost no excitation.

8.4. The Effect of String Stiffness on the Excitation of Strings

When one pulls a real string aside by means of a knifelike plectrum, the stiffness of the string prevents it from assuming a sharply marked triangular shape of the sort which has been sketched in the top line of figure 7.8 in chapter 7. Figure 8.8 shows the nature of the deflection of a real string as it compares with that of the

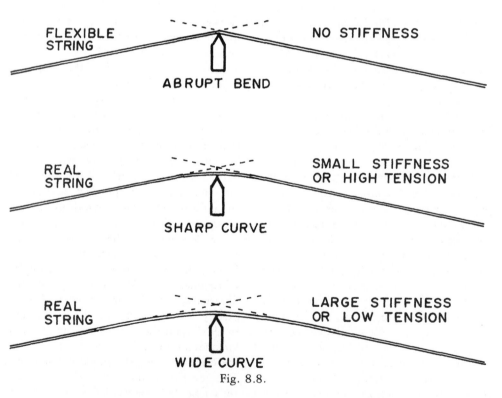

Fig. 8.8.

idealized flexible string that we have discussed so far. The top diagram shows how a completely flexible string under tension bends abruptly around a sharp-edged object. The center diagram shows that a string having small stiffness or one under great tension bends in a smooth curve around a sharp object, the bent region being restricted to a short distance on either side of the edge. The bottom diagram indicates that a very stiff string or one under relatively low tension bends around a deflecting object in a smoother curve of considerably greater extent.

One can see curvatures of this sort by using a magnifying glass to examine the strings of a guitar at the point where they run over the bridge and at the fixed nut at the far end of the neck. The curvatures observed for the bass strings differ from those of the treble strings, and one also finds differences between nylon and steel strings.

There is a close relation between struck and plucked strings, so it is at least plausible that the presence of curvature at the plucking point will eliminate the higher modes from the vibration recipe in a way that is similar to the elimination resulting from blows by a soft or round-faced hammer. The mathematical analysis of the effect is not particularly easy, nor is it a simple matter to outline the arguments in a book such as this. We will therefore content outselves with the following summary of the results:

1. The presence of string stiffness will greatly reduce the excitation of higher modes in a manner similar to that resulting from the use of wide plectra or hammers.

2. Increasing the string tension and/or reducing the string stiffness will make the vibration recipe of a real string behave progressively more like that of a flexible string.

One finds that because of stiffness effects in guitar strings, there can be very little excitation of modes above about serial number 40 or 50 (depending on the type of string). This is true even if such excitation is otherwise permitted by the plectrum width.

8.5. The Upper Limits of the Vibration Recipe: *A Summary*

Our analysis of the excitation of plucked and struck strings has had only four major ideas running through it. Because of their direct musical importance and because of their wider implications, we should review these ideas and put them in a broader context.

The first major idea is that the strength of excitation of a string mode caused by either plucking or striking the string with a narrow object is proportional to the relative excursion of that vibrational shape at the point of excitation. Disturbing the string at any nodal point for a certain mode thus gives zero excitation to the mode. Excitation is, on the other hand, at a maximum when the string is impulsively disturbed at any points of large oscillation (which are found to lie between the nodal points). Systematic application of this idea to each characteristic vibrational mode belonging to a string allows us to deduce the entire vibrational recipe resulting from an impulsive excitation.

The second major idea is that the vibrational recipe associated with excitation by an extended plectrum or hammer may be deduced by suitably adding the recipes belonging to a set of closely spaced narrow exciters arranged to give the string the same initial state as that produced by the actual exciter. We found also that this idea of superposing the effects of impulses distributed along the string could be adapted to the case of impulses distributed over a short period of time.

The third major idea is that regardless of the nature of the excitation, if it is distributed along the string, modes whose hump length is comparable to the width of the distribution will not be excited. The exact numerical relationships vary from case to case, but the effect of exciter width in eliminating the higher-numbered modes is always found. An exactly similar relationship is found between the duration of a hammer blow and the period of oscillation of a given mode of oscillation. Modes whose periods are shorter than the impact time are weakly excited.

The fourth important idea appearing throughout chapters 7 and 8 is that the vibration recipe of any *plucked* string has the amplitudes of its first, second, third, fourth, and nth modes reduced by the factors $1/1^2$, $1/2^2$, $1/3^2$, $1/4^2$, . . . , $1/n^2$, . . . ; on the other hand, the recipe of a *struck* string has a set of reduction factors which run 1, 1/2, 1/3, 1/4, . . . , $1/n$, . . . for the successive modes. This pair of effects is present over and above any complication produced by the size and hardness of the exciter or its point of application.

There are analogous though more complicated reduction factors to be found in the two-dimensional case of a drumhead or a soundboard, as well as for the impulsive excitations of rooms. At this point, however, we will not need to know much about them beyond the fact that the higher frequency modes are less well excited than are the lower ones, just as in the case of strings. Furthermore, the re-

duction takes place more rapidly in the case of plucked (initial displacement) excitations than it does when a metal sheet is struck with a hammer or when a firecracker is set off in a room.

The first three of our set of four major ideas listed above will carry over unchanged to the behavior of soundboards, rooms, etc., and we will make constant use of them and of their further implications throughout our work. The last section of this chapter will provide several examples of their utility in helping us to understand the excitation of various sorts of stringed instruments.

8.6. Examples, Experiments, and Questions

1. The highest pitched string on a steel-stringed guitar provides us with an excellent experimental subject for the exploration of many phenomena which we have met in this chapter and in chapter 7. For example, we found that plucking a string *precisely* at its midpoint gives rise to a vibration whose recipe contains only the odd-numbered modes. Listening experiments with the guitar also inform us that the tone we hear in this case is peculiar and hollow-sounding. Furthermore, we discover that plucking only half a finger's width off-center almost completely eliminates the special hollow quality of the tone. As we move our plucking further and further away from the center of the string, the remaining tone color changes are relatively slight until we get very close indeed to the fixed string ends. (When the string is plucked exactly 1/3 of the way from one end, which eliminates modes 3, 6, 9, etc., from the recipe, it gives a sound which is only a little dif-

ferent from that arising from nearby plucking points.) The perceptual status of a sound that is lacking even-numbered harmonic partials is quite different from that of any other sounds. Even a very small addition of the even harmonics (produced by plucking off-center) will essentially destroy the special status. Excitation arithmetic based on a plucking point that is 1 cm away from the center point of a 60 cm string shows us that the lower seven members of the normalized vibration recipe have the following initial amplitudes: 1.000, 0.026, 0.111, 0.013, 0.040, 0.009, 0.020. Notice how small the amplitudes of the even-numbered modes are compared to their odd-numbered immediate neighbors. According to our analysis so far, the normalized recipe produced by plucking at the exact center is found by replacing all the even-numbered mode amounts by zeros.

2. Let us continue our experiments with the top string of a guitar in order to study the effects of damping various sets of modes selectively. Thus, if one first plucks the string (at any normal spot) and then lightly touches the *exact* midpoint of the string with the corner of a soft foam sponge, modes 1, 3, and 5 will die away quickly, leaving modes 2, 4, 6, . . . to ring on in essentially their normal fashion. This effect of selective damping comes about because all odd-numbered modes have a large excursion at the midpoint, so that they can rub away their oscillations by friction against the piece of foam. On the other hand, for even-numbered modes the string is at rest at the mid-point, so that there is no retarding effect exerted upon them by the sponge.

What happens to the pitch of the sound of this plucked string when we apply our sponge damper? When the

string is first plucked, its vibration recipe contains components oscillating at 329.6/second and its (very nearly) whole-number multiples. Such a collection made up of a fundamental and its harmonics has the 329.6/second repetition rate which we associate with the note E_4 just above piano middle C. After the damping has had time to take effect, we are left with components whose frequencies are $2 \times 329.6 = 659.2$/second and its whole-number multiples, and we say that the pitch has gone up an octave from E_4 to E_5.

If an exactly similar experiment is carried out with the damping sponge applied exactly 1/3 of the way along the string from either end, we find that only modes numbered 3, 6, 9, 12, . . . survive undamped, giving us a perceived pitch very close to the one tabulated for B_5, essentially a musical twelfth above the original pitch of the string. What would we hear if dampers were simultaneously applied to the string at the midpoint and 1/3 of the way along it?

Let us now notice what happens when the sponge is kept lightly in contact with the string *before* it is plucked. For an instant after the string is plucked we hear the original pitch of the normal string, but this version of the sound appears to die away almost at once to leave a more persistent tone at the higher pitch. We have here a spectacular example of changes produced in the nature of a sound as it dies away if the various modes of vibration have different halving times. Our ears are by how sufficiently educated to listen for the less marked but musically important changes that take place when a single key of the piano is struck and held down until all vestiges of the tone have died away.

3. There are many more ways in which we can use selective damping techniques to check up on the effects of plucking point on the excitation of various string modes. For example, if the string is plucked exactly at its center, we have been led to expect complete silence to result if the damper is also applied at the string's midpoint. In actual fact, the experiment works well when it is tried, provided one is careful to pluck and to damp the string *precisely* at the midpoint.

The duration of a hammer blow and its effect on the excitation of various vibratory modes can easily be studied with the help of a collection of pencils (with and without erasers), rubber balls, and steel balls. These can be bounced off different spots on tuning forks, glockenspiel bars, and the like, and note taken of the modes which are or are not excited by collision with a given object. Since many mode frequencies have been given throughout the book for objects of this sort, it should prove possible (by cross-checking of experiments) to prepare a table giving quite accurate estimates of the collision time T_h belonging to various objects that can be used as musical hammers.

4. In section 8.1 we explored the behavior of a string when two plectra act upon it simultaneously. We found that the two can either aid one another in exciting a given mode, or tend to counteract one another, depending on their distance apart along the string (compare the bottom two parts of fig. 8.3). Exactly similar phenomena take place when the player of a double-pickup electric guitar throws the switch to combine the signals from both pickups. For example, it is not hard to show (with the help of assertion 4 in sec. 8.1) that regardless of their position along the string, the pair of pickups produce *no signal whatever* at the frequency of a mode whose hump length matches the spacing between the pickups. Disconnecting either pickup will then restore the signal to whatever level is appropriate to the location of the functioning pickup.

There are many experiments which a thoughtful listener can carry out with the help of a two-pickup electric guitar and his ears. He can search for variations on the guitar experiments already described in this chapter and the last, making use of his newly added ability to detect (pick up) the vibrations at well-defined points on the string, while varying the plucking and damping points. One can use two small magnets in combination with the guitar string itself to form a generator of electrical signals (see experiment 5 at the end of chap. 7); this permits an even wider variety of experimentation. Turning one magnet end for end changes the additions to subtractions and vice versa when one looks into the combined effect of two magnets acting on a single string.

Let us consider the implications of what happens to the electrical recipe when both pickups are connected to the amplifier. We have learned that even if all the modes of a string were excited equally well (could this actually be done?), the electrical recipe associated with a single pickup would have irregularities in its overall pattern. This is because the sensitivity of the pickup to a given modal vibration depends on its position relative to the humps and nodes. When two pickups are connected together, we find that the recipe belonging to their joint output is even more irregular than that of either one. Over and above the fluctuations in strength of the various components as they come from the individual pickups is the fact that the pickups aid one another in responding to certain modes (giving an unusually large output signal) and for other modes they cancel one another out. A close cousin to this phenomenon besets the recording engineer when he records a performance by means of several microphones connected to his tape machine via a mixing panel.

9

The Vibrations of Drumheads and Soundboards

By now we have accumulated a considerable fund of knowledge about characteristic vibrations and how they may be selectively excited or damped out. So far our chief examples have been based on more or less close relatives to vibrating musical strings. These stringlike objects are what are often called one-dimensional vibrators. The vibrating string has a length but no appreciable breadth, in contrast to its two-dimensional cousin, a woven carpet with strings running lengthwise (the warp) and crosswise (the woof). The carpet is an object having both length and breadth. The air in a room, or some jelly in a bowl, can serve as an example of the three-dimensional objects in which oscillations can take place.

9.1. Unraveling the Mode Shapes of a Glockenspiel Bar

Let us use the glockenspiel bar first described in section 5.1 as our introductory example of vibrations that involve two dimensions. We should first focus our attention on the sound recipe component whose frequency is 1046/second. Since it is the lowest frequency component in the

set, we are fairly safe in assuming it to belong to the first (and most simply shaped) of the characteristic vibrational modes of the bar. If we move the hammer over the surface of the bar while continually tapping it, we notice that the resulting sound is particularly loud when one strikes near the middle of the bar and fairly loud when one hits near the ends. There are two places somewhat in from the ends where the hammer seems to be unable to excite mode 1. The upper part of figure 9.1 summarizes the results of these experiments. The shading is heaviest in those parts of the bar where it is most strongly excited by tapping, and becomes less pronounced in those regions where the excitation is found to be least. If we recall that the strength of excitation is greatest at those points where the vibration is of largest amplitude and is least at the positions of the nodes, we are encouraged to believe that mode 1 of our bar has a vibrational shape of the sort shown in the lower part of figure 9.1. That is, the bar bows back and forth in a simple curve, with nodes at the points where we found the weakest excitation. Let us confirm this by an experiment with selectively applied damping. Resting a finger on the bar at any point that moves

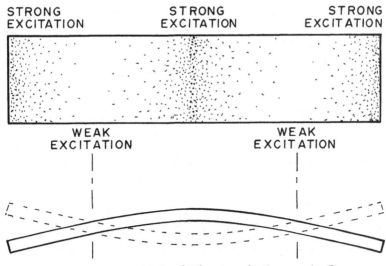

Fig. 9.1.   Lowest Mode of Vibration of a Rectangular Bar

will tend to damp out the vibration, whereas application at one of the two presumed nodal positions will leave the oscillation almost undisturbed. Testing in this manner shows this to be true and we may realize (a little sheepishly) that the experiment hardly needed to be carried out, since the soft felt strips on which the bar normally rests are already located at spots chosen to give minimum frictional damping to the mode 1 vibration.

Let us continue our study of the bar's vibrations by looking for mode 2. Every detective knows that even a partial description helps him track down a suspect, so we should guide our study by means of the best description of mode 2 that is available to us. To begin with, we have already learned its frequency, via observation of its pitch. This lets our ears pick out the relevant component of the sound. In the second place, we have noticed in a general way that any given mode of oscillation seems to have one more hump in its characteristic vibrational shape than does the next lower mode in the

sequence. Another way to express the same idea is to say that a given mode has one more node than its predecessor. Following up this clue, we make a sketch like that shown at the top of figure 9.2 for the probable vibrational shape of mode 2. This sketch suggests that there are four regions along the bar where tapping will strongly excite mode 2. It also suggests that a finger laid on the bar in its exact center will assure us that mode 1 will be effectively removed from the vibration recipe, leaving mode 2 undamped. In other words, we have found a probable way in which to separate mode 2 from mode 1 in our experiments. Now that we know what to do, we can place a finger on the middle of the bar and tap everywhere else with the hammer. The middle part of figure 9.2 shows the regions in which mode 2 turns out to be strongly excited, and those where it is only weakly set into motion, if at all. Comparison with our sketch of the presumed vibrational shape shows that the original guess was good. Further confir-

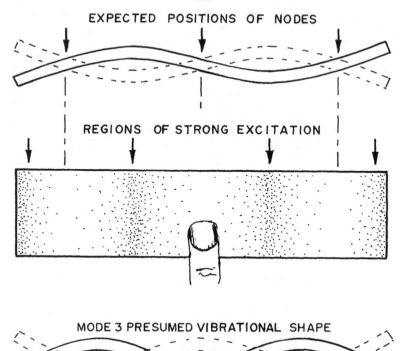

EXPECTED POSITIONS OF NODES

REGIONS OF STRONG EXCITATION

MODE 3 PRESUMED VIBRATIONAL SHAPE

Fig. 9.2. Rectangular Bar: Modes 2 and 3

mation of its correctness can be found by moving the finger to one or another of the presumed nodal spots, or even by using two or three fingers at the same time as dampers. Now that we really know what is going on, we can go back and discover that all of this can be verified by listening experiments alone. One merely taps all over the surface, while ignoring the low-frequency sound component belonging to mode 1.

By now we can lay a trap for mode 3 with the help of a sketch of the sort shown in the bottom part of figure 9.2. Here we have provided an assumed vibrational shape with three humplike curves instead of one or two, and we expect (for example) that tapping at the exact center

of the bar will give strong excitation of the 3906/second oscillation belonging to mode 3. We also expect that putting a pair of fingers symmetrically on the bar at points fairly near the center will effectively kill off modes 1 and 2 (look back at figs. 9.1 and 9.2 to see why), and leave mode 3 relatively free to vibrate. When we actually try the experiment, however, it is clear that something has gone wrong. The frequency component belonging to mode 3 is not heard. However, in the course of tinkering around (with the idea that our fingers are not quite properly placed) we notice that the pitch associated with mode 4 *can* be detected when the bar is tapped. Further investigation confirms that our presumed vibrational shape belongs in fact to mode 4, and that mode 3 has somehow managed to elude us.

The fact that mode 4 turned up in clearcut fashion in the shape expected for mode 3 shows that we have a fairly good, but not complete, understanding of vibrational mode shapes for a bar. At this point the experienced experimentalist will resort to a kind of educated messing around. He knows that the sound of mode 3 will disappear if the bar is struck at the position of a node; he knows also that in the case at hand mode 3 does not make its appearance when the bar is struck at its center, at least when fingers are laid on the bar at two points near the center. Removal of the fingers does not bring in the sound of mode 3. Tapping all over the bar, with no fingers on it at all, brings to light a pattern of mode 3 excitation of the unfamiliar sort shown in the top part of figure 9.3. There is clear evidence that striking the bar anywhere along its two mid-lines (shown dotted) fails to excite mode 3. Striking anywhere near the four corners of the bar gives rise to a strong mode-3 frequency component. Now that we have found some good clues as to what is going on, it takes only a few moments to confirm the hints gathered so far about mode shape: putting damping fingers anywhere along the two mid-lines will leave mode 3 intact, but will kill off

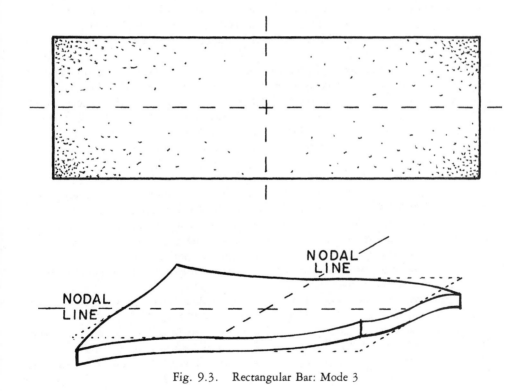

Fig. 9.3. Rectangular Bar: Mode 3

the other modes (except at the positions of *their* nodes).

We have already found that in any mode there are regions of strong vibrational disturbance (humps) separated by places in which there is no motion at all (nodes). We also have noticed that the system always moves in opposite directions on the two sides of a node. This observation that the mechanical motion on one side of a node is opposite to that on the other will allow us to unravel the vibrational shape of our bar. A glance back at the upper part of figure 9.3 suggests that the bar vibrates with each quarter of the bar moving in the opposite direction to its adjacent neighbors', as shown in the lower part of the figure. An easy way to visualize this sort of motion is to take a rectangular strip of cardboard and twist its two ends back and forth around an axis running through the long mid-line of the rectangle.

We have run through a series of experiments with the vibrational behavior of a bar partly as a way to introduce the nature of two-dimensional vibrations, and partly as an illustration of the enormous investigational power that is conferred on us when we have a general understanding of vibrational modes. With nothing but a mallet and our fingers we have acquired a great deal of detailed information about a bar; it would require rather elaborate equipment to add anything quantitative to our stock of knowledge at this point, but there is considerable practical use that can be made of the qualitative sort of information we have so easily discovered in the preceding paragraphs.[1] We shall see, for example, how violin makers and the makers of wind instruments can use methods similar to these to guide the ad-

justment of the characteristic frequencies of their wooden boxes and air columns to enhance their instruments' musical functioning.

9.2. Mode Shapes of a Rectangular Plate Having Free Edges

In the last section we carried out an experimental investigation of the first few modes of a glockenspiel bar and discovered a mode whose peculiar twisting motion was quite different from the ordinary bending implied by an analogy between bars and strings. We will now elaborate on this analogy to understand better the vibrations of a two-dimensional plate. When we look at a rectangular plate, it is easy to image two ways in which it can behave in simple, barlike fashion (i.e., like modes 1, 2, and 4 of the glockenspiel bar). Figure 9.4 shows two examples of each of these two families of bending vibration. The plus and minus signs on the rectangles are a mathematician's way of indicating which way the adjacent vibrational humps are bulging. On the left we find what have been called modes 1 and 2 of the glockenspiel bar, and on the right are exactly the same shapes, except this time we might say that the bar appears to have become wider than it is long. Let us see if we can find a way to estimate the frequencies of these newly recognized modes of oscillation.

The complete set of glockenspiel bars, taken together, indicates that short bars have higher characteristic frequencies than do long bars. Close inspection shows that each bar in the upper octave is about 70 percent of the length of its namesake an octave lower. As a result, the top C

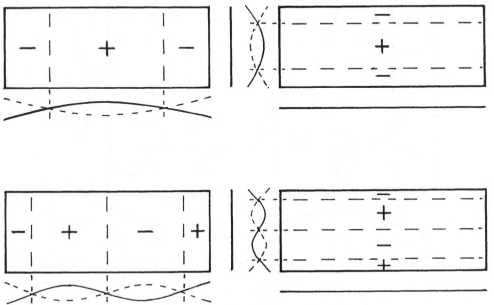

Fig. 9.4. Pairs of Similar-Appearing Modes

bar is approximately half as long as the bottom C bar two octaves lower (since $0.7 \times 0.7 \cong 0.5$). In other words, halving the length of a bar will raise its frequencies about fourfold. Since the bar shown in figure 9.4 is drawn so that its length is 2.5 times its width, we may expect then that the vibrations shown on the right-hand side will have frequencies that are more than four times those belonging to the left-hand ones. A simplified calculation of the ratio shows as a matter of fact that it is greater than 6 to 1, making the lowest of the right-hand vibration frequencies higher than the fourth characteristic frequency belonging to the left-hand set of oscillations.

Digression on Wooden Plates.
Wood has a pronounced grain, which results in its bending stiffness being much greater in one direction than the other. If for example a plate whose proportions are similar to those of figure 9.4 is cut out of wood with the grain running lengthwise, the low stiffness of the wood for bending modes of the right-hand type so far reduces their frequencies as to make them comparable to their counterparts on the left-hand side.

By tinkering around with the analogies between bars and rectangular plates we have come up with two conceivable families of natural modes of vibration. In one family the humps are arranged along the length of the plate, with nodal lines

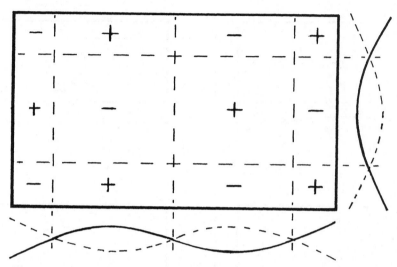

Fig. 9.5. A More Complicated Mode of Vibration of a Rectangular Bar

crossing it (as shown on the left side of fig. 9.4). In the other family, the humps run crosswise on the plate, with longitudinal nodal lines (right side of fig. 9.4). Ordinary curiosity prompts the question as to whether vibrations are not somehow possible in which there can be humps running both ways. Our recollection of the twisting mode illustrated in figure 9.3 confirms that the question is by no means absurd. Tapping experiments, or other, more formal studies of the vibrations of a rectangular plate, show that our expectations are correct. Mode shapes exist that have humps running both ways, such as the one shown in figure 9.5. This particular mode has features that are reminiscent of modes 1 and 2 of the bar (shown in figs. 9.1 and 9.2). It turns out that the natural frequency belonging to any one of these more com-

plicated modes *is always higher than that of either of its "ancestors."* This should not surprise us, since we have always found that increased complexity in the vibrational shape (i.e., increased numbers of humps separated by increased numbers of nodal regions) is associated with higher frequency. Notice also that each mode could be given a definite name, constructed out of the names of its ancestors. For a string or a narrow bar, we found that simply giving the serial number of the mode was sufficient to let us know its characteristic shape. In the two-dimensional world of a rectangular plate, we can similarly indicate a mode's shape by naming its longitudinal and transverse ancestors. If the vibrations of figures 9.1 and 9.2 are named modes 1 and 2, then the one shown in figure 9.5 is called the (2, 1) mode.

Let us now go back to the peculiar twisting mode of vibration of a glockenspiel bar. In chapter 5 we gave this mode the name *mode 3* simply because its characteristic frequency was third in line when measurements were made. In section 9.1 above we were able to figure out the vibrational shape of this mode (see fig. 9.3). Notice that its vibrational shape does not have ancestors among the tribe of one-dimensional modes, as the above discussion might lead us to expect. Its lack of such ancestors is the reason this mode is sometimes mislaid in textbook discussions of bar vibrations. This mode is also the one whose frequency is an exception to the formula given in the digression above. Despite its lonely position in the world of mathematical physics, the frequency of this twisting mode turns up as an important guide to the violin maker as he carves the top and bottom plates of his instruments to their correctly graduated thicknesses. For wooden plates that are two or three times as long in the direction of the grain as they are across it, and for uniform plates (i.e., without grain) that are roughly square, this mode turns out to have the lowest frequency of the entire set. Anyone who wishes to give his own hands a tangible feeling for the truth of this remark need only cut out a square of sheet metal (for example, 16 to 20 gauge, a hand's breadth across) and compare the feeling of stiffness it gives when it is twisted with what is felt when an attempt is made to bow it into a shape similar to that of mode 1 of a bar. In section 6.1 we learned that the frequency of oscillation of a mass on its system of springs is high if the stiffness coefficients of the springs are high, whereas the frequency is low if the springs are easily deflected. Our hands find it easy to notice

that a sheet's twisting stiffness is enormously lower than is its bending stiffness, which leads us to expect that the twisting mode will oscillate more slowly than the bending one.

9.3. The Effect of Various Boundaries

In chapters 7 and 8 we confined our attention to vibrations of wires such as those whose ends are fixed to the frame of a piano or the body of a guitar. In chapter 5 and again in the first section of the present chapter we have dealt with the vibrations of a bar that is free at its ends, as well as its cousin, a plate whose edges are left free. The front plate of a guitar, the soundboard of a piano, or the stretched leather head of a kettledrum are, on the other hand, vibrating systems whose boundaries are more or less fixed. We should therefore seek to adapt what we have learned about the characteristic vibrations of free-edged rectangles for use with sheetlike objects whose boundaries are fixed.[2]

It is possible to categorize the boundary conditions at the edges of a sheet into three limiting main types. We must not forget that in the real world one is certain to meet systems having various other sorts of boundaries. However, it is helpful to notice that the influence of these other kinds of boundaries on the characteristic vibrations is more or less similar to that of one or another of our prime categories. Let us set down descriptions of our three major boundary conditions in the form of numbered statements, each with its own illustrative examples:

1. Free edge. No externally applied constraints are placed on the edge, which is therefore free to move back and forth under the influence of the rest of the plate. The free-edge rectangular plate discussed in the previous section provided us with many examples of this sort of vibration.

2. Clamped edge. Here the whole perimeter is clamped as in the jaws of a vise. Not only is the edge fixed so that it cannot move, it is also held so that it cannot tilt up and down at the boundary. In forming a hump, the material must curve away from the flatness imposed on it by the clamp. A strip

of steel clamped at both ends provides a clear, one-dimensional example of a clamped boundary. The upper part of figure 9.6 illustrates the mode shapes belonging to the first two characteristic vibrations of such a bar. To emphasize the generality of our classification, the bar thickness varies along its length. Experiments 1, 2, and 3 at the end of chapter 4 were performed on a closely related system—a hacksaw blade with one end clamped in a vise, the other end being left free.

3. Hinged edge. If one arranges a hinged fastening for the edge of a plate or bar, it is kept from moving back and forth as in case 2 above, but it is no longer constrained from tilting. The lower part of figure 9.6 shows the first two mode shapes for a nonuniform bar

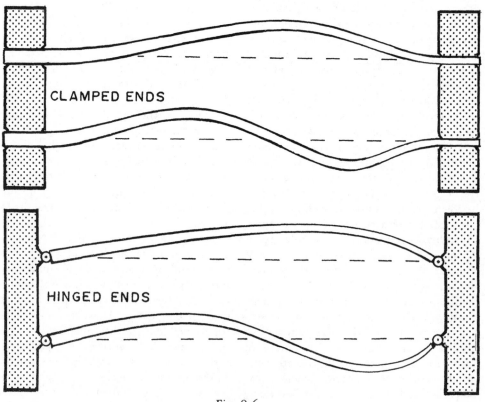

CLAMPED ENDS

HINGED ENDS

Fig. 9.6.

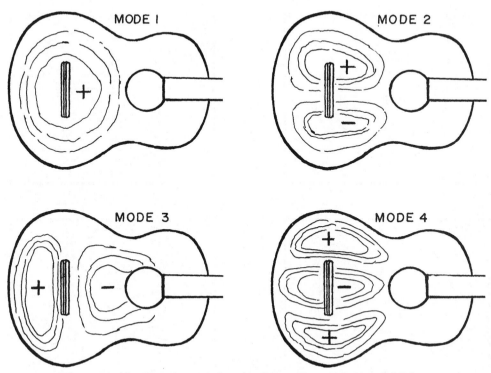

Fig. 9.7. The First Four Modes of a Guitar Plate with Clamped Edges

with hinged ends and contrasts them with those for the clamped bar shown in the upper part of the diagram.

Figure 9.7 shows the vibrational shapes of the first four modes of a guitar front plate mounted in a frame that clamps its edges firmly.[3] The shapes of the various modes here are not wildly different from what we would expect from a rectangular piece of wood, which is shown in figure 9.8. We may note in passing that the shapes belonging to modes 2 and 3 in figures 9.7 and 9.8 would appear in reverse order if the plates had been made not of wood (having a grain that runs from left to right in the diagram) but rather of some material having equal stiffness in both longitudinal and transverse directions.

We should also compare the two parts of figure 9.6 to notice that the general shapes of the various vibrational modes are only slightly changed when we shift from clamped to hinged boundaries. We can see this better in figure 9.9, the top part of which shows the characteristic shapes of the first four modes of a circular plate whose edges are solidly clamped. The lower part of the figure shows similarly the vibrational shapes that belong to the same plate when its edges are fixed to its mountings by means of a hinged joint.

We have met many examples of the idea that the more bending there is in a mode shape the higher the corresponding

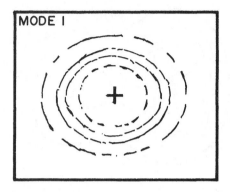

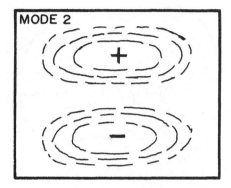

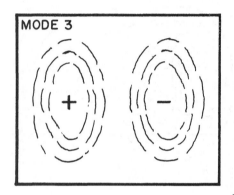

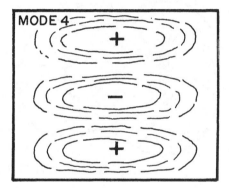

Fig. 9.8.

frequency. Because of the additional bending that is found at the edges of a clamped plate, we therefore expect the natural frequencies of its various modes to be somewhat higher than those of its hinged-edge counterpart. We can go farther yet, and expect that the difference between the two cases is less for high-numbered modes than for the lower ones because the bending associated with the ever-increasing number of humps will tend to drown the relatively constant amount of bending forced by a clamped edge. Such expectations are borne out in practice. Mode 1 for a clamped disc oscillates at a frequency 76 percent higher than is the case for a disc with a hinged boundary. The increase is 45 percent for mode 2, 32 percent for mode 3, and falls to 17 percent at mode 9. Similar changes are observed for rectangular plates, or for plates of any other shape, for that matter.

It is not difficult to recognize the connection between our discussion of clamped plates and the properties of soundboards on pianos and harpsichords. We have already met the free-edged plates by way of the glockenspiel, and one can go on to realize that cymbals, gongs, and even bells are progressively more arched versions of the same thing, somewhat in the way that the U-shaped tuning fork is an arched cousin to the free-ended bar. It is perhaps not so easy

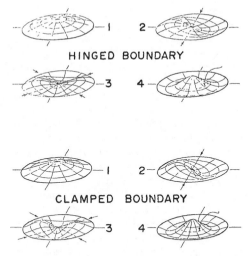

HINGED BOUNDARY

CLAMPED BOUNDARY

Fig. 9.9. Comparison of Modes of Vibration of Discs Having Clamped or Hinged Boundaries. Adapted from *Vibration and Sound* by Philip M. Morse. Copyright 1936, 1948, by the McGraw-Hill Book Company, Inc. Used with permission of the McGraw-Hill Book Company.

to understand the amount of attention that has been devoted to the hinged-edge plates. A close look at a violin or cello will reveal why: a groove runs all around the edges of both the top and the bottom plates of the instrument, and into this groove are inlaid decorative strips of hardwood. The fiddle maker has to make sure that he does not wedge these decorative strips (called the purfling) in too tightly or attach them with too much glue, for by so doing he could spoil the tone of his instrument. The purfling grooves provide a thin, hingelike anchorage for the edges of the plates. Too much stiffness imposed by wedging changes the plate modes from a sort that approximate hinged-edge modes to ones that are characteristic of boards having clamped edges.

Digression on Neglected Violins.

A violin that has not been played for a long time sometimes becomes unresponsive and has an unpleasant tone. One of the ways in which this can happen is for the purfling to become stuck too tightly in its grooves. Very loud and vigorous playing of chromatic scales for a few minutes on such a violin will often shake loose the impediments and allow its plate modes to revert to their original, properly adjusted state.

9.4. Adjustment of Frequency Relations by Variations of Thickness

We have progressed far enough in our study of musical acoustics to have some appreciation for the possible importance of arranging our vibrating objects to have suitable patterns of characteristic frequencies. Not only does the perceived pitch of a composite sound depend on the frequency relations that exist between its components, but also we have had hints that the clarity of a sound or its apparent persistence may also depend on these relations (see, for example, experiment 4 in chapter 5 where we listened to the sounds made by snapping the keys on a normal and on a slightly modified flute). It turns out that many kinds of musical instruments depend for their excellence upon the careful adjustment of their characteristic frequencies. The reasons this adjustment must be made and the means used to achieve it differ as we go from drums to violins and guitars and thence by way of the human voice to the wind instruments. There are, however, a few basic principles common to all adjustment procedures that can be explained easily at this point in our study of two-dimensional vibrators.

In the present section we will sketch out two ways in which variations of thickness from point to point on the surface of a plate or membrane can alter its natural frequencies. We then will devote the section that follows to a description of the way the pitchless thump of an ordinary drumhead is converted into the clear, ringing tone of a properly tuned kettledrum.

A flexible membrane such as a drumhead is related to a circular plate in the same way that a flexible string is related to a bar. The analogy is closest if the plate and the bar have hinged rather than clamped boundaries. In either case we should recall that the spring forces which try to restore the plate to flatness are produced by the stiffness of the material. The flexible string and membrane are, on the other hand, lacking in stiffness, so that they must be pulled tight at the boundaries in order for their tension to supply the restoring force.

Interestingly enough, the vibrational shapes of a circular membrane under tension are exactly the same as those of a plate having hinged edges (see the upper part of fig. 9.9). Despite this similarity of vibrational shapes, the two sequences of characteristic frequency ratios are not at all alike, as the following tabular comparison shows:

Mode number	Membrane	Plate
1	1.000	1.000
2	1.593	2.092
3	2.135	3.427
4	2.295	3.910
5	2.653	6.067

Notice how much farther apart the plate's lower few frequencies are in comparison with those of a membrane. This qualitative observation applies not only to circular objects, but also to surfaces having boundaries of any shape whatever.

Digression on the Average Spacing of Successive Natural Frequencies.

In addition to the contrast between the first few frequency ratios described above for membranes and plates of any shape whatever, it is possible to make general assertions about the behavior of the high frequency modes. Once we get above about serial number 5 in the sequence of modes, we find in the case of a vibrating plate that the difference between successive characteristic frequencies is roughly constant, whereas for membranes this difference becomes progressively smaller. These generalizations are once again independent of the shape of the vibrating object. We find that some of the features which distinguish the sound of a concert grand piano from that of a small spinet arise as a result of these general properties as they apply to soundboards of various sizes. We will also meet a cousin to the membrane generalization when we compare the acoustics of a small music studio with that of a large concert hall.

Let us ask now what the effect is of sticking a small lump of wax onto a plate at some point. In section 6.1 we learned that the frequency of any characteristic sinusoidal oscillation was determined jointly by the stiffness coefficient S of some sort of spring and by the amount of moving mass M which is oscillating back and forth, according to a formula which is reproduced here:

$$f = \sqrt{S/M} \text{ times a numerical constant}$$

In a book such as this it is not possible for us to work out the detailed interpretation of this formula for the case where M stands for the mass of a diaphragm. We can however readily understand that increasing M by the addition of a lump of wax of mass m will lower the frequency. Furthermore, we should now have enough understanding of vibration to realize that adding the wax at a point of maximum excursion will produce maximum effect on the frequency. Adding the wax on a node will, however, produce no frequency change at all, since in this case the mass remains stationary and does not have to be dragged back and forth as a part of the oscillation. Furthermore, if we add several tiny lumps of wax, the net shift of the various natural frequencies is simply the aggregate of the changes produced by each lump acting separately.

Lord Rayleigh (whom we first met in chap. 5 in connection with his work on bells) has provided the world of physics with some extremely powerful mathematical procedures which not only permit calculation of the effects of loading a membrane or plate, but even allow us to discover some universally applicable answers giving us the order of magnitude of the effect without the need for further calculation.[4] The following set of three assertions is based on application of Rayleigh's methods, and is able to give us numerical information to combine with what we have already learned:

1. Attaching a lump of mass m to some point on a plate will lower the vibration frequency of its characteristic modes.

2. The effect of such a lump on a given mode is the maximum if the load is attached at a point of maximum excursion. There is no effect if the lump is attached on a nodal point or line.

3. Attaching a lump at a point of maximum excursion will make a fractional change in frequency that is equal to about twice the fractional increase of total mass produced by the addition of the lump. That is, for each mode:

$$\left(\frac{\text{maximum possible frequency reduction}}{\text{original frequency}}\right)$$
$$\cong 2\left(\frac{\text{added mass}}{\text{original diaphragm mass}}\right)$$

This approximate result holds for systems with boundaries of any shape.

Let us illustrate these assertions with the help of a simple example. Suppose a 1/2-gram lump of wax is attached at the exact center of a thin disc of sheet iron whose diameter is 10 cm (a hand's breadth) and whose thickness is 0.025 cm (1/4 the thickness of a dime). It has a first-mode frequency of vibration of 250/second. Assume that the disc is clamped at its circumference. The mass of such a disc is close to 15 grams, so that assertion 3 tells us that the fractional change in frequency produced by the 1/2-gram load has an upper limit of about 7 percent, as shown by the following arithmetic:

$$\left(\frac{\text{maximum possible frequency change}}{\text{frequency}}\right)$$
$$\cong 2\left(\frac{0.5\,\text{grams}}{15\,\text{grams}}\right) = 0.067$$

That is, mode 1 for a loaded disc has a natural frequency of about $250 - 16.7 = 233.3$/second. A musician listening to the sound of our disc would say that the pitch of mode 1 was originally a little above B_3 (next to piano middle C) and that the added wax lowered the pitch by slightly more than a semitone, to a spot just above $A_3\sharp$.

We now turn to a consideration of mode 2. Figure 9.9 shows that when a disc vibrates in its second mode, it has a nodal line running across its diameter, so that our lump of wax is sitting at a spot where it remains stationary. Mode 2 is, according to assertion 2, *not altered at all* by the addition of the wax. Reference to the table of frequency ratios given earlier in this section shows that mode 2 for this plate has a natural frequency of

$250 \times 2.092 = 523$/second, which is associated with a pitch that is a trifle lower than C_5.

The musical interval between the pitches for modes 1 and 2 was originally about a semitone more than an octave (from B_3 to C_4 approximately), while the addition of the wax stretches this interval so that it becomes about *two* semitones plus an octave (mode 1 being close to A_3, while mode 2 is still very nearly C_5). We must understand clearly that the change we have been discussing might be either desirable or undesirable in a musical sense. The real point of our example is to show that it is possible to adjust the relations between modes if musical need arises.

Let us look briefly at one more example of the effect of loading a diaphragm. Suppose that instead of putting the wax at the center of the disc, we put it about halfway out toward the rim, so that it now sits near a point of maximum excursion for mode 2. It is now mode 2 that has its frequency lowered by about 6.7 percent, to 488/second. Meanwhile mode 1 is altered to a considerably smaller extent, because the wax is at a point of relatively small excursion. Numerical application of Rayleigh's method to this case is beyond our scope, but it turns out that mode 1 has its frequency lowered by only about 1 percent, to 247.5/second. In this second case, then, the musical interval between the first and second modes becomes a shade less than an octave (reaching from almost exactly B_3 to a little below B_4).

From a musical standpoint, our two examples have shown us that simply by moving an applied load from one point to another on a vibrator we are able to widen or narrow the musical interval between two modes. If for some reason a craftsman decided to arrange mode 1 and mode 2 for a clamped disc so that they would fall exactly an octave apart, he could apply a lump of wax to the disc, and then move it in and out radially until the desired pitch relation were obtained. Another way to do the same job would be to try different-sized lumps of wax attached at a fixed radial position, again choosing the one that gives the desired two-to-one frequency relationship.

Digression on Eccentric Loading.

We have just described how to lower the mode 2 frequency by application of a lump of wax part way out from the center, in the manner shown in the left-hand part of figure 9.10. The alert reader may ask about the case shown in the right-hand part of the figure. Here we again have mode 2, but this time its nodal line runs through the location of the wax, so that no *frequency change is expected! We seem to have found two answers to a single physical problem. The resolution to the apparent paradox is not difficult however, if we recall from section 6.4 that whenever a particle is added to a system of masses and springs, a new mode of vibration becomes possible (see fig. 6.8). In the case at hand, we originally had what was called mode 2 for the plate, and the addition of a mass causes this mode to become two distinct modes of roughly the same frequency. The vibrational shapes of these paired modes are in fact exactly those shown in figure 9.10. One of the characteristic frequencies (in this special case) turns out to be exactly equal to that of its plate-alone ancestor, while the other one lies somewhat lower. All the old rules about excitation points hold in the new situation, so that if we strike along either one of the two nodal lines shown, only the other mode will be excited. Striking at any other point will excite greater or lesser amounts of both modes.*

Up to this point we have confined our attention to the effect of adding lumps of

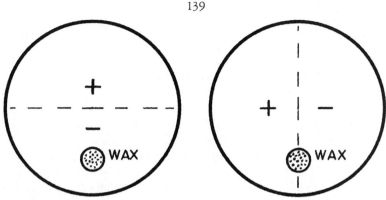

Fig. 9.10. Vibrational Shapes of Two Forms of Mode Two for a Loaded Disc with Clamped Edges

wax or other forms of mass-loading onto a vibrating plate, tacitly assuming that the added load did not change the spring stiffness of the system. When, however, we think about the effect of altering the thickness of a diaphragm or plate, it is at once obvious that we are changing not only the mass of the plate but also its stiffness. Our general formula for the vibration frequency of an object, $f = \sqrt{S/M}$ (times a numerical constant), implies that thinning the plate at some point not only reduces the moving mass M and so tends to raise the frequency (as we have already seen), but also reduces the stiffness coefficient S, which tends to lower the frequency. We find then that it is necessary to find out which of these two contrary effects predominates, and by how much.

Rayleigh's method of analysis allows us to deduce that when one cuts away material at some spot on a plate, the amount of frequency lowering produced by the stiffness reduction is almost exactly three times the amount of frequency raising associated with the loss of mass. The frequency alteration that we actually obtain is then the result of a large change in one direction which is partially offset by a smaller change in the opposite direction.

Let us summarize what happens in this contradictory-sounding situation by means of a fourth assertion that supplements the three that were set down earlier in this section.

4. Scraping off a small amount of mass from some spot on a plate reduces the plate thickness locally. When this is done at a point of maximum excursion, the combined effect of the resulting mass and stiffness changes is such as to lower the vibrational frequency by an amount equal to about four times the fractional decrease in the plate mass. That is, for each mode of vibration:

$$\left(\frac{\text{maximum possible frequency reduction}}{\text{original frequency}}\right) \cong 4\left(\frac{\text{reduction of mass}}{\text{original plate mass}}\right)$$

Notice the similarity of this assertion to assertion 3, and note its relationship to assertion 1. Here, however, we find a *reduction* in frequency arising from the thinning of a plate, contrary to the implications of assertions 1 and 3, which suggest an increase. It should be clearly understood that assertion 2 stands *almost* unaltered when we take stiffness changes into account. We give here the modified version:

2a. The frequency change due to localized stiffness changes is a maximum if thinning is done at a point of maximum bending. There is little or no effect if the thinning takes place at a nodal point or along a nodal line.

Note that assertion 2 says that mass changes have their maximum effect where the plate excursion is largest, while 2a associates the effect of stiffness changes with points of maximum bending. It is an interesting problem for the mathematician to satisfy himself that (for plates with clamped or hinged edges) the regions of maximum bending (curvature) and of maximum excursion (deflection) are distributed quite similarly over the surface of the plate. Similarly the nodal lines for zero bending closely match the nodal lines of zero displacement. This permits us to treat both forms of assertion 2 as being equivalent in their practical implications.

We can neatly illustrate the interplay between assertions 3 and 4 and their connection with the implications of assertions 2 and 2a by describing how a guitar or violin maker who had acquired enough understanding might put these ideas to practical use. We will take it for granted that this craftsman already knows that the front and back plates of a good instrument must be carved in such a way as to give them certain specified characteristic frequencies (measured before the plates are glued into the completed instrument). We assume also that he has a fairly clear notion of the characteristic vibrational shapes belonging to the desired frequencies, and that he knows that a plate that is slightly too thick but otherwise in good proportion will have *all* of its characteristic frequencies coming out a little too high. To begin with, our craftsman can experiment on his plate with lumps of wax, adding mass but not stiffness, to get the various vibration frequencies shifted from where he finds them to where he wishes them to be. In carrying out this program, he can use whatever understanding and sophistication is available to him. He will, in other words, make use (consciously or unconsiously) of the implications of our various numbered assertions to guide him in putting his loadings at points of large vibration of the modes whose frequency he wants to alter the most, arranging them at the same time to fall near the nodal lines of the modes whose frequencies are nearly satisfactory to him. All this preparatory tinkering can be done with confidence and safety, since any errors or misjudgements can be corrected simply by moving the offending pieces of wax.

Once the wax has been arranged to give all the characteristic frequencies their proper values, our craftsman is ready to proceed to the more permanent part of his labors. Having noted the position of a particular lump of wax, he picks it off and weighs it. He can then carefully carve away at his plate to thin it in the region where the wax had been, making careful observations of the various natural frequencies, and watching them shift toward their corrected values as the changes due to his carving take the place of the changes that were originally produced by the lump of wax. As a piece of insurance, our craftsmen might also weigh his plate from time to time as he carves to make sure that he is not thinning the wood too much. He would expect that his correction process will be complete when the mass of wood removed is equal to half of the mass of wax that produced the same effect (compare the numerical factors belonging to the mathematical expressions in assertions 3 and 4 to learn the reason for the difference between the masses of wood and wax that cause the same change). At this stage of the process we see before us a plate with part of its surface thinned by carving, while other parts of it are still loaded with pieces of wax. Recall that this plate, despite its motley and untidy appearance, is still one whose natural frequencies have been adjusted by the skill of its maker to the values which he believes will ultimately lead to a good instrument. The process of picking off pieces of wax and carving away wood where the wax had been attached can be carried on slowly and carefully until all the wax has been removed. By now, at least in principle, the plate is finished, with all its characteristic modes of vibration adjusted perfectly.

Digression on the Effect of Loading a Membrane.
You may be wondering why this whole section devoted to the effect of added mass has been so carefully restricted to a discussion of plates and diaphragms, rather than of stretched membranes such as those used as drumheads. It looks as though the whole argument could equally well apply to membranes. There are, however, certain subtle quirks in the nature of a membrane which lead to a very surprising phenomenon: adding a lump *of mass appears to* raise *the frequencies of the normal modes! We cannot take time here to account for this peculiar phenomenon, although a distant cousin to it will show up when we consider the interaction of a piano string with its soundboard. Meanwhile we can console ourselves with the knowledge that one of the very few mistakes ever made by Lord Rayleigh led him to miss this backwards-appearing behavior.* [5]

9.5. An Example: *The Kettledrum*

The orchestral kettle drum (a set of kettle drums is called the *timpani*) provides us with a good practical example of the way in which the behavior of a membrane comes to be adjusted for musical purposes. This drum consists of a more or less hemispherical shell of metal (usually copper) over which is mounted the "head," a membrane of calfskin or plastic sheet about 0.2 mm (0.008 inches) thick. Provision is made for tuning the pitch of the drum by adjusting the overall tension of the head, as well as for making corrections to the tension at a number of points around its periphery. We have recently seen the vibrational modes of a membrane in the upper part of figure 9.9 and can find the frequency ratios of the first five modes in section 9.4. Because of our musical orientation, we should be disturbed to realize that these ratios do not appear to have the whole-number relationships which so often are found among the partials of musical tones. Let us see how it comes about that the sound of a complete kettledrum acquires these useful relationships.

In his classic book, *Theory of Sound* (1877), Lord Rayleigh sketches the earlier scientific history of vibrating membranes in general and goes on to describe some of his own investigations on kettledrums. Because of its brevity and admirable clarity, it is worthwhile to quote:

In the case of kettle-drums the matter is further complicated by the action of the shell, which limits the motion of the air upon one side of the membrane. From the fact that kettle-drums are struck, not in the centre, but at a point about midway between the centre and edge [actually about a quarter of the way in from the edge], we may infer that the vibrations which it is desired to excite are not of the symmetrical class. The sound is indeed but little affected when the central point is touched with the finger.

Under these circumstances the principal vibration (1) is that with one nodal diameter and no nodal circle [this is mode 2 of the membrane—see fig. 9.9], and to this corresponds the greater part of the sound obtained in the normal use of the instrument. Other tones, however, are audible, which correspond with vibrations characterized (2) by two nodal diameters and no nodal circle, (3) by three nodal diameters and no nodal circles, (4) by one nodal diameter and one nodal circle. By observation with resonators upon a large kettle-drum of 25 inches diameter the pitch of (2) was found to be about a fifth [frequency ratio of about 1.5] above (1), that of (3) about a major seventh [1.89 ratio] above (1), and that of (4) a little higher again, forming an imperfect octave with the principal tone. For the corresponding modes of a uniform perfectly flexible membrane vibrating *in vacuo*, the theoretical intervals are those represented by the ratios 1.34, 1.66, 1.83 respectively.[6]

Notice how carefully Rayleigh distinguishes the behavior expected of an idealized membrane from that of one mounted as the cover on a tankful of air. In the years since Rayleigh, only a few people have wrestled with the problem of how the enclosed and the external air act to modify the membrane vibrations; to this day the problem has not yet been completely dealt with. My own interest in the subject was stimulated by a letter I received in 1962 from the distinguished South African ethnomusicologist, Percival Kirby, who had an earlier career as the leading timpanist in Britain.[7] Kirby gave an admirably clear description of his own observations of the sounds from a kettle-drum and of the corresponding vibrational shapes of its head. He asserted that

by skillful adjustment of tensions around the drumhead it is possible to produce a sound whose lowest two components have a frequency ratio of *exactly* 1.5. This ratio he deemed essential, along with a 2-to-1 relationship and several other "in tune" ratios.

Kirby was most critical of Rayleigh's experiments. In his letter he wrote:

I know that he and his brother, the Hon. Richard Strutt, conducted the experiments themselves, and without the aid of an expert player (Richard Strutt told me this himself. . . . Strutt rather choked me off when I gently suggested that there were certain things which they had overlooked). . . . [Moreover, the drum was] a battered one at that, if one may believe George Bernard Shaw, who, on page 126 of his *London Music in 1888–89*, calls it "a second-hand kettle-drum".

Kirby's letter was intended to interest me in the problem, and the following paragraphs outline what I have learned since by talking with timpanists, by reading, by making experiments, and by doing a certain amount of calculation myself.

First we may ask why some variant of the single-hump lowest vibrational mode of the membrane is not heard. Rayleigh's comments give some hint, but even a direct blow at the center of the head fails to elicit more than a pitchless thwack. The answer is to be found in the presence of a vent hole in the bottom of the bowl. The ostensible reason for it is to equalize the air pressures inside and outside the drum as the weather changes. If the hole were closed, the added spring force distributed over the surface if the drumhead due to the compression and rarefaction of the enclosed air would raise the frequency of the oscillation in question, in a manner that was worked out some years ago by the American physicist, Philip Morse (the inertia of the enclosed air turns out in this case to have negligible effect). However, the vent hole prevents the frequency change phonomenon and gives rise instead to a very heavy damping of the mode, because of the viscous friction in the air as it is pumped in and out of the kettle by the vibration of the drumhead. One learns that conscientious and skillful drum makers carefully adjust the size of the vent hole so as to give the best tone—and we find that the musically optimum size is essentially that which is efficacious in killing off mode 1.

Mode 2 of the drumhead is the one whose frequency is associated with the pitch to which it is tuned. This mode has two humps in its vibrational shape, one of which moves up while the other moves down, and vice versa. Motions of this sort excite a back-and-forth sloshing motion of the air contained in the kettle, a sloshing very similar to that of tea rocking in a teacup. It is significant that Rayleigh gives extended and careful attention in his book not only to the vibrations of isolated membranes, but also to the oscillations of air in a spherical cavity. His ability to choose and elucidate the basic ingredients of complex acoustical systems is what has preserved his book as a standard reference for nearly a century. An exact analysis of the mutual influence of the two-hump oscillatory mode of the drumhead and the sloshing mode of the air would be extremely difficult to carry out. However, I have found it possible to work out a simplified version of the problem which shows that the resultant combined motion takes place at a frequency

that is considerably lower than that of the air or the head taken in isolation. I have also verified that for mode 2 there is no variation of air pressure at the position of the vent hole, and therefore no dissipation-causing oscillatory flow of air through it. This is true too for the other musically significant modes.

The other modes of vibration of the drumhead also are influenced by the sloshing air motions within the shell to a musically significant degree, but the changes are considerably less than those described in the preceding paragraph. My various calculations give us a better understanding of how the kettle helps move the drumhead frequencies to their observed values (given below).

Digression on the Intertwining of Air and Drumhead Properties.

It is important for us not to fall into the trap here of thinking of air modes and drumhead modes as being actually distinct systems that keep their separate identities. The air and the head make up a single system the two parts of which are of equal importance in determining the frequencies and overall vibrational shapes. The springiness and mass coefficients of the two parts are inextricably intertwined in the mathematics, just as are the corresponding coefficients of the two masses in the systems discussed in sections 6.3 and 7.1.

Actual measurements of sounds from a drum tuned to C_3 (130.8/sec) were carried out in 1973 using a tape recording made in Cleveland's Severance Hall, with Cloyd Duff, timpanist of the Cleveland Orchestra, playing one of his own very fine instruments. The frequency ratios of the first ten recorded components of the complete sound follow:

Component	Ratio	Component	Ratio
P	1.000	U	2.494
Q	1.504	V	2.800
R	1.742	W	2.852
S	2.000	X	2.979
T	2.245	Y	3.462

We notice at once that Kirby's claims for the true nature of the sound are quite correct: for example, P, Q, and S have almost exactly the specified relationship. Looking back at what we learned about pitch perception in chapter 5, we are struck by a remarkably clear pair of patterns in the sound of a kettledrum. Components P, S, and X form an almost precise set of harmonics whose fundamental component is 130.8/sec. These three components together then define a tone whose pitch is the nominal C_3 to which the drum is tuned. Components Q and X also fit together as fundamental and second harmonic of a tone whose repetition rate is close to 196/sec, having the pitch name G_3. There is yet another way in which the extreme orderliness of the sound may be displayed: components P, Q, S, U, and X range themselves as second, third, fourth, fifth, and sixth harmonics of a tone whose pitch is C_2, exactly an octave below the nominal pitch C_3. No mention has been made yet of components R, V, W, and Y. These are scattered around in the tone as a sort of flavoring, and are not always particularly heard as separately pitched sounds in their own right.

We will return in chapters 14 and 15 to a closer examination of the musical implications of sounds having multiple patterns of regularity in the frequency ratios of their component partials, but we should at least comment here that the timpani produce an interesting mixture of diversity and unity in the perceptual im-

pressions they give. The tone can simultaneously serve as a single low-pitched sound and as the two parts of the musically important tonic-dominant relationship. Musicians who enjoy number games may also notice that component T has almost exactly the same frequency ratio (1.5) to component Q as Q does to P.

You may at this point be wondering whether the acoustical regularities described above are essential to the tone of a good drum as the player alters its tuning over the half octave of its usable range. After all, it is not obvious that the influence of the air in the kettle of fixed size can produce a proper modification of the membrane vibrations as the tension is varied over what turns out to be a range of nearly two-to-one. It was a particularly challenging part of my mathematical analysis to verify that the air in kettles of normal proportions is in fact able to preserve the desired relationships to a considerable degree of accuracy over the tuning range. The varying degree of perfection in preserving the correct air-to-membrane relationships is what explains the observation by musicians that every drum plays best at one particular frequency in its range of usability. We also come to understand better why only a few variants among many possibilities for kettle shape give a musically acceptable result.

It is not sufficient merely to get the overall skin tension correct for the desired pitch of the kettledrum, one must also make small additional changes in the tensions produced by the various screws around the periphery of the drum. Cloyd Duff has a particularly apt word to describe this process of subsidiary adjustment which compensates for the inherent irregularity of the skin and for the possible eccentricity of the kettle rim. When everything is in perfect adjustment, the drum is said to have been "cleared." It is a revelation to listen to an expert such as Duff "clearing" a good drum, making the tone ring with smoothness and clarity. This clearing in fact is a process of persuading the partials to more closely match the ideal. As a matter of fact, Duff apologized for his drum's lack of tonal clarity—a season's hard use had battered the skin to a point where he no longer considered it possible to bring it into proper adjustment.

9.6. Examples, Experiments, and Questions

1. The general nature of the oscillations of two-dimensional objects can be explored very conveniently with the help of a teacup, a washbasin, or a bathtub filled with water. As a way to get started in your researches, re-read the descriptions of experiments using a water trough given in section 6.6 and try to devise their two-dimensional analogues. You will also find it worthwhile to seek trends in the variation of mode shapes as the shape of the container is altered. A rather challenging project would be to seek out the kinships and contrasts between water-surface oscillation shapes and those characteristic of clamped, hinged, or free-edged plates having the same boundary shape as the water surface. Your acquaintance with the basic principles of vibration physics may allow you to discover many useful relationships.

2. The strings of a guitar provide an excellent laboratory for experiments on the effect of loading a vibrating system at different points. First lower the pitch of one of the strings by slacking its tension, until it is halfway down to the pitch of the next lower string. Then increase the tension of this lower string until it plays at exactly the same pitch as its slackened neighbor. One of these strings can then serve as a reference against which the other one can be tested. Wrap a short length of soft copper or lead wire closely around one of these strings exactly at its midpoint, and notice how all the odd-numbered modes are lowered in frequency, leaving the even-numbered ones unaltered. Next, slide the wire wrapping to a point exactly one-third of the way from one end of the string. Why do you expect a lowering of all the characteristic frequencies except for modes 3, 6, 9, . . . ? Is mode 2 affected more, or less, than mode 1? (Note: the factors of two and four relating the fractional change of frequency to that of the mass in assertions 2 and 4 found in section 9.4 are halved when one is dealing with their one-dimensional analogues.)

From time to time musically inclined engineers undertake to counteract the smoothly varying part of the inharmonicity of piano strings by adding a small mass to a carefully chosen point very close to the fixed end of the string. The nature of the piano string inharmonicity is described briefly at the end of section 5.4. Make careful sketches of the first half dozen modes of a piano string, and verify the plausibility of this sort of project.

3. In section 5.2, we met the clock chime, made up of a set of steel rods, each one clamped at one end. The fact that these rods are thinned by grinding near the clamped end gives them a set of characteristic frequency ratios that are intermediate between those of a uniform bar clamped at one end and a bar attached to its support by means of a hinge. For the bar in our example the frequency ratios referred to mode 2 come out thus:

	P	Q	R	S	T
clamped uniform rod	0.16	1.00	2.80	5.57	9.07
clamped and thinned rod	0.03	1.00	2.92 & 2.94	5.90	9.84
hinged rod	0.00	1.00	3.24	6.76	11.57

Why does frequency P fall all the way to zero in the case of the hinged rod? Verify by means of freehand sketches that the characteristic vibrational shape belonging to Q has one node, that for R has two nodes, and so on for modes S and T (for the moment we ignore the fact that two frequencies are listed under R). The thinning of the rod was done by grinding it away roughly, so that in the thinned region the rod is not perfectly round. Vibrations excited in one plane involve the bending of a thicker and stiffer rod than those excited in a plane at right angles to the first. As a result there are two complete sets of vibrations which the hammer can excite. By chance, only the two R components were different enough to be noticed separately in my measurements. If you simplify things by assuming the rod to be thinned in a perfectly symmetrical fashion, you might find it possible to work out some sort of thinning procedure (at points along the rod) by means of which components Q, R, S, and T could be modified to work them toward a whole-number relationship such as 1, 3, 6, 9. In the light of your present understanding, figure out some of the ways in which such a sound would be perceived. Why might it not give as successful a *bell* sound as does the original?

4. The calfskin head of a kettledrum cannot, by its very nature, have a uniform density and strength. The region which came from along the animal's backbone and shoulder is distinctly different from the skin from the sides. There is also a difference between the neck and rump regions. While additions of mass in *lumps* on a membrane give peculiar alterations in modal frequencies, smoothly varying additions of mass over the surface can be dealt with by means of the methods outlined in section 9.4. Left-right symmetry of the skin and increased density along the backbone will lead to a frequency for component P, when it is excited by a blow at a point on the backbone line, that will differ from that produced by a blow one quarter of the way around the periphery of the drum. Assuming the tension to be uniform, you will be able to figure out which striking point gives the lower frequency. Note that the heavier skin lies along the nodal line in one case but not in the other (see the Digression on Eccentric Loading in sec. 9.4). Figure out how the timpanist might vary the tension around the head to minimize the effect of skin nonuniformity described above. Can you convince yourself that adjustment of tone P will pretty well take care of the rest of the sound? How would the timpanist go about guiding his adjustments? For an earlier example of the effects of frequency ratio on clarity of tone, refer back to the experiments with snapping keys on a flute that were described in experiment 4 in section 5.9.

5. Alterations in shape and size of a guitar bridge or of the braces glued to the inner surface of the top plate can make profound changes in the instrument's tone and response. You can get an initial view of what is going on by figuring out

the alterations to the mode frequencies for the guitar plate shown in figure 9.7. Notice that adding various wood parts does not particularly alter the *damping* (frictional force) acting on the vibrating system; it merely changes its stiffness and mass coefficients. Notice further that adding mass to some point of a vibrating plate does not necessarily reduce the amplitude of the vibrations at the point relative to the motion at other points on the plate's surface. To see this, compare the amplitudes of motion at various points along the tapered chain with corresponding points on the uniform chain of figure 6.9.

Notes

1. While the basic behavior of vibrating bars is quite straightforward, the mathematical physics of their description is quite complicated. Different readers may find one or another of the following references accessible. They are all worth at least a cursory examination because of the variety of diagrams and the references to musical implications. Lawrence E. Kinsler and Austin R. Frey, *Fundamentals of Acoustics*, 2d ed. (New York: Wiley, 1962), chap. 3; Horace Lamb, *The Dynamical Theory of Sound*, 2d ed. (1925; reprint ed., New York: Dover, 1960), pp. 126–35; and Philip M. Morse, *Vibration and Sound*, 2d ed. (New York: McGraw-Hill, 1948), pp. 157–70.

2. Morse, *Vibration and Sound*, chap. V, "Membranes and Plates." Many students of musical acoustics will find Morse's mathematical discussion difficult, but anyone will find rewarding the beautifully executed diagrams of various types of vibrations that are possible on round and rectangular objects. See also John Tyndall, *Sound*, 3rd ed. rev. and enlarged (New York: Appleton, 1896), pp. 170–79. This nineteenth-century book is a classic, devoted to the nontechnical exposition of acoustics. For present purposes this book is particularly useful for its pictures of various vibrational shapes that result from the simultaneous excitation of several modes on a plate, as well as for a clear account of how one can go about deducing these *combined* shapes from the shapes of the characteristic modes themselves. See also Alfred Leitner, "Vibrations of a Circular Membrane," *Am. J. Phys.* 35 (1967): 1029–31.

3. This figure is based on photographs obtained by E. V. Jansson of the Speech Transmission Laboratory, Royal Institute of Technology, Sweden, which are published in an article, "A Study of Acoustical and Hologram Interferometric Measurements of the Top Plate Vibrations of a Guitar," *Acustica* 25 (1971): 95–100.

4. G. Temple and W. G. Bickley, *Rayleigh's Principle and Its Applications to Engineering* (New York: Dover, 1956).

5. E. T. Kornhauser and D. Mintzer, "On the Vibration of Mass-Loaded Membranes," *J. Acoust. Soc. Am.* 25 (1953): 903–6.

6. Lord Rayleigh [John William Strutt], *The Theory of Sound*, 2 vols. bound as one, 2d ed. rev. and enlarged (1894; reprint ed., New York: Dover, 1945), I:348.

7. P. R. Kirby was the author of *The Kettledrums* (London: Oxford, 1930), which is considered by timpanists to be one of the basic books about their instrument.

10

Sinusoidally Driven Oscillations

When one plucks a guitar string or strikes a piano string with its hammer, the string is given a complicated motion made up of a collection of characteristic sinusoidal oscillations belonging to the string. We have already investigated this sort of composite motion in considerable detail. We have also seen that soundboards and other two-dimensional objects respond to excitation in a similar fashion. We should now inquire about the way forces exerted by any one of the characteristic sinusoidal oscillations of one object (for instance, a piano string) excite the vibrations of another object (for example, the soundboard on which it is mounted). In simplest terms this question can be reduced to one about the behavior of a single spring-and-mass system when it is driven by a sinusoidally varying force. Once we understand what goes on here, it will prove easy to generalize in familiar ways to learn what takes place when a more complicated system (having several characteristic modes) is sinusoidally driven. Each of these modes will respond to the driving force in the same basic way.

Many coffee drinkers have observed that the liquid in a cup has a side-to-side sloshing mode which oscillates with a frequency of about two repetitions/second. This mode is, as a matter of fact, a very close cousin to the single mode of oscillation that was found to take place in a U-tube filled with water (see sec. 6.1 and fig. 6.3). The coffee drinker may also know from experience that if he waves his filled cup gently to and fro at a frequency that is even approximately equal to the natural frequency of the fluid, the coffee oscillates ever more wildly, and soon slops out of the cup. That is, repetitive excitation of an object can build up a very large amplitude of oscillation if the excitation frequency is roughly equal to the natural vibration frequency of the object.

10.1. Excitation of a Pendulum by a Repetitive Force

Let us think about an easily studied example of sinusoidal drive. Figure 10.1 shows a board suspended like a pendulum from screw eyes in a door frame and connected by means of a long string of rubber bands to a crank that is rotated by a geared-down variable-speed motor. If the hanging board is long enough to reach nearly to the bottom of a door frame of

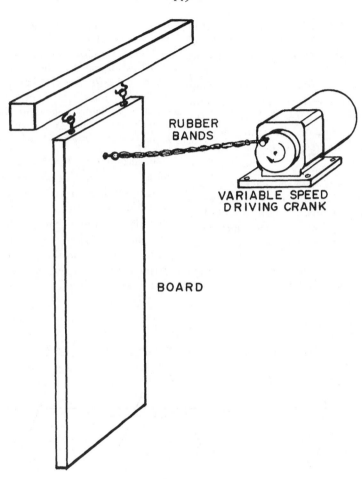

RUBBER
BANDS

VARIABLE SPEED
DRIVING CRANK

BOARD

Fig. 10.1.

ordinary size, we find that its natural swinging frequency is somewhat less than 0.4 repetitions/second (2 oscillations in 5 seconds).

When the motor is running, the circular motion of the crank gives rise to a regularly repeating cycle of increasing and decreasing tension in the rubber bands, so that the board is subjected to a repetitive driving force which varies in step with the crank's revolution rate. If the rubber band is long, this varying force is quite accurately sinusoidal in its nature. It is our expectation that if the motor is run so that the crank makes about 0.4 revolutions/second, the pendulum will be caused to swing with a considerable amplitude. We also find it plausible to expect that a faster or slower motor speed will give rise to a much smaller response on the part of the board, since we expect that the driving force might get out of step with the board's swinging from time to time.

Now that we have our expectations somewhat organized so that we know what to look for in the behavior of the board, let us turn on the motor and see what actually happens under a variety of conditions:

1. Regardless of the crank's rate of revolution, we find that whenever the motor is switched on, the board starts out with a random-appearing initial motion which eventually settles down to a steady sinusoidal oscillation.

2. This steady, final oscillation always takes place at exactly the driving frequency set by the motor, independent of the natural frequency of the pendulum itself.

3. The amplitude of this steady-state sinusoidal oscillation depends on the relationship between the frequency of the driver and that of the pendulum. The amplitude of the pendulum's oscillatory response to the driver is at a maximum when the driving frequency matches that of the pendulum.

Figure 10.2 shows examples of the messy beginnings that are characteristic of the response of an oscillator to a sinusoidal driving force. The top part shows the sort of thing that can happen when the motor's driving frequency is lower than the pendulum's characteristic frequency (35 percent of it in the present example), while the lower part shows a

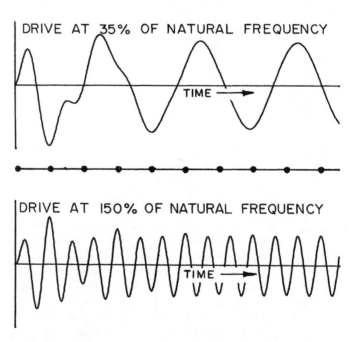

Fig. 10.2. Initial Response of an Oscillator to Sinusoidal Driving Forces above and below Its Own Natural Frequency

typical response for the case where the drive frequency is well above the natural frequency (1.5 times as large). The horizontal dotted line drawn across the middle of the figure between the two parts indicates the natural frequency of oscillation of the system if it were left free to take its own way. Notice in the upper and lower sections of the figure that after the completion of the complicated initial part of the motion (the *transient,* as it is technically labeled), the motion settles down to a sinusoidal oscillation that agrees in frequency with that of the driver.

Figure 10.3 shows diagrammatically the relationship described in assertion 3 above. The amplitude of the pendulum's eventual sinusoidal response is weak if the driving frequency is very much larger or very much smaller than the natural

frequency, and the response is very strong when the two frequencies match reasonably well.

If we continue our study of the sinusoidally driven steady-state oscillations of the pendulum, we can record four more observations whose essential features are shown in the four parts of figure 10.4.

4. When the motor's driving frequency is much lower than the pendulum's own characteristic frequency, we find that the pendulum moves almost exactly in step with the applied force. The pendulum is observed to move toward the motor during the part of the cycle when the rubber band is most stretched, and away from the motor when the rubber is least stretched.

5. When the pendulum is driven at a frequency that is near to, but lower than, its natural frequency, the pendulum lags behind slightly in its motion, always coming to the

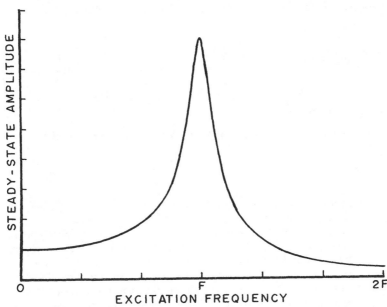

Fig. 10.3. The response of a driven oscillator becomes very large when the excitation frequency matches the natural frequency of the oscillator.

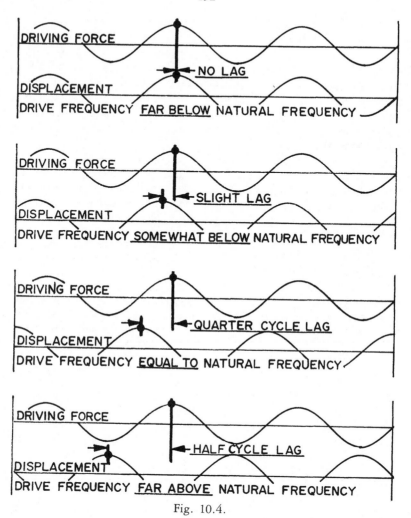

Fig. 10.4.

end of its swing and reversing its motion slightly after the driving crank has stopped its progressive stretching of the rubber bands and has begun to let them relax.

6. When the motor drive frequency is exactly equal to the pendulum frequency, the lagging behavior of the pendulum is more manifest. The pendulum reaches its mid-swing position when the rubber band arrives at its state of maximum tension. In other words the pendulum lags one-quarter cycle behind its driving force.

7. At the highest driving frequencies the lagging is complete, so that the motion runs exactly half a cycle behind the driving force. That is, we see the pendulum moving away from the motor when the rubber bands are given their maximum tension, and toward the motor as the pull is relaxed.

10.2. Properties of the Initial Transient Motion

Let us turn our attention now to a closer examination of the complicated-looking initial (transient) motion of the pendulum. Repeated trials, in which the pendulum starts from rest and the drive motor is started to run always with the same revolution rate, seem to give randomly differing initial motions even though the eventual steady-state motion is always the same. This variation of the start-up motion is upsetting to minds accustomed to associating cause and effect, so it would be a good idea to look a little closer at what we have been doing. In our initial experiments the crank rotation would begin from whatever random angle it was left at when the motor was last switched off. If we now make sure that the crank is always started from the same angle, then all the details of the pendulum motion will reproduce themselves from trial to trial, allaying our scientific discomfort.

Because we find that the complicated initial motion of a sinusoidally driven pendulum eventually sorts itself out into a smooth sinusoidal motion, we are led to speculate that perhaps the complexity is something that dies away in a manner similar to the familiar dying away of an ordinary free oscillation. Perhaps we will find that the driven oscillator will sort itself out more quickly when the damping is adjusted so as to make the characteristic free oscillations die away quickly. This is a possibility which we can test by arranging some sort of variable damping for our pendulum, so that the halving

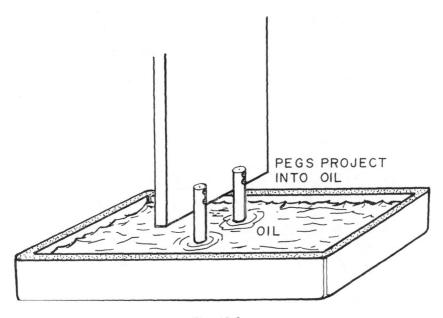

PEGS PROJECT
INTO OIL

OIL

Fig. 10.5.

time of the free oscillation amplitude can be varied (see sec. 4.8 and fig. 4.6).

Figure 10.5 shows how our pendulum board can be supplied with an adjustable friction of a suitable kind for these experiments. One or more wooden pegs are attached to the bottom of the board and allowed to project down into a shallow tray filled with water or oil. Varying the number of pegs, the depth of their immersion in oil, or the viscosity of the fluid (see sec. 6.1) will allow us to obtain any desired halving time for the pendulum's characteristic free oscillations. Experiments using the motor drive will now be able to show us that our suspicion was correct about the relation between the duration of free oscillation and that of the

complex initial part of the driven oscillation.

The influence of viscous damping on the duration of the initial transient is shown in figure 10.6. The top part of this figure is a reproduction of the top part of figure 10.2. The driving frequency is 35 percent of the pendulum's natural frequency, and (we can say it now) the oil damping is such that the amplitude of free oscillation falls to one half in the time of 1.32 periods of the characteristic oscillation. The lower part of the figure shows what happens when the damping is doubled to make the halving time 0.66 periods (1.32 divided by 2). Heavily damped oscillators do indeed settle down to their steady-state vibrations much

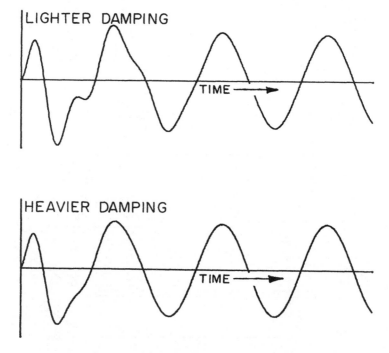

Fig. 10.6. The Influence of Viscous Damping on the Duration of the Initial Transient

more quickly than do lightly damped oscillators.

So far we have not found out exactly what is going on during the time of the initial transient, even though we do know that it dies away at the same rate as does a free oscillation of the pendulum. We can examine the transient part of the motion in the same way we did in the latter part of section 3.4 in which we worked at sorting out the nature of a skillet clang.

We find that the initial transient is *in fact* the combination of a damped oscillation of the free type on top of the steady oscillation that is the eventual survivor! The nature of this assertion can easily be seen from figure 10.7, in which the oscillation already shown in the top parts of figures 10.2 and 10.6 is shown along with its two newly discovered ingredients.

It is a little hard to use our pendulum for a direct experimental proof of the

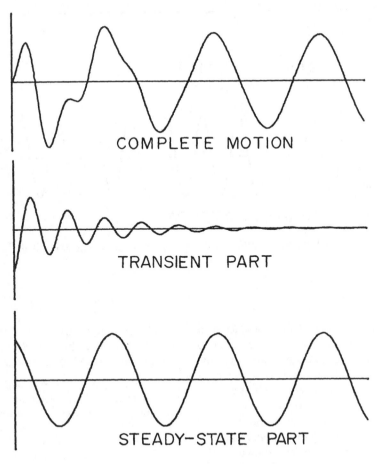

COMPLETE MOTION

TRANSIENT PART

STEADY–STATE PART

Fig. 10.7.

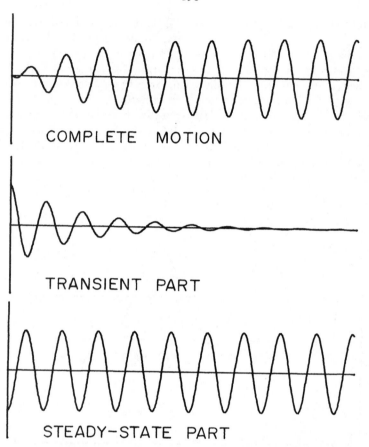

COMPLETE MOTION

TRANSIENT PART

STEADY-STATE PART

Fig. 10.8. Initial Transient When Driving Force Is Equal to the Natural Frequency

presence of the damped free oscillation in the initial transient. However, in order to illustrate what is going on, we can show an interesting special case—that in which the frequency of the driving force is exactly equal to the natural frequency. The upper part of figure 10.8 shows how the transient develops in this special case, with the two ingredients of the transient shown in the lower two lines. Let us record our new

knowledge (gained from figs. 10.6, 10.7, and 10.8) as the eighth member of our collection of numbered observations.

8. The complex initial transient motion of a sinusoidally driven pendulum is always made up of a damped oscillation running at the natural frequency of the pendulum, plus a driven oscillation that takes place at the driving frequency. This latter oscillation is all that persists after the transient has died out.

10.3. The Influence of Variable Damping on the Steady Response

In the course of our experimenting we have half-noticed a number of subsidiary things whose importance begins to grow as we get a deeper understanding of what is going on. For one thing we realize that while changes in the damping have a major influence on the duration of the initial transient, they have a curiously small influence on the amplitude of the final steady-state oscillation, as long as the driving frequency of the motor is not very close to the natural frequency of the pendulum. In other words, what we might call the skirts of the response curve in figure 10.3 apparently are little influenced by changes in the damping, whereas the central portion is considerably changed. We need therefore to go back and repeat the experiments of the sort that gave us figure 10.3, with the pegs and the oil tray arranged to give us various amounts of damping. The results of these additional experiments are summarized in figure 10.9. The tallest curve in this figure represents the behavior of a system having half the damping of the pendulum whose starting behavior is shown in the top part of figure 10.6. The second tallest curve is calculated for the

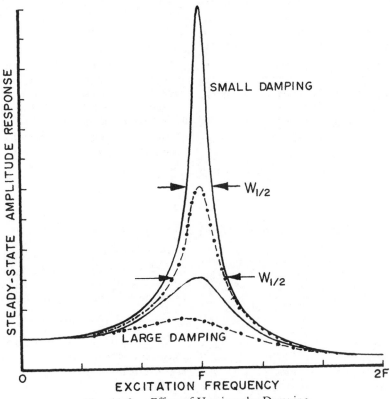

Fig. 10.9. Effect of Varying the Damping

same damping as that assumed in the upper part of figure 10.6. The third tallest response curve in figure 10.9 belongs to the pendulum whose initial behavior is shown in the lower part of figure 10.6 (for which the damping was doubled). The lowest curve shows what one gets when the damping is again increased twofold. Our informal impressions are well confirmed, and certain quantitative relationships are also made visible between the maximum response observed when the driving frequency matches the pendulum's natural frequency and the amount by which the response is reduced when the driving frequency is altered by a small amount. In terms of the *picture* we can say this more easily by talking in terms of the relationship between the *height* of the response curve at its tallest peak and its *width* in the neighborhood of this peak. Let us define a *half-amplitude bandwidth* or resonance width $W_{1/2}$ as being the range of driving frequencies within which the pendulum swings with a steady-state amplitude of at least half the maximum it can attain (the maximum being indicated by the height of the resonance peak in our diagram). These bandwidths are indicated in figure 10.9.

Digression on Various Definitions for the Bandwidth.

There are a number of ways in which engineers and physicists describe the relation between the strength of maximum response and the range of driving frequencies over which a driven oscillator shows appreciable response. Each of these ways has a certain simplicity or computational convenience for a particular set of practical problems. Our definition of $W_{1/2}$ (sometimes written FWHM, i.e., full width at half maximum) corresponds to what electrical engineers would call the 6-dB bandwidth; it is 1.732 times as large as the 3-dB bandwidth to

which they are more accustomed. Our choice has been made chiefly for conceptual simplicity in a book where we do not plan to do a lot of computation. Our definition has, however, certain other virtues which will become apparent in due course. You might find it worthwhile at this point to review the way in which the strength and duration of a hammer blow was described in section 8.2, since there is a striking similarity between figures 8.7 and 10.9.

Inspection of the curves depicted in figure 10.9 shows us that if the damping is increased by an amount sufficient to halve the amplitude of maximum response, the corresponding bandwidth $W_{1/2}$ has been doubled. This observation can be put together with our earlier ones to form a pair of interlocking numbered observations as follows:

9. As one increases the damping D of a pendulum, we find that variations of halving time $T_{1/2}$ for *free* oscillation and of maximum response amplitude A_{max} for sinusoidally *driven* oscillation run exactly parallel. Mathematically speaking, both damping $T_{1/2}$ and A_{max} are inversely proportional to the damping.

$$T_{1/2} = \frac{\text{constant}}{D} \qquad \text{and}$$

$$A_{max} = \frac{\text{another constant}}{D}$$

10. As the damping of a pendulum is increased, we find that the half-amplitude bandwidth $W_{1/2}$ grows in a way that is directly proportional to the damping. That is:

$$W_{1/2} = \text{a constant times } D$$

Let us combine the results summarized in assertions 9 and 10 into a formula that is convenient in many real-life situations. Our intuitions can be comfortable with the notion of describing the damping of an oscillator in terms of the number N of free oscillations it makes during the time $T_{1/2}$ that is required for the amplitude to die away to one half. In the same spirit, we can define a *percentage band-width* (PBW) that tells us the range of excitation frequencies over which our oscillator will respond with at least half its maximum amplitude, the range being expressed as a percentage of the natural oscillation frequency:

11. The percentage bandwidth PBW gives a measure of the selectivity of the response of an oscillator to an externally applied sinusoidal force. It may be expressed in terms of the number N of its *free* oscillations that must elapse for the amplitude to decay to one half, as follows:

PBW = (38.2/N) percent

Our list of eleven numbered observations adds up to a heavy dose of physics. It is time to put some of it to use in a musical context in order to clarify its meaning and to show some of its utility.

Digression on Frequency Labeling.
So far in this book, we have always been very explicit in talking about frequencies and repetition rates. We have made a habit of spelling out our exact meaning by means of expressions like "oscillations per second" or "repetitions per second." By now we are familiar enough with these ideas that it is convenient and safe to follow the engineering custom of writing the two-letter combination Hz to represent the written-out version. Thus we can say that the musical tone A_4, which is the note sounded by the oboist when an orchestra tunes, has a 440-Hz repetition rate, and that the second, third, and fourth (etc.) harmonics of a 100 Hz fundamental are found at 200 Hz, 300 Hz, 400 Hz, ... The letters Hz come from the name of Heinrich Hertz, who is honored as the first to observe the electromagnetic waves whose application in television and radar is familiar to us.

Musicians sometimes use the 440-Hz tuning fork to check up on how well they are in tune in a way different from the usual one of striking the fork to set it in motion. The oboist, for example, will play his A in front of the fork in the expectation that acoustical forces exerted on the fork by the fundamental component of this tone will drive the fork into oscillation in the way we have been discussing. If he plays a little bit sharp (or flat), the driving frequency will be above (or below) the fork's natural frequency, and so the response of the fork will be small (after the transient has died out). If the oboe tone is right on pitch, the fork will respond strongly, telling the player he is doing well. It takes about 5 seconds after a tuning fork is struck for its vibratory amplitude to die away to one half, so that the number N of oscillations taking place in this time is:

N = 2200 (= 440 osc/sec times 5 sec)

The formula in observation 11 implies that when an oboist tries to get his fork to sing, he must be in tune within a percentage margin of error of only:

PBW = 38.2/2200 = 0.017 percent

This corresponds to a pitch error of less than 0.003 semitone! The conclusion that follows from this little calculation is that a musician must be very good indeed if he is to persuade the fork to respond to his blandishments. In the real world of the musician's studio, however, we find that his life is a little bit simpler than this even though the physics of what goes on is somewhat more complicated, as the following anecdote will show.

10.4. A Flute Player's Unplanned Experiment

Several years ago my daughter, who is a serious and competent flute player, was checking up on her tuning with the help of a tuning fork. I overheard her playing the A_4 in long and short toots, first sharp, then flat, then slowly varying in pitch. It was not possible for me to hear the fork, but it did seem a little odd that these tuning experiments went on so long without the pitch settling down in the quick and tidy fashion I was accustomed to hearing. Then I heard an anguished (or perhaps only puzzled) call for help: "This tuning fork has gone crazy!" It seems that the fork would sometimes respond strongly to tones that were off pitch by as much as a third of a semitone. Even more upsetting to my daughter was the fact that the fork seemed to put forth the accustomed 440-Hz sound even when it had been stimulated by an out-of-tune note from the flute. From the heights of my superior knowledge of physics I was not surprised that the fork would ring on pitch when left to its own devices—it was simply finishing off its starting transient after the original stimulus was gone. The fact that the fork would respond appreciably to an out-of-tune flute note was less quickly understood. I knew that the PBW for a tuning fork is only a fraction of one percent, which at first makes the idea of strong response here rather surprising. However, there is a good explanation.

A short toot of sound lasts only a small fraction of the time it takes for a tuning-fork transient to die out. As a result, the fork is started into its initial complex wiggles and then is deserted by the flute to make its ordinary free decay (on pitch).

A random set of short notes from the flute is quite likely to start up a strong initial vibration of the fork, regardless of the pitch relation between the fork and the flute. This can be true even though the eventual response of the fork to the *sustained* sound of an out-of-tune flute will be miniscule. My daughter and I also confirmed experimentally that a flute tone having unsteady pitch would excite the fork fairly well, as long as the pitch would "visit" the exact value reasonably often.

The chief practical conclusion that can be drawn from these informal experiments is the following: if one wishes to use the excitation of the fork's vibration as a criterion for the accurate tuning of a musical instrument, it is necessary to play long, steady tones whose duration is several seconds (a time comparable with the decay time of the fork). The fact that a tuning fork will sing softly and steadily in one's studio during a practice session is a respectable check on the correctness of every A_4 that comes along in the music (and therefore an indication that the other notes are reasonably correct as well). However reassuring this sort of a check may be, we must always remember that these tuning notes come and go quite rapidly, so that there is considerable latitude to the response of the fork in such a playing situation.

10.5. Steady Excitation of a System Having Two Characteristic Modes of Vibration

In previous chapters we learned that a vibratory system possesses one or more characteristic modes of oscillation. Each of these modes has its own frequency, decay time, and vibrational shape. In the case of impulsive excitation (as by plucking or striking), we found that once the act of excitation has taken place, each mode carries out its own sinusoidal motion independently of the others. The disturbance taking place at any point in the system can then be calculated by simply adding up the motions that are associated with the various modes. We can now extend these ideas to a description of the response of the individual modes of a system when a long-continued sinusoidal driving force is applied in place of an impulsive excitation.

Consider a hypothetical mechanical setup of the sort sketched in the upper part of figure 10.10. Here we have two equal masses, m_1 and m_2, joined into a chain by three equal springs. The ends of the chain are anchored to solid supports.

We will drive this chain by means of a long, weak spring (or rubber band) that connects m_1 to a driving crank whose rate of rotation can be controlled. This system is the two-mass (and therefore two-mode) elaboration of the single-mode driven oscillator we have studied so far in this chapter. The lower part of figure 10.10 reminds us of the vibrational shapes that are characteristic of the two modes of this system of springs and masses—a system we first met in section 6.3. For convenience in describing our later investigations, we will assume that the spring stiffnesses have been chosen to produce a first-mode characteristic frequency of 10 Hz, which implies (for the case of two equal masses and three equal springs) that the second mode has a natural frequency of 17.32 Hz. We will also suppose that the viscous damping exerted on the

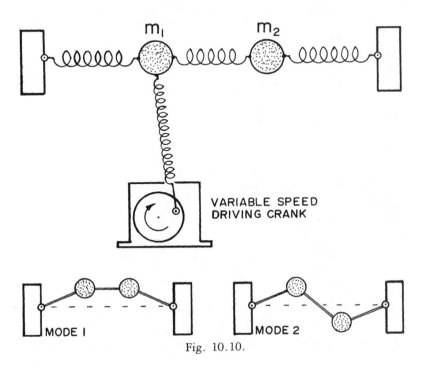

VARIABLE SPEED
DRIVING CRANK

MODE I

MODE 2

Fig. 10.10.

masses by the surrounding air is such that the amplitude of each mode dies away with a halving time that is 0.567 seconds; this is the time required for mode 1 to make 5.67 oscillations.

Let us confine our attention initially to the directly driven mass m_1, which when driven will presumably behave very much like the pendulum we studied earlier. Because each vibrational mode has all the ordinary properties of a single oscillator, we may expect that a steady driving of our system at a very low frequency will produce only a small excursion of m_1. As the drive motor is speeded up to the neighborhood of 10 Hz (the frequency belonging to mode 1) we presumably will observe a large amplitude motion for m_1, with a subsequent decrease in amplitude until the drive frequency is in the neighborhood of 17.32 Hz, where mode 2 is expected to respond most strongly.

The heavily dotted curve in figure 10.11 shows what we would in fact observe for the steady-state amplitude (A_1) of the driven mass as the driving frequency is varied. Qualitatively what can be observed is very much in accordance with assertions 1 through 9 that were found to apply to a single-mass oscillator. Closer inspection shows a number of significant differences. For example, the widths $W_{1/2}$ of the two response peaks are not quite consistent with what one calculates from the decay time and the formula in assertion 11. The calculated widths are shown in the diagram. These small discrepancies need not disturb us particularly, however, because we realize that m_1 is actually participating in two different modes of oscillation simultaneously. For example, when the drive motor is running at 5 rev/sec, the mode 1 aspect of m_1's response is that corresponding to driving at half the 10 Hz frequency natural to this mode. The other

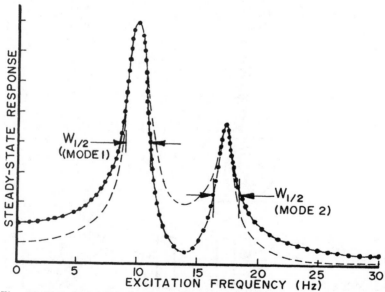

Fig. 10.11. Response of a Two-Mass System Observed at the Driven Mass

contribution to the motion comes from the fact that the system is being driven at about 29 percent ($5/17.32 = 0.29$) of the second-mode natural frequency. What one observes is the *sum* of these two types of response.

Something new happens when the drive motor is run at a speed that lies *between* the two natural frequencies. Observation 7 tells us that when mode 1 is driven well above its natural frequency, the driven mass moves so that it lags nearly half a cycle behind the driving force, which means that when the drive spring pulls, m_1 moves away from the crank. On the other hand, the mode-2 aspect of the motion keeps in step with the drive force, with only a slight lag. Since m_1 is being asked to move in two contrary directions at the same time, the magnitude of actual motion will be the numerical difference between the corresponding distances.

If there were almost no damping at all, the contrary effects of mode 1 and mode 2 on the motion of the driven mass would almost completely cancel one another at a 14.14 Hz driving frequency, where the responses of the two modes are equal. Because of the lags produced by damping, the cancellation is not in fact complete. Figure 10.11 shows however that the amplitude of motion is at a minimum at this driving frequency. We also find here that the mass moves in such a way that it lags almost exactly a quarter cycle behind the driving force, just as is the case when the drive frequency matches one of the natural frequencies. The presence of a quarter-cycle lag near the frequency of minimum response, as well as at maximum response, is a general and useful property of many vibrating systems. We should therefore provide our-

selves with two more numbered assertions that extend our formal understanding into the territory of systems having more than one mode:

12. The motion of every mass of a sinusoidally driven complex system reaches maximum amplitude when the driving frequency is close to any one of the system's natural frequencies. In many cases this motion is out of step with the driving force by a quarter cycle.

13. At certain frequencies lying *between* those frequencies that are characteristic of the system's vibrational modes, the motion of all masses has a minimum amplitude. At these frequencies of minimum response, the masses again usually have a motion that is one-quarter cycle out of step with the driving force.

Let us transfer our attention briefly to the steady-state oscillations of the other member (m_2) of our pair of masses. The dashed curve in figure 10.11 shows that m_2 also has the expected two-peaked behavior, although the details are not the same for m_1. For one thing, the asymmetries of the two peaks are more or less reversed from what we found for m_1. Below 10 Hz, m_2 moves with a much smaller amplitude than does m_1. Between the 10 Hz and 17.32 Hz frequencies of maximum response, m_2 moves with a much larger amplitude than does m_1, while at frequencies above 17.32 Hz it has a much more restricted motion.

Another way to look at the whole behavior is to consider the vibrational shapes associated with the settled-down sinusoidal oscillation produced by different driving frequencies. Figure 10.12 shows these shapes for a number of driving frequencies. When m_1 is driven at frequencies of 4 and 8 Hz, we find the two masses vibrating with slightly un-

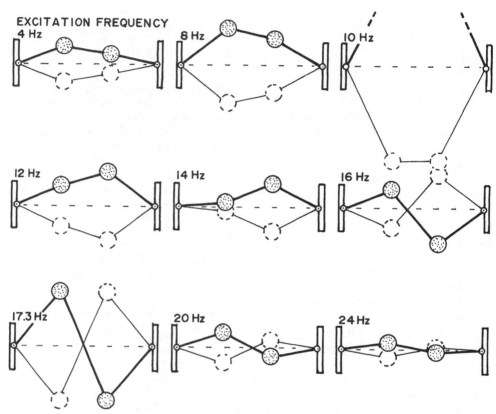

Fig. 10.12. Vibrational Shapes versus Excitation Frequency for a Two-Mass System

equal amplitudes in an overall shape that is reminiscent of the free vibration shape for mode 1 (look back to sec. 7.1 and fig. 7.2 to review how one superposes the characteristic mode shapes to get things of this sort).

At 10 Hz, where mode 1 responds most strongly, our driven vibration seems to have a pure mode-1 vibrational shape of very large amplitude—there is no asymmetry here even though a certain amount of mode-2 excitation is present! The explanation of this phenomenon is a little beyond our scope, but it has to do with the way in which the half-cycle lag of mode 1 combines with the nearly zero

lag of mode 2 at this frequency, as discussed in assertion 6 above.

At driving frequencies above 10 Hz we find that the vibrational shape will change, as expected, from something reminiscent of mode 1 to something more like mode 2 as we approach the second charateristic frequency. Here at 17.32 Hz we again find a large and completely symmetrical shape, this time of pure mode-2 type. At higher frequencies yet, the size of the overall disturbance becomes progressively less, but it always preserves its mode-2 character, with the two masses moving in opposite directions.

10.6. A Summary of the Properties of a Sinusoidally Driven System

We have now completed a rather grueling investigation of the properties of a sinusoidally driven system having several characteristic modes of vibration. Because in the future we will need to refer back repeatedly to our collection of numbered assertions, it is worthwhile at this point to summarize the main ideas we have developed.

When one starts to drive a system of springs and masses at any frequency, there is an initial transient which is enormously complicated, since it is made up of the already complex transient motions belonging to each separate mode of oscillation. We therefore have present in the vibrational recipe not only the driving frequency but also the (decaying) complete collection of characteristic frequencies, *exactly as in the case of impulsive excitation.*

Once the transient has died out, all parts of the system will settle down into a steady oscillation at exactly the driving frequency. The overall vibrational shape of this oscillation is one whose ingredients are the individual shapes characteristic of the various natural modes of vibration. The amounts of these ingredients that are present and the degree of lag between the motion of these components and the driving force can be found from the general properties of each mode taken as an isolated pendulum. When the driving force varies at a frequency close to one of the natural frequencies of the system, the resultant vibrational shape of the system is (very nearly) that of the corresponding mode.

The response peaks belonging to the various characteristic modes are not in general symmetrical when one looks at the response of a complex system. Furthermore the widths $W_{1/2}$ of these peaks are very nearly (but not exactly) equal to those belonging to the modes if they could be studied in isolation. For this reason, we can treat the easily observed peaks as though they belonged to the individual modes. As a matter of fact, there are certain physical systems (some of musical interest) where the spacing between the response peaks and other features of the system make even the slight discrepancy disappear.

Digression on terminology.

Curves showing the response of a system to a sinusoidal driving force are often referred to as resonance curves *or* response curves. *Peaks in such curves are usually called* resonance peaks, *or simply the* resonances of the system. *If one records the response of a system at the same point where the driving force is applied, the response curve is often referred to as a* driving-point response curve. *If, on the other hand, one records the motion of some part of the system other than at the driving point, the response curve is called a* transfer response curve. *Thus the dotted curve in figure 10.11 shows the driving-point response of a two-mass chain, since it shows the motion of the mass m_1 to which the driving force is applied. The dashed curve in this figure, on the other hand, is a transfer resonance curve showing what happens to mass m_2 when m_1 is being driven.*

10.7. The Transfer Response of a Tin Tray

In the earlier parts of this chapter we have taken the description of the response of a single mass and spring (pendulum) to sinusoidal driving forces and adapted it to the case of two (or more) masses coupled in a chainlike structure. Let us now look

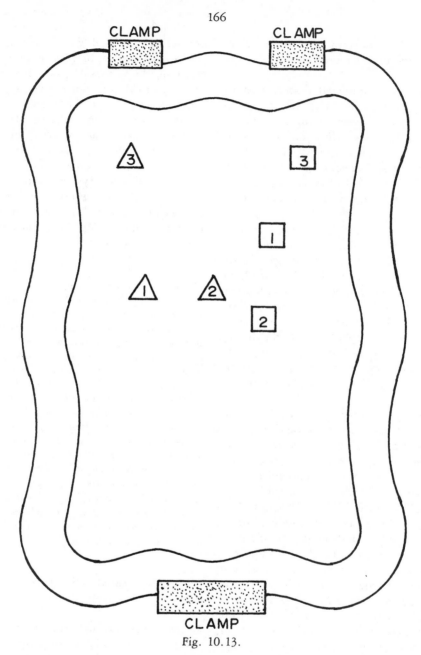

Fig. 10.13.

briefly at what happens when we attach a magnetic driver at one point and a motion detector at another point of a metal serving tray (a two-dimensional plate of the sort we studied in chapter 9). Not only will our observations have a direct bearing on the way in which the soundboards of pianos and the front plates of guitars and violins respond to the strings' driving forces, it will also prepare us for the greater complexity found in sound transmission between musical sources and the listener in a room.

Figure 10.13 shows the tray clamped at three points along its edges. The numbered triangles show the spots at which electromagnetic motion sensors were successively located, while the numbered squares show in similar fashion the points where a driver was located. Response curves for the tray are easily obtained. One has only to connect the loudspeaker-like driver to an oscillator and the motion detector to an amplifier and a strip-chart recorder. Figure 10.14 shows four such recordings obtained with various combinations of the driver and the detector positions. The first thing we notice about these (transfer) response curves is that the

curves look very different from one another. Tall peaks and low squiggles appear to be randomly distributed over the 0-300 Hz frequency range of the measurements. Closer examination shows that at least small traces of a tall resonance peak are found at the corresponding frequency on all the charts. For example, in the upper left-hand recording (chart A) one finds, at a point just above 70 Hz, a small downward step marked by an arrow and the letter P. In chart B this point is visible as a small response peak, as a taller one in chart C, and as an upward step in chart D. Another example of this sort of behavior is found for a driving frequency just above 170 Hz. The arrows labeled Q mark the corresponding points on the four recordings.

It is not at all difficult to understand why these transfer response curves should

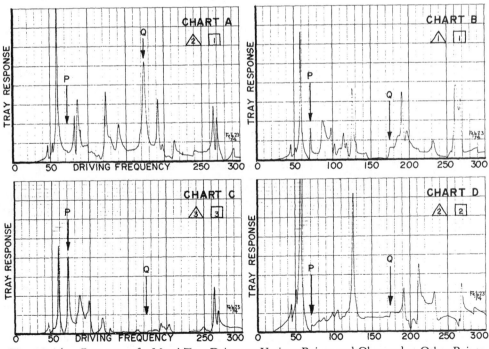

Fig. 10.14.   Response of a Metal Tray Driven at Various Points and Observed at Other Points

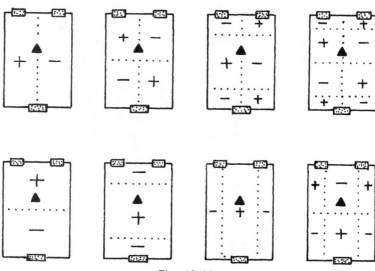

Fig. 10.15.

look so different from one another when we recall that the detector is blind (or deaf?) to any of the tray's vibrational modes which have a nodal line running through the detector position. For example, figure 10.13 shows that detector position 2 lies on the midline of the tray, and it follows that the detector at this position becomes totally insensitive to plate modes of the sort sketched in the upper part of figure 10.15, whereas it is particularly sensitive to the excitation of modes of the sort sketched in the lower part of the figure. In exactly similar fashion, the ability of the driver to excite a given mode depends on its position relative to the nodal lines and humps belonging to this mode's characteristic shape. In other words, all the rules of the game of excitation and detection that we discovered in chapters 7, 8, and 9 for struck and plucked objects apply almost unchanged when we make use of a sinusoidal excitation. We must always remember, however, that no matter what the frequency of the driving force, all of the modes are excited somewhat, so that the degree of the steady-state response observed at any given point depends on the summation of the responses of all of these modes, with proper account being taken not only of the fact that the predominant contributors are those whose natural frequencies approximate the driving frequency, but also of the presence of varying amounts of lag between stimulus and response.

Quite aside from fluctuations in the number of plate modes which happen to lie close enough to the driving frequency to be appreciably excited by it and from accidents of driver and detector placement which may affect the behavior of any one of these modes, we can expect quasi-random fluctuations in the observed response because of the accidental way in which the different active modes may happen to reinforce or cancel each other at the point of observation. Figure 10.16 illustrates this in schematic fashion for a rectangular

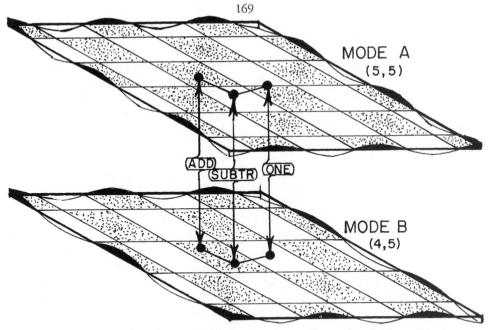

Fig. 10.16.   Effect of Superposing Two Modes as Observed at Different Places

plate for the case where only two of its characteristic modes (labeled modes A and B) are excited. The upper part of the diagram indicates the vibrational shape belonging to mode A, which has five humps each way; the lower part shows the corresponding shape for mode B, which has four humps one way and five the other. (On our metal tray, the frequencies corresponding to these modes would differ by only a few Hz.) The shaded areas on these diagrams show those parts of the plate that are momentarily deflected upwards, while the unshaded portions indicate those regions that are bulging downwards. The grid of straight lines delineates the node arrangements for our idealized vibrations. The pairs of black spots located vertically above one another call attention to three typical things that can happen as one surveys the vibrational amplitude over the

surface of the plate. There are places where the two modes give deflections of the same sign, so that the net disturbance is very large; there are spots where the two modes give opposite and essentially equal disturbances, which therefore cancel one another out to give a negligible detector signal even though the actual disturbance over the plate as a whole is very large; and finally there are places where one mode contributes alone to the detector signal because we are located on a nodal line of the other mode.

Looking back over our experiments with the steady-state transmission of sound from one point to another on a metal tray, we are left with a sense of basic simplicity in the way the resonant behaviors of many modes add up to relate the driving force at one point to the resulting response of the plate at another point. We are also left with a feeling of dismay over the enormous complexity of behavior that can result from these simple basic phenomena. We come to realize that altering the position of either driver or detector can drastically alter the nature of the transfer response curve. Because everything depends on the addition of many small contributions to the response, as well as on those of one or two large contributors, we find a few spots on the tray where the detector will discover a particularly strong vibration and a few spots where the disturbance is almost nil. At a slightly different driver frequency, the arrangement of the points of strong and weak response will be totally altered. In general, the overall patterns of response will have no particular resemblance to the characteristic vibration patterns of the modes which make them up.

10.8. Some Musical Implications

The thoughtful reader may ask whether irregularity of response of a plate is a good thing or a bad thing from a musical point of view. He then would be likely to ask how the nature of these irregularities might be controlled for musical purposes. The answer to the first question does not exist in any simple form. We have already had hints of the fact that the excellence of a guitar or violin rests in large measure on the details of the excitation of plate modes. Irregularity turns out to be a requirement, but it must be controlled by methods such as those described in the latter parts of chapter 9. The exact placement of the soundboard resonances of a piano or harpsichord turns out to be much less critically involved in the musical nature of the instrument, but we shall see that the average difference in

frequency between adjacent modes is of considerable importance.

The transmission of sound from one point to another in a room is another example of the transfer response of a multi-resonance system (this time a three-dimensional one). The irregularities of this transmission process in a room, which we will take up in the next chapter, have a great deal to do with the way in which the voices of musical instruments are easily recognizable. The manner in which these voices keep their identities when sounding together and yet manage to combine in various musical blends turns out to be based in part on the properties of rooms and in part on the ways in which the human nervous system deals with complex sensory patterns. Many different sorts of acoustical messages come from the instruments to our ears, and our minds simultaneously process these incoming messages in a variety of ways.

10.9. Examples, Experiments, and Questions

1. The lowest mode of vibration of a certain guitar top plate has a frequency of 185 Hz and a half-amplitude bandwidth $W_{1/2}$ of about 11 Hz (see figure 9.7). This means that if someone were to finger the note $F_3\sharp$ on the instrument and pluck the string, the first string mode would be at the frequency of maximum excitation of the plate mode. Verify for yourself that the fundamental components of the tones $F_3\natural$ and G_3 will not give any particular excitation to this plate mode. Notice that when one plays $F_2\sharp$ at the lower end of the guitar's range, this same plate mode responds strongly to the second harmonic

component of the string's vibration recipe. One can be sure (from the relationship of the bridge to the region of large plate motion) that the string is well able to drive the mode in question. Assuming that the string itself vibrates for a long time, it is possible to figure out how long it takes for the plate mode's starting transient to die away. Try to use the relations described in section 10.3, statements 10 and 11, to work out this problem.

2. Guitar plate modes 2 and 3 (figure 9.7, p. 133) may be expected to be only weakly excited by the bridge (why is this so?). However, these modes will play some role in determining the tonal flavor of the guitar sound. Mode 2 has a frequency of 287 Hz and $W_{1/2}$ is again about 11 Hz. The fact that this resonance falls between two playing notes makes its tonal influence somewhat different from that of mode 1.

Mode 3 for this guitar has a characteristic frequency of 460 Hz and $W_{1/2} =$ 18 Hz. For what notes of the guitar scale can you expect this mode to be active? Notice that the note $F_2^{\sharp}$ can have its sound altered by effects from plate mode 3, along with those from mode 1.

3. When one strikes the G_4 key of a well-tuned piano, the strings vibrate with the following list of harmonically related characteristic frequencies: 392, 784, 1176, 1568, 1960, 2352, . . . Hz (we are ignoring the slight inharmonicity of real strings here). All of these components serve to drive the soundboard, and thence everything else that it is connected to, including other strings. If we slowly but fully depress the key for G_3 in order to raise the damper for that note without striking the strings, we supply ourselves with a system whose natural frequencies are as follows: 196, 392, 588, 784, 980, 1176, . . . Hz. Striking the G_4 key (while the G_3 key is still being silently depressed) and releasing it quickly will provide a short burst of excitation to the even-numbered modes of the G_3 strings, and these will continue to sing after the direct sound of the G_4 strings has been killed off by their damper touching them on the release of the key. Why do we hear a pitch belonging to G_4 coming from the open G_3 string in this experiment? Reversing the experiment, so that the G_4 key is held down and the G_3 key is struck briefly, produces a closely similar result, with a similar explanation. Your understanding of what is going on here will be improved if you observe what happens when G_3 is replaced by $F_3^{\sharp}$ or $G_3^{\sharp}$, with the G_4 key being used as before.

4. Another experiment on the piano that is closely related to the one just described is the following. Hold down the G_3 key and briefly strike the D_4 key, which produces excitation whose frequency components are 293.7, 587.3, 881, 1174, 1468, 1761, 2055, . . . Hz. In this case, you will hear a clear, ringing tone whose pitch is an octave above D_4! Figure out the resonance and perception reasons for this phenomenon.

11

Room Acoustics I: Excitation of the Modes and the Transmission of Impulses

A room is a three-dimensional region containing air. Air in a room (or elsewhere) has elasticity—a fact recognized by anyone who has checked a bicycle tire for proper inflation by pressing it with his thumb. The fact that air has mass is perhaps less easily appreciated, but we might remark that the air in a filled balloon generally weighs a little less than the balloon rubber itself. In any event, the fact that a volume of air possesses both mass and elasticity tells us that modes of oscillation are possible in a room, with each of these modes having its own vibrational shape and characteristic frequency. The ideas that we have so carefully developed concerning the response of oscillatory modes to impulsive and sinusoidal excitation keep their validity for oscillations in air, including those telling us that excitation is at a maximum when we drive the system at points of maximum oscillatory disturbance and that it is at a minumum at the nodes.

11.1. Sound Pressure: *A Way of Describing the Characteristic Oscillatory Modes of Room Air*

Most microphones have a diaphragm that is pushed back and forth by the air pressure variations associated with the sound which reaches them, so that their output electrical signals are a direct measure of the *pressure* exerted by the air molecules. Our own hearing apparatus has a similar behavior, in that our nervous system operates upon signals passed to it via motions of the eardrum caused by inward and outward forces exerted on it by the air. For this reason acousticians have found it natural and convenient to focus their attention on the oscillatory pressure associated with sounds, whether in rooms or in the air columns of wind instruments.

The fact that oscillations of the air in a room are most conveniently studied and described in terms of sound pressure variations rather than mechanical displacements of the molecules means that we should find out how to translate the language of our earlier descriptions of phenomena into the newer form. A convenient way to accomplish the change in viewpoint is to make use of the phenomena described in connection with the third experiment of section 6.6. This experiment had to do with the one-dimensional sloshing of water in a trough closed at both ends. Here we noticed that, for each characteristic mode of oscillation, the oscillatory shape belonging to the horizontal motion of the water was quite different from that of the water-level variation. In particular we noticed that the nodes for horizontal motion were near points of maximum up-and-down motion and vice versa. If we were to install small, fast-acting water pressure gauges in the bottom of this trough we would notice that the fluctuations of water level above and below "mean sea level" correspond exactly to the fluctuations of water pressure measured by the gauges above and below the mean value associated with the depth of quiescent water. The relationship between these water pressure variations (which we also visualized directly in terms of the water's depth) and the variations in horizontal water flow associated with a particular sloshing mode in the water is *identical* with the relationship that holds between air pressure and air flow in the corresponding sloshing mode of air in a straight-sided pipe that is closed at both ends. Because of this identity, the diagrams drawn in figure 6.13 for each characteristic mode to show water height can equally well be used to show variations of pressure in an air-filled pipe.

It is a simple matter to adapt pictures of one-dimensional sloshing modes in a trough to their two-dimensional analogues in a swimming pool (of whatever shape!). In a similar manner one can adapt pictures of pressure disturbances in a pipe or a one-dimensional room (which is a room having a very low ceiling and very small width) to those belonging to a two-dimensional room (one having a very low ceiling but appreciable width and length) and thence to the somewhat more abstract three-dimensional room, having a normal proportionality between length, width, and height. In other words, we can draw diagrams showing characteristic shapes of oscillatory *pressure* variations in room modes in exactly the same way as we earlier drew diagrams showing the oscillatory variations of *displacement* in the characteristic modes of strings and drumheads. Figure 10.16 can be understood to represent the water surface shape for two modes of water oscillating in a rectangular swimming pool. It can then also be taken as a picture of the air pressure distribution for these same modes in a two-dimensional room.

11.2. Excitation of Room Modes by a Simple Source

In earlier chapters it was not particularly hard for us to visualize the impulsive excitation of a plucked or struck string or the sinusoidal excitation of a hanging board pushed by means of a motor-driven crank and some rubber bands. The impulsive and sinusoidal excitations of air in a room can similarly be made understandable with the help of a couple of introductory experiments.

When a balloon is pricked, one hears a pop as the air compressed within it is abruptly released into the room. A more violent version of the same mechanism for impulsive excitation of air modes takes place when one sets off a firecracker in a room. The rapid, explosive burning of gunpowder releases a sudden burst of hot gas into the room. Notice that in both cases additional gas has been injected into the room from a small source.

For sinusoidal excitation of the room air we need only arrange some sort of pump which alternately injects air into the room and extracts it from the room at the desired driving frequency. A "muscle feeling" of what is involved is easily attained. One has only to raise his tongue to close off the back of the mouth cavity and then move the tongue back and forth, alternately expelling and taking in air through pursed lips in a manner reminiscent of the way a swimmer spouts a mouthful of water. The maximum frequency of oscillation that is possible for this sort of crude, physiological pump can hardly be above a sluggish 5 Hz. Loudspeakers work in the same manner to push air in and out, but at a wide range of frequencies. Most home loudspeakers have a movable paper cone mounted on the front side of an otherwise sealed box. When electrical signals from the amplifier cause it to move in and out, the cone is acting exactly like a pump piston, which provides us with a very direct and literal example of what is meant by a source.

In our earlier investigations it was very natural to talk about the strength of the excitative stimulus in terms of the magnitude of the force (either impulsive or sinusoidal) that was exerted on the vibrating object. The need for similar terminology to describe the strength of the excitative influence on air moving within a cavity led acousticians to borrow the term *source strength* from the study of fluid mechanics. To specify the strength of any device acting as a source of fluid, one makes a statement about the rate at which the fluid issues from it (for example, the water faucet in a kitchen is an adjustable source of water whose strength may conveniently be said to range from zero when it is closed to several cupfuls per second when it is fully opened). In the case of a sinusoidally operating pump, the flow takes place alternately in an outward and an inward direction, with the

flow rate passing through its maximum outward value before it falls to zero and then reverses toward a maximum inward rate. Such an oscillatory flow device is customarily described in terms of the maximum value of the flow rate (either inward or outward), just as in the past we have described the sinusoidal motion of a pendulum in terms of its maximum displacement on either side of the midpoint. You will recall that in all cases of sinusoidal disturbance we have found it convenient to describe its vigor in terms of its amplitude, which is the maximum value of the oscillatory disturbance.

In acoustics, what is known as a *simple source* (of given strength) is one whose aperture is very tiny compared with the distance between nodal regions of the characteristic room oscillations. An easy way for us to understand the meaning of the term is to relate it to things we have already met in connection with our study of strings in chapter 7. There we spoke of the excitation of strings by narrow plectra and sharp-edged hammers. For room acoustics, then, the simple source is the exact analogue of narrow hammers and plectra. Moreover, the changes in room excitation brought about by widening the source aperture are exactly like those which were described in chapter 8 for the excitation of strings by widened hammers.

Digression on Loudspeakers.

The behavior of a real loudspeaker as a generator of sound is not quite like the behavior of the simple source we have just described. For one thing the speaker cone is fairly wide, so that at high frequencies it spans a number of humps in the vibratory pattern of the air, therefore failing to drive them effectively (see secs. 8.1, 8.2, and 8.5). Furthermore, the loudspeaker cone acts like a mass mounted on a spring, giving it its own resonance behavior. The suitable coordination of these two phenomena with those that are primarily electrical in nature is a serious problem for a loudspeaker designer, but not one that we need to concern ourselves with here. Suffice it to say that with suitable equipment it is possible to arrange small, pumplike devices that allow us to study the properties of rooms and the air columns of musical instruments in terms of their pressure response to excitation by a simple source.

Now that we have described the simple source as a basic device for the excitation of the vibratory modes of air in a room and contrasted its properties with those of the familiar loudspeaker, we can adapt some of the principles studied in earlier chapters to the new physical situation. Following custom, we will do this by means of a set of numbered assertions:

1. A given oscillatory mode in a room is maximally excited by a simple source if the source is located at one of the points of maximum pressure variation belonging to that mode. There is no excitation at all if the source is located at the position of a pressure node (see assertions 1, 2, and 3 in sec. 7.2).

2. Sinusoidal excitation of a mode by means of a simple source produces a maximum oscillatory pressure amplitude when the excitation has a driving frequency that matches the natural frequency of the mode (see assertion 3, sec. 10.1, also fig. 10.3).

3. Lightly damped room modes, when started and then left to "ring," will run for many oscillations before the pressure amplitude has fallen appreciably. Such modes respond strongly to the excitation frequency only when the excitation frequency closely matches the characteristic frequency of the mode. Put another way, when the damping is low, the halving time $T_{1/2}$ is long and the half-amplitude bandwidth $W_{1/2}$ is narrow (see assertions 9 and 10 in sec. 10.3, also fig. 10.9).

4. Each particular room mode responds sinusoidally to some extent regardless of the driving frequency. The resulting oscillation will have the characteristic shape belonging to the mode and (after the initial transient has died down) will oscillate at the driving frequency (see fig. 10.2).

5. All of the transient behavior of room air responding either to sinusoidal driving by a simple source or to impulsive excitation by explosions shows pressure variations which follow all the rules that we discovered earlier for the mechanical oscillations of masses, strings, bars, plates, and membranes (review sec. 10.6).

11.3. Detection of Room Modes by a Microphone or by the Ear:
Interchangeability of Source and Detector

In the previous section we learned that the oscillatory pressures associated with the motion of air in a room are excited by a simple source of sinusoidal air flow in a manner we should find quite familiar since we have met it several times earlier in this book. We turn our attention now to the detection of these modes by a small microphone or by the human ear. It seems almost a triviality to point out that the amplitude of the microphone's electrical signal will fall to zero when the microphone is located at the position of a pressure node; conversely, the signal will be of maximum size if the microphone is moved to a point in the room where the pressure variations belonging to the mode are at a maximum. Such a point of maximum pressure variation in the room is often said to be at a pressure *antinode*. In our more informal terminology, it could be described as being at the highest point of a hump in the characteristic vibrational shape for the mode in question.

We are now in a position to recognize formally a connection between the physics of the pressure variations which we have been discussing and the perceived response to these variations which comes about when a human nervous system processes the signals coming to it from the ear. Since ears are like microphones in being sensitive to oscillatory pressure variations in the atmosphere, we would expect to hear a loud sound when our ears are located at an antinode and complete silence when they are placed at a node. If we could in fact excite the room modes one at a time by means of a simple source, this is exactly what we would observe. One ordinarily does *not* find points of silence in rooms, or points of sharply marked maximum loudness. The reasons for this lack are to be found partly in the physics of rooms in which many modes are excited simultaneously (as described later in this chapter) and partly in the way our hearing mechanism operates (see chap. 12).

You may wonder why acousticians are in the habit of referring to oscillatory variations of air pressure as *sound pressure.* In its original meaning, the word "sound" referred to a particular kind of *perceived* signal—the one received by the ears of a living creature. As men came to understand the connection between certain kinds of vibration and the sounds they heard, the vibrations themselves were referred to as sound. Now and then the question is posed: "If a tree falls in the forest and there is no one around to hear it, is there really a sound?" The answer, of course, depends on the special interests of the questioner. To someone confining his interest to the vibrations of objects and the resulting pressure variations in the air, there is indeed a sound.

On the other hand, the student of perception might assert (perfectly correctly) that if no auditory signals are being processed in a nervous system, then there is no sound. Musicians are of course vitally concerned with both the generation and the perception of sound, which is why we find ourselves continually moving back and forth between the two viewpoints.

We close this section with an observation which has remarkable consequences both for the physicist and for the perception psychologist. Everywhere in this book we have noticed that the modes of oscillation characteristic of any system are most favorably excited as precisely the same points as those where oscillation is most strongly observable. In other words, there appears to be a considerable similarity between the efficacy of excitation and the ease of detection of an oscillation. This similarity is actually complete: the points of excitation by a simple source and of detection by a small microphone are *precisely interchangeable.* This relationship is indicated schematically for a one-dimensional room in the upper part of figure 11.1 If a simple source is located at one point in a room (call it point A) and a small microphone is located at another point (point B), then the pressure signal at B due to the action of a flow source at A is exactly the same as the pressure signal to be observed at A if the source is moved to B (see the lower part of fig. 11.1). This assertion seems particularly shocking when one realizes that it implies that a listener seated on stage in a concert hall will hear from a violinist in the balcony exactly the same sounds he will hear if the player and listener take up their more normal positions! In actual fact, the two versions will not sound exactly alike. This is partly because a violin

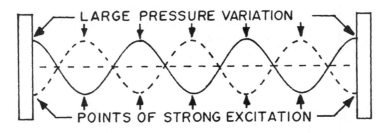

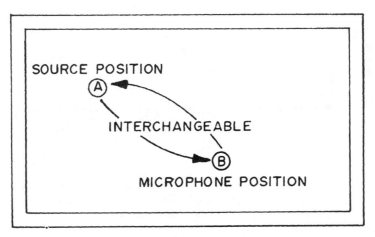

Fig. 11.1.

does not act quite as a simple flow source and partly because we use two ears for our listening, ears that are separated by a fairly solid skull, but the difference arises chiefly as a result of the way our nervous system operates.

11.4. Measured Steady-State Response Curves for a Room

In the previous sections of this chapter we simply reviewed the excitation and detection of room modes taken one at a time. Our experiments in chapter 10 with the metal tray have already given some indication of what can happen when the disturbance at some point is made up of the superposition of vibrational shapes belonging to several modes. Except for those of us who sing in shower enclosures or telephone booths, our experience is mainly with rooms large enough to have scores of modes that are strongly excited, even by a source that generates an oscillatory flow at only a single frequency.

Figure 11.2 presents a graph of the average number of room modes that lie close enough to a given (sinusoidal) excitation frequency to be excited to more

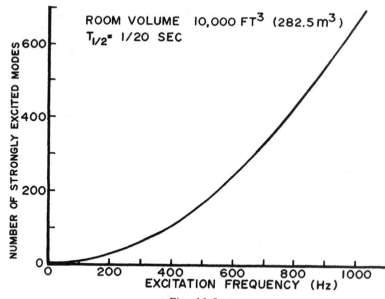

ROOM VOLUME 10,000 FT³ (282.5 m³)
$T_{1/2} = 1/20$ SEC

NUMBER OF STRONGLY EXCITED MODES

EXCITATION FREQUENCY (Hz)

Fig. 11.2.

than half their maximum amplitude. The curve is calculated for a typical, well-cluttered, medium-sized room of 10,000 cubic feet (282 cubic meters) volume whose modes are damped enough to make them die away in amplitude with a halving time $T_{1/2}$ of 1/20 second (giving them a half-amplitude bandwidth $W_{1/2}$ of very close to 7.6 Hz). The figure shows that for any excitation frequency above about 200 Hz, several dozen of the room modes are willing to be strongly excited by the source.

Digression on the Number of Strongly Excited Modes for Any Room at Any Frequency.

Figure 11.2 can easily be adapted to give the numbers of actively excited modes at a given frequency in rooms of any size and with any amount of damping. The curve can also be made to give information for higher frequency sounds. First of all, the number of active modes at any frequency is proportional to the volume of the room. Because of this, if we compare a million-cubic-foot concert hall with the 10,000-cubic-foot room described above, we can expect to have a 100-fold increase (1,000,000 ÷ 10,000) in the number of active modes at any given frequency. Secondly, an increase in the damping raises $W_{1/2}$ proportionately (see assertion 10 in sec. 10.3) and so makes a corresponding change in the number of modes that can be excited. Finally it is a fact that the curve in figure 11.2 is one that rises proportionately to the square of the frequency. As a result, at a frequency that is, for instance, ten times any of the listed ones, the number of strongly excited modes is increased 100-fold (10 × 10).

Let us now see what actually happens when a simple source is arranged to excite my laboratory room, whose volume is nearly that assumed in figure 11.2 (78 percent of it) and whose damping is exactly the same. I should remark that musicians find the room a pleasant one to

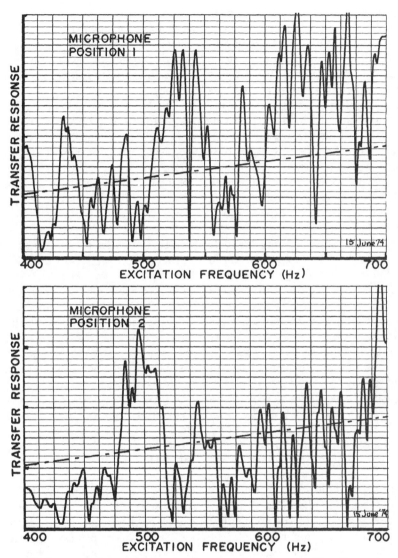

Fig. 11.3. Variation of the Signal Detected at the Microphone at Two Points in a Room as the Excitation Frequency Is Varied

play in and that it is particularly satisfactory for instruments that play above the note A_3, whose fundamental frequency component lies at 220 Hz. Figure 11.3 shows two transfer response curves measured for this room over the restricted frequency range from 400 to 700 Hz. In both cases a carefully checked simple source was located on the floor exactly in one corner of the room; however, the detecting microphone was moved several feet between the two tracings. Notice first of all that the sound pressure amplitude recorded at the microphone position is extremely variable as the steadily operating simple source runs through its range of frequencies. Notice also that the curves for the two microphone positions have no similarity in the arrangement of their peaks and dips. This is in contrast to the way in which various small details of the resonance peaks kept reappearing in all of the resonance curves of our metal tray (see fig. 10.14). The explanation is as follows. The individual resonances of the tray modes were separated widely enough (a few Hz apart) in comparison to their half-amplitude widths ($W_{1/2}$) that we could see their separate contributions on the chart; in the room, however, over the frequency range of interest the resonances are so closely spaced that a very large number of modes are appreciably excited at any driving frequency. In this room, for example, at a 400-Hz excitation frequency there are about 110 modes whose characteristic frequencies lie close enough (within about 4 Hz on either side) to be strongly excited by the source. What we are seeing in the response curve, then, is the randomly varying combination of these strongly excited modes as "heard" by the microphone (look at fig. 10.16), along with the more smoothly varying contribution from the "tails" of the resonance curves of tens of thousands of other room modes which, though they are only weakly excited, make up, through sheer numerousness, an appreciable part of the measured response. If I had made hundreds of tracings, each with the microphone in a different position in the room, numerical averaging of the magnitude of the responses would have

given a rising straight-line graph for the aggregate behavior of the room, as is shown by the dashed lines on the two parts of figure 11.3 (see also the remarks made in connection with fig. 11.6 in sec. 11.8).

This average curve for the response of a room to driving by a simple source can actually be calculated by correctly integrating the contributions of all the thousands of weakly responding high-frequency modes with those of the more obvious modes that have strong responses when taken one by one.[1]

In section 9.4 there is a digression pointing out that the frequency difference between successive resonances of a plate is constant as one explores ever-higher modes of vibration, whereas for a membrane this spacing gets smaller at high frequencies. We have found that rooms have a somewhat similar behavior in that the frequency spacing between successive resonances becomes less and less as we study the higher frequencies. It is this that gives rise to the sharply increasing number of strongly excited modes at high frequencies that is implied by figure 11.2. Ordinary ideas about the regularizing effects of averaging many numbers might lead us to expect that the response curve should become smoother at high frequencies if there are more strongly driven modes to contribute to the behavior. Such is not the case, however, as we can verify at a glance if we examine figure 11.3. The general wiggliness is no less near 700 Hz than it was near 400 Hz, despite the fact that there are more than twice as many active modes at the upper end than there are at the lower. About twenty years ago, it was discovered that under the conditions of our experiment the mean spacing of the peaks in the random fluctuations of a response curve depends chiefly on what we have called the halving time $T_{1/2}$ for the decay of oscillations.[2] A long decay time is associated with a steady-state pressure-response curve which has many squiggly peaks over any interval of frequency, and a short decay time is associated with a smaller number of wiggles. The heights and depths of the wiggles, however, do not depend on the size of the room or on the halving time! The fact that our response curves are uniformly wiggly over their entire frequency range is then merely an indication that the decay time is nearly the same for all modes over the measured frequency range.

11.5. The Influence of Furniture and Moving Objects on Room Modes

In the preceding section we learned that the observed response at any point in a room varies wildly as the excitation frequency is changed. Our earlier studies of the influence of added mass, etc., on plates and drumheads suggest that the presence of furniture and people in a room will rearrange the frequencies of the various modes and also change the oscillatory pressure distributions which characterize them. Such alterations to the individual room modes turn out to be small in magnitude. Whatever is observed in the room comes about, however, through the piling up of many thousands of strongly and weakly excited modes, nearly all of which are altered to some extent, and one does in fact observe a quite significant net effect.[3]

The upper part of figure 11.4 shows what the microphone response signal looked like when I walked *slowly* around

my laboratory room and back to my starting place. In this experiment the corner-mounted source was running at a particular frequency near 600 Hz (the microphone position was the same as in the lower part of figure 11.3). The graph shows a certain amount of fluctuation in the microphone signal as my body altered the arrangement of the characteristic patterns of the room modes. In the middle part of the trace we see that my perambulations took me into a region that had a particularly large influence. It is a matter of pure chance that this region happened to lie clear across the room. Notice that the pressure signal was the same after my return to the starting point as it had been originally; you may also realize from the horizontality of the trace in the immediate neighborhood of the starting point that in this region of the room small changes in my position have almost no effect on the detected acoustic signal.

Look now at the lower part of figure 11.4. In making this curve, the source and detector positions were left unchanged, as was my point of departure for the room circumnavigation. The chief alteration was a small change (some 5 or 10 Hz) in the excitation frequency. The new frequency was critically chosen to give an especially small response at the microphone position. The electrical drive to the source was also turned up, so as to bring the level of the microphone signal back approximately to its value at the beginning of the first experiment (the sound to my ears under these conditions was almost unbearably loud). The chart recorder trace made under these conditions shows enormously large and complex fluctuations in the microphone signal. Experiments like these, where one looks into changes in the sound transmis-

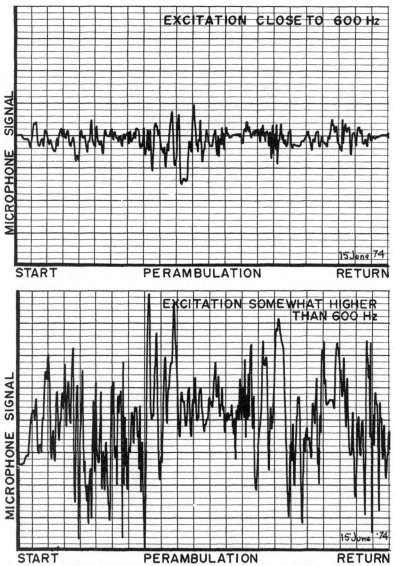

Fig. 11.4.   The Effect of Someone Walking Around in the Room on the Detected Signal. *Upper trace*, the fairly uniform transmission observed at a selected frequency for which the transmission to the microphone is particularly strong; *lower trace*, the much wilder fluctuations observed for a nearby frequency that produces particularly small transmission to the same microphone position.

sion that are associated with changes in the arrangement of the room, show a number of features which I will summarize as follows:

1. For any particular frequency of excitation and source location there are microphone positions in a room at which the detected sound pressure is particularly insensitive to the effects arising when objects are moved around in the room. There is generally a strong transmission of sound to the microphone at such positions, and things are little changed if the frequency is altered slightly.

2. For any given excitation frequency and source location, there are a few microphone positions in the room at which sound pressure amplitude is extremely low. These regions are very small (about fist-sized for frequencies in the neighborhood of 500 Hz). When objects are moved around in the room there are enormous fluctuations in the microphone signal. The positions in the room of such points of minimum sound pressure and wild signal fluctuation are considerably displaced if a small change is made in the excitation frequency.

11.6. Room Response: *Some Apparent Problems*

We have so far given our attention to the way in which steady-state responses of many modes combine to give the microphone signal in a room. We have yet to look at the related problems of the starting transient, the decay of sounds in a room when sinusoidal excitation is shut off, and the related responses of the room to impulsive excitation. Before taking up these matters, however, we should pause briefly to glance at some of the problems which steady-state room behavior might raise in the mind of a musically oriented reader.

In chapters 7 and 8 a great deal of care was invested in the explanation of various vibration recipes produced when strings are struck or plucked in various ways. As a reader you were entitled to deduce from this that what we call tone color was somehow associated with these vibration recipes, and that skillful manipulation of the recipes belonging to different musical instruments is one of the resources of composers and performers.

Even without worrying about the detailed manner in which an actual musical instrument acts as a sound source in the studio or concert hall, we may be led by figures 11.3 and 11.4 to fear that the properties of rooms may somehow destroy all possibility for well-defined tone color. Depending on where the listener sits (and also, by symmetry, on where the source is located), the strengths of the various partial components of the tone apparently can have almost any relationship whatever to one another at the listener's ear. Furthermore, if either the player or the listener moves to another part of the room, these relative strengths will be reshuffled into yet another new and random arrangement!

It is of course a fact that for many centuries music has been satisfactorily performed in rooms. It is also a fact that most of us quickly recognize the individual voices of our friends and even of particular musical instruments when they are heard in rooms. Obviously there are some gaps in our understanding of what is going on. Some of these gaps belong to the territory of physics and will be filled somewhat later in this chapter. Other pieces of missing information will be supplied in chapter 12, where we will consider how our ears not only cope with but also exploit the sound-pressure complexities of a room. Meanwhile, let us look at one semi-practical implication of what we have learned so far.

In section 11.4 it was remarked that an arithmetical average of a room's response behavior observed at many different points gives a good representation of the output from the source. This might lead us to leap to the conclusion that connecting together the outputs of a whole set of microphones which are placed throughout the room would allow one at least to record something that is not "spoiled" by the vagaries of room acoustics. This turns out not to be true, because the electrical adding-up of a set of *sinusoids,* one from each microphone, each with its own amplitude and degree of lagging behind the driving stimulus, is not at all the same thing as sitting down with pencil and paper to average the measured *amplitudes* of these same sinusoids. As a matter of fact, if you feed two or three microphones together into a commercial microphone mixing circuit and record the combination, the resulting signal will normally have an *increased* irregularity when compared with a recording made with any one of the microphones used alone (there was mention of this same phenomenon in the final experiment in chapter 8 having to do with the use of dual pickups on an electric guitar). Because of the symmetry that holds between point sources and small detectors, we should realize that the use of several interconnected loudspeakers in the room will for the same reasons fail to increase the regularity of the excitation process. I hasten to add that at this stage it is premature to say whether the use of multiple, interconnected microphones or of similarly related loudspeakers is good or bad. One merely has to remember that the steady-state transmission of sound be-

tween source and microphone is made (if anything) more irregular by any reduplication of source or detector.

11.7. Transient Response of Rooms to Sinusoidal Excitation

So far in this chapter on room acoustics we have confined our attention to microphone signals picked up under steady-state conditions. All changes of frequency, microphone position, or my own position as an adjustable perturbation of the room modes were made very slowly, and the system was left running long enough that the initial transient behavior had time to decay away. We will now focus our attention on the transients themselves. We recall from section 10.2 that when a single mode of oscillation is excited by a sinusoidal driving mechanism, the initial motion of the vibrating object can be a very messy-looking combination of a steady oscillation at the drive frequency plus a damped sinusoid characteristic of the free oscillations of the mode. However, if one drives the mode at precisely its own natural frequency, the initial transient can have a tidy-looking motion (see fig. 10.8). When one thinks about the initial behavior of a room when it is driven by a sinusoidally varying flow, it is not obvious what sort of microphone signal to expect. Will the fairly orderly-looking response of the set of strongly excited modes (whose frequencies match that of the driver) predominate in the observed microphone signal? Will the aggregate effect of the thousands of off-resonance modes pile up to give some recognizable pattern? Will the whole thing degenerate into hopeless complexity? The fact that the percussionist can make use of elaborate rhythmic patterns in his playing and the fact that a competent instrumentalist exploits variations in the phrasing and articulation of his successive notes certainly suggest that there must be some sort of regularity in the transient behavior and that this regularity is something our ears have learned to use.

Figure 11.5 shows what happens in my laboratory room when the excitory signal is first switched on and then turned off a few tenths of a second later. The source and the microphone are located where they were during the making of figure 11.4. In all these cases the drive frequency was close to 600 Hz. The vertical displacement of the oscilloscope spot is a measure of the sound pressure at the microphone, while the horizontal axis is marked off in 1/10-second intervals (compare these pictures with those taken with the microphone placed near a tuning fork, figure 4.2). The top picture in figure 11.5 was made using the same driving frequency used in making the top tracing of figure 11.4. The oscilloscope trace begins at the left at the instant the excitation was turned on, and we can see that the sound-pressure amplitude grows to nearly its full value in the course of the first 1/10 second. The source was turned off after a little more than 0.55 seconds, as shown by the fact that the sound begins to die away at a point lying between the fifth and the sixth timing marks. After this time the sound pressure fades out in a manner very reminiscent of the decay of a single mode, with a halving time of about 1/20 second (a half square on the oscilloscope grid). The narrow, blurry stripe that runs along the last 0.2 seconds of the trace shows merely that the room's ventilating system supplies a little stray noise which covers up the last vestiges of the decay. If one were to see this picture by itself, it would be easy to decide that the first of our rhetorical questions has an affirmative answer: the build-up and the decay of sound in a room *are* dominated by the strongly excited modes, which somehow manage to give a total response that looks like that of a single spring-mass system taken by itself. However, we have two other oscilloscope pictures to think about.

The bottom one of the three oscilloscope traces in figure 11.5 shows the room response when the driving frequency is altered by only a few Hz to give it the value used in making the lower chart re-

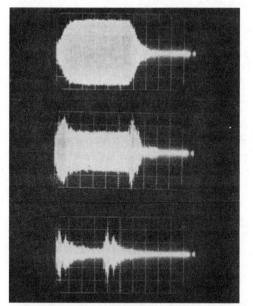

HORIZONTAL SCALE   0.1 SEC/DIV.

Fig. 11.5.   Transient Behavior at One Point in a Room for Three Nearby Frequencies. *Upper trace,* made under the same conditions as upper trace in fig. 11.4; *lower trace,* made under the same conditions as lower trace in fig. 11.4; *middle trace,* conditions midway between the other two.

cording of figure 11.4. You will recall that at this excitation frequency the microphone signal was particularly tiny. When the tone is switched on we find an almost immediate ragged burst of sound arriving at the microphone, and then this drops away over the next few tenths of a second to an amplitude only about twice that of the background noise in the room. The excitation is turned off 0.37 seconds after it begins and, immediately *following* this switch-off, the microphone receives a second irregular burst of sound which decays to leave only room noise.

The middle picture in figure 11.5 shows the build-up and decay of sound at the microphone position when the source frequency is set at a value intermediate between those used for the other pictures. To produce this picture, the excitation was shut off 0.43 seconds after it was switched on. Notice that the overall shape of the response is midway between those shown in the other two pictures. There are initial and final bursts of large amplitude sound, although they are smoother and less pronounced than in the bottom picture. After the initial transient has settled down, the steady-state response shown here for the room is intermediate between that shown for the other two excitation frequencies.

Let us distill the information that can be gleaned from the comparison of figures 11.4 and 11.5 into a set of numbered statements:

1. The transient behavior observed at any point in a room after the excitation is turned off is very similar to that observed immediately after the source is turned on.[4]
2. The duration of the onset and decay transients is as long as, *or longer than,* what one might expect on the basis of the known halving time for individual room modes.

3. When the excitation frequency is set at a value that makes the microphone signal insensitive to the position of objects moving around the room, the onset and turn-off transients have a form very similar to the build-up and decay of a single mode acting by itself. The steady-state signal at the microphone is relatively strong under these conditions.
4. When the drive frequency is set to produce maximum sensitivity of the microphone signal to rearrangements of the furniture, the onset and turn-off transients are in the form of irregular bursts of sound. During the steady part of the excitation the microphone signal is particularly small.
5. At driving frequencies other than those described in statements 3 and 4, the transient behavior is intermediate between the two extreme forms.
6. Moving the source and the microphone to new positions in the room causes a total rearrangement of the frequencies at which the various forms of transient and steady-state response take place.

Before we leave the subject of the transient response of rooms to sinusoidal driving for a look at their response to impulsive sources, we should see how much we can figure out about *how* the air modes work together to produce the phenomena described above. Statement 1 can be understood if we recognize that shutting off a steadily running source at some instant is exactly equivalent to leaving it running while starting up an immediately adjacent second source at that same instant. The new source must be arranged to suck in air at those precise instants that the original one is ejecting air, and vice versa. If we think about the room's response to this late-starting (and reversed) source acting by itself, we should expect a new transient that is exactly like that belonging to the first except for the interchange of positive and negative pressure maxima in the course of each individual oscillation. After this transient has died out, the effects of the two sources exactly cancel each other out everywhere in the room to produce silence. In other words, we can think of the start-up transient as being due to the initiation of an indefinitely continued excitation, while the shut-off transient can be thought of as the start-up transient of a later, reversed-phase source which also continues indefinitely, eventually canceling the first one.

Statement 2 is somewhat harder to make something of. However, we can get an idea of what is important by recalling that all of the *strongly excited* room modes have approximately the same frequency (within about 3.8 Hz of each other in our example). Because they run at nearly the same frequencies, their individual transient responses will tend to pull out of step with one another; this has a noticeable effect over any period of time that is longer than their individual halving times.

In a book of this sort there is really very little that can be said of an explanatory nature about statement 3. We will have to content ourselves with remarking that the experiment is done at a frequency for which there are *many* ways in which the room modes can respond to the driver to give essentially the same microphone signal.

Statement 4, on the other hand, is amenable to a slightly more detailed explanation. To produce zero response at some point in the room during steady excitation, there has to be an extremely precise adjustment if the aggregated and reasonably stable contributions of the thousands of off-resonance modes are to cancel exactly the combination of the relatively fewer strongly excited modes.

During the onset and turn-off epochs every one of these modes is undergoing its individual transient oscillation, with each transient oscillation including a good helping of the mode's own characteristic frequency component along with the driven component whose magnitude was so carefully adjusted. It is the collection of individual mode transients, then, that gives rise to the bursts of sound at the microphone when the source is first turned on and when it is shut off.

Statement 6 is merely a reminder that the pressure variations detected by a microphone at some point in the room are the result of superposing the contributions of many modes. The amount of each mode's contribution depends not only on the position of the microphone relative to the nodes and antinodes of that mode's oscillatory pattern, but also in the same way on the position of the source.

11.8. Response to Impulsive Excitation I: *Signal Delays and Reverberation*

In this section we will look into the way a room responds to an impulsive flow excitation and learn of a new phenomenon in the evolution over time of the pressure distribution. This phenomenon is observable not only in a room, but also in certain one-dimensional objects such as piano strings and straight-sided pipes containing air (the phenomenon in its simplest form does *not* take place in two-dimensional objects!).

The top part of figure 11.6 shows the particular variety of impulsive flow behavior that I have arranged as a stimulus to the laboratory room. The laboratory source is electrically driven in such a way that it first sucks air *into* itself briefly and

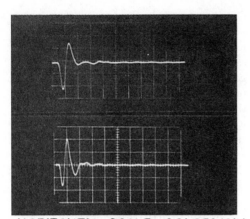

HORIZONTAL SCALE .OOI SEC/DIV

Fig. 11.6. *Top,* impulsive flow pattern of a source; *bottom,* corresponding pressure signal at a nearby microphone.

then *expels* some air before settling down into inactivity. The downward dip at the left-hand end of the oscilloscope trace indicates the sucking-in phase of the action while the succeeding upward hump shows the pumping-out action. The oscilloscope is set up so that each square of rightward motion represents the passage of 1/1000 second (1 millisecond) of time, which means that the complete in-and-out flow impulse takes place in about 1.5 milliseconds.

The lower part of figure 11.6 shows the *pressure* disturbance recorded when the microphone is placed immediately next to the flow aperture of the source. The fact that the initial twitch of the oscilloscope trace is downward agrees well with our intuitive idea that a sudden extraction of air from a region should momentarily lower the atmospheric pressure there. Beyond this point, however, our intuitions fail us: the pressure signal is not a copy of the flow signal—not only does it have a different shape, it also seems to have acquired one additional wiggle! The

proper explanation of this phenomenon is not something we can give in this book, but we should know that the effect is a consequence of the three-dimensionality of the room and is closely related to the linearly rising *averaged* room response that was shown by the dashed lines in both parts of figure 11.3 (see sec. 11.4).[5] An experiment using the same flow source signal to excite the modes of a long, air-filled pipe (a one-dimensional room) would show not only a pressure disturbance that is an exact copy of the flow disturbance, but an *averaged* "room" response that neither rises nor falls as the frequency is changed.

Figure 11.7 shows (top trace) the microphone signals recorded with the micro-

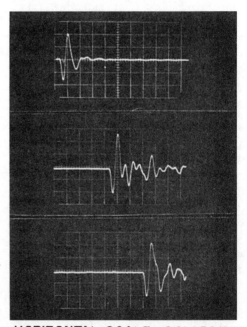

HORIZONTAL SCALE .OOI SEC/DIV

Fig. 11.7. Microphone Signals in a Room Measured at Varying Distances from the Source

phone right next to the source aperture, (middle trace) those recorded with the microphone a few feet away from the source in the middle of the room, and (bottom trace) those recorded with the microphone at a greater distance from the source. In all three cases the horizontal motion of the oscilloscope spot was electrically initiated an instant (about 0.0005 seconds, or 0.5 milliseconds) before the flow started. As in figure 11.6, each division along the horizontal scale represents 1 millisecond of time. Comparison of these three pictures shows us that impulsive excitation of the room modes gives rise to a curious phenomenon. The separately started sinusoidal oscillations of these modes pile up on each other in all parts of the room in such a way that the more distant the microphone is from the source, the longer it takes after the impulse for the microphone to "find out about it" by recording a pressure variation. It turns out that the speed with which the initial part of the message runs outward from the source to the microphone is the same for all directions of travel in the room; it is also the same for all sorts of excitations. This speed at which the front ends of signals travel in a room is what is formally known as *the speed of sound in air*. In a reasonably warm room the speed of sound has an easily remembered round-number value of 345 meters/second (i.e., 1133 feet/second). Measurement of the middle picture in figure 11.7 shows that the microphone waited almost exactly 4 milliseconds for its message, whence we deduce that it was located a distance of $345 \times 4/1000 = 1.38$ meters, or 4.53 feet, away from the source. Similarly, there is a delay of 6.3 milliseconds associated with the microphone signal in

the lower picture, so the distance traveled was 2.17 meters (7.14 feet).

It takes only a cursory examination of figure 11.7 to show us that the pressure disturbances picked up by the microphone at various distances from an impulsive source are not at all the same, even though repetitions of the excitation always produce identical signals at a given location (as long as no one moves himself or the furniture). We do observe, however, that the very first part of the signal preserves its shape fairly well. Let us look once more at the pressure signal picked up at the more distant microphone position. This time we will use a slower horizontal traverse rate for the oscilloscope spot, so that the traces show the pressure variations over a longer time interval.

The top part of figure 11.8 shows the microphone signal at the 2.17-meter distance, using a time scale in which each square represents 20 milliseconds. This

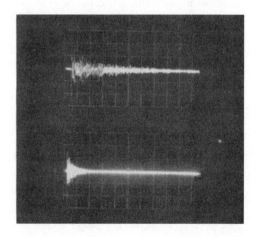

**UPPER TRACE   .020 SEC/DIV
LOWER TRACE   0.10 SEC/DIV**

Fig. 11.8.   Decay of an Impulsive Sound in a Room

trace covers a time interval twenty times longer than before, so that the beginning of the microphone signal lies near the left side of the picture instead of being past the middle as it was in the lower part of figure 11.7. In the new picture the whole pattern is compressed so that we can no longer make out the details of the individual wiggles. We can, however, see a larger, though irregular, pattern which dies down in a way reminiscent of the decay of sound from a struck skillet or from a room after sinusoidal excitation is shut off.

The lower part of figure 11.8 confirms that the decay pattern shown in the figure resembles that for a struck skillet. Here the trace speed has been cut down so that each square represents 100 milliseconds (identical to the 1/10-second-per-division rate that was used in making the pictures in figure 11.5). The halving time for the whole messy decay of sound from impulsive excitation is the same as that measured using sinusoidal excitation, an observation that is not surprising when we recall that in both cases a collection of room modes has been set into oscillation and then allowed to die away freely, each mode according to its own tendency.

We can now draw together the results of our observations of rooms in the form of three numbered statements. The section will then close with a careful definition of the term *reverberation time,* which is an important part of the room acoustician's working vocabulary.

1. The pressure signal observed in the immediate neighborhood of a simple source acting in a three-dimensional room has a shape that is descended from but not identical with the flow pattern of the source output itself. In a one-dimensional room (a pipe), however, the two patterns are alike. (Both these state-

ments are subject to a simple limitation which will be made clear in section 11.9)

2. The signal from a microphone that is placed some distance away from a simple source will detect the beginning of the excitatory signal only after a short delay time. This is because the room modes combine in such a way that signals travel in the room with a velocity of 345 meters/sec (1133 ft/sec).

3. The decay of sound after excitation, as observed at some point in a room, is of the same general type whether the excitation began impulsively or sinusoidally. This decay is in general quite ragged, but, taken overall, it has a form reminiscent of that found for the dying-away of the sinusoidal oscillation of a single characteristic mode.

If one makes observations of the decay of sound at many points in the room and with shifts of furniture, source position, etc., it is possible to construct a room-average decay curve for the sound amplitude. This decay curve shows a definite halving time behavior. That is, the instants of successive halvings of the *averaged* amplitude during the decay are observed to occur at equally spaced intervals of time. It is possible to show mathematically that the averaged halving time just described is very nearly equal to that of the room modes that were most strongly excited by the source. Sound engineers and the designers of concert halls make use of a somewhat simpler way of getting a value for the average halving time for modes whose frequencies lie near a certain one. They drive the source by means of an electrical signal in such a way that its vibration recipe contains many components of roughly equal amplitude whose frequencies lie within a range of about 12 percent above and a similar amount below the frequency of major interest (occasionally the limits are increased to about 19 percent). The sound pressure decay curve observed when such an excitation is interrupted can then be measured to find the halving time. For historical as well as practical reasons having to do not only with wave physics but also with the mechanisms of hearing (see chap. 12), acousticians are in the habit of specifying the *reverberation time* T_{rev} rather than the halving time $T_{1/2}$ that has been our choice so far. This reverberation time is defined as the time required for the averaged sound pressure in a room to die down to *one-thousandth* of its initial amplitude, instead of half its initial amplitude, as we specified for $T_{1/2}$.[6] There is a very simple relationship between $T_{1/2}$ and T_{rev}. The reverberation time is almost exactly ten (9.97) times the halving time, and it follows that the bandwidth $W_{1/2}$ over which a given mode is strongly excited can be calculated by means of a simple formula:

$$W_{1/2} = (3.8/T_{rev}) \text{ Hz}$$

11.9. Response to Impulsive Excitation II: *Reflections and Scattering*

In section 11.8 we found that the aggregate behavior of the room modes is such that when they are impulsively excited it takes a little while for the disturbance to become detectable at any point away from the source. Figure 11.7 illustrated for us the fact that while the travel time for the *initial* part of a disturbance was well-defined in terms of what we identified as the speed of sound, the shape of the pressure impulse did not seem to be preserved to any recognizable extent as it traveled through the room. It is the purpose of this section to show in simple fashion how these distortions of shape

come about, and also to lay the groundwork for an explanation in chapter 12 of how the ear manages to disentangle the "true" nature of the pulse from the distortions and distractions that seem to overlay it.

To begin with, let us imagine a large, uncluttered room which has such enormous dimensions that impulsive pressure messages from the source do not reach the walls during the whole time that we pay attention to the source and its signals. In practice one could use an aircraft hangar or an athletic field house for such experiments, making sure that the source and the microphone are up on tall poles to keep them away from the floor and ceiling. (One might consider using the whole outdoors as an analogue to our enormous room, with the source and the microphone perhaps being hung in midair by means of balloons!) In such a large room, we would find that the shape of the pressure signal remains unchanged whether the microphone is placed next to the source or far away from it. In this sort of room all three pulse shapes recorded as in figure 11.7 would have the same dip-peak-dip shape as the one appearing in the top picture. The amplitudes of the observed signals, however, would decrease with distance in such a way that at 5 meters the amplitude would be only 1/5th of that measured at 1 meter. If the room is big enough to permit observations at 100 meters, the amplitude of the (still undistorted) pressure impulse would be only 1 percent of the 1-meter value.

If our experiments had been carried on within a few meters of one wall of a huge room, we would find that a second (undistorted) pressure signal would make its appearance at the microphone. To produce such a pair of signals, the original impulse travels past the microphone (making the first pulse) to the wall and is reflected back to the microphone, in the manner sketched in the top part of figure 11.9. The time delay between the first and second appearances of the disturbance is simply the time required for sound to make one round trip from microphone to wall and back. The pressure amplitude of the second pulse is reduced relative to the first for two reasons, first because it has traveled an additional distance in making the round trip to the wall and back, and second because of dissipative effects produced during the reflection process (by, for example, porosity of the wall).

We are now in a position to understand the simplest way in which the pulse observed by a microphone in an ordinary room can have a different shape from the one sent out by the source. The microphone need only be close enough to a wall for the front end of the reflected pulse to arrive before the tail end of the original pulse has gone past. The microphone then responds to the sum of the two pressure signals that act upon it, which means that we could calculate the resulting signal by use of the graphical methods developed in section 4.5. The lower part of figure 11.9 shows an example of such calculation. Notice how the earlier part of the composite signal is a perfect match for the original pressure wave, while the later parts have a strongly modified shape.

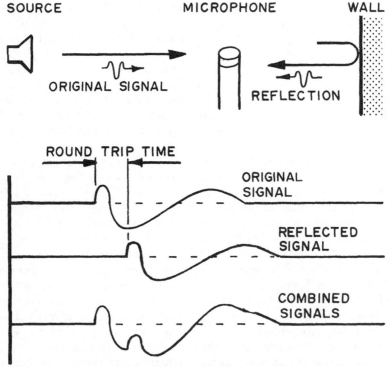

Fig. 11.9. Superposition of an Impulse and Its Reflected Echo

In an empty room having perfectly flat walls, the microphone receives first the direct sound from the source and then the six reflected sounds coming from the floor, ceiling, and four walls, plus an ever-weakening train of successive re-reflections as the original impulse travels around in the room. It is the superposition of these multiple reflections that accounts in large measure for the grassy, irregular appearance of the pictures in figure 11.8. We should note, however, that in such a room the actual *shape* of each individual reflected pulse would always match that of its ancestor, the direct sound. The eventual complications in the shape of the pressure disturbance would arise solely from the adding up of successively delayed overlapping replicas of the original impulse.

In any real room, one is not dealing with a simple, flat-walled rectangular box. There is always furniture in it, and people are present along with musical instruments, scientific equipment, books, record players, and the like. In a concert hall one also finds many sorts of architectural details, chandeliers, catwalks, and spotlights, not to mention human beings. Sound that is reflected or, more properly, scattered from these irregularities does *not* preserve the shape of the original impulse. Furthermore, we find that even very small objects can scatter a rather considerable amount of sound, in ways that have a noticeable effect on what is heard in a musical performance. Suppose that the object, or *scatterer* as it is usually termed, is a compact object whose crosswise dimensions are much less than the distance which sound travels in the time required for the completion of one hump in the oscilloscope pattern for the original pressure disturbance. An object of this sort acts somewhat like a new but enslaved additional source that generates a modified version of the original pressure wave; this modified wave leaves its birthplace to travel pretty much in all directions along with its more ordinary, undistorted cousins. As an example of what we are talking about, notice that the pressure impulse shown in the lower part of figure 11.6 has humps, each of which has a duration of about 0.0005 seconds. Scattering objects that behave toward this sound in the manner just described would have to be smaller than 0.17 meters (0.0005 sec times 345 m/sec), or about 7 inches across, which is roughly the size of a man's head. If the source had produced the same *shape* of pressure disturbance, but had taken twice as long in doing so, then objects up to about double this size would produce scattering of the kind under discussion.

Digression on the Waveform of Disturbances Scattered by Small Obstacles.

For an impulsive type of original disturbance, the newly created scattered pressure wave acquires two more humps than the number possessed by its pressure ancestor,[7] in somewhat the way that the original pressure disturbance coming from the source acquires one more hump than was present in the pattern of air flow ejected by the source. We also find that rapidly wiggling impulses incident on the scatterer give rise to very much stronger scattered pressure disturbances than do more slowly oscillating ones.

A larger object, such as the oscilloscope that sits on a cart in my laboratory or the television set in someone's living room, acts differently upon many sounds which reach it because it does not meet the smallness criterion specified earlier.

Instead of making neat reflections of the sound without changing its shape on the oscilloscope screen as would a large wall, or strewing a newly created impulse about itself as would a small object, a large object produces a *somewhat* distorted reflection of the original disturbance. This reflection does not, however, spread out evenly throughout the room but rather tends to concentrate more or less in the directions in which light would go if a lamp placed at the sound source were to shine its rays on mirrors fastened to the sides of the object. There is also a certain tendency for acoustic shadows to form behind such objects, a tendency that is not apparent with small scatterers.

We have now met the last of the contributors to the elaborate behavior of rooms when they are subjected to impulsive excitation, so it is appropriate to consolidate everything with the help of a set of summarizing remarks. The pressure disturbances caused by impulsive excitation of a room by a simple source (which disturbances we can record by means of a microphone) are controlled in various ways:

1. The original pressure impulse travels to the walls (and other large, flat objects) and is reflected from them without change of form. The reflected signals are then detected by the microphone along with the original signal from the source. The nature of these reflections is strictly analogous to the reflection of light from an ordinary mirror.

2. Compact, small, solid objects act somewhat as new sources of sound that originate new impulses of modifed shape whenever an impulse is incident upon them.

3. Articles of furniture that are somewhat larger display a behavior that is intermediate between that described for large, flat walls and that for small, compact objects.

4. In the absence of any obstacles, acoustic pressure impulses travel across the room with unchanged form at the speed of sound, which is 345 m/sec (1133 ft/sec). Out-of-doors or in a one-dimensional room with straight-sided walls (a uniform duct or one having a uniform taper), the impulse also travels unchanged with this same speed.

5. The pressure amplitude of a given impulse arising from a simple source becomes less and less as it continues its travels about in the room. For one thing, the amplitude decreases to a value inversely proportional to *total distance traveled;* for another, porosity (etc.) of the walls or scatterers will also take its toll, resulting in further reduction of the reflected or scattered amplitudes. If this latter process alone were present, then a simple source would produce a sound whose decay observed at one point in the room would show a true halving or reverberation time behavior. The presence of the distance effect modifies the nature of the observed decay somewhat.

6. All of the transient behavior which we have described in terms of traveling impulses can also be dealt with entirely upon the basis of our knowledge of the characteristic oscillatory modes of the room. Similarly all of the steady-state behavior of rooms can be worked out using traveling impulse methods. The two different-appearing viewpoints are *entirely equivalent*. It is merely a matter of mathematical or intuitive convenience which method one chooses in a particular situation. One must, however, be very careful to be strictly consistent when trying to switch from one viewpoint to the other in midstream.

In closing this section I should like to emphasize that while there are certain great similarities between the behavior of sounds in large rooms and their behavior out-of-doors, it is extremely hazardous to pursue the analogy between them unless one is capable of working out everything in each situation. The difficulty arises chiefly through the fact that the outdoors acts simultaneously like a room of infinite reverberation time, since it never "fills up" with sound, and like one having zero reverberation time, since there is no "ringing on" of the modes after the source is turned off.

11.10. Examples, Experiments, and Questions

1. It is possible to get a good idea of the way in which room modes behave one by one if you can find a sufficiently small, hard-walled room to sing in as you move around. Once you have found two or three singing pitches that make the room resound strongly it is easy to verify that there are points in the room where the excitation and response are particularly strong, and others where they are weak. It requires the help of a friend listening in the room to verify that the points of strong excitation are also points of loud sound. If the room is of fairly rectangular shape and lacking much furniture, you will find that the interaction of both source and detector with any one of the modes is strong near the walls, stronger yet in a corner between two of them, and strongest of all at the junction of three of the boundaries of the room. Perhaps you will be able to figure out why this is so. Save your conclusions so as to compare them with the discussion of this point that appears in chapter 12.

2. The slow build-up and decay of sound in a small room can also be experimented with. It is worth playing with the effects of changes in the room decay time by bringing in some cushions, carpeting, bedding, etc.

3. Many experiments on the excitation of sounds in a room may be carried out at home with the help of the family hi-fi set using a test tape or a record that gives sinusoidal tones. Ignore the directions that come with such tapes or records and simply use the sounds as something to listen to as you move around the room or as you sit still and a friend moves around. Don't forget to distinguish between what you hear when two sound sources are in action (the so-called "stereo" mode) and when one loudspeaker is in action by itself. Confine your present attentions to the latter. Also, do most of your experimenting with one ear plugged by a finger, in order to reduce the complications that arise through your neurological processor. A better but more elaborate way to do the experiments would be to carry the microphone of a tape recorder around the room, holding it at arm's length to reduce the complicating effects caused by scattering from your body. Listening to the recorded sound by means of headphones will reduce the efficiency with which your nervous system "covers up" the fluctuations, so that what you hear will better match what we are talking about in this chapter (chapter 12 deals further with these matters). Be sure that your tape recorder does not have an automatic level control, lest its operations succeed in eliminating everything that is being sought.

4. While much of what is important in the home playing of recordings depends upon the activities of our nervous system, it might be interesting for you to prepare for the discussion of these matters by reading and thinking about the relation between what we have learned so far in this book and the commonly available popular literature and advertising about high fidelity systems. In particular, you might at this point focus attention on the possibility of constructing an "equalizer"

to make the sound produced in the room on playback into an accurate match of that which the microphone picked up in a concert hall.

5. Hi-fi addicts commonly talk about something they call the "standing waves" in a room. These turn out to be evidences of individual modes that lie at low enough frequencies to be separately excited. In my laboratory room, for example, one must explore the frequency region well below 100 Hz to find much of this sort of behavior. Use figure 11.2 and the dimensions of your own living room to help you figure out the frequency domain in which so-called standing-wave behavior is to be expected in it. Notice that phenomena associated with these individual modes can be observed everywhere in the room, so that it might be sensible to install an equalizer that can minimize their effects. Why is it *not* true that putting partitions and hard-surfaced furniture into a room can "break up the standing waves"? What will be the effect of bringing in porous items such as sofas, curtains, and carpeting on these separately observable low-frequency room modes? What about the effect at higher frequencies, where the room response becomes more a matter of statistics?

Notes

1. Philip M. Morse and K. Uno Ingard, *Theoretical Acoustics* (New York: McGraw-Hill, 1968),

pp. 576–99. In particular, see figures 9.17 and 9.18.

2. M. Schröder, "Die Statistischen Parameter der Frequenzkurven von grossen Räumen," *Acustica* 4 (1954): 594–600.

3. P. E. Doak, "Fluctuations of the Sound Pressure Level in Rooms When the Receiver Position Is Varied," *Acustica* 9 (1959): 1–9; Richard V. Waterhouse, "Output of a Sound Source in a Reverberation Chamber and Other Reflecting Environments," *J. Acoust. Soc. Am.* 30 (1958): 4–13; R. H. Lyon, "Statistical Analysis of Power Injection and Response in Structures and Rooms," *J. Acoust. Soc. Am.* 45 (1969): 545–65; and David Lubman, "Precision of reverberant sound power measurements," *J. Acoust. Soc. Am.* 56 (1974): 523–33. There is a great deal of active research going on today on the ways in which sound distributes itself in rooms.

4. M. R. Schroeder, "Complementarity of Sound Buildup and Decay," *J. Acoust. Soc. Am.* 40 (1966): 549–51.

5. Morse and Ingard, *Theoretical Acoustics*, pp. 556–57, and Waterhouse, "Output of a Sound Source."

6. Leo L. Beranek, *Acoustics* (New York: McGraw-Hill, 1954), pp. 291–94. Chapter 10 of Beranek's book gives a good summary of the engineering approach to the behavior of sound in an enclosure.

7. We have here a phenomenon that is found everywhere in wave physics. A simplified manifestation of it is commonly known as "Rayleigh scattering." See Lord Rayleigh [John William Strutt], *The Theory of Sound*, 2 vols. bound as one, 2d ed. rev. and enlarged (1894; reprint ed., New York: Dover, 1945), II:272–82, and also Morse and Ingard, *Theoretical Acoustics*, sec. 8.2, pp. 418–41. The current acoustical literature contains reports on the behavior of sound scattered by objects of many shapes and many gradations of surface elasticity and porosity.

12

Room Acoustics II: The Listener and the Room

When one first learns about the complicated and irregular manner in which sound gets from one part of a room to another, it is tempting to conclude that music lovers who insist on hearing music under the best of all possible conditions should hire musicians to play in a room lined with elaborate arrays of rock-wool wedges arranged to prevent any echoes from bouncing off the walls, floor, and ceiling (such a room is known as an *anechoic chamber*). Furthermore, the listener might, if he were an absolute fanatic about "correct" sound transmission (and rich enough to afford it), insist that no one else but himself could come to the concert. He would object to having company, of course, because of the way in which his fellow listeners and the chairs they sit upon would scatter the sound. When one looks into what actually happens in such surroundings, it turns out that he would find himself feeling frustrated and insecure, and his musicians would feel even more so.

It is true that scientific investigators can sometimes simplify the analysis of their experiments if sounds are sent from source to listener in an anechoic chamber. They can often further simplify their labors by working with electrically generated sounds supplied directly to the ears by means of headphones. However, it is

almost universally true that the human ear's ability to discriminate small changes of pitch, loudness, or tone color, or otherwise to "make sense" out of combinations of signals, is immensely better in a room than it is under acoustically more sterile surroundings.

Resolution of the apparent paradox implied in the foregoing two paragraphs depends on the fact that musical sounds are continually changing in pitch, in time, in loudness, and in the way the various instruments join their voices together. Not only that, but the musicians themselves are continually moving, as are their listeners. Our nervous system is admirably suited to the job of exploiting these changes: it uses them, instead of being confused by them. This is the reason that our ears can outdo our laboratory instruments in many situations and for many purposes. In this chapter we will look at a few examples of what the ear can do and examine some instances of the way in which these abilities can be put to use.

12.1. Hearing Sustained Sounds in a Room

Suppose that (for example) a trumpet player sounds a long, steady note upon his instrument as he stands on the stage of a concert hall. If he is playing A_3 (which is a note having a repetition rate of 220 Hz), then the room is being driven by a source (the open end of the trumpet bell) having a vibration recipe whose components have frequencies of 220, 440, 660, 880, 1100, 1320, . . . Hz. It is a property of trumpet bells that they behave almost exactly like simple sources for frequency components below about 1200 Hz, while radiating higher frequencies more in the fashion of an extended source. This means that the half-dozen lower components listed above may be expected to behave in the room almost exactly as would our carefully built laboratory source. Measurements made upon sounds *within* the trumpet show us that any particular instrument played at a given loudness by almost any reasonably competent player acts as an extremely well-defined excitatory source. That is, source strengths belonging to each partial are definite, and the ratio between the amplitude of the first (harmonic) partial and those of the second, third, etc., partials are also well-defined and reproducible. All of this is to say that when a trumpet is played, the *excitation* acting on the room has a very stable and definite nature.

In section 11.4 we learned that at the listener's ear, the sound pressure associated with any partial is ill-defined indeed. Any point in the room where the ear might find itself has its own relationship between source strength and measured sound pressure, this relationship being different for every frequency component that may be emitted by the source. The vibration recipe that relates the amplitudes of the partials in our trumpet tone at a listener's ear will therefore differ wildly from point to point

in the room. One's right ear might for example be at a spot where the collection of room modes excited by the first partial combine to give a particularly large amplitude, yet at this same point the pressure amplitude associated with the second partial might be very small. At the location of the left ear the situation might (by chance) be reversed, so that the fundamental component of the trumpet tone would be represented with less-than-average strength while the second partial would have a greater-than-normal pressure amplitude. Even though it looks at the moment as though chaos would rule the situation, we have here the physical basis for one of the ways in which ears go about making sense of a trumpet tone or other sound. Let us state it as the first of three assertions describing aspects of human interaction with sound in a room:

1. Our nervous system is able to operate in many ways simultaneously. One of the things it is able to do is to make a preliminary assessment of the strength of the partials of a musical tone by forming a kind of averaged amplitude measurement based upon the different signals received from the two ears (see sec. 11.4 and the last paragraph of sec. 11.6).

This assertion, when applied to actual hearing in the concert hall, is helpful only for sorting out partials whose frequencies are higher than about 1000 Hz. Let us go back to the physics laboratory to find the cause of this 1000-Hz limitation.

Imagine that the *sound field* of a room has been explored by means of a slowly moving traveling microphone which uses a fixed excitation frequency. Measurements of this sort give wiggly-looking chart recorder traces whose appearance is almost exactly similar to the traces shown in figure 11.3, except that in the present example the horizontal axis of the chart represents the traversal of the microphone rather than a progressive variation in the excitation frequency. Our new kind of chart recording is a way of showing the fluctuation observed in the sound pressure as the microphone visits various parts of the room. Comparison of traces obtained with different excitation frequencies shows us that high frequency excitation is associated with closely spaced random wiggles in the sound pressure trace, whereas at low frequencies one must move the microphone much farther to get from one part of the fluctuation to the next. In the precise but rather terse jargon of the statistician, our results can be summarized by saying that the auto-correlation distance for sound-pressure fluctuations in a room is about one-half of the wavelength belonging to the excitation frequency. Before we can say this in plain English, we should first observe

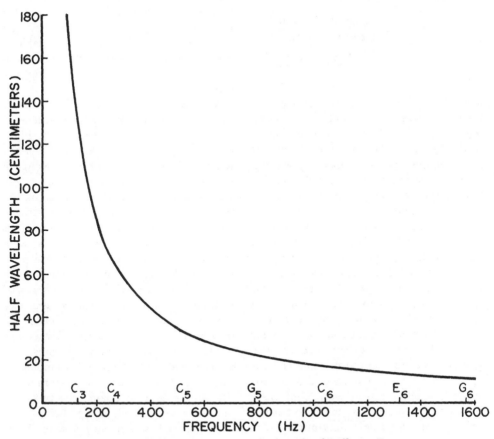

Fig. 12.1.   Half Wavelengths in Air for Sounds of Different Frequency

that in this context the word "wavelength" means the distance through the air in the middle part of an uncluttered room that a sinusoidal acoustic disturbance travels in the time of one complete oscillation. The width of what we have called a hump in the characteristic vibrational shape of the room mode turns out to be equal to one-half of the wavelength we have just defined. Figure 12.1 shows the relationship between frequency and this half wavelength, with a few note names added to show the pitch relationship of various frequencies. The curve is calculated from the formula:

$$\text{half wavelength} = \frac{\text{speed of sound}}{\text{frequency times 2}}$$

$$= \frac{345 \text{ meters/sec}}{2f}$$

The phrase *half wavelength* directly connotes the width of a hump in a room mode, and, if we could excite one of these modes by itself, the travels of our microphone would give us a smoothly varying trace on the chart, with each hump following the next in proper order. Under these conditions a look at any point on the trace lets us predict accurately what the trace will look like farther along. In an actual room, however, the superposition of contributions from thousands of modes leads to a great irregularity. A look at one part of the chart tracing then lets us "predict" only a very short way ahead. The statistician's statement merely tells us that the relationship between two points a half wavelength or more apart is totally random: there is no chance of telling the sound pressure at one of these points on the basis of what we find at the other point. Between points much closer together than a half wavelength, how-

ever, it is possible to make rough predictions. An approximate measurement of the human head to find the distance between our ears may be used along with the wavelength data of figure 12.1 to show that only at frequencies above 1000 Hz are ears spaced so as to get independent views of the room sound for averaging purposes. (The actual figure is affected not only by the minimum half wavelength as measured between the ears through the head but also by acoustic properties of the head.) We can also deduce from the figure that at the 220-Hz fundamental frequency of the trumpet tone the ears are close enough together that they receive rather similar messages from the room and therefore are unable to eke out extra information about the trumpet by use of an amplitude-averaging process.

We have just been discussing one of the ways in which our two ears can work together in an effort to extract the high-frequency part of the "true voice" of the steadily blown trumpet from the welter of sound in the room. It does not take a very great leap of the imagination to recognize that if we simply sway around a little in our seats while the player sounds his trumpet, we supply each of our ears with an interestingly varied set of sound pressure samples which can be melted down into an improved average for each partial making up the tone. There are two aspects to this improvement. First of all, moving one's head puts the ears at new positions. For all ordinary swayings, this directly adds only a restricted amount of additional low-frequency information, for the same reasons as before: the two samples are taken too close together to do a good job on low frequency sounds. There is an additional and fairly considerable effect, however: the displacement of one's head and shoulders alters the characteristic frequencies of the various room modes by a very tiny amount and so makes small changes in the individual responses to excitation (as we learned in sec. 11.5). Measurements show, however, that even in a concert hall of considerable size, the *reshuffling* of room statistics by a moving listener can increase the fluctuations at his ears enough to provide them with almost as much averaging material at 500 Hz as they get at 1000 Hz! As an additional help to the listener, we have the normal swaying of the musician himself as he plays (remember there is complete similarity between what goes on at the source position and what goes on at the detector). If there is an audience, its movements serve to make an enormously effective addition to the net fluctuations that are available for averaging by our hearing mechanisms.

We will close this outline of how ears operate on a steadily maintained sound with a simple example of how all these phenomena are put to use, plus two more summarizing statements. When a conductor wants to know how a chord sounds from his orchestra, he is very likely to start it playing and then pace around a little, either on the podium or out in the hall. Usually this is a completely intuitive action on his part, and he has little conscious awareness of all the peculiar acoustical things that are going on. The sensible fellow simply listens to the sound and makes his decisions. Earlier we made a statement that the human nervous system is able to make running averages from the signals arriving at the two ears, to deduce more precisely the true nature of the sound recipe. We can now extend this statement a little:

2. Our nervous system is able not only to make running averages of the signals at the two ears as a means for determining the strengths of various partials, but also to pile up information from both ears over a short period of time and average all of it, so as to exploit fluctuations arising from moving objects in the room. The listener only feels secure and certain about a sound if he has the chance to exploit most of the physical opportunities for making averages.

3. The human body is of such a size that ordinary small motions of a listener or player are sufficient to provide appreciable help to our aural averaging mechanism—for steady sounds only—for frequency components above about 500 Hz.

12.2. The Role of Early Reflections: *The Precedence Effect*

One almost never meets with long, steady sounds in a musical performance, so that the listener's ear is offered all the complexities of start-up and decay of sound in the concert hall on top of those belonging, so to speak, to the middle portions (in duration) of the notes as they are played. It was this middle part that we were dealing with in the preceding section of this chapter. We will now look at some of the things that happen when our trumpet player attacks (starts) each note and when he cuts it off or shifts to a new note in the music. Actually, there are two parts to the beginning and ending phenomena. The trumpet itself begins and ends its notes in its own characteristic way that is somewhat under the player's control, and then the room operates upon these beginnings and endings in ways that we explored in chapter 11. At the moment we wish to confine our attention to the latter set of phenomena since our present concern is with the interaction of room acoustics with the hearing process. Because of this, we will temporarily pretend that trumpet tones are started and stopped by electrical means in some prompt but featureless fashion.

When our musician sounds a note, each sinusoidal component launches itself from the bell and travels through the room. If we confine our attention briefly to the lower-frequency partials, those for which the trumpet acts like a simple source, we find that they are sent out *with equal strength in all directions.* Each of our ears is supplied with the direct sound within a few milliseconds, and is also supplied with the six first echoes off the walls, floor, and ceiling of the room (a few more, reasonably orderly, additional echoes will also come in, but they need not be dealt with separately). Recall from section 11.9 that pressure disturbances reflect from large, flat walls without change of form; this is simply another way of saying that reflection takes place without altering the relative strengths of the partials. In the initial stages of the room transient, then, our ears are supplied with half a dozen *repetitions* of the actual sound recipe of the trumpet, and, to the extent that our nervous system can exploit this, it will already have acquired a good view of what the player is doing for comparison and checking against information it will gather later on during the middle part of each tone. Furthermore, the *stopping* of a sound produces what we might call "un-echoes" that provide the ear with information that is more or less identical with that presented during start-up (see the explanation of this phenomenon in sec. 11.7). This duplication provides further trustworthy data for our neurological grinder to operate upon.

The high-frequency partials of a trumpet tone (and those from many other instruments) do not excite the room modes in the manner of a simple source. In particular the sound leaving the bell does not spread out evenly in all directions through the room. In the case of a trumpet, the high frequencies are launched so that the start-up disturbance propagates mainly in the direction in which the bell is pointing. If the player happens to point his instrument directly at us, then the first news of the tone to arrive at our ears has a very much stronger representation of high-frequency components than do the later-arriving, reflected sounds. Under these conditions we get an *aggregate* impression of the sound that is somewhat different from what is received by the majority of listeners in the room, for whom the higher partials are less strongly but similarly represented in both the direct and the reflected initial sound.

Now that we have outlined some of the physics involved in getting the start-up and shutting-down parts of the trumpet tone to our ears, it is time to sketch a few of the things which our ears do as they go about performing a synthesis of the information that comes to them. Our story goes back to the middle of the nineteenth century when the American physicist Joseph Henry (who is best known today for his researches in electromagnetism) was led, in connection with his duties as secretary of the newly founded Smithsonian Institution in Washington, to make a study of the acoustics of lecture halls. The result of his investigation were published in an interesting paper entitled "Acoustics Applied to Public Buildings," which was reprinted as a part of the 1856 *Annual Report* of the Smithsonian. Among other things in this report, Henry describes experiments in which he determined the smallest time delay that would permit the human ear to perceive the returning echo of an impulsive sound as an entity distinct from the original sound. We can understand Henry's interest in this question when we realize that human speech consists of a rapid succession of impulsive sounds and that, if the room is large enough for us to hear the various echoes separately, the echoes may prove to be a distraction and a hindrance to our understanding. Figure 12.2 illustrates the sort of things that Henry was concerned about. He found that if the reflected sound has traveled an extra distance of about 60 feet (call it 20 meters) as compared with the direct sound, it can just barely be heard separately from its ances-

tor. Larger path differences make the separate sounds more clearly distinguishable and so increase the danger of their confusing the listener. Let us say this in another way: the speed of sound in air being about 345 m/sec (1133 ft/sec), it is possible to calculate that we can separately perceive an impulsive signal and its reflection if the time delay between them is much more than about 60 milliseconds. We will not look here into the ways in which a properly designed hall can sometimes be arranged to permit satisfactory communication even when its size is larger than the limits implied by the foregoing numbers. Instead we will focus our attention on how our ears deal with reflected sounds which reach them with

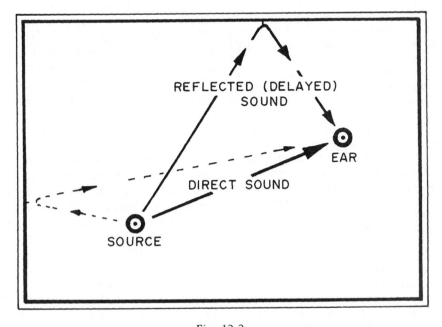

Fig. 12.2.

time delays that are less than about 35 milliseconds.

In the 1930s William Snow and John Steinberg of the Bell Telephone Laboratories found that when the same sound reaches our ears from two sources at different distances, we hear the sound as though it all came from the nearer source, rather than from the two places at once, or from some imaginary spot between them.[1] This work attracted relatively little attention. Later discoveries have stemmed mostly from an account published in 1951 by Helmut Haas of the University of Goettingen.[2] It turns out that our nervous system can combine a whole collection of early echoes into a single perceptual whole. The following numbered statements set forth a description of the phenomenon, which is properly referred to as the *precedence effect:*

1. The human ear will combine a set of reduplicated sound sequences and hear them as though they were a single entity, provided (a) that they all arrive within a time interval of about 35 milliseconds of the arrival of the first member of the set and (b) that the sound pressure recipes of all members of the set are sufficiently alike.
2. The singly perceived entity is heard as though all of the later arrivals were piled upon the first one without any delay. That is, the perceived time of arrival of the set is that belonging to the first version of the sound, and the loudness of this first sound appears augmented.
3. The apparent position of the source of this perceived sound coincides with the position of the source whose sound arrives first, regardless of the true direction of arrival of the later sounds (see sec. 12.3).
4. The functioning of the precedence effect persists even when the later arrivals in the set of sounds have pressure amplitudes that are larger than that of the first signal, provided these amplitudes are no more than about three times that of the first sound.

Notice that statements 1, 2, and 3 tell us that our nervous system's processor has in fact been set up so as to exploit all the the transient sound pressure data which a room offers to it when music is played. In other words, practically all of the descriptive material about trumpet sounds given in the earlier parts of this section reappears in condensed and generalized form in the numbered statements.[3]

As a way to consolidate our understanding of the precedence effect, let us go beyond our description of how a trumpet tone travels to the listener's ear to a brief glance at the way one goes about designing a modern loudspeaker system for a church or for an outdoor orchestra shell. We will, however, continue to postpone any discussion of the perceived effects of reverberant sound in the room, whose influence may well be felt for several seconds, long after the precedence phenomenon has ceased to function.

Suppose we have to deal with a church whose nave is so long that the minister's voice does not reach his congregation with loudness sufficient to make the sermon understandable. For one thing, the spreading out of the sounds from the speaker's mouth (which functions acoustically as a simple source) leads to small pressure amplitudes at a distant listener's ear. Furthermore, the size of the room is such that the early echoes (of comparable amplitude) arrive well after the 35-millisecond precedence limit, so that they become annoying and distracting in the fashion that worried Joseph Henry. For example, a single echo whose amplitude is equal to that of the original sound would produce about a 50 percent disruption of speech intelligibility if the delay time is 100 milliseconds. Suppose now we start our engineering job by installing above the minister's head and a little behind it a loudspeaker, chosen to project most of its sound down the length of the hall. This will permit approximately threefold reinforcement of the sound (see statement 4), as long as the minister's direct voice can be heard at all in the absence of this reinforcement. An arrangement of this sort will assure that at least the closer segment of the congregation gets enough sound for it to hear what is going on. They will not be aware of the loudspeaker if it is a good one, because its output sound recipe will closely match that of the preacher and also because the sound from it has to travel slightly farther to the listener's ears than does the direct sound from the pastor's mouth.

If the church is a very large one, we will have to take additional measures to provide adequate sound farther back. A few carefully chosen, small, non-directional loudspeakers can be installed, spaced along the side walls toward the back of the room. These loudspeakers would call attention to themselves if they were simply connected to the same amplifier that drives the directional speaker at the front of the church (because they would then supply the first-arriving signals). We can, however, make them unobtrusive and at the same time useful if each one is driven via a properly chosen electronic delay circuit to make sure that a listener gets the minister's initially reinforced voice signals slightly *before* the same message issues from the local loudspeaker (see statement 1 in this section). As before, the sound pressure due to the local loudspeaker must be arranged to be

no more than three times the amplitude of the direct sound (in agreement with statement 4.). The reason that *nondirectional* loudspeakers must be used along the walls is to be found by implication in statement 1. For successful operation, the recipe reaching every listener's ear must be a good match with the original sound (otherwise the loudspeakers will be perceived as sound sources in their own right). It is necessary to use nondirectional loudspeakers because directional loudspeakers have a path of strong transmission, and at the edges of this path the sound recipe is drastically altered. Listeners who (unavoidably) are seated a little out of the direct line of aim of such a loudspeaker would, as a result, fail to get any benefit from the precedence effect, since the loudspeaker sounds would regain their individuality.

12.3. Localization by the Ears of Sound Sources in a Room

When we listen to music in a concert hall or converse with a friend in a noisy room, it is possible for us to focus our attention on particular sources of sound with an accuracy that is often astounding. We can usually perform these feats with more confidence of success in a room than we can outdoors, because we are able to put together all sorts of clues concerning what the source is doing and where it is doing it from the way in which its sounds are reflected and scattered by the room. The fact that we can manage pretty well at all this even when using only one ear gives us our point of entry into some understanding of what is going on.

From the physicist's point of view, the simplest clues to the position of a musical source to be expected for monaural (single-ear) listening are the time relations between the arrival of the direct sound and the first half dozen echoes which come to the ear. Some knowledge of the way in which sound spreads around the listener's head as it undergoes scattering can also suggest the availability of additional directional clues. The amplitudes and shapes of these pressure signals depend on the direction from which they come to the head.

It would be an oversimplification, however, merely to compare the times of arrival of an impulse at each ear, one of which may be closer to the source than is the other one. The listener's head scatters the sound in such a way as to alter the shape of the impulse, and we have just learned that another way to describe this scattering process is to say that the acoustic pressure distribution at various points around the head is different for high-frequency signal components from what it is for low-frequency ones. We may clarify the meaning of all this by making an oscilloscope picture of the direct sound impulses recorded by two tiny microphones located a headwidth apart in the room and comparing it with a picture of the impulses recorded by the same microphones when a human head is interposed between them.

The upper part of figure 12.3 shows how the two microphones respond to the direct sound from a source that is obliquely located about 2 meters away (compare these pictures with those of fig. 11.7). The top trace belongs to the microphone which we will shortly associate with a listener's left ear, while the lower trace shows the pressure variation at the right ear. Because the impulse begins slightly earlier in the lower trace, we can

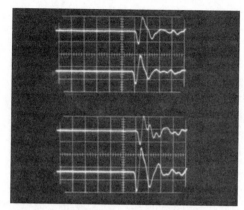

HORIZONTAL SCALE .OOI SEC/DIV

Fig. 12.3. Signals at a Pair of Closely Spaced Microphones with and without a Listener's Head between Them

deduce that the source is located somewhat to the "listener's" right. The shapes of the impulses recorded by the two microphones are, of course, very much alike, since they both are responding to the direct sound from a source. The lower part of figure 12.3 shows how the two signals are altered when a human head is interposed between the microphones. The most obvious change is the growth of the gross magnitude of the "right-ear" signal, without a corresponding decrease of signal at the (nominally shadowed) "left ear." It only takes a moment more to notice that in addition to the amplitude change there is a rather drastic modification of the wave form observed at each microphone. Since the two microphones are located almost exactly at the ears of my experimental subject we are entitled to make the following generalization (which is the first of a set dealing with sorting out sounds in a room): [4]

1. Because of the presence of the listener's head, the pressure signals arriving at his ears

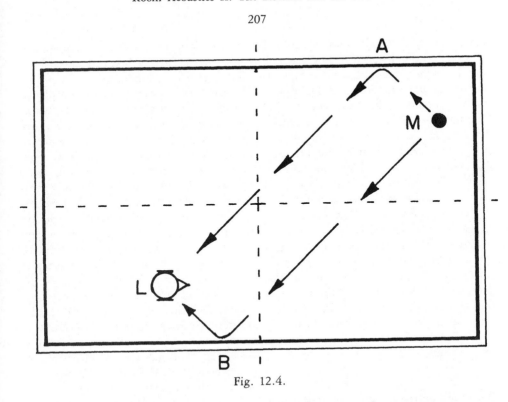

Fig. 12.4.

are not identical with those that would be measured by small test microphones in the absence of the head. However, the relations between the actual ear-arriving signals and the disturbances otherwise present in the room are definite for a given person's head, making it possible for him to exploit the relationship.

The example shown in figure 12.4 will illustrate some of the possibilities for direction finding that are inherent in the behavior of sound in a room. Here we have a musical source M at one spot near one end of a bare, rectangular concert hall, and a listener L at another point. The diagram shows the listener facing forward in the hall (as indicated by his pointed nose). Suppose for the moment that he has a plug in his right ear so that he can only make use of sounds arriving at his left ear. If the impulses coming to him by reflection from the side walls (via the two paths MAL and MBL) are simultaneous, this tells our listener that the two paths are of equal length and that therefore the musician is symmetrically located as far to the left of the hall's midline (shown dotted) as the listener is seated to its right. The reflections from front and back walls will show up in the ear at very different times because of their very different travel distances. The fact that one of these reflections arrives almost immediately after the direct sound is a clue that the player is seated close to the front wall.

Let us return our attention to the signals which come to the ear by reflection from the side walls. Suppose that the source is displaced from its symmetrical position to one slightly more to the left (as seen by the listener). Now we find that the earlier-arriving signal travels via path MAL and produces a large impulse at the eardrum, while the later arrival (coming via MBL) is smaller in amplitude. It is the presence of the human head that alters the relative strengths and shapes of the earlier and later members of our almost-coincident pair of echoes, and so allows them to provide information about which side the source lies relative to the point of symmetry.

When our listener has both his ears open, he can add enormously to his ability to cross-check and reconfirm the deductions he has made, since the right-ear signals from the side walls are very like the ones on the left; all that changes is the order of arrival of the larger and the smaller signals.

Digression on the Description of Two-Ear Effects in Terms of the Sinusoidal Components of a Signal.

While we have not been very explicit about saying so up till now, it is a fact that any sort of signal may be separated into a collection of long-continuing sinusoidal partials. This is true even for impulsive sounds and for the beginnings and endings of ordinary musical sounds. Because of the general applicability of the sinusoidal recipe idea, we should notice that the two impulses recorded at the listener's ears in figure 12.3 may be described in terms of the relative strengths of the various partials as observed by the two ears. For example, when sounds come past the head from a direction about 60° to the listener's left, partial components having frequencies near 600 Hz have amplitudes 1.8 times as strong at the left as at the right ear. For components near 3000 Hz, the ratio is closer to 3.6.

There is one more piece of wave physics we should notice before going on to

see what our nervous system is able to do with all the intertwined directional hints that are made available to it. In chapter 11 we learned that various-sized objects reflect or scatter sounds in different ways, depending on the wiggliness of the impulses arriving at them. As was remarked earlier in this section, we can think about all of this in terms of the scattering (etc.) of the individual sinusoidal components of the sound recipe. While we have not met very much in the way of quantitative information about these processes, everything has in fact been predicated on the assumption that the scattering object is at a considerable distance from the source. It is important to know that at closer distances (less than one wavelength), the details of scattering and the pressure relations around one's head become strongly modified. The messages a musician's ear receives will be affected by his own head differently for messages arriving from (1) the instrument of the player seated next to him, (2) the more distant players in the orchestra, and (3) events at the back of the hall.

Let us now turn our attention away from the physics of sound localization in a room and investigate the extent to which our ears can process the cryptic information that is made available to them. Laboratory experiments carried on over many years unite in showing that our nervous system does in fact make use of the various kinds of physical information coming to it. Formal experiments concur with everyday experience in showing that a listener who is free to move his head around can do better than one who is not, and that binaural listening is immensely more informative than is monaural. The correlation of the sound recipe information coming to us (see the description in sec. 12.2 above) with the operation of our straightforward localization machinery helps us follow the various orchestral voices with confidence and accuracy, especially when we can also make use of information coming to us through our eyes as we watch the players perform.[5]

Listeners who attend many "live" concerts and, more particularly, musicians who play such concerts often feel that listening to music through headphones is an uncomfortable and frustrating experience. This is particularly the case when they are provided with electrically generated signals or those recorded by using electrically mixed signals from microphones placed immediately next to each player (who may even be placed in an isolation booth). The reasons for this discomfort and reduced ability to hear subtle details should be clear to us by now: the headphone signals and the recording technique deprive us to a greater or lesser extent of a wealth of cross-coupled, interrelated, and reiterated clues as to what the sound sources are doing.

It is precisely because our hearing processes are so clever at taking involved hints that the perception psychologist makes use of headphones in his experiments. He is trying deliberately to exclude all but one form of signal at a time from the ear, in the hope that he can learn step by step from a study of our responses to each aspect of the total acoustic signal met in the world at large.

Let us end this section now with four additions to our set of remarks which sum up our ability to track down an interesting sound and hear it in the midst of a crowd of competing sounds.

2. While it is not literally true, one can stay reasonably close to the truth by assuming initially that if an acoustic signal has distinctive features in its sound pressure makeup at the eardrums, then our neurological processes will be able to discover these features and recognize the signal by making use of them.

3. Our auditory apparatus is able very quickly to "learn" the scattering behavior of nearby objects and the acoustic changes produced by moving the listener's head, and can separate the characteristic nature of these changes from the identifying features of the original sound.

4. The human nervous system is so organized that, in making its recognitions, it can make simultaneous use of several kinds of auditory information coming to it.

5. We are also able to collect information over a short period of time (as when one moves one's head) and put all of this information together into a single percept. We can also combine such dribbled-in data with the sets of data that come in simultaneously as described in comment 3 above.

The precedence effect described in the preceding section and a modern cousin to Joseph Henry's echo experiments provide us with an interesting way to review the implications of the above remarks. When a sound comes to us, we first make a very quick and perhaps rough determination of the position of the source and of the kind of sound that it is generating, basing our determination on the first-arriving train of signals. We then make use of the precedence effect in taking the later part of the sound arriving during a 35-millisecond time interval to reconfirm and elaborate our picture of what is going on. (It is interesting to speculate on the physics and the physiology that led us to evolve the particular time of 35 milliseconds for the data accumulation process.) We must not forget, however, that while one part of our processor is melting together the signals over this interval of time, other parts are busily looking at everything through a fine-grained frequency and time analyzer that extracts the pieces of primary information that are being put together. It turns out that one can some-times make distinctions between signals that differ from one another in the details of their variations down to a time dif-ference of 30 millionths of a second!

Looking at the longer-term parts of what goes on, we notice that Henry's echo experiments involve the detection and processing of two similar events which arrive 60 milliseconds or more apart. The fact that these are really heard separately is confirmed by experiments in which someone who is talking is supplied with a delayed earphone version of what he is saying. When the delay is much more than about 60 milliseconds, the conflict between what the subject hears and what he is trying to say makes it im-possible for him to talk properly. Perhaps some of you have noticed a similar dif-ficulty when making a long-distance tele-phone call—occasionally there is an elec-trically produced echo in the earpiece whose delay is sufficient to cause dif-ficulty. By the way, the speech difficulty produced by late echoes is greatly reduced if the echo's component recipe has been drastically altered in the course of the echo process, even though the echo taken by itself may remain perfectly in-telligible.

12.4. Some Examples of the Interplay between Room and Ear

The first three sections of this chapter have sketched out some of the ways in which the wave physics of rooms and of scatterers provides our ears and nervous system with perception material out of which they can build a trustworthy audi-tory composite. In the exposition of the basic ideas there was little chance to pro-vide everyday examples of how everything fits together. We are now in a position to understand several interesting illustra-tions of actual auditory behavior in a room. For later convenience in referring to these examples, each one will be given an alphabetical label and a short title.

A. Flutter Echoes. If you clap your hands while standing near the middle of a reasonably uncluttered rectangular room, you may hear a sort of whine or buzz which quickly dies away. If the room is very large, the sound resolves itself into a rapidly repeating series of echoes whose repetition time is equal to the time it takes sound impulses to make the round trip from (for example) one wall to the opposite one and back. Because this sort of large-room echo sometimes reminds one of something fluttering (repetition rates of a few per second), the whole phe-nomenon is given the name flutter echo. In my living room the series of echoes repeats fast enough to produce a sound whose pitch is a little above that of the note C_2, having a repetition rate close to 65.4 Hz. A little arithmetic using the 1133 ft/sec value for the speed of sound confirms that this particular train of echoes is one that runs between floor and ceiling, these two being 8.5 feet (2.6 me-ters) apart.

It would be worthwhile at this point to go back and reread section 2.3 on the repetition rates of various rhythmic pat-terns so that you can understand why a listener whose ears are fairly near the floor or ceiling assigns the pitch in accordance with the number of round trips made per second, rather than twice this value. In brief, the explanation is that we recognize true repetition times and count each pair of downward- and upward-traveling im-pulses as a repetition (see figs. 2.2 and

2.3). A microphone placed exactly midway *would* receive "identical" pressure signals from the upward- and downward-moving impulses, and if one were to listen to the resulting electrical repetition rate, the perceived rate would in fact be double. However, if I stand so as to put both my ears exactly halfway between the floor and the ceiling, the perceived repetition rate does not double. Since my head and body, like most people's, are unsymmetrical, there is an alternation between the shapes of the signals produced at my ears by the upward and downward impulses. Obviously the repetition rate could only be perceived as doubled if the equally spaced signals matched each other exactly. It must be admitted that the clear-sounding echo heard near the floor is heard less clearly when both ears are at mid-room. Apparently there is enough symmetry to confuse the hearing process slightly. This little "theory" is immediately confirmed when I tilt my head so one ear is somewhat above the other. The clarity of perception is at once restored because the two ears can now make an easy distinction between impulses traveling in the two directions. Incidentally, we have so far ignored the fact that there are really *two* series of echoes going on in the room. One of these is descended from the first echo from the ceiling, while the other one follows the first echo from the floor. Perhaps you can figure out why our general line of argument so far needs only the most trivial alterations to make it apply to the true situation.

There is no flutter echo to be heard associated with wall-to-wall reflections in my living room because of the irregular scattering that is produced by furniture, doors, windows, and fireplace. All of these objects are of intermediate size compared with the wavelength of the sound, and so conspire to destroy rapidly any semblance of regularity in the reflected sounds. Now and then one does, however, find a bare room in which two or even three flutter echo repetition rates can be discerned. The association of these echoes with the pairs of boundary surfaces can sometimes be sorted out by experiments in which doors or windows are opened and closed, as well as by listening experiments in various parts of the room.

When one attempts to follow the course of a flutter echo by means of a microphone and an oscilloscope, it is unusual to find more than one or two recognizable members of the train of echoes we have been discussing, despite the fact that they may be clearly audible for some time. In my living room, for example, they can be heard for somewhat more than half a second, which corresponds to about 30 recognizable repetitions. (By the way, in many situations such as this where a single loud sound source shuts off, we can hear the signal dying away over a time interval that is a reasonably good approximation to the reverberation time for 1/1000 amplitude decay, as defined at the end of section 11.8. We will discuss the reasons for this somewhat surprising fact in chapter 13.) The reason why the oscilloscope trace is rapidly cluttered into unrecognizability is simple: all the scattered impulses that propagate hither and thither in the room pile up on top of the regularities, and obscure them from our eyes. The explanation for the ability of our ears to track the flutter despite all these distractions is less straightforward. Basically it is a matter of our ability to recognize a chain of repetitive regularity as a characteristic feature of complex sounds. The precedence effect can help explain this. The ear could perfectly well take the first dozen impulses and understand them as what we have called the "initial sound," and then fuse in several of the later echoes (about 35 millisecond's worth) to reinforce the impression. This process can operate over the whole decay, with earlier parts always serving as the hook upon which the later parts are hung.

B. *Perception of Articulated Trumpet Notes Recorded in a Large Hall.* Not long ago I had occasion to carry out a series of acoustical experiments in collaboration with the well-known trumpet virtuoso Edward Tarr. One small part of our observations is worth describing here because it gives an illustration of how well our ears can extract musically interesting information from the sound field of a large hall. Mr. Tarr stood at the front of the hall, a large, high-ceilinged room with a volume of somewhat over 400,000 cubic feet (11,300 cubic meters) and a reverberation time of about 2.5 seconds in the frequency range particularly inhabited by trumpet sounds. I listened on the main floor of the auditorium and also made a tape recording of the sound there. As a preliminary to our other work, we verified the existence of various steady-tone fluctuation phenomena involving the movement of listener and player (as described in chapter 11). Our present interest centers, however, on several sequences of repeated tones on one pitch, starting slowly, about two per second, and working up to something close to 9 per second. To my ears, these accelerating sequences of notes sounded as crisp and clean as one should expect from a first-class player who was thoroughly prepared for a concert that evening. It was also perfectly possible to tell when the player changed his mode of separating successive sounds (usually called *articulation*) from what is known as single tonguing to double tonguing. It should be explained that a good player is able to minimize the differences between the two articulations enough that the changeover is unnoticeable to anyone who is not looking for it. In other words, I could hear a rather subtle change in the way notes were started and stopped. It was also possible to make out small, random irregularities of articulation, which are inevitable when many repeated notes are sounded with no musical context to guide their timing. None of these details will come as a surprise to those of my readers who are musicians.

We know enough by now about room acoustics to presume that an oscilloscope display of the tape-recorded version of these trumpet sounds would look pretty irregular. Because of the hall's 0.25-second amplitude halving time (deduced from the 2.5-second reverberation time) we are correctly led to expect that even at the slowest tone repetition rate (two per second), the sound hardly has a chance to decay during the brief interruption of excitation that comes between tones. One sees a clearly marked but rough and irregular-looking pulsation in the pattern and this pulsation keeps in step with the series of audible tones. The oscilloscope traces associated with rapidly repeating parts of the tone sequences form, on the other hand, such a jumble that even the overall pulsation in amplitude is hardly visible.

We should be impressed by the contrast between the distinctness of the auditory impression produced by the trumpet tones and the messiness of the recorded pressure wave forms that are its acoustical ancestors in the room. In section 12.1 we learned that a trumpet produces very definite and repeatable wave forms in its function as a sound source, so that the tape-recorded irregularities must be attributed to the properties of the concert hall. In section 12.3 we also learned of a number of ways in which our two ears can work together to unravel some of the room's acoustical complexity. The example we have been considering is a tape of a trumpet tone (responding to the hall in which it was recorded), a tape which was then listened to and analyzed in my laboratory room. This poses questions having to do with the effects of two different surroundings acting on the original sound. Let us review the situation briefly: use of a single microphone eliminates all of the two-ear, head-effect information from the recording. On playback the sound issues from a single loudspeaker that serves to excite the oscillatory modes characteristic of an entirely different room. In this room the listener plausibly enough attributes the sound to the loudspeaker itself, and he has no trouble recognizing the tone color, articulation, playing style, etc., as they were originally heard in the concert hall! In short, it is a successful recording. Once again, the listener in the laboratory feels deprived if he must sit very still or if he is restricted to the use of only one ear, but basically he is able to cope with the combined properties of two rooms as they are connected by a single track of tape. In an informal way such an experiment verifies that it is possible to record sounds in one room and to play them back, meaningfully, in another one. Our thinking about this possibility may leave us with a somewhat greater sense of wonder at what the human brain can do.

C. A Harshness Problem of Certain Loud-speaker Systems. Musicians and others who are more used to listening to live sounds than to their recorded counterparts sometimes complain bitterly of a particular sort of harshness in the sounds produced by elaborate sound systems. This is an effect which they do not perceive when they use lesser equipment. Understandably, complaints of this sort are likely to enrage the owner or designer of the troublemaking equipment, leading him to provide all sorts of laboratory evidence to prove its perfection. Let us look at one way in which this sort of contretemps can come about. We will restrict our attention to single-channel rather than the so-called stereo or quadriphonic modes of listening, since the problem is one which arises in each channel by itself without much regard to the presence of the other channels.

The fixed principles underlying the design of all cone loudspeakers set upper and lower limits to their efficient functioning. A loudspeaker's acoustic output into a room is minuscule for all frequencies below the natural frequency (resonance) determined by the cone mass acting with the elasticity of its supports and of the air within the cabinet. This puts a lower limit to the frequency range over which a given loudspeaker can be used. Above this lower limit a properly designed loudspeaker can provide a fairly constant (averaged) sound pressure in a room for all excitation frequencies up to a certain value. The high-frequency limit to the sound output is reached when the cone spans several humps in the modal patterns for the room. A neater way to express this criterion numerically is to relate the circumference of the speaker cone to the wavelength of radiated sound. High-frequency sounds whose wavelengths are shorter than about half the circumference are more and more poorly radiated. For example, a simplified loudspeaker having a rigid cone about 30 cm (12 inches) in diameter has a circumference of a little less than one meter (call it 3 feet). Such a loudspeaker will already begin to show some reduction in sound-production ability at 700 Hz (refer to fig. 12.1 for the relation between frequency and half wavelength). An octave higher, at 1400 Hz, the averaged amplitude set up in the room is reduced fourfold, and similar decreases take place for successive doublings of the frequency. An additional phenomenon takes place for sounds whose frequencies lie above the limit for uniform output: the sound no longer spreads uniformly throughout the room, but rather gathers itself into increasingly narrow beams that travel out along the axis of the cone, having the same auditory significance that was discussed for trumpet sounds in section 12.2.

The designer of a wide-range loudspeaker system is expected to devise something that will provide uniform averaged excitation throughout the room at frequencies ranging from about 40 Hz up to about 15,000 Hz. To do this he generally chooses a relatively large loudspeaker with a cone massive enough to resonate below 40 Hz and with a circumference that permits it to work fairly well up to about 1500 Hz. He then adds another loudspeaker, much smaller in diameter, that behaves well over the remaining high-frequency part of the desired range. Sometimes three loudspeakers are used to share the duty instead of only two. In order to make this composite system work properly it is necessary to provide *crossover networks* whose duty it is to steer the low-frequency partials of the electrical drive signal predominantly to the low-frequency loudspeaker (the *woofer*), the remaining components being sent to the speakers designed to deal properly with the middle and high frequencies (the *midrange speaker* and the *tweeter*). Figure 12.5 shows the general way in which the various parts are installed in a loudspeaker cabinet, and the way in which the crossovers and the driving amplifier are connected.

A composite loudspeaker system can

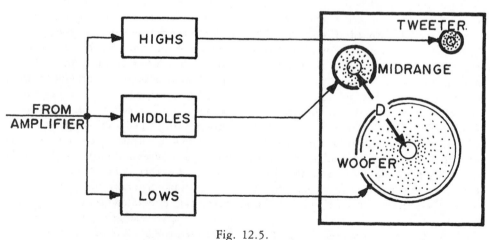

Fig. 12.5.

give trouble when the loudspeakers are driven by sinusoidal components oscillating near the crossover frequencies at which one of the speakers gives up its predominance to another one. Near crossover, the speakers have approximately equal source strengths and (if the design is even roughly correct) they are acting in step as they inject and abstract air to and from the room. Suppose now that the distance D between the two sources is equal to a half wavelength (or any odd multiple of it) at the crossover frequency. The effect of one of the speakers on almost any given room mode is then opposite to the effect of the other source, because they are bound to be acting on points in the characteristic mode pattern having opposite directions of oscillation. In the half-wave case they are acting on opposite sides of a nodal line (review the explanation of fig. 8.3 in sec. 8.1 for a one-dimensional example of what is going on). Our basic explanation implies that in the neighborhood of crossover there is a particular frequency at which the system totally fails to excite the room! In practice, various details of the speaker cone shapes and their differing sizes conspire with the effects of room shape, speaker cabinet structure, and furniture to replace this phenomenon of complete failure with one in which every conceivable sort of excitatory irregularity can manifest itself with particular obviousness. Since everything that comes to the listener's ear is processed through the coupling of loudspeaker to room, the irregularities described above become an inextricable part of the original sound. Our ears can cope with the vagaries of the room itself because we can move around in it and so dissolve each irregularity in the sea of its neighbors. The motions of everyone in

the recording studio similarly provide something for our ears to chew upon while they extract the music from the studio's properties. Through all of these processings the loudspeaker continues to make its presence felt, as it operates inexorably and impartially on singer, violin, and flute. Our highly developed abilities for localizing anything having a stable acoustical nature are trapped into the job of discovering the loudspeaker instead of the music it is supposed to reproduce.

Luckily not very many loudspeaker systems are built with an interspeaker distance of (for example) 8.6, 25.9, or 43.3 cm which would combine with a 2000-Hz crossover frequency to produce the most obtrusive effect. Other spacings between loudspeaker elements produce lesser effects, but they may still be discernible. Overall, you will perhaps recognize the phenomenon described above as one more manifestation of the general principle that the irregularity of response in any vibrating system is increased if two or three exciters are connected together or if the signals from two or three microphones are added together.

There is yet another way in which obtrusive effects can arise from a multiple-loudspeaker system. Electrical crossover circuits that are used for selecting the frequency components sent to each speaker are commonly designed on the assumption that each loudspeaker has electrical properties that do not change as the frequency is varied. In fact, these properties usually change a great deal and in a way that sometimes permits the nominally inactive parts of the system to leak appreciable sound when the excitation frequency is far from the crossover value. If this is the case, our irregularity phenomenon can appear several times over.

We should take a moment now to ask how it is that the various difficulties described above can sometimes escape the attention of a competent and conscientious audio engineer as he makes his tests. First of all, it has become customary for him to make loudspeaker measurements in an anechoic chamber, with the help of a microphone and a chart recorder. He does this in order to avoid the transmission irregularity of a room. Such tests are equivalent to tests made out-of-doors, and so miss almost all hints of the two-source mode excitation phenomena that are the troublemakers. To be sure, there are sharply marked irregularities in the directional behavior of the steady sound emitted into an anechoic room near the crossover frequency, and these arise from the same causes as does our phenomenon, but since the sound is monitored in only a few directions, it is easy to miss the anomalies, especially if one is not aware of their significance. It is true that some manufacturers use a reverberant room for measurements of what is called the power response. They may still miss spotting the crossover irregularity phenomenon if they use an electrical drive signal containing a mixture of many frequencies instead of using a single-frequency sinusoid. The mixture provides the microphone with a kind of average over the loudspeaker system's acoustical irregularities. This averaging technique is very familiar in acoustics, and was inspired by the room-response averages that are obtained with the help of a similar type of excitation (described near the end of sec. 11.8).

Before leaving this topic we must see why the particular problems described so far are less likely to arise when the cheaper sort of loudspeaker system is used. In the very simplest case, the manufacturer makes do with only a single loudspeaker in the cabinet, and ekes out a slightly wider range of effective sound production by playing various games with the cone shape. Since the distance D is zero in this case, there is no difficulty with cancellation across nodal lines. A somewhat more elaborate system (which is also found in certain high quality, expensive loudspeakers) uses a woofer loudspeaker to take care of the low frequencies, letting its acoustical output die away naturally for the highs (the electrical drive to it remaining active). There is a tweeter provided as well, with a simple electrical device which lets it receive an increasing amount of the electrical power as the frequency rises. The most common of these devices causes the tweeter to oscillate about halfway out of step with the woofer at the crossover frequency instead of being exactly in step. That is, the tweeter cone is momentarily at the extremes of its motion at instants when the woofer is in mid-swing, and vice versa. Excitation of the room modes under these conditions is not quite as strong under favorable conditions as when the more normal in-step excitation is used, but we find that the drastic consequences of matching D with the crossover frequency half wavelength are almost completely eliminated, to the greater comfort of sophisticated listeners. I should remark here that devoted audiophiles who are not bothered by the crossover phenomenon provide us with an additional example of the way in which our auditory system works. We are good at hearing what interests us partly because of the recognition facilities described already and partly because the nervous system is enormously skilled at shutting out all sorts of distracting and unwanted data.

D. *Unexpected Observations on Visiting an*

Anechoic Chamber. Some years ago a European colleague took me into the magnificent anechoic chamber at his laboratory. This chamber was an enormous room lined with sound-absorbing wedges on all its surfaces, including the bottom one. In such installations one walks and sets up equipment on a net made of taut steel cables stretched across the room half way between floor and ceiling, so as to keep everything far away from the room boundaries. While I followed my friend toward the center of the room, the normal oppressive feeling one gets in such rooms developed at first, and then something else called itself to the attention of my ears. On a hunch, I asked my guide to stop and turn around so he faced me. I then held out my hands about a foot (30 cm) apart and said, "I get the strong impression that there is some object about this big on the wall behind me." My friend looked up beyond my shoulders toward the wall in some astonishment. There was indeed a small loudspeaker box hanging there, out of my sight, but whose size was about as I had indicated. Nothing else was in the room. How did this object make its presence and its size known so quickly?

It is not difficult to understand how the existence and position of the loudspeaker in the room were signaled to my ears. We were talking as we walked in, and, because of the perfection of the room for its purpose, sound scattered from the loudspeaker box was the only indirect signal to reach my ears. The direction from which it came and the time delay between it and the direct sound of our voices was sufficient information about the location of the scatterer.

The possibility of making a rough size estimate on the basis of sound scattered back toward us by the loudspeaker box is also fairly easily understood. The two of us in the room had speaking voices pitched somewhat below C_3, where the repetition rate is about 100 to 130 Hz. For simplicity let us assume the rate to be 120 Hz, so that the sounds in the room were constructed out of varying amounts of sinusoidal components at 120, 240, 360, 480, . . . Hz. All but the lowest three of these partials have frequencies above 400 Hz. All of the higher-frequency partials were equally well scattered back toward their source by a box of the size in question. The first partial, on the other hand, was scattered to my ears with about a sixteenfold reduction relative to the higher partials, while the second partial suffered a reduction of about fourfold in the scattering process. This particular depletion of the strengths of the lower partials in the scattered sound depends characteristically on the size of the box. The changeover from strong discrimination to uniformly returned sound takes place at lower frequencies for large boxes than it does for small ones (the change occurs somewhat above the frequency whose wavelength corresponds to the "circumference" of the scatterer if it is of compact, roughly spherical shape). Apparently it is possible unconsciously to learn the relation between changed recipes for scattered sound and the size of the scatterer. Furthermore, it is possible for us to do this in the course of everyday activities—one does not need to practice in an anechoic chamber (I have been in such chambers only briefly, on half a dozen occasions spread over many years). A few minutes after our unexpected contact with the properties of scattered sound in a really good echo-free room, I was in another, less elaborate chamber where I was totally unable to sense a much larger object by means of my hearing. By all ordinary standards the second room was a good one, but there was enough scattering from various small objects in its structure to completely drown any interpretable signals from the test scatterer. The ease with which size and position estimates can be made is a tribute to the cleverness of the human nervous system. Blind people often become extremely skilled at such activities; relatively few of the rest of us practice enough or have sufficient confidence in our ears to exploit their capabilities fully.

12.5. Examples, Experiments, and Questions

1. Joseph Henry's echo experiments are easily repeated and will provide you with a convenient place to begin in developing a conscious awareness of how your ears function with delayed sounds. Do your experimenting in a wide parking lot (or better, on a grassy lawn) bounded on one side by a wide, flat wall to use as a reflector. It is worthwhile to provide yourself with one or two sources of impulsive sound. For example, a metal bucket struck on its bottom by a stick serves well to provide sounds having a reasonable amount of lower-frequency components (below 500 Hz) in its recipe. A sound source whose recipe is concentrated more toward the higher frequencies can easily be made from two strips of thin wood tightly bound together at one end with rubber bands in the manner shown in figure 12.6. Hold the bound end of this device in one hand and smartly strike the other end flat against the heel of your other hand to generate a sharp cracking of sound. Clapping with cupped or flat hands is another (less loud) way of generating the two kinds of impulse.

Using first one and then the other of these sources, find the shortest distance from the wall at which you must stand for the echo to be clearly distinguishable by your ears. Don't forget that during the echo delay time the sound must travel the round-trip distance from you (functioning as both source and listener) to the wall and back. For making rough estimates of time and distance, you may find it worthwhile to recall that sound travels about the length of a man's foot in the time of one millisecond.

Once your ear has become experienced in listening to the echo, repeat your experiment with the help of a talkative friend who keeps up a running conversation as he walks with you toward and away from the wall. To hear the echo of his voice under these circumstances is a little more difficult, but still possible.

2. If the surroundings are quiet, there is another sort of experiment you can do with the help of a reflecting wall outdoors. Close your eyes and try walking toward the wall from a distance of 3 or 4 meters (10 to 15 feet). If there is a hard pavement underfoot, the sound of your footsteps may generate sufficient impulsive sound; otherwise, clap your hands at the rate of one or two per second. With only a little practice you will be able to use the reflected sound as a means to sense the presence of the wall and even to gauge your distance from it reasonably well. Very few blindfolded people would walk right into a collision with the wall under these conditions. Sightless persons, and those who are otherwise motivated to develop their skills in using reflected sounds for distance estimation, find it possible to use the reflected sounds of their own footsteps, conversation, or a tapping cane as a basis for such estimations.

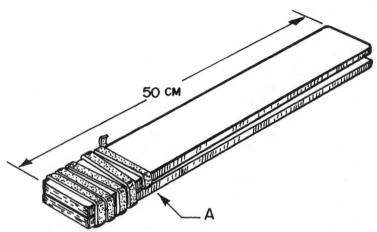

Fig. 12.6.   A Slap Stick for Producing Impulsive Sounds. At the point marked A, a strand of rubber runs between the strips of wood to act as a spacer.

I have suggested experiments of the sort described in the preceding paragraph to call to your attention the fact that even at the short times that lie within the domain of the precedence effect (where the return signal may not be heard in its own right), other parts of our brain can put the echo time delay information to good use for distance measurement purposes.

You might try to repeat the wall-approach experiments using impulsive sounds produced by a friend standing still at some distance from the wall. If you have success in this enterprise, it may very well be possible for you to navigate near the wall upon the basis of clues arising from the stray sounds which are produced by passing cars or distant machinery. Why might one expect, on the basis of these experiments, that it would be easier to make wall-distance estimates in a large, bare room than next to a wall outdoors?

3. Try to devise scattering experiments analogous to the reflection experiments described in experiment 2 above. Trees, architectural details, people, and parked automobiles can all be used, each one showing its own relationship between sound wavelength and the amount scattered in a given direction. As a start, drive down a quiet street with only the right front (and then only the right rear) window open. Focus your attention on the different ways that tire noise is scattered in through the window by the curbstone, fire hydrants, trees in the lawn, bridge rails, and the like. For present purposes you may assume the rushing sound of tire noise to be made up of almost equal amounts of all possible frequency components.

4. In one of his experiments, Joseph Henry observed that he could stand outdoors at a distance of 100 feet in front of a steadily talking man and understand what he had to say, whereas the words were intelligible only to a distance of about 30 feet when he stood behind the speaker. The influence of the human head

is such that voice partials below 100 Hz are radiated uniformly in all directions. Those partials having frequencies near 200 Hz are radiated to produce a larger sound pressure amplitude in the forward direction than in the backward direction, with a measured forward-to-backward amplitude ratio of 1.5 to 1. For voice partials near 1000 Hz the forward-to-back ratio is about 3 to 1, and above about 5000 Hz the ratio is approximately 8 to 1. Knowing that out-of-doors the amplitude of any given partial falls inversely as the distance between source and detector, you may be able to figure out what frequencies among the various voice partials of the sound output from a man's voice are *predominantly* associated with the intelligibility of what he has to say. The male voice may be taken to consist chiefly of sinusoidal components whose frequencies are whole-number multiples of about 100 Hz.

Recalling that the roles of mouth and ear are quite interchangeable as far as physics is concerned, you might expect the front-to-back amplitude ratios given above to appear consistent with the 60-degree left-and-right ear amplitude data given in the digression in section 12.3. Compare these two sets of figures, with the help of diagrams of a spherical head provided with a mouth and two ears, to verify that the data are inconsistent. Perhaps you can invoke your knowledge of the actual structure of the human head to explain the discrepancy.

5. A two-channel ("stereo") home music system can provide the basis for many room-acoustics experiments. Set the system to the "mono" mode, in which the two loudspeakers are fed identical signals (regardless of whether the source is mono or stereo). Verify that you identify

the *nearer* of the two loudspeakers as the source of the whole sound, while the other one is essentially inaudible. If there is a balance control that adjusts the relative amplitudes of the signals sent to the two speakers, you will also be able to verify that (in accordance with the precedence effect) the ear's localization on the closer source persists even when the farther source produces a somewhat larger amplitude signal at your ears.[6]

Notice how ambiguous the position of a radio announcer's voice can become if you sit at equal distances from the two mono-connected loudspeakers. The apparent source seems to skip about the room, or from one loudspeaker to the other. Some of the skipping around comes from small inequalities between the loudspeakers, and some from scattering effects from furniture in the room. For many people, especially those who have cultivated their ability to localize ordinary sound sources, the sound of an announcer's voice coming from two loudspeakers is upsetting; it seems to come from nowhere because of the conflicting cues supplied to the two ears. These effects are present in some degree when one listens to music through two loudspeakers in the mono mode. Why would there normally be less confusion with music than with the voice?

6. Use your present understanding of room acoustics and perception to think through the implications of the following varieties of two-channel recording and playback. Some of your deductions may be at variance with the opinions expressed in the hi-fi literature, but be courageous and postpone all attempts to resolve the discrepancies until later!

A. A recording is made of a string quartet playing in a concert hall, using a pair of small microphones mounted at ear position on a dummy head placed among the human members of the audience. The recording is played back using high-quality earphones properly fitted to the listener's head. How does the playback compare with what the listener would hear if he were present in the audience?

B. A recording is made using a dummy head as in A above, and it is played back over a pair of good loudspeakers in someone's living room. Why would the listener's position not make a drastic difference to the nature of the music as heard? Hint: localization in *space* is not particularly important to classical music, even though the ability to follow the different voices is generally of great value.

C. A recording is made by means of a pair of microphones spaced about 3 meters (10 to 12 feet) apart on a stage, arranged so that the musicians are seated at the apex of a roughly equilateral triangle, the microphones being at the other two corners and well up away from the floor. Compare what you would expect to hear using headphones with what would be heard by a listener in the audience (for whom there is no electronic reinforcement system).

D. A recording is made as in C and is played back as in B. Verify by your analysis that the formal cues to localization discussed in this chapter cannot function in this recording and playback context. This is not to say that the nervous system fails to construct a mental "picture" of the concert hall. The listener is functioning in the same way as does a sophisticated viewer who can see and appreciate the solidity of objects drawn by an artist despite deliberate violations of the rules of photographic perspective.

E. Figure out why the announcer's voice on stereo broadcasts is almost invariably routed to either the left or the right channel, but not to both. Even when two microphones are used to pick up the voice, one for each loudspeaker, the effect tends to be unsatisfactory in the listening room. Why should the announcer's speech sounds give trouble when the singing voice seems to work fairly well under stereo broadcast conditions?

7. An ordinary small microphone is almost exactly the detecting analogue of the simple source of sound in that it is equally sensitive to sounds coming to it from all directions. It is also uniform in its response to all frequencies. Sound engineers from time to time make use of special microphones that "hear" well only those sounds coming from a certain direction. These have uniform frequency response only in their preferred direction (review the discussion of loudspeaker directionality in the church acoustics discussion above). Each directional microphone has its own characteristic way of altering its response as the source is approached, whereas nondirectional microphones display essentially no change in their detection characteristics when used close to a source. As a result, music simultaneously recorded close up on two adjacent microphones, one one-directional and the other nondirectional, will differ noticeably from one version to the other. It is not, however, meaningful at this point to make any statement about the relative "fidelity" of the two recordings (should one perhaps mount pressure microphones on a rubber dummy head?!).

Notes

1. This work was never written up at the time. A later report, which includes some important

comments on the problems of stereo reproduction, is in William B. Snow, "Effect of Arrival Time on Stereophonic Localization," *J. Acoust. Soc. Am.* 26 (1954): 1071–74.

2. Helmut Haas, "Über den Einfluss eines Einfachechos auf die Hörsamkeit von Sprache," *Acustica* 1 (1951): 49–58.

3. Heinrich Kuttruff, *Room Acoustics* (New York: Wiley, 1973). Kuttruff in chapter VII, "The Subjective Effect of Combined Sound Fields," gives a good summary of the ideas we have been discussing. A good general account of the practical implications of room acoustics is to be found in Vern O. Knudsen and Cyril M. Harris, *Acoustical Designing in Architecture* (New York: Wiley; London: Chapman & Hall, 1950).

4. E. A. G. Shaw, "Transformation of sound pressure level from the free field to the eardrum in the horizontal plane," *J. Acoust. Soc. Am.* 56 (1974): 1848–61. See also Jack Hebrank and D. Wright, "Spectral cues used in the localization of sound sources on the median plane," *J. Acoust. Soc. Am.* 56 (1974): 1829–34.

5. Robert M. Lambert, "Dynamic theory of sound-source localization," *J. Acoust. Soc. Am.* 56 (1974): 165–71.

6. The home music industry has the notion that we localize sounds by making use only of loudness relations between various signals that arrive at our ears. An interesting study of the relationships between arrival time and signal strength is that of John D. Gilliom and Robert D. Sorkin, "Discrimination of Interaural Time and Intensity," *J. Acoust. Soc. Am.* 52 (1972), 1635–44. See also the carefully written pioneering paper by J. C. Steinberg and W. B. Snow, "Physical Factors" (paper from Symposium on Wire Transmission of Symphonic Music and Its Reproduction in Auditory Perspective), *Bell System Tech. J.* 13 (1934): 245–58.

13

The Loudness of Single and Combined Sounds

We have had occasion earlier in this book to deal in a preliminary way with the relationship between perceived pitch and the repetition rates of various components of a sound. While the detailed relationship between pitch and frequency is somewhat complicated, we have seen that, overall, physical stimuli having high repetition rates give rise to pitch sensations at the high end of the musical scale. We have also noticed indications of a relationship between a sound's vibration recipe (the strengths and frequencies of its various components) and what the musician calls the timbre or tone color of a sound. In this connection we find that it is necessary for our ears and their associated nervous system to process a great deal of room-acoustics information on the way to deducing the characteristic "voice" of an instrument. In a similar vein, we have learned of the processing that is done so that the beginnings and ends of musical notes can be recognized as a part of music. In summary, then, we have given thought to three of the four aspects of a single sound as it interests a musician: pitch, tone color, and duration. The present chapter is devoted mainly to an examination of the remaining aspect—the loudness of the perceived sound as it is determined by its mechanical correlates, which are the magnitudes of the various components and the relationships among their frequencies. Our study will also reveal some basic phenomena that govern the aural interactions between sounds from different instruments.

13.1. Thresholds of Hearing and Pain for a 1000-Hz Sinusoid

We have already learned in chapter 12 that the ear (like most microphones) is a pressure-measuring device in which the eardrum is alternately pressed inward and pulled outward in response to the oscillatory fluctuation of pressure above and below the normal atmospheric pressure of the room. Let us provide ourselves with a few reference values for the magnitude of these pressure variations as a guide to our future understanding, and as a way to impress upon ourselves the enormous range of acoustic pressures with which our ears can deal. The normal operating pressure in an automobile tire, for example, arises because the air within it has been compressed to a volume that is about 35 percent of its original value. This is an everyday illustration of the fact

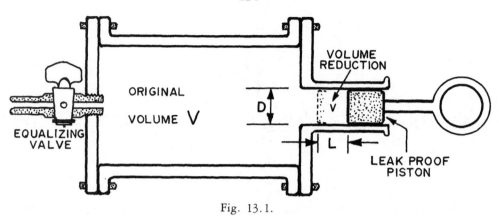

Fig. 13.1.

that when a confined quantity of air is compressed into a smaller space, its pressure rises. We can make use of this basic idea to help ourselves imagine the pressure amplitudes of various sounds. Figure 13.1 shows an airtight tank (of original volume V) which is filled with air to atmospheric pressure via an equalizing valve. When the valve is closed, a leak-proof piston of diameter D is pushed in a distance L so as to reduce the total volume of the tank by an amount v; this causes the pressure to rise by a small amount p above the original atmospheric value p_a. The relationship between a small volume change and the resulting small pressure change may be illustrated by means of an example: a 10-percent reduction in the volume raises the pressure by an amount equal to 10 percent of the original atmospheric pressure.

Suppose we listen to a 1000-Hz sinusoidal pressure oscillation with both ears open in a very quiet room and reduce the pressure amplitude of the sound progressively until it is barely audible. One could ask what is the diameter D of a piston and the length L of its displacement that will produce in a 1-liter tank (holding about a quart) a *steady* pressure change that is equal to the amplitude of the barely audible acoustic pressure signal which oscillates at 1000 Hz. The answer is surprising: if our imaginary pump has a piston whose diameter is equal to that of one of my hairs—0.006 cm—one would have to move this tiny piston forward only 0.01 cm, somewhat less than twice its own diameter, to produce the desired pressure change. This movement of the pump will produce a volume change of only one part in about 3.5 billion. Under the influence of oscillatory changes of pressure having this amplitude, the eardrum is pushed back and forth a distance that is considerably less than the diameter of the atoms making up the air, and yet this minuscule disturbance is something we can hear!

When the pressure amplitude is increased to a value 100-fold larger, we will hear our 1000-Hz sinusoid with a loudness that is roughly comparable to that of a normally struck tuning fork held a handspan from the ear. A further increase of 100-fold (to a pressure amplitude 10,000 times the detectable limit) brings us into the range set up everywhere in a studio or a large living room by a flute player sounding his notes at what he would call a *mezzo-forte* dynamic level. If we increase the electrical driving signal to our sound source 100-fold further, making it so that the sound pressure at the listener's ear is a million times greater than the threshold value, he will complain of uncomfortable loudness and may stuff fingers in his ears to try to shut out the unwanted sound. Let us summarize what is shown by such a series of experiments done with a single component sound.

1. At 1000 Hz, for normal healthy ears working together, the minimum audible sound pressure amplitude at the threshold of hearing is about 1/3,530,000,000 of atmospheric pressure. We will take this value as our reference in all future work (see sec. 13.2 for further details).

2. A 100-fold increase in the amplitude above the reference value brings us to the lower region of musical loudness, and a 10,000-fold increase in amplitude puts the sound into the middle of the musical loudness range.

3. The *threshold of pain* is found to lie at pressure amplitudes 1,000,000 times larger than the reference value if we make our observations at a frequency of 1000 Hz.

4. The extent of the amplitude range for music shows that the enormous physical variation in amplitude does not manifest itself as an equally enormous variation in the perceived loudness.

13.2. The Decibel Notation and Its Application to Acoustical Signals

It is commonplace to make use of the term "decibel" in today's discussions of acoustics in the popular press as well as in technical articles. We have reached the place in this book where the term needs to be explained and a preliminary indication of its usefulness sketched out. A device whose readings are normally given in decibels, the sound level meter, will be described in section 13.8.

The *decibel* and its close cousin the *neper* were terms invented by telephone engineers who sought a convenient way to deal with the gain and loss of wave energy as it is transmitted successively through one member after another of a communication chain of telephone cables, switchboards, equalizing networks, repeater amplifiers, and the like. The decibel is *not* a *quantity* of sound (or of electrical energy); in essence it expresses an energy flow *relationship* between any two signals.

Physicists and engineers are very much concerned with the concept of energy flow. This is a unifying concept of enormous power which can help clarify the nature of many processes. The physics involved in the transfer of heat energy from a glass of lemonade to the ice cubes which melt as they cool it is nearly identical with what happens in the transformation of chemical energy from my supper into muscular energy that is deposited in the spring of my watch when I wind it; some of this energy is in turn converted into acoustical energy which I can perceive in the form of a ticking sound.

Many of the physicist's measuring devices are directly sensitive to energy; however, the microphone and the ear are not. Furthermore, our hearing process itself does not, at the level of our concern, give a measure of acoustic energy. It is for this reason (chiefly) that we have evaded the concept of energy so far in this book. It will suffice for us to note in passing that the energy involved in any vibrational process is proportional to the square of the amplitude of the vibration.

Because of this, a 2-fold increase in amplitude involves a $2 \times 2 = 4$-fold increase in the energy, while a tripling of the amplitude is associated with a 9-fold increase in energy. It naturally follows that a 10-fold energy change calls for a $\sqrt{10} = 3.162$-fold increase in the amplitude—a figure which turns out to be very useful in discussions of acoustic energy.

If a telephone amplifier is said to have a *gain* of 10 decibels, the engineer is telling us that the signal energy associated with every sinusoidal component sent down the cable connected to its output is 10-fold larger than the signal energy component coming to it from the input cable. If the two cables are alike, we can also recognize that the amplitude of the output signal from this amplifier will be 3.162 times larger than the amplitude of the signal coming in. Two such amplifiers cascaded will of course produce a $10 \times 10 = 100$-fold increase in energy at the output, and an engineer speaking decibel language will tell us that the combined amplifier has an energy gain of 20 decibels (abbreviated *dB*). We notice furthermore that the output amplitude of the two amplifiers in cascade is 10 times larger than the input signal amplitude. In general, whenever the signal energy flow is increased by 10 dB, the associated oscillatory amplitude goes up by a factor of 3.162. A 20-dB increase, therefore, corresponds to a $3.162 \times 3.162 = 10$-fold increase in amplitude.

Figure 13.2 presents a curve giving the amplitude ratios between two signals when the decibel relationship between them is given. To help yourself to understand the use of the curve, it would be worthwhile to examine the figure to verify that a doubling of amplitude corresponds very nearly to a 6 dB change, and

tripling it corresponds to a change of almost 10 dB, while an 8-fold increase in amplitude may equally well be said to involve an increase of 15.6 dB. Notice that a 1 dB change corresponds to a 1.1220-to-1 amplitude ratio—in other words, the amplitude is increased by 12.2 percent.

Let us go back now to the 1000-Hz experiments described in section 13.1 to see how the decibel notation can be applied to them. The 100-fold increase of oscillatory pressure amplitude above the threshold of audibility which was described as giving a tuning-fork-like gentle sound can now be said to correspond to an increase of 40 dB. The next step up in amplitude was to a value 100-fold larger, so we can say that the mezzo-forte sound has a level 40 dB above the previous one, or a sound pressure 80 dB above our reference value. Finally, we notice that the pain threshold at 1000 Hz is found 120 dB above our reference.

Let us now see in a more formal way exactly what the sound engineer is talking about when he specifies a *sound level* in decibels (at any single frequency). There is an internationally agreed-upon reference sound pressure amplitude for all acoustical measurements in air which we may write as: $\sqrt{2} \times 0.0002 = 0.000283$ dyne/cm². The factor of $\sqrt{2}$ that appears here arises because engineers do not customarily describe an oscillatory signal in terms of its amplitude, choosing instead to specify what they call its "rms amplitude." One may specify the amplitude of any acoustical signal in decibel form. When, for example, one writes "the sound pressure level is 97 dB re 0.0002 dyne/cm²," or, more compactly, "the SPL is 97 dB," the word *level* or its initial letter serves as a tipoff that the standard reference pressure is to be assumed.

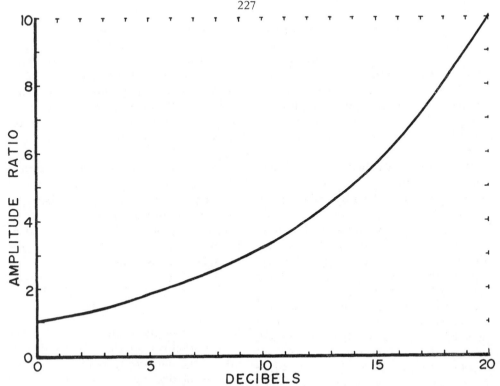

Fig. 13.2.   Amplitude Ratios Corresponding to Given Decibel Differences

We can use the facts presented so far along with figure 13.2 to translate an SPL (sound pressure level) of 97 dB into a ratio between the pressure amplitude of that sound and the amplitude of the agreed-upon standard reference sound. For simplicity, we can deal with the 97 dB in two parts: 97 dB = (80 + 17) dB. We have learned already that an 80-dB level difference corresponds to an amplitude ratio of 10,000 to 1, while figure 13.2 tells us that a 17-dB level change is associated with a ratio of 7.08 to 1. As a result, 97 dB corresponds to a 7.08 × 10,000 = 70,800-to-1 amplitude ratio between the pressure amplitude of the sound in question and the standard reference amplitude.

The standardized reference amplitude used in calculating SPLs is in fact identical with the 1/3,530,000,000th of atmospheric pressure given in section 13.1 as being at the threshold of audibility. This particular reference was chosen to make it easy to recall roughly where it lies in the gamut of our hearing. Another fact worth remembering is that a 1000-Hz sinusoid has a pitch that lies slightly above B_5 (which is the B just above the treble staff).

So far everything has been fairly straightforward. Changes in the sound level at our ears could easily be related to changes in the gain of the earphone driver amplifier: the signal flows along a single path from the oscillator, via the gain control and amplifier, through the earphone and into our listener's ear. Suppose, however, we have our listener sitting in a room in which there are two loudspeakers. Now there can be two paths to the listener's ear, and the initial simplicity of the decibel approach breaks down. Let's see what happens in this slightly more complex case.

If we assume that the listener is reasonably far away from the two loudspeakers, his ears are supplied with a piled-up aggregate of the steady-state room mode response to each loudspeaker. When we take into account that our two ears are able to provide us with a good "averaging" (both temporal and spatial) of the sound field in their neighborhood, we find that, if a single speaker is used and the amplitude of the cone's motion is doubled, the SPL at the listener's ear will go up 6 dB (in agreement with the predictions of figure 13.2). If, on the other hand, each of the two loudspeakers when acting alone is set to produce the same SPL averaged by the listener's ears and they are turned on together, then the statistical combination of one set of room responses with the other leads to a 3 dB rise in the SPL.

More generally, if we have several *distinct* sources A, B, C, . . . in the room (having the same, or different frequencies) which have various pressure amplitudes p_a, p_b, p_c, . . . as measured at some point in the room, then the statistically averaged net pressure amplitude p_{net} at that point turns out to be equal to the square root of the sum of the squares of the different amplitudes, as shown in the formula:

$$p_{net} = \sqrt{p_a^2 + p_b^2 + p_c^2 + \ldots}$$

(In a multi-path signal system of this sort involving the statistical transmission process, or when the components have differing frequencies, the decibel description becomes complicated. One must first convert each SPL to its corresponding pressure amplitude, combine these by our formula, and then find the SPL belonging to p_{net}.)

Let us conclude this section with a piece of arithmetic showing a curious property of the formula given above for pressure amplitudes. Suppose that p_a has a magnitude of 5 units, with p_b and p_c having a size of 2 and 1 units. Then the formula looks like this:

$$p_{net} = \sqrt{5^2 + 2^2 + 1^2} = \sqrt{25 + 4 + 1}$$
$$= \sqrt{30} = 5.48$$

We see from the arithmetic that if one contribution is more than about twice the others, the statistically averaged net pressure is hardly bigger than that of the largest contributor. In the case at hand the increase is slightly less than 10 percent. We must remember, however, that our ears keep track of a lot of things that a measuring microphone cannot. If, for example, the weaker signal p_b happens to arrive earlier than the strong one p_a (as in a sound reinforcement system based on the precedence effect), we will *attribute* all the sound to the source for p_b. The perceived loudness of such a combined sound will, on the other hand, be based on p_{net} in a way that we will take up in sections 4 and 5 of this chapter.

13.3. Hearing and Pain Thresholds at Various Frequencies

Section 13.1 pointed out that the healthy human ear is incredibly sensitive to a sinusoidal pressure signal having a frequency of 1000 Hz. That section also showed that increasing the pressure amplitude of a 1000-Hz tone causes it to become progressively louder, the point of discomfort being reached when the amplitude is about 1,000,000 times larger than the minimum audible value. In section 13.2 we learned that acousticians have chosen for their laboratory purposes a reference pressure amplitude whose value was selected for convenience to be very close to the minimum audible value at 1000 Hz. The decibel sound pressure level (SPL) is then a way of specifying the *ratio* of any given sound pressure amplitude to this reference pressure.

So far in this chapter we have confined our attention to what happens at 1000 Hz, a frequency that has a rather restricted utility in music! Let us now ask what minimum sound pressure amplitude is required if our ears are to hear something at other excitation frequencies. Suppose we measure the minimum SPL required at a healthy listener's ears for him just barely to detect the presence of sounds of various frequencies. Because our interests are directed mainly toward sound as it is heard in a musical context, our experimental listener is permitted to use both his ears and to move around freely as he sits in a large, reverberant room. Figure 13.3 summarizes the results of experiments carried on throughout the world over a period of many years, as discussed in Recommendations 226 and 454 of the International Standards Organization (ISO).[1] The horizontal axis of this graph covers a range of frequencies extending from

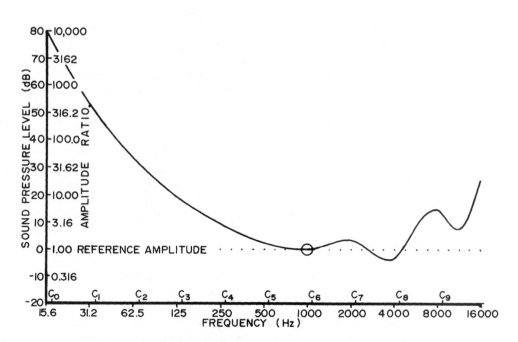

Fig. 13.3.   Threshold of Hearing for Two-Ear Listening

20 Hz to 16,000 Hz, plotted so that the various octaves of the musical note C fall at equally spaced points along the axis, just as they do along the piano keyboard. The vertical axis of this graph is marked to show the relation, expressed in decibels, between a given sound pressure amplitude and the conventional reference pressure described in section 13.2. The corresponding amplitude ratios are also shown on this axis.

By looking at figure 13.3 we can verify immediately that at 1000 Hz the threshold of hearing is almost precisely equal to the reference amplitude. That is, the threshold SPL is zero dB and the amplitude ratio is 1.000. At an excitatory frequency of about 125 Hz, 3 octaves lower, the curve shows that the barely audible SPL is 20 dB; in other words, if we are just barely to hear anything at 125 Hz, an oscillatory acoustic pressure amplitude is required that is ten times as large as that which was sufficient to produce an audible signal at 1000 Hz. Down at 24 Hz we hear nothing unless the sound pressure is increased to a value 1000-fold larger (60 dB SPL) than that required for detection at 1000 Hz. The overall sensitivity of our ears falls rapidly as we test them with lower and lower frequencies.

We can similarly examine figure 13.3 to see what happens above 1000 Hz. At 2000 Hz, the minimum audible pressure amplitude is 150 percent of that measured at 1000 Hz, whereas only about 80 percent as strong a signal is required for audibility at 4000 Hz. In other words, our ears are slightly more sensitive at 4000 Hz (the first partial of notes lying near the top of the piano) than at 1000 Hz. To continue, at 8000 Hz the minimum amplitude is 5 times the 1000-Hz value, while at 16,000 Hz it must be

increased to an SPL of about 26 dB (a 20-fold amplitude increase). The wiggles in the sensitivity curve at high frequencies are produced partly by natural-frequency resonance effects in the listener's ear canals and partly by perception games our neurological processor plays when faced with the interaction of the two sound pressure signals received at the two sides of the listener's head.

Looking at the general shape of the threshold curve in figure 13.3, we notice that, roughly speaking, the healthy ear is quite sensitive over a frequency range between 250 Hz and 6000 Hz; beyond these frequency limits the sound pressure must be increased considerably if anything at all is to be heard.

We must be careful not to take the standardized curve of figure 13.3 too literally: it is in fact compiled for people with extremely good hearing. If you bring people in off the street and measure their hearing, three-quarters of them will require about ten times the signal amplitudes given in the curve. For the younger of these people, the *shape* of the curve tends to resemble the curve in figure 13.3, though it is displaced upward to larger sound levels, but as one grows older in our noisy culture, the part of the threshold curve above about 4000 Hz (the right-hand quarter of fig. 13.3) rises much more steeply, so that the pressure amplitude required for audibility at 10,000 Hz may rise to values comparable to those required at 20 Hz! Individual variations are extremely large at all ages. When I was a sophomore in college, I was one of two or three people in a large physics class who could easily hear sounds having frequencies above 25,000 Hz produced in a big lecture hall by striking the ends of short steel bars arranged to make a sort of glockenspiel. There were others in the group who could not hear similar bars if they vibrated above 4000 Hz.

We will close this section with one further observation: the sound pressure amplitude that produced a feeling of pain and discomfort at 1000 Hz is very nearly the same as that which produces discomfort at all other frequencies. This amplitude is about 1,000,000 times the reference value, giving it an SPL of 120 dB.

13.4. Variations in the Perceived Loudness of a Single-Component Sound: *Sones*

We have so far learned that the sound pressure required for mere audibility is very large at low and at high frequencies as compared with what it takes in the range from 250 to 6000 Hz. Let us now turn our attention to the way in which the *perceived loudness* of a sound changes if we supply our ears with a variable frequency signal of constant sound pressure level. We shall not take time to describe the many ingenious psychoacoustic experiments that were done in order to set up a scale relating the loudness of the sounds we hear (a *perceived* attribute) to the acoustic pressure amplitudes of the disturbances which give rise to them.[2] However, it is important to realize that the ability to make meaningful calculations of loudness is one of the foundations of the modern, highly developed practice of noise control engineering. It is this ability to predict the loudness of sounds separately and in combination that makes possible some of the legal requirements

currently being developed in the interests of environmental health and safety. We will borrow from this body of knowledge only certain parts that bear upon our particular musical interests.

We have introduced the idea of a sound pressure level, which provides a means for comparing the physicist's measured quantity (sound pressure) with a suitably chosen numerical reference value (1/3,530,000,000 of an atmosphere). Similarly, to measure human perception of sounds we need to provide ourselves with a standardized unit of perceived loudness—the *sone*. If a listener with healthy hearing sits in an anechoic chamber facing a distant loudspeaker, he will hear a sound whose loudness is defined as 1 sone when a source having a frequency of 1000 Hz produces an SPL of 40 dB at his ear. There are many situations, particularly in music, in which loudness figures expressed in sones obey ordinary additive arithmetic (as decibels do not) in the sense that the loudness of a 2-sone source combines with that of a 3-sone source to produce a sound which we perceive to be equal in loudness to a source whose loudness was separately determined to be 5 sones. Similarly, there are ways to predict how much it is necessary to turn down the amplitudes of a *set* of contributing loudspeaker sources so that their net loudness as perceived will match the loudness of any one of the sources when it is operated by itself. The implications of these various possibilities will become clearer as we make use of the loudness scale and its connection with the frequencies of various sound components and their amplitudes.

Figure 13.4 presents a family of curves giving the variation of loudness in sones when the listener in a room is presented

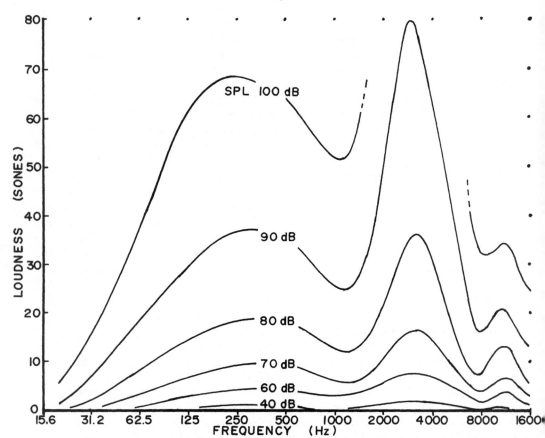

Fig. 13.4. Loudness (in Sones) of Single-Component Sounds in a Room as a Function of Frequency. Each of the curves is marked with the sound pressure level (decibels) of the stimulus. Note that a 10-dB increase in SPL approximately doubles the loudness as long as the signal is about 40 dB above threshold.

with sounds from a perfect loudspeaker sinusoidally driven to produce constant (room averaged) SPL at his ears. I have calculated the curves upon the basis of ISO recommendations 126, 454, and R 131.[3] Let us follow the 80 dB SPL curve first, which corresponds to a pressure amplitude that is 10,000 times the conventional reference value. The loudness of this sound is very small at a

20-Hz frequency, as one would expect, since figure 13.3 shows that an 80-dB SPL is only a little above the audible threshold at this frequency. When the frequency is raised to the region between 250 and 500 Hz (corresponding to pitches near the middle of the piano), the loudness rises to about 18 sones. The loudness dips to 13 sones near 1000 Hz, and then shoots up to 34 sones near 3000

Hz before falling away in wiggly fashion at higher frequencies.

Our perception of the loudness *variations* associated with uniform sound pressure excitation at our ears differs when the chosen sound pressure is high from that observed when it is low. For example, the loudness change between 1000 Hz and 3000 Hz is only about 4 sones when the ear is driven by a sinusoid having a pressure amplitude 1000 times the reference value (SPL = 60 dB), whereas between these same frequencies the loudness changes by a much larger amount, 64 sones, when the SPL is 90 dB. If you have a test record that provides a constant amplitude sinusoidal signal of steadily rising frequency, you can observe this difference yourself. Quite aside from the fine-grained irregularities associated with the statistics of room acoustics, you will barely be able to perceive the loudness peaks and dips when the recording is softly played, whereas you will become drastically aware of them when you turn up the volume to make a loud repetition of the same test. The easy availability of commercial *equalizer circuits* sometimes tempts an unwary listener into adjusting his playback system to produce an equally loud sound at every frequency when it is fed from a test tape, instead of making sure that the equalizer compensates for variations in loudspeaker efficiency to assure uniform sound pressure response at all frequencies. The equal-loudness type of adjustment leads to the production of curious-sounding music when ordinary records are played. In particular, records played under such conditions appear to have an unnatural amount of bass and treble sound, plus a lack of what the record reviewers sometimes call "presence" (associated with the general

signal level in the region between 3000 and 4000 Hz). The explanation is straightforward: since our nervous system is built to deal with and even exploit the loudness variations shown in figure 13.4, use of an equal-loudness filter creates a conflict within our auditory apparatus; it suppresses the work done by the recording engineer as he strives to recreate in your living room the sound pressure arrangements that his microphones detect in the concert hall, leaving your ears to carry out their natural operations in the room as they do in the concert hall.

While the curves shown in figure 13.4 cover the main range of sound pressures commonly found for the partial components of musical sounds, it is useful to know how to adapt the diagram for use with higher ranges of SPL. We may make use of the fact that, at any frequency, raising the SPL by 10 dB (increasing the pressure amplitude by a factor of 3.16) approximately doubles the numerical value (sones) of the perceived loudness. To the extent that this approximation is valid, if we want to make the figure apply to sound pressure levels 10 dB higher, we can relabel each of the curves accordingly and replace the 10, 20, 30, . . . sone sequence of numbers along the diagram's left-hand side by the sequence 20, 40, 60, . . . sones. The results of such a relabeling procedure are accurate within 15 to 20 percent over the middle part of the diagram, as long as one deals only with SPLs above about 60 dB. However, this shortcut procedure fails badly for SPLs lower than 60 dB, especially at low and high frequencies. This is because the perceived loudness at the frequency extremes falls away rapidly as one reduces the SPL toward its value at the threshold of audibility (zero loudness).

13.5. Loudness of Combined Single-Component or Narrow-Band Noise Signals Having Identical or Different Pitches

Now that we have provided ourselves with an initial view of the relationship between the sound pressure amplitude and the loudness of a single sinusoidal component at different frequencies, we are in a position to compare the loudness changes produced when one varies the amplitude of a single source with the changes arising when different numbers of equal-strength sources are used, all of them running at the same frequency. From this we will go on to investigate what happens when sources having different pitches are combined.

The upper curve in figure 13.5 shows the variation in loudness, expressed in sones, produced when the excitation amplitude of a single source is progressively increased. We assume that the initial amplitude is such as to produce a loudness of one sone. Notice that the amplitude must be more than tripled for the loudness to rise to 2 sones, and a loudness of 4 sones is not reached until the amplitude is increased tenfold. The lower curve in figure 13.5 shows the loudness variation produced when a room has sources added to it one by one, all sources running *at the same frequency* and arranged (when acting separately) to have a loudness of 1 sone. The single-source and multiple-source curves differ because of the statistical way in which the sound pressures from several

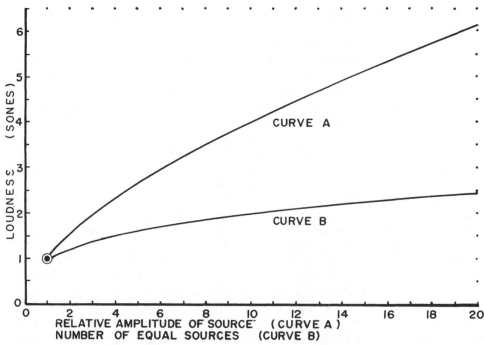

Fig. 13.5. Changes in Loudness. *A*, produced by changes in the amplitude of a single source; *B*, produced by changes in the number of identical sources.

sources combine, as shown by the square-root formula given in section 13.2. It is at once apparent from the striking difference in appearance between the two curves that loudness grows only slowly as more and more equal sources are brought into action. It takes 10 sources running together to double the loudness, and 100 would be required to quadruple it!

So far we have limited our consideration of loudness effects to a simple 1000-Hz tone. You may recognize, however, that a single musician, who may well be able to vary the sound pressure output of his instrument over a 20-fold range, provides a far greater dynamic range than a composer could obtain by orchestrating different numbers of players who are all constrained to play with a fixed amplitude. The fact that in orchestral music many players are given the same part has a musical function other than the quite limited one of achieving a wider dynamic range.

We are ready now to investigate the combined loudness produced in our hearing by a pair of signals having different pitches. Our nervous system has two fairly distinct ways in which it combines such sounds to produce a sensation of loudness, one or the other of these ways being chosen according to the nature of the signals themselves and the setting in which they are heard. We shall begin with the simpler one, which has had by far the most study devoted to it partly because of its scientific implications and partly because it is the one having most to do with such applications as noise control. First we will consider a slightly messy-looking pair of signals which nevertheless have reasonably well-defined frequencies, and later we will adapt our discoveries to the musically important

case in which two *sinusoids* are combined. To begin, then, we will consider what happens when each of our pair of acoustical signals is constructed out of a very large number of sinusoidal components whose frequencies are randomly chosen but constrained to be within about 10 percent of a particular *center frequency;* in this case, the two signals have their groups of components clustered about different center frequencies. It turns out that the loudness of each of these groups (which are usually referred to as being *narrow-band noise signals*) is equal to that of a single sinusoidal component having the same SPL and whose frequency matches the center frequency of the group. A narrow-band noise signal of this kind is perceived as a sort of rushing or hissing sound that has a fairly definite pitch. Composers of electronic music often make use of such sounds, and, at a humbler level, similar sounds can be heard when someone tries unsuccessfully to play a flute or blow across the top of a bottle.

Let us assume that each of our signals is arranged to produce a loudness sensation of 13 sones when it is turned on by itself. If one of the two groups has a center frequency lying above about 300 Hz and the other one has a center frequency at least four times as great (two or more octaves higher), then the two loudnesses are found to add arithmetacally when both sources are in operation, giving a total of 26 sones. When the pitches of the two "tones" are this widely spaced, any two loudnesses will add similarly; for example, a 13-sone signal sounded along with one having a loudness of 5 sones will produce a composite sound whose loudness is 18 sones.

Suppose now that the center frequencies of the two 13-sone groups are brought closer together. When the pitch interval between them is about an octave, the combined loudness is found to have reduced itself from 26 sones to something close to 24 sones, as shown by the solid curve in figure 13.6. (At present we will ignore the existence of a spiky protrusion shown at the left-hand end of the otherwise smooth trend of the curve.) When the two sounds are brought into a half-octave pitch relationship (6 semitones apart, an interval of an augmented fourth), we find that the combined loudness is only

about 20 sones. Looking further at the curve, we notice that if the two components have about equal center frequencies, their joint loudness is 16 sones. This agrees with predictions which could have been made on the basis of figure 13.5, which showed that two equal sources combine to give a 1.23-fold increase (equal to 16/13) in loudness.

By examining figure 13.6 we can also realize that if the frequencies of the two groups are initially made identical and are then progressively separated, there will be essentially no change in loudness until

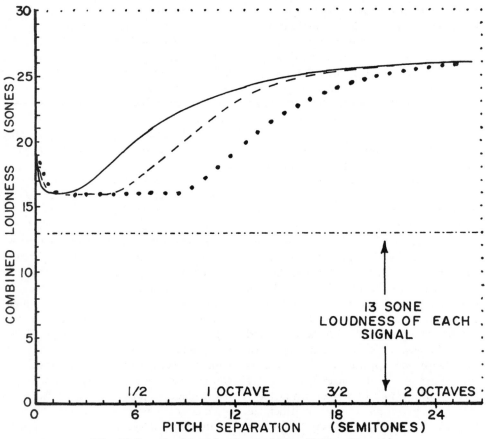

Fig. 13.6.   Combined Loudness of Two 13-Sone Sinusoids

they are more than about 3 semitones (a minor third) apart! Historically, experiments of the sort implied here gave psychoacoustics its first hint that in some ways our nervous system processes closely grouped sinusoidal components as though they were indistinguishable. This phenomenon also helps to demonstrate that sounds in various frequency ranges are parceled out for processing to different parts of the auditory system. The frequency range within which a pair of sinusoidal groups must lie if they are to show these lumping-together effects is known as the *critical bandwidth*. [4] By the way, it is this melting together of the loudness perception of signals having roughly the same frequency (well within the critical bandwidth) that explains why we could replace a single sinusoid by a narrow-band noise of the same combined SPL.

For our purposes it will be sufficiently accurate to use critical bandwidths that follow ISO Recommendation 532. Here all the critical bandwidths for sounds above 280 Hz are quite accurately conventionalized as being 1/3 of an octave wide (4 semitones, an interval of a major third). In the frequency region from 180 to 280 Hz the bandwidth is 2/3 of an octave wide (8 semitones, an interval of a minor sixth), and below that the critical bandwidth is treated as extending over a full octave.

The dashed curve in figure 13.6 shows how the critical bandwidth phenomenon influences the loudness summation of our two 13-sone components when the lower one has a frequency of about 200 Hz, while the dotted curve does the same for a lower component having a frequency near 100 Hz. Spikes similar to the one drawn for the solid curve are also associated with

the dashed and dotted curves. The implications of, and reasons for, these spikes will be taken up in the next section of this chapter.

Sounds made up of harmonically related components (i.e., those having frequencies that are whole-number multiples of a fundamental pitch-giving frequency) are musically very important. Let us consider briefly the loudness of a very similar kind of sound—one made up of a set of narrow-band noises whose center frequencies are harmonically related. For definiteness we will assume that it consists of five of these noise-partials (as we shall call them) having center frequencies at 300, 600, 900, 1200, and 1500 Hz. We will further assume that each noise-partial has a loudness of 13 sones when heard by itself.

We start by asking about the loudness of noise-partials 4 and 5 when taken together in the absence of the other components. It turns out that the pitches of these two are separated by only 4 semitones (1/3 octave—a major third). Figure 13.6 shows therefore that they combine to give a loudness somewhat above 17 sones.

Let us now transfer our attention to the way that noise-partials 3 and 4 would combine in the absence of everything else. These two, having center frequencies of 900 and 1200 Hz, have pitches that are 5 semitones apart (a perfect fourth), and we learn from figure 13.6 that their combined loudness is close to 19 sones. I should remark at this point that due to a phenomenon known as *upward masking,* the presence of the lower-pitched component has the effect of reducing the loudness with which the upper component is heard. The reverse effect, downward masking, is only slight. The net effect of the masking is that the 19-sone loudness of our two noise-partials may be thought of (but only very crudely) as being produced by the *arithmetical addition* of a 13-sone lower component to an upper component whose loudness is reduced by masking to 6 sones.

Looking back to noise-partials 4 and 5 we notice in similarly crude terms that upward masking has reduced the loudness contributed by the 1500-Hz component to $17 - 13 = 4$ sones, a value about 1/3 of its loudness when heard alone. In similar vein, number juggling of the interaction between noise-partials 2 and 3 (separated by 7 semitones) reduces the loudness of the upper component to about 7 sones, or a little more than 1/2 its original loudness.

It is possible to put all of this masking arithmetic together and construct a simple though admittedly very rough arithmetical procedure for calculating the total loudness of a sound made up of no more than 6 or 8 harmonically related noise-partials. I shall give the formula first and then explain it, along with its limitations.

We assume that sound pressure measurements have already been made of the various noise-partials, and that each one of these harmonically related narrow-band noise components has been properly converted into sones with the help of figures 13.4 and 13.5. In terms of these loudnesses S_1, S_2, S_3, . . . , the total loudness S_{tnp} of the collection of noise-partials can be calculated from the formula:

$$S_{tnp} = S_1 + 0.75S_2 + 0.50S_3 + 0.50S_4 + 0.30S_5 + 0.20 \times (S_6 + S_7 + S_8)$$

For the collection of five 13-sone components we have been talking about, the total loudness is given as:

$$S_{tnp} = 13 + 9.75 + 6.5 + 6.5 + 3.9$$
$$= 39.65 \text{ sones}$$

In other words, the five equally loud components are predicted to give a sound that is about 3 times as loud as any one of its components. Our crude formula assumes (a) that the first (fundamental frequency) noise-partial is the loudest of the set, (b) that the loudnesses of the second, third, fourth, and fifth noise-partials do not fall much below the proportions $S_1/4$, $S_1/6$, $S_1/8$, and $S_1/10$ when they are compared with the fundamental component—if they decrease much more rapidly than this, some of them may have so little strength as to be totally masked by their lower-frequency neighbors—and (c) that the loudnesses of the 6th and higher components, if present, are quite small. The use of this formula will be illustrated in section 13.6, where its predictions are compared with those of a formula that applies to sounds made up of harmonically related sinusoidal components.

The phenomena described in this section are relatively insensitive to the means whereby they are studied. One can use earphones and anechoic chambers, or signals transmitted by a loudspeaker in one part of the room to a listener seated in another part.[5]

13.6. The Combined Loudness of Two or More Sinusoids; Relationships Advertised by Beats

In several ways, the discussion of loudness effects in section 13.5 had the appearance of a detour, or of a leap from the simplicity of single-frequency effects into the complexities of signals having whole groups of frequency components. Our need to ignore the spike poking up from the smooth curves of figure 13.6 added yet another bit of mystery to the proceedings. We are now in a position to go back and fill in the gaps and explain why the detour was necessary. We will begin by learning the origin of the spike at the zero-octave (equal-frequency) end of the curves in figure 13.6.

For experimental definiteness we should start out by imagining our listener wearing an earphone on one ear and an earmuff on the other, so that sound signals come only to one ear. If the electrical signal driving the earphone is made up of sinusoidal components having equal amplitudes but slightly different frequencies, our listener will notice a periodic alternation of loud sound and silence. It is easy to see how the phenomenon takes place: at those instants when the loud tone in heard, the two signals are in step, and they act together in driving the earphone's diaphragm back and forth. Under these conditions the diaphragm is oscillating with twice the amplitude it would have if only one signal were impressed upon it. Since one of the electrical components is oscillating with a higher frequency than the other, the periodic forces exerted by it on the diaphragm come at progressively earlier and earlier instants as compared with the forces produced by the other signal component. Eventually, one of the components will advance to the point where it is pushing on the diaphragm when the other is pulling. The net result is that the diaphragm is no longer in motion and so ceases temporarily to act as a sound source. As time goes on, the higher frequency component continues to gain on the other one, until they are once more acting in unison upon the diaphragm. This alternate growing and shrinking of the amplitude of motion of a single object that is acted upon by a

pair of sinusoidal forces having somewhat different frequencies is generally referred to as the phenomenon of *beating*. The two components are said to "beat together," and the rate at which the resulting oscillatory amplitude grows and shrinks is known as the *beat frequency*. It can be shown by simple mathematics that the beat frequency is equal to the difference between the frequencies of the two original stimuli. When I strike two tuning forks, one giving the 440-Hz sinusoid that is our current pitch reference for the note A_4 and the other giving the older 435-Hz reference frequency, the two sound pressure signals act on my eardrum to provide me with a tuning-fork sound that goes through $440 - 435 = 5$ cycles of waxing and waning in every second.

Let us return now to our loudness experiment. Whenever the two sinusoids find themselves in step, the ear is momentarily provided with an acoustical signal whose pressure *amplitude* is double that which either component can produce by itself—and thence arises an increase in *loudness* of nearly 50 percent (see fig. 13.5). As the two sinusoids run progressively farther out of step, the loudness diminishes, until the sinusoids cancel enough to produce a sound pressure that is below the threshold of hearing. The beaded curve in figure 13.7 shows the calculated variation in loudness for an earphone experiment done with two beating sinusoids, each one of which by itself has a sound pressure sufficient to give a 13-sone loudness. According to this calculation there would be momentary periods of silence, interspersed between swellings of sound. Note that there are considerable intervals of time during which the loudness is more than the 16-sone value implied by the solid curve in figure 13.6.

When the beats take place slowly

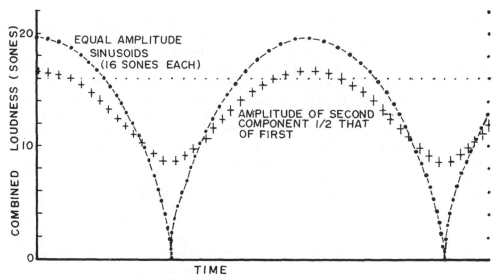

Fig. 13.7.   Variation in Loudness As Two Sinusoids Beat

enough (once a second or so), we do in fact hear variations of the sort predicted. However, when the frequencies of the two components differ by 5 to 15 Hz, the individual variations of loudness during the beat cycle are too rapid to be heard separately, and they average out to give a rough, rolling sound whose loudness is somewhere between the 16-sone value predicted by narrow-band noise experiments and the 19.7-sone loudness predicted by the slow beats calculation.

The curve drawn by means of crosses in figure 13.7 shows the variation in loudness produced at very slowly beating frequencies when one component's amplitude is as before but the other's is half as large. This of course implies an amplitude ranging from one 1.5 times that of the original sinusoid to one that is 0.5 times as large, varying as the two components run in and out of step. Notice that the loudness variation during a beat cycle is much less now that the two compo-

nents are of unequal size, since they can never combine to produce silence.

It should be fairly clear that beats between two equal large-amplitude signals are much more obtrusive than those between a weaker pair of signals, simply because the range between maximum loudness and utter silence is greater in one case than in the other. We similarly expect beats between unequal sinusoids to be more prominent when the separate components are loud than when they are fairly soft (but not much below 40 dB SPL). Near the threshold of hearing the beating may again be more clearly heard because of the altered way in which our ears relate loudness to sound pressure in this region of very soft sounds.

Let us summarize the salient features of the beat phenomenon as it takes place between two sinusoids fed directly to our ears.

1. When two sinusoidal driving forces that have roughly equal frequencies are brought to

act upon a single object, they alternately aid and counteract one another as the two oscillations run in and out of step. The swelling and shrinking of the resulting vibration amplitude is called beating. It takes place at a frequency equal to the difference between the two driving frequencies.

2. The beat phenomenon manifests itself most prominently when the two driving forces have equal amplitudes, so that they alternately produce complete cancellation and double amplitude response.

3. To the extent that beats are prominently heard between two sinusoidal components, their combined loudness will be greater than that predicted on the basis of narrow-band noise experiments.

4. The perceived sensations arising from the phenomenon of beats are much more strongly marked when they arise from large amplitude sinusoids than when weak signals are used. This variation may reverse its trend, however, as we approach the threshold of hearing.

We have now familiarized ourselves with the concept of beats between sinusoidal components and looked briefly at its implications in a single-earphone laboratory experiment. Let us use our knowledge to figure out what is to be expected when sinusoids from two different sources are supplied to our ears in the more normal listening environment of a room. Points in the room exist where only one of the components is strong enough to be heard, and nearby points where only the other one is appreciable (refer back to fig. 11.3). At most points in the room both components are audible, however, and the beat phenomenon will remain perceptible as our heads and bodies move around to explore the sound field in our neighborhood. For many of us the beats heard by a single ear between two sinusoids in a room tend to be slightly less prominent than those we get in earphone experiments. We find, however, that if both ears are available for use, our nervous system is able to recognize the beat regularities as an essential part of the signal of interest. As a matter of fact, someone listening in a room is often able to hear the higher-pitched and the lower-pitched sinusoids as distinct entities *along with* the beating sound (which generally is heard to have its own, intermediate pitch). This is in contrast to what happens in an earphone experiment. Here, if the two sinusoids are of equal strength, one hears only a beating, intermediately pitched sound. If the components are not of equal amplitudes, the beat is still audible and we generally hear a sound whose pitch is approximately that of the stronger original sinusoid. Overall, then, the fluctuation phenomena in a room permit us to separate out and perceive many things which are not otherwise distinguishable.

We have already learned from the earphone experiment one way in which the presence of beats can enhance the net loudness of two sinusoidal components over that expected on the basis of noise-partial measurements. The presence of fluctuation phenomena in a room will further increase their loudness, both because the sounds' irregularities serve to call attention to them and because various aspects of the sounds are made manifest one after the other in some random sequence. There is a more formal way to say all this, by making use of the concept of masking.

The phenomenon of masking is greatly weakened by the presence of room-caused fluctuations in the sound pressure amplitudes of all components. At one instant a super-strength bit of the upper component is being picked up along wth a vanishingly small amount of the lower component; under these conditions masking obviously cannot take place at all. At some other instant, to be sure, the upper component may be weakened into inaudibility, in part because of an increased amplitude for the lower component. Over any short period of time, the flickering relationships between the sinusoids leave us with overall loudness impressions which are relatively little influenced by masking of the sort measured in earphone experiments.

Consideration of the influence of room acoustics on the perception of beats and on the extent of masking explains the little spike appearing on the loudness curves of figure 13.6. Two sinusoids of nearly the same frequency combine in a room to produce a considerably louder sound than do two noise-partials having similar center frequencies. As the two sinusoids in a room are progressively separated in frequency, the net loudness falls away somewhat as the beats become too fast to hear; however, the loudness does not revert all the way back to the smooth curve of figure 13.6 because masking is still somewhat in abeyance. Experiments using narrow-band noise-partials do not suffer the influence of beats for a very simple reason. Noise-partials are constructed out of so many closely spaced components that loudness fluctuations due to any pair of them are drowned out by the presence of all the other pairs. It is very rare for a set of randomly related influences to combine with zero resultant! The whole subject of the masking behavior of sounds in rooms is a portion of psychoacoustics that begs for detailed study by a skilled experimentalist, but we can at least summarize what is known by

setting down here four more items to add to our group of assertions detailing the loudness behavior of sinusoidal components:

5. The statistical consequences of listening to a pair of sinusoidal excitations of nearly equal frequency in a room are such as to permit the distinct recognition of beats even when the averaged amplitudes of the two excitations are quite different.

6. In a room one can often recognize the upper and lower frequency components as sounds in their own right, along with their beating combination, even though the beating combination is the only signal that is heard when one listens through an earphone.

7. The masking effects of one sinusoid on another (at any frequency) are drastically reduced when one listens to them in a room; however, narrow-band noise signals mask each other in very much the same way whether we listen to them via earphones or in a room.

8. The presence of audible beats among the components of a sound has the effect of increasing the perceived loudness of the sound.

Item 7 in our summarizing list suggests that we consider the possibility of *ignoring* masking effects as a shortcut to a formula for calculating the loudness of a sound made up of sinusoidal components whose frequencies are widely enough separated for them not to beat. That is, for listening in a room, we are led to consider the following formula for the total loudness S_{tsp} in sones produced by a sound constructed out of sinusoidal partials having loudnesses S_1, S_2, S_3, . . . :

$$S_{tsp} = S_1 + S_2 + S_3 + \ . \ . \ . \ \text{sones}$$

This differs from the formula given in section 13.5 for the total loudness S_{tnp} arising from a collection of noise-partials by giving equal weight to contributions from all components rather than a decreasing importance to the higher frequency ones.

I have carried out a simple experiment to illustrate the difference between the two loudness formulas, the results of which will be described next. Two signals (call them J and K) were alternately presented to the listener's ears via a loudspeaker in my laboratory room. The strength of signal K was adjusted to make its loudness match that of signal J, to the satisfaction of a listener who was free to move around.

Signal J consisted of three sinusoidal components each having an SPL of 70 dB (as measured in the room), their frequencies being in the exact harmonic relationship of 200, 400, and 600 Hz. With the help of figure 13.4 we find that the separate loudnesses S_1, S_2, and S_3 are about 8.5, 10, and 8.5 sones, so that the loudness S_{tsp} predicted for the aggregate of these sinusoidal partials is:

$$S_{tsp} = 8.5 + 10 + 8.5 = 27 \text{ sones}$$

Signal K was constructed out of three equal-strength noise-partials each having its sinusoidal components spread over a 1/3-octave range. The center frequencies of these groups were at 200, 400, and 630 Hz, so as to give a good correspondence with the frequencies of signal J. When the loudness of this signal was adjusted to match that of signal J, the measured SPLs of each of the noise-partials were found to lie close to 75 dB. From figure 13.4 we deduce the corresponding loudnesses to be about 12, 13.5, and 13 sones. The overall loudness S_{tnp} given by the formula of section 13.5 then becomes:

$$S_{tnp} = 12 + (0.75 \times 13.5) + (0.5 \times 13)$$
$$= 29 \text{ sones}$$

This calculated figure for the loudness of three noise-partials is only about 7 percent higher than the one obtained from the loudness of the three sinusoidal components of signal J. Since the two sounds were adjusted to be equally loud, we have verified the need for two separate formulas for the two kinds of signal.

Recall that the SPL for a *single* sinusoid will match that of a *single* noise-partial when the two are adjusted for equal loudness. The fact that we require louder noise-partials than sinusoids to produce the same aggregate loudness is clear evidence of the difference in masking produced by the two kinds of signals under room-listening conditions.

There is one more piece of information that can be wrung from this same experiment. If the whole-number relationship between the partials in signal J is slightly deranged, for example by setting the frequencies at 200, 396, and 605 Hz, we hear fairly slow (4 to 13 Hz) beats among the components. The explanation of this somewhat unexpected phenomenon will have to wait until chapter 14, but its presence allows us to verify item 8 in the list of summarizing remarks. When a loudness match is made between the set of not-quite-harmonically related components (each having a 70 dB SPL as before) and the set of noise partials, we find that the SPL of the latter must be raised yet another 2 dB. In other words, the presence of beats has raised the loudness of signal J from about 27 sones to about 31 sones! I should remark that the *overall* SPL of signal J was not changed when the frequencies were altered, which tells us that whatever gives rise to beats is not an additional collection of sound components that reach the measuring microphone. In other words, the increased loudness is not a result of additional signals which somehow have appeared in the room air and whose loudnesses therefore need to be included directly in the calculations.

In this section we have learned that the loudnesses of sinusoidal components of a sound add up quite simply in the ear of a listener when he is permitted to make use of the sound transmission properties of a room. That is, the masking effects that are always observed when noise-partials are combined and (to a lesser extent) when sinusoids are combined in earphone or anechoic chamber experiments do not play much of a role for sounds heard in a room. We have also learned that the presence of beats can make considerable additions to the perceived loudness of a sound made up of sinusoidal components. At the very end of the section our attention was drawn to a new phenomenon: the presence of audible slow beats between sinusoids whose frequencies are over 100 Hz apart. As we will learn in chapter 14, this phenomenon has several modes of occurrence and several points of origin. We will also learn of its central importance to the way in which we recognize musical relationships.

13.7. A Loudness Experiment Comparing Two Saxophone Tones

In the spring of 1971, Mark Gridley, a talented professional jazz musician who at the time was also a graduate student working on problems of auditory perception, asked me for help in achieving a louder and more penetrating tone from his tenor saxophone. The simplest of the acoustical options that suggested themselves to me involved a tiny and easily

made change in his instrument's mouthpiece which would increase the strength of the second harmonic component along with the strengths of some of the higher partials. When the instrument was altered in this way, its sound more successfully met Gridley's musical requirements and he used it in his playing engagements.

Because we shared an interest in the perceptual and acoustical aspects of this musical problem, Gridley and I decided to make a few measurements on his instrument both before and after the change was made. Since the experiments provide a small-scale but typical example of how one deals with musical instruments in the laboratory, I shall describe what we did and why, with emphasis for present purposes on the loudness aspects of the study. I will mention various details having to do with the physics of the saxophone itself without giving an explanation for them, since that can wait for our later, more specific discussion of the woodwinds. For example, I will at this time merely assert that the sound pressure recipe obtained from a woodwind by means of a microphone placed next to the first open tone hole gives a fair imitation of the recipe one gets from a painstaking averaging process based on microphone measurements in a room. In other words, a microphone placed in this way allows us to record a sound similar to the one our hearing mechanism puts together as we move around in a room. The imitation works best if we listen to this sort of recording as it is played back in room surroundings rather than through earphones.

Using a microphone in the manner described above, we recorded on one channel of a stereo tape recorder several repetitions of the sound of the written note G$_3$ (fundamental frequency 174.6 Hz; we are dealing with a transposing instrument) as it was played on the saxophone using the unmodified mouthpiece (call this tone Q). The modification was then installed and a series of tones was once again recorded, this time on the other channel (tone R). In both cases Gridley was instructed to play at what he called a *mezzo-forte* dynamic level. I played the two channels of our tape back through an adjustable band-pass filter (also known as a wave analyzer) to measure the amplitudes of the various sinusoidal partials of both the

modified and the unmodified saxophone tones, and verified that Gridley's playing was stable and well-defined, so that we were not in danger of being led astray by chance variations in his performance. Figure 13.8 summarizes the results of these measurements.

The heavy black dots in figure 13.8 show the relative amplitudes of the fundamental and harmonics of tone Q. In the figure this fundamental is shown as having an amplitude of unity. We can see that the second harmonic (partial 2) has an amplitude that is 92 percent of partial 1, whereas partial 4 has an amplitude that is only about 7 percent as strong. To

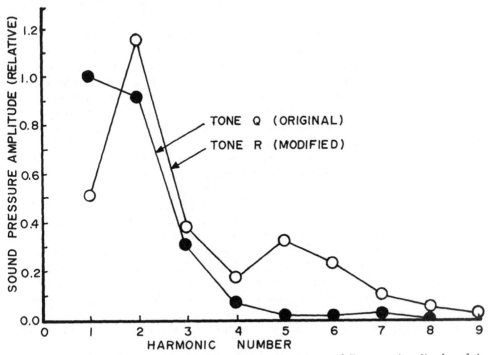

Fig. 13.8. Effect of Mouthpiece Modifications on the Measured Pressure Amplitudes of the Spectrum of the Note G$_3$ on a Tenor Saxophone. While the net SPLs of these spectra are identical, tone R is noticeably louder than tone Q.

guide your eye, these dots are connected by solid lines, so that the "shape" of the overall recipe (or spectrum, as it is sometimes called) can clearly be seen. As we shall see, this shape is typical of the low-register tone of a single-reed woodwind; three or four of the lower frequency partials are reasonably strong, the higher ones falling away very rapidly. (The chief error arising from the use of a microphone on the outside of the tone hole is an underrepresentation of the strengths of the higher partials, in this case numbers 4 and higher. A more accurate representation can be obtained by putting a probe microphone into the tone hole.)

The open circles connected by dashed lines in figure 13.8 show similarly the pressure amplitudes of the partials making up tone R. For convenience in calculation I have adjusted all of the amplitudes of tone R relative to those of tone Q in such a way as to give them the same overall SPL (calculated using the formula for the combination of several components given in sec. 13.2). Notice that in tone R, partial 1 is quite weak, partial 2 is strong, and partials 5 and 6 have particularly large amplitudes when compared with their predecessors belonging to tone Q.

Let us now compare the loudnesses of these two tones, on the assumption that component 1 of tone Q has an SPL of 80 dB (which gives a net SPL for the whole tone that is close to 86 dB in both cases). We find the loudnesses of the various components (as calculated with the help of figs. 13.2 and 13.4) to be as follows:

The total loudnesses given at the right-hand end of the lists are found by simple addition, in accordance with the formula given in section 13.6 for sounds having exactly harmonic partials listened to freely in a room. We see here that two sounds having equal SPLs (the engineer's measure of the overall sound pressure) can be made to have quite different perceived loudnesses, simply by rearranging the strengths of the partials.

According to the calculation described above, tone R is $72/54 = 1.33$ times as loud as tone Q. Figure 13.5 tells us that a similar increase in loudness could have been achieved by having 2.6 players sounding their *mezzo-forte* tones in the same room. A piece of arithmetic based on the fact that the loudness of a sound doubles if the SPL is raised 10 dB allows us to predict further that playing back tone Q with an SPL 4 dB *higher* than that of tone R should make them sound equally loud. It is this prediction that Gridley and I set out to test next.

Figure 13.9 shows the arrangement we used to play back our tape recording of tones Q and R for a test of our loudness predictions. These tones were fed from the two channels of the playback machine via a pair of attenuators to a device known as a *soft switch* that feeds the two tones in alternation, for approximately one-second intervals, to an amplifier and loudspeaker system set up in my laboratory room. The soft switch quickly and smoothly turns down the amplitude of one signal, waits an instant, and then turns up the other one. Each of these

Component	1	2	3	4	5	6	7	8	9	Total
Tone Q	17	19	9	3	2	2	2	0.3	—	54.3 sones
Tone R	12	22	11	6	7	5	3.5	3	2.5	72.0 sones

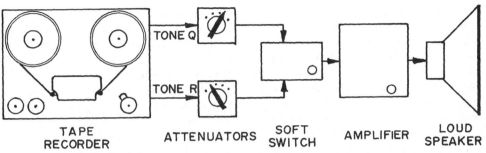

TAPE RECORDER   ATTENUATORS   SOFT SWITCH   AMPLIFIER   LOUD SPEAKER

TONE Q

TONE R

Fig. 13.9.

amplitude changes takes place over a period of 25 or 30 milliseconds, thus preventing electrical clicks and room echoes from confusing the listener's loudness judgments. While listening to the alternating sequence of tones Q and R, our listener could play with the two attenuators, adjusting them until the two signals sounded equally loud to him. People who tried our loudness balancing experiments on the before-and-after saxophone tape with one ear stopped up or with the head held in a fixed position found the task quite difficult, and many of them gave quite variable responses under these conditions. The problem was compounded if they were forced to use earphones. If on the other hand they could sway or move around in the room a little, our subjects found their task relatively easy. While there were small differences in the settings made by different people, they all preferred settings which gave about 4 dB difference between the SPLs measured for the two tones at the position of the listener's ear, in agreement with the prediction of our calculation.

It is possible to squeeze a little more information from the results of this saxophone experiment. The player was instructed to sound his instrument at a *mezzo-forte* level in making both tone Q

and tone R. In other words, he was asked, in musical terms, to make equally loud sounds. When I went back to measure the signal levels actually recorded on the original tape, tone Q had an SPL that was somewhat more than 2 dB above that belonging to tone R. In other words, the increased efficacy of tone R at the player's ears led him to generate it on a smaller scale of sound pressure; the player governs the vigor of his blowing and therefore the loudness of the sounds he generates at least in part on the basis of direct acoustical messages arriving at his ears.

13.8. The Sound Level Meter

An increasingly familiar instrument today as we become more concerned about the control of noise in the environment is the *sound level meter,* a compact device having an acoustical function somewhat analogous to that of the light meter used by photographers. It is from the dial readings of the sound level meter, expressed in decibels, that the general public has come to consider the word decibel to represent a measure of loudness. Let us see in fact what the instrument is, and what its readings mean.[6]

In the 1930s, when the sound level

meter first began its development, it was hoped that if a microphone connected via a special amplifier to an electrical meter were given the same variation of *sensitivity* with frequency as is characteristic of the ear, the net sound pressure readings displayed on the meter would be a good measure of the perceived loudness of the sound. While the original hope was not fulfilled, instruments designed in accordance with this plan have nevertheless proved to be very useful, and it is worthwhile to review the thinking of its originators.

Already in the thirties it was known that, at low sound levels, not only do our ears fail to hear very low- and very high-frequency sound components (see fig. 13.3), but also the loudness of the still-audible components near the limits of hearing are reduced in comparison with those in the 500-to-4000-Hz frequency range. On the basis of this information, it was (very plausibly) presumed that these ill-heard components would contribute little to the net loudness, and should therefore be prevented from having much influence on the electrical device's meter reading. In line with this thinking, the instrument had built into it an electrical circuit having a rolloff in its low-frequency response such as to reduce the transmission of 100-Hz components to 10 percent of their original amplitudes (20 dB attenuation). The reduction at 200 Hz is to 28 percent of the original amplitude. From 500 Hz to about 2000 Hz the response is reasonably uniform; at 5000 Hz, there is a reduction to 70 percent. This particular sort of circuit was intended to approximate the behavior of the ear for sounds having sound pressure levels near 40 dB. The indicating meter itself was designed to give a measure of

the net sound pressure of all the sound components reaching it through the response-adjustment circuit (weighting network), this net sound pressure being electrically arranged to agree with calculations like those described at the end of section 13.2. For reasons chiefly connected with the electrical engineering convenience of its designers, the meter was calibrated to indicate in decibels the SPL of the modified net sound pressure.

To identify the readings made with an instrument arranged as described above, a meter reading of 47 is commonly said to show a "sound level of 47 dB-A," or an "A-weighted sound level of 47 dB" ("sound level" is often abbreviated SL). In either case the letter A identifies the transmission characteristics of the particular network that has been described.

Continuing our study of the design of a sound level meter, we find that two additional weighting networks are usually provided. The B-weighted circuit attenuates the 100-Hz components to about 56 percent (5 dB reduction) as compared with 1000-Hz components. The high-frequency components are treated in almost exactly the same way as in the A-weighting circuit. This B-weighting was intended to approximate the hearing characteristics of our ears for sound components having SPLs in the region of 70 dB. The C-weighting circuit has almost uniform transmission of low-frequency sound components (no attenuation) and provides slightly less attenuation for high frequencies than is the case for the other two networks. The intention here was to represent our hearing for SPLs close to 100 dB.

From what has gone on earlier in this chapter, you may already have realized why a sound level meter tested on a variety of real sounds is not able to give a true measure of loudness. For one thing, it has no way to take care of masking, or of beats. Even if the weighting networks of a sound level meter reading *were* able to take proper account of the way in which various sound components interact to determine the loudness of a sound, the use of a decibel scale on the meter itself causes trouble. Equal increases in decibel readings *do not at all* produce equal increases in perceived loudness, even for single-component sounds. Figure 13.10 illustrates this fact by presenting the actual relation between the perceived loudnesses (expressed in sones) and the SPLs that give rise to them, at 125 Hz and at 4000 Hz. The data for this curve are contained in figure 13.4, as you can verify by

reading upward along vertical lines at the two frequencies. In the simplest of worlds, then, to get a numerical measure of loudness, one would take the decibel readings of a sound level meter and then use curves such as those in figure 13.4 to convert these numbers into sones. This does in fact work pretty well in the case of single sinusoids or their equivalent noise-partials.

By now you will be wondering why the sound level meter has come into common use, despite its limitations as a measurer of loudness. In crudest terms we recognize that sounds having a large sound level reading on the meter will in general also sound loud to our ears. Also, sounds having SLs of above about 120 dB will tend to be painful.

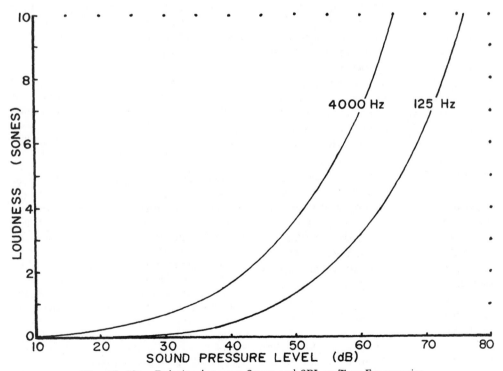

Fig. 13.10.   Relation between Sones and SPL at Two Frequencies

At a more sophisticated level, we learn that many industrial and other environmental sounds and also *averaged* speech are made up of thousands of randomly arranged sinusoidal partials whose measured amplitudes do not vary abruptly as we shift our wave analyzer from one frequency setting to a nearby one. For *broad-band continuous-spectrum* sounds of this sort, a sound level meter can be used to get reasonably sensible results as a loudness measuring device if the differently weighted readings are used in conjunction with curves similar to those in figure 13.10. Furthermore, comparison of the A-, B-, and C-weighted sound levels can tell the experienced user a great deal about the strengths of the low-frequency (well below 1000 Hz) components of a sound as they compare with the amplitudes of the components lying above 1000 Hz. For example, as I read aloud and compare the different SLs produced by my voice with the A, B, and C settings of the meter, it turns out that the B-weighted sound level is about 4 dB below the C-weighted level, while the A-weighted level is nearly 8 dB lower still. This is consistent with the fact that (when averaged over a long series of words) my voice sounds are constructed out of harmonics of a fundamental that is roughly 100 Hz. The first 8 of these harmonics have about equal amplitude, and the higher components fade away (on the average) in a smooth manner (9 dB per octave) that gives the 16th harmonic a pressure amplitude of about 35 percent of the low-frequency components, while the 32nd harmonic is down to 12.6 percent in amplitude.

For many legal purposes, such as defining the tolerable noisiness of truck engines (or a neighbor's air conditioner), careful studies are made by experts using *both* sound level meters and the most elaborate analysis equipment that is available. Since truck engines all make pretty much the same *kind* of noise, it then becomes possible to tell the policeman what combinations of readings from the simple meter correspond to unacceptable levels of real noisiness.

We can learn to estimate SL readings by ear, simply by practice with a sound level meter, in very much the way that a carpenter learns to estimate the sizes of his boards, or a photographer to decide on a suitable exposure setting. Curiously enough, it is very much easier to learn SL estimations for broad-band noise sounds than it is for sounds made up of a few sinusoidal partials. It is also easier (at all sound levels) to estimate A-weighted readings than the other two types. To give you a basis for estimating, here are a few typical readings.

(a) As I sit here at home in the suburbs with the windows open on a summer day, the A-weighted SL is a little over 30 dB, while the B- and C-weighted levels are both about 10 dB higher. When a not particularly quiet refrigerator starts up in the next room, all levels go up about 10 dB.

(b) Quiet conversation at arm's length is carried out at a level of about 60 dB-A; the relation of the corresponding B-weighted and C-weighted levels is similar to that described earlier in connection with the measurements for reading aloud.

(c) Chamber music in a small auditorium averages out to have an A-weighted SL of 75 to 85 dB at the listener's ears, although the fluctuation in level during performance may be considerable. The players themselves generally operate in a region of much higher sound level. The violin is particularly prone to produce large sound levels at its player's left ear, while the flute player's right ear can be similarly assaulted as it is provided with sound levels of 90 to 100 dB-A. A good piccolo strongly played can easily exceed its player's pain threshold.

(d) The noise of a large truck starting up produces about 80 dB-A at curbside. A very different distribution of sound components gives rise to a similar level next to a crowded outdoor swimming pool, where the chief contributors to the measured sound level turn out to be teen-age boys!

(e) A jet airplane flying low overhead can give rise to a 120-dB-A sound level on the ground.

(f) The dial tone of a telephone produces a sound level a little above 80 dB-A when the receiver is pressed closely to your ear.

13.9. Examples, Experiments, and Questions

Many of the phenomena described in this chapter can be observed today with the help of very simple equipment. For example, oscillators can be fed in various ways to the two channels of an ordinary stereo hi-fi system to provide sound sources in the listening room. A thoughtfully used sound level meter can be employed to provide sound pressure data. The simpler "stops" of most electronic organs can also be put to good use, since these produce sounds made up of relatively few harmonically related partials, and these sounds are available over a wide range of fundamental frequencies. If you plan to experiment with more than one organ note at the same time, however, you should restrict your combinations to unisons, fifths, octaves, and perhaps twelfths. The old rotating-disc type of Hammond organ is *not* suitable for experiments at this stage, nor are any of the ordinary woodwind, brass, string, or keyboard instruments. These have various acoustical complexities that might obscure the phenomena we are currently pursuing.

You can also use some of the following paper-and-pencil experiments to sharpen up or test your comprehension of the ideas sketched out in this chapter.

1. Imagine that, while you are listening in an ordinary room, your ears are supplied with a tone whose partials have the following harmonically related frequencies: 62.5, 125, 187.5, 250, and 312.5 Hz. Each of these partials has a pressure amplitude corresponding to an SPL somewhat less than 20 dB. (a) Use figure 13.3 to help you decide on the audibility of each of these partials taken by itself. (b) Look back to the discussion of how we assign pitch to a collection of harmonically related sounds (see secs. 5.6 and 5.7), and then make use of figure 2.1 to work out the note name we would give to this very soft sound.

2. Suppose the SPLs of each of the components of the sound described in question 1 were raised to 75 dB. Make an estimate of the total loudness of such a sound by finding S_{tsp}, expressed in sones (you will need to make use of fig. 13.4).

3. Verify from the curves of figure 13.10 that while equal increases in the decibel level do not produce equal steps of increasing loudness, it is true that the loudness very nearly doubles whenever the SPL is increased by 10 dB, as was pointed out in section 13.4.

4. Assume that you are supplied with a roomful of sound made up of two sinusoidal partials whose frequencies are 250 and 500 Hz (an octave apart). Consider two versions of this sound: the first gives the components equal amplitudes and SPLs of 80 dB; in the second version, the

lower component has an SPL of 82.4 dB, that of the higher one being 74 dB. The SPL of the total signal in both versions is the same—83 dB. You will find that the loudness of version 1 is greater than that of version 2. See if you can understand why, on the basis of the summarizing information contained in figure 13.10. Would it change things if the two components had their amplitudes reversed?

5. Mathematically inclined readers may wish to know how the loudness of a single sinusoid (or the corresponding narrow-band noise-partial) is related to its pressure amplitude. For a signal whose pressure amplitude p is more than 100 times (40 dB above) the threshold value p_{thr} for that frequency (see fig. 13.3), the loudness S in sones is quite accurately given by the following formula:

$$S = (p/100 \, p_{thr})^{0.6}$$

This relation does not however hold for fainter sounds. For example, in the immediate neighborhood of threshold the formula becomes:

$$S = (p/22 \, p_{thr})^2$$

As one goes up in sound pressure from threshold, the 22 in the denominator grows smoothly toward 100, and the exponent 2 shrinks to its eventual value of 0.6 that applies for all sound pressures that are more than 40 dB above threshold. The mathematical form of these relations between a sensation and its physical stimulus is typical of many aspects of our sensory activities.

6. In the mid-1800s Gustav Fechner followed up a proposal by E. H. Weber in asserting that any sensation (e.g., loudness) evoked by a stimulus increases by a constant amount whenever the stim-ulus is increased by a constant factor. Despite the fact that the hypothesis is not supported by experiment, it has exerted an enormous intellectual attraction for philosophically inclined scientists, to the point that one often hears of the "Weber-Fechner Law." [7] You might verify that this "law" implies that the loudness variation obeys the formula:

$$S = \text{a constant} \times \log (p/p_{thr})$$
$$= \text{another constant} \times (\text{SPL-SPL}_{thr})$$

This is an expression that is entirely incompatible with the formulas given above in question 5.

7. A tone made up of 8 exactly harmonic partials has a fundamental frequency near 250 Hz. For simplicity we will assume that all the components are of equal strength, having individual SPLs of 80 dB. Suppose now that this tone is played with a vibrato, so that the frequencies of components rise and fall together with a repetition rate of a few times per second. (a) Verify that if the amplitude of this fluctuation is 2 percent, the first partial is "visiting" a frequency region that extends 5 Hz above and below 250 Hz, the fourth partial covers a range of 20 Hz on each side of 1000 Hz, and the 8th partial oscillates over a region that extends 40 Hz on either side of 2000 Hz. (b) Figure out informally why the loudness of this sound might well be increased for a listener in a concert hall as a result of the vibrato. As a help in this, look at the vibrato-caused *fluctuations* in loudness of at least the 1st, 4th, and 8th partials, as implied by the 80-dB curve in figure 13.4. Don't forget also to keep in mind that due to room acoustics there are random fluctuations of signal amplitude produced at all the component frequencies.

Notes

1. These International Standards are interesting reading. They can be obtained from: International Organization for Standardization, 1 Rue de Narembé, Geneva, Switzerland. A brief but clear introduction to the subject of loudness estimation is to be found in sections I through IV of the Hewlett-Packard *Acoustics Handbook* (Palo Alto, Calif.: Hewlett-Packard Company, 1968). See also chapter IV, "What Do We Hear?" in the charming paperback book, *Waves and the Ear*, by Willem A. van Bergeijk, John R. Pierce, and Edward E. David, Jr. (Garden City: Doubleday Anchor Books, 1960).

2. S. S. Stevens, *Psychophysics: Introduction to Its Perceptual, Neural, and Social Prospects*, ed. Geraldine Stevens (New York: Wiley, 1975). In Stevens's book such experiments and similar ones having to do with human response to many other sensory inputs are clearly described by the man who did the most to develop them.

3. The information consolidated in figure 13.4 is more usually presented piecemeal. See, for example, the Hewlett-Packard *Acoustics Handbook*, figures 1 and 2, plus the table in Appendix A; or van Bergeijk, Pierce, and David, *Waves and the Ear*, figures 4.2 and 4.3.

4. Jerry V. Tobias, ed., *Foundations of Modern Auditory Theory*, 2 vols. (New York: Academic Press, 1970); see volume 1, chapter 3, "Masking," by Lloyd A. Jeffress, and chapter 5, "Critical Bands," by Bertram Scharf. See also Arnold M. Small, Jr., "Pure-Tone Masking," *J. Acoust. Soc. Am.* 31 (1959): 1619–25.

5. While the subject has developed considerably in the past two decades, two basic papers on the calculation of loudness of complex sounds are still worth reading. They are: E. Zwicker and R. Feldtkeller, "Über die Lautstärke von gleichförmigen Geräuschen," *Acustica* 5 (1955): 303–16; and S. S. Stevens, "Calculation of the Loudness of Complex Noise," *J. Acoust. Soc. Am.* 28 (1956): 807–31.

6. Leo L. Beranek, *Acoustic Measurements* (New York: Wiley, 1949); see chapter 20, "The Sound Level Meter." Section V of the Hewlett-Packard *Acoustics Handbook* gives a good description of a number of sound level meters and discusses loudness meters as well.

7. A brief but crystal clear outline of the origin and nature of Fechner's ideas and of the developments which follow them is to be found in Bertram Scharf, "Laws That Govern Behavior" (review of *Psychophysics* by S. S. Stevens), *Science* 188 (23 May 1975): 827–29.

14

The Acoustical Phenomena Governing the Musical Relationships of Pitch

In chapter 13 we met the phenomenon of beats which can occur between two sinusoidal components. It does not take very much imagination or experience to realize that a musician can use the beat phenomenon as a guide in the adjustment of the frequency of one source to that of another. For example, an oboist who wishes to check the accuracy of the A_4 which he will give to the orchestra can strike a tuning fork and play his tuning A with it to make sure that the fundamental component of his tone matches the 440-Hz sinusoid generated by the fork. If he is playing accurately in tune, the two signals will not beat together. If he is either a little sharp or a little flat, beats will be heard, and he simply makes frequency adjustments to reduce the beat frequency until it disappears. We have already learned that our ears are particularly well-fitted to detect beats when they are heard in a room, since in such surroundings the amplitude fluctuations of the two sounds are bound to make them equal for at least part of the time, thereby producing the most prominent sort of loudness variation.

In the next-to-last paragraph of section 13.6 it was mentioned in passing that there are certain additional frequency relations (other than near equality between the sinusoids) that can sometimes give rise to audible beats. We need to provide ourselves with some knowledge of the frequencies at which these additional, and perhaps unexpected, beats are located, and should also learn of the general way in which a mechanical system can give rise to them.[1] Not only will this complete the formal system of information we need to understand the principles governing musical pitch relationships, but it will further provide us with an eventual entryway into an understanding of how the wind instruments and the members of the violin family go about producing their sustained tones.

14.1. Heterodyne Components: Their Detection and Frequency Relationships

A very simple experiment will help us begin the formal search for the extra beat frequencies touched on in section 13.6. A reasonably strong, one-component (i.e., sinusoidal) signal at a frequency of (for example) 400 Hz is supplied to a single, high-quality earphone mounted on a listener's head. The other ear is blocked off or (better) supplied with a steady, broadband noise signal of sufficient magnitude to mask any stray sounds that may be leaked to it. In addition to the strong, fixed-frequency signal that is fed to the main earphone, we also provide it with a much weaker sinusoid whose frequency and amplitude are both adjustable. For reasons which will become apparent in a moment, this weaker, adjustable sound is usually called the *search tone*.

A preliminary scan, carried out as the frequency of the search tone is varied from 400 Hz on up, shows signs of the beat phenomenon in the immediate neighborhoods of 400, 800, 1200, . . . Hz. In other words, beats are found at frequencies that are harmonics of the main excitation frequency. We have clear evidence, then, that new, harmonically related frequency components have somehow been created from the original single-component excitation, and that these new components have been called to our attention by their beatings with the search tone.

In section 13.6 we learned that beats have maximum prominence when the amplitudes of the two components are equal, which permits the loudness of the combined sound to drop all the way to zero once during each cycle of the beat. This fact suggests that if we adjust the amplitude of our search tone to maximize the prominence of the beating it makes with one of the new components, then the amplitude of the search tone will be exactly equal to the amplitude of the unknown signal. Such adjustments prove to be easily attained, and the resulting amplitude measurements are reproducible and well-defined.

Digression on a Refinement of the Search-Tone Technique.

Julius Goldstein, while at M.I.T. and the Harvard Psychoacoustics Laboratory, developed an interesting variant of the search-tone technique for measuring amplitude. He uses a search tone whose frequency is exactly equal to that of the main signal, and then adjusts its phase (slides it over in time) to where its pressure variations act in a direction to counteract those "belonging" to the component under study. All that remains then is to adjust the search-tone amplitude so that continuous silence results at the search-tone frequency.

Amplitude measurements of the extra components of the sort we are dealing with here have been made for many years using variants of the search-tone technique. Let us provide ourselves with a few of the numbers Goldstein found from his careful measurements that tell how the amplitudes of these extra components vary.[2] If the SPL associated with the main (400-Hz) component is 95 dB within the earphone, the 800-, 1200-, and 1600-Hz components will have amplitudes that are approximately equal to each other; for cancellation, the search tone amplitude must in all three cases be at an SPL of 75 dB. In other words the newly created sounds are cancelled by means of a search tone whose pressure amplitude is 10 percent of the main signal. When the main tone has its amplitude reduced to 1/2 of its original value (to 89 dB SPL), the 800-Hz second-harmonic search tone must be reduced fourfold (to an SPL of 63 dB) to produce cancellation, and similar measurement reveals that the 1200-Hz and 1600-Hz components are now down to 1/8th and 1/16th of their original values (to SPLs of 57 and 51 dB). If our main tone is supplied at the musically more relevant but still fairly high SPL of

75 dB, we find that the harmonics are cancelled by SPLs of about 55, 35, and 15 dB. For most purposes it turns out that, at sound levels of 75 dB and lower, we can ignore all but the second harmonic contribution, the others being so weak (close to the threshold of hearing) as to play only the most feeble role in what we hear musically.

By now you will be wondering where these extra components come from. Use of a probe microphone and wave analyzer to study the sounds actually produced by the earphone show (if the earphone is a really good one) no sign of the mysterious components. However, if we use surgical techniques to probe within the fleshy parts of the middle and inner ear, evidence of the extra vibration components is readily found, although their amplitudes do not vary with the strength of ex-

Suppose we supply our earphone with not one but two strong sinusoidal components, and then repeat our search-tone survey to discover what new components have made their appearance. Let us use the letters P and Q to stand for the frequencies of the two externally supplied sinusoids. If P is applied by itself, we have already learned to expect the presence of additional components having the harmonic frequencies 2P, 3P, and 4P, so that the complete list of components present in the ear is: P, (2P), (3P), (4P), . . . I have put parentheses around the new components to distinguish them symbolically from their externally applied ancestor P. When P and Q are sounded together, our list of what we will call *heterodyne components* can be arranged together with their ancestors in a tabular schema as follows:

Original Components	Simplest Heterodyne Components	Next-Appearing Heterodyne Components
P	(2P)	(3P)
		(2P + Q), (2P − Q)
	(P + Q), (P − Q)	
		(2Q + P), (2Q − P)
Q	(2Q)	(3Q)

citation in exactly the way implied by the search tone measurements. Deeper probings, using electrical instruments to detect the actual impulses sent to the brain by the auditory nerves, confirm that the hearing mechanism itself is creating new components. Furthermore, we learn that both the mechanical and the neurological parts of our ears take part in this creative process. The basic physics that leads to these creative processes will be outlined in section 14.2. Meanwhile we will continue with our exploration of the phenomena they give rise to.

In the first column, we find the two components P and Q which make up the original sound. In the second column we find the expected double-frequency heterodyne components (2P) and (2Q); in addition one can usually discover two more heterodyne components having frequencies that equal the sum (P + Q) and the difference (P − Q) of the original signals. In the third column we find (3P) and (3Q), as expected, along with a set of four heterodyne signals that are the result of what we might facetiously call the interbreeding of P and Q.

Notice that all the heterodyne components in the middle column have frequencies that are constructed out of sums and differences of *any two* objects (or their duplicates) taken from column one. Similarly you will notice that the third column is inhabited by creatures resulting from the joining of *three* items (or their duplicates) from column one. Another way to say this is to point out that the third column can be put together arithmetically by combining a frequency from the second column with one from the first. We could continue these numerical games indefinitely; for example, the objects in a fourth column would be made by combining (by addition and subtraction) frequencies from column one with those in column three.[3] For musical purposes involving our ears, it turns out that the second column provides us with almost everything of interest, while the third column makes its appearance only rarely. Beyond this, the auditory effects are musically negligible.

Digression on Negative Frequencies.

The statement that one of the heterodyne components we should expect has a frequency $(P - Q)$ seems straightforward enough if P happens to be 276 Hz and Q is 192 Hz, so that $(P - Q)$ gives us $(276 - 192) = (84)$ Hz. What, on the other hand, would we get if P is 276 Hz, as before, and Q is 320 Hz? $(P - Q)$ then becomes $(276 - 320) = (-44)$ Hz. The fact that the difference comes out negative is not relevant to our purposes in this book. It is the magnitude of the frequency difference that matters to us here, so we can drop the minus sign. This does not mean the minus sign can always be ignored. You might wish to consider the following brief example of negative frequencies having distinct physical meaning. Imagine a crank-driven pendulum of the sort that was shown in figure 10.1. As the crank rotates, *the pendulum is driven at a frequency equal to the rotation rate. If the drive crank is made to revolve in the opposite direction (e.g., clockwise instead of counterclockwise) the pendulum is being driven at a negative frequency.*

What we have called heterodyne frequencies are sometimes referred to as combination tones, summation or difference tones, subjective tones, intermodulation components, and occasionally even beat tones. I have avoided these names for several reasons and adopted a rather unfamiliar (though technically exact) engineering name. One reason for this choice is that I wish to restrict our usage of the word *tone* to sounds made up of a set of exactly harmonic partials—we need such a term because of the way our hearing machinery groups such partials into a single auditory whole (see secs. 5.2 and 5.6). The heterodyne phenomenon has to do with the generation of new partials; whether these combine with other things to produce a perceived musical tone as defined above is a separate question. Another reason for choosing the engineer's word *heterodyne* is that we will have occasion to meet examples of the same basic physics in situations outside of the human ear, making it advisable to avoid confusions that might otherwise arise between mechanical phenomena and their perceived correlates.

A very simple example of the way in which the existence of heterodyne components can influence the musical responses of our ears follows. Suppose we listen to a sound made up of two partials whose frequencies are 400 and 600 Hz. The simplest heterodyne components that have the 400-Hz partial for one of their parents are the following:

(400 + 400) = (800) Hz; also (400 ± 600) = (1000) Hz and (200) Hz. Similarly, the only heterodyne offspring of the 600-Hz partial not already listed is (600 + 600) = (1200) Hz. Let us now list all of the components present in the ear in order of increasing frequency:

(200), 400, 600, (800), (1000), (1200) Hz

Out of a pair of original components, our ears have constructed the first six members of a complete harmonic series! It does not matter particularly how strong these various components are, or whether all of them are simultaneously present in the ears of a listener as he moves about in a room. His auditory system will recognize the frequency relationships in this sequence of components and will perceive them in aggregate as a sound whose pitch belongs with the 200-Hz fundamental frequency. (We have here an example of one way in which our hearing mechanism sets about playing pitch-assignment games to discover the hidden tune described in experiment 2 of section 5.9.) Before we go on to a study of the mechanical influences that give rise to heterodyne components, we should set down in order a group of assertions summarizing and slightly extending the knowledge of heterodyne components that we have acquired so far in the chapter:

1. The ear shares with various other systems the ability to generate within itself new heterodyne components in response to externally supplied signals.
2. Out of a very large class of *possible* heterodyne frequencies within the ear, we shall (for simplicity) generally confine our attention to those which are equal to the sums and differences between the applied signal frequencies, including doublings. Not all of these

will be separately audible without help from a search tone.
3. The amplitudes of the heterodyne components depend on the amplitudes of the original input signals. As a rule, strong original components give rise to strong heterodyne descendants, but some heterodynes (particularly those associated with neurological effects) do not disappear rapidly as the stimuli are reduced.
4. Heterodyne components with frequencies below about 20 Hz are inaudible, for very much the same reasons that make externally supplied sounds inaudible when their frequencies are low.

There is a fifth assertion to be made which is almost self-explanatory in the light of what we already know. I will follow this additional assertion with a specific example to illustrate its meaning.

5. If two heterodyne components happen to be close together in frequency, they themselves can beat in exactly the way that was described in section 13.6. It is also sometimes possible for a heterodyne component to beat with a nearby ordinary component that is supplied from outside the ear.

Suppose we have a stimulus made up of three sinusoidal components, P, Q, and R, which have frequencies of 200, 396, and 605 Hz. Heterodyne components (Q − P) = (196) Hz and (R − Q) = (209) Hz are close enough together to beat, the rate of beating being 13 Hz. Similarly (Q − P) is able to beat with P itself at a 4-Hz rate. There are several other possibilities for beats in this collection, which you may wish to work out. Notice that this example is exactly the one used to introduce the existence of the unexpected beats that were first described near the end of section 13.6.

14.2. Mechanical Origins of the Heterodyne Components

Heterodyne components are often produced as part of the response of a mechanical system driven by oscillatory forces. The reasons for this creative process are not too difficult to grasp if we make use of a suitably chosen mechanical model. A long steel bar clamped at one end in a vise and then plucked will vibrate predominantly in its lowest-frequency mode of oscillation (discussed in chap. 6; see also the first 3 examples in sec. 4.9). If we could somehow attach a pen to the vibrating tip of the bar, it would trace out a wavy, accurately sinusoidal curve on a piece of strip chart paper pulled steadily past it.

If instead of clamping the bar in an ordinary vise, we fasten it in the manner shown by the top part of figure 14.1, the vibration will no longer be sinusoidal under all conditions. If the bar is plucked very gently so that it is given only a small amplitude of oscillation, it will move sinusoidally and act as though the vibration length extends from the bar's tip back to the point marked A, where it touches the mounting. Plucking the bar more vigorously gives rise to a different motion: during the upward part of its swing, the bar moves away from the point A and swings farther than otherwise before com-

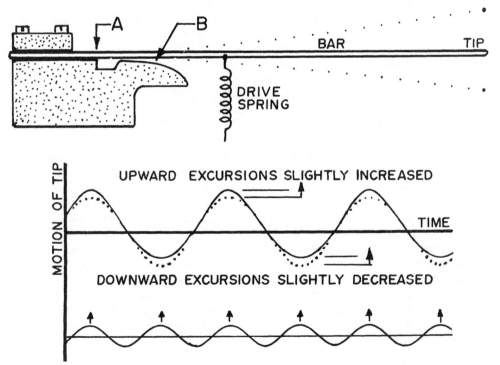

Fig. 14.1. A Vibrator Whose Motion Is Not Quite Sinusoidal

ing to rest because the moving part is now longer and therefore less stiff; during the downward swing, the bar moves "normally" at first, and then begins to roll down firmly against the curving ramp B. Because of this ramp, the moving part of the bar is progressively shortened, and therefore stiffened. As a result its tip fails to come down quite as far at the limit of its motion as it would if the clamping were of a more normal type. Overall, then, the peculiarly clamped bar departs from sinusoidal motion by swinging upward a little farther than normal, and by swinging downward a little less far. The exact details of the alteration depend of course on the proportions and shape of the clamp. The middle part of figure 14.1 compares the sinusoidal vibration expected from a normally clamped bar with the motion of our modified one.

The motion of our oddly clamped bar is clearly repetitive, and we have been at some pains to notice that it is not sinusoidal. We learned in section 5.5 that a nonsinusoidal but repetitive motion is made up of a set of *harmonically* related components whose amplitudes are such as to make them add up to give the observed overall motion. When taken together the lower two parts of figure 14.1 show that a double-frequency sinusoid can combine with the fundamental frequency sinusoid to produce a *wave form* (chart recorder trace) that is peaked at the tops and flattened at the bottoms of the up-and-down oscillations, in general agreement with the way our bar is observed to move. To summarize: our bar, whose clamping arrangements make its stiffness vary from one part to another of the oscillation, has a first mode characteristic oscillation that is not sinusoidal. The vibration is made up of a fundamental

frequency component plus a set of harmonics. The same remark applies to any one of the higher modes as well, if we set that mode into motion *by itself*.

Suppose we now arrange to excite the bar sinusoidally by driving it from a rotating crank via a long spring or rubber band (see figs. 10.1 and 10.10 for earlier examples of such a driving system). Let us assume that the first mode characteristic frequency of the bar is 20 Hz; this puts mode 2 above 120 Hz, far enough away that we can ignore its influence in what follows.

When the drive motor is running slowly so that it applies a sinusoidal driving force to the bar at a frequency well below the 20-Hz natural frequency, the steady-state driven motion will be of relatively small amplitude (see sec. 10.3 and 10.6). However, if (in our machine) this amplitude happens to be sufficient to lift the bar off of the step at A on its upward swing, and to roll it down on the ramp at B during the downward swing, then the driven motion will not be sinusoidal. Harmonics of the driving frequency will be detectable in the oscillation.

Figure 14.2 shows the resonance curve obtained by measuring the overall amplitude of the (generally nonsinusoidal) oscillation of our bar when it is driven at various frequencies. The tall response peak corresponding to an excitation frequency of 20 Hz is completely expected; the bar is responding strongly to excitation near its natural frequency. The little response peaks at 6.67 (= 20/3) Hz and at 10 (= 20/2) Hz show something new. As the driving frequency is slowly raised, these humps show that the bar is able to respond fairly strongly to the third and then to the second harmonic heterodyne components arising from the

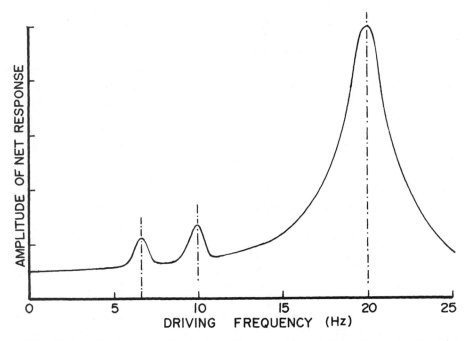

Fig. 14.2. The Response Curve of the Nonsinusoidal Oscillator Shown in Fig. 14.1

driving frequency! If we were to watch the motion of the bar when it is driven at frequencies somewhat above or below 6.67 Hz, the motion would be predominantly sinusoidal at this driving frequency, with only a small admixture of higher harmonics being manifest. At exactly 6.67 Hz, however, the oscillation would look quite peculiar—the predominant component in the vibration recipe would be the 20-Hz third harmonic of the driving frequency. In other words we would find the bar vibrating strongly at a frequency that is different from the driving frequency! Similar behavior would be observed for excitation in the neighborhood of 10 Hz, where the bar is swinging predominantly in response to

the self-generated second harmonic of the driving frequency.

By now it will not be difficult for you to predict what will happen to the response of the bar if it is driven simultaneously by two springs attached to driving cranks running at different frequencies. If we call the two driving frequencies P and Q, then the list of excitation frequency components acting on the bar includes (among others) the heterodyne components listed in the schema given earlier in this section. The bar will respond strongly and in step with any one of the heterodyne components that happens to be close to its own 20-Hz natural frequency. If, for example, P has a frequency of 9 Hz and Q is about 30 Hz,

the (P − Q) heterodyne component is at
21 Hz and so will give a strong excitation
to the bar. In similar fashion, if P = 7 Hz
and Q = 11 Hz, the (P + Q) heterodyne
will set up a fairly large 18-Hz steady-
state vibration in the bar. We have already met the possibility of strong response to the 2P or 2Q heterodyne components as well.

We are now in a position to pull
together and elaborate our various mechanical and acoustical observations on
the heterodyne phenomenon. For one
thing, we might notice that heterodyne
effects did not call attention to themselves mechanically until we made some
alterations to the spring behavior of the
vibrating bar. Let us look a little more
closely at this behavior, making use of an
apparatus of the sort shown in the upper
part of figure 14.3. If one adds weights in
succession to the upper pan in the manner
illustrated, the bar will be deflected upwards to successive positions of equilibrium. If the same weights are hung directly on the bar, as shown by the dotted
lines, the bar will be deflected downward.
The lower part of figure 14.3 shows how
the upward and downward deflections of
the bar depend on the number of weights
applied. For a bar that is normally
clamped, the deflections are shown by the
solid dots, and for one mounted as shown
in figure 14.1, by open circles. Notice
that for the normal bar, successive additions or removals of equal weights produce equal *changes* in deflection, as indicated by the double-headed arrows
marked A in the diagram. (This is just
what we learned to expect in section 6.1
for a spring capable of producing sinusoidal motion.)

The modified bar shows a different behavior. The deflections produced by add-

ing a single weight on either pan are essentially the same as for the normal bar.
However, the deflection (marked B on the
diagram) produced by adding the fifth
weight on the upper pan is considerably
larger than the corresponding deflection
for the normal bar (marked A). On the
other hand the modified clamping leads
to a reduction in the deflection associated
with the addition of a further weight to
the lower pan. Overall we find that a normally clamped bar shows deflections that
are exactly proportional to the applied
load and that the line drawn through the
various experimental points is *perfectly
straight*. For the peculiarly clamped bar,
the deflections depend on the load in a
more complicated way (whose causes are
obvious to us here), so that the curve of
deflection-versus-force is not a straight
line. This *nonlinearity* in the graphical relation between stimulus and response is
the general property we are seeking for an
explanation of the heterodyne phenomenon. Let us summarize what we have
learned in this section in a set of numbered statements:

1. A nonlinear (nonproportional) relationship between a stimulus and its corresponding response implies that the net response of the system to several stimuli is not
the sum of the responses as measured separately. In a non-linear system the whole response is not simply the sum of its parts.

2. When a nonlinear system is subjected to
sinusoidal forces, heterodyne components are
generated. (This is a special way to say what
appears in statement 1.) The frequency relations of these heterodyne components are
always those described in the schema given
earlier, *regardless of the nature of the nonlinearity*
(neurological or mechanical).

3. The amplitudes of the heterodyne components generated by a nonlinear system depend on the details of the nonlinearity and (in

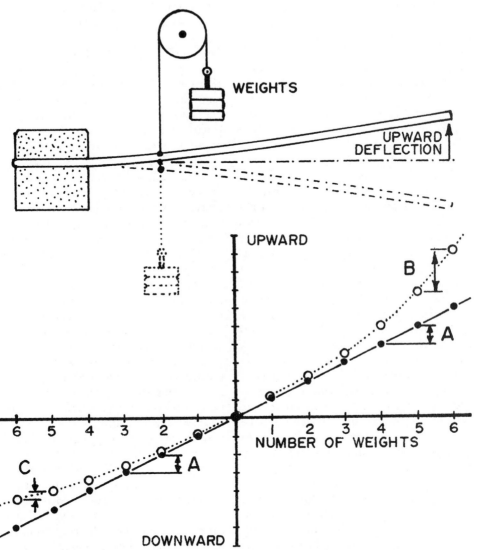

Fig. 14.3. Apparatus to Study the Nonlinear Behavior of a Spring

general) on the amplitudes of the excitatory forces.

Notice that everything we studied through chapter 12 was predicated on the assumption of linearity in the relation between the stiffness forces acting in our vibrating systems and the deflections of their various parts. The very existence of characteristic modes of vibration and the possibility of superposing freely chosen amounts of them to make up a desired vibration recipe depend on the linearity of the system. If the various springs belonging to a vibrating system are almost linear in their force-versus-deflection characteristics, the system *usually* behaves very much like a linear one; one does, however, meet exceptions upon occasion. The mathematics and physics of almost-linear systems built up of many springs and masses have unfortunately been given very little study to date, although they abound in curiosities and paradoxes.

As long as we confine our attention to linear (or very-nearly-linear) systems, the fact that characteristic modes of vibration exist and that each one of these possesses all the oscillation properties (no more and no less) of a *single* spring-mass system gives us enormously powerful tools for understanding many kinds of acoustical systems. The usefulness of these tools is particularly great because of our ability to build up vibration recipes by simply adding up the contributions of the various modes. One may at first feel quite frustrated to learn that the existence of nonlinear effects can destroy this whole beautiful structure. It is true that the mathematics of nonlinear systems can be enormously complicated. There are, however, methods for dealing simply and effectively with many nonlinear systems of musical interest (e.g., wind instruments). Once one learns how to do this, it proves possible to get an extremely good general idea of what is going on, without having to use much more than the basic principles outlined in assertions 1, 2, and 3 above. Of particular utility is assertion 2, which tells us that the heterodyne frequencies one gets in any given situation can always be calculated by a standard arithmetical procedure whose only drawback is its tediousness.[4]

14.3. The Musical Tone: *Special Properties of Sounds Having Harmonic Components*

Over and over in this book we have referred to sounds having a definite repetition rate. The fact that such sounds have harmonically related component frequencies gives them certain arithmetical simplicities that have attracted the attention of thinkers since the time of the ancient Greeks. We realize, of course, that mathematical simplicity in itself is almost irrelevant to the study of acoustics or of music. On the other hand, we have noticed that many musical instruments generate such sounds, which does give us a good reason to make a close study of their properties. Another reason for our interest can be found in the fact that the perceived pitch of a set of harmonically related partials remains remarkably constant when a few of these partials are eliminated. We learned of this durability very early in the book, and have just learned how the existence of heterodyne effects helps us to understand the acoustical reasons for this durability. These heterodyne effects also provide clues as to why the ear tends to group the miscellaneous partials of a bell or chime sound into groups when assigning their pitch.

In the previous section of this chapter, I made a definition: we would henceforth reserve the word *tone* to refer to sounds having harmonic partials. For emphasis, I will often refer to such sounds as *musical tones,* not with the purpose of denigrating other kinds of sound or of implying that music cannot be made from them, but rather to underline the fact that harmonically related complexes of partials have a *very special perceptual status* that happens also to make them useful in music. It is the purpose of this section to make clear the nature of this special status.

In seeking to clarify such a status, let us start out by providing a single-component sinusoidal excitation for our ears via a loudspeaker in a room. If the sound pressure is low, we will hear a soft, cooing sound whose loudness may vary as we move about. When the source amplitude is progressively raised, we perceive a louder sound, but its nature is still clearly identifiable as being made up of a single sinusoid. This identification persists despite the fact that increasing amounts of second, third, and fourth harmonics are being generated by our auditory nonlinearities. As we move around in the room, or as someone varies the strength of the originating sound source, there will be (more or less random) variations in the sound pressure signals at our ears; however, the strengths of the various heterodyne components will grow and shrink *exactly in step* with these variations in accordance with the amplitude relationships given in Goldstein's work, which was mentioned in section 14.1. Because there is an exact "tracking" of the original amplitude variations by the heterodyne amplitudes, these harmonics are merely a part of what we always process, and so they usually escape conscious notice. Most of us are not aware of these additional components until our attention is called to them by the use of a search tone or the like.

Suppose now that our sound source is modified so that it adds a small amount of second harmonic to the original sinusoid, and perhaps also a lesser amount of third harmonic. Many listeners will hardly notice the addition of these extra

components in the original signal. If they are introduced very gradually, their presence is easy to overlook because they seem so natural and familiar! You will occasionally find someone with a good sense of tone color who will tell you that the sound "appears" to be louder, even though you may have taken pains actually to *reduce* the loudness by turning down the amplifier gain in accordance with the principles outlined in section 13.6. Such a person is using indirect words to describe the fact that his processor expects to receive higher harmonics when the external sound pressure is made larger. His cautious use of the word "appears" is a sign that all is not tidy in his processor. When he moves around the room, the amplitudes of the upper partials within his ear no longer exactly track the amplitude of the fundamental. The explanation is simple—each one of these internal components is now made up of the superposition of the externally supplied signal plus the heterodyne components (these do not beat, since they are of precisely the same frequency). The ear is not forced to recognize a drastic difference between the sound of a loudly played sinusoid and that of a tone made up of harmonic partials, since *the list of frequency components is the same in both cases.*

Let us alter the circumstances of our experimentation now, to the extent of supplying *almost* harmonic instead of exactly harmonic components to our ears. Suppose we have a strong lowest partial at 256 Hz accompanied by a second partial whose frequency is 502 Hz and a third partial at 747 Hz (call these components X, Y, and Z). These three components are located more or less where the ear "expects" to have harmonics belonging to a

250-Hz sinusoid. If X, Y, and Z are of sufficient amplitude, they generate many kinds of heterodyne components. For the simplest example, $(Y - X) = (252)$ Hz, $(Z - Y) = (245)$ Hz, $(Z - X) = (497)$ Hz, and $(X + Y) = 752$ Hz. Also present in this simple version are the double-frequency components $(2X)$, $(2Y)$, etc. In the neighborhood of 250 Hz, then, the ear is provided with the following group of components: (245), 250, and (252) Hz; similarly, near 500 Hz we have (497), (500), and 502 Hz; and near 750 Hz we also find a (752)-Hz component. The presence of a sound having *almost-harmonic* components, then, provides the ear with little clumps of components whose members may or may not beat noticeably. In any event the clumps themselves have a slightly more orderly harmonicity in their center frequencies than do the original components that gave rise to them. Sounds of this quasi-harmonic sort tend to be heard very much like musical tones, although they may not seem quite so "clear" (refer back to the flute-key-snapping experiment described in sec. 5.9).

The most important conclusion to be drawn from our study so far of tones constructed of harmonic partials is that our auditory system tends to process the whole collection as a unit. Sources like the tuning fork with its widely spaced, inharmonic characteristic frequencies are on the other hand recognized as generating two separate sounds. When a violin is played, we simply notice a series of auditory units (notes), each one having a "tone color" characteristic of the instrument. The partials of each note do not normally come to our attention as individuals. When two instruments play different notes, we habitually and automatically group the interwoven sets of harmonic partials into two separate sounds, recognizing one from each instrument. Doing this does not depend upon using our hearing to localize the two instruments in different parts of the listening room. The ability to group a collection of partials into harmonic subsets is marked enough that a listener presented with inharmonic partials from a clock chime has no trouble in collecting them into two approximately harmonic groups, to each of which he assigns a pitch and each of which he identifies as a separate tone (see secs. 5.2 and 5.6).

14.4. Pitch Matching: *The Unison and Other Special Intervals*

Back in chapter 2 we chose a conventionalized set of reference sounds having precisely specified *frequencies* against which we could compare other sounds for the twin purposes of frequency measurement and of assigning pitch names to these sounds. Nothing was said then about the origin of the set of reference pitches beyond the assertion that they belong to the arrangement known to musicians as an equally tempered chromatic scale. At that time it was pointed out that sounds having a fast repetition rate are perceived as having high pitch, while slow rates are associated with low pitch. However, there was no guarantee that the sequence of mathematically determined reference frequencies would necessarily give our ears a uniformly spaced set of pitch impressions. Equal changes in frequency (a physical quantity) do not give equal changes in pitch (a perceived attribute); this should not surprise us since we met the same sort of thing in the relation between acoustic pressure amplitude and loudness. Moreover, the frequency-versus-pitch relationship of a single sinusoid can be quite different from that belonging to sounds made up of several partials. We have already looked into these matters in some detail as we studied clock chimes, bells, and guitar strings in chapter 5. Section 14.3 of this chapter also has a bearing on these matters. As we explore questions of pitch relations in more depth in this chapter, we will continue to make a distinction between tones whose harmonically related components are generally heard as a group and sounds with less orderly arrangements of components which may be heard either separately or collected into several more or less ill-fitting subgroups.

We often need to be able to say in a well-defined manner that the pitch of some unknown sound agrees with that of a reference sound that lies (say) 60 percent of the way between A_4 and $A_4\#$. The same mathematics that tells us how to divide up each octave of our reference scale into 12 semitone steps tells how each semitone step can be divided into 100 units that are usually called *cents*. For example, the pitch name G_4 belongs with a conventional repetition frequency of 392 Hz; the next step in the scale is $G_4\#$ at 415.3 Hz. Clearly the round-numbered frequency of 400 Hz is associated with a pitch intermediate between these two. Suitable calculation shows that the pitch name for 400 Hz is $G_4 + 35$ cents. In similar vein 500 Hz corresponds to $B_4 + 21$ cents, and 435 Hz corresponds to $A_4 - 20$ cents.

In section 10.4 we learned what can happen when a flute player attempts to set her playing frequency by trying to excite a tuning fork into oscillation at its own natural frequency. At the beginning of this chapter we noticed that an oboist can adjust his tuning by achieving what is called zero beat between the sound of a tuning fork and the fundamental partial of his tone. It is important for us to realize that, in all strictness, tuning procedures such as these do not actually make a match of *pitch,* but rather they produce a matching of *frequencies.* Most of the time in musical surroundings, pitch-matching and frequency-matching procedures lead to similar results, but not always. For example, the pitches of chimes and bells (secs. 5.2 and 5.3) are easily matched by a listener who alternates their sounds with sounds from a reference keyboard. There is no reason to expect the partials making up these sounds to match the partials of the reference sounds, however, and there is therefore no possibility of devising a zero-beat procedure for deducing the pitch in this case. Another illustration of the difference between pitch matching and frequency matching is found in subsection A below. The subsections that follow demonstrate the special nature of the unison, the octave, and other intervals whose musical importance we will continue to examine from time to time throughout the rest of this book.

A. Pitch and Frequency Comparison of a Buzz and a Sinusoid. Some time ago I set up and tape-recorded a little experiment to illustrate the distinction between pitch matching and frequency matching. The experiment contrasted the behavior of an electrically generated buzz made up of about 25 equally strong harmonic partials with that of a single sinusoid of adjustable frequency, both being presented to the ear via a loudspeaker. The buzz was arranged to have a repetition rate of 261.6 Hz, which has a pitch name of C_4.

The two signals were alternately connected to the loudspeaker by means of the soft switch described in section 13.7. To begin with, I slowly varied the frequency of the sinusoid up and down in the neighborhood of 261 Hz until its pitch was matched to my satisfaction with that of the alternately presented buzz. When the tape of this part of the experiment was played for a classroom full of music students from Case Western Reserve University and the Cleveland Institute of Music, there was general agreement that my pitch matching had been accurate. This agreement shows that we were all operating pretty much alike in the way we heard the two sounds. I might add that there was agreement even from several musicians in the group who, because of a distrust of technology, were sometimes disinclined to take my word for matters concerned with musical relationships.

The next part of the experiment and of the tape was to feed the buzz and the carefully pitch-matched sinusoid to the loudspeaker simultaneously. The class was stunned to hear a beat taking place at about a 3-Hz rate, with the sinusoid now sounding sharp in pitch relative to the buzz. This phenomenon could have been presented in another way, by showing that when a buzz and a sinusoid having equal 261.6-Hz repetition rates are listened to alternately, they are heard as differing in pitch by nearly 20 cents. All of us agreed, on the other hand, that the two sounds when presented together had acceptable pitch matching only when they were adjusted to have identical repetition rates. Let us distill the results of this experiment and some related ones into the first of a set of numbered statements:

1. Pitch-matches between alternately presented sounds do not always agree with matches made when the sounds are presented together.

2. Pitch equality of two sounds heard simultaneously is attained at the same time that their repetition rates are equalized. The physicist's zero-beat condition matches the musician's equal-pitch condition, provided we deal with musical tones—i.e., sounds having harmonic partials.

3. If one uses a pair of *tones* in which only the first few partials have appreciable strength, the two methods of pitch matching (alternation, and superposition, of sounds) give almost identical results, without much regard for the details of vibration recipes or the sound pressure level. This is particularly true of sounds heard in a room.

4. Most of the tones that one meets in ordinary music behave as described in statement 3.

B. Beat Phenomena and the "Almost-Unison" between Two Musical Tones. Suppose we supply our ears with two tones, labeled J and K, one having its four harmonic partials (J_1, J_2, J_3, and J_4) based on a 250-Hz fundamental frequency, the other having its four harmonic partials (K_1, etc.) based on 252 Hz. Beats can take place in the neighborhood of four frequencies. If we set heterodyne effects aside for a moment, the beating pairs are as follows:

Tone J	250	500	750	1000 Hz
Tone K	252	504	756	1008 Hz
Beat frequency	2	4	6	8 Hz

As one pulls the two tones into closer agreement, the strongly marked beat between the fundamental components eventually becomes so slow as not to be easily heard (recognizing it turns into a feat of memory!). The second and higher harmonics are still beating vigorously, however, so that our attention is drawn to them as the next guide to the tuning process. This successive transfer of auditory attention to beats of the higher partials is very useful because it provides ever finer indications as we approach an exact match. For instance, an almost unhearable 1/4-Hz beat (one beat every four seconds) between the fundamental components is associated with an easily detected rate of 1 Hz (one per second) at the fourth harmonic.

Heterodyne components are present to a varying extent in the sound of an almost-unison. These change what we hear by adding more things that can beat in the neighborhood of each component frequency. Here are a few examples:

$$(J_2 - K_1) = (248) \text{ Hz},$$
$$(K_2 - J_1) = (254) \text{ Hz}$$
$$(J_3 - K_1) = (498) \text{ Hz},$$
$$(K_3 - J_1) = (506) \text{ Hz}$$

You have probably noticed that two of these components beat near the fundamental and two near the second harmonic. I have worked out the very simplest (sum-and-difference) heterodyne frequencies that arise through the interaction of the partials of tones J and K. In the list shown below, numbers representing heterodyne frequencies are enclosed in parentheses, while those belonging with the original tones J and K are underlined. The components clump themselves into groups, each one of which is given on a line of its own.

1st clump: (244), (246), (248), _250, 252_, (254), (256), (258) Hz
2nd clump: (496), (498), _500_, (502), _504_, (506), (508) Hz

3rd clump: (748), _750_, (752), (754), _756_, (758) Hz
4th clump: _1000_, (1002), (1004), (1006), _1008_ Hz
etc.

We see at once that to whatever extent heterodyne components are generated, there is a great increase in the complexity of the beats to be heard in the neighborhood of each harmonic of the original sounds. Instead of the original beat frequency, we get harmonically related clumps of beats regardless of the complexity of the way in which they are generated. This sort of elaboration can sometimes fuzz up the clarity with which the beats are heard.

The exact way in which we respond perceptually to the heterodyne-induced complexity has never been properly studied, but it is possible to make some experimentally-based summarizing statements that can be added to the list begun earlier in this section:

5. The presence of heterodyne components for tones having only two or three strong partials apiece intensifies and makes more audible the beats produced by a slight departure from equal frequencies.

6. A pair of tones with slightly different fundamental frequencies, each having a large number of strong harmonics, may not be heard as giving very clear beats. The resulting large collections of heterodyne components grouped near each harmonic can become confusing to the ear.

7. Because of the dependence of many heterodyne effects on the amplitudes of the originating components, a given pair of tones may behave either as in statement 5 or as in statement 6, depending on the loudness with which they are heard.

We have collected several pieces of information by now on the way our ears perceive the composite sound of two close-together musical tones. On the basis of this information I would like now to show what happens when an almost-unison draws closer and closer to its steady partner, unites with it, and then little by little moves away. This description will prove useful to us as we continue in our investigation of these special relationships.

If the fundamental frequencies of two tones are separated by more than about 30 Hz, sounding them together generally produces an effect that may be a little rough, but otherwise is not particularly noteworthy. As the repetition frequencies of the two tones are brought closer together, we begin to hear beats between members of the fundamental-frequency clump of components. The repetition rate of these beats within the clump is equal to the beat frequency of the fundamental components. The clarity of these beats at first grows as the frequency match becomes better; then they become too slow for easy recognition, and our attention shifts to the more easily heard second-harmonic collection of beats. As long as the heterodyne effects are not too strong (in the sense of statement 6 above), a musician desiring to bring the two tones into a *unison* (equal-frequency) relationship has clear messages as to what needs doing. He simply strives to make whatever beats he hears take place at the lowest possible frequency. If he overshoots the zero-beat adjustment, the beats start up again. In any case, the perfect unison is perceptually an extremely well-defined relationship, closely hemmed in on either side by more-or-less complicated collections of beat phenomena. If we progressively raise the frequency of one tone from below that of a stationary

tone, passing through equality and going on up, our sensory impressions can be summarized as follows:

BELOW → $\underbrace{\text{UNISON}}$ → ABOVE
nondescript   beats ‖ beats   nondescript

The unison is the first of several *special relationships* we will be dealing with. In each case the relationship advertises itself to the listener's nervous system as giving a particularly identifiable sound that is *narrowly* confined between regions in which a collection of beats can be heard. It does not matter whether the beats take place between the partials of the original sounds, between their heterodyne components, or in some crisscross fashion. When musical tones are used (those having only harmonic partials, according to our narrow definition) every kind of beat goes to zero frequency as the tones approach one of these special relationships. At the present moment I am particularly interested in the objective existence in our perception of certain acoustical phenomena, since these provide an important clue to why these special relationships are important in music.

C. The Octave Relationship. Musicians of all periods and all places have tended to agree that when they hear a tone having a repetition frequency double that of another one, the two are very nearly interchangeable. This similarity of a tone with its octave is so striking that in most languages both tones are given the same note name. In fact, even notes that are several octaves apart are called by the same name, with more or less confusing adjectives being appended to tell us which particular octave is meant. One of the noteworthy attributes of the octave relationship is its behavior as an example of the perceptually special relationships that we defined above while looking at the unisons and near-unisons of two tones.

The special relationship between tones whose repetition frequencies differ by a factor of two is advertised to our ears by the collections of beats that group themselves immediately to either side of the exact interval. Let us look at the clumpings of components that might beat together when a tone P made up of four harmonics of 200 Hz is sounded along with a tone Q whose four components are multiples of 401 Hz. First we glance at the originating components by themselves:

tone P 200 400 600 800
tone Q   401   802 1203 1604

Out of the sequence belonging to P we find that only the even-numbered (2, 4, 6, . . .) harmonics have counterparts in the harmonics of Q with which they can beat. If we ignore heterodyne components for the moment, there are only half as many cues to call our ears' attention to the special relationship of the octave as there are for a unison. The scarcity of cues seems particularly acute if the tones are of the musically familiar sort possessing only three or four partials of appreciable amplitude. Let us tabulate the clumps of components that are available for processing when the simplest type of nonlinear (heterodyne) effect is taken into account as well:

1st clump: (199), _200_, (201), (202) Hz
2nd clump: (399), _400_, _401_, (402), (403) Hz
3rd clump: _600_, (601), (602), (603) Hz
4th clump: _800_, (801), _802_, (803), (804) Hz
5th clump: (1000), (1001), (1002), (1003), (1004) Hz

6th clump: (1200), (1201), (1202), _1203_, (1204) Hz
7th clump: (1402), (1403), (1404) Hz
8th clump: (1600), (1602), (1603), _1604_ Hz
etc.

As before, our list has not been carried out to frequencies higher than those present in the original sound. Heterodyne components exist beyond this, of course, but their numbers thin out rapidly and so give a relatively small contribution to the audibility of a tuning error.

The first thing that strikes us in looking at the list of components is the large number of them in each frequency clump. We also notice that these clumps are located at frequencies that are harmonics belonging to the tone P. When we take heterodyne effects into account, it is clear that (on paper at least) there are actually more kinds of "messages" available to our ears to establish the special relationship than there are in the case of the unison! We also notice that when we obtain a zero-beat condition by adjusting the fundamental frequency of Q to exactly 400 Hz, the vibration recipe, or spectrum of P and Q taken together, is simply an extension of the harmonic series belonging to P. This fact helps us to appreciate the close relationship between members of an octave pair, in a way that reminds us of the manner in which our ears recognize the relationship between a single musical tone and the aggregate effect produced by a single loud sinusoidal component and its internally generated collection of harmonics.

D. The Musical Fifth. A pair of tones separated by what musicians call the interval of a fifth provides our next example of a strongly marked special relationship and introduces us to a whole hierarchy of similar though less strongly identifiable pairings. A fifth can be defined very simply (on paper) as two tones whose fundamental frequencies are in the ratio of 3/2. As was the case with unisons and octaves, when the special relationship is approached it advertises itself by the presence of beats. Since the places at which the beating occurs tell us a lot about the special relationship, once again we will consider an almost-tuned interval consisting of two tones, M and N, each consisting of 4 harmonic partials:

tone M	200	400	600	800
tone N	301	602	903	1204

If the two sequences of strong harmonics were extended past the fourth one, we would notice that every second partial of tone N is in a position to beat with every third partial of tone M. In our musically realistic simplification we find only one such beating pair—the 600-Hz third partial of M and the 602-Hz second partial of N.

When the simplest heterodyne effects are calculated as before, it turns out that the clumps of beating components arrange themselves as multiples of 100 Hz (in our particular example):

1st clump:	(99), (101), (103) Hz
2nd clump:	(198), _200,_ (202) Hz
3rd clump:	(299), _301,_ (303) Hz
4th clump:	_400,_ (402), (404) Hz
5th clump:	(499), (501), (503) Hz
6th clump:	_600, 602,_ (604) Hz
7th clump:	(701), (703) Hz
8th clump:	_800,_ (802), (804) Hz
9th clump:	(901), _903_ Hz
10th clump:	(1000), (1002), (1004) Hz
11th clump:	(1101), (1103) Hz
12th clump:	(1200), (1202), _1204_ Hz

Notice that these frequency clumps are arranged in a harmonic series based on a

fundamental frequency half that of tone M, and also that any _lack_ of accuracy in setting an exact 3/2 frequency ratio will be called to our attention by a total of 12 clumps. Of these, 9 clumps contain 3 components (such as clumps 1 and 12) and 3 more clumps are each made up of 2 components (as is clump 7). (You may wish to verify that when the octave relationship is described in this way, it advertises itself by 1 triple-component clump, 3 quadruple-component clumps, and 4 clumps which are quintuple.)

Let us consider the auditory and physical meaning of the harmonically related clumps. If the sound of M plus N is supplied to us electrically from two perfectly steady oscillators feeding the same loudspeaker, it is possible to play a rather interesting game with our ears. Suppose first that M and N are in an _exact_ 3/2 frequency relationship, and that we walk into the room where this composite sound is already being generated. Our ears are presented with a set of components having frequencies of 200, 300, 400, ———, 600, ———, 800, 900, ———, ———, and 1200 Hz. This collection of interlaced original components is itself a fairly complete harmonic series. Because heterodyne components will fill out the series (regardless of their mode of production), the collection will almost invariably be perceived as a single 100-Hz tone, a phenomenon we first took note of back in chapter 5 and then explained in section 14.1 of this chapter.

Suppose now that while we are in the room, the oscillator belonging either to tone M or to tone N is turned off and then turned on again (preferably with the help of a soft switch or a fader). When both tones are again in operation, many of us would discover to our surprise that there are "really" two tones being played in the room, even though things are *acoustically* back where they started. The reason is clear: shutting off tone N eliminates the 300-, 900-, and 1200-Hz components, and weakens the 600-Hz one, leaving tone M clearly audible. The act of turning N on again calls attention to the systematic relationship of the partials that are being restored. The heterodyne components will also rearrange themselves in a characteristic way during the turn-on, a way which our ears have heard many times in the course of ordinary listening.

If we go through the whole experiment again, with separate loudspeakers being provided for the two tones, or if one of the tones is given a slight vibrato, our ears are not so easily fooled into hearing the combined tones as a single entity which is pitched an octave below M. However, we can often hear this lower tone as an additional tone having a 100-Hz repetition rate, especially if it is called to our attention by the momentary operation of an auxiliary tone generator tuned to 100 Hz. We shall formally call this third sound the *implied tone*, which arises in this case from the components of tones tuned accurately in a 3/2 ratio. This particular implied tone is in an octave relationship to the lower of the original tones, and so "hides" behind it. You may recall some passing remarks on this subject in connection with the sound spectrum of the kettledrum (see sec. 9.5).

Digression on Sum and Difference Tones.
We have just learned the possibility of hearing something I have called an implied tone that can arise when two tones having a special (zero-beat) relationship are sounded together. Let us take a moment to see what happens if the two original tones are not in special relationship of this sort.

For example, we take tones V (200 Hz and three more of its harmonics) and W (273 Hz and its harmonics). The simplified list of heterodyne components starts out (19), (54), (73), (127), (146), . . . Hz. Out of this list, we find three components that are harmonic multiples of the 73-Hz component. This sub-collection of harmonics can usually be heard as a rather rough-sounding low-pitched tone, along with the original tones V and W. Let us give this new tone the temporary letter name T. There is one more harmonically related collection of four components to be found in the complete list of simplest-type heterodynes, this one being the set of harmonics of 473 Hz (call this tone by the name S). Chiefly because of upward masking effects caused by tones V and W and because of distractions arising from a large number of heterodyne components which do not organize themselves into any sort of recognizable pattern, this collection (473 Hz and its harmonics) is normally inaudible, although an adjustable search tone having two or three harmonics may smoke it out.

A little arithmetic shows that the unclear but audible new tone T always has a fundamental frequency T_1 equal to the difference $(W_1 - V_1)$ between the fundamentals of V and W. Similarly, the collection we have just named S has a fundamental frequency S_1 equal to the sum $(V_1 + W_1)$. Musicians have been aware of what we have called tone T at least since the baroque era (it is sometimes said that such tones were discovered by the violinist Tartini). Hermann Helmholtz, whose name is as famous in acoustics as it is in optics, electromagnetism, and thermodynamics, was the first to give a general explanation of these tones in terms of heterodyne components. It was he who first referred to the lower one as the difference *tone. The other tone is by analogy called the* summation *tone. A great deal of confusion exists in the literature, caused chiefly by the almost-universal tendency of scientists and musicians to talk interchangeably about single-component sounds and those made up of a set of harmonics. Another cause for misunderstanding arose from ignorance or neglect of masking and the distractions produced by the other, unclassifiable heterodyne components that are generally present. Helmholtz's essentially correct physics regarding these new tones was challenged* *for many years because of the experimental fact that the* perception *of summation tones by our ears is not normally possible, even though their components are detectable within the ear.*

I should close this digression with the remark that if our randomly tuned tones V and W are progressively moved toward a special relationship with one another, the difference tone, the summation tone, the unclassifiable other components, and the partials of the original tones all align themselves progressively into a single harmonic relationship—the one associated with what we have named the implied tone!

E. *Other Special Relationships.* The most direct way to introduce a number of other special relationships between musical tones is to describe a demonstration experiment which I have carried out upon several occasions. Two adjustable-frequency oscillators are connected to loudspeakers. The oscillators are internally constructed in such a way as to provide sound signals having three or four exactly harmonic partials of appreciable strength. The convenient way to do this is to modify an electrically generated sinusoid by a suitably designed nonlinear device which produces the higher components by heterodyne action (see sec. 14.2). The only other equipment needed is a device for frequency measurement and perhaps an auxiliary oscillator and loudspeaker for use as a search-tone generator. One oscillator is turned on to produce an unvarying tone whose repetition rate is somewhere between about 250 and 1000 Hz (or in the range C_4 to C_6), which keeps all of the tone's partials in the frequency region where our ears work best. Let us call this the reference tone.

In the presence of a group of people (musicians or otherwise), I set the frequency of the other oscillator to some random value and ask one of my listeners to tune it either upward or downward until he finds a nearby setting that shows the distinguishing marks of a special relationship. That is, he is asked to look for a beat-free setting, narrowly confined between two restricted regions in which a wide variety of beats take place. The experimenter never has to search far to locate one of these special settings, and everyone in the room agrees with him when zero beat is properly achieved. The musicians in the group will recognize and give names to most of these special relationships, just as they call the equal-frequency special relationship a unison, the 2/1 relationship an octave, and the 3/2 relation a fifth.

Table 14.1 summarizes the results of experiments of this general sort. At the

Table 14.1

Frequency Ratios for Specially Related Tone Pairs

Ratio	Musical Name	Cents	Indicators
1/1	Unison	000	1 quintuple
			1 sextuple
			1 septuple
			1 octuple
2/1	Octave	1200	1 triple
			4 quadruple
			3 quintuple
3/2	Fifth	702	3 double
			9 triple
4/3	Fourth	498	12 double
			1 triple
5/3	Major sixth	884	14 double
5/4	Major third	386	10 double
6/5	Minor third	316	6 double
7/4	—	969	6 double
7/5	—	583	4 double
8/5	Minor sixth	814	3 double
7/6	—	267	3 double

top of the list is the most well-defined relationship, the unison, followed in order of decreasing definition by the octave, the fifth, etc. The first column in the table gives the frequency ratio between the fundamentals of the fixed (or reference) tone and the adjustable tone.

The second column in table 14.1 gives the interval names which musician-listeners will *invariably* give to the different special relationships. Whenever I have had someone carry out this experiment, everyone in the room has been completely satisfied that the so-called special relationships coincide *exactly* with the musical relationships implied by the customary names, provided that the oscillator settings produce beat free sounds.

The third column tells the pitch relationship of the two tones expressed in terms of the equal-tempered comparison scale that is illustrated in figure 2.1. You will recall from the early part of this section that each octave is divided up into 12 chromatic steps, each one containing 100 cents. It is for this reason that the 2/1 (octave) relationship can be said to represent a musical interval of exactly 1200 cents. The special relationship having a 5/4 frequency ratio calls for the adjustable tone in our experiment to have a named interval that is $400 - 386 = 14$ cents lower than the fourth chromatic step in the equal-tempered reference scale.

The fourth column in table 14.1 gives an indication of the definiteness of the relationship by telling how many components are collected into the various clumps that can beat when things are out of tune. For example, we already noticed in subsection D above that errors in the 3/2 relationship are heralded by beats in 9 clumps each having 3 components (a tri-ple indicator), plus 3 clumps each containing a pair of components (a double indicator). Looking down this column from top to bottom will clearly show the hierarchical order of the special relationships. Note that the 8/5 and 7/6 relations shown at the bottom of the table are recognizable only with difficulty when no more than 4 harmonics are strong in the original tones.

It is an easily verifiable fact that if one sets up the two oscillators to give a frequency ratio of 1.25992 (corresponding to an equal-temperament interval of exactly 400 cents), instead of our experimentally verified 1.25000 ($= 5/4$) ratio (386 cents), everyone notices the resulting beats, and all the musicians in the group will say that an out-of-tune (sharp) major third is being sounded. When I tell my musician experimenters that the 400-cent interval is the equal-temperament version of the major third, they typically react with skepticism or dismay. They respond in even more intense fashion to the extremely rough-sounding combination whose frequency ratio is 1.26563 ($= 81/64$) which spans an interval of 408 cents. This particular ratio, which is the product of 2000-year-old arithmetical ingenuity, is called a Pythagorean third.

When I sound the equal-temperament and Pythagorean major thirds by means of two electronic tone generators, the usual question is "What makes anyone think that those are acceptable tunings?" My response at this stage is to point out that a laboratory experiment is not quite the same thing as a musical performance. There are many ways in which the auditory physics of our special relationships works itself out when we listen to the various sounds of actual musical instruments. We will shortly learn, for example, that the smoothly varying *in*harmonicity of piano and harpsichord partials slightly changes the frequency ratios of the special relationships, and that other randomly appearing inharmonicities present in these instruments can cause even further alterations in the relationships (see sec. 5.4). Moreover, the practical acceptability of "errors" in the setting up of special relationships differs among the various families of instruments, for reasons which we will learn as we continue through the book.

Laboratory instruments can easily be set up to display the special relationships. Our success in showing these relationships using actual musical instruments is quite variable, ranging from fairly easy to almost impossible. The woodwinds, played without vibrato, are closely followed by the brasses in their ability to display the relations disclosed by our laboratory instruments. Two vibrato-free voices trail in the clarity with which they show them. Electronic and pipe organs are not very suitable, chiefly because it is not easy to retune them for experimental purposes. I have already suggested why the piano and the harpsichord are not useful for our experiments at this stage, and as we shall see the bowed strings are not appropriate for such experimenting because of the astonishing weakness of beats they display between closely spaced components.

There are many reasons why musicians sometimes use frequency relationships other than those implied so far in this chapter. For one thing, in solo performance or when two instruments are sounded alternately, the direct comparisons we have been discussing may not

exist. For another, there are cases where special relationships exist to connect three or more tones which do not seem closely related when they are taken two at a time. As we shall see, the equal-tempered tuning used for many keyboard instruments is a choice that is obviously a compromise. As with most compromises it has weaknesses, but it gives great flexibility particularly in modulation, and its weaknesses can even be turned into strengths on occasion.

Written music is a generalized set of performing directions in the sense that much is left unspecified, which assumes that suitable choices will be made by a musically sensitive performer. Some of these choices are culturally conditioned, and can easily change in the course of time. Pitch indications and the musical relationships which they imply are very often of a different sort, since they are influenced if not dominated by the perceptual effects of physical relationships between the various sets of partials. When a violinist or wind instrument player learns to read music, he learns very early that each note corresponds to a particular set of finger positions, lip tensions, bow pressures, and the like. To be sure, these maneuvers get the pitch of his tone close to where it should be, but he is then expected to adjust the pitch until it is exactly "right" in the context of the sounds of his fellow players. (As we will see in chapter 15, another guide for the player is the sound left over in the room from his immediately preceding notes.) It has been the purpose of this chapter to indicate the nature of one of the acoustical relationships available for the use of the player as a *guide* in adjusting the pitch relationships of his musical performance.

Let me close this section with a few more summarizing statements dealing with these matters.

8. Musical note names and the words describing pitch relationships may have different meanings in different contexts.

9. The performing musician uses the written notes to get himself close to the required pitches. He then listens and exerts whatever skill he has to set them accurately in their own context.

10. Acoustical cues similar to those which single out the special relationships normally provide the basis for the correction process mentioned in statement 9.

11. Pitch relationships based on acoustic cues are the guideposts of music since their exact or approximate presence is generally perceived with extreme speed. They are physical and neurological in nature, and not culturally determined.

12. Statement 11 should not be interpreted to mean that a composer or player is wrong if he knowingly chooses to avoid specially related sounds. Such avoidance in itself may gain auditory impact because it contrasts with the various special, neurophysics-based relationships between tones that are exploited in music.

14.5. Examples, Experiments, and Questions

1. We get a strong sense of pitch from a tone made up of a set of harmonic partials, even if several of these (including the fundamental component) are missing. The nonlinear production of heterodyne components gives us a clue to the way our ears can do this. To get a good idea of the effectiveness of this process, do the arithmetic to verify that even the simplest of the heterodyne components arising from an original stimulus made up of 200-, 500-, and 600-Hz partials join with these original components to give a complete set of 100-Hz harmonics. Work them out for the first through at least the eighth harmonics. Notice also that, for any more or less complete musical tone, every *adjacent* pair of partials produces a fundamental frequency heterodyne component, so that all parts of the tone "point" to the fundamental as an important frequency.

2. The low notes on a clarinet seldom sound as low in pitch as the corresponding notes on any other instrument. The listener tends to place the clarinet an octave too high. Even musicians are surprised to learn that the bottom note of the little E♭ soprano clarinet is the same as the bottom note of a violin (G_3— 196 Hz). The sound pressure recipe for the low notes of a really good clarinet shows strong odd-numbered partials and weak even-numbered ones. Let us play a game with this fact by pretending that the even partials are nonexistent, so that the clarinet's note G_3 is imagined to have a recipe made up of components at 1, 3, 5, and 7 times the 196-Hz fundamental. In simplest terms, the ear can be imagined to act on this spectrum to generate double-frequency as well as sum-and-difference heterodyne components. Verify that *all* of these generated components are found at *even* multiples of the fundamental frequency, where the instrument itself is presumed to make no contribution. Notice also that, contrary to the normal case, adjacent partials in the (hypothetical) original tone all produce heterodyne components at the frequency of the *second* harmonic rather than the first. In other words, the he-

terodyne components provided by our ears make up the complete set of harmonics of a tone whose pitch is an octave above that of the clarinet, and these even-numbered components lack any direct contact with the original clarinet partials. Speculate on the possible connection between this fact and the octave error that is often made.

3. Consider the following experiment made with the vibrating bar shown in figure 14.1. To begin with, suppose that it is running steadily under the influence of a 40-Hz sinusoidal force. Because it is driven so far above its 20-Hz natural frequency, it has only a small amplitude of vibration (as implied by fig. 14.2). Suppose now that it is abruptly plucked and released while the 40-Hz driver continues in operation. Figure out why the 20-Hz damped (transient) oscillation normally expected of a plucked bar fails to die away as usual, while the bar continues to oscillate steadily and with an appreciable amplitude having the 20-Hz component predominant in the vibration recipe. The bar will continue to vibrate in this peculiar fashion as long as the 40-Hz driving force is kept in operation. Hint: what are the simplest heterodyne frequencies that one would expect to get between the initially plucked 20-Hz vibration and that due to the 40-Hz sinusoidal driving force? Could a similar oscillation be maintained if the driver were to be run at a frequency of 60 Hz?

4. I am often asked how it is that our ears are so sensitive to and offended by the smallest traces of nonlinear distortion in an amplifier and loudspeaker system, when the heterodyne components generated within our own ears by aural nonlinearities seem to be useful rather than destructive. Consider what happens when music is played through an imperfect loudspeaker system: the heterodyne components produced by the loudspeaker and sent into the room are then acted upon by our ears, and so are reworked and entangled among themselves and among the desired partials of the music itself.[5] This redoubled modification of the music by two sets of nonlinearities produces an enormous increase in the number of components that are competing for our auditory attention. There is often very little pattern to the signals, and whatever patterns exist among these components are unfamiliar to us and not of the sort normally connected with music. The unfamiliarity itself is an additional source of confusion and distraction.

In recent years, musicians have begun to use electronic nonlinearities deliberately to put together new sounds. Whether these are the result of the fuzz-tone box used by rock guitarists or of the modulators dear to more academic musicians, their musical usefulness generally depends on the processing of only selected parts of the total sound, or on using very simple sounds in the first place. If this initial simplicity is absent, our ears respond to the results as being just one more undistinguishable jumble, instead of coping with and enjoying some newly invented auditory combinations.

5. A good introduction to the existence and nature of special intervals and of difference tones can be achieved with the help of two piccolo or soprano recorder players; flutes (which sound an octave lower) will work but are not so well suited for a first hearing. Once you have learned to hear consciously what is going on in an especially simple situation, it

will not be difficult to become aware of the same phenomena in other surroundings.

(*a*) Ask the players to provide you with a unison, played *fortissimo* and without vibrato on the note F_6. This is the second-register F on either instrument. Until the players settle down to match their instruments exactly, you will be supplied with a wonderful variety of beats between the pairs of partials having frequencies that are almost equal.

(*b*) Next ask the louder of your players to shift down an octave to allow you to hear the beating results of bringing the F_5-to-F_6 octave in and out of tune.

(*c*) Now arrange for the F_6-to-C_7 fifth to be played. Don't seek the implied tone yet—simply make yourself aware of the collections of beats which manifest themselves when the players are out of tune with one another.

(*d*) Do the same for the F_6-to-B_6b interval of a fourth and also the F_6-to-A_6 major third.

(*e*) You are now ready to seek an easy difference tone (see Digression in sec. 14.4, part D). Ask the two players to stand with their instruments near one another. You should at first stand so that one ear is directly exposed to the sounds of both instruments. The F_6-to-B_6b fourth is to be played, with the player of the lower note slowly varying his pitch up and down a little. Listen for a harsh-sounding tone located about a musical twelfth (an octave plus a fifth) below F_6—that is, in the neighborhood of C_5. You may find it helpful momentarily to sound C_5 softly on a piano as a way of telling your ears where to listen. One identifying mark of the difference tone is

that its pitch rises as the Bb player plays flatter, and vice versa. Notice that when the F and the Bb are in a beat-free relationship, the difference tone is exactly at C.

(*f*) You are now ready to pursue the difference tones associated with the F_6-to-C_7 interval of a fifth, and the major third that relates F_6 and A_6. In the first case the difference tone wanders near F_5 and in the second one you should listen yet an octave lower, in the neighborhood of F_4. Note that when these intervals become beat free and have everything lined up, what you are hearing is the implied tone described in 14.4, subsection D.

(*g*) If you have gotten so that you can hear all of the relationships described so far, you are ready to try the minor third, F_6 to A_6b, and the 7/4 frequency ratio. This last one can be sought by having one player sound D_6 while the other one pulls his pitch slowly down from C_7 for a match when he comes down 30 cents (about a third of the way) toward B_6.

Notes

1. Alexander Wood, *The Physics of Music*, 6th ed., rev. J. M. Bowsher (New York: Dover, 1961), pp. 83–89. A 7th edition is now available (New York: Wiley, Halsted Press, 1974).

2. J. L. Goldstein, "Aural Harmonics," *Research in Progress*, Report 48, Laboratory of Psychophysics, Harvard University, June 1967.

3. See the article, "Aural Combination Tones," by Julius L. Goldstein, in R. Plomp and G. F. Smoorenburg, eds., *Frequency Analysis and Periodicity Detection in Hearing* (Leiden: A. W. Sijthoff, 1970), pp. 230–47.

4. A good survey of heterodyne phenomena in the ear can be found in four papers by Donald D.

Greenwood: "Aural Combination Tones and Auditory Masking," *J. Acoust. Soc. Am.* 50 (1971): 502–43; and three that appear together in *J. Acoust. Soc. Am.* 52 (1972): 1137–67: "Masking by Narrow Bands of Noise in Proximity to More Intense Pure Tones of Higher Frequency;" "Mask-ing by Combination Bands;" and "Combination Bands of Even Order."

5. See Alf Gabrielsson and Håkon Sjögren, "Detection of Amplitude Distortion in Flute and Clarinet Spectra," *J. Acoust. Soc. Am.* 52 (1972): 471–83.

15

Successive Tones: Reverberations, Melodic Relationships, and Musical Scales

The perceivable physical relationships between pairs of tones, which were the subject of our explorations in chapter 14, closely parallel the relationships that musicians and composers find musically interesting. It is possible to extend our study of the way sounds are transmitted from musical instruments to our ears by studying under what conditions these physical relationships or cues are weakened, and by noticing what changes in the musicians' actions result from the reduction in the audibility of the cues.

In the present chapter we will first examine how the reverberant properties of a room influence and extend the usefulness of our acoustically special relationships, after which we will look into the basic nature of musical scales. This represents a shift of our attention from superposed tones to a study of the way in which successive tones are related. The rest of the chapter will be devoted to examples that will illustrate how music is affected by some of the simpler physical relationships between tones.

15.1. Reverberation Times and the Audibility of Decaying Sounds in a Room

When two or more musical tones are sounded together in a room, their special relationship is sometimes emphasized and sometimes obscured by the fact that the beginnings and endings of the tones come to our ears in ways that are different from the manner in which their middle portions arrive. The physics of these effects and some of its auditory implications have already been outlined in chapters 11 and 12, but we should review the essential points before turning to new things.

When a musician plays a tone, the listener first learns of it from the directly propagated sound that comes to his ears. Through the working of the precedence effect, this first message is combined in our ears with the first few echoes and perhaps some scattered sound as well, extending over a time of about 30 to 50 milliseconds. All this can also be said (more clumsily) in terms of the thousands of vibrational modes of the room air which are undergoing their initial transient oscillations excited by the instrument as it acts as a multifrequency set of acoustic sources.

After the first few tens of milliseconds, on the other hand, the behavior of a room is easier to describe in terms of piled-up collections of modes than it is in terms of multiple reflections. We learned in section 11.7 that the overall behavior of sound in a room shows an irregular growth from the time the source is switched on until a steady state is reached; this is followed by a progressive decay when the source is switched off. An assertion was made in section 11.8 that it is convenient to specify this buildup or decay in terms of the reverberation time, defined as the time required for the averaged sound pressure to die down to 1/1000th of its initial value. The main reason for choosing this manner of specifying the decay time is connected with a historical observation of the way in which our ears respond to a decaying sound. Let us consider a practical situation in which we listen to this decay.

Suppose we are standing in a concert hall and are equipped with a stopwatch and either a strong-voiced whistle or a nearby oscillator-and-loudspeaker system. If the sound source is turned on for 5 to 10 seconds and cut off abruptly, we can hear the sound that fills the room decaying progressively. Once the sound has become very gentle, it seems to disappear quite abruptly, because the dependence of our loudness sensation on sound pressure is different below 40-dB SPL from what it is at higher levels. It is possible to use the stopwatch to measure the time interval over which the tone is audible without strain. A very useful accident is the fact that this *audibility time* agrees quite well with the reverberation time defined by physicists and engineers. Quite aside from the numerical agreement, we should ask how it comes about that the duration of the audible sound after the source is shut off appears to be quite constant for any particular hall and frequency of excitation, even when the amplitude of the original excitation is varied severalfold. Moreover, the period of audibility does not change much when the background noise level in the hall is altered by turning the ventilating system off or on.

One possible explanation for the good match between the time of audibility and the physicist's reverberation time is that perhaps a reasonably high SPL at the listener's ears maintained for a few seconds might shift the threshold of hearing upward from its normal pressure amplitude to a value that is very nearly 60 dB below the SPL of the excitory sound. According to this hypothesis, the time required for the sound to decay from any given initial SPL at our ears to a just-audible sound level matches the time for a decay of 60 dB down to the shifted threshold. We may recall that the formally defined reverberation time corresponds to a 1000-fold change in sound pressure amplitude, and this 1000-fold change can equally well be expressed as a 60-dB change in SPL. If this preliminary hypothesis is to work, it has one more requirement: the initial SPL of the excitation must be more than 60 dB above the net SPL of the room noise measured within a critical bandwidth at the frequency of excitation. If this requirement is not met, the time of audibility would be expected to extend only until the sound weakens enough to drown itself in overall noise.

Unfortunately, this beautifully simple theory collapses when a direct experimental test is made of the underlying assumptions (a) that there is a significant shift of threshold and (b) that the threshold shift always rises to a value 60 dB below the SPL of the original excitation. As a test, I arranged to feed a 500-Hz sinusoid to a loudspeaker in my laboratory room via a switch-controlled attenuator which permitted an abrupt reduction in the SPL at my ears after they had been exposed for a few seconds to a loud initial sound. When the higher SPL in the range of 70 to 90 dB was switched abruptly to a level 65 dB lower, my mildly deafened ears were left briefly in silence (for about 1/10th of a second) after which the loudness of the weaker signal quickly restored itself to normal. A repetition of the experiment using a 75-dB attenuator produced similar results—my ears merely took a little longer to recover enough to hear the 3-fold-smaller signal pressure amplitude. These experiments show that exposure of the ears to a few seconds of loud sounds does indeed raise their threshold. However, recovery from a few seconds of exposure is essentially complete within half a second, so that the phenomenon is of too brief a duration to explain the success of source-and-stopwatch measurements of reverberation times in the range from 1 to 10 seconds.

Audibility time measurements using the source-and-stopwatch method may seem rather informal, but they turn out to be a reliable way to investigate the properties of a room. For the measurements to give stable results, one finds that the initial SPL needs to be about 80 or 90 dB above threshold (corresponding to a loudness of tens of sones). After a lapse of one reverberation time, the SPL is, of course, down to 20 or 30 dB. This puts the loudness below 1 sone, in a region of sound pressure where the perceived loudness falls away with particular rapidity as the signal approaches the threshold of audibility (see the end of sec. 13.4 and also example 5 of sec. 13.9). Perhaps our ears are responding to this abrupt change in the *rate* of loudness decay, as the signal dives below the level of ambient room noise (typically in the range of 20 to 30-dB SPL in a critical bandwidth).[1] Lest this rough-sounding guess at an explanation seem too approximate to be plausible (particularly because

of the cavalier way in which 10-dB variations in SPL are bandied about), I should tell you that a 10-dB change in the audible span of SPLs (e.g., a change of span from 60 dB to 70 dB) will result in a change of only about 16 percent in the time during which the decay is audible.

The source-and-stopwatch method for estimating audibility times goes back to Clement Sabine,[2] who founded the formal subject of room acoustics in the years between 1895 and 1915. The method has proved useful ever since, despite the lack of a good psychoacoustic explanation for its stability or for its connection with the more mechanically defined reverberation time. One reason for its usefulness (pointed out by Sabine himself) is that our ears are not confused or distracted by the normal irregularities of the decay pattern, irregularities that are very difficult to average out when laboratory instruments are used.

My colleague Robert Shankland has made very effective use of a set of easily portable organ pipes in his source-and-stopwatch studies of the reverberation properties of concert halls, auditoriums, and religious buildings in Europe as well as in North America. He finds that with practice it is possible to measure audibility times with a repeatability of about 10 percent. Several of his co-workers including myself have repeatedly verified that our separate judgments in a given room are mutually consistent, and that we can return to a hall after a lapse of some years and obtain essentially the same figures. During the past 20 years Shankland and I have repeatedly compared these auditory results with carefully carried out experiments using various electronic sound sources, a wave analyzer, and a high-speed level recorder. It is difficult (especially when using a tape recorder to store the data for leisurely study in the laboratory) to make an accurate measurement of a decay curve over the full 60-dB range required by its definition. We have done this complete wide-range analysis on more than one occasion, and have verified the general agreement between the properly measured reverberation time and the simpler auditory result.

Electronically measured reverberation time estimates are ordinarily made on the basis of a restricted decay range of only 40 or 50 dB, which is likely to result in an overlong value for the reverberation time. This is because of the way in which a level recorder computes the net SPL of a rapidly decaying sinusoid (or narrow-band noise signal) in the presence of various kinds of electronic and room noise.

Certain instruments are in use today that estimate the reverberation time on the assumption that the whole decay takes place in a way that is exactly consistent with the initial quarter or third of it (15- or 20-dB decay). While clever design can provide enough averaging of the room response in such a device to give consistent results from trial to trial, an estimate based on the early part of a decay can seriously misrepresent (usually by underestimating) the true reverberation time, particularly in certain kinds of rooms. These matters have been well-understood for forty years.

The foregoing paragraphs have shown us (among other things) that while the idea of a reverberation time is conceptually quite clear, it is not at all easy to get an accurate measure of either the sound pressure or the auditory version. However, most of the approximate methods described manage to provide useful *comparisons* of the reverberation time for a given frequency of excitation in one room with that for another frequency, as a guide for acoustical planning and correction. For musical purposes, of course, the choice is clear—we usually want to know how long a given sound persists audibly in the room, so that in all strictness what I have referred to as the audibility time is in fact the most relevant figure. For the sake of simplicity, however, and to follow a traditional usage which is not particularly misleading, we shall henceforth exploit the rough equality of the audibility time and the reverberation time and refer to them both as reverberation times.

15.2. The Effect of Room Reverberation and Noise on Musical Pitch Relationships

In chapter 14 we learned of a set of perceptually definite special relationships between pairs of musical tones. We also learned that these relationships are recognized by musicians as being a familiar part of their profession. It is possible to say that in chapter 14 we studied some of the acoustical guideposts for the construction of musical harmonies. Having just reviewed and extended our knowledge of how sounds tend to persist audibly in a room after their sources are shut off, we are now in a position to investigate some of the acoustical guideposts that are available to a musician intent on producing melodies—the way in which *successive* tones are related to one another.

To introduce and illustrate these concepts I shall follow our usual custom of tracing out the results of a series of carefully chosen experiments, experiments which you might want to reproduce for

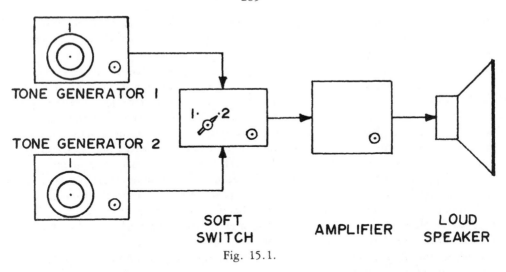

TONE GENERATOR 1

TONE GENERATOR 2

SOFT
SWITCH

AMPLIFIER

LOUD
SPEAKER

Fig. 15.1.

yourself. We will make use once again of a pair of electrical tone generators whose vibration recipes contain appreciable amounts of only the first few harmonics. Figure 15.1 shows how a soft switch can alternately feed one or the other oscillator to an amplifier-and-loudspeaker system. The soft switch assures that the two tones can be alternated promptly and cleanly without the harsh cracklings and poppings that might otherwise accompany the electrical changeover. Marks made with a grease pencil on the frequency dials of the oscillators give us a convenient way to record the settings corresponding to any interesting frequencies that may be discovered. We will assume that the equipment is set up in a fairly large room whose reverberation time is at least 1/3 of a second.

We start our experiments by choosing a basic pitch toward the lower end of the playing range of tone generator number 1. Let us choose this basic pitch in such a way as to make it match one of the Cs of the reference scale of pitches; e.g., it

might have a repetition rate (fundamental frequency) of 261.6 Hz or of 523.2 Hz. The next thing we do is fool around with the complete system, switching back and forth between the reference tone produced by tone generator no. 1 and various randomly set tones from tone generator no. 2. This is a way not only to familiarize ourselves with the machinery, but also to get our ears accustomed to hearing and recognizing the reference tone.

If the room has a reverberation time of one or two seconds (as is characteristic of a small concert hall), our random experimenting will make us aware of all kinds of momentary beats and roughnesses which make their appearance every time one tone is exchanged for the other. The explanation of these roughnesses is straightforward: the reverberant sounds of the paritals belonging to the earlier tone are beating with the newly-set-up partials of the second tone; every decaying partial is at some instant equal in amplitude to its growing successor, and at that time beats against it with maximum auditory effect. A similar remark applies to any heterodyne components that may be produced between tones exhibiting roughness or beating.

During the changeover of room response from one tone to the next, our ears are supplied with both tones simultaneously. In a room having a long reverberation time, there is a long interval during which "successive" tones are audibly overlapping. In a room with highly absorptive walls and therefore a short reverberation, intercomparison of the two tones takes place only during a very brief period. Once we have recognized that successive sounds in a room always overlap to some extent, it is an easy matter to verify experimentally that the special relationships discovered in chapter 14 for pairs of superposed sounds continue to advertise themselves to at least a limited extent between successive sounds in a room. This observation is important enough that we should dignify it and its direct consequences by means of some numbered statements:

1. When one long tone quickly follows another one in a reverberant room, the growth of one tone and the decay of the other overlap sufficiently at our ears that it is possible for us to recognize at least the strongly marked special pitch relationships described for concurrent sounds in chapter 14.

2. As the room's reverberation time is reduced, the overlap time between successive sounds at our ears is also reduced. This weakens the clarity and certainty with which we can recognize any special pitch relationships. We lose recognition of these relationships in order, beginning at the bottom of the list given in table 14.1.

3. For any given reverberation time, there is an upper limit to the rapidity with which tones can follow one another and still show a relationship. This is because in rapid playing

the remnants of several earlier tones may be hearable, and so can confuse the auditory picture.

A fair question to ask at this stage in our experimentation is whether we are really using reverberant sound as a way to relate one tone to the next; perhaps there is something else going on which gives us some clues, or perhaps our upbringing is such that the special relationships have become drilled into us simply from our exposure to music from the time of babyhood. Our everyday experience immediately provides us with one clue—singers and instrumentalists enjoy performing in a reverberant environment, whether it is while taking a shower or playing in a "live" concert hall. Their confidence is heightened by such surroundings and so, as a matter of fact, is their accuracy in achieving the desired pitch relationships, provided the speed of the music is moderate enough that the constraints of statement 3 do not take appreciable effect.

Both the presence and the absence of reverberant cues can demonstrate how we rely on them in musical situations. Some years ago I inveigled a professional musician friend into being a subject for several experiments in the course of which I did not always tell him what I was actually up to. One experiment required him to set two tone generators to various musical intervals (chiefly 3rds, 4ths, and 5ths) that I might specify at random. This experiment was done in my laboratory, where the reverberation time is only about 1/3 of a second, so that the amount of overlap between successive tones is extremely short. As long as my friend shifted from one tone to the other without leaving an intervening period of silence, he had little difficulty in setting any desired interval to his own satisfaction. He would switch back and forth between the tones, adjusting the frequency of one until the interval sounded "right" to him. By actual measurement of his settings I was able to verify that he almost always arranged the tones to agree exactly with what we might expect from the concurrent-tone experiments of chapter 14. My friend became a little impatient with my delighted announcement of each of his "successes." Did I not take it for granted that a musician of his stature would be able to do such easy things?

While I was attempting to explain my scientific interest in the experiments we had just completed, I unobtrusively connected an electrical generator of *white noise* to a separate loudspeaker and gradually turned up the volume so that the room was filled with a gentle hissing, rushing sound of the sort one gets from an FM radio receiver that is tuned between broadcast stations. A white-noise signal, when analyzed, proves to be made up of thousands of overlapping sinusoidal components having all possible frequencies, all with equal amplitudes, each component running randomly out of step with all the rest. My purpose was to provide an overall masking signal of sufficient strength that reverberant sounds would be almost completely lost in the hissing background noise. My victim noticed the presence of noise, which I passed off as a temporary fault of the equipment, and then I requested that he repeat the preceding set of experiments. The task proved very difficult for him, and while he was often able to make "correct" settings (his word for it), he worked slowly and his confidence in their accuracy was greatly reduced. He then realized that the noise was causing his trouble and expressed interest in the fact that what he

called the "distraction" of the noise could cause such difficulty, even when the tones themselves were clearly audible. He did however point out that it is hard to perform in a noisy, crowded nightclub, thereby demonstrating clearly that he had already faced the problem of masking noises in the course of his professional career.

We learn from experiments such as this that it is possible to set the simpler musical intervals between successive tones even when the reverberation is masked. We already know, for that matter, that music can be played outdoors where there is no chance of making direct comparisons between the tones. Are we able to do this on the basis of physical clues other than the ones considered so far, or is it simply that a trained ear can memorize the intervals in the way that a toolmaker's eye learns to recognize the inch or millimeter sizes of the objects he work with? Further experimentation shows us that a little of both is going on.

Let us give our main attention here to the nature and operation of aids to tuning (other than reverberant overlap) which are available in the acoustics of an interval-setting experiment. In experiments using headphones or under other nonreverberant conditions, it is possible for most of us to set reasonably accurate facsimiles of the special intervals between tones. While it is possible to do this with normal, multicomponent tones, our ability to do it is greatly weakened when single-component tones are used. One musician-victim of such an experiment with pure tones was quite frightened to discover that the intervals seemed too vague to him—he would set and reset, never feeling sure of what he had done. Furthermore, he tended always to set the intervals wider than those associated with his expected simple, whole-number frequency ratios. My friend feared that some ear disease was about to rob him of his livelihood. The poor fellow was somewhat relieved to discover that if he sang in unison with the first note, or an octave below, and then tried to set the second tone, things went much better. He was also relieved to find that when I turned up the loudness of the sounds, much of his skill seemed to return. It appears that temporary auditory patterns are set up in our nervous system by the components of the first tone, and that useful comparisons may be made between them and corresponding patterns belonging to the second tone. For example, while setting a musical 5th, we may be recognizing the equality of frequency of the 3rd, 6th, etc., harmonic partials of the lower tone with the 2nd, 4th, etc., partials of the upper tone. When we are supplied with single sinusoids, the patterns are too simple to be useful, and we have trouble unless the sounds are loud enough to produce harmonics within the ear by heterodyne action (which action brings back the recognizable patterns once again). Singing the tones provides an analogous restoration of the patterns. We can now set down additional members of our list of summarizing statements about the recognition of musical intervals between successively presented tones:

4. The acoustically definite special relationships found for superposed tones can continue to guide the intervals set between successive tones even in nonreverberant surroundings, as long as one tone follows the other with reasonable promptness (i.e., with a delay of less than about half a second).

5. When the sound pressure is kept low, interval-setting between sinusoids presented one after the other is quite difficult to accomplish, even for a skilled musician.

6. Single-component sounds that are loudly played (at SPLs above about 80 dB) generate enough harmonic components within the ear to permit interval-setting that is almost as good as that described in statement 4 above.

7. The intervals set while listening to low-SPL sinusoids or to normal tones presented with a large intervening period of silence tend to be wider than those governed by the physical relationships discussed in chapter 14. However, the frequency ratios that any one listener sets are not very well defined. The settings vary from trial to trial.

15.3. Introduction to Musical Scales

In most cultures, music is built around a set of sounds having well-defined pitches. One finds that the most-used of these pitches are connected in a manner strongly reminiscent of what were termed special relationships in chapter 14. From the acoustical point of view this parallelism is not surprising, since these special relationships call attention to themselves perceptually in many concurrent ways— by beats among the partials and by the production of orderly sets of heterodynes between superposed sounds, by similar comparisons in the reverberant sounds in a room, or by the weaker clues arising from the recognition of matches between parts of the earlier (remembered) and presently heard auditory patterns.

In any system of music it is customary to arrange the chosen set of tones in order of rising (and sometimes descending) pitch to make something called a *scale*. There are many such scales known to musicians and a part of their craft is to use the scale that suits their aesthetic purposes. I do not wish to imply that all music must have the notes of its scale based on our collection of acoustic cues, nor do I wish to suggest that all of the cues present themselves in every musical situation. On the other hand it is important to recognize that these cues provide musical guideposts for the performer and that these are sufficiently clear-cut that their influence is found wherever there is music. How the musician responds to these influences is of course strongly affected by the culture and traditions of his environment.

There are many ways in which one can "derive" a musical scale as an exercise on paper. There are also many ways in which a musician might discover the tones of a scale in the course of experiments with different sounds from his instrument. Let us see how we might experiment in a reverberant room to lay out the most familiar scale used in Western music and its extension to a chromatic scale. We will need to pick out only enough tones for our scale to span a single octave; because of the near identity of any tone with its octaves, each tone within the original octave implies its brothers in all other octaves.

To lay out our musical scale we will use an apparatus like that sketched in figure 15.1, which has its number 1 tone generator tuned to the note C. Using this apparatus we can make alternated-tone experiments of the sort described in section 15.2, marking the tuning dial of generator 2 to correspond to the easily recognized and strongly marked intervals of a major 3rd, a 4th, a 5th, a major 6th, and an octave, all in relation to the reference tone. When this work is completed,

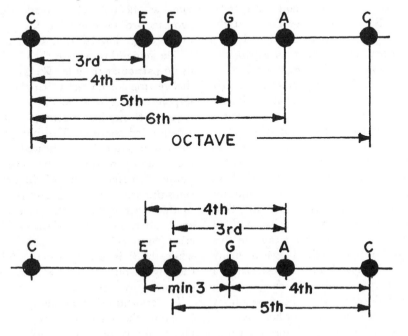

Fig. 15.2. Step I in the Building of a Musical Scale

we will have obtained an orderly series of pitches that musicians will recognize as being the reference tone C plus E, F, G, A, and the octave C, which together make a fairly complete C-major scale. We can match up these note names with the musically defined (beat-free) intervals we found in chapter 14, arranging them in a row along a line as shown in the upper part of figure 15.2. The reason for the irregular spacing of the labeled dots along the line will become apparent very shortly. This part of the experiment and its tabulation completes what I shall call Step 1 in the construction of our scale.

Let us pause now to "play with" the tones we have selected in Step I, to see if there are any relationships between pairs of the newly selected tones in addition to their basic relations with the reference tone C. The lower part of figure 15.2 reveals that there are many such relationships. For example, we find that the upper C of our scale is related to F by a 3/2 frequency ratio, which corresponds to a beat-free interval of a 5th. From E to A, and from G to C, the intervals are exactly a 4th, while between F and A we have a major 3rd. We also can recognize that the much less well-advertised but still exactly beat-free interval of a minor 3rd separates the tones E and G, and is also the interval between A and the C above it. We have discovered something rather significant here—not only can we make zero-beat transitions from C to any other note in the collection, but also transitions of this same kind are possible between many pairs of the newly defined notes. Using a tune that employs only this set of tones, a singer would feel secure as he moved from one of these tones to another. All he would need to do is to measure each new note accurately from the last one.

Anyone knowing the musical alphabet will notice that two tones are missing from our collection—the tones named D and B. Step II of our scale construction involves finding the settings for these two tones. Since C is a 4th below F, we are led (by analogy) to try tucking in a D that is a 4th below G. An equally plausible way to get a D would be to locate it a perfect 5th below A. The upper part of figure 15.3 shows us that these two Ds (indicated by open squares) *are not the same*—they differ by 22 cents, corresponding to a 1.27-percent discrepancy in frequency. If we were to sound the lower one of these Ds against G, or the upper one against A, strong beats would be heard. If the lower C of our scale is C_4 at 261.6 Hz, the two Ds would differ in frequency by nearly 4 Hz! It turns out that the tuning discrepancy here is the same as the one which made the Pythagorean 3rd unacceptable in the experiments of section 14.4, subsection E.

The remaining note of the C scale gives us no particular trouble. We find that the dial setting for an exact 5th above E corresponds precisely with the setting required to produce an interval of exactly a major 3rd above G. This note, which is the sought-after B, is indicated in the figure by an open square. The lower part of figure 15.3 shows some of the exact relationships that connect B and the two Ds to the other notes of the scale as developed so far. The lower of the two Ds is in exact minor-3rd relationship with F, while the B is exactly a major 6th above the higher-pitched D. We do not find any other strongly marked relationships.

In performing situations in the key of C major, the apparent difficulty with the Ds would cause little trouble to most singers, violinists, or wind instrument

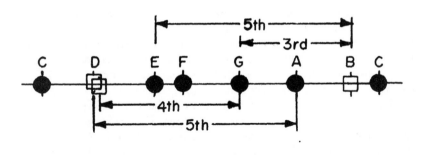

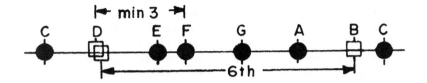

Fig. 15.3.   Step II in the Building of a Musical Scale

players as long as they were playing solo music. An unaccompanied player, performing slow-to-moderate sequences of notes in a reverberant room, tends (often unconsciously) to use the pitch flexibility of his instrument to get D from any of its predecessors by means of a beat-free (special) frequency relationship, in order to satisfy himself and his listeners. When he leaves this D, he will be led similarly to make a special-interval jump to the next note in his music (the interval being measured from the D). In faster music, a skillful musician may not do quite this, partly because he may sense that a long sequence of exact-interval jumps to and from an ambiguously defined note like D can pull the whole scale around, with rather confusing results for any listeners who can remember the pitches of several of the preceding tones!

Step II of our construction of the notes of a C-major scale was completed when the two missing notes of the major scale were filled in. The basic notes discovered in Step I are indicated in the figures by means of black dots, while the subsidiary (shall we call them second-generation?) tones appear as open squares. As we continue to experiment with various relationships between the tones discovered so far, it becomes apparent that there are some more gaps that can be filled. In Steps III and III-A I propose to outline *one* way of filling these gaps. This method in its simplest form would prove not quite workable for playing actual music, but it will serve to illustrate the nature of the problems which must be dealt with. For example, our list contains no tone that lies a beat-free 4th above F, nor one that is an exact major 3rd below F. The open triangles appearing in the top line of figure 15.4 show how all but one of the new tones might be fitted into the scheme of things. Notice that once again there is an ambiguity in defining one of the tones: what a musician would call A♭ lies an exact major third below the upper C, whereas going up an accurately tuned major 3rd from E brings us to a G♯ that is somewhat lower. The frequency discrepancy between these two tones fitted between G and A is 2.4 percent, somewhat larger than the one discovered between the two versions of D. We have already mentioned the simpler aspects of a soloist's problems with the paired tones, so we shift our attention to another such ambiguous pair, which (as Step III-A of our procedure) concludes our investigation into the construction of a scale by filling the gap remaining between F and G. The cardinal relationships involving this F♯-G♭ pair are shown in the lower part of figure 15.4.

If we were to explore systematically all the relationships between the notes of the scale as constructed so far, it would turn out that the resolution of each discrepancy by inserting yet another tuning for the notes of the scale would lead to a never-ending proliferation of notes. For practical music the competent soloist does what he can to reconcile the discrepancies. His problems while doing this are not terribly serious for a number of reasons which are well worth discussion.

Earlier in this section we learned that a musician who is given plenty of time to experiment and recheck in reverberant surroundings will set very accurate intervals of the beat-free special type. As the need for speed increases, or as the room becomes less reverberant mis-settings of pitch become less easily detected, and so are less of a problem to the player. Because the sound level is always greater at the player's ears than at the listeners', the player normally has more elaborate checks

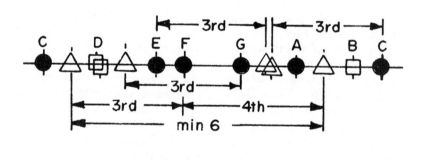

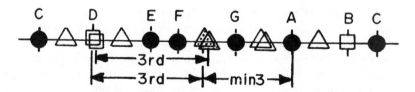

Fig. 15.4. Steps III and III-A in the Building of a Musical Scale

on his tuning success than does the audience. If he is reasonably competent, he generally has the advantage of being better tuned than his audience demands!

Let us close this section with the usual set of numbered statements that summarize and emphasize the salient points that we have studied:

1. A series of tones that all hold a strongly marked relationship to a single reference tone (the *tonic*) forms a five-note scale, each of whose members is in various special relationships to some other members of the set.

2. The scale can be filled out by choosing additional tones that are in special relationships to the original tones, even though they may not have a clearly marked relation to the tonic.

3. It is categorically impossible for exact beat-free relationships to be maintained between *all* members of a scale set up by any given succession of special intervals.

4. Because of the limited possibility of detection of tuning discrepancies of the sort implied in statement 3, the solo performer makes the best reconciliation he can, subject to the musical context and the nature of his training.

5. The performer can normally detect any discrepancy in tuning with more sensitivity than his listeners, so that he is in an advantageous position to make corrections that will be acceptable to them.

15.4. The Function of Equal Temperament for Adjustable-Pitch Instruments

In section 15.3 we became aware of the impossibility of maintaining a consistent set of frequencies for the scale of tones used in a solo performance. The inevitable discrepancies that arise in the tuning of any note when it is approached from some earlier member of a melodic sequence display themselves most strongly when slow music is played in reverberant surroundings. The practical difficulties associated with these discrepancies are, however, not particularly serious, because the acoustical conditions which display the problem most clearly are also the most favorable for helping the performer to detect and correct or disguise them.

Most of the tuning cues available for guidance in tuning successive tones in a melody are simply weakened versions of the ones which govern the tuning of superposed tones. Because of this, we recognize that when two or more players attempt to maintain beat-free pitch relations between the sounds they produce at any instant while playing successive notes chosen from some scale, the discrepancy problems are greatly magnified and, unless the players are skillful, chaos can result.

Without concerning ourselves here with the historical development of the subject,[3] let us see how this problem is dealt with today by musicians performing on adjustable-pitch instruments such as the woodwinds and brasses and also (to a lesser extent) on the bowed strings. Basically they are provided with a set of tones whose frequencies make a reasonable approximation to those needed for the notes desired. The music is written to identify these approximate notes, merely as a matter of convenience. It is then the duty of the players to cooperate in making fine adjustments on their pitches, to the extent permitted by their skills and demanded by their listeners. The approximate fixed scale is, in other words, used as a reference system and as *a point of departure*. It is kept more or less clearly in the minds of the players, but it may not be directly on display for the audience.

Let us see how to lay out this fixed chromatic scale, taking inspiration from the particular scale that we worked out in section 15.3. By now we are familiar enough with the nature of the beat-free musical intervals to recognize that they relate pairs of musical tones via the ratios between their fundamental frequencies. For example, the perfect 5th is identified with a $3/2 = 1.5000$ frequency ratio, while the major 3rd belongs with a ratio of $5/4 = 1.2500$ (see table 14.1). Following up this recognition, simple arithmetic shows that the frequency ratios between *successive* named members of our experimentally constructed scale lie between limits of about 1.04 and 1.07. In particular, the musical intervals between adjacent pairs E and F and between B and C turn out to have a frequency ratio of $1.0667 \ (= 16/15)$, whereas the ratio corresponding to the interval from C♯ and the lower of our pair of Ds is 1.0417, and the interval between F and its next upper neighbor is 1.0547. Let us take our courage in hand and inquire about the musical consequences of constructing a scale in which all the steps correspond to a single one of these frequency ratios. In words more familiar to contemporary musicians, we are asking about the consequences of constructing a scale having *equal temperament*.

Going through the sequence C, C♯, D, . . . C involves twelve upward steps, so we can inquire about (for example) what happens if we multiply the C♯-to-D interval 1.0417 by itself twelve times. If the answer is exactly 2, we have found the desired equally tempered semitone; if it is not, we shall have to seek further.

Here are the results of carrying out these multiplications for the three semitone ratios given in the paragraph above:

$$1.0417 \times 1.0417 \times 1.0417 \times \ . \ . \ .$$
$$(12 \text{ times}) = 1.6327$$

$$1.0547 \times 1.0547 \times 1.0547 \times \ . \ . \ .$$
$$(12 \text{ times}) = 1.8947$$

$$1.0667 \times 1.0667 \times 1.0667 \times \ . \ . \ .$$
$$(12 \text{ times}) = 2.1702$$

Clearly, the first two of our candidates are unsuccessful because they are too small. In the first case the 12-fold multiplication leaves us about a minor 3rd short of the desired 2-to-1 octave ratio, while the second one is nearly a semitone short. The third ratio is too big, since it leads to a 12-step sequence that is a little more than a semitone wider than the 2-to-1 ratio we seek. In this day of pocket calculators you might wish to inch your way down by small decrements from the overly large 1.0667 ratio to verify that the desired ratio for equal temperament is 1.059463. That is, if any given fundamental frequency is multiplied successively by this number, it will give the frequencies of the various equally tempered semitones that we have been seeking; the number 1.059463 multiplied by itself twelve times is equal to two. The frequencies listed for the set of reference tones in figure 2.1 were calculated in exactly this way, beginning with the 261.6-Hz frequency that belongs with the note C_4.

In section 14.4 it was explained that each interval of the 12-step equally tempered octave is divided up into 100 subintervals called cents. The frequency ratios for 10-cent increments within any given equally tempered semitone are listed in table 15.1.

Table 15.1

Frequency Ratios for 10-Cent Intervals

Interval in Cents	Frequency Ratio
0	1.00000
10	1.00579
20	1.01162
30	1.01748
40	1.02337
50	1.02930
60	1.03526
70	1.04126
80	1.04729
90	1.05337
100	1.05946

We should now check up on how well the relations between members of equally tempered scales match the special intervals that are so important to music. We can refer back to table 14.1 to learn about the discrepancies. The unison and the octave were matched in setting up the temperament, so there is no error there. The musically definite 3/2 ratio (the perfect 5th) turns out to be an interval of 702 cents, meaning that the equal-temperament approximation to the 5th is 2 cents narrower than the corresponding perfect 7-semitone interval. The 4/3 ratio of an exact 4th corresponds to an interval of 498 cents; i.e., it is 2 cents narrower than the 5-semitone exact interval. These errors are very small indeed. Calculations based on table 15.1 show that for notes near A_4 (440 Hz) a 10-cent error corresponds to a fundamental frequency change of about 2.5 Hz. A 2-cent error in this region of the scale then amounts to a frequency discrepancy of about $(2/10) \times 2.5 = 0.5$ Hz. The fact that most of the special intervals fall in this manner very close to whole-number mul-

tiples of 100 cents shows that equal temperament is basically a good approximation. The equal-temperament approximation to the beat-free interval of a major 3rd (4 semitones) is the least accurate of the ordinary intervals. Here the error is $400 - 386 = 14$ cents, which gives a frequency error of about 3.5 Hz near A_4. Before we go on to other things we should also notice that the unnamed 7/4 and 7/5 special frequency ratios listed in table 14.1 are 20 or 30 cents away from any note of the equally tempered series, and as a result lack familiar musical names.

We come now to a very important relationship that exists between equal temperament and the musically exact intervals that are preferred when time and circumstances permit. In figure 15.3 we met the fact that two Ds made their appearance. One of these proves to be 4 cents higher, and the other is 18 cents lower, than the D belonging to equal temperament. A tabulation comparing similarly the location of a given equally tempered note with the places it would need to be to permit perfectly tuned transitions to it from *any other note* in the scale shows that the most-needed settings gather themselves roughly into three groups. One group extends over a range of about 7 cents clustered at a point about 12 cents below the equally tempered setting; a similar group collects around a setting that is 12 cents above equal temperament, and a third collection of settings is found in the immediate neighborhood of the equal-temperament note. We can understand from this threefold grouping why it is that many musicians form the habit of "thinking" a note sharp or flat relative to equal temperament. While playing, such a musician starts with the written note, recognizes from the context whether it should be played in the upper, the middle, or the lower group, and finally zeroes in to a more exact setting if there is time.[4] If there is not time or if the listening conditions are not suitable, he nevertheless has gotten within a very few cents of the true setting, and by very simple means. Most players are unaware of the arithmetic of what they are doing, but because of long habit they will almost always go up or down in pitch by about 10 cents if asked to play a little sharper or a little flatter— just the amount needed to shift from one to another of the groups. Because of the need to move up or down a little from equal temperament and because the instruments do not "sing" well if their pitches are pulled too far above or below their own inherent tuning, the players on wind instruments take pains to find instruments that are built to play most naturally in accordance with the needs of the middle cluster of tunings. Many brass players also exploit the added refinement permitted by lever-controlled small motions of various value slides on their instruments. This allows them to adjust the "singing" pitches of their horns to the music as it progresses.

15.5. Basic Scale Relations in the Music of India

The way musicians in India deal with their musical scales provides us with a number of insights into how the influences of vibration physics and of the human hearing mechanism show themselves in the music of another culture. The Indian musician works within a musical structure built around a basic seven-tone (plus octave) scale of natural notes that interestingly enough matches the relations we met in constructing the C-major scale. In the Western tradition, when a musician wants to speak of a scale (a system of pitch relationships) without committing himself to any particular one (e.g., the major scale beginning on the note G), he uses the general note names do, re, mi, . . . which are familiar to most of us. A similar set of note names is used in India. Both sets of names are given below, along with the serial numbers of the notes in the ascending scale and our letter names for the case in which the first note happens to be C:

Serial number 1 2 3 4 5 6 7 8
Indian name *sa re ga ma pa dha ni sa*
European
    name   do re mi fa sol la ti do
Letter name   C D E F G A B C

Indian music theory allows the 2nd, 3rd, 6th, and 7th notes to be flattened a semitone, while the 4th can only be sharpened. The words *komal* and *tivra* are interchangeable with our words *flat* and *sharp*, so that if *sa* has a pitch that matches C, then *komal re* is what we would write as D♭ and *tivra ma* is F♯. When we transcribe all of the possible note names into the C scale, it turns out that they arrange themselves into a complete chromatic scale, as follows:

    C D♭ D E♭ E F F♯ G A♭ A B♭ B C
In our music, the possibility of writing either D♭ or C♯ for the second step of this scale is a musician's way of reminding himself of the most important pitch relationships between this note and the other ones in the particular piece of music. In figure 15.4 this note was deduced by measuring down a major 3rd from F; the musical contexts in which

this sort of reference is found would lead musicians to name the note D♭. If, on the other hand, I had chosen in the example to measure up a major 3rd from A, the correct name for the note would have been C♯. The same thing goes on in Indian music; the rule that certain notes can be flattened and only one sharpened is simply a reflection of the way in which the music is put together. We must always remember that note names with sharps and flats are merely indications of what needs to be done. The exact pitch the musician is to seek depends on the other notes of the music, both melody and accompaniment.

The Indian classical musician almost invariably plays to the accompaniment of a continuous set of drone pitch references, usually provided by the four successively plucked strings of a *tambura*. Chaitanya Deva, in his excellent book *Psychophysics of Music and Speech,* describes the tonal background provided by the tambura as follows:

According to the notes used in the *raga*, the tambura is tuned in one of the following ways:

Pa_1 Sa Sa Sa_1; Ma_1 Sa Sa Sa_1; Ni_1 Sa Sa Sa_1
G_1 C C C_1 F_1 C C C_1 B_1 C C C_1

(The last is not very common). The last two types of tuning are absent in the Southern system of our music.[5]

Here the subscript 1 on a note indicates that it belongs to the octave below the octave that contains notes lacking the subscript. Deva goes on to say that the first 9 string partials are audible to the player, and points out the curious fact that the strengths of these partials depend very little on the point where the strings are plucked (contrary to what we should

expect from our studies in chapter 7). The grazing contact of the strings as they touch the curved surface of the bridge gives rise to harmonically related heterodyne frequencies that have the overall effect of filling in any gaps in the generated vibration recipe. This is quite analogous to the way the internal nonlinearities of our ears reconstitute any missing harmonics in the sounds that come to them.

Tuning clues provided by the tambura are used very consciously by the player, especially if his own instrument lacks drone strings. Some years ago in Delhi, I met a professional player of the North Indian flute who in the course of our conversation was unwilling to sound his instrument in my presence without a reference drone of some sort. This was despite the fact that I had just heard him play beautifully in public, and had come round to tell him so. He explained that since he had just heard me achieve accurate intervals on his flute without a drone, my acute ear was bound to discover any errors he might make. You will notice that in spite of the disclaimer, he was perfectly sure of his sense of pitch in judging my own efforts on an unfamiliar instrument. Despite the differences in the kind of music we were accustomed to play, there was complete agreement about the intonation of the notes we used.

Listeners brought up in the European tradition of music often get the impression that Indian music abounds in all sorts of microtonal intervals, although the notation system would tend to show the lack of substantive existence of such notes. (It is true that certain notes in certain *ragas* are to be played slightly sharp or flat to increase the emotional effect of the mood of the *raga*. However, in present-day musical usage such alterations are becoming rarer.) The explanation for the impression of microtonal intervals is to be found in the way an Indian classical musician opens his pieces with a slow *alap,* in which the notes of the ascending and descending scale are presented in all sorts of contexts to establish their positions and relationships. One way in which the player establishes these guideposts is by wandering subtly around in their neighborhood, teasing the listener for a while before the tone is finally presented. As the music progresses, this evasion and skirting of the special pitch relationships becomes more and more elaborate, to the point where it becomes almost a game between the player and his listeners. It is considered to be in good taste for the audience to exclaim in surprise at the player's tricks during the performance, or to murmur its relieved approval when he finally "comes home" to the formal pitch. The musician thinks of all this pitch wandering as skillful decoration which he learns to do, in much the same way as a jazz musician learns which notes to depress microtonally in pitch in order to create the "blue" notes. The Indian musician has obviously learned that the possibility of contrast between the perceptually marked relationships and the vast array of unmarked ones is a powerful resource in his music. I have a tape recording made of a singing lesson broadcast over All-India Radio in which one can hear the contrast between the teacher's purposeful variations about each note in a short sequence before coming solidly onto it, and the much more tentative and unsteady efforts of his two pupils. It is a typical music lesson, complete with admonitions to end up exactly on the pitch of the *ma* (a fourth) or the *pa* (a

fifth), and explanations of the proper way to approach them. It was very easy to make measurements on this tape to verify the accuracy with which the various pitches were finally settled.

In Western music, pitch wanderings for effect are also present, but are usually much more limited in extent. The vibrato, the most familiar (to us) of these wanderings, can be somewhat confusing to an Indian musician. A brief wavering of pitch as someone comes on or off a note is perfectly familiar to him as a musical device, but the steadily maintained vibrato used by singers in particular causes him puzzlement. He thinks of it as some peculiar sort of trill and is surprised to find the microtones it implies in a musical culture which looks to him rather rigid, because we almost always make abrupt transitions from one note to another, without the slides that for him are an integral part of music. I have been asked how the Western performer who uses vibrato knows how much above and below the basic pitch he is supposed to go, and how fast the variations should be!

15.6. Other Reasons for Departures from the Special Intervals of a Scale

As one participates in, listens to, or makes measurements on the tuning of notes in music from all over the world, it quickly becomes apparent that the acoustically conditioned special intervals do not always govern performance practice. One universal reason for this we have already met in the last section—the player may choose to depart from formal tunings as a technical resource that contrasts the in-tuneness of one note (i.e., the presence of the tuning cues which define it) with the out-of-tuneness or non-tuned-ness of other notes which may advertise themselves either by strong beats or by the absence of any particular tuning indications.

Another reason for departures from the special relationships is to be found in situations where the player is performing in nonreverberant surroundings, or as a soloist with a large orchestra whose complex sounds can form a masking background in a fashion similar to that described for white noise in section 15.2. As we noted earlier, in passing, if we are deprived of the clear messages produced by beats between overlapping partials, most of us will tend to set our musical intervals a little bit wider than otherwise. The amount of this reference-free interval stretching varies from person to person, and also changes with a given person's state of health or mood. The effect is particularly large in the case of sounds having but a single component, which will be explained in example 4 of section 15.7.

Music played on instruments having a *large* number of strong, harmonically related partials is sometimes liberated from the constraints imposed by the special intervals, in part because the harmonically related clumps of beating partials which advertise them become so extensive as to confuse their message. For the closer intervals such as the minor or the major 3rd, the adjacent clumps may even overlap, producing near-total obliteration of the special relationship. An acoustically related property of violin and cello tones makes beats between their partials almost inaudible, permitting the player great latitude in his choice of pitch (an explanation of the detailed nature of this will be found later on in sec. 24.5).

In chapter 16 we will learn how the mechanical nature of the sounds produced by the various keyboard instruments influences the way that we hear them and therefore the ways in which they are tuned. As we progress to a study of other instruments (including the bowed strings) we will learn of reasons peculiar to each type that lead their players to use stretched or compressed intervals in their solo playing; these departures occur to an even greater extent during warmup and while the unaccompanied musician is practicing his exercises for tone and technique.

Among the wind instruments in particular, the musician quickly finds the playing pitch at which his instrument "sings" best. The pitches that are associated with best tone, promptest response, steadiest frequency, and widest dynamic range do not always exactly coincide with equal temperament or with its special-interval relatives. The musician playing in musically unconstrained circumstances will tend to let the instrument take its own way, playing each note at the pitch where the instrument sings best, provided of course that these pitches are not *too* irregular in their departures above and below the formally desired tunings. While I will leave a detailed discussion of these matters to later chapters, one example would be appropriate at this point. There are several cases (e.g., clarinets of the German Oehler system and the French-type Boehm system) in which two common forms of an instrument show opposite tendencies in the trend of the scale, one normally giving narrowed intervals when allowed to find its own pitches, the other giving wide intervals. Players who switch back and forth from one to the other have little more difficulty in adjusting their tuning than do those who specialize in only one variety. We shall see that the good-response cues available to the player are generally so strong (on a reasonably good instrument) that he can repeat his *pitches* far more accurately (even from day to day) when asked to get the best *tone,* than when he is asked to concentrate his attention on pitch alone. This fact has proved to be of enormous utility in guiding our researches into the ways in which wind instruments actually work, and of even greater significance in controlling the adjustments which improve their overall behavior. It gives us a stable and well-defined basis for measurement, which turns out to transcend historical, cultural, and stylistic boundaries.[6]

15.7. Examples, Experiments, and Questions

1. The simplest musical implications of room reverberation and background noise were well-illustrated at a concert given in Cleveland by the Netherland Chamber Choir a few years ago. During the first half of the concert, those of us who had already heard this expert and musically sensitive group in person or on records were a little disappointed with the performance. The voices did not blend well and chords seemed vague. The singers themselves were visibly ill at ease and the entrances of various solo voices were slightly hesitant and sometimes a little off-key. Because the group is highly professional, the performance continued in an acceptable if not excellent style until intermission. After intermission, everything was changed, and we were presented with a striking series of difficult compositions, perfectly sung.

A noisy air conditioner left on during the first half of the concert was the cause of the trouble. Its noise masked the reverberant cues normally available to the musicians. Let us examine the situation a little more closely. The A-weighted sound level in this particular empty hall is about 45 dB when the air conditioner is running. The presence of an attenuating audience makes almost no change in the measured sound level. The noise level from the machinery itself is reduced somewhat by the sound absorption that an audience provides, but the inevitable sounds of people moving, shuffling their programs, etc., bring the level back very nearly to the original empty-hall value. If we assume that the SPLs achieved by the choir range from 65 to 90 dB, we might expect that the musicians would have very nearly their accustomed amount of reverberation overlap in which to match their successive tones. Therefore, if one examines only the A-weighted sound level in the hall, one wouldn't expect the air conditioner to have much adverse effect on successive tones as heard by the choir. Similarly, the possibility of matching the superposed tones of each chord would also seem to be unaffected by the presence of a little room noise.

However, when we learn that the C-weighted noise level due to the air conditioner is 75 dB, our view of the concert changes drastically. The 30-dB excess of the C-weighted level over the A-weighted reading shows the presence of enormous amounts of low-frequency noise (see sec. 13.8), which is placed where it can mask the reverberations of the bass and tenor voices directly and also cover up the implied tones produced by practically any combination of musical parts. With the air conditioner turned on, the musicians were deprived of a large share of the subtle messages that normally tell each part of the choir what the other parts are doing. Several members of the choir told me later of their feelings of dismay and insecurity during the first half of the concert. They also expressed their enjoyment of the acoustics of the hall itself when the mechanical noise was reduced. This satisfaction with the hall was reiterated during a second visit by the group some years later (though they recalled their earlier encounter with the air conditioner as one of their more traumatic experiences).

2. In music theory the relationship between two (or more) tones is said to have been *inverted* when the lower tone is exchanged for its own higher octave. Thus the interval of a 5th between C_4 and G_4 inverts to give a 4th when we compare G_4 with the C_5 above it. Refer back to table 14.1 and verify that despite the fact that octaves are almost completely interchangeable when we are dealing with a single tone, the clarity with which a given interval is advertised need not be at all the same as that associated with its inversion. Look first at the following practical example: someone desiring to play a well-tuned $A_4\flat$ as a minor sixth above C_4 would find the placing of the note quite indefinite as compared with the same $A_4\flat$ when it is measured down a major 3rd from C_5.

3. I recently wasted some time trying to work out the tuning relationships of the Indian *jal tarang*. This is a tuned bell instrument made up of a set of chinaware bowls which are carefully adjusted for pitch by pouring water into them. Frustration arose because I naïvely forgot that the perceived pitches of bells are not related in any simple way to the frequencies of their partials (see chap. 5), and my

measurements of the first-mode frequencies of the bells gave little interpretable information. Perhaps you can devise a simple and workable technique whereby the *pitch* relations of these bells could be measured, or those of the Javanese *gamelan,* which is made up of a set of irregularly cast brass bars reminiscent of a glockenspiel. What special property of the sound spectrum of our Western glockenspiel allows it to be tuned by simply adjusting the lowest frequency modes of its bars?

4. You will recall from chapter 13 that equal increments of acoustic pressure amplitude (or of SPL) failed to give equal increases in loudness. We face the same sort of problem once again in connection with the relation between pitch perception and vibratory frequency. From the point of view of psychoacoustics the two problems are quite analogous. In the case of sinusoids, it is possible to arrange a sequence of equally spaced increments of perceived pitch (expressed in *mels*).[7] This mel scale is not at all in agreement with the musician's sequence of equally tempered (equal-frequency ratio) pitches. Suppose for example that we were to build a sine-wave electric organ, with each note being tuned in unison with the corresponding equally tempered note of an ordinary organ (so that successive keys produce sounds whose frequencies are raised by successive increments of almost exactly 6 percent). The perceived pitch change associated with playing C♯ after C near the middle of the keyboard would be heard as a rise of about 2 mels. At the bottom end of the keyboard the pitch change from one note to the next (again a 6-percent change in frequency) would be perceived as a rise of only about 1 mel. At the top end of the sine-wave organ

keyboard, however, the equal-tempered semitone step corresponds to a pitch rise of about 12 mels. To reiterate: when one is dealing with sinusoids, the equally tempered frequency scale is not an equal-step *pitch* scale. To get an equal-tempered sinusoid pitch scale, it would be necessary to stretch the traditional 2-to-1 frequency ratio for a perceived octave somewhat in going down from the middle toward the lower part of the keyboard, and to shrink it drastically on the way to the upper part. Such an equal-pitch-increment scale would be torn apart by fights between heterodyne components if we were to try to play music with it at any reasonable sound pressure level.

The situation with tones having harmonic partials is much more straightforward. We have already learned that pitch-matchings between successive and superposed tones are in agreement when the tones consist of a few strong partials. We have also given great attention to the way in which such sounds display their interrelationships, and have learned that an equally tempered scale (constructed using equal frequency ratios) is at the very least a good working approximation to what is needed. Notice that all this did *not* require us to produce a sequence of equally spaced pitches!

You may find it interesting and worthwhile to play around on a piano or, better, an electric organ, comparing the *pitch* changes you perceive for any given small musical interval (e.g., one to three semitones) at various points of the complete scale. You will find that over most of the keyboard, the pitch changes corresponding (say) to a semitone sound pretty much the same. Among the lowest notes a keyboard semitone begins to sound a little narrow in pitch, though by no

means to the extent found with sinusoids. At the top end of the keyboard once again the semitone ratio gives a slightly narrow-sounding pitch change compared with what you get over the middle two-thirds of the instrument's range. In other words, you can verify that, over the range in which music is played, each musical interval corresponds fairly well to a particular perceived pitch change, regardless of the absolute frequencies of the notes being compared. All this seems so obvious that many people take it for granted, and they miss the point that music based on special intervals could exist whether or not each of these intervals always implied the same change in perceived pitch.

5. I have sometimes been asked for a simple piece of evidence that music of all sorts depends on the *ratios* between frequencies rather than on the frequencies themselves. You might wish to work out a good answer to this question, built around the fact that a piece of music sounds perfectly well in tune (with itself) when it is played on an out-of-adjustment record player so that everything is run through too fast or too slow. A more historical answer can be built around the fact that in Bach's day much music was played using scales based on a 420-Hz frequency for A_4, whereas in late nineteenth-century Britain the reference frequency was 453 Hz, and in this country it rose as high as 461 Hz before dipping to 435 Hz, being at present a shade above the nominal 440-Hz value. All the music works perfectly well in all these tunings (provided the sopranos don't break on the high notes or the pianos lose their tone on the low ones, etc.). Can you go on to prove that these conclusions apply equally well to music which is *not* based on any system of spe-

cially marked relationships? Hint: make use of the fact that for ordinary musical tones having only a few strong partials the perceived pitch will change for all the notes by roughly the same amount when their frequencies are altered by a given ratio (see the latter half of example 4 above).

Notes

1. Recent experiments lend support to this interpretation of the phenomenon. See A. Kotschy, T. Tarnoczy, and K. Vicsi, "Subjective judgment of artificial reverberation processes," *J. Acoust. Soc. Am.* 56 (1974): 1192–94. See also Eric Young and Murray B. Sachs, "Recovery from sound exposure in auditory-nerve fibers," *J. Acoust. Soc. Am.* 54 (1973): 1535–43.

2. Wallace Clement Sabine, *Collected Papers on Acoustics* (New York: Dover, 1964). The earlier papers give a particularly rewarding look into the methods of a thoughtful and skillful investigator as he devises methods for the study of new phenomena. Sabine's comments on fluctuation phenomena in a room and on the musical implications of room reverberation foreshadow much of what we are discussing in this book.

3. A basic source for information on this is Hermann Helmholtz, *On the Sensations of Tone,* trans. Alexander Ellis from 4th German ed. of 1877 with material added by translator (reprint ed., New York: Dover, 1954). See part III, "The Relationship of Musical Tones," and parts of Appendix XX, "Additions by the Translator." See also Alexander Wood, *The Physics of Music,* 6th ed., rev. J. M. Bowsher (New York: Dover, 1961), chapter 11, "Scales and Temperament," and C. A. Taylor, *The Physics of Musical Sounds* (New York: American Elsevier, 1965), chapter 8, "Combinations of Notes." This chapter in Taylor's book contains a particularly interesting way of displaying the influence of heterodyne components.

4. Experiments by Paul Boomsliter and Warren Creel give us very important information on what a musician actually does about tuning. My discussion in this chapter is strongly influenced by these data, although I do not completely accept their published interpretation. Paul C. Boomsliter and Warren Creel, "The Long Pattern Hypothesis in Harmony and Hearing," *J. Mus. Theory* 5, no. 2 (1961): 2–30, and Paul C. Boomsliter and Warren Creel, "Extended Reference: An Unrecognized Dynamic in Melody," *J. Mus. Theory* 7, no. 2 (1963): 2–22. See also the synthesis of a different line of thinking about musical perception provided in Ernst Terhardt, "Pitch, consonance, and harmony," *J. Acoust. Soc. Am.* 55 (1974): 1061–69.

5. B. Chaitanya Deva, *Psychoacoustics of Music and Speech* (Madras: The Music Academy, 1967), p. 19. There is a great deal in this thoughtful and well-informed book to repay a reader, even if he has no particular interest in Indian music as such. Some readers may also wish to become acquainted with G. H. Ranade's book, *Hindusthani Music: Its Physics and Aesthetics,* 2d ed. (1951: reprint ed., Bombay: Popular Prakashan, 1971). The relationship between music in India and music in the West is very well summarized by Roger Ashton, "Basic Details of Variance Between Music in India and the West," in *Music East and West* (New Delhi: Indian Council for Cultural Relations, 1966).

6. The foregoing remarks disagree somewhat with the conclusions drawn by the authors of the following thoughtfully written papers: J. E. F. Sundberg and J. Lindqvist, "Musical octaves and pitch," *J. Acoust. Soc. Am.* 54 (1973): 922–29, and Frans Fransson, Johan Sundberg, and Per Tjernlund, "The scale in played music" (in English), *Svensk tidskrift för musikforskning* 56/1 (1974): 49–54. I believe that they have not taken sufficient account of the (sometimes unavoidable) tuning errors that are normally found in the instruments they studied.

7. S. S. Stevens and J. Volkman, "The relation of pitch to frequency: a revised scale," *Am. J. Psychology* 53 (1940): 329–53.

16
Keyboard Temperaments and Tuning: Organ, Harpsichord, Piano

In chapter 15 we investigated the general way in which a musician guides his tuning while playing on adjustable-pitch instruments. We learned in particular that there is *no possibility* of devising a fixed set of musical tones all of whose members will fit together neatly in accordance with the special relationships discussed in chapter 14. We found that woodwind and brass players prefer for practical purposes to use instruments tuned in equal temperament (with equal frequency ratios between adjacent semitones) whose notes can then be pushed up or down a little in pitch to meet the exigencies of the music.

We must now turn our attention to the problems of musicians who perform on keyboard instruments, where pressing on each key gives rise to a sound of fixed pitch, with no possibility during performance of sliding the pitch up or down according to musical need. After all that has been said so far about the care with which good musicians adjust their playing pitches when such adjustments are possible, you are bound to be curious about the manner in which acceptable music can be extracted from nonadjustable instruments such as the pipe organ, the piano, the harpsichord, or the clavichord. We will find that there are slight

differences in the ways in which the various kinds of keyboard instruments are tuned in order best to satisfy essentially identical musical requirements. Satisfying these requirements proves to be more difficult on the pipe organ than it is on instruments that work by plucking or striking strings.

Let us look ahead briefly into the manner in which the present chapter is put together. First we will look at a number of ways of dealing with the pipe organ tuning problem. This investigation is relatively straightforward, because we are dealing with the relations between sustained musical tones whose partials are in exact harmonic relationship. On the other hand, in sounds made by plucked and struck strings, the impulsively excited partials die away in time, and they are not quite harmonic in their frequency relationships, thus altering the way in which musical relationships arrange themselves. We will need therefore to extend our knowledge of the vibration physics of such strings before continuing with an account of the ways in which tuning procedures laid down for pipe organs adapt themselves for use with the stringed keyboard instruments. The chapter closes with a discussion of some of the musical implications of these adaptations.

16.1. "Just" Scales: The Conventional Basis for Keyboard Tunings

By the end of the seventeenth century, the pipe organ and various other keyboard instruments had become well-established in European music. In order for this to occur, musicians had been forced to devise tuning procedures for these instruments that would minimize the musical drawbacks arising from the nonadjustability of their pitches. Musicians guided their tuning efforts by keeping in mind an idealized pair of so-called *just scales* that are very closely related to the chromatic scale we devised in chapter 15 on the basis of our special frequency relationships. Frequency relationships between a reference note (the tonic) and the

son for this conventional choice is partly historical and partly a result of the greater frequency of occurrence (in the key of C) of intervals relating D with G than of intervals connecting D with A. We are already aware of reasons why both Ds are important in even the simplest of music. You will recognize that aside from the major 2nd and the major 7th, all of the just intervals measured from the tonic C correspond exactly with the well-marked beat-free relationships that we met first in chapter 14 (see table 14.1). We have, on the other hand, considerable freedom in placing the D and the B (relative to C) since the zero-beat relationship between C and either of these two notes is very weak—traces of the direct relationship can only be demonstrated under loud playing conditions using specially chosen vibration recipes for the tones.

Let us now look at the analogous just tunings for the minor scale:

1/1	10/9	6/5	4/3	3/2	8/5	9/5	2/1
unison	major 2nd	minor 3rd	perfect 4th	perfect 5th	minor 6th	minor 7th	octave
C	D	E♭	F	G	A♭	B♭	C

various members of the major scale in just tuning are written out as follows (note names are given for a scale beginning at C):

Referring again to table 14.1, we find here the lower of our two tunings for D, the upper one of our A♭/G♯ pair, and a new sort of B♭ that is exactly a minor 3rd

1	9/8	5/4	4/3	3/2	5/3	15/8	2/1
unison	major 2nd	major 3rd	perfect 4th	perfect 5th	major 6th	major 7th	octave
C	D	E	F	G	A	B	C

The major second (9/8 frequency ratio) that is chosen for the just major scale corresponds exactly to the *upper* one of the pair of Ds we discovered earlier. The rea-

above G. There are of course many ways in which a given note may be defined via its relations with other notes. For example, music theorists recognize two varieties of minor 7th besides the 9/5 ratio listed above; one of these, the grave minor 7th (having a frequency ratio of 16/9), is what we had settled on for a B♭ in chapter 15, while the harmonic minor 7th (7/4 frequency ratio) is one of the special intervals listed in chapter 14.

It is possible to work with our rather good compromise tunings as long as one is willing to restrict his composing and playing to the major keys of C (no sharps or flats), G (one sharp), F (one flat), D (two sharps), and B♭ (two flats). These compromise tunings will also be successful for use in the corresponding minor keys whose key signatures also contain no more than two sharps or flats. That is, the compromise *fixed* tunings give a close approximation to the desired just intervals in certain scales. Some of these tunings also serve well for music written in three sharps or three flats, but beyond this the approximations become progressively less acceptable to the listener.

The other major compromise tuning, equal temperament, has no perfectly tuned intervals except the octave. Some of its scale errors are quite large, and they are irregularly arranged relative to just tuning. In marked contrast to other systems, equal temperament uses an individual compromise mistuning for each particular type of interval, and these interval mistunings remain exactly the same in all playing keys. One thing that makes the equally tempered system practical is the fact that the important and strongly marked interval of the fifth closely approximates the special relationship that is the fifth of just tuning.

16.2. A Tuning Procedure for Setting Equal Temperament

Discussions of keyboard instrument tunings quickly become sterile exercises in arithmetic if they do not include workable methods for "setting" the desired temperament *and for testing whether it has actually been obtained.* In this section I shall describe a simplified tuning and checking procedure for setting equal temperament on an electric or pipe organ whose sustained tones are made up of exactly harmonic partials. Later on in this chapter we will learn how such procedures may be adapted to the tuning of the harpsichord and other instruments where the effects of string inharmonicity must be taken into account.

The equally tempered scale is a good place to begin learning how to tune— first, because of its predominance in today's music, and second, because one can carry out its tuning by means of an entirely repetitious procedure. In "setting" this temperament we make use of the fact that its approximate fifths are all alike, and are very close to but not exactly equal to their beat-free counterparts; i.e., the equally tempered frequency ratio between the two tones is 1.4983 instead of the exactly beat-free ratio of $3/2 = 1.5000$. In other words, we set a series of intervals each of which is smaller than a perfect fifth by 2 cents (see sec. 15.4). Since we will be using only fifths to do our tuning (along with beat-free octaves), we should verify that if we write down the note names for a series of fifths beginning with C, all the notes of the chromatic scale will appear, in the sequence C, G, D, A, E, B, F♯, C♯, G♯, D♯, A♯, F, C.

Suppose that the repetition rate for C_4 is set to 261.63 Hz by means of a tuning fork. The equal-temperament G_4 above it is then supposed to have a fundamental frequency of $261.6 \times 1.4983 = 392.00$ Hz.

Let us refer back to part D of section 14.4 to see what is to be expected from a not-quite-perfect 5th in the way of beats. We noticed there that for exact beat-free tuning of a musical 5th, the third harmonic partial of the lower note should coincide with the second partial of the note a 5th higher. In the example demonstrating the effect of a slight mistuning, we found that the 600-Hz third harmonic of tone M (whose fundamental is 200 Hz) and the 602-Hz second harmonic of tone N (301 Hz) differed by 2 Hz. Notice now that in every clump of beating components (heterodyne and original) the intercomponent beats take place at 2 Hz *or at one of its whole-number multiples.* That is, in the first clump (near 100 Hz) there are 2-Hz beats between the 99- and the 101-Hz components, and also between the 103- and the 101-Hz components; the remaining possibility for beating here is the 4-Hz (twice 2 Hz) rate associated with the 99- and 103-Hz pairing. In a more general way, we can say that for a mistuned 5th, whether we focus our attention on beats among members of a low-frequency clump or on those among members of a high-frequency clump, the *repetition rate* of the beats in the clump will equal the frequency difference between the third partial of the lower tone and the second partial of the upper one.

In tuning G_4 to C_4, then, we wish to listen for a beat repetition rate running a trifle slower than one per second:

$$(3 \times 261.63) - (2 \times 392.00) = 0.89 \text{ Hz}$$

We must of course make sure that G is tuned on the *low* side of the zero-beat in-

terval. (By the way, it is advisable to use the diapason stop or another of similar tone color when setting the scale, in order to make sure that there are sufficient harmonic partials in the tones to establish the musical relationships, but not so many as to obscure them. (The trompette stop, e.g., is built of tones containing far too many strong partials for easy tuning.)

The next step is similarly to tune D_5 relative to the newly set G_4. In equal temperament, the fundamental frequency of D_5 is $392.00 \times 1.4983 = 587.33$ Hz, so that the desired beat repetition rate between G_4 and D_5 is:

$$(3 \times 392.00) - (2 \times 587.33) = 1.34 \text{ Hz}$$

It is a good idea to keep all one's tuning in the same general pitch region; therefore, our next step is to tune a beat-free (2-to-1) octave down from D_5 to D_4 before we continue by setting the A_4 on the basis of the lower D. Figure 16.1 sets forth the first few members of the tuning sequence written out on the musical staff. The numbers in parentheses give the beat repetition rates telling how much below zero beat the upper member of each note pair is to be tuned. You may find it interesting to work out why there are two alternating sequences of slow and fast beats, each sequence rising in rate by about 12 percent as we go through the tuning series.

Digression on the Use of a Metronome to Define Beating Rates.
Relatively slow beating rates of the sort used to adjust tempered intervals are somewhat hard to determine with the unaided ear. If, however, you set the ticking rate of a metronome to correspond to the desired beat frequency, a few seconds of listening to its rhythm will educate your ear for the job it is

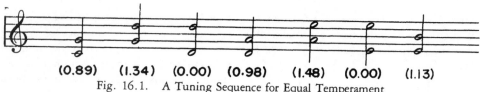

(0.89)   (1.34)   (0.00)   (0.98)   (1.48)   (0.00)   (1.13)

Fig. 16.1.   A Tuning Sequence for Equal Temperament

supposed to do. It is not difficult to work out the metronome setting corresponding to the desired beat frequency, since the device is calibrated in ticks per minute, which is 60 times the desired number of beats per second. For example, the metronome setting for the 0.89-Hz beating rate for the $C_{\sharp}$-to-G_4 interval is $0.89 \times 60 = 53.4$ ticks/minute, while the 1.34-Hz beat relating D_5 to G_4 corresponds to 80.4 ticks/minute. Few metronomes are accurate within 10 percent, so there is no sense in carrying out such detailed calculations. The first setting should be thought of as being close to 55/min and the second close to 80/min. Metronome inaccuracies of the sort referred to here cause little trouble, because one should use the metronome only to start the tuning procedure. As we shall see, the procedure itself always contains its own provisions for checking and correcting errors as they arise.

You are likely to discover, soon after starting a tuning series of the sort described above, that your ears are able to guide you quite well in setting intervals that sound "equally out-of-tune" without any need for you to count beats. For this reason I do not need to set down beating rates beyond the first few notes. As you proceed, however, it is a good idea to keep checking back over the intervals set earlier to remind your ears of the correct (consistent) out-of-tuneness. Also, as soon as you pass E in the sequence, it is possible to listen for the very rapidly pulsating sound associated with the fast beating of the widened major thirds that are typical of equal temperament. Each newly tuned 5th can be checked against the note a major 3rd below it, providing a means of

watching the consistency of the tuning while it is in progress. If you wish to count beats for these 3rds (they tend to be too fast for easy counting), you can listen for a $(5 \times 261.63) - (4 \times 329.63) = 10.37$-Hz beat repetition rate for the beats arising between the components belonging to C_4 and E_4, corresponding to the frequency difference between the 5th partial of C_4 and the 4th partial of E_4. Similarly, you will find an 11.64-Hz beat repetition rate when D_4 is compared with $F_4\sharp$. Once you have learned what to listen for, your attention should be focused on the nature of this sound rather than on its beat repetition rate.

If you have carried out a consistent tuning along the lines sketched above, its ultimate correctness will be proven by testing the final F-to-C interval in the complete sequence. Since you started with C and worked around to F by a long series of tunings, one more tuning of the sort you have been doing should bring you back once again to the original C (or its exact octave). If the tested F-to-C interval comes out narrow, your fifths have not been sufficiently shrunken, and it will be necessary to start over again with a *slightly* faster beating rate than what you assumed at the start (your metronome may have been inaccurate, or mis-set). Once the "circle of approximate fifths" is made to close at the octave by a properly uniform set of shrunken intervals, you will have achieved equal temperament. Any given interval between pairs of tones should then sound pretty much the same, no matter where you test it in the span of a little more than an octave that you have freshly tuned. That is, all the semitone intervals are supposed to sound "like" each other, as do the whole-tone intervals, minor thirds, major thirds, fourths, etc. It is worthwhile to make comparisons by alternating the notes of a pair as well as by sounding them together. Once you have checked over the various intervals, it is time to tune all the rest of the keyboard by means of beat-free octave settings based on the tempered scale that we have set up starting from C_4. This completes the tuning.

I hope most of my readers can experiment with actual tuning, and will trust their ears as they try to set a temperament. But you are presumably also curious about just how much each equal-tempered interval departs from the corresponding justly tuned interval, and in which direction. Table 16.1 shows in the right-hand column the discrepancies (ex-

pressed in cents) between equal temperament and just tuning. A positive number indicates that equal temperament is sharp; a negative one indicates a flat tuning. You can see here why certain intervals sound smoother or rougher than other intervals of the equal-tempered scale.

Many musically inclined people will feel quite unhappy with the results of tuning an organ for the first time by the procedure outlined above, and will find it hard to believe that they have done it correctly. Most of us are not used to paying such close attention to intervals sounded on keyboard instruments; moreover, the systematically arranged beats that arise on an instrument producing sustained tones with harmonic partials make the discrepancies particularly obvious. The tuning situation, furthermore, is far removed from music-making, in which so many tones are present and so much is constantly changing that our attention seldom dwells long enough on a particular

Table 16.1

Tuning Errors for Two Different Temperaments (*Expressed in Cents*)

Interval	Werckmeister III							Equal Temperament
	Tonic Note:							Error for Any Particular Interval Is Identical in All Keys
	C	G	F	D	B♭	A	E♭	
Major 2nd	−10	−10	+7	−5	zero	zero	zero	−12
Major 3rd	+6	+11	+6	+9	+11	+14	+17	+14
Major 4th	zero	+5	zero	+5	zero	+5	zero	+2
Major 5th	−5	−6	zero	−5	zero	zero	zero	−2
Major 6th	+6	+10	+11	+7	+7	+14	+22	+16
Major 7th	+6	+3	+6	+9	+6	+14	+11	+12
	Tonic Note:							
	A	E	D	B	G	F♯	C	
Minor 3rd	−6	−11	−9	−17	−7	−14	−22	−16
Minor 6th	−6	−6	−11	−11	−17	−9	−22	−14

two-note interval to question whether it is precisely in tune. Interestingly enough, a clever combination of three or more equally tempered tones often produces a much more "in-tune" overall effect than one would expect from an examination of these tones played two at a time. The proliferation of sevenths, ninths, and more and more complex chords from the time of Beethoven through the Romantic and Impressionistic eras and into the present can be attributed at least in part to the ubiquitous use of the equally tempered modern piano. Composers for present-day keyboard instructions exploit the possibilities of equal-tempered tuning, just as earlier composers exploited the differing inequalities of the tunings of the their time. We will take a step in the direction of explaining these remarks in the next section as we look at one of the keyboard tunings whose utility is restricted to only a few tonalities.

16.3. A Useful Unequal Temperament: *Andreas Werckmeister III*

We have seen that tuning a keyboard instrument in equal temperament gives one the ability to play equally well in all scales. This versatility is paid for by the presence of tuning errors that are relatively large (compared to beat-free tuning), although the important interval of the fifth is quite well approximated, so that one of the acoustical underpinnings of the scale is solidly present. A different approach to the "engineering design" of a keyboard temperament is to work for the best approximation possible over a restricted set of scales, with a group of several somewhat more out-of-tune fifths buying more accuracy in the overall tuning in these keys.

In this section we will look at a temperament devised by Andreas Werckmeister in 1691. This particular temperament (known as Werckmeister III) is sometimes used today for tuning pipe organs of the baroque type, and is also often applied to harpsichords and other old instruments. The actual tuning procedure outlined here was described to me by Herman Greunke, an associate of the tracker-organ builder John Brombaugh.

One begins the Werckmeister III tuning by setting the C_4 reference note (for example at 261.63 Hz) and tuning E_4 a perfect (zero-beat) major third above it. This E will serve as a temporary checkpoint in setting the next part of the scale. Following this a series of four contracted 5ths are tuned (C to G, G to D, D to A, A to E), very much as in setting up an equally tempered scale, except that here one must shrink the tuning of each of the four intervals enough for the resulting E to be identical with the checkpoint E we have already set. Each member of this set of carefully mistuned 5ths has a frequency ratio of 1.4952 (5.5 cents short), so that the G_4 needs to have a fundamental frequency of $1.4952 \times 261.63 = 391.20$ Hz, and the first beating repetition rate to listen for will be at $(3 \times 261.63) - (2 \times 391.20) = 2.49$ Hz. This is considerably faster than the 0.89-Hz beat we met first in setting up an equally tempered scale. In the Werckmeister III tuning procedure, the second beating rate, between G and D, turns out to be 3.72 Hz.

Now that the initial set of tempered (modified) 5ths has been tuned and checked against the initial setting for E_4, we must retune E by raising it enough to make it a perfect, beat-free 5th above the A that has already been determined. We can then use this newly set E as the reference point for tuning B a beat-free 5th above it.

The basic scale is completed by tuning a downward sequence of perfect 5ths, beginning from C thus: C, F, Bb, Eb, Ab, Db, Gb (making the usual octave skips to stay in the middle of the keyboard). It is not useful to try checking up on this scale by continuing on down a 5th from Gb to Cb, because this last note on the instrument has already been tuned as a B by another route. The Cb obtained by going down from C by perfect 5ths is not supposed to agree with the B lying a perfect 5th above our modified E!

The main part of table 16.1 shows the discrepancies in cents between the Werckmeister III temperament and just tuning for the keys in which it is intended to be useful. In the key of C major we find that the major 2nd is 10 cents flat (as compared with 12 cents in equal temperament). That is, both tunings split approximately in half the 22-cent difference between the 10/9 and 9/8 ratios that we found for our second note in the major and minor just scales (see sec. 15.3), making a more useful overall approximation than would result from either "exact" tuning used by itself. In C major we notice that the Werckmeister major 3rd is only 6 cents sharp, rather than 14 cents sharp as it is in equal-temperament 3rds in all keys. The 4th turns out to be exact (beat-free) in the key of C, while the crucial 5th is 5 cents flat. Looking over the rest of the table, we notice that the various other keys display errors of a very similar nature: the notes are typically a half dozen cents sharp or flat, the errors being differently distributed in the different keys. We can use the Werckmeister III temperament as a typical representative of the tribe of workable unequal temperaments, and any conclu-

sions we draw about its musical implications will apply with only minor modifications to many other temperaments. In section 16.8 you will find directions for setting up two more temperaments with which to experiment.

16.4. Some Musical Implications: *Key Mood and Modulation*

In the baroque era musicians were vividly conscious of the changes of flavor or mood produced when a piece of music is transposed from one key to another. There are many ways in which the acoustics of our ears and of our musical instruments can give rise to these changes. At the present moment, however, we will confine our attention to the changes of key color or flavor produced on the organ family of instruments where (to first approximation at least) the tone colors and loudnesses of the individual notes of a scale are essentially identical. These mood changes are also important for the stringed keyboard instruments.

Table 16.1 has shown us that for an unequal temperament the errors of tuning relative to the just scale differ from one key to another. Whether or not we take the just scale literally as the model of perfection, the table shows clearly that the beats (and other evidences of musical relationship) that are heard when any set of intervals is sounded will change from key to key. This fact is sufficient to establish that music played in different keys will give different overall impressions.

Beyond the changes in the musical relationships between tones in the music caused by these differing frequency relationships, we discover a different kind of change that can occur in organs of the older sort, known as *tracker organs*, in which the flow of air to the various pipes is controlled by slide valves operated directly by mechanical linkages to the keyboard. On such organs, the valves may be opened more or less promptly depending on whether they are worked by stronger or weaker fingers as the player presses the long white keys or the short black ones of the keyboard. The patterns of finger motion and of long and short levers on the keyboard are altered when one plays in different keys, so that there are fairly well established changes in the patterns governing the way the individual pipes break into song. That is, small but characteristic irregularities in the starting-up and shutting-off times of the notes join the small and characteristic pitch irregularities resulting from the tuning procedures in defining the musical personality of a given key signature. When one plays upon an organ tuned in equal temperament that is provided with electrical or pneumatic air valves, there is essentially no characteristic musical flavor associated with the various key signatures, at least as they arise from simple pitch and timing changes.

When in the course of a piece of music the composer shifts (*modulates*) into another key, the listener is subjected to an auditory process that so to speak releases him from the musical expectations associated with the original key, while a new set of expectations is sketched out belonging to the new key. The process of modulation itself (however it is carried out) has a musical interest in its own right, and for a time the listener retains his memory of what went before, even as he becomes accustomed to what is new. Just as a pan of lukewarm water may feel hot to a hand that has earlier been dipped in ice water, or cold to a hand that has

been immersed in hot water, so also the musical flavor of a given new key signature will depend to some extent on the key which the music has just left.

When one is using equal temperament, the aesthetic impact resulting from modulation from one key to another is not nearly as strong as it can be in the unequal temperaments, and the effect is temporary, lasting only as long as the listener can retain some kind of aural recollection of what came before. Music played on an unequally tempered organ shows in addition the longer-term change of flavor arising from the acoustical relationships between notes that are systematically altered by the key change. It is ironic that in equal temperament the increased freedom to modulate from one key to another one far distant from it is purchased at the expense of a lost distinction between these keys.

It should be clearly understood that the problems of producing good music on sustained-tone instruments having notes of fixed pitch are by no means insuperable, although they do pose a challenge to the skill and imagination of the composer. The following anecdote will perhaps help you to understand the situation. I recently had occasion to hear a concert which I tape recorded for acoustical reasons with the permission of the performer. The program included the following three compositions for pipe organ: *Toccata per l'Elevatione* from the *Messa delli Apostoli* (1635) by Girolamo Frescobaldi; *Prelude and Fugue in A major* (BWV 536) by J. S. Bach; and *Etude I* (1967) by Gyorgy Ligeti. The first of these pieces contained a number of sustained major thirds, which work perfectly well on an organ tuned to one of the unequal temperaments common in the seventeenth century, but which fight unmercifully on today's equally tempered instruments. During the playing of it the audience stirred uneasily, and, when I have played the tape, numerous musicians (including pianists and harpsichordists) have asked me what terrible thing went wrong with the organ. Most are incredulous when the explanation is given, even when they listen to the piece by Bach played the same evening on the identical organ, sounding in the Bach like the admirable instrument it is. Bach arranged for his thirds to come and go, well disguised by their musical context. Even close listening does not bring out the roughnesses that we know are present in the bare interval. The third composition, a modern one, directly exploits the roughness of equally tempered thirds. One long-held chord follows another without let-up in a slow and hypnotic progression of changing registrations, pitches, and beating intervals.

16.5. Vibration Physics of Real Strings

So far in this chapter we have been dealing with the organ, which produces sustained tones made up of partials having a whole-number relationship. It is time to turn to keyboard instruments that make their sounds by plucking and striking stretched strings, so we can look into the way the complexities introduced by such things as string stiffness and the decay of the tone affect music. Back in chapter 7 we learned that a vibrating guitar or piano string has characteristic vibration frequencies that are *almost* in a whole-number relationship. Studying the causes of this inharmonicity can lead us to a bet-

ter understanding of the musical properties of such strings.

Consider a perfectly flexible round string of length L and radius r, which is stretched between rigid supports under a tension T. The density of the string material is d. The formula for the nth natural frequency f_n of such a string is:

$$f_n \left(\begin{matrix} \text{flexible string} \\ \text{under tension} \end{matrix} \right) = n \left(\frac{1}{Lr} \right) \sqrt{\frac{T}{d}} \sqrt{\frac{1}{4\pi}}$$

For such a string we see that $f_n = nf_1$; i.e., the natural frequencies form an exact harmonic series. We also notice that the frequencies are all inversely proportional to the vibrating length L, so that a 5-percent increase in length gives rise to a 5-percent decrease in each natural frequency, and a doubling of the length lowers the resulting tone by an octave—provided we keep the tension unchanged. An exactly similar set of remarks applies to the result of changing the radius r of the string. We notice, on the other hand, that the frequencies are proportional to the square root of the tension; as a consequence of this it would be necessary to quadruple T in order to raise the pitch of the plucked string by one octave, and to produce a 5-percent change in frequency one would have to alter the tension by very nearly 10 percent.

Any real string used in a musical instrument has some stiffness, so that if it were not under tension it would act like a very long, thin bar hinged at its two ends (see chap. 9, sec. 3 and fig. 9.6). Once we know the behavior produced by the elastic forces arising from the tension and from the barlike stiffness of the string, it is not difficult to work out the behavior of a real string where the vibration is governed by the joint action of these elastic forces. Consider a bar of length L and radius r, fastened by hinges at its two ends to a solid anchorage; the stiffness properties of the material of this bar are expressed in terms of its "modulus of elasticity" Y, and d once more stands for the bar's density. The nth characteristic frequency of the bar is given by the following formula:

$$f_n \text{ (hinged bar)} = n^2 \left(\frac{r}{L^2}\right) \sqrt{\frac{Y}{d}} \left(\frac{\pi}{\sqrt{2}}\right)$$

Here we notice that $f_n = n^2 f_1$, so that a bar whose first mode frequency f_1 is 100 Hz will produce components at $2^2 \times 100 = 400$ Hz, $3^2 \times 100 = 900$ Hz, etc., instead of the 100-, 200-, 300-, . . . Hz sequence of the flexible string. That is, the natural frequencies for a bar are much more widely spaced than they are for a string. We also notice that the frequency varies inversely as the square of the bar's length, so that doubling the length moves the sound down two octaves in pitch (a relationship we have already noted in connection with glockenspiel bars; see sec. 9.2). Observe that the bar's radius appears upstairs in the formula here, instead of in the denominator, so that an increase in the thickness of the bar raises its frequency instead of lowering it as is the case for a flexible string under tension.

It happens that the characteristic vibrational shapes for string and hinged bar are exactly alike (sinusoidal), even though the frequency relationships are wildly different. In the nineteenth century, the French physicist Felix Savart pointed out that because of the identity of vibrational shape there is a very simple way to find the frequency of vibration of a rod moving under the influence of both kinds of elastic forces. The nth mode of vibration

(having n sinusoidal humps in its characteristic shape) has a frequency which is equal to the square root of the sum of the squares of the frequencies belonging to the two simpler cases. That is:

f_n (stiff string under tension)

$$= \sqrt{f_n^2(\text{flexible}) + f_n^2(\text{bar})}$$

We met a very similar mathematical relationship in section 9.2 in the Digression on Rectangular Plate Frequency.

For musical strings where the stiffness contribution to the frequency is very small compared with that produced by the tension, we can make use of a simplified version of the formula given above:

$$f_n\left(\begin{array}{c}\text{stiff string}\\\text{under tension}\end{array}\right)$$

$$= nf_1\left(\begin{array}{c}\text{flexible string}\\\text{under tension}\end{array}\right) \times (1 + Jn^2)$$

Here we recognize that $f_1 \times (1 + J)$ is the first mode frequency, where J is a numerically small coefficient that contains the influence of the stiffness. Notice that the term (Jn^2) gradually raises the successive frequencies above the nf_1 harmonic series values expected for a musically simple sound source. The value of J turns out to be:

$$J = \left(\frac{r^4 Y}{TL^2}\right) \left(\frac{\pi}{2}\right)^3$$

which shows that (for a given playing frequency) the inharmonicity is reduced if one uses the longest, tautest, and slenderest string that meets all the other requirements which may be laid down upon a musical string. For a typical grand piano, such as the one described under "Piano Manufacturing" in the Encyclopedia Britannica, the tension is roughly constant for all the strings across the main span of the keyboard (about the weight of a man), and the strings used for playing C_4 are proportioned to make J close to 0.00016. On such a piano, as one goes along the scale from note to note, the value of J grows quite smoothly, increasing by a factor of about 2.76 for every octave one goes up and decreasing by the same factor for every octave down (until one reaches the copper-wound bass strings that are designed by a different set of rules).

It is worthwhile here to compare the harmonically related frequency components produced by a pipe organ tuned to C_4 with the nearly harmonic frequency components produced by a piano string whose first mode has the same frequency:

ends. Figure 16.2 contrasts the mode-4 vibrational shapes for a wire having hinged ends with those for a wire having clamped ends. The figure also suggests to us that in a fairly correct metaphorical sense we can think of the clamped-end bar as acting like a hinged-end bar having a somewhat reduced length L_c. Mathematical enquiry into the nature of the vibrations of a taut musical string with clamped ends shows that we do in fact come back to exactly the formula given above, with the L replaced by the shortened length $L_c = L \times (1 - \sqrt{J})$. Because of this similarity between the frequency ratios associated with the two kinds of string anchorage, we can safely make use of the results obtained earlier without worrying too much about the degree of

Component:	1	2	3	4	5	6
Piano string:	261.63	523.51	785.91	1049.23	1313.23	1578.68 Hz
Pipe organ:	261.63	523.26	784.89	1046.52	1308.15	1569.78 Hz
Discrepancy:	000.00	0.25	1.02	2.71	5.08	8.90 Hz

This list of frequencies should make us suspect that many of the musical relationships heretofore signaled to our ears by beats between sets of harmonically related components will take on quite a different aspect when we listen to piano strings. Before we look into these musical consequences, we should collect a little more information about the nature of real strings in a musical instrument.

So far we have looked at what physics has to tell us about strings attached under tension to immovable mountings by means of hinged joints. On a piano, a harpsichord, or a guitar, we notice that the ends of the string act more like clamped bars than they do hinged ones, so that the vibrational shapes include an almost undeflected section at the string

clamping produced at the string ends of a real instrument.[1]

The fact that strings are coupled to a soundboard at one end means that the anchorage at that end is not absolutely rigid. We know enough about the vibrations of plates and membranes (see sec. 10.7) to realize that if some particular natural frequency of the string happens to coincide with one of the characteristic vibration frequencies of the soundboard, the bridge is likely to be driven into an oscillation having appreciable amplitude. This resulting motion of the soundboard and bridge (at the driving point) will of course be quite small if the string's excitation is applied near a node, and quite large if it acts near an antinode for the board's vibration. It is very easy for us to

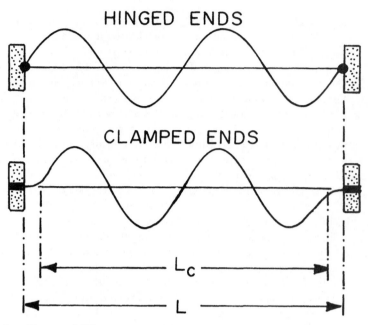

Fig. 16.2. Shortened Vibrating Length Produced by Clamping a Wire at Both Ends

work out the influence of soundboard motion on the natural vibration frequencies of the string itself if we remember that any given vibrational mode of the soundboard can be represented at the driving point in terms of a simple string-and-mass system chosen to have the proper natural frequency, damping, and "wave impedance"—a concept whose meaning we will explore in chapter 17. For the present it will suffice for us to imagine that the string is anchored at one end to a massive block that is free to slide vertically on a smooth rod under the influence of a pair of springs and the oscillatory up-and-down forces exerted on it by the vibrating string. The upper part of figure 16.3 shows such a system provided with a string of length L vibrating in its second mode. This diagram shows the

relation between the position of the sliding mass M and the string's own displacement for the case where the driving frequency F_S of the string mode is less than the natural frequency F_M of the block when it is allowed to oscillate under the influence of the springs alone. Under these conditions, the mass moves upward in response to an upward pull from the string, and downward a half cycle later in the oscillation when the string force on the block has a downward component (see statement 4 in chap. 10, sec. 1). A glance at the right-hand end of our diagram shows us that the string takes on a shape that is similar to that of a simple string anchored rigidly at points separated by a distance (L + C). That is, we can say metaphorically that if $F_S < F_M$, a spring-mass anchorage makes

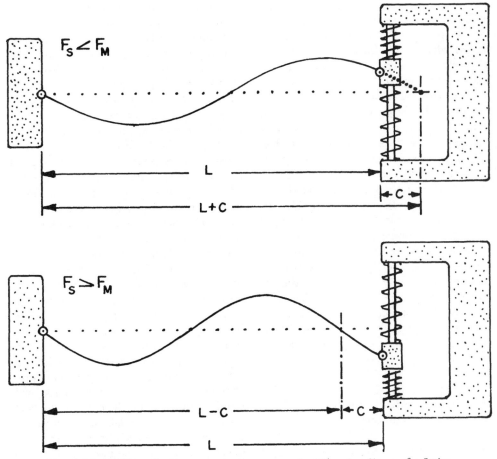

Fig. 16.3.   Effect of a Resonant Anchorage on the Vibration Shape of a String

the string act as though it is elongated by an amount C, so that this particular natural frequency of the string is lowered relative to what it would be if the anchorage were immovable.

If by chance the string vibrates with a frequency F_S that is larger than F_M, the block will oscillate in the direction opposite to the driving forces acting on it (see statement 7 in chap. 10, sec. 1). That is, the block finds itself below its mid-position when the string is pulling upward, as is shown in the lower part of figure 16.3. We recognize from this diagram that if $F_S > F_M$, the string acts as though it were shortened to a length $(L - C)$, so that this string mode has its natural frequency raised.[2]

We are now in a position to understand the peculiar and changing relationships between the characteristic frequencies of the guitar strings described in section 5.4. The guitar string frequencies were very nearly in a harmonic series, and we see now that the ratios are widened progressively because of the effects of string stiffness. The irregularities in the observed frequency sequence can similarly be understood to arise from the influence of guitar body resonances that happen to be near one or another of the string mode frequencies. Retuning the string to a new pitch produces little change in the stiffness effects but does rearrange the interaction of the body resonances with those of the string. The characteristic frequencies of piano and harpsichord strings exhibit similar irregularities that arise from the effects of soundboard resonances. The larger the soundboard, however, the more its resonances tend to overlap, and this overlapping smoothes out and dilutes the irregularities to such an extent that only traces of them are detectable in grand pianos (see the first digression in sec. 9.4, and the closely related digression in sec. 11.4).

16.6. Temperaments for Stringed Keyboard Instruments

The fact that piano and harpsichord strings have inharmonic partials means that we should not directly transfer to these instruments the tuning procedures described for pipe organs. Let us, by means of labeled subsections, make a quick survey of what kinds of things must be dealt with.

A. *Pitch of a Single String Sound*. Since the partials making up the sound of a plucked or struck string are inharmonic, we should not expect the pitch of the sound to correspond very well to that belonging to a harmonically related set of components having the same fundamental frequency. I have made a simplified calculation of the pitch relation between the harmonically related components of a normal musical tone and a sound whose first six partials have the slightly inharmonic component frequencies listed in section 16.5 for a C_4 piano string ($f_1 = 261.63$ Hz). Assuming all six partials to be equally important in determining the pitch, one finds that the normal tone must have its pitch raised about 4 cents (so that its f_1 is raised to 262.24 Hz) if the two are to agree when presented alternately. In the next paragraph and in section 16.7 I will present some little experiments to illustrate the qualitative correctness of this calculation.

Jont Allen of the Bell Telephone Laboratories was kind enough to make for me some computer-generated tape recordings of certain "guitar twangs"; one of these has a typical inharmonicity pattern of the sort we have been discussing, and a second tape carries a pattern in which the sign of J is reversed so that the upper components run *flat* relative to the harmonic series, rather than sharp. In both cases, the upper partials are arranged to die away more quickly in time than the lower ones, so that the initial parts of the impulsive sounds contain many inharmonic partials, while later on in the decay our ears are audibly supplied with only the first one or two components (which are very nearly harmonic in their relationship). Listening to the tape of the decay of the "normal" (stretched inharmonicity) twang, one hears a distinct and rather quick falling-off of pitch (equivalent to several cents), while there is an equally distinct and rapid rise in pitch as the sound with compressed inharmonicity dies away. Furthermore, the initial pitch impression for the stretched-inharmonicity string is distinctly higher than that of the other version. Sounding the two tape segments together gives a very peculiar impression: there is a sort of out-of-tuneness apparent at first which is a little ambiguous because the lowest components of the two sounds are identical in frequency, while the second and higher partials diverge symmetrically from one another, above and below their harmonically expected positions. As the sounds decay, however, the pitches appear to merge in the normal fashion.

Piano and harpsichord strings normally do not display to our ears the peculiar time variation behavior described in the preceding paragraph. As a matter of fact, most people would say that the tones of plucked or struck strings, if they change at all, seem to rise slowly in pitch as the tone dies away (see sec. 17.2 in the next chapter). The listening conditions for a real tone, however, are quite different from those for the computed twang as it exists on tape. After a musical string is excited in a complicated way, it sets up what we might call a two-dimensional, reverberant sound field in the soundboard. The soundboard in its turn communicates via the elaborate motion of dozens of its vibrational modes with thousands of room modes. As a result of all this complexity, the strengths of the various partials fluctuate wildly as they arrive at our ears during the earlier as well as the later parts of the sound, giving quite a different sort of signal to our neurological processors from that produced by the laboratory tape. For our initial investigations we will set aside these complications and proceed as though the pitch of a piano or harpsichord string remained fairly independent of time as the tone decays. However, we are not always justified in assuming that the musically relevant pitch is to be associated with the fundamental component of the sound in the simple way that holds for harmonically related musical sounds. That is, an oboist playing exactly at A-440 with his set of precisely harmonic partials should not expect to feel that he is perfectly in tune with a piano string tuned to give a 440-Hz first-mode frequency component (more on this in sec. 16.7).

B. The Piano Tuner's Octave. Up until now we have defined the octave experimentally in terms of a beat-free condition between *all* the partials of the upper musical tone and the *even-numbered* partials of the lower tone. We were also secure in the knowledge that any heterodyne components that might come into existence would fall into the same beat-free relationship with everything else. It is manifestly impossible to get similarly thoroughgoing beat-free relationships between the components of two piano or harpsichord tones that are to be an octave apart. On the other hand we know from practical experience that pianos and harpsichords are eminently useful as musical instruments, and that in tuning them it has always been possible to achieve string settings that serve perfectly well as octaves in a musical context. Let us see what actually happens when one tunes a single string belonging to C_5 so that it matches a single string belonging to C_4 on a grand piano of good quality. If a competent tuner sounds the two notes alternately or together and tunes the upper one until it "sounds right," we find that while the beats are not all removed, there is a distinct and well-defined reduction in the aggregate amount of "tonal garbage" to be perceived when the fundamental component of C_5 on a good piano is set about 3 cents higher than twice the fundamental component of C_4. Such a tuning leads to the following frequencies and beating repetition rates for the lower few partials:

C_4:	261.63	523.51	785.91	1049.23	1313.23	1578.68 Hz
C_5:	----	523.70	----	1048.81	-----	1571.11 Hz
Beat frequency:		+0.19		−0.42		−7.57 Hz

This is the "piano tuner's octave" for the piano under discussion. If the careful tuner is dealing with a piano having a different inharmonicity factor J, or if a soundboard resonance moves one of the string partials a little, he will choose a different setting in his efforts to clean up the interval. It is to be emphasized that the tuner always seeks the same goal—that of the least obtrusive beating and roughness in his octave—whether he is working on a pipe organ, on a concert grand, or on some ratty little miniature piano whose strings are stiff and short and whose soundboard is too small. In the first case he can achieve perfection, in the second he can work toward the best, but in the last one all he can hope to attain is a condition of least badness. It is important for us to keep in mind everywhere in this section and in those that follow that we are considering the relations between single strings without taking account of the effects arising from double and triple stringings used for most of the individual notes of a normal instrument. The effects of multiple stringing will be dealt with in chapter 17.

The piano tuner's octave is a true musical interval in the sense that it is properly defined by a well-marked perceptual relationship between two tones, a relationship whose existence is advertised by sharply increased roughness of sound when small errors are made in the setting. In the middle ranges of a good instrument the cues are almost as clear-cut as those associated with musical tones constructed of harmonic partials. They are less clear-cut at the ends of the keyboard scale where the string inharmonicity is considerably larger. I should remark that octave settings between two "negative-J" tones adapted by re-recording from those provided by Jont Allen are as well-defined as those based on the more normal inharmonicity. In this case, however, the ratio between the two first components f_1 is less than 2.

C. "Perfect" Fifths and Thirds on the Piano. In the earlier parts of this chapter we saw that the design of a practical keyboard temperament revolves around modifications of the fifths and the thirds. We need to understand how these modifications are adjusted for use on stringed keyboard instruments. In the middle part of a grand piano scale, the condition of least roughness is obtained for a musical fifth when mode 1 of the upper note of the pair is tuned about 1 cent higher than 3/2 times the mode-1 frequency of the lower note. A typical setting of this sort gives a beat frequency of only 0.2 Hz (high) between mode 3 of the C_4 string and mode 2 of the G_4 string, while mode 6 of the C_4 is lower than G_4's mode 4 by 0.9 Hz; we see from this that, in the mid-range of the piano, a "perfect" fifth (i.e., one having least roughness) often turns out to be a slightly smoother interval than the piano tuner's octave! We should not forget, however, that the perturbing effect of a soundboard resonance on one of the string modes could destroy the possibility of a good fifth.

For the particular instrument we are considering, the "perfect" third is found (in the middle of the keyboard) to produce its minimum beating condition when mode 1 of the upper note is set about 3.5 cents higher than the 5/4 ratio that relates this mode to mode 1 of the lower member of the pair. Once again the structure of the instrument and the position in its scale will lead to individual variations in the frequency ratios that make for the best tuning of various thirds.

D. Setting Temperaments on a Piano or a Harpsichord. It is necessary in setting any of the temperaments used for keyboard music to work around a series of tempered fifths whose intervals are shrunken more or less to meet the requirements of the chosen tuning system (Werckmeister, equal temperament, etc.). For example, in section 16.2 we learned that to obtain equal temperament on a pipe organ one starts by setting the C_4-to-G_4 interval narrow enough to produce beats having a repetition rate of 0.89 Hz, followed by a G_4-to-D_5 interval that beats at 1.34 Hz, etc. On a piano or harpsichord, use of these same beating repetition rates gives a circle of fifths that closes reasonably well in going from the final F back to C, although the actual frequency ratios are distributed through the scale a trifle differently. The particular distribution comes about from the inharmonicities of the octaves and the fifths, which influence the tuning in ways that differ for the two kinds of intervals. We see here why it is essential that every tuning procedure have its own built-in checks for consistency.

Every respectable piano and harpsichord has its own smooth trend of inharmonicities produced by string stiffness and its own set of larger or smaller irregularities of mode frequency arising from soundboard resonances. As a result, every note must be tuned to its own predecessor and reconciled with the requirements laid on it for agreement with other notes in the scale.[3]

Every piano tuner meets instruments which he cannot tune satisfactorily. Errors in the design, or the effects of rust on a string, for instance, might throw things off in such a way that the tuner would find that a satisfactory C_4-to-G_4 tuning tuning followed by satisfactory octave tunings C_4-to-C_5 and G_4-to-G_5 would lead to a totally unacceptable relationship between the resulting C_5 and G_5. Problems of this kind are particularly likely to occur in the smallest pianos, where the strings are short (and stiff) and the small soundboard has distinct and well-separated resonances with which the string can interact without benefit of statistical averages. On better instruments, the tuner can usually work out (not always consciously) an acceptable compromise, and on a really fine instrument the tuning goes quickly and easily to a successful conclusion.

If one listens closely to a good piano or harpsichord after it has been carefully tuned, its scale sounds quite even. Careful measurements of the mode-1 frequencies of its strings (the rest of the sound being filtered out to prevent errors in the electronic measurement) show, however, a small but significant irregularity in the frequency ratios. We find that, over a period of years, the irregularities tend to recur as the instrument is tuned and re-tuned, showing that they are in fact the result of dealing with the quirks of the individual notes.

16.7. Further Musical Implications and Summary

The presence of a slight inharmonicity in the frequency relationships between components of harpsichord or piano tones has, as we have seen, two major consequences for music. First, the sharply marked, beat-free indications of the special musical relationships become more diffuse, turning into minimum-roughness relationships instead. Secondly, these special relationships no longer correspond to simple numerical values between the frequencies of the fundamental (first mode) components of the two tones. We find however that the same basic procedures that work for setting temperaments on a pipe organ adapt themselves perfectly well to the tuning of other keyboard instruments. The tuner himself does not have to change his mental processes when he shifts from instruments whose tones contain harmonically related components to those having slightly inharmonic partials, as long as the inharmonicity is predominantly of a smoothly progressive type.

The modified form of equal temperament that is used on pianos and harpsichords generally proves more successful in practical music than does the strict version found on the pipe organ. One realizes immediately that the decay of sounds from struck or plucked strings will in itself reduce the audibility of whatever roughness and beats are present as compared with what one hears coming from a sustained-tone instrument. At a subtler level, we recognize that the less well-marked nature of musical relationships between inharmonic tones will also reduce the noticeability of any discrepancy. The way in which this works and also the way in which the general nature of the inharmonicity can influence the success of a temperament will be illustrated in the next paragraph.

A piano tuned to equal temperament by properly shrunken "tuners' fifths" displays major thirds that have a shimmering brightness rather than the almost pounding sound arising from the orderly and harmonically related beats which exist between components in a pipe organ sound. There is no corresponding pattern to the intercomponent beats between the piano tones, so that our attention has relatively little to focus upon. Furthermore, we find that the main reference cue for the musical interval—the beat between the fifth partial of the lower note and the fourth partial of the upper one—is distinctly slower on the piano than on the organ. For example, sounding C_4 with E_4 usually shows a discrepancy of about 8.2 Hz on a piano, instead of the 10.4 Hz value we found in section 16.2 for the beat repetition rate for an equally tempered third using tones with strictly harmonic partials. As a general principle, then, we realize that built-in temperament errors designed to be on the wide side of "perfection" will have their out-of-tuneness mitigated by the presence of string inharmonicity, while the narrow intervals will be made slightly worse. It is instructive to look over the Werckmeister III tunings of table 16.1 in the light of this remark.

Let us close this section with brief glances at some of the things that happen when a stringed keyboard instrument plays next to a woodwind whose sound spectrum is made up of precisely harmonic components. Suppose for example that a flutist plays a mezzo-forte G_4, maintaining it accurately in tune with the G_4 produced by a single harpsichord string (whose inharmonicity is very similar to that of the strings we have been discussing all along). The flute is sounded steadily, and the corresponding harpsichord key is struck repetitively at the rate of about 2 per second, so that the tone is restored quickly after each dying away. Repeated trials show that players and listeners are only satisfied with the tuning when component 1 of the harpsichord is closely matched (well within 1/2 Hz) to component 1 from the flute. Our ears do not seem to give much importance to the various other beats between the partials; even the 1-Hz beat that is verified to exist between the two second components seems not to bother our ears! I should remark further that if the unison here is mistuned, we become aware of distinctly audible beats whose rate correlates with the error between the bottom components of the two tones. If, however, the harpsichordist sounds one more note after the flutist has shut off his well-tuned tone, this last note sounds a trifle sharp to our ears (a few cents) compared with the flute, which tells us that the *unaccompanied* plucked sound has its pitch assigned differently via the pattern of harmonic components it most closely matches (see sec. 14.4, part A, and 16.6, part A), rather than on the basis of only its lowest component.

The next experiment we are led to consider is a measurement of the G_4 which a flute player produces when he is asked to play a perfect 5th above C_4 on the harpsichord. Following a procedure exactly

like the one described earlier, we find to our surprise that a well-defined auditory zero-beat condition is obtained when the flute's first partial has a frequency exactly 3/2 that of the harpsichord's first partial! This is despite the fact that our measuring equipment clearly displays a discrepancy close to 1 Hz between partial 2 of the flute tone and partial 3 of the harpsichord sound. It is not easy to understand the origin of the perceived beats that serve as our guide in tuning a perfect 5th between a flute and harpsichord. No doubt it has to do with our neurological recognition of quasi patterns among the physiological and neurological heterodyne components, patterns that become more orderly as one approaches the zero-beat condition. Notice that our observations of the flute-harpsichord unison can also be looked at from the same point of view. Presumably we are faced with the creation of some version of the "implied tones" discussed in part D of section 14.4 and in the Digression on Sum and Difference Tones that appears there. We are left, however, with the unanswered question why and how the ear manages not to construct equally convincing regularities and patterns out of the relationship of string mode 2 (etc.) to the various harmonic components of the flute tone.

Let us close this section by summarizing in more explicitly musical terms our observations about the relation of harpsichord or piano tones to each other and to tones having harmonic partials, setting the observations out in numbered sequence for easy reference:

1. The presence of string stiffness causes the tones from piano or harpsichord strings to be made up of slightly inharmonic partials. The predominant effect is a gradual raising of the upper component frequencies relative to

the harmonic series. There is also a small but sometimes significant effect due to the possible interaction of some resonance of the soundboard with one or another vibration mode of the string.

2. Special musical relationships such as the octave or the fifth are found between sounds from pairs of impulsively excited strings. These relationships are (as usual) signalized by the presence of beats when there is a tuning error. The beats do not however disappear completely when the "exact" relationship is attained, as they do in the case of sounds made up of harmonic partials.

3. Pianos, harpsichords, and the like are tuned in any desired temperament upon the basis of the minimum beating relationships described in statement 2 above. However, the actual frequencies of the sound components for the notes of a given instrument will not necessarily coincide with those that are correct for an instrument of different basic design. In particular, the tuning will be quite different from that (determined by the same criteria) of an organ, whose tones are made up of harmonic components.

4. The overall scale (in any temperament) is stretched on the stringed keyboard instruments as a result of tuning notes whose partials are progressively sharper than a harmonic series. One finds similarly that an instrument giving sounds whose partials run *closer* together than the harmonic series can also be tuned in various temperaments. These are found to be compressed relative to the tunings of harmonically related tones. The overall stretching or compressing of a scale is the direct result of inharmonicity. There is no fixed preference for one or the other on the part of the listener; he will always prefer to hear tunings based ultimately on minimum-roughness relationships between two tones at hand.[4]

5. Partly because of the rapid decay of impulsive string sounds and partly because of the "stretching" nature of the inharmonicity, equal temperament gives somewhat less discordant results in pianos and harpsichords

than it does in pipe organs, where one is dealing with sustained tones having harmonic components.

6. When the tones of an impulsively excited string are presented alternately with tones containing harmonic partials, the string sound is perceived to be a few cents sharper in pitch if the lowest partial of one tone has the same frequency as the lowest partial of the other.

7. When the sound of a repeatedly excited string is superposed on the sound of an instrument having harmonic partials, experiment shows that our ears apply the minimum-beat criterion in a way that requires the fundamental components of the two tones to have simple, whole-number frequency ratios exactly like those that are found between pairs of ordinary (harmonic) musical tones. This is despite the fact that a great many "disorderly" components are present in the ear.

8. Exact frequency relationships for special intervals may vary from special case to special case in a musical context when impulsive and mildly inharmonic string sounds are combined with one another or with more ordinary musical sounds. However, errors in setting these special relationships always advertise themselves in the same manner—by the presence of beats and roughness. In other words, the musician always recognizes the problem in the same way and solves it in the same way, but his answers understandably come out different in different circumstances.

16.8. Examples, Experiments, and Questions

1. Here is a procedure for setting up a keyboard to give just intonation. Set A_4 to the desired reference, e.g., 440 Hz, and tune F_4 a minimum-beat major third below and $C_5\sharp$ a minimum-beat major third above the reference A_4. After doing this, tune the following sequences of per-

fect fifths: F, C, G, D; A, E, B, F♯; C♯, G♯, D♯, A♯. See if you can decide which key signature is the one in which the just tuning is exact. You will find that a keyboard set up in this way also works quite well in a number of other keys.

2. Mean-tone tuning is the usual name for temperaments that produce perfect major 3rds, along with pretty good 5ths and 4ths (review table 16.1, and note that the Werckmeister tuning given in sec. 16.3 is *not* a strict mean-tone tuning). The following procedure will give a strict mean-tone temperament. Set C_4 as the tuning reference at about 263 Hz, so that the whole scale will lie at a pitch that is comfortable for musicians using today's woodwinds tuned around A-440. Set E_4 a minimum-beat major 3rd above C_4, and continue to follow the Werckmeister procedure through the generation of the tempered-5ths sequence: C, G, D, A, E. Check that the E is essentially beat free next to the C. Tune the *upper* one of the following pairs to give minimum-beat major 3rds: D-F♯, G-B, A-C♯; tune the *lower* one of the following pairs to give minimum-beat major 3rds: D-B♭, A-F. For your final 3rds, you have a choice of setting E♭ by measuring down from G or tuning D♯ up from B, which will give you one of the remaining notes, and a choice between taking A♭ from C or setting G♯ from E to supply the other one. The choice made here is obviously governed by the keys you intend to use for your music-making.

3. In the descriptions of all of the non-equal-temperament tuning procedures given in this chapter, it was necessary to specify the note name for the tuning fork reference pitch. This was done so that the properties of the various key signatures would have the desired musical rela-

tionships with one another. One would need both an A and a C tuning fork to be able to set up all the temperaments discussed in this chapter. Why would it be possible, on the other hand, to tune in equal temperament using as a reference a tuning fork having any note name whatever? Can you devise a Werckmeister tuning procedure in which the key of E major displays all the properties normally associated with C major? What would D minor sound like in such a tuning?

4. The frequency ratios between successive components in a tone having harmonic partials are closely related to the special intervals that we have found to exist between musical tones. For example, the perfect fifth is implied by the 3/2 frequency ratio between partial 3 and partial 2, and the major third is implied by the relation between partials 4 and 5. Setting aside the fact that musical relationships hold between *tones* and have little relevance between sinusoidal single components, verify that the note names that can be associated with the harmonic components of C_4 are as follows:

1	2	3	4	5	6
C_4	C_5	G_5	C_6	E_6	G_6

What names are similarly associated with partials 7, 8, 9, and 10?

5. Until fairly recently the Hammond electric organ produced the tones of its scale in the following ingenious way. Associated with each note named on the keyboard is a rotating wheel that electromagnetically generates a *sinusoid* whose frequency is the conventional frequency in the equally tempered scale. If there were nothing more to the instrument than a loudspeaker connected to play these various sinusoids as the keys are pressed, very little of musical interest could be

achieved (see however item 4 in sec. 15.7). To get musically useful tones, this type of Hammond organ is arranged to borrow "harmonically" related sinusoids from the upper parts of the keyboard when any note is played. Thus, pressing the C_4 key feeds the loudspeaker with sinusoids belonging to the notes named G_4, C_5, etc., as given in the list at the end of item 4 above. Verify that because of the nature of equal temperament, partials 2, 4, 8, 16, . . . are exactly harmonic, partials 3, 6, 12 are slightly flat (2 cents) relative to strict harmonicity, while partials 5 and 10 are inharmonic by being 14 cents sharp. What is the inharmonicity of the 9th partial? The tone color of such a collection of partials is somewhat peculiar, but you can verify that this organ has one remarkable musical feature—the major thirds are considerably smoother than on any other kind of organ, and the fifths are very good also. What happens to some of the other important musical intervals? You might find it worthwhile to construct a table of clumps of beating components for this instrument analogous to those set forth in section 14.4, part D, and in table 14.1.

6. A skilled oboist performs with a keyboard instrument tuned to the accurate version of the equal temperament that is appropriate to its nature (pipe or Hammond organ, small or large piano, etc.). Why is it very unlikely that the oboist will himself be playing in equal temperament?

7. Consider a piano tuner who shows up for work with some sort of electronic frequency-measuring device as one of his tools. Why might this be an acceptable aid in setting the basic temperament for a medium-sized piano or harpsichord but probably inappropriate for a concert grand instrument? Could he use unstretched equal temperament for setting the center octave? What about setting the temperament of a small, cheap piano? Can the tuning of the rest of the keyboard above and below the temperament octave be safely carried out with electronic help on any instrument?

8. In part 2 of section 15.7 we noticed that the musical relationships are not the same in an interval such as the fifth (e.g., C_4 to G_4) and in its inversion (G_4 to C_5). At that time we were concerned only with sounds with harmonic partials. Follow up on these observations to figure out the qualitative effect of string inharmonicity when keyboard temperaments are set by *mixtures* of upward and downward intervals (of the sort described in parts 1 and 2 of this section). Some modern tuners set piano temperaments by the alternate use of fifths and fourths. They will obtain a tuning that is slightly different from that produced by those of their colleagues who employ upward fifths alone, along the lines suggested in section 16.2.

9. Repeat experiments 3 and 4 in section 10.9, and extend them to the case where the B_6 key is held down while the G_4 key is struck and released. Why does one expect very little response in this case?

10. The question often arises as to the proper way to lay out the frets for a guitar whose "open" string length is L_0. You will not find it hard to verify that the frequency formula in section 16.5 for a flexible string implies that the frets will give an equally tempered chromatic scale if each successive string length is shorter than its predecessor by the factor $(1/1.059463)$. The presence of inharmonicity can be thought of as effectively

altering the string lengths. Try to figure out then why the frets on a real guitar should always be farther from the bridge than those calculated by the simple formula, with the alteration becoming increasingly large for the higher notes on the string. How would you tilt the bridge to minimize the errors on a guitar caused by its use of strings of various thicknesses?

Notes

1. A paper giving the most complete account of the basic physics of stiff strings in theory and in experiment is that of R. S. Shankland and J. W. Coltman, "The Departure of the Overtones of a Vibrating Wire from a True Harmonic Series," *J. Acoust. Soc. Am.* 10 (1939): 161–66. See also Robert W. Young, "Inharmonicity of Plain Wire Piano Strings," *J. Acoust. Soc. Am.* 24 (1952): 267–73, and Harvey Fletcher, "Normal Vibration Frequencies of a Stiff Piano String," *J. Acoust. Soc. Am.* 36 (1964): 203–9.

2. Detailed calculations of the effects described above have been made by many people during the past century. One of the earliest to carry them out was Lord Rayleigh [John William Strutt], as reported in his book *The Theory of Sound,* 2 vols. bound as one, 2d ed. rev. and enlarged (1894; reprint ed., New York: Dover, 1945), I:200–204.

3. A basic paper on the systematic effect of string stiffness on the trends of tuning in pianos of different sizes is that of O. H. Schuck and R. W. Young, "Observations on the Vibrations of Piano Strings," *J. Acoust. Soc. Am.* 15 (1943): 1–11. It is interesting to contrast the tuning trends observed by Schuck and Young with those of H. Meinel, "Musikinstrumentenstimmungen und Tonsysteme," *Acustica* 7 (1957): 185–90, and with those in the paper by Young and by Fletcher mentioned in note 1 of this chapter. The data presented in all of these papers also contain clear (though unrecognized) evidence of the random shifts caused by soundboard resonances, along with the smooth trends associated with string stiffness.

4. There are many ways in which this remark can be verified. An experiment that bears on these matters can be found in the paper by Frank H. Slaymaker, "Chords from Tones Having Stretched Partials," *J. Acoust. Soc. Am.* 47 (1970): 1569–71.

17

Sound Production in Pianos

In the second half of chapter 16 we examined the interplay between the physics of vibrating strings and the tuning behavior of various kinds of keyboard musical instruments. In the present chapter we will turn our attention to the way in which the strings of a piano, harpsichord, or clavichord communicate their carefully tuned vibrations to the soundboard and thence to our ears. Thus we will be focusing our attention on the nature of the sounds produced by these intruments. In broad outline, the chapter will begin by examining the requirements that must be met by a string belonging to a note in the middle of the piano keyboard. This is followed by an account of what is accomplished by the use of more than one string per note and a description of the changes and compromises necessary for satisfactory production of lower and higher tones. Having dealt with sounds produced on the piano, we will be ready in chapter 18 to adapt our understanding of these basic principles to the clavichord and the harpsichord.

17.1. The Soundboard As Seen by the Strings; *The Concept of Wave Impedance*

Anyone looking into a grand piano will notice that each note in its scale has one or more strings stretched across a soundboard in the manner shown in figure 17.1. The so-called vibrating length of the string extends from a rigid *capo d'astro* bar (or from a fixed *agraffe*) which is found at the keyboard end, to the bridge,

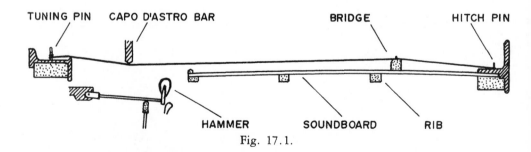

Fig. 17.1.

which is elastically supported by a broad, thin soundboard. A hammer is arranged to excite this length of string by striking it at a suitably chosen point near the fixed end. Not shown in the figure is a felt damper that normally rests on the string near the hammer to keep it from vibrating when it is not in use.

In chapters 7 and 8 we learned some of the basic principles guiding the excitation of string modes by hammers of various sorts acting at various distances from the fixed end. Now it is time to look at the way in which these characteristic vibrations of the string are communicated to the soundboard and thence to the concert hall. The string and the soundboard meet by way of the bridge, so we need to know what sort of a termination the string "sees" as it looks at the place where it runs over the bridge. The bridge actually functions acoustically as a part of the soundboard, which is attached to its lower side. The soundboard is a two-dimensional wave-carrying medium of the sort we first met in chapter 9. Carefully profiled ribs run across the grain on the underside of the soundboard to make its stiffness approximately the same across the grain as it is lengthwise. We have already acquired at least a general idea of the way in which such a uniform two-dimensional object will respond to an excitation applied at some point on its surface (see figs. 10.13 and 10.14). In section 16.5 we also learned a little about how the driven motion of the soundboard can react back on the string to alter its natural frequencies.

There is more to what the string sees at the bridge end than just bridge and soundboard. There are some 240 other strings running over the top surface of the bridge, and these also form a kind of two-dimensional wave-carrying medium that is "visible" to our vibrating strings, albeit in a more limited way because waves are not able to run easily in a crosswise direction from string to string. (There is only the bridge to connect them to each other, with no ribs to equalize what we might in this case call the cross-grain and along-the-grain properties of the system.) The fact that most of the strings are damped by pieces of felt need not concern us at present, any more than does the question whether the edges of the soundboard function as hinged or as clamped boundaries.

The playing string, the bridge-plus-soundboard, and the sheet of silent but downbearing strings can each be thought of as a wave-carrying medium. Acoustical theory tells us that any wave-carrying medium can be characterized fully by two specifications: the velocity with which waves are propagated along the medium, and the wave impedance. We will briefly review the first and more familiar of these before considering the idea of wave impedance.

When any sort of acoustic disturbance is made at one point in a wave-carrying medium, it takes a little while for the disturbance to make its appearance at another point a little distance away. The rate at which the disturbance travels from its source to the point of observation is what is known as the speed of sound or *wave velocity* (for example, we learned in sec. 11.8 that the speed of sound in air is about 345 meters/sec). The wave velocity always depends on the springiness or elasticity with which one small part of the medium acts on its neighbors during a disturbance; the wave velocity depends also on the inertia of the material (i.e., the amount of mass belonging to each of these small parts). These are related to each other by the following formula:

$$\text{wave velocity} = \sqrt{\frac{\text{springiness}}{\text{inertia}}}$$

Question 2 in the final section of this chapter will help you understand why this formula for the wave velocity (the speed of sound) looks so remarkably like the formula found in section 6.1 for the natural frequency of oscillation of a spring-and-mass system.

The second concept we need for an understanding of how a struck string communicates with the soundboard is the idea of *wave impedance*. When a disturbance is set up in some medium and travels to the boundary between it and some other medium (as when disturbances travel along a slender wire to a thicker wire or a soundboard), a certain fraction of the disturbance is transmitted into the new medium and the remainder is reflected back into the original medium. The amplitudes of the reflected and the transmitted waves, and also the amounts of energy carried by them, all depend on the ratio of the wave impedances of the two media.[1] If these impedances are very different, there is almost complete reflection, with only a small share of the total energy being sent on. On the other hand, if the two media have wave impedances that are approximately equal, then there is very little reflection and the disturbance is almost completely transmitted across the junction. It turns out that wave impedance depends on the same two properties of the medium as does wave velocity, although they are arranged differently, thus:

wave impedance

$$= \sqrt{\text{inertia} \times \text{springiness}}$$

Digression on Terminology: Wave Impedance vs. Characteristic Impedance.

In order to keep things clear for the less technically oriented readers of this book, I have chosen to use the slightly old-fashioned name wave impedance *rather than the more current term* characteristic impedance. *Everywhere else in this book, the perfectly customary adjective* characteristic *has been reserved for use as a way to advertise certain attributes of some mode of vibration belonging to a particular finite system of springs and masses. Thus, for a given system, its entire behavior can be understood in terms of its modes of vibration, each of these having its own characteristic frequency of vibration, its own characteristic vibrational shape, and its own characteristic (internally caused) damping. These characteristic properties are determined jointly by the nature of the vibrating medium and by the way in which its boundaries are constrained. It is only under very special circumstances that one finds a characteristic vibration taking place in an infinitely extended system, and then it exists only in a restricted region of it. The wave impedance, on the other hand, is a way of specifying (along with the wave velocity) one of the attributes of the wave-carrying medium itself, without reference to its boundaries. As a matter of fact, one of the easy ways to measure a wave impedance is to experiment on a very extended piece of material and to conclude the measurements before any echoes can be returned by its boundaries (see sec. 17.4 below for an example of this). I might remark that those of us who use today's more conventional terminology in our daily work are in the habit of identifying the special attributes of bounded systems by use of the German prefix* eigen- *in place of the English word* characteristic *that we employ in this book.*

Let us illustrate the ideas of wave velocity and of wave impedance by considering the case of waves on a flexible string made of some material whose density is d and whose radius is r (i.e., cross-sectional area $= \pi r^2$). The string is long, and it is kept under a tension T.

wave velocity $= \sqrt{\dfrac{T}{(\pi r^2 d)}} = \left(\dfrac{1}{r}\right)\sqrt{\dfrac{T}{\pi d}}$

wave impedance $= \sqrt{(\pi r^2 d)T} = r\sqrt{\pi T d}$

Here the tension T serves to supply the springiness, and the product $\pi r^2 d$ will be recognized as the mass per unit length, which is a measure of the relevant inertia property of the string. Notice that we can trade tension for density or radius while keeping the impedance the same, but it is not possible at the same time to preserve the speed unchanged.

An analogous but somewhat simplified formula for the wave impedance of a soundboard at its driving point is:

wave impedance
$= t^2 \sqrt{Y_w d_w} \times$ (a numerical constant)

Here t is the thickness of the board, d_w is the density, and Y_w is the modulus of elasticity for the wood.[2] We will assume that the ribs and bridge have been so designed that they properly take care of the difference in stiffness in the two directions relative to the grain, and that the thickness t is also properly averaged to take these extra pieces into account. I should remark that the wave impedance of the board taken by itself is very considerably larger than that of a string.

We must also consider, besides the playing string and the soundboard, the aggregate influence of the damped and inactive strings. Their influence is best thought of in two parts. The simplest but least important part is the wave impedance of the collection considered as a peculiar two-dimensional sheet; this turns out to depend on the strings' spacing along the bridge, and it has a magnitude only three or four times the impedance of a single string. The second and rather larger influence comes from the way the *downward* pull of the slanting strings between bridge and hitch pins alters the elasticity of the otherwise slightly arched soundboard, subtly modifying the soundboard wave impedance formula given above.

The string layout between the bridge and the hitch pin is illustrated in the top part of figure 17.2. This silent portion of the string (which is provided with a damping strip of felt) has a length Q and a "downbearing" P that is carefully proportioned to vary along the scale of any properly made instrument. Makers of the finest instruments find that the downbearing must be meticulously adjusted string by string on each individual piano, as a part of its final regulation. Errors in the trend of relationship among P, Q, and the string tension can cause as much trouble to the overall sound of the piano as can errors in the stiffness and curve of the bridge, or in the thickness of the soundboard. If the ratio P/Q is locally too small, the instrument acts somewhat the way it would with a thin spot in the soundboard. Notice that the downbearing is not simply a matter of getting adequate contact between the bridge and the strings; the string tension acting together with the offset on the bridge where the string runs zigzag past two steel pins is already quite sufficient for this contact, as is suggested by the lower part of figure 17.2.

The wave impedance ratio between the struck string and the soundboard must be chosen to meet two conflicting requirements. First of all, there must be suf-

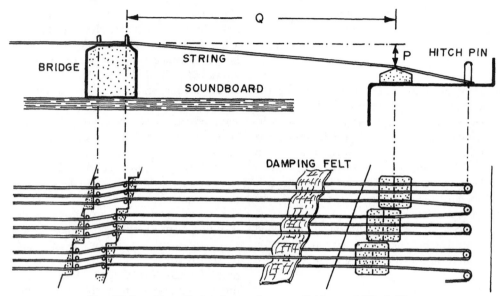

Fig. 17.2.   Piano String Layout between Bridge and Hitch Pin

ficient transmission of vibratory energy from the string to the soundboard that our ears are ultimately provided with a sound of satisfactory loudness. If the soundboard were a plate of steel 4 cm thick instead of a wooden board about 1 cm thick, its wave impedance would be increased several hundredfold and we would hear almost nothing from the soundboard, nor would the string produce much sound directly in the air. If on the other hand the disturbance excited on the string by the hammer were communicated to the soundboard at too rapid a rate, these vibrations would die down so quickly that we would hear little more than a tuned thud, a louder version of what is produced by hitting a note while a wadded handkerchief is firmly pressed against the vibrating part of the string next to the bridge. We also want the

soundboard impedance to be high enough that its resonances will not play an unacceptably large role in the tuning of individual string modes, a phenomenon that we met in section 16.5.

Digression on the Vibrational Modes of Segments of a Larger System.
In chapter 6 and in the latter half of chapter 10 the idea was developed that any finite-sized system of springs and masses would have its own particular set of characteristic vibrational modes, these modes being attributes of the system as a whole. This implies that it makes no sense to consider apart from the whole a particular mass or even a subset of masses as a separate vibrational system. In this chapter I have apparently violated this principle of the unified behavior of a complete system by discussing the string modes and the soundboard modes as though these were in fact separable. Let us see why this very convenient separation of ideas

proves to be acceptably accurate as a piece of physics. If a certain complete system (e.g., string and soundboard) consists of two parts or regions with drastically different wave impedances, the communication of vibrations from one of these parts to the other is small enough that the two behave very much as though they were fully isolated. When this condition is met, then, it is possible to pick out of the complete set of characteristic modes a subset in which the overall vibrational shapes ordain that the predominant share of the vibration takes place in the high-impedance region, while the remaining modes involve chiefly the rest of the system, which is constructed of low-impedance material. Once the approximate vibrational shapes associated with each region alone are well understood, it is then easy enough to correct for the mutual influence of the two regions. It is in precisely this spirit that we corrected the string mode frequencies for the effect of soundboard resonances in section 16.5; the soundboard has a wave impedance so much higher than that of the strings that we are justified in thinking of them as quasi-separate entities. Notice, however, that the wave impedances of the bridge and the soundboard are similar enough that we would not be justified in dealing with them separately—the two act together with the ribs as a single wooden vibrating system (see sec. 9.5 for another example of a two-part system that cannot be dealt with piecemeal).

17.2. The Proportions of a Mid-Scale Piano String and the Necessity for Multiple Stringing

In section 16.5 we learned that the stiffness of real strings gives rise to a slight inharmonicity in the ratios between their characteristic frequencies and that this inharmonicity was less in long, taut, thin strings than in short, slack, thick ones. We have seen how a *small* amount of string-type inharmonicity serves a useful purpose—it can help disguise the necessary errors of keyboard temperament or

can even convert some of these errors into musical virtues. Moreover, numerous experiments have shown that a certain amount of inharmonicity is necessary if the listener is to be satisfied that what he hears is an impulsively excited string sound. Nevertheless the history of keyboard instrument development from the earliest times reveals an intense though not always conscious interest in reducing the inharmonicity. Because of this, we will begin our discussion of the proportioning of mid-scale strings by postulating that their tension is to be made as large as is reasonably possible, short of breaking the string. On the basis of this choice, the vibrating length L of the string turns out to be a fixed length that is independent of the string's thickness. This is the reason that the length of the C_4 string is close to 62.5 cm for all steel-strung pianos. The minimum inharmonicity associated with a string tightened nearly to breaking tension depends in a simplified way on its radius r and length L as follows (compare with the formula for J given in sec. 16.5):

$$J_{min} = \left(\frac{r^2}{L^2}\right) \times (\text{a numerical constant})$$

This suggests that we should use the thinnest possible string, since L has already been fixed by the frequency requirements laid down for the string. However, if we make the string too thin we are speared on the other horn of our dilemma. The transmission of vibration from our string to the soundboard is proportional to the wave impedance ratio, and so depends on the wire radius and soundboard thickness (as influenced by the ribs) in accordance with the expression:

$$\left(\frac{\text{string wave impedance}}{\text{soundboard wave impedance}}\right) =$$

$$\left(\frac{r^2}{t^2}\right) \times \text{(a numerical constant)}$$

This relationship holds only if the string tension is always maintained fairly close to breaking. The equation indicates that making the wire thin will mean that it will be able to drive the soundboard to only a small fraction of its own amplitude, so that only very weak sounds will be radiated into the room.

Some numerical values for the soundboard and strings of a real piano should be of interest at this point. A good piano has a soundboard made of beautifully finished spruce that has a density d_w close to 0.4 grams/cm^3. The soundboard is often tapered and is generally thinner at the bass side, but in the main its thickness is a little less than 10 mm. The radius of the C$_4$ string is close to 0.5 mm, and its density d is close to 7.8 grams/cm^3. A single such string on a piano having a soundboard of this description sustains its tones very acceptably and shows tuning behavior almost identical with that described in chapter 16. However, the loudness of the sound of the single string is inadequate and the tone lacks a certain liveliness that we have become used to in pianos having three strings instead of one for most of the keyboard notes. An obvious way of simultaneously meeting the least-inharmonicity requirements (which call for thin strings) and the loudness requirements is to use several strings, each of which will have acceptable inharmonicity and each of which can join with the others in driving the soundboard to a greater vibrational amplitude. The physics of the multistring piano note turns out to have surprising aspects that lead to two important features of the tone of a piano; a description of these matters is the subject of the next section.

17.3. The Effect of Multiple Stringing on the Sound of the Piano

We will introduce ourselves to some of the consequences of multiple stringing on a piano with the help of experiments you can easily try. Repeatedly strike the C$_4$ key of a piano while alternately pressing and releasing a finger (or pencil eraser) against two of the three strings, so that part of the time only one string is free to vibrate and the rest of the time all three strings are sounding. With any reasonably well-tuned piano, the perceived loudness at your ears (expressed in sones) should be roughly 40 percent higher when three strings are active than when only one is producing a sound (see curve B of fig. 13.5), which is a quite significant change. The next experiment consists in verifying in a crude and informal way that the total audibility time of the decaying tone is roughly the same whether three strings are active or only one. So far everything appears to be in accordance with our expectations. We also notice that the tone is a little thinner and perhaps less interesting when only one string is allowed to sound than it is when all three are set into vibration. To be sure, if the piano is badly out of tune the three strings will beat against one another to give the jangling sound conventionally associated with a barroom piano, while on a freshly tuned instrument there is only a hint of beats among the lower partials and a pleasantly shimmering suggestion of beating among the higher ones.

In 1959 Roger Kirk of the Baldwin Piano Company reported the preferences of a large group of people for the tuning relationship among the three strings of each so-called unison of a piano.[3] He found that

> the most preferred tuning conditions . . . are 1 and 2 cents maximum deviation among the strings of each note in the scale. Musically trained subjects prefer less deviation . . . than do untrained subjects. Close agreement was found between the subjects' tuning preferences and the way artist tuners actually tune piano strings.

He also found that a piano tuned so that the group of strings for each note of the scale covered a spread of 8 cents was acceptable to many listeners, and that the overall spread between the lowest and highest frequency strings was of more importance than the tuning of the intermediate string. The beat frequencies between the first five components (partials) of two C_4 strings tuned 2 cents and 8 cents apart are:

Component:	1	2	3	4	5	
2-cent difference:	0.30	0.61	0.91	1.20	1.50	Hz
8-cent difference:	1.21	2.42	3.53	4.80	6.10	Hz

Notice first of all that with the 2-cent detuning the beating rate for the first pair of partials is quite slow, as are those for the second and third pair of partials. As a result the tone sounds reasonably smooth when played by itself. The 8-cent spread gives a rather brighter sound, but it is not yet the sort of jangle one gets with a spread of 15 to 20 cents.

When we use a 2-cent detuning between strings, the 0.91-Hz beat frequency belonging to its set of 3rd components is just able to cover up the 0.89-Hz beat that one uses in setting the equal-temperament fifth to G_4 (see sec. 16.6, part D). Note that partial 2 of the G_4 strings will have a similar beating rate to obscure further the departure from just tuning. With the 8-cent inter-string spread, on the other hand, the fifths become pretty diffuse.

Let us turn now to the interval of a major third in equal temperament. Using a 2-cent detuning, the fifth component group of C_4 has within it a 1.5-Hz maximum beating frequency, as does the fourth component group of the note E_4 if its strings similarly have a 2-cent detuning spread. Taking these together we see the possibility of beat frequencies as high as $1.5 + 1.5 = 3$ Hz among the components upon which the interval is chiefly based. In section 16.7, we learned that the beating rate for a piano tuner's third in equal temperament is about 8 Hz, a little more than twice the smearing produced by the detuned unison. If the spread among members of a three-string "unison" were increased to 8 cents, the beating would become rapid enough to drown the temperament error completely. Clearly there is a trade-off of musical virtues between the two kinds of unison spread as one compares various musical intervals. In any event we have provided ourselves with another reason stringed keyboard instruments are so well-adapted to musical performance, despite the problems with fixed pitch that at first seemed insurmountable.

As a practical matter it proves to be exceedingly difficult to tune a set of unison strings to a true zero-beat condition (one even meets cases where it is literally impossible to do so). The question arises then whether or not people's preference for a slight detuning of the unisons is simply a favorable response to the most familiar type of sound, or whether something more fundamental is involved. Kirk finds that piano tuners and musicians are unanimous in their verdict that too-close tuning gives a tone that not only sounds dead but dies away too rapidly. Laboratory measurement confirms the auditory impression we gained in our initial experiments that slightly detuned (normal) strings die away in about the same total length of time as a single one of these strings when the other ones are prevented from vibrating. However, when three strings are tuned *exactly* together they will actually die away much more rapidly. The presence of other precisely in-tune strings encourages each string to transfer its vibration more rapidly to the soundboard and thence to the room! Let us first make use of our knowledge of wave impedance to verify its consistency with these observations and then go on to an example of the same kind of physics displayed in an everyday experience far removed from acoustics.

In section 17.1 we learned that the wave impedance of a string is equal to the square root of the product of tension T and mass per unit length ($\pi r^2 d$). How do we find the corresponding impedance for a triplet of identical strings acting together? The top part of figure 17.3 indicates the appearance of our three strings as they are normally seen in a piano. The middle part of the diagram shows them moved so close together that they are on the verge of touching. If they were *identically* tuned strings, they would stay precisely in step with one another, and there

would be no frictional or other force acting between them to change things in case they did touch. In other words, the three closely spaced strings will behave exactly like their more separate cousins. In particular, the aggregate impedances are the same in both cases. The bottom part of figure 17.3 shows the last step in our imaginary set of transformations: here the strings are fused together into a ribbonlike whole, with no change of total mass or tension. An extension of our former reasoning shows that this new sort of string also retains the acoustical properties of its ancestor at the top—as long as we confine ourselves to vibrations of the normal type (up and down, as shown in the diagram).

Having done a little thinking about three strings acting precisely together, we are now ready to calculate. Clearly, the total tension acting on our composite string is three times the tension acting on each of the original strings, so we must write 3T under the square root sign where formerly there was a T. Similarly, any short length of the composite has precisely three times the mass of a corresponding length of ordinary wire, so we must also write $3(\pi r^2 d)$ in place of $\pi r^2 d$ in the formula. Putting all this together, we get:

$$\begin{pmatrix} \text{wave impedance} \\ \text{of a tricord} \end{pmatrix} = \sqrt{3(\pi r^2 d) \times 3T}$$

$$= 3 \times \begin{pmatrix} \text{wave impedance} \\ \text{of a single wire} \end{pmatrix}$$

This shows us that three strings acting precisely together produce a threefold increase in the wave impedance, and thus a threefold increase in the amplitude of the bridge motion, which ultimately leads to a threefold reduction in the decay time of

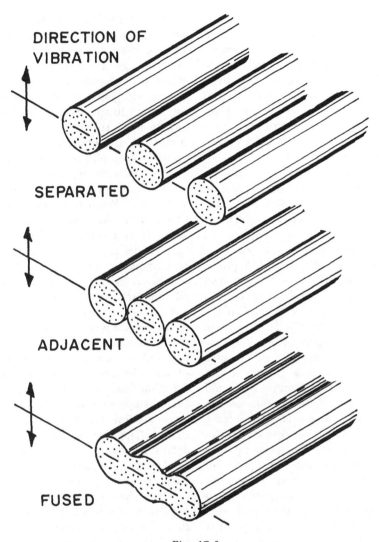

DIRECTION OF
VIBRATION

SEPARATED

ADJACENT

FUSED

Fig. 17.3.

the vibration. You might find it worth-while to deduce this last assertion on the basis of the principles outlined in section 6.1.

The expected difference in sound between a struck single string and a perfectly tuned triplet of strings is not hard to figure out on the basis of what we have just learned. First of all, the tone of the precisely tuned triple strings will die away much more quickly, which matches actual experience. Second, we would expect on the basis of curve A in figure 13.5 that the perceived loudness of the tone (as expressed in sones) would be very nearly doubled because of the threefold increase in source (soundboard) amplitude. The tone would not actually appear this much louder, however, because a short or decaying sound always sounds less loud that a steady one. In the three-string case the increased rapidity of the decay partially offsets the perceived effect of the larger amplitude.

We seem by now to have left the slightly detuned strings of a real piano in a sort of unexplained limbo between the single string and a perfectly tuned triplet. The true behavior of detuned triplets will be easy to understand once we have looked at the everyday example I promised a few paragraphs ago. Suppose you have undertaken to push your friend's small car along a fairly level road. If the rolling friction of the car is large, you may find it barely possible to keep the vehicle rolling, and yet you will be able to move the car quite a distance under these conditions without much strain and without becoming winded. Suppose on the other hand that you have acquired a helper in the pushing, so that the two of you together can get the speed up to a fast walk. Pushing at this faster pace will soon leave you winded and panting for breath, even if you are not pushing any harder as an individual than you were during the solo performance. The point is this: the energy you expend in pushing with a certain force over a given distance will be spent in a much shorter time if your friend helps you make the trip more quickly. The rate at which *you* work is increased because of the cooperative presence of your friend.

The translation of this example to the case of vibrating strings is easy: one string pulling up and down on the sound-board and moving it corresponds to you pushing on the car alone. If two strings are less than precisely in tune with one another, the situation is like the case where your car-pushing friend sometimes pushes with you and sometimes pushes in opposition to you. In a semi-disorganized situation like this there is no absolute coherence to the undertaking and the aggregate accomplishment is simply equal to the sum of the separate contributions.

Daniel Martin and his research group at Baldwin Piano Company have shown that a very characteristic feature of the sound from a piano is a dual decay pattern.[4] This is the second musically important result of the use of multiple strings. A blow from the hammer starts all three strings off exactly in step with one another, so that they radiate strongly to the outside world. Initially, then, each partial dies away quickly at about the rate expected for strings that are in precise unison. However, because of their slight detuning from one another, they soon get out of step, so that we might say that there are eventually three solo performances. The vibration of each string then decays on its own in isolation at the single-string rate, and close cousins to ordinary beats are produced for us to hear.

When the strings of the C_4 note on a good piano are tuned to a total spread of about 2 cents, the net sound pressure due to all the partials (see sec. 13.2) shows the presence of fast decay for about 1 second out of the total time of 20 seconds (crudely speaking) that is required for the net pressure amplitude to be reduced to 1/1000th of its initial value.

I will close this section with a brief explanation of the pitch rise that is often perceived in a piano tone as it dies away. To begin with there is a clearly audible change in tone quality, explainable in part by the fact that the lower-frequency partials become unimportant and then inaudible more quickly than do the higher partials, simply because of the greater sensitivity of the ear at high frequencies (see fig. 13.3). Furthermore, the amplitude of the lowest partial generally falls away more quickly than the higher partials, chiefly because the slow beating rate between the strings for this component keeps their vibrations in step for a longer time, during which they suffer the accelerated decay characteristic of the cooperative effect. This gives us an additional, mechanical reason to expect a listener's attention to transfer itself to the higher partials of a decaying tone. Because of string inharmonicity, these higher partials heard by themselves imply a higher pitch than that which our ears assign when they base their "calculation" on the lower partials (see also sec. 16.7). However, the decay patterns of individual notes of a keyboard scale differ enough from note to note, even on a very fine instrument, that we should not expect the invariable presence of a pitch rise during the decay of every tone.

17.4. The Action of Piano Hammers

General principles were developed in chapter 8 to guide our understanding of vibration recipes produced when strings are struck at various places by various kinds of hammers. In particular we found that the duration of contact in a hammer blow exerts a considerable influence on the number of characteristic modes that are excited. Modes having frequencies high enough that one or more of their oscillations could take place during the contact time are, as a result, only weakly excited. On a piano the time of contact is only partly influenced by the softness of the hammer felt; the predominant influence arises from the way the string itself pushes back against the hammer. Our thinking about this influence can conveniently be divided into what we might call an elastic version and a wavelike version, the second version being used to refine our conclusions from the first.

If someone were to force a piano hammer slowly and progressively into the exaggerated position shown in the upper part of figure 17.4, the tension of the deflected string would act on the hammer, exerting a downward restoring force whose magnitude would grow as the hammer is displaced farther and farther upward. It should be apparent from the diagram that the greater slant of the shorter, left-hand segment of the string means that this segment exerts the major portion of the restoring force. For example, on a piano string whose hammer strikes at a distance H equal to 1/9th of the string length L, the two forces are in the ratio $(L - H)/H = 8/1$, meaning that in this particular case the restoring force of the short segment acting on the hammer will be eight times as great as that of the long segment.

If one strikes a piano key, the system of levers called the action accelerates the hammer to some final speed and then releases it, allowing it to continue freely upward until it strikes the string. When contact is made with the string, the hammer's upward motion persists, but the string exerts an increasingly large downward force on it as already described. If we temporarily set aside the force exerted by the longer portion of the string, it is apparent that the hammer and the shorter

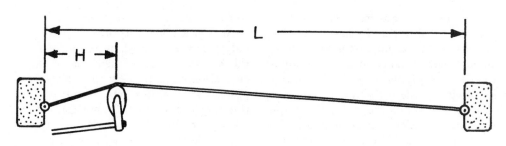

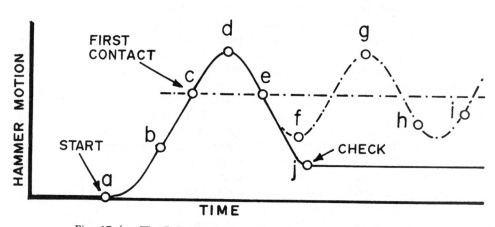

Fig. 17.4. The Behavior of the Piano String at the Striking Point

segment H of the string together constitute an elementary spring-and-mass system. The natural frequency f_H of this system is determined by the string tension T, the length H, and the mass M of the hammer, as follows (see sec. 6.1):

$$f_H = \left(\frac{1}{2\pi}\right)\sqrt{\frac{T}{MH}}$$

The lower part of figure 17.4 shows the motion of the hammer head (a) as it leaves its original rest position when the key is first pressed, and then as it continues to accelerate under the influence of the player's finger until the instant (b) when the action releases it. Following its release by the action, the hammer swings freely upward toward the string and meets it at (c), after which the string forces convert the motion into an up-and-down movement of oscillatory type (c), (d), (e). If the hammer were somehow to glue itself now to the string, the oscillation would continue in the manner indicated by the dotted curve and the letters (f), (g), (h), and (i). In fact, the hammer comes loose from the string after about half a cycle of oscillation, at the instant marked (e), and then falls back down until (j) when it is caught and arrested by what is known as the check.

Clearly, if our calculation is correct, the all-important time of contact T_c between hammer and string is about equal to one-half the time required for one oscillation of the hammer bouncing on its "spring," which is the string length H. When we modify the formula for f_H to take into account the three strings which act together on any given hammer, we get:

$$T_c = \left(\frac{1}{2}\right)\left(\frac{1}{f_H}\right) = \pi\sqrt{\frac{MH}{3T}}$$

Notice that, according to this formula, increasing either the hammer mass M or the striking distance H will lengthen the time of contact T_c and thus reduce the number of higher partials excited in the tone, as explained in chapter 8. The "elastic" version of the hammer recoil analysis is now complete, and we must consider next how the wave behavior of disturbances on the long segment of the string alters the conclusions we have drawn thus far.

A hammer interacts with the longer segment $(L - H)$ of a piano string in a way that can easily be understood if we begin by imagining the string to be extremely long, so that the hammer rebounds from it before an echo returns from the far end. For instance, it would take six seconds for an echo to return from the far end of a set of C_4 piano strings one kilometer long (about 0.6 mile). During the time the hammer is touching the strings we have already noticed that it feels a springlike force exerted by the short string segment H. Wave physics tells us that as the hammer

launches waves down the long segment of the strings, another force (in addition to the springlike force) acts to make the hammer feel exactly as though it were immersed in and plowing through an extremely viscous fluid. As a result, the half-oscillation discussed earlier is damped (in the manner described in sec. 6.1). In this case the lost oscillatory energy is transmitted out along the strings (for eventual return) instead of being frictionally dissipated. The viscous dissipation coefficient D defined for a spring-mass system in section 6.1 proves to be exactly the aggregate wave impedance of the long segments of the strings (see sec. 17.2)!

You may find it helpful to know that the combined wave impedance of three C_4 strings is roughly equal to the viscous coefficient D associated with two of your fingers moving broadside through a bowl of molasses left outdoors in January. Despite the numerically large size of the viscous damping coefficient just described, calculation shows that the wave-type damping on a piano hammer produces only a few percent diminution in the amplitude of any *one* of its oscillations, so that the formula of our original, simple estimate of the hammer contact time T_c does not yet need changing.

Having considered how the long string segment feels to the hammer before an echo has time to return, we are now ready to follow the progress of the half-sinusoidal pulse impressed by the hammer blow on the long side of the strings as it travels to the far end and back. Figure 17.5 indicates that a completed upward blow from the piano hammer produces an upward pulse that travels to the bridge end and is then reflected back toward the hammer. Because the bridge has

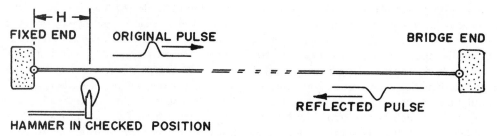

Fig. 17.5.   Reflection of the Hammer Impulse

a very large wave impedance compared with that of the strings, this reflected pulse has very nearly the same amplitude as the original, but it is inverted. As long as the hammer is thrown clear in advance of the reflected wave (as is the case for notes below about C_5 on a piano), the pulse runs back and forth over the whole length of the strings, being reflected and re-reflected at the two ends. This particular motion is exactly the one we described in chapter 8, using language that details the motion in terms of the vibration recipe belonging to a given hammer blow at a particular point on the three strings (see secs. 8.2 and 8.3 and also statement 6, sec. 11.9).

For the upper two octaves of the piano scale, the inverted pulse returns before the hammer has left the strings, and so adds its forces to those exerted by the short string segments H. As a result, the hammer is thrown off the strings earlier than otherwise, thus shortening the time of contact.

It is time now to go back and refine our view of what is happening on the short length H of the strings during the hammer blow. These do not really act ex-actly like the simple spring we assumed originally. The disturbance on this is actually a peculiar train of impulses rapidly echoing between the *capo d'astro* bar and the hammer itself (at C_4 these impulses make about four complete round trips during the time we calculated earlier for T_c). When the net effect of these rapid echoes is properly worked out, we find we must change the half-sinusoidal hammer motion assumed earlier, which takes place between (c) and (e) in figure 17.4. The hammer motion is now seen to have a new but similar shape that looks as though it were made of roughly straight line segments, each lasting the time it takes the impulses to make one round trip between the fixed end and the hammer. The time of contact T_c estimated earlier remains fairly accurate, however, as do our earlier conclusions about the effect on it produced by echoes coming back from the bridge.

The not-quite-sinusoidal (segmented) hammer motion can be thought of as a combination of the original sinusoid and an additional bouncing motion. This bouncing motion is of course caused by string vibrations set up in the short string length H during the time of hammer contact. These vibrations form a harmonic series whose frequencies are L/H times as high as the corresponding modes of the complete, full-length strings. During the course of the blow, then, the new high-frequency oscillations of the hammer and of the short part of the string are given to the complete strings in addition to the more familiar components of the vibration recipe. It is somewhat shocking to realize that these extra components fill in the otherwise expected gaps in the recipe produced when the hammer strikes at nodal points at various modes. For example, in chapter 8 we learned that a simple, nonsegmented blow from a mathematically idealized hammer 1/4th of the way from one end of a string would eliminate modes 4, 8, 12, etc., from the recipe. A real hammer blow restores these missing components. We have here the explanation of the century-old observation that a piano-type hammer strikes in such a manner that no modes are ever missing from the recipe of a piano tone.[5]

17.5. Scaling the Strings of a Piano

The piano that has been studied so painstakingly thus far in the chapter would be of rather limited musical usefulness, for the simple reason that it can do little more than play the note C_4! The extension of the basic design to the high and low limits of the scale is influenced by constraints of a mechanical sort and also by the fact that our hearing changes drastically as we go to these extremes. For example, the fundamental components

belonging to the top octave (from 2100 to 4200 Hz) span the most sensitive range of our hearing, while the fundamentals of the lower notes (from 27.5 Hz) are only weakly heard under ordinary playing conditions.

The formula given at the beginning of section 16.5 for the vibration frequency of a flexible string suggests that for every octave one goes up in pitch, the string length might be halved (if the tension and string size are kept fixed). We will see in a moment why it proves better on a piano to reduce the lengths by a factor close to 1/1.88 per octave, so that if we start with our 62.5-cm C_4 string, the C_8 string (four octaves higher) has a length close to $62.5/(1.88)^4 = 5.00$ cm, instead of the 3.91-cm string length calculated on the basis of four successive halvings. In a similar vein, experience has shown the advisability of reducing the string diameter by a factor of about 0.946 per octave from the 1-mm diameter at C_4, making the top string a little under 0.79 mm in diameter. Strings proportioned thus have to be pulled to slightly lower tension at the top of the scale than at C_4.

As we have already learned in chapter 16, the inharmonicity of constant-tension strings proportioned in this way rises 2.76-fold for every octave we go up. For example, at the top note (C_8), mode 2 is more than 50 cents sharp compared with mode 1, instead of the 0.83-cent widening associated with C_4. If many string partials for C_8 were excited, the tone would be quite harsh ("metallic," i.e., reminiscent of the vibrations of steel bars), so the softness of the hammer felt must be carefully adjusted to give a suitable contact time during the blow in order to produce a tone of acceptable quality.

I will say little about the trend relating the upper strings' wave impedance to that of the soundboard beyond remarking that at C_8 the string impedance is only about 75 percent of the value at C_4, which reduces the transfer of vibration from string to soundboard by the same factor. Perhaps the increasing sensitivity of our ears for higher-frequency sounds calls for a reduction in the actual amount of vibration transmitted to them by the topmost strings. Another reason for reducing the string-to-soundboard coupling is that it leads, as we have already seen, to longer ringing of these strings. Recall that even so, the sound from these strings decays so rapidly that dampers are not normally provided for them.

The true challenge to the piano maker's skill lies in the notes below C_3. Even on a full concert grand with an overall measure of nine feet, the bottommost strings must be made less than half the lengths implied by the scaling rules used above C_4 if the instrument is to have dimensions less than those of a battleship. For example, the bottom note (A_0) on a Baldwin concert grand I have examined has a string length close to 203 cm, instead of 486 cm. The same note on the six-foot-long model L Steinway grand in my living room has a somewhat shorter length—a little over 137 cm. On some small spinet pianos, the bottom string is a troublemaking 95 cm, only 20 percent of the "ideal" length.

How does one strive to meet the requirements for acceptable (if not good) tone, sufficient power, and adequate duration of sound in the lower strings? The need for acceptable tone implies not only a tolerably low value for the string inharmonicity factor J, but also a properly proportioned relationship among the ham-

mer's mass, breadth, and softness, the string tension, and the point at which the hammer strikes the strings. To get sufficient power with an adequately long decay time one must in addition arrange to get a correct ratio between the wave impedances of the string and the bridge.

The formula given in section 16.5 for the natural frequencies of a flexible string suggests immediately that a proportional increase in string thickness will automatically offset a reduction in its length. For example, if we were to preserve our usual constant tension, the bottom string of our concert grand would have a diameter that is $486/203 = 2.39$ times the 1.22-mm diameter of the full-length string called for by our basic mid-scale design. Such a 3-mm "string" would in fact be an impractically thick rod having nearly half the diameter of the tuning pins! The inharmonicity of this rod would be so large that it would emit a clanging sound when struck. The piano maker in practice avoids a great deal of the inharmonicity problem by using a slender steel string (to support the tension) which is wound with one or more layers of copper wire, so as to raise the mass per unit length without adding much stiffness. On a concert grand, carefully designed bass strings of this sort are held under a tension that is about 50 percent larger than the mid-scale value. We find then (on the Baldwin concert grand, for example) that J calculated [6] for the bottom string has a surprisingly low value, about equal to the inharmonicity coefficient belonging to C_3 in the main part of the scale. On the smaller pianos, however, the problem remains serious, and what passes for good tone cannot be obtained from a bottom string shorter than about 130 cm. On the smallest spinets, J for the bottom string can be as much as ten times the concert grand's value.

Of particular concern to the piano maker is the problem of making a smooth transition from the full-length plain wire strings to the sequence of shortened wound strings that function for the lowest notes of the scale. Let us see how the problem is dealt with in the Steinway mentioned earlier. On this instrument the lowest triple set of plain wires is found at B_2. The next note down the scale, B_2b, is provided with a pair of copper-wound wires having a length of about 91 cm. I have used the wire sizes and playing frequencies of these two sets of strings to calculate that the tension in the wound strings is 60 percent higher than in the plain ones, the latter being about 10 percent slacker than normal because they are already 10 cm shorter than the basic scaling rules would call for. The calculated string tension shows a rather large jump, so I checked the correctness of this calculated change in tension by comparing the pitches of sounds produced by plucking the nonplaying lengths of these strings between bridge and hitch pin. The copper windings of the B_2b string do not extend into this region, and the core wire diameter is equal to the wire size for B_2.

As one slowly plays down the chromatic scale in the vicinity of the break between nonwound and wound strings, one notices a slight but progressive deterioration of the tone below F_3, where the strings first begin to fall short relative to properly scaled lengths of the sort used in the upper half of the instrument. The main alteration in tone is due to a growing inharmonicity associated with both a shortening of the string and the concomitant reduction of tension. The change of tone one hears in going between wound and nonwound strings is relatively small, the inharmonicity increase due to the greater stiffness of wound strings being offset by the increase in their tension. The calculated inharmonicity factors match within 5 percent across the break, which is less than the 9 percent change from note to note of the normal scaling!

The question of suitable gradation of string and soundboard wave impedance across the break is our next concern. Because the wave impedance depends on $\sqrt{(\text{inertia}) \times (\text{elasticity})}$, it is apparent that in going from the "properly scaled" F_3 down to the slightly slack strings at B_2, we have a reduction of about 5 percent in the string impedance. Across the break, from the three slack wires at B_2 to the two wound and very tight strings at B_2b, there is a 40 percent upward jump in wave impedance. Let us resort once again to observation in order to find out how the maker has dealt with these nonuniformities.

On the Steinway in my home there is a trend of progressive increase in the decay times measured for sounds from *single* strings belonging to the notes running from F_3 down to B_2. The falling sequence of wave impedances for these strings, all mounted in a row on the same bridge, leads us to expect a 5 percent increase in decay time, roughly the observed amount. We must now compare the decay time for a single wound string belonging to B_2b with a plain string belonging to B_2; these two strings are found to vibrate for roughly the same lengths of time. On the other hand, the fact that the B_2b strings have a 40-percent higher impedance might lead us to expect them to spill their excitation into the soundboard at a fast enough rate that they would become effectively silent in only about 70 percent of the time required for the B_2 strings. The initial appearance of conflict between observation and acoustical theory is easily resolved, however, if we look into the piano. The wound strings are mounted on their own separate bridge. This bridge is designed to be stiffer and more massive, which makes the wave impedance of the soundboard to which it is glued look considerably larger to its strings than that of the lighter and more flexible structure seen by the plain wire strings. We have here a good example of the way in which painstaking traditional craftsmanship has learned over many years of experience to meet musico-acoustic design requirements, some details of which we have come to recognize scientifically only in recent years.

17.6. The Sound of a Piano

In the preceding sections of this chapter we have looked at many of the ways that changes in the mechanical structure of a piano can give rise to changes in the vibration recipes of its strings. We have also considered the changes in the rates at which the various components of these recipes decay after a key is struck. We will now look briefly at what happens in the soundboard when a string is put into vibration, and we will also consider the way the soundboard communicates with our ears via the room air.

When the soundboard is excited by the string where it runs over the bridge, each frequency component excites several char-

acteristic vibrations of the soundboard in a manner exactly similar to how a small loudspeaker excites the characteristic modes of a room. We have a similar spreading-out of the initial signals throughout the region, similar scattering caused by discontinuities, similar reflection from boundaries, and the sort of irregular growth and decay behavior that is similar to what we studied in chapter 11. However, the manner in which sounds are communicated from a soundboard to a room depends significantly on a pair of differences between the overall behaviors of vibrations excited on a two-dimensional soundboard and in a three-dimensional room.

We learned from section 11.4 and figure 11.2 that, in a given room, if a particular sinusoidal excitation runs at a high frequency it finds a great many room modes to "talk" to and to excite strongly, but it will find only a few if the excitation frequency is low. In other words, the average spacing between adjacent characteristic frequencies of the room becomes progressively less as we turn our attention to the higher modes. On the other hand, in section 9.4 a digression on the average spacing of natural frequencies told us that the mean spacing between adjacent characteristic frequencies of a given soundboard is essentially constant at all frequencies. Thus the statistical smoothing effect of many simultaneously excited modes acts differently on the *steady-state* responses of the two systems as we consider low and high frequencies. Another important difference between soundboards and rooms is associated with their *transient* behavior. The speed of sound in air is a constant (345 meters/sec), regardless of the excitation frequency. As a result all sinusoidal components of an impulsive signal travel at the same speed from source to reflector, or from scatterer to scatterer (see sec. 12.4, part A, for an example). However, on a soundboard (or along a bar), the speed of sound is not constant (as pointed out in sec. 17.1), but rather rises as the square root of the frequency. Because of this, the different partials of a string tone run out across the soundboard at different rates (e.g., the second partial takes only 70 percent as long to traverse a given distance as does the fundamental, while the fourth partial takes only half as long).

If the speed of sound on a soundboard were a constant nearly equal to its speed through the air in the room, the transfer of excitation would still differ from the transfer from a small loudspeaker in the room to its listener. The sound pressure amplitude produced at any point in the room has an extremely complicated relationship to the amplitude of the string vibration that caused it. We have only to think of each tiny moving patch of the soundboard as a small pump to realize that the complete board acts as a vast multitude of *simple sources* (see sec. 11.2) that run not necessarily in step and have many different amplitudes. We have already read in part C of section 12.4 of the complications arising when a mere two sources, the woofer and tweeter of a loudspeaker system, are given the same signal to radiate, so it is easy to understand why the ordinary sound pressure recipes even for adjacent piano notes look unrecognizably different from one another when measured, though they may sound very well-matched to our ears. Whether one makes his observations with the piano in an anechoic chamber or in a reverberant room, using one microphone or the combined results of many, the "overall" measure-

ment usually drowns itself in a collection of overlapping signals. Our nervous system, on the other hand, processes sound in several ways simultaneously and also keeps track of many things as they develop in time. Those parts of the welter of signals that we can process and "make something of" are the ones that usually end up being of musical importance. They are important precisely because they are recognizable perceptual elements and as such are available for artistic manipulation. Because the laboratory apparatus functions differently, keeping excellent track of things our ears lose entirely and yet obliterating things that we hear very well, an experimenter in musical acoustics must often do a great deal of careful listening before he decides on what to measure, and then he must arrange things in such a way as to focus the "attention" of his apparatus sharply on a particular musical aspect of what is going on.

Despite the almost frightening complexity of the detailed behavior of a soundboard in its role as mediator between piano string and room air, it is possible to set down some numbered statements that describe the common elements of those piano sounds to which our ears predominantly respond in a musical context.[7] These statements are restricted to matters other than the roles of inharmonicity and of multiple string detuning. Unless otherwise stated, the assertions apply to tones that are played mezzo forte, with the tones being measured in ways that tend to give particular importance to the earliest few seconds of the sound.

1. The joint effects of hammer breadth, softness, striking point, and return echoes on

the string lead to piano tones that, for notes from the bottom of the scale up to about C_2, are made up of many (20 or 30) partials having significant strength in the room. That is, these partials average out to have pressure amplitudes that are more than 3 to 5 percent of the average amplitude of the three or four lowest-frequency partials.

2. Between G_2 and C_5 the sound pressure recipe typically contains partials of appreciable amplitude only up to about 3000 Hz. This means that at G_2, 25 or 30 partials are tonally significant; at G_3 the number is about halved; at C_5 only 5 or 6 partials play much of a role in the sound.

3. For notes above C_5 (fundamental frequency near 523 Hz) the number of significant partials decreases progressively, until at C_8 (near 4200 Hz) the fundamental is accompanied by very little more than the second partial.

4. For notes below C_2, the first few partials of a tone may have roughly equal amplitudes; however, because of the insensitivity of the ear below 60 Hz, the lowest-frequency partials of these tones contribute very little to the perceived loudness.

5. Along with the components having sharply defined frequencies (associated with the string vibrations), the piano produces a very considerable amount of fairly diffuse sound made up of closely spaced, even overlapping frequency components arising from (a) the thumping blow of the hammer as transmitted to the frame by the short part of the string and to the soundboard by the initial impulse carried to it by the longer string segment, (b) the short-lived oscillations of all the damped strings that are impulsively excited via the bridge motion at the beginning of the tone, (c) the analogous, higher-frequency sounds associated with the "inactive" string lengths between bridge and soundboard, and (d) the excitation of fairly long-lived oscillations in the topmost strings of the scale, which are not provided with dampers. Predominant among the sounds described in (c) is the contribution from the strings whose long part has been struck by the hammer. In many pianos the frequency of this contribution is harmonically related to that of the played note.

6. Due in part to the momentary compression and hardening of hammer felt in the course of a vigorous hammer blow, the vibration recipes associated with *fortissimo* playing show an augmentation of the strengths of the higher partials relative to the lower ones. This means that the number of significant partials in a given tone is increased when it is loudly played. The converse behavior is observed at the limits of *pianissimo* playing.

7. After a key is struck, the reverberative sound builds up in the soundboard, whence it radiates into the room. Each component of the sound comes out in its own way, but when our ears consider the sound in the aggregate, they are chiefly sensitive to the fact that there is an initial burst of sound associated with the combined effects of the struck strings and the various short-lived components listed in statement 5. At C_4 this burst builds up in roughly 0.03 seconds. During the next few tenths of a second the short-lived components disappear, leaving the string sounds to decay in the manner described below. The time scale of these developments is longer when low notes are sounded and shorter for high notes. This is in part because as we go from one part of the scale to another, the predominantly excited components have different frequencies and therefore different "spreading times" across the soundboard.

8. The decay of any given partial in a piano tone has a complicated nature (see secs. 17.2 and 17.3). Taking the sound as heard overall, we find that 20 seconds is a good round number for the time required for the aggregate sound pressure of C_4 to fall to 1/1000th of the original sound pressure. As we go up to about G_7, the corresponding decay times become progressively shorter, decreasing by a factor of about 0.66 for each octave. Above G_7 the decay times become very much shorter, falling to a value of less than 0.5

seconds at C_8. Going down the scale below C_4, we find that the decay times become gradually longer, growing by a factor of about 1.2 for each octave.

9. When a key is released, the damper falls into place, but it is unable to kill off the string oscillations immediately. Each partial decays at its own rate, because of the varying efficacy of damper action on each string mode. A characteristic part of the piano sound is the quickly damped tail at the end of each tone. The fundamental component disappears in a few tenths of a second, usually leaving the higher partials softly audible for several seconds.

10. Both top and bottom surfaces are active in coupling the soundboard vibrations to the air. When the cover is lowered, there is a distinct change in piano tone, because the top surface of the soundboard now communicates with the broad but not very high channel of air between it and the lid. Signals produced by parts of the soundboard far back in this channel take longer to come out into the room than do those which arise in regions near the open edge of the lid. The impulsive parts of the piano tone are influenced by the fact that in a narrow (almost two-dimensional) channel of air, a given frequency component is transmitted in several "propagation modes" each having its own (frequency-dependent) velocity. As a result of the altered coupling to the room, the build-up processes described in statement 7 are rearranged and spread over a longer period of time. Piano makers recognize the existence of a lid angle giving "best" tone in a concert hall. Curiously enough, the props installed on the piano to adjust the lid angle do not always provide this "best" angle.

17.7. Examples, Experiments, and Questions

1. Find a freshly tuned piano and play the bottom note A_0 along with its octave, A_1. Get a fairly clear impression in your ears of the joint sound of these two carefully adjusted notes. Next listen to sounds produced by the two strings when you lightly touch the exact center of the A_0 string with a finger tip so that its odd-numbered modes are quickly damped out. You will be surprised at how many hitherto inaudible beats become easily apparent, producing a very rough sound. When the string is damped in its exact center, only those partials of A_0 remain which *directly* compare themselves with the partials of A_1 (see the digression on sounds with only even harmonics in sec. 5.5, and also experiment 2, sec. 8.6). If a piano tuner were present, he could retune A_0 so as to make the beats less noticeable in the altered circumstances, but then the normal A_0-to-A_1 octave tuning would become unacceptable. See if you can find some acoustical reasons why the presence of the odd-numbered partials in the normal tone of A_0 leads the tuner to provide a setting different from the elementary minimum-beat conditions which we might naïvely expect. At the bottom of the keyboard, tuners generally check not only the octave, but also double octaves, as they proceed. They usually play their pairs of notes alternately as well as together. Why is this an admirable practice?

2. The number of round trips per second (shall we call it the echoing rate?) which a disturbance can make on a string of length L is $v/2L$, where v is the wave velocity for disturbances on this string. Replace the v in this echoing rate formula $v/2L$ with the formula for the wave velocity of a flexible string given in section 17.1. Verify that the resulting formula for the echoing rate is exactly the same as the formula set forth at the beginning of

section 16.5 for the mode-1 vibration frequency of a flexible string. To say there is a pulse echoing back and forth on a string is simply another way of saying that a repetitive process is going on, one which therefore can be described in terms of a set of harmonically related sinusoidal components. These components are the ones we have studied so much already from quite a different viewpoint. They are of course associated with the various vibrational modes of the string. In the real world of piano strings, the wire has stiffness, which means we cannot (strictly speaking) calculate a simple echoing rate. This is because a given impulse does not preserve its shape as it travels along the string, so that the disturbance on the string is not of a strictly repeating nature. As a result its recipe cannot be based on harmonically related frequencies. The reason for the changing form of the traveling impulse is that the various sinusoidal components making it up do not all travel at the same speed on a stiff string (see the remark about wave speed on a soundboard in sec. 17.1). It is the stiff string characteristic frequencies, therefore, which are the proper basis for constructing a vibration recipe.

3. A number of practical advantages are obtained from the practice of multiple stringing on pianos. Some very fine pianos are built using four instead of three strings on each note in the main part of the scale. You may find it interesting and worthwhile to speculate about the acoustical consequences of adding strings in this way. Assume first that no *other* changes are made in the instrument, and consider such matters as hammer rebound time, string impedances, tuning spread, etc., as they influence the overall tone. Why would it be very difficult to arrange for the use of multiple strings at the extreme bass?

4. Flat steel ribbons used instead of sets of round wires would appear to allow the piano maker convenience in adjusting the relations between inharmonicity, wave impedance, and the effect of string tension on hammer rebound. He would have ribbon thickness, width, and length at his disposal. The simple string frequency formula in this case becomes $f_n = (n/2L)\sqrt{T/(twd)}$, where t is the ribbon thickness and w is its width. See if you can verify that the wave impedance becomes $\sqrt{Ttwd}$. The inharmonicity coefficient J uses the thickness t instead of wire radius r (the width w being irrelevant), and the numerical factor takes on a slightly larger magnitude. See if you can come up with a list of arguments for and against the use of tapelike strings in a piano.

5. Many people find it possible to pick out fleeting parts of a musical sound if their ears have once been told what to listen for. The various impulsive sounds coming at the beginning of a piano tone may be separated one from another by your ears if you will produce each one by itself before listening for it in a normally produced sound. For example, knock repeatedly at some point on the bridge by tapping with the eraser end of a vertically held pencil, and become familiar with the woody thump that results. Listen for this same thump when you play a vigorous note on some key whose strings pass over the bridge at your thumping point. Play only very short notes so that the sustained part of the tone does not distract you. Notice that the pitch of the thump varies with the position of the striking point along the keyboard. Now run your fingers lightly and quickly across a range

of playing strings. Do this near the bridge and listen for the brief, harplike glissando that results. If you run upward in pitch along the top octave of damped strings it may be possible to imagine that the sound is reminiscent of someone whispering the word "whee!" After running your fingers back and forth across these strings and sounding them at random, you will probably be able to pick out their collective sounds when one of these triplets of strings is struck a short, sharp blow with its hammer in the normal way. The ringing of the damped strings is easily audible, and will be quite recognizable. Now see if you can hear these same sounds when the piano key is held down after each blow. Other aspects of the piano's initial tone can be tracked down with the help of similar ear-training experiments. You will also find it worthwhile to listen to a number of notes, each one being played by itself and allowed to die away. Damping one or two of the strings belonging to the individual note will produce tonal changes which will repay your close attention.

6. In 1949, Franklin Miller, Jr., of Kenyon College proposed that adding one or more lumps of material to a piano string might usefully reduce its inharmonicity and so improve the tone (see sec. 9.6, part 1).[8] The reduction of frequency produced by loading a wire is one-half the shift associated with a similar loading on a plate (see sec. 9.4, assertion 3). You may wish to experiment by wrapping a few centimeters of wire solder *tightly* around a piano bass string near one end or the other. Why will wrapping it at a point 1/10th of the way along produce the desired result, a progressively greater alteration (lowering) of the first five modes? From your knowledge of

hammer dynamics you may be able to decide whether it is better to add the load at the bridge end of the string or at the hammer end. Even though the steady-state motion (made up of the modified string vibrations) can be made more nearly repetitive (i.e., more harmonic) by the use of an added mass, the initial echoing after the hammer blow will include among other things an early echo due to partial reflection from the added mass plus a later, modified pulse returning from the string termination. How will this affect the early impulsive part of the piano tone? Do you think that a normal bass string has its inharmonicity raised or lowered by the fact that the copper windings do not extend all the way to the two ends?

Notes

1. A. P. French, *Vibrations and Waves* (New York: Norton, 1971), pp. 259–64.

2. Eugen Skudrzyk, *Simple and Complex Vibratory Systems* (University Park: Pennsylvania State University Press, 1968), p. 253.

3. Roger E. Kirk, "Tuning Preferences for Piano Unison Groups," *J. Acoust. Soc. Am.* 31 (1959): 1644–48.

4. Daniel W. Martin, "Decay Rates of Piano Tones," *J. Acoust. Soc. Am.* 19 (1947): 535–41.

5. Hermann Helmholtz, *On the Sensations of Tone*, trans. Alexander Ellis from 4th German ed. of 1877 with material added by translator (reprint ed., New York: Dover, 1954). See Appendix V, "On the Vibrational Forms of Pianoforte Strings," and Appendix XX, section N, part 2, "Harmonics and Partials of a Pianoforte String Struck at One-eighth of Its Length." For references to more modern work see A. B. Wood, *A Textbook of Sound*, 3rd rev. ed. (1955; reprint ed., London: Bell, 1960), pp. 100–101, and E. G. Richardson, ed., *Technical Aspects of Sound*, 3 vols. (Amsterdam: Elsevier,

1953), I:464–68. The reader should be cautious in accepting the correctness of some of the work referred to by Wood and Richardson. To make matters worse, the summary of it given by Richardson is garbled at several points.

6. This calculation is based on equation 28c in the paper by Harvey Fletcher, "Normal Vibration Frequencies of a Stiff Piano String," *J. Acoust. Soc. Am.* 36 (1964): 203–9. The effect of a winding taper at the string ends is incorrectly given by Fletcher as the explanation of certain inharmonicities that are in fact due to soundboard resonances.

7. Some of the information presented here is taken from the article by Daniel W. Martin (see note 4 in this chapter). Most of the remainder is to be found in Harvey Fletcher, E. Donnell Blackham, and Richard Stratton, "Quality of Piano Tones," *J. Acoust. Soc. Am.* 34 (1962): 749–61. A less technical account of this same work is given by E. Donnell Blackham, "The Physics of the Piano," *Scientific American,* December 1965, pp. 88–99. The dependability of some of the conclusions drawn in these two papers is reduced by the fact that one of the pianos was badly out of tune at the time the experiments were done, thus deranging the excitation and decay processes of the strings, as well as the frequencies of their partials.

8. Franklin Miller, Jr., "A Proposed Loading of Piano Strings for Improved Tone," *J. Acoust. Soc. Am.* 21 (1949): 318–22.

18

The Clavichord and the Harpsichord

The clavichord and the harpsichord developed earlier than the piano. We will devote only limited attention to the first of these, chiefly as a way to help us use our knowledge of piano-hammer dynamics to understand some of the tonal attributes of the harpsichord.

18.1. The Clavichord

On a clavichord each key forms a simple rocking lever whose far end carries a wedge-shaped metal *tangent* that rises up against the string. We might think of the tangent as being a narrow and hard piano hammer, but unlike a piano hammer, the tangent is not released by the action to fall away from the string. The sounding length of a clavichord string is the part between tangent and bridge, while the short portion of the string (marked H in the top of fig. 17.4) is provided with a strip of damping felt to keep it more or less silent. We can use the lower part of figure 17.4 to help ourselves visualize what happens when a clavichord key is pressed. The tangent (carrying its own mass plus those of the key and the player's finger) rises toward the string along the curve (a) (b) (c), exactly as does

the hammer on a piano. Once contact is made, the string and tangent remain together and move up and down in an oscillatory manner very similar to what is indicated by the letters (d), (e), . . . (i). The chief difference between what is sketched in the figure and the motion of a tangent is that the steady pressure of the player's finger causes the whole bouncing oscillation to take place above and below an average position somewhat above the original string position (c). Also, this oscillation is fairly heavily damped (chiefly by the player's finger). The formula in section 17.4 for the oscillating frequency f_H of a hammer bouncing on its string applies to the present situation as well, and we can understand from it why the large mass M of tangent-plus-key-plus-finger joins with the clavichord's low string tension T' and relatively long, felt-damped string length H to give the tangent a very low bouncing frequency. The period of oscillation ($1/f_H$) of this bouncing is several tenths of a second instead of the few hundredths of a second that it is on a piano.

The tangent's oscillation is exceedingly slow in comparison to the string's musical vibrations. The initial kink imposed on the string at the instant of contact can therefore be thought of as echoing rapidly back and forth along a string whose "fixed" end at the tangent is gradually moving upward and downward. According to wave physics, the string modes that combine to give such a motion follow a recipe that is almost identical with the recipe of a string plucked *very* close to one end by a narrow plectrum. In other words, all the lower-numbered modes decrease with mode number very nearly as $1/n$ (instead of $1/n^2$) up to that mode whose wiggliness has a curvature matching the curve produced by the stiffness of the string at the plucking point (see sec. 7.3, sec. 7.4, part 6, and sec. 8.4).

The actual vibration recipe of a clavichord string is not quite like that described in the preceding paragraph. During the earliest instants after the tangent touches the string, the contact force is not very large, so that each of the first few echoes returning from the bridge actually makes the string jump off the tangent momentarily once per cycle of the lowest string mode. These jumps are rapidly damped out, however, because at each jump a considerable amount of wave energy escapes past the tangent to be eaten up by the felt damper on the string beyond. What we hear then is a very brief "tzip" of sound at the beginning of each tone. The components of this initial sound are of course in *exact* harmonic relationship to the echo repetition rate. The sustained portion of the clavichord sound quite resembles the tone of a harpsichord, though it is considerably softer.

18.2. The Harpsichord

The harpsichord has enjoyed a long period of popularity that extends to the present day. Its development began well before 1600 and peaked during the first half of the eighteenth century. Even in the early part of this period the art of harpsichord building and design was well developed and sophisticated, and the harpsichord gave way to the piano only when the latter instrument was improved to the point where it became competitive. Fine harpsichords made as long ago as 1618 by the Ruckers family show much of the subtlety of soundboard-ribs-and-bridge design and string scaling that we find in today's pianos. Wire of brass, iron, and steel was available in accurately graded sizes for use by early harpsichord builders. The predominant British and German system of the eighteenth century gave 9.4 percent reductions in going from one numbered size to the next, so that there were eight wire sizes for each doubling of diameter, quite enough to take care of the necessary changes for scaling harpsichord strings.[1]

Let us make a quick survey of the relation between the note C_4 on a particular Ruckers harpsichord and the same note on a typical grand piano of today. On the old instrument, the string length is slightly greater—70 cm instead of 62.5—as comports with a lower overall tuning based on an A_4 setting near 410 Hz. The steel strings for this note have a diameter of 0.32 mm instead of the piano's 1 mm, and the harpsichord's string tension is about 11 percent of that used on a piano. This reduction in string tension is almost entirely attributable to the use of thinner strings rather than to limitations of strength in the materials. Typically, for each octave one goes up from C_4, the strings are 50 percent as long as the corresponding ones in the lower octave, in contrast to 53 percent on the piano. The diameter of a harpsichord string will be 73 percent of the measure of its mate an octave lower, while on a piano the higher note has string diameters that are 94 percent of those for the note an octave below it. As we go down from mid-scale, the bass strings of a harpsichord grow according to the rule described for the upper scale. The soundboard on this harpsichord has a thickness varying between 2.5 and 3 mm, in contrast to a thickness near 10 mm that is typical of a piano.[2]

The mounting of light, low-tension strings on a thinner soundboard gives a string-to-soundboard wave impedance ratio for the harpsichord that is higher by a factor of 1.3 than the ratio between a single string and the piano soundboard. This might lead us to expect the decay time on a harpsichord to be about $20/1.3 = 15.4$ seconds (see statement 8, sec. 17.5; why is it correct here to use the single-string rather than the triple-string wave impedance for the piano?). I find by informal trial on a similarly proportioned modern harpsichord that the apparent persistence of the overall tone is in fact much less than this, the time being on the order of half a dozen seconds. However, the above prediction based on wave impedance ratios is oversimplified, since it does not take into account the damping of string vibrations by viscous friction in the surrounding air. This damping has only a small role to play in the behavior of a piano string, but it cannot be ignored on the harpsichord.

In 1856 the distinguished British physicist Sir George Stokes worked out the theory of such air damping of string vibrations by viscous friction, and showed among other things that the vibrations of small-diameter wires are more quickly damped than are those of large wires (halving the diameter halves the decay time). He further showed that the high-frequency modes die away more quickly than do the lower ones (doubling the frequency reduces the decay time by about 70 percent). If we confine our attention to the lowest-frequency component (mode 1) of sounds from the two instruments, it is possible to reconcile their decay times reasonably well by including the effects of air friction.[3] Numbered statement 4, below, implies the resolution of any remaining discrepancy in the perceived decay times.

Digression on Archimedes and Mersenne. *The inverse relationship between vibration frequency and both string length and diameter was recognized long ago by Archimedes (287-212 B.C.), at least in the sense that halving either dimension would raise the pitch by an octave. The fondness of Greek intellectuals and their successors in Europe for simple ratios as a means for expressing the perfection of nature obscured for many years the fact that the vibrations of bars and those of water in a cup do not follow such relationships, and (in particular) also obscured the square-root relationship between string tension and vibrating frequency. It is perhaps significant that the Frenchman Marin Mersenne (1588–1648), who is credited today with scientifically clarifying the nature of string vibrations, lived at a time when craftsmen were already very expert in making use of musical strings. Mersenne was quite aware of the influence of stiffness on the effective lengths of strings. We should realize, however, that the class of ideas implied by our term* wave impedance *did not become well systematized until the latter half of the nineteenth century, following the laying of the Atlantic telegraph cable.*[4]

We are now in a position to describe the tonal nature of the harpsichord sound, which we will do chiefly by comparing it with what we already know of the sounds produced by the piano and the clavichord.

1. When a harpsichord key is depressed, the plectrum is in contact with the string for a short time before the string slips off of it to vibrate freely. During this short contact time, small-amplitude but audible clavichord-like vibrations are set up on the portion of string between plectrum and bridge, and also in the part between plectrum and fixed string end. In particular, the sound begins with a brief but complex buzz as the echoing impulses on both sides of the string cause it to tap against the plectrum. The sound recipe also contains harmonic components belonging to the characteristic vibrations of the short and long portions of the string acting independently. These are not generally in tune with the note eventually to be produced, the exact frequencies depending on the position of the plucking point along the string.

2. Once the jack has pulled the string aside and released it, ordinary plucked-string vibrations of the sort discussed in sections 7.3, 8.1, and 8.4 are set up on the whole string. Furthermore, the string shapes and velocities that are present on the two sides of the jack before the string slips clear now become free to travel up and down the length of the entire string. The presence of these additional vibrations means that, as in the case of the piano tone, the complete recipe has in it modes of vibration that have nodes at the plucking point.

3. When the player releases a key, the plectrum brushes past the string slightly before the damper comes down into action. During this interval of time an extra bit of sound arises from the momentary tapping (buzzing) of the string as the plectrum slips past it. Because this tapping takes place between the string and a relatively hard, narrow object, a great many of the string modes are excited to appreciable amplitude. This is particularly true because, in contrast to the effect of a single, metallic tangent blow, we have

here repeated blows, all exactly in step with the natural vibrations of the string. The duration of the tapping excitation is somewhat longer than that of its clavichordlike predecessor during initial plucking. The brief chirp that one generally hears at the end of a harpsichord tone is compounded out of the main tone plus the components added on the plectrum's return trip, these being permitted to decay over a period of 1/4 to 1/2 a second after the relatively narrow damper comes into action.

4. Besides the expected brief ringing after the damper touches the string, there is one more aspect of the damped sound of a harpsichord string that helps to establish the musical personality of the instrument. Since the damper is firm and narrow, the segment of string between the fixed end and the damper vibrates briefly at its own natural frequencies. In general the pitch of this short sound is not in any musical relation to the main tone. One finds, however, that certain strings of a harpsichord scale have their dampers located close to a node for one of their higher partials (typically the 5th, 6th, or 7th). For these strings, then, our ears are provided with a more lingering, harmonically related reminder of the main tone, which may last for a second or two.

5. The tone color and (to a slight extent) the loudness are both altered when a key is struck more or less hard. That is in part due to changes in the amount and duration of the clavichordlike fraction of the tone. The remaining contribution comes from changes in the relative amounts of soundboard and damped-string sound that are produced in comparison with the relatively fixed amplitudes of the main string sounds (see sec. 17.6, statement 5).

6. The sound pressure recipe for a harpsichord note contains a much larger number of important partials than does the tone of a piano. The effect of frictional damping by the air on the slender strings of a harpsichord causes the high-frequency components of its tone to die away very much more quickly

than do the lower partials, so that the perceived duration of the tone as a whole is very short. During the decay, the tone color changes because the vibration recipe rapidly loses its higher partials, exactly the reverse of the way in which piano tones are heard to survive longest via their higher partials.

7. Due to the slenderness of harpsichord strings, the inharmonicity of the partials of a harpsichord tone is generally very much less (e.g., 1/14th as large at C_4) than that found on a piano. The musical effect of the greater harmonicity is not particularly apparent, however, because partials 2, 4, 6, . . . of the harpsichord tone have, very crudely speaking, the same frequency shifts at C_4 due to inharmonicity as do partials 1, 2, 3, . . . of the piano tone. The harpsichord's larger string impedance relative to that of its bridge also increases the random inharmonicity due to soundboard resonances. The harpsichord tone thus collects by means of its large number of important partials an aggretate inharmonicity that does not differ much from the inharmonicity associated with the fewer partials in a piano tone. Tuning discrepancies are perhaps a little harder to detect in the more diffuse but shorter-lived sound of a harpsichord.

18.3. Examples, Experiments, and Questions

1. On large harpsichords one finds stops that give the player a choice of varying tone colors. One of these stops arranges for the strings to be plucked a considerable distance from their fixed ends. Another arrangement presses a small block of felt against each string very near to the fixed end, so as to damp its vibrations lightly. See how many musical implications you can draw from the acoustical changes produced by these stops. Consider in particular that the influence of the added felt block at the end of the

string increases progressively as we go to the higher modes.

2. Most harpsichords have at least a pair of strings for each note of the main scale, and the player has the option of plucking one or both of these. For both mechanical and tonal reasons, the distance between the fixed string end and the plucking point is different for the two strings. If both strings of a pair could be plucked exactly together, the acoustical consequences would be very similar to those associated with multiple stringing on a piano. In practice the strings are not released precisely together, which at the very least eliminates the rapid initial decay. Think about the auditory consequences of having strings excited a few hundredths to one-tenth of a second apart. Consider next what goes on if only one string of a closely tuned pair is excited directly by the player, the ordinary damper being lifted for both. Each vibrational mode of the plucked string then drives its originally silent counterpart into transient motion fo the sort described in chapter 10. As the driven oscillations of the second or "sympathetic" string build up, they in turn start driving the soundboard, and so produce a certain share of the audible sound. See if you can figure out why the vibrations of the plucked string may die out very rapidly at first, and yet leave us with an actual swelling of audible sound. What sort of tonal effect would you expect from the fact that the sympathetic string receives an initial impulsive excitation when the first kink arrives at the bridge after the plectrum slips free of the other string?

3. Harpsichords are usually provided with a set of so-called "four-foot" strings in addition to the normal "eight-foot" ones that provide the basic scale. The

four-foot strings are tuned to sound an octave above their nominal note names. Thus the C_4 key of a harpsichord keyboard can pluck strings tuned to 261.6 Hz and also one tuned to 523.2 Hz. On the Ruckers harpsichord described earlier, the string lengths of the four-foot strings are approximately half those of their eight-foot brothers. The wire sizes are not quite the same, however: at C_6 the wires are alike, at C_4 the higher-pitched string is about 10 percent thinner than the lower, while at C_2 (the bottom note), the four-foot string is about 20 percent smaller. The thinner, high-pitched set of strings thus runs at a reduced tension, so that at C_6 the wave impedance is 90 percent of the eight-foot value; at C_4 and at C_2 the figures are close to 80 and 70 percent. See what you can predict about the loudness and sustaining power of the four-foot strings, taking account of the fact that we hear better at high frequencies and also considering the fact that the short strings run over their own slender bridge, after which they are anchored with large downbearing directly to the soundboard in the region between the two bridges. The four-foot strings are generally plucked a little closer to their centers than is customary for the full-size strings.

4. Some concerts of baroque music are played at today's pitch, based on A-440, while at other times the choice favors a reference frequency near 415 Hz, which is a semitone lower. Harpsichords are sometimes built so that either pitch can be selected by mechanical transposition, the keyboard being slid sideways to operate on different plectra and strings. On other instruments it becomes necessary to retune the strings themselves to shift from high pitch to low pitch or vice versa.

Consider what happens to a satisfactory high-pitch instrument when the string tension is slackened about 12 percent to bring it to the lower tuning. What will happen to the decay time of the tones and to their loudnesses? (Be careful here—there are several aspects to the physics and also to the perception process.) How will the stiffness and soundboard-resonance contributions to the inharmonicity be changed? What musical consequences will these have? The initial thump from the soundboard and frame will have an audibly different relationship to the main sound. A serious builder of harpsichords might find similar cogitations useful in suggesting ways to guide his proportioning of string gauges and lengths, soundboard thickness, bridge and rib dimensions, downbearing angles, etc., when he adapts a successful design intended for one tuning to the construction of an instrument tuned to the other pitch.

5. Unlike the piano, the bottom surface of a harpsichord case is closed by a large board traversed by several stiffening ribs mounted on its inner surface from one side plank of the case to the other. Soundboard vibrations communicated to the somewhat compartmentalized air cavity within the case are radiated into the room via the long, narrow opening left at the keyboard end of the soundboard. The overall balance of sound from different parts of a harpsichord scale (both loudness and tone color) can be influenced by the acoustical relationship of the air cavity modes to those of the soundboard (see sec. 17.6, part 10, concerning the lid on a piano). The effect is particularly noticeable at the bass end of the scale. Refer back to section 9.5 and see how much of the discussion there of the interaction of

kettledrum cavity and drumhead can be adapted to the present situation. Why could the cutting of a hole in the case bottom, or of an elaborately carved "rose" in the soundboard, be expected to produce tonal changes?

6. One occasionally meets notes on a harpsichord that "beat with themselves" even when only a single string is permitted to vibrate. The simplest way in which this phenomenon can come about is the following. At the bridge, the stiffness of the anchorage appears considerably greater to a string that vibrates from side to side in a horizontal plane (parallel to the soundboard) than it does to a string vibrating more normally in a vertical plane. Because of this, any given mode of oscillation will have a slightly higher frequency when excited in a horizontal plane than in a vertical (see sec. 16.5). Furthermore, we find that the plane of oscillation for such a string will slowly rotate, at a rate equal to the frequency difference between the two versions of the mode. As a result, an initial vertically oriented oscillation produced by normal plucking will slowly rotate a quarter revolution into a horizontal oscillation (which cannot drive the bridge) before continuing another quarter revolution, at which time it will again become a vertical

oscillation, etc. Verify that the sound waxes and wanes, as a result of this rotation, at twice the frequency we normally would associate with ordinary beats between the modes. Why is this whole phenomenon most likely to manifest itself for string modes whose frequencies lie close to resonances of the soundboard? Can you figure out why even a slight kink put into a wire during installation can give rise to a similar kind of beating sound?

Notes

1. Kenneth Bakeman, "Stringing Techniques of Harpsichord Builders," *Galpin Soc. J.* 27 (April 1974): 95–112.

2. Friedrich Ernst, "Four Ruckers Harpsichords in Berlin," trans. David Jones, *Galpin Soc. J.* 20 (March 1967): 63–76, and J. H. Van der Meer, "An Example of Harpsichord Restoration," *Galpin Soc. J.* 17 (February 1964): 5–16.

3. A. B. Wood, *A Textbook of Sound*, 3rd rev. ed. (1955; reprint ed., London: Bell, 1960), pp. 109–110. See also Irving B. Crandall, *Theory of Vibrating Systems and Sound* (New York: Van Nostrand, 1926), pp. 124–33.

4. A fascinating account of the historical development of these ideas is to be found in Sigalia Dostrovsky, "Early Vibration Theory: Physics and Music in the Seventeenth Century," *Archive for History of Exact Sciences,* in press.

19

The Voice as a Musical Instrument

The preceding chapters of this book have concentrated on impulsively excited tones that die away—clangs, drum thumps, guitar pluckings, and the sounds made by the stringed keyboard instruments. It is now time to consider sound sources that are capable of producing a sustained tone. This chapter will be devoted to the human voice, after which we will take up the orchestral brasses, woodwinds, and stringed instruments. (In chapter 16 we devoted some attention to two sustained-tone instruments—the pipe organ and its electronic counterpart—but our interest was restricted to the pitch relationships of their sounds, and we took no account of the ways in which these sounds are generated.)

In the present chapter we will consider how voice sounds are generated and how these sounds are modified in the mouth and nose cavities before being radiated into the room, after which we will look into some of the implications of these operations for speech and for music. Our interest in the sound production processes of the voice is twofold. On the one hand, the singing voice has considerable musical significance; on the other hand, several of its acoustical aspects provide us with a particularly good introduction to much

that is important in the nature of woodwinds, brasses, and bowed string instruments.

19.1. The Voice: *A Source of Controllable Sound*

One has only to listen for a moment to a singer to realize that the voice is a sound source whose pitch is controllable. In physical terms this means that the human voice can produce acoustic signals having repetition rates that can be varied over a large range. The fact that a singer can enunciate different sustained sounds (e.g., one vowel or another) while maintaining his pitch suggests further that the other important aspect of a sustained sound—the amplitudes of its sinusoidal components—is subject to control. It may seem curious in a book on musical acoustics that we will be giving a fair amount of attention in this chapter to speech sounds, particularly vowels. They prove to be useful to a study of musical acoustics for two reasons. First, they are a musical element of singing quite aside from their information-carrying function. Second, the ways in which recognizable word sounds are shaped out of the original relatively featureless vibration recipe from our vocal cords can give us considerable insight into acoustic connections between tone color, pitch, and the strengths of the partials we hear.

The relationship between vowel sounds and tone color can be illustrated if we imagine building a pair of musical keyboard instruments; one instrument uses the sound component recipe for a particular vowel sung at C_4 as a basis for constructing its tones (by transposition), while the other similarly made instrument uses the recipe for a different vowel sung at the same pitch. We would be unanimous in recognizing that the two instruments have distinctly different tone colors, even though very few of us would recognize that the sounds from the two keyboards were copies of spoken vowels. Contrast this with what happens when two of your friends sing or enunciate a wide variety of words at a wide variety of pitches; their voices will retain some kind of overall tone color or flavor through all this that allows us to recognize them as the voices of specific people. Obviously musical sounds, including voices, have a

tone color that is connected in a nontrivial fashion to their vibration recipes, quite aside from processing complications introduced by room acoustics.

It is fortunate indeed for our present purposes that the human voice mechanism separates itself very easily into unambiguously recognizable functional parts, each of which can be thought about in isolation. Once we have examined the various parts separately, we can put everything back together to make the central part of what Peter Denes and Elliot Pinson of the Bell Telephone Laboratories have called the speech chain.[1] In our investigations in this chapter we will focus our attention almost entirely on the vibration physics of vocal sound production; this means that we plan to ignore the mental and neurophysiological processes governing the selection and formation of voice sounds.

Figure 19.1 is a block diagram of the voice mechanism as it concerns us. The labels within most of the boxes give ordinary names to the various physiological objects with which we are dealing, while the words written above these boxes de-

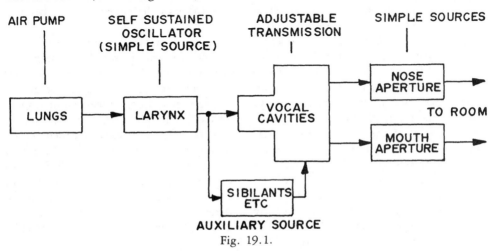

Fig. 19.1.

scribe the acoustical function or nature of these objects. The box marked "sibilants, etc.," does not quite fit into the labeling scheme just described. It serves simply as a graphical device for reminding us that the production of sounds like *s, sh, k, t,* and *th* involves an auxiliary, broadband (multicomponent) random source which can be located almost anywhere within the vocal cavity region. When speech sounds are made, the larynx may or may not itself be vibrating to produce an oscillatory flow of air; it is this choice that makes the distinction between the voiced and the unvoiced consonants.

We may quite properly think of the larynx as being what we defined in chapter 11 as a simple source. This simple source feeds into a small, very elongated (i.e., more or less one-dimensional) room of complex shape formed by the vocal cavities. Our study in chapter 11 of the acoustical response of rooms to excitation by such a source should have prepared us for the idea that the sound pressure at any given point in the vocal cavity (away from the source) will depend drastically both on the excitation frequency and on the point of observation. We should also recognize that (wherever we observe it) the acoustical response will be particularly large if the excitation frequency components of the source match one or another of the characteristic vibrational modes of the cavity.

Over and over in this book we have met examples of the way in which alterations in the structure of a vibrating object, and more particularly of its boundaries, can alter the frequencies of its characteristic modes. In the course of speaking or singing, one continually alters the shape of one's vocal cavities. The production of each particular vowel or consonant is associated with a fairly well-defined shape for the cavities, and therefore with a particular pattern of strong and weak responses to the various sinusoidal components of the airflow controlled by the vocal cords.

As we explore what happens inside the vocal cavity to the sound produced by the vocal cords, we will confine our attention to what happens at the mouth aperture. (The nose aperture, which is also used separately or with the mouth, has very similar properties; therefore we need make no further mention of it.) At the mouth opening, the oscillatory flow of air depends on the relation between the excitation frequency (from the larynx) and the various resonances of the vocal cavity. The mouth, of course, also has acoustical importance since it serves as the source for sounds as we hear them in the room. (The specific things going on acoustically inside the vocal cavity that we do not have time to explore are well understood. Research is done by using a tiny probe microphone to measure the sound pressure set up at various points inside the vocal cavity; also, motion pictures have been made of the movements of the vocal cords.)

In the next two sections we will first consider the way in which the flesh folds that are known as the vocal cords set themselves into oscillation at a frequency corresponding to the speaker's or singer's desired pitch, and then we will enquire into the particular ways in which the resulting oscillatory flow from the larynx has its vibration recipe modified on its way through the vocal cavities to the room and thence to our ears. The various patterns of these modifications are what make different voice sounds recognizable.

19.2. The Larynx: *A Self-Sustaining Oscillatory Flow Controller*

The vocal cords, which do the actual vibrating in the larynx, are flaplike folds of muscle attached to the interior of the larynx in such a way as to produce a slit-like opening through which air can pass. The cords are capable of assuming a wide variety of shapes and spacings. When we breathe normally, they pull themselves back out of the way, so as to leave an unobstructed air passage. When we whisper, they are held close enough together that air flowing between them generates a rushing or hissing sound made up of roughly equal amounts of all possible frequency components ("white" noise); the vocal tract can operate on this random collection of closely spaced sinusoidal components to produce intelligible speech, even though the sound has a radiated sound pressure spectrum in the room quite different from that of normal speech. When one phonates (produces vocal sound) normally, the cords are given a shape and spacing that permits the aerodynamic forces which arise from the air flowing between them to set them into oscillation. However, the speed of the airflow only slightly influences the frequency of this oscillation; the predominant control comes from the mass of the vocal cords and the muscle tension set up in them. The oscillation of the cords is of such a nature that they alternately approach one another and recede, bringing about a corresponding oscillatory decrease and increase in the amount of air that is permitted to flow between them. Not only can the speaker choose the frequency of oscillation of the cords (and so the pitch of the resulting sounds), he can also choose to have the cords swing with sufficient amplitude that they can press together during a controllable portion of each oscillatory cycle. Under these conditions, the flow consists of momentary puffs of air whose duration can be adjusted more or less independently of their repetition rate. As a result the singer is provided additionally with an adjustable recipe for his internal sound source, and therefore with one of his means for altering the tone color of his music.

As an initial step in our quest for understanding how the air passing between vocal cords can maintain their oscillations, we should remind ourselves of a few facts about the motion of fluids and some of the initial consequences of these facts. Most of us are quite familiar with these facts in an everyday way, even if we have not thought about them formally or tried to describe them in words. Because of their basic importance to our understanding of many things we will examine in the rest of this book (not just in connection with the maintenance of oscillations), I shall set down these basic ideas as the first few members of a set of numbered statements to which we can easily make reference whenever the need arises.

1. Fluids (including air) tend to flow from regions of high pressure toward regions where the pressure is low.

2. As a consequence of the influence of pressure on fluid flow, we recognize that if we see an increasing flow velocity of a fluid as it moves from one point to another in its travels, we can deduce that the pressure at a high-velocity spot must be lower than at the low-velocity point from which the fluid came. One cannot speed anything up without arranging to have an excess of force acting behind it.

3. When a fluid flows steadily and continuously in a long duct, we expect the velocity

of flow to be higher in any narrow parts of the duct than in the wider parts.

Statement 3 is simply a recognition of the fact that, for fluid flowing in a leak-free duct, a fixed volume of fluid passes any given point per second. Where the pipe cross-section is large, many small "chunks" of the slow-moving fluid travel abreast of one another; in the narrower parts these must run quickly through the constriction in single file.

4. A joint implication of statements 2 and 3 is that we should expect the fluid pressure in the narrow parts of a long duct to be lower than it is in the broad parts.

The argument leading to statement 4 runs thus: in a leak-proof pipe any given small chunk of fluid (which you might wish to identify by squirting in a tiny droplet of ink) finds itself accelerating to a higher velocity as it enters a narrow region, and then slowing back down as it continues on into a broader part of the duct. Looking at things from the point of view of the small piece of fluid, we realize that it will not change its state of motion unless a force acts on it. It speeds up as it enters a constriction; therefore, the pressure behind it must be greater than in the constricted region it is approaching. Similarly, it slows down as it leaves the constriction; therefore, an excess pressure must be acting on its front surface to retard it. The quantitative expression of statement 4 and an elucidation of some of its remarkable consequences were first worked out by the Swiss physicist Daniel Bernoulli in 1738. The formal expression of our statement 4 is known as Bernoulli's Theorem for Steady Flow.

5. The presence of viscous friction that is normally found in a fluid and between the fluid and its containing walls does not change the *qualitative* correctness of statements 1 through 4. However, it leads to a reduction in the total amount of fluid that passes through the system per second under the influence of a given driving pressure of the source.

We are now provided with the information needed for a look at the vocal cords in their role as oscillators. If a mechanical engineer were asked to design a simplified machine that worked in much the same way as the vocal cords, he might very well come up with something of the sort shown in figure 19.2. Air from the lungs flows in the diagram from left to right through a large-diameter duct (A) which corresponds to the windpipe or trachea. The air then flows through a constriction (B) and out again into an enlarged portion of the duct (C), which is the beginning of the vocal tract. The upper boundary of the constriction consists chiefly of a mass M mounted on a spring having a stiffness coefficient S, the mass being free to oscillate smoothly up and down along a carefully fitted guide. This guide is made leak-proof by means of some grease, which also serves to lubricate the guide. Our engineer has chosen to represent one of the two vocal cords by this spring-mass system (with viscous damping D provided by the sealing grease). The other cord would move symmetrically with the first under the influence of similar forces, and so can be left out of our initial consideration.

If no air is sent through our iron larynx, it is easy for us to see that the natural frequency of oscillation of the mass M is proportional to the quantity $\sqrt{S/M}$, and that if it is pulled aside and released, the oscillations will die away with a halving time proportional to M/D

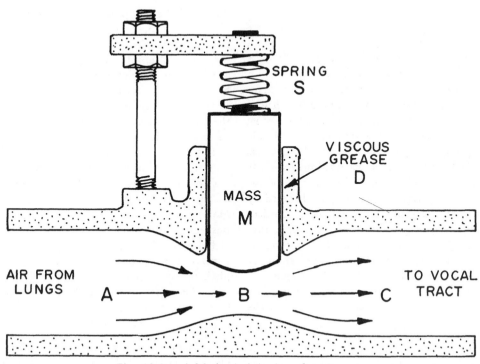

SPRING
S

VISCOUS
GREASE
D

MASS
M

AIR FROM
LUNGS

A →

B →

C

TO VOCAL
TRACT

Fig. 19.2. A Mechanical Analog of the Larynx

(see sec. 6.1). It is this natural frequency which the singer changes as he shifts from one musical pitch to another.

If the airstream is turned on, we recognize on the basis of statement 4 above that the air pressure at (B) will be reduced relative to what it is both at (A) and at (C). If the mass moves downward, further constricting the opening, two opposing things will happen. Narrowing the aperture will increase the speed of the air motion at (B), as a result of which the pressure here is also reduced, thus tending to suck the mass even farther down. On the other hand, the added frictional resistance produced in the narrowed opening will (if the lung pressure is kept the same) reduce the total volume of air that flows past per second. As a result, the flow-dependent pressure will not change in quite the way we would otherwise expect. When everything so far is taken into account, we find that the presence of flowing air causes M to feel an aerodynamic force that has two recognizable components: a steady inward force, plus one which fluctuates as the mass vibrates in and out. We shall call this last, fluctuating part the oscillatory Bernoulli force.

Let us see how the presence of flow can be expected to modify the sinusoidal oscillation which would normally result from the interaction of the spring with the mass. The steady part of the flow-induced force pulls M in against the elasticity of the spring to a new equilibrium position in which the aperture is slightly reduced. We find further that as the mass oscillates, the other flow-induced force component acts against the spring as an additional force tending to pull the mass further away from its altered equilibrium position. It is thus perfectly permissible for us at this stage in our thinking to consider the joint action of the spring and the airflow as being equivalent to the action of a single spring having a somewhat smaller stiffness coefficient. The conclusion follows then that the natural frequency of oscillation of our imitation vocal cord is slightly lowered by the existence of an airflow past it. Notice, however, that we have not yet found anything that can counteract the damping effect of the lubricating grease. In other words, we have not yet discovered any means whereby the flowing current of air can initiate or maintain oscillations of the vocal cord.

Let us digress a moment now and examine the motion of a child on a swing, and notice what we must do while pushing him. This examination will suggest to us what to look for in the larynx, which is a device whose cords are of course known to oscillate. As a child swings back and forth, we recognize first the springlike restoring force that arises from the joint effect of his weight and of the oblique rope which supports him. As we learned in chapter 6, this force acts in a direction opposite to the child's displacement; it determines the frequency of oscillation according to a familiar formula. Once the child is pulled to one side and released, he swings in ever-decreasing arcs; the decrease is the result of the viscous friction of the air through which he moves (see fig. 10.5). Notice that the viscous friction is a damping force that acts in a direction opposite to the *motion* of the child. The contrast between the restoring force and the damping force can be made clear if we realize that the restoring force is zero at midswing, where the damping force on the rapidly moving child reaches a maximum. Conversely, the damping force falls to zero as the child comes to rest at the limits of his travel, which are the points at which the restoring force has its largest value.

If we wish to maintain the swinging motion of the child, it seems pretty obvious that it is necessary to do our pushing in the direction of the child's motion. More accurately, we realize that if we push on him over an appreciable fraction of the time of one cycle, at least the *predominant share* of our pushing should take place in the helpful direction. Let us distill these ideas into the sixth of our numbered statements:

6. Because the damping force on a vibrating object always acts to oppose the motion of the object, any successful attempt to maintain the oscillation requires the application of a periodic force that acts (at least predominantly) in the same direction as the motion.

Let us now go back to our artificial larynx to seek the missing force contribution that meets the requirements laid down in statement 6. Our model at this point is too simple in that it takes insufficient account of the fact that the airflow is by no means steady: it increases and decreases as the valve opens and closes. In the case of unsteady flow, Bernoulli's theorem does not quite hold true. Because of the inertia of the moving air, the velocity of air flowing through a constriction cannot instantaneously readjust itself as the aperture is changed. In other words, the sinusoidally varying aperture determined by our oscillating mass has

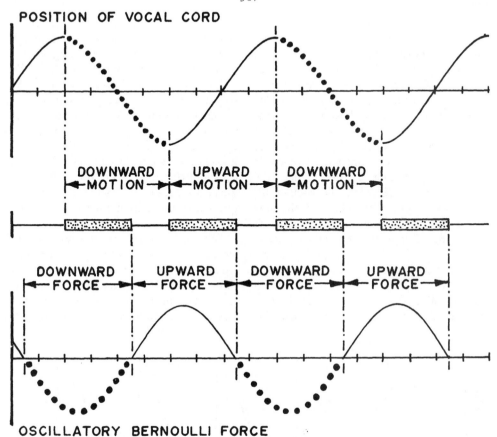

POSITION OF VOCAL CORD

DOWNWARD MOTION — UPWARD MOTION — DOWNWARD MOTION

DOWNWARD FORCE — UPWARD FORCE — DOWNWARD FORCE — UPWARD FORCE

OSCILLATORY BERNOULLI FORCE

Fig. 19.3. Relationship between the Position of the Vocal Cord and the Aerodynamic Force Acting on It

passing through it an airflow whose variations lag behind by a small amount.

Figure 19.3 will allow us to see how the oscillation is maintained. At the top of the diagram we see a curve that represents the sinusoidal up-and-down oscillations of the mass M. The bottom part of the figure shows the corresponding variation of the flow-induced oscillatory Bernoulli force that acts upon it. Notice that the force reaches its upward and downward maxima at instants of time that are slightly later than those at which the maximum excursions of the mass itself take place. To help us recognize the relationship between the Bernoulli force and the direction of motion of M, all parts of the displacement curve that correspond to downward motion are so labeled, and they are also drawn using a beaded line. In similar fashion, those parts of the force curve that represent a downward urging on the mass are labeled and drawn with a beaded line. The parts of the two curves corresponding respectively to upward motion and upward force are also labeled, and are drawn using plain lines. In the middle area of figure 19.3 we find a series of shaded boxes which call our attention to those periods of time during which the Bernoulli force acts in the *same direction* as the motion of the vocal-cord surrogate M. These are the times during which the force contributes to the maintenance of oscillation. Notice that these intervals of "helpful" interaction are longer than the intervening periods during which the force tends to diminish the oscillation. The net action is therefore of the sort needed for the maintenance of oscillation, according to the requirements of statement 6.

Detailed study of our mechanical model of the larynx shows that it has all of the major properties of the real larynx, but lacks some of the subtler features.

James Flanagan and his co-workers at the Bell Telephone Laboratories have found, however, that almost everything can be well accounted for with only a slight elaboration of our simple machine.[2] All that is required is the provision of two adjacent movable lumps of matter, each with its own spring and damper, plus a coupling spring between them. This makes the whole larynx model into a cousin of the two-mass chain, with consequences some of which you will be able to guess with the help of what is said in sections 6.3 and 10.5.

We will close this section with a brief look at the actual flow patterns (and their sinusoidal components) that come through the larynx to act as a sound source for the rest of the vocal system.[3] The patterns range between the two lim-

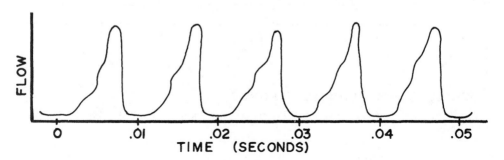

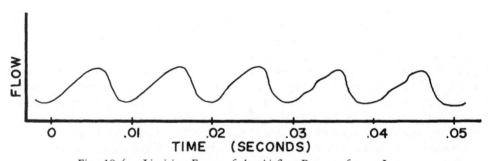

Fig. 19.4. Limiting Forms of the Airflow Patterns from a Larynx

iting forms shown in figure 19.4. The top part of the figure shows the successive puffs of air produced when a man sings a note a little above G_2 (100 Hz) with a relatively high breath pressure and fairly close initial spacing of the vocal cords. Notice first of all that the successive puffs of air are quite uniformly spaced (0.01 seconds apart), giving a well-defined repetition rate. This tells us that the partials are harmonically related. During each puff, the flow rises fairly slowly to its peak, and then decreases more rapidly. Notice further that the flow ceases completely for about one-third of each cycle, during the interval when the two cords have pressed themselves together.

The lower part of figure 19.4 shows the other extreme in voice production. A gentle stream of air is sent past the cords, flowing just strongly enough to keep them vibrating. The cords do not close completely, however, so that the flow is never shut off altogether. The waveform here is not as spiky as before, being shaped more like a slightly skewed sinusoid. We will postpone until later in the chapter any consideration of the implications of the slight irregularities existing between successive pulsations.

The vibration recipes for the two flow patterns illustrated in figure 19.4 differ chiefly in the relative amplitudes of the first half dozen pairs of corresponding partials. In the spiky waveform, partials from 1 to about 6 are of roughly equal amplitude, whereas above this the amplitude of the nth component is about $1/n^2$ as large as that of the first partial. In the more rounded signal, the 100-Hz fundamental component is considerably stronger than the other harmonic components, say 4 or 5 times the amplitude of partial 2, after which the amplitudes fall

away with extreme rapidity.

For ordinary speech we may safely assume a pattern of flow intermediate between the two we have just considered. This intermediate pattern has a slightly skewed triangular shape. The flow is reduced to zero only momentarily, and the pattern shows a slightly rounded peak at the top. This shape is almost precisely what one sees at the start-up of a guitar string that is plucked somewhat to one side of center. This means that if we want the recipe for a typical intermediate voice sound, we can take over exactly the same recipe described in section 7.2, as modified by the corner-rounding explained in section 8.4. That is, the amplitude A_n of the nth harmonic partial is primarily related to the fundamental amplitude A_1 by the formula $A_n = A_1/n^2$, with a few partials being weakened because their nodes (in time now instead of in space along the string) lie near the top corner of the waveform (the analog of the plucking point). A communications engineer would describe a recipe like this as having a few "zeros" in it, with the shape being outlined by an "envelope" that falls at the rate of 12 dB per octave.

19.3. Sound Transmission through the Vocal Cavities and into the Room

The vocal tract, which extends from the larynx to the mouth (and/or nose) aperture, has the duty of transforming the rather simple airflow spectrum provided by the vocal cords into the recognizable acoustical patterns needed for speech and music. We have already learned in broad outline that the larynx, acting as a source, feeds one point in an elongated, roughly tubular, one-dimensional "room" whose set of natural frequencies can be adjusted (by movements of the tongue, lips, etc.). The mouth aperture is a sort of window at the far end of this room, acting in its turn as a simple source for the excitation of the vibrational modes of the three-dimensional room in which we can imagine we are listening.

The pressure variations produced by the larynx in the vocal tract, and thence the strength of the resulting source at the mouth, depend in a simple way on the adjustable resonance properties of the vocal tract. The pressure amplitudes produced for the various voice partials in the room surrounding the listener do not, however, have a simple proportionality to the strengths of the corresponding airflow components from the mouth. Simple sources radiating into a three-dimensional room have the fundamental property (mentioned earlier in connection with the discussion of figure 11.3) that the room-averaged sound pressure resulting from a given source strength is larger for high-frequency sources than for those oscillating more slowly. More precisely, for every doubling of frequency, there is a doubling of sound pressure in the room, provided the source strength is kept constant. A telephone engineer would say that the sound pressure in a room due to a constant-strength source rises at the rate of 6 dB/octave. The physical explanation of this relative emphasis at high frequencies is to be found in the rapidly increasing number of off-resonance room modes whose collected responses make up so much of the sound in a room (see sec. 11.4). There is no corresponding increase in the number of modes at high frequencies in a one-dimensional (i.e., long and narrow) room, which explains why we do not find a similar "treble boost" taking place at the junction of larynx and vocal tract.

In addition to the systematic effect of the mouth's radiation behavior on the sound pressure recipe, we need to take into account the fact that our ears themselves have progressively greater sensitivity for high frequencies (up to about 3500 Hz) than they have for lower frequencies. In what follows, both effects will be taken into account, and the discussion will be confined to the loudnesses, expressed in sones (see secs. 13.4 and 13.6), of the individual voice partials that someone would perceive if they came to his ear one by one, on the assumption that he is listening only a short distance away from the mouth of the singer or the person speaking. We will give the name *loudness recipe* or *loudness spectrum* to the description of the strengths of the various partials calculated in this way for a given vocal tone.

The top part of figure 19.5 shows the loudness recipe that is typical of the vowel [ah] steadily pronounced as in the word *father* by a man who pitches his voice 35 cents above G_2.[4] The sinusoidal components of his voice sounding at this pitch will be exact multiples of 100 Hz. If the fundamental component of this sound reaches the listener's ear to produce a loudness of a trifle over two sones (as shown), the second partial would be heard at about 4.2 sones, etc. Notice that partial number 7 is very loud. We notice further that the loudness of the 11th partial is also greater than that of its adjacent neighbors. In similar fashion the 26th harmonic is also emphasized in the overall loudness spectrum of our 100-Hz tone.

The lower half of figure 19.5 shows the loudness spectrum associated with a 220-

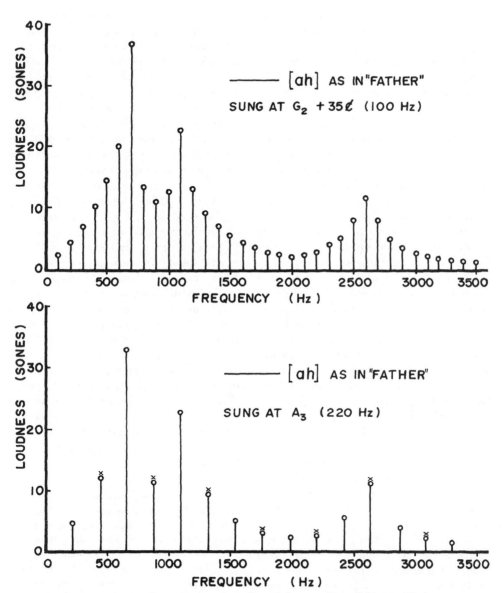

Fig. 19.5.   Loudness Recipes for a Vowel Sung at Two Different Pitches

Hz (A₃) tone produced by the same man if he keeps his jaw, tongue, and lip positions unchanged from those used for the 100-Hz tone. The pitch of this tone is somewhat more than an octave higher than the first, but we would still agree that the same [ah] vowel is being produced. Notice that the overall shapes of the two spectra are quite similar. In both cases we find a particularly strong component in the region from 600 to 700 Hz, another near 1100 Hz, and a third one lying near 2600 Hz that is louder than its neighbors. In between these loud components we find weaker ones, and the strengths of these in the two tones are quite similar as long as we confine our attention to some particular frequency region. For example, the 20th partial of the 100-Hz tone and the 9th one of A-220 both lie close to 2000 Hz and have loudnesses of about 2 sones.

The common element of the two differently pitched [ah] sounds that we have examined is the presence of especially strong components near 700, 1100, and 2600 Hz, and the existence of frequency regions near 900 and 2000 Hz and below about 300 Hz in which the partials are especially weak. The explanation of these peaks and dips in the loudness spectrum is easy to find—the peaks correspond to the characteristic frequencies of the particular vocal tract air column used by our subject when he is asked to pronounce the vowel [ah], and the dips arise from the tendency for cancellation between the in-phase responses of a higher mode driven below resonance and of a lower mode driven above its natural frequency. These matters were carefully discussed in section 10.5.

What is often called the spectrum envelope of the [ah] sound is a smooth curve drawn to indicate the pattern of loudness of this vowel, regardless of what fundamental voice frequency is used for its production. This spectrum envelope is almost exactly the ordinary resonance response curve measured between the point of original excitation and the position of the detector. Figure 11.3 is an example of such a curve measured between two

points in a room, while figure 10.14 shows the corresponding transmission for vibration between points on a metal tray. In this chapter we are using a slightly modified version of these transmission curves, since we want to make allowance for the properties of the ear itself.

The middle part of figure 19.6 is the loudness spectrum envelope for [ah]; the top and bottom parts of the figure show the corresponding envelopes for the vowels [oo], the middle sound of the word *pool,* and [ee], whose sound is found in the word *feet.* Each recognizable vocal sound that we produce is associated with its own particular arrangement of characteristic mode frequencies for the vocal tract, and each of these is brought about by a particular shaping of the air column.

We are now in a position to summarize and slightly extend the basic ideas of vocal sound production as we have met them so far. This summary is an abbreviated paraphrase of the opening remarks in the present-day classic study, *Acoustic Theory of Speech Production,* by the Swedish scientist Gunnar Fant, who is director of the Speech Transmission Laboratory at the Royal Institute of Technology in Stockholm.[5]

1. The vocal cords oscillate at a frequency determined primarily by their mass and tension, with frictional losses being restored by means of aerodynamic (Bernoulli) forces produced by the stream of air from the lungs.

2. This oscillation of the vocal cords transmits roughly triangular puffs of air into the vocal tract. The repetition rate of these puffs is equal to the vibration rate of the cords. The vibration of the cords, and therefore the shape of the resulting puffs, varies slightly from cycle to cycle, even when an attempt is made to generate a perfectly steady sound.

3. A voice source (as heard in the room) is characterized by a spectrum envelope. Each

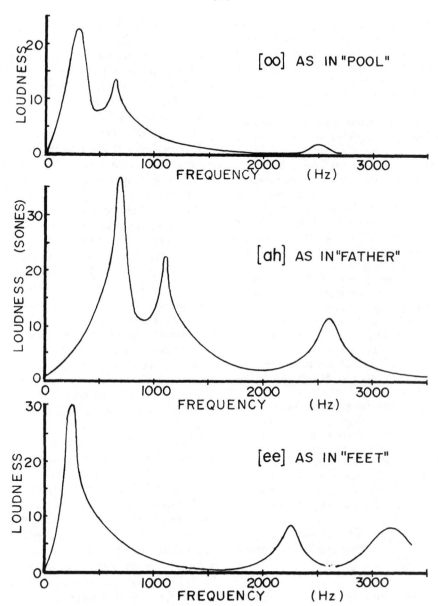

Fig. 19.6. Loudness Spectrum Envelopes for Three Vowels

vowel (and consonant) sound that one may wish to produce has its own characteristic spectrum envelope. The peaks and dips of any such spectrum envelope are determined by the frequencies of the characteristic vibrational modes of the corresponding vocal tract configuration.

4. The peaks that are observed in the spectrum envelope are called *formants*. Conventionally one assigns an identifying serial number to these formant peaks, formant 1 being the one having the lowest frequency.

5. For males the first formant peak of any vocal sound lies in the frequency region between 150 and 850 Hz, the second in the range between 500 and 2500 Hz, and the third and fourth in the 1500-to-3500-Hz and 2500-to-4800-Hz regions.

6. As a consequence of the one-dimensional, long and narrow nature of the vocal tract, the average spacing of the formant frequencies is roughly constant. Its length is such that for males the average spacing is about 1000 Hz. Because of these limitations, it is not possible for a person to achieve every arbitrarily chosen pattern of formants within the ranges given above.

7. Two people uttering the "same" sound will generally use slightly different formant frequencies, partly because of differences in their regional accent, and partly because of differences in the dimensions of their vocal tracts. Women's formants generally lie about 17 percent higher, and children's about 25 percent higher, than those typical of men.

8. The first three formants dominate the recognizability of speech, and much intelligibility is retained if only two formants are present.

The importance of the formant peaks, and in particular of the frequencies of these peaks, suggests that a sound made up of a few inharmonically related sinusoids each of which is matched to one of the formant frequencies of a particular vowel might be heard as giving that par-

ticular vowel. For example, we might guess that the [ah] sound could arise from the simultaneous sounding of components at 700, 1100, and 2600 Hz, or that [oo] would be produced by components at 300, 625, and 2500 Hz. This does not in general prove to be the case.

We consider next the much more serious problem of the possibility of ambiguity in the recognition of a given formant pattern, and learn of the way in which our ears exploit the information available to them to resolve the ambiguity. Suppose for example that our experimental subject is asked to produce exactly the same [ah] sound that led to the spectra shown in figure 19.5, except that he is to use a frequency of 440 Hz as the fundamental frequency rather than the 100- and 220-Hz values he used before. For a man to sound a 440-Hz tone generally requires a shift to what is called the *falsetto,* a type of sound production that is understandable in terms of a double-mass vocal cord model in which the motion is a combination of mode-1 and mode-2 oscillations. The relationship between walking and running is an analogous piece of physics in which we recognize differing combinations of two characteristic modes of oscillation. The loudness spectrum for the higher-pitched 440-Hz sound is readily deduced from the one appropriate to the 220-Hz tone an octave lower: one has only to obliterate the odd-numbered components from the lower diagram in figure 19.5. Elimination of the odd components appears (at least on paper) to do a rather destructive thing to the recognizability of the formant pattern, since the strong components at 660 and 1100 Hz are eliminated, along with the noticeably weak one close to 2000 Hz. The remaining partials (harmonics of 440 Hz) are indicated in the diagram by crosses drawn above each one of them, so that your eye can more easily visualize a rather broad implied formant hump extending from around 200 Hz to nearly 1500 Hz, together with a spike at 2640 Hz belonging to the strong 6th harmonic of the 440-Hz tone. Comparison of this implied spectrum envelope with the envelope given for [oo] at the top of figure 19.6 shows that the two have a very similar appearance. This means that these two vowels would be hard to distinguish when spoken at a pitch corresponding to 440 Hz. There would of course be no difficulty in distinguishing the 440-Hz version of [ee] from the other two sounds.

The resolution of the ambiguity proves to be straightforward. The fact that the repetitive motion of the vocal cords is not precisely regular (due in part to inescapable muscle tremor and in part to certain aerodynamic instabilities of flow) means among other things that there is a continual fluctuation of the fundamental frequency—a sort of random vibrato. A typical extent for this fluctuation is 0.5 percent, corresponding to variations of 2.2 Hz, 4.4 Hz, and 6.6 Hz at the first three harmonics of 440 Hz. Since the component near 440 Hz is fluctuating a little in frequency, the strength of this partial also fluctuates as the excitation slides up and down on the resonance curve of the vocal tract. For instance, an upward fluctuation of frequency brings this component closer to the first formant resonance, and so increases the loudness of what we hear. At 440 Hz, then, our ear is supplied with the information that the spectrum envelope curve is steeply rising toward high frequencies (verify this by looking at the slope of the curve for [ah] at 440 Hz in fig. 19.6). This tells

our ears that a formant peak lies a little above 440 Hz. In an exactly similar fashion, fluctuations of the 880-Hz second partial inform us that in this neighborhood the spectrum envelope is roughly horizontal (i.e., this component lies at either the top of a formant peak or at the bottom of a dip in the spectrum envelope). To continue, the downward slope to the response curve brought to light by fluctuations of the third harmonic (around 1320 Hz) implies the existence of a formant peak lying below this frequency. Let us put these various pieces of information together now to see how completely the ambiguity has resolved itself. The behavior of partial 1 tells us there is a peak on the high-frequency side of it. This missing peak must lie between partials 1 and 2 since partial 2 could not possibly be at the top of a peak and still match partial 1 in loudness. A similar argument establishes the presence of formant 2 between partials 2 and 3.

There is an even more clear-cut way in which our hearing process manages to keep track of the formant locations that might otherwise sandwich themselves between the voice harmonics. In speaking and singing, one is constantly going from one sound to another, and each formant moves smoothly from its position for one part of the utterance to that belonging to the next part. If the pitch is maintained constant throughout, we have the spectrum envelope moving past the fixed voice harmonics to plot out their shapes in time, just as we earlier found that pitch fluctuations are able to explore the shape of a fixed formant pattern. In actual speech and singing, of course, both processes are going on continually as we raise and lower the pitch of our voices and simultaneously change the formant patterns belonging to the separate parts of the words we are enunciating.

19.4. The Male Voice and the "Singer's Formant"

The bass-baritone voice can be thought of as a musical instrument whose lowest note has a fundamental frequency lying in the region of 80 Hz (near E_2), with its top note (near F_4) having a fundamental in the neighborhood of 350 Hz. In this section we will seek some of the musically relevant elements that characterize the tones of this vocal instrument (which elements are typical also of the higher male voices), and learn how the singer can make alterations in his mode of tone production. We will ignore the verbal communication aspects of singing, considering only those musical effects that might be noticed by a listener who is not acquainted with the language being sung.

The relatively stable and featureless source spectrum generated in a singer's larynx is operated on by his vocal tract to produce the elaborately shaped and rapidly varying audible spectrum that comes to our ears as the singer goes from note to note and from vowel to vowel (see secs. 19.2 and 19.3). While we are listening to a singer, our nervous system (in the midst of its many other duties) deduces a kind of running average and seeks correlations over successive brief but overlapping spans of time; this continual processing gives us a good perceptual idea of the common element in the singer's varied sounds, this common element being the source spectrum generated by his larynx. When the puffs of air are short and spiky, we say that the singer is using a light or bright voice. The darker voice colors are associated with a rounded, smoothed-out pattern of airflow (see fig. 19.4).

Digression on the Extraction of Average Properties: The LTAS.

The following laboratory technique is based on a much simplified cousin of the way in which our nervous system works to extract the common elements of a sound. A sound is tape-recorded over a suitably chosen interval of time; this tape is then made into a loop and played over and over into an electronic analyzer that picks out successive frequency bands (say 50 or 100 Hz wide) and measures the aggregate strength of the partials lying within them, averaging the results of each measurement over the entire duration of the passage. If we wish to apply this procedure to a singer's voice, the recording must be long enough that the singer has had time for several repetitions of a substantial fraction of his voice's repertory of pitches and vowels. Under these conditions, the long time average spectrum (abbreviated LTAS) gives us something that is a close cousin to the larynx spectrum as modified by the "treble boost" property of the mouth-to-room coupling. The peaks and dips of the vocal tract transmission for various enunciations tend to average themselves out when various pitches are sung in an LTAS, leaving evidence of their statistical aggregate in the form of a somewhat accentuated region near 450 Hz, analogous to the mouth-aperture trend toward accentuated high frequencies that was just mentioned. (While the LTAS technique has many uses in the study of musical sounds, one cannot use it trivially to deduce such things as the flow spectrum at the reed end of a woodwind, or the force spectrum at the bowing point of a violin, despite their apparent analogy with the excitation spectrum from the larynx.)

In the above digression and the immediately preceding paragraph we have considered an aspect of vocal sounds whose description remains fairly constant even when the singing pitch is altered. It proves possible to make statements of the sort, "we learn from a certain singer's LTAS that the higher partials of his voice become successively weaker at the rate of 12 dB/octave," without having to specify the repetition rate of the source. The musical relevance of this possibility comes at present from the fact that our hearing mechanism is able to extricate an auditory version of this same information. It is time now to look at the interplay between a constant element of a given vowel (its formants) and the variations in pitch that are the basis of singing.

The fact that the upper two-thirds of the bass-baritone singing instrument's range overlaps the lower third of the 150-to-850-Hz range of the first voice formant guarantees the impossibility of specifying the amplitude relation between successive partials measured in the room without also specifying the singing pitch. Thus we deduce from figure 19.6 that the 700-Hz first formant for the vowel sound [ah] lies three octaves plus about a semitone above the 80-Hz bottom note singable by a typical male voice, so that the strongest partials of the E_2 note (as we hear it) will be the 8th and 9th. On the other hand, the top note of our hypothetical male singing instrument has a 350-Hz fundamental frequency, so that when it sounds [ah] while singing F_4, this same first formant will cause the 2nd partial to come to our ears most strongly.

We, as listeners experienced with human speech, would have no difficulty in recognizing the vowel [ah] as produced by our singer at either of the above-mentioned pitch extremes. On the other hand, as musicians interested in tone color who imagine ourselves to be listening to abstract sounds, we might not be willing to say that the singer produces

the same tone color when he sings [ah] at the bottom of his range as he does at the top of it. Let us sharpen up the contrast between the musical and verbal versions of our perceptions with the help of an example mentioned early in section 19.1. Suppose we tape record the sound of a singer producing the sustained vowel [ee] at the pitch C_4, and then play this tape back at various speeds so as to transpose the tone to all the semitones of the musical scale. In this process the formant frequencies (peaks in the spectrum envelope) are transposed to higher and lower frequencies, along with the partials of the tone itself. An engineer would say that the spectra of the resulting tones all have the same shape, and he could deduce from the bottom curve in figure 19.6 that the fundamental component (which was originally at 261.6 Hz) is more than 3 times as loud as partial 2 and about 15 times louder than partial 3 (lying near 784 Hz); partial 6 is almost inaudible since it lies at the dip in the formant curve (near 1570 Hz), while partials 8 and 9 straddle the second formant peak and so are about as strong as partial 3. If this description omits the frequency designations (which were purely explanatory) leaving only the serial numbers of the various partials and their relative strengths, the above statements remain true for the entire scale of transposed notes, as already noted by the engineer.

As long as we do not wander more than an octave or two on our scale above or below C_4, our musical ears would agree with the engineer's description given above in the sense that they would recognize that all these [ee] sounds have a rather constant tone color. At a subtler level of listening we would detect a slow trend toward what many people would call brightness or lightness in this sort of sound as we go up the scale, and a corresponding darkening as we go down. This description of relative lightness or darkness, however, is not associated with quite the same sort of acoustical change that we find associated with these adjectives when a singer changes the excitation recipe from his larynx.

If we change our mode of listening to that used in recognizing human speech, we find, on the other hand, that the sound of our tape playbacks would *not* preserve the [ee] vowel character very far as we go up or down in the scale from the C_4 starting point. This is because in playback the formant frequencies themselves are being shifted, thus destroying the identifying marks of the vowel. To be sure, no trouble at all comes from going up or down the scale by a major third because this leaves us within the 25-percent range spanned by the average formant frequencies of men, women, and children. Experiment shows, however, that a 50-percent shift of the formants by the transposition of our tones up or down by a musical fifth will change speech sounds enough to hinder intelligibility seriously.

Opera singers and others who perform with large orchestral accompaniment have developed several very interesting ways of coping with the problem of being heard recognizably. While parts of the two phenomena I shall describe here have been recognized for several decades, our understanding of their implications has been clarified greatly by the recent work of Johan Sundberg at the Speech Transmission Laboratory in Stockholm.[6]

Let us first investigate the acoustical nature of the singer-versus-orchestra audibility problem, so that its solution can be made intelligible. To begin with, we must be aware that the shape of the long time average sound pressure spectrum (LTAS, see the previous digression in this section) of orchestral music is very much the same, whether one measures a Mozart violin concerto or an operatic overture by Wagner. There are of course small differences, and loud passages in particular have an LTAS with a slight increase of their high-frequency components relative to the low-frequency ones. We can describe the sound pressure level (decibel) version of the orchestral LTAS by saying that it rises quickly from low frequencies to a peak near 450 Hz, and then falls away with an average slope of about 9 dB/octave. The actual measured spectrum can be translated into the corresponding loudness curve, which gives at any frequency the loudness that that particular segment of the spectrum would have if it were heard by itself. We find here that the peak at 450 Hz has now become very marked indeed, falling to half loudness on the two sides of the peak at about 150 and 900 Hz. The loudness is roughly constant from 1000 Hz to about 2500 Hz, above which it decreases steadily to nothing at the upper limit of hearing. A typical example of this behavior is shown by the smooth curve in figure 19.7.

The LTAS for ordinary speech and ordinary singing (but not for singing in the large-scale, operatic style) has a shape that is roughly similar to what we have just described as belonging to an orchestra. This remark provides us with at least an indication that a singer might have problems being heard; he apparently does not sound very different (in one sense) from the orchestra, and it is unlikely that

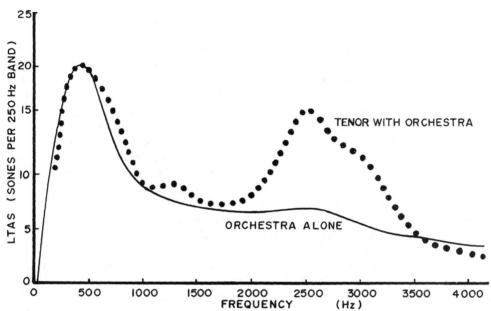

Fig. 19.7.   Long Time Averaged Loudness Spectrum for an Orchestra with and without a Singer

he can overpower it through sheer vocal exertion. If the LTAS of an orchestra and an ordinary voice are quite similar, we would expect a certain amount of masking to take place (see chap. 13). When one listens in a room to pairs of *sinusoids,* fluctuations in the transmission of both the masking and the masked sound from source to our ears normally make masking unimportant. However, when there are *many components* from various sources having frequencies within the ear's critical bandwidth (about four semitones) centered around the frequency of the test sinusoid, masking can be a problem. Sundberg has found in a preliminary way that, for a single sinusoid to be audible in the presence of a noise source whose spectrum has been given the same shape as the orchestral LTAS, this single sinusoid

must have a pressure amplitude roughly equal to the aggregate masking sound pressure of the noise that is within the critical bandwidth surrounding the sinusoid. In a musical surrounding one might expect the highly organized harmonic components of the singer's voice to survive masking somewhat better than this, because they can advertise themselves quite well as a single entity: that is, they have exactly synchronized beginnings and endings, precisely tracking vibratos, and well-defined patterns of swelling and diminishing as the formants change during articulation. All these things prove to be somewhat effective, particularly since many of these patterns of change are quite different from those that help characterize the various orchestral instruments. Nevertheless, the sheer weight of numbers leads to trouble when one man tries to make himself heard above the sounds from many. Furthermore, the overall similarity of the orchestral LTAS and its *ordinary* vocal counterpart guarantees that at no place in the frequency range do the voice partials have a chance to predominate over their orchestral setting, and so "carry" their weaker brothers to our attention.

The first of the acoustical alterations cultivated by the operatic singer to help him in the audibility contest is his habit of singing with a vocal cord placement and lung pressure relationship that produce short, sharp puffs of air in the output of his larynx. By this means he can, as we have seen earlier, strengthen the upper partials in his voice. The increased audibility of these upper partials helps us to follow the rest of his voice components through the orchestral sound.

The second large-voice acoustical phenomenon we will consider is the so-called *singer's formant*. At least 25 years ago it was noticed that skilled male operatic singers did not sing words with quite the arrangement of formants that they would use in speaking those same words. Many of these differences are relatively small, and for present purposes unimportant. However, there is one very significant alteration that turns out to contribute enormously to the audibility of a singer who competes with an orchestra. Tucked in among the other formants of his voice is a very strongly marked *extra* one lying somewhere in the region between 2500 and 3000 Hz. When we measure the various speech sounds one by one in an operatic singer's voice, we find that this particular formant has a frequency that is independent of the placement of the other, more ordinary formants. The enor-

mous contribution of the singer's formant to his audibility can readily be understood by comparing the loudness LTAS for ordinary music (solid line in fig. 19.7) with the one obtained by Sundberg for the tenor Jussi Björling singing with loud orchestral accompaniment, which is shown as the beaded line in figure 19.7.

The fact that the singer's formant is independent of the placement of the other formants tells us that this formant arises from resonances in some part of the vocal tract that somehow escapes the influence of the ordinary changes in its shape. We can make good use of the ideas of wave impedance (which were first met in section 17.1) to help ourselves find the origin of the singer's formant. The vocal cords form an adjustable closure at the bottom of a small tube (the larynx tube) which is a little more than 2 cm long. The larynx tube has a slight bulge at its lower end, and its upper end opens into a somewhat enlarged throat region which then connects with mouth and nose cavities. The operatic singer has learned to exaggerate the change in cross-section that exists at the junction of the larynx tube and the throat, thus increasing the discontinuity of wave impedance between the two ducts. The second digression in section 17.1 explains that if two parts of a large system have drastically different wave impedances, it is permissible to think about the characteristic frequencies of each part more or less independently. Sundberg has shown that the first characteristic mode of vibration of air in the short larynx tube is associated with the singer's formant. The excitation in the short tube is given its acoustical identity by the trained singer's ability to provide a strong discontinuity in the cross-section at its upper end. If the discontinuity is not emphasized, the larynx tube is merely part of the "room" of irregular shape called the vocal tract. If we like, the operatic singer's larynx tube can be thought of as a miniature vocal tract in its own right, whose upper end serves as a kind of mouth which excites the long narrow room provided by the rest of the vocal tract. In this way of looking at things, the singer's formant is the first formant of the miniature vocal tract. In other words, the oscillatory flow recipe from the larynx is first given, in the short tube of the larynx, a strongly peaked boost in the 2500-to-3000-Hz region before it is passed on for a more familiar type of processing by the rest of the vocal system.

To summarize, the trained operatic male voice is produced by a singer who has learned to cope with his orchestral accompaniment by means of several changes in his acoustical output. First of all, he can generate a flow pattern from his larynx whose higher partials become progressively weaker at a more gradual rate than those used in ordinary speech or in a smaller-scale type of singing. In addition, he has learned (sometimes at the expense of a certain amount of strain, or even discomfort) to pull the lower end of his vocal tract into a shape that permits the production of the singer's formant. Finally, he tends to use a fair amount of vibrato, which adds a great deal of recognizability to the various sinusoidal components of his voice by providing them with a synchronized pulsation in frequency and amplitude (as they sweep across their various formants). Such synchronized variations in an otherwise complex signal are of course exactly the sort of things our auditory recognition machine works well upon. The synchronized pulsations of vibrato are one more common element in

the singer's sound which we can seize upon as our ears pursue his voice through the music.

The special skills of the male operatic singer have, as we have seen, a particular value to him in his chosen profession, but they are not an entirely unmixed blessing. The singer's formant, whose frequency is essentially unchangeable, can become a harsh and obtrusive element sawing away on the listener's consciousness. This harshness can be avoided to some degree if the performer is artistic enough to vary his singer's formant from nothing on up to its maximum prominence, changing its magnitude as his musical surroundings change. Similarly, his customary form of vibrato, which runs continually and at its own pace completely independent of the rhythmic pattern of the music, can give great audibility to his voice precisely because of the individuality of its pattern. However, any piece of music is likely to require a resourceful musician to employ once again the full range of variation, from no vibrato at all, through one which comes and goes during the longer notes, to the more fixed variety whose function we have already described. In short, maximum audibility is not automatically advantageous—a voice whose rich variability is skillfully made to appear and disappear in various ways provides a marvelous vehicle for the display of true artistry.

19.5. Formant Tuning and the Soprano Singing Voice

The soprano singer uses tones from the upper portion of the range for human voices. The relationships between a soprano's relatively high voice frequencies and those of the formants she uses for speech will help us understand several of her practices that are quite different from those of her male colleague. A particularly striking practice of some sopranos will be the subject of this section.

One evening in the fall of 1971 my wife and I noticed an arresting and most attractive quality in the sounds we heard in a recording by the soprano Teresa Stich-Randall as she performed the aria *Porgi amor* from Mozart's opera *The Marriage of Figaro*.[7] Whenever a note of the aria persisted a little, she seemed to be "tuning" one or another of the vowel formants to a harmonic component of the voice spectrum. It did not seem possible for her to start each note with this formant matching already complete, but the adjustment would take place rather quickly, making the tone "bloom" in a most pleasing way. Enquiry among singers shows that this mode of singing is not in general consciously cultivated. As a matter of fact, only a few singers do it with the precision that first brought it to our attention. Many listeners also seem to find it difficult at first to focus their attention on these acoustical changes, though most will say they find the resulting tone color admirable. It was easy for me to recognize this soprano's tuning process, since it was simply a new example of what I am accustomed to listen for as I alter the resonances of musical instruments by shading a woodwind tone hole with my finger or by moving an object in and out of the bell of a woodwind or a brass instrument. Such effects are important when I am asked to work on an instrument, because they act as a guide to more permanent adjustments to its physical structure.

To help us see what is going on when a singer tunes her formants in the way we noticed on the recording, we will look at a specific example. We will suppose that our soprano, while singing a word having the vowel sound {oo}, comes to rest on the note B_4b in the middle of the treble staff. At this point she is producing a tone made up of harmonic partials whose frequencies are 466.2, 932.3, 1398.5, . . . Hz. Clearly, the first partial of her voice lies somewhat above the 350-Hz position we would expect her to give formant 1 (17 percent above the 300-Hz value shown in the top part of fig. 19.6 for a male voice). The singer alters her tongue, jaw, and lip positions a little bit from her normal way of producing the {oo} sound, in such a way as to raise this formant to match the fundamental component of her voice sound. Our meticulous singer is next called on to sing a word having the vowel sound {ah} while producing the note D_5, whose frequency components lie at 587.3, 1174.7, 1762.0, . . . Hz. While sustaining her note she can make a small downward adjustment in the frequency of her 1287-Hz second formant to make it coincide with the second voice partial.

In 1972 Johan Sundberg made a set of observations on the way a professional soprano placed her formants while singing various vowels. He found that singers tend to align their formant frequencies in approximately the way just described, although his experimental subject did not align her formant tunings as closely as do certain singers whom I have noticed. However, the general behavior observed by Sundberg is entirely consistent with the possibility of exact tuning.[8]

Figure 19.8 shows the kind of things that a soprano can do if she wishes (and is able) to make close tunings of her own voice formants to the voice frequencies

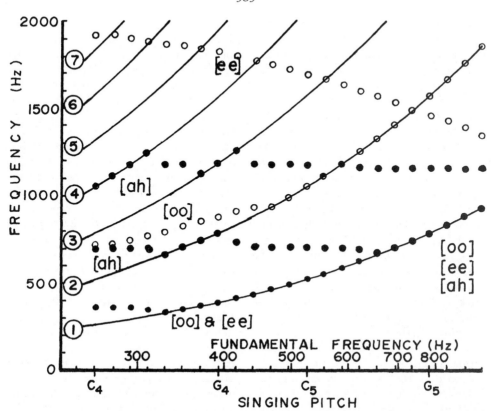

Fig. 19.8.   Influence of Voice Harmonics on the Formants of Various Sung Vowels

required by the musical circumstances. Marks for the chromatic scale notes between C_4 and $A_5\sharp$ are arranged along the bottom axis of the figure, along with an indication for the fundamental frequencies belonging to these notes. The vertical axis is marked off with a frequency scale to indicate the voice-partial frequencies, and those of various formants. The solid-line curves that rise toward the right show the trend of the fundamental frequency and of its harmonics as one sings up the scale. Each curve is numbered at its left-hand end to indicate the harmonic to which it refers.

The sequence of dots along the lowest part of the graph shows the way in which

the frequency of formant one varies if one sings either [oo] or [ee] up the chromatic scale between C_4 and $A_5\sharp$. This formant frequency is about 350 Hz for all notes below $D_4\sharp$, and therefore is not close to any of the voice harmonics. When the singer gets to E_4, formant one for these two vowels has a frequency that matches that of her voice fundamental. As she sings further up the scale, she opens her mouth progressively wider, moves her jaw, etc., to keep formant one in tune with partial 1, even though their frequency rises from 329.6 Hz all the way up to 932.3 Hz. In other words, over a great part of her singing range a soprano is able to strengthen partial 1 by letting it ride on the peak of the first formant of either [oo] or [ee].

The next progression of dots above the one we have just discussed shows what happens semitone-by-semitone to formant one of the vowel [ah] as our fine-tuned singer progresses up the scale. Below E_4, this formant cannot be brought into tune with a voice partial. From E_4 to about G_4 it is possible for vocal-tract adjustments to be made matching formant one with the frequency of the singer's second partial. Above this point in the scale, there is no reasonable way to bring the first formant belonging to [ah] into resonance until we come to E_5. Beyond this the voice fundamental has risen sufficiently that it can be used to guide the matching of the first formant of [ah] as well as those belonging to the [oo] and [ee] sounds recognized earlier.

Just above the dots showing the first-formant behavior of [ah] we find a similar sequence for the variation of formant two belonging to [oo]. This formant can come under the control of the second voice harmonic from about $A_4\sharp$ all the way to the top of the range. Notice that above $A_4\sharp$ the singer has the possibility of keeping *both* fundamental and second harmonic of her singing pitch in tune with formants of [oo]. Whether she does this, or picks one or the other, or tunes neither to the formants of [oo] presumably would depend on her skill and also on the time available. There is also the possibility that for some singing pitches it is not physiologically possible to attain both matchings simultaneously.

The second formant of [ah] jogs along in the general neighborhood of 1200 Hz over the whole singing range, although it becomes a candidate for tuning below $D_4\sharp$ and in the immediate neighborhoods

of G_4 and D_5. Sundberg found no evidence for an attempt at tuning the second formant of [ee], as indicated by the gently sloping row of dots at the top of the diagram. He finds this same lack of influence of upper partials on the tuning for the second formants of two or three other vowels, all of which lie very close to that shown for [ee]. This observed lack of influence of the higher partials is consistent with my own experience in the adjustment of wind instruments. If one can get two or three air column resonances accurately lined up with the lower partials of the sound spectrum, the listener and the player are very pleased with the result. Evidence in support of this observation can be traced in instrument making and performance practice at least back to 1720.

Let us ask now what musical resources are made available to a singer who can tune one or two of her vowel formants to match at least approximately the harmonic components of the note she is producing. Sundberg points out that the most obvious advantage that comes from even an approximate tuning of the first formant is a very large increase in the loudness of the sound a singer can achieve for a given vocal effort. Not only will this be of use when she must compete with strong accompaniments, but also in more normal musical surroundings it has the advantage of increasing the range of dynamics that she can produce between a just-audible *pianissimo* and the *fortissimo* level that corresponds to the maximum effort of which she is capable.

There is a subtler effect of considerable musical importance which can be noticed when there is exact tuning of any formant. We learned earlier in this chapter that the inherent unsteadiness of the vocal cord oscillations gives rise to minute fluctuations in both amplitude and frequency of the sinusoidal components of the airflow recipe. In the closing part of section 19.3 we noticed that fluctuations in the frequency of a voice partial located on the sloping side of a formant peak give rise to fluctuations in the amplitude of the component as it is given to the room. In other words, there is more amplitude unsteadiness to be detected in the radiated sound than is present in the original excitation recipe from the larynx. When, however, the voice partial finds itself perched at the rounded top of a formant peak, the frequency fluctuations no longer give rise to additional amplitude variations, and the tone takes on a particular smoothness and fullness. Once again it should be remarked that my first awareness of the perceptual importance of an altered relationship between the two kinds of source unsteadiness came from study of the analogous behavior of orchestral wind instruments. This also led to the development of a simple but highly precise method for the measurement of air column resonance frequencies.

Whether or not a singer tunes a formant precisely to a voice partial, we recognize that her use of vibrato will have a very marked effect on the overall tone. The vibrato is of course a smoothly varying fluctuation in frequency which varies almost sinusoidally half a dozen times per second. This makes for a corresponding variation in the loudness of any partial that lies on the side of a formant peak. If the vibrato centers itself to vary equally on either side of a formant peak, the loudness drops briefly twice per cycle of the vibrato, as its excitation frequency slides down alternately on the two sides of the formant peak.

19.6. Intermediate Voices and Various Musical Implications

You will perhaps be wondering by now whether the male singer tunes formants to the harmonic partials of his voice after the manner of the soprano, and you may also be curious to know whether she borrows his custom of generating a singer's formant. The answers to these questions lead us toward an understanding of the ways in which tenors and altos cope with the musical demands made on their voices, which lie acoustically in the region between the high and low voices we have been studying.

Because the male voice has formant peaks whose widths are comparable to the distance between its closely spaced harmonics (see the top part of fig. 19.5), very little change in the loudness of such a voice would be expected when formant tuning takes place. The loudness contributed by a pair of partials that straddle a formant peak is not very different from that produced when one of these lies exactly on the peak while the other one is displaced some distance down along the shoulder. To be sure, we can expect to find in the low voice a slight and rather pleasant change of tone color caused, in passing, by ordinary vowel changes and by vibrato, as discussed in earlier sections.

The soprano makes almost no use of the singer's formant that is an important resource of the male singer. We have learned that her habit of formant tuning already gives her a powerful weapon in the battle for audibility (quite aside from its important aesthetic function). Thus she has no particular reason to seek additional reinforcements. Sundberg finds in addition that the muscular requirements that must be met to produce the singer's formant are sometimes incompatible with the adjustments that many of these same muscles must make in tuning the formants.

Singers whose voices lie between the bass and the soprano are apt to borrow heavily from the techniques used by their higher- and lower-pitched neighbors. Thus the alto will frequently use the singer's formant. In the same way one gets more than a hint of formant tuning when tenors and altos use the higher parts of their registers, where the technique becomes acoustically more effective.

Most singers, throughout their musical range, constantly (though usually unconsciously) manipulate the vocal tract formants to place their frequencies at musically useful spots. These modifications in formant frequencies provide the major explanation for the difficulty we often have in understanding the words of a song. The patterns we are accustomed to use for the identification of spoken words are modified in music to meet other requirements. Often the words used in a musical setting require a high degree of understandability (for instance, in musical comedy, light opera, and *lieder* singing). In this type of music the singer and the composer both face an extremely difficult challenge, quite aside from the question of competition with an accompaniment, since both must constantly work toward getting the right word sounds together with the right pitches.

Before we leave the singers for a study of other musical instruments, we should notice one more feature of their tone production which is of considerable musical importance. The inherent unsteadiness of the vocal cord motion produces, as we have seen, a slight fluctuation in the amplitudes and frequencies of the various voice partials, even when there is no deliberate vibrato. It is useful to recast our description of the resulting sound by recognizing that each unsteady partial is in fact a closely spaced clump of randomly arranged steady sinusoids; the strongest members of these clumps have very nearly the nominal frequency of the partial, with weaker components being spread over a narrow surrounding region of frequency. For some voices, each of these narrow-band clumps of sound is spread across a pitch range of about 15 cents; for others it is as narrow as 5 cents. My own voice lies in the middle of this classification.

We have already learned in our study of the piano the useful consequences of having multiple clumps of partials (see sec. 17.3). For singers the same consequences are manifested, but in a broader and smoother way. The beat phenomenon (which is so pronounced between pairs of sinusoids) is very little heard between the sounds of two slightly mistuned clumps of partials. For this reason, then, slight errors of tuning between two singers produce far less clashing and roughness than would arise, for example, from similar errors in the tuning of two electric organ tones whose partials are made up of single sinusoids. Curiously enough, the slight smearing of the partials of a singer's tone does not prevent the production of audible heterodyne components (see chap. 14). As a matter of fact, the production of difference tones, as defined in the digression in section 14.4, is particularly easy to demonstrate with the help of two sopranos.

The following example will show how the natural small fluctuations of the voice affect the generation of heterodyne components. Suppose we feed two clumps of components, P and Q, to a nonlinear device such as the human ear, P being centered at 300 Hz and Q at 450 Hz. Let us assume for the sake of numerical simplicity that in both cases the smearing width of the clumps is one percent, so that in P the components are spread over a range of 3 Hz, while in Q they extend over 4.5 Hz. The simplest heterodyne components that are born of this pair of sounds are clumps which are centered at the following frequencies:

$$2P = 600 \text{ Hz}, 2Q = 900 \text{ Hz}, (P + Q)$$
$$= 750 \text{ Hz}, (P - Q) = 150 \text{ Hz}$$

The extent of the smearing of the resulting partials at these various locations depends jointly on the widths of the ancestral clumps and on the details of the strengths of the partials which are distributed within them. The spread of the heterodyne clumps at 600, 900, etc., Hz might be something like the following: 4.2, 6.4, 5.4, 5.4 Hz. In every case the width of a heterodyne clump is somewhat broader than the widths of its ancestors.

If you refer back to our investigation in section 14.4 of the special relationships between musical sounds, it will be apparent that the broadening of spectrum components into clumps by voice instabilities by no means destroys these relationships. It does, however, remove the clear-cut, all-or-nothing nature of the beat-free intervals, converting them into a sort of pastel version. This gives the composer a range between consonance and dissonance as he writes his chords, making many things musically possible that are not successful when he writes for instruments whose tones are made up of strictly sinusoidal (single-component) partials.

19.7. Examples, Experiments, and Questions

1. Close your lips around one open end of a long piece of tubing with a 20-to-25-mm diameter and sing a slowly rising *glissando* from your bottom note. You will find certain sharply defined pitches at which it is essentially impossible to produce any sound at all. Your vocal cords will insist on jumping to either a higher or a lower frequency of oscillation in a most unsettling and unfamiliar manner. For a pipe that is 150 cm long, a voice will act in this way at frequencies close to 90, 185, and 265 Hz (only the highest of these is likely to be reachable by a woman); if the pipe is 100 cm long, the disruptions occur near 130 and 250 Hz; for a 50 cm pipe, the effect takes place at a lowest frequency near 245 Hz.[9] You may wish to verify that, as the piece of tubing is progressively shortened, its disruptive effects become progressively weaker, and the frequencies at which they occur rise above 1000 Hz, which carries the phenomenon out of the singing range for most of us.

The upsetting effects produced by a piece of pipe on the vocal cord oscillations take place at very narrowly defined frequencies, between which nothing unusual is noticed in the "feel" of the experimenter's larynx. Since the effect disappears completely as the pipe is shortened, it was indeed correct in section 19.1 to treat the vocal cords as a normally autonomous self-oscillating system which is not itself much influenced by the varying acoustical properties of the vocal tract to which it is coupled.

2. Several experiments having to do with formants can be done with a piece of hard-walled tubing about 15 cm long

with a diameter large enough (50 mm or so) to fit around your ear while you press the pipe airtight against the side of your head. With the pipe in place, listen to the rushing sound produced by its response to random noise in the room as you progressively close off the open end by sliding the flat of your hand across it. The resonances of the cavity impose on the room noise a spectrum envelope having formantlike behavior, so that you hear something like a progression of whispered vowel sounds. The lowest three formantlike frequencies associated with this cavity will be close to the following values:

Wide open end:	520, 1560, 2600 Hz
Half the end area blocked:	412, 1357, 2425 Hz
Three-quarters blocked:	374, 1310, 2390 Hz
Nine-tenths blocked:	321, 1259, 2359 Hz

The last of these will give you a rough imitation of an [oo] sound, even though the formants do not coincide with those given in the top part of figure 19.6.

3. If you sing a vowel sound in the presence of a piano whose dampers are lifted, many of the strings will be set into vibration. When your tone ceases, these strings will be heard to give back a crude but often recognizable echo of your vowel. This phenomenon can be exploited in many ways. For instance, you could hold down only the key whose note name is the same as that of the tone you sing, on the assumption that the various string modes will respond to your sound. Why will this experiment work better if you simultaneously hold down three keys, corresponding to the pitch of the note you

are singing plus the ones a semitone above and below? Numerous other combinations of selectively damped or undamped strings will suggest themselves for your experimentation.

4. Playing back various long-sustained vowels on a tape recorder at a speed greater or less than that used in recording them can make quite startling changes in what they sound like. For example, playing [ah] back at half speed turns it into [oh] despite the fact the first-formant frequencies for these two vowels are in the ratio 0.77, while the second formant ratio is 0.7, and the higher formants have ratios close to unity. The tape recorder running at half speed of course produces a ratio of 0.5 for all frequencies. Do you expect that a double-speed playback of [oh] will necessarily give an [ah]?

5. Deep-sea divers must work under conditions in which the atmosphere they breathe is under very high pressure. To prevent "the bends," this atmosphere generally has helium gas mixed in with the oxygen that is necessary to sustain life. In such an atmosphere, the speed of sound and hence the frequencies of the voice formants are raised considerably. In contrast to this change, why would you expect only a small change in the oscillation frequency of the diver's vocal cords, and so also in the pitch of his voice? There is a considerable disruption of the intelligibility of speech when diving, caused in part by the changes listed above and in part because the production of consonants is deranged through changes in the air viscosity and density. Taking everything into account, would you expect greater disruption of speech intelligibility for men or women divers? Would you expect the diver to have trouble understanding what he hears over the

telephone from his helper who is at the water's surface?

6. Sound spectrographs are immensely useful laboratory tools for displaying visually the changing patterns of strong and weak partials in the sounds of human speech. It is inherent in the nature of these devices that sufficient speed to follow rapidly changing sounds is attained at the expense of an ability to measure accurately the frequencies of the individual partials; a sound spectrograph shows only the general outline of the behavior of the formants.

From comic strips and television shows one sometimes gets the impression that prints generated by the sound spectrograph can be used to identify criminals in the same dependable way that is possible with fingerprints. You might find it interesting to list for yourself a few of the important aspects of human speech recognition which cannot be displayed by such a device. It turns out that the most dependable identifications are made by expert human listeners who supplement the evidence of their ears with several instruments, including the spectrograph.[10]

7. It is sometimes possible to describe the tone quality of musical instruments by telling what vowel their tone imitates (e.g., the [aw] sound attributed to the English horn). This occasionally tempts people to draw the erroneous conclusion that the spectrum of the instrument resembles that of the vowel. In the late nineteenth and early twentieth centuries, studies of human speech were generally able to uncover only the strongest formant (usually the first), which led to a particularly trivial characterization of instrumental tone color. A vivid example of the acoustical disparity between a musical sound and its vocal imitation is the "whee" sound that was attributed (in part 5 of section 17.7) to the sound of brushed-across piano strings. When one enunciates this word, the first formant starts near 300 Hz, rises steadily to about 700 Hz, and then falls to 250 Hz. The second formant meanwhile starts at 650 Hz, rises above 1000 Hz, and then dips to 900 Hz before rising fairly smoothly to 2250 Hz. The third formant has a slowly rising trend from 2500 Hz to about 3200 Hz. Meanwhile, the sound spectrum of the stroked upper strings of a piano has a fundamental component that steadily rises from about 2100 Hz at C_7 to about 4200 Hz at C_8, while the second harmonic covers a similar variation at double frequency, ending up at 8400 Hz. It would be interesting to know how our nervous system operates on such complexities to give us impressions of speechlike sounds when we listen to musical instruments.

Notes

1. An introduction to the speech process is to be found in their paperback book of this title. Peter B. Denes and Elliot N. Pinson, *The Speech Chain* (Garden City: Doubleday Anchor Books, 1973). Another introductory paperback is that of Peter Ladefoged, *Elements of Acoustic Phonetics* (Chicago: University of Chicago Press, 1962).

2. J. L. Flanagan, K. Ishizaka, and K. L. Shipley, "Synthesis of Speech from a Dynamic Model of the Vocal Cords and Vocal Tract," *Bell System Tech. J.* 54 (1975): 485–506. See also Arend Bouhuys, ed., "Sound Production in Man," *Annals of the New York Academy of Sciences* 155 (1968): 1–381.

3. See, for example, James L. Flanagan, *Speech Analysis, Synthesis and Perception*, 2d ed. (New York: Springer-Verlag, 1972), pp. 49, 233, and 250. This book is one of the basic sources of information today about the mechanisms of human

speech. See also Gunnar Fant, *Acoustic Theory of Speech Production* (The Hague: Mouton, 1970), p. 271. This is the other major reference book on the speech process.

4. J. L. Flanagan, "Voices of Men and Machines," *J. Acoust. Soc. Am.* 51 (1972): 1375–87, and James L. Flanagan, "The Synthesis of Speech," *Scientific American,* February 1972, pp. 48–58. The curves in figures 19.5 and 19.6 are calculated on the basis of data found in Fant, *Acoustic Theory of Speech Production,* pp. 109, 110, and 126. See also Flanagan, *Speech Analysis,* pp. 276–82.

5. Published at The Hague: Mouton, 1970.

6. J. Sundberg, "A Perceptual Function of the 'Singing Formant,' " Royal Institute of Technology (KTH), Speech Transmission Laboratory, Stockholm, *Quarterly Progress and Status Report,* 15 October 1972, pp. 61–63, and also Johan Sundberg, "Articulatory interpretation of the 'singing formant,' " *J. Acoust. Soc. Am.* 55 (1974): 838–44.

7. *Teresa Stich-Randall Sings Mozart Arias* (phonograph recording), Westminster WST-17046.

8. J. Sundberg, "Formant Technique in a Professional Female Singer," *Acustica* 32 (1975): 89–96. See also Huston Smith, Kenneth N. Stevens, and Raymond S. Tomlinson, "On an Unusual Mode of Chanting by Tibetan Lamas," *J. Acoust. Soc. Am.* 41 (1967): 1262–64.

9. Bertil Kågén and Wilhelm Trendelenburg, "Zur Kenntnis der Wirkung von künstlichen Ansatzrohen auf die Stimmschwingungen," *Archiv für die Gesamte Phonetic* 1 (1937): 129–50.

10. Richard H. Bolt, Franklin S. Cooper, Edward E. David, Jr., Peter B. Denes, James M. Pickett, and Kenneth N. Stevens, "Identification of a Speaker by Speech Spectrograms," *Science* 166 (17 October 1969): 338–43; Michael H. L. Hecker, *Speaker Recognition: An Interpretive Survey of the Literature,* ASHA Monographs No. 16 (Washington, D.C.: American Speech and Hearing Association, 1971); and Harry Hollien, "Peculiar case of 'voiceprints' " (letter), *J. Acoust. Soc. Am.* 56 (1974): 210–13.

20
The Brass Wind Instruments

The orchestral brass instruments and the human speech system are acoustically similar: both have a flow-control device that admits puffs of air into an elongated air column whose open far end acts as a source that excites acoustic disturbances in the surrounding air. In both cases the performer controls the pitch of his tones by making adjustments to the tension and inertia of a pair of fleshy folds (either the singer's vocal cords or the brass player's lips). In both cases the placement of resonances of the air column (contained either within the vocal tract or within the flaring brass tube) is critical to the production of musically useful sounds. However, we must be careful not to take the analogy too far.

In the voice system, we observed that the vocal cords oscillate autonomously, with no appreciable influence exerted on their motion by the vocal tract. Quite the contrary is true in the playing of brass instruments: the player's lips have a motion that is very strongly influenced by the acoustical properties of the air column to which they are connected. That is, the mechanical shape of a trumpet (and hence the location of its characteristic frequencies) has a direct influence on the shapes of the puffs of air which enter its mouthpiece. The brass instrument's air column has a dual function, then: not only does it (like the vocal tract) transmit sound components selectively from the flow source to the room, it also plays a large role in determining the nature of the incoming flow pattern itself.

In most of this chapter we will concern ourselves exclusively with what goes on *inside* a brass instrument; only when we reach section 20.8 will we finally compare the pressure amplitudes for the various partials measured in the mouthpiece cup (where they control the oscillation of the lips) with those that are observed out in the room where we hear the music.[1]

20.1. A Model of the Brass Player's Excitation Mechanism: *The Water Trumpet*

A brass instrument consists of a long and carefully shaped metal duct coupled to a flow-control mechanism which converts a steady wind supply from the player's lungs into oscillations of the air column contained within the duct. The flow of air from the player passes between his lips, which open and close rapidly in response to the acoustical variations within the

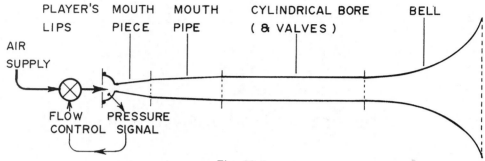

Fig. 20.1.

mouthpiece and so admit a periodically varying flow of air into the mouthpiece. The air column, on the other hand, is kept oscillating in its longitudinal vibratory motion because of these periodic puffs of air supplied to it via the lip-valve.

As shown in figure 20.1, all brass instruments consist of a mouthpiece (which generally has a cup and a tapered back bore), a mouthpipe (which also has a carefully controlled taper), a main bore (which is either cylindrical or conical), and a flaring bell that forms the exit from the interior of the horn into the space around the instrument. It is possible to reproduce the complex shape of such an air column in the form of an open channel filled with water (see part 3 of sec. 6.6). Water waves moving in such a channel of varying cross section obey precisely the same equations as do the sound waves that oscillate along an air column of varying cross section: the lengthwise swinging of air in the horn is replaced in the water model by sloshing water, and our lips are replaced by a flow-control valve.

Figure 20.2 shows an example of an air column visualized in terms of its water equivalent, which we might call a "water trumpet." In this machine we have arranged to have a water supply valve that opens progressively as the water level rises at the "mouthpiece" end of the trough; this supply valve reduces the flow when the float moves downward. We need not assume at this point that the flow through the valve is ever cut off entirely—all that is required is that an increase of flow into the channel take place

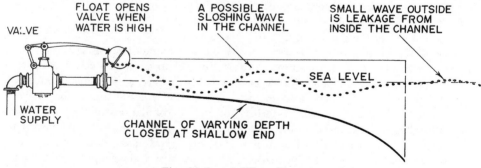

Fig. 20.2.   A Water Trumpet

when the water at the valve end is above "sea level" and a decrease of flow take place when the water level is low. In section 19.2 we learned that in order to maintain an oscillatory motion, such as that of a child swinging, one must apply the excitation at properly timed instants during the swing. Notice that our flow-control valve is arranged to meet this same requirement for maintaining the oscillation of water in the channel. At instants during the sloshing when water is collecting at the trough end, the valve injects yet more water there, to enhance the piling-up of fluid. Similarly, at times of low water, the injected flow is reduced below the average rate and causes a temporary deficit in the otherwise steady (non-oscillatory) flow of water that would run along the trough and out if the valve were held at its sea-level position.

In 1877 the German physicist Hermann Helmholtz added an appendix to the fourth German edition of his classic work, *On the Sensations of Tone;* this appendix gives a brief but complete analysis of the way in which a pressure-controlled valve collaborates with a single, longitudinally vibrating mode of the air in a duct to maintain it in oscillation.[2] Our water trumpet, as described so far, is an exact equivalent in water of the system analyzed by Helmholtz, as we can easily verify with the help of some ideas sketched out earlier in section 11.1. In that section we recognized that when water sloshes back and forth longitudinally in a duct, the alternate piling up and lowering of water near the closed end also gives rise to fluid pressure variations at the bottom of the trough; the water pressure there varies above and below the average value (corresponding to the pressure measured at the bottom

when the water surface is at rest). These pressure variations are of course the consequences of the highly visible oscillatory changes in the height of the water. It should be obvious that the water trumpet is a device in which the entering fluid flow is controlled by pressure variations at the input end of the trough. The brass-player's lips perform an almost strictly analogous flow-control function as they open and close under the influence of the acoustic (i.e., oscillatory) pressure variations that take place within the mouthpiece cup. For brevity and general applicability to woodwinds as well as brasses, we will generally refer to the flow controller as a *reed-valve* or a *lip-valve* (this reed- or lip-valve should not be confused with the valves on brass instruments that add varying amounts of tubing to the overall length of the instrument).

Let us summarize our conclusions so far in the first member of a set of fundamental principles governing the self-sustained oscillations of an air column acting in collaboration with a pressure-operated flow controller:

1. A pressure-operated reed-valve will collaborate with an air column to favor the maintenance of oscillation at frequencies closely matching one or another of the natural frequencies characteristic of the air column itself.

So far we have said nothing about what determines the shapes of air columns that are useful for making good brass instruments. If we proceed upon the basis of what we have learned so far, it would seem possible to make a usable horn by choosing an air-column shape whose characteristic frequencies possess almost any desired musical relationship. For example, mode 1 could be located at 110

Hz, presumably to play A_2, with mode 2 placed at 196 Hz to provide us with G_3, while modes 3 and 4 might be located at 294 Hz and 523 Hz to provide the notes D_4 and C_5. Certainly a musician might make a choice of frequencies more suited to his convenience, but the choice de-scribed here might be expected at least to play one or another of these notes. This expectation proves to be false, for reasons that will appear in the next section along with a rather neat way of gaining several significant advantages.

20.2. Multiple-Mode Cooperations:
Regimes of Oscillation

A trombonist trying to play the hypo-thetical instrument described in the last section would meet many difficulties. The notes would be hard to start, they would be unsteady, and they would be ex-tremely fatiguing to play over any length of time. The sound would be rather dull and muffled as well. Our musician would probably plead with us that if he is to be deprived of his noble and responsive trombone, he should at least be permitted to use a garden hose instead of the balky horror we have given him.

Let us examine more closely the phys-ics of what takes place as a player's lips collaborate with one of the modes belong-ing to the hypothetical instrument pro-posed above, in the hope of finding out how a real trombone happens to work so much more satisfactorily than does our initial invention. Harking back to our study of the vocal cords, we can recognize that a pair of lips vibrating at 196 Hz in collaboration with mode 2 of our column will admit a repetitive train of puffs whose flow recipe includes harmonic par-

tials at 392 and 588 Hz (etc.) in addition to the 196-Hz fundamental component that excites air-column mode 2. The ad-ditional components in the flow recipe arise from the fact that even if the player's lips were to move sinusoidally as they open and close,[3] the airflow through them is not normally sinusoidal, because of the nonlinearity of the valve-control characteristic. The upper harmonic com-ponents in the flow contribute nothing to the maintenance of oscillation and are therefore a drain on the physical resources of the player. As a matter of fact, for cer-tain shapes of air column, these compo-nents can end up exerting a disruptive ef-fect on the original oscillation in a way that is reminiscent of the disruptions pro-duced in the vocal cord oscillations when pipes of certain lengths are sung into (see example 1, sec. 19.7).

Suppose we alter the shape of our pecu-liar horn in a metal-worker's analog to the formant-tuning procedure employed by some soprano singers. If we raise the frequency of mode 3 (or lower that of mode 4) to place it at 392 Hz, then the already existing second harmonic in the flow spectrum will be able to excite this altered mode, so that there would now be two oscillations taking place in the air column, either one of which might main-tain itself according to the fundamental principle enunciated in statement 1. These would synchronize themselves, be-cause they both act on the same lip-valve, causing it to produce a much stronger and more spiky airflow pattern than be-fore. Our trombone player would be somewhat happier with this modified in-strument than he was before. The 110-Hz[1] A_2 note would be as bad as before and the newly arranged G_4 at 392 Hz would be no better, but G_3 would play at least plausibly, because it would now be produced with oscillatory contributions to the reed motion coming from two air-column modes running at harmonically related frequencies. A redesigned air column that somehow provides two or more harmonically arranged modes to help the production of *each* of the notes to be played would begin to seem quite usable to our musician.

The usefulness of the harmonically related air-column resonances in fostering stable oscillations sustained by a reed-valve was first pointed out by the French physicist Henri Bouasse in his book *Instruments à Vent,* the two volumes of which appeared in 1929 and 1930.[4] These volumes contain what still constitutes one of the most thorough and dependable accounts of the acoustics of wind instruments, despite the fact that Bouasse had some misunderstandings about the mouthpieces and bells of brasses. The second of our set of statements is a slightly elaborated version of the observation he made on the properties of musical wind instruments:

2. If the reed-valve is nonlinear (i.e., if the flow through it varies in a way that is not simply proportional to the acoustic pressure which controls it), then oscillation is favored if the air column has one or more natural frequencies that correspond to one or more of the higher partials of the tone being produced.

All of the instruments (string as well as wind) that we will consider in the rest of this book function in a manner that is consistent with the requirements we have laid down in statements 1 and 2. Because it is not always possible to arrange precise matching of air-column (or string) resonance frequencies with harmonics of the tone that is to be played, we need to pro-

vide ourselves with a means for discussing such matters as the relative ease with which the instrument produces its different sounds, the loudness and pitch stability of various notes, the variation of both playing pitch and sound spectrum as the loudness is altered, and the nature of the sound-pressure spectrum generated within the instrument.

As a first step in setting up the basis for our discussion, we must recognize that when we make use of a lip- or reed-valve and an air column, the independent existence of the various characteristic air-column modes (which so far in this book we have assumed) is destroyed by the mutual influence these modes have on one another via the nonlinearly shared flow through the reed-valve. The heterodyne frequencies generated at the valve by a pair of oscillatory components can themselves stir up air-column oscillations that alter the lip or reed motion. The valve and the air column must therefore mutually adjust themselves to produce a definite multifrequency oscillatory state which we shall call a regime of oscillation. We will devote the third of our set of statements to a formal definition of this term:

3. A *regime of oscillation* is that state of the collective motion of an air column in which a nonlinear excitation mechanism (the reed) collaborates with a *set* of air-column modes to maintain a steady oscillation containing several harmonically related frequency components, each with its own definite amplitude.

As will become increasingly apparent in the pages to follow, the word *regime* was chosen deliberately, to call attention to what we might imagine to be political negotiations that go on simultaneously at various frequencies between the air column and the reed, as changing musical conditions give dominance to different members of the regime.

20.3. Acoustical Measurements and Playing Experiments on Simple Air Columns

The vibration of a brass-player's lips is controlled by a basic property of the air column; this basic property is the acoustic pressure developed in the mouthpiece in response to the stimulus of a pulsating flow of air injected from the player's lungs. Let us see how this response at the mouthpiece end of the air column might be measured in the laboratory by methods that are independent of the complications engendered by the interaction of the air column with the player's lips. Figure 20.3 shows in simplified form how an oscillatory pump can feed the mouthpiece cavity via a capillary tube such as one might cut from a hypodermic syringe. The pump cylinder produces sinusoidal variations of air pressure at the driving motor's frequency; these pressure varia-

tions give rise to a small flow into and out of the mouthpiece. A tiny microphone is placed inside the mouthpiece to measure the amplitude of the pressure fluctuations. This microphone gives us the desired response information, which can be displayed on a graph as a function of pump driving frequency.

Digression on Air-Column Excitation Methods.

In excitation machines that are used in the laboratory, the crank-driven pump of figure 20.3 is replaced by some variation of a loudspeaker. Such a driver is then monitored and controlled by an auxiliary microphone which maintains constant flow stimulus as one sweeps automatically through the interesting range of frequencies. In the 1950s, Earle Kent and his co-workers at C. G. Conn Ltd. in Elkhart, Indiana, developed the capillary excitation method to a degree of precision which has never been surpassed. Up until 1968 I made great use of an adaptation of their equipment. More recently I have also used an apparatus in which a closely controlled excitatory diaphragm acts directly on the air column, which gives certain advantages. One piece of my newer equipment is based on a design by the Czech engineer Josef Merhaut, and the other one is an adaptation of the work of John

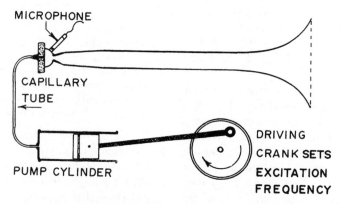

Fig. 20.3.   Excitation Mechanism for Study of Pressure Response of an Air Column

Coltman of the Westinghouse Research Laboratory in Pittsburgh. In every case the excitation devices function exactly as do the acoustic sources described in section 11.2.[5]

Suppose we mount on our laboratory machine a duct (of uniform cross section) that is long enough for us to complete our measurements before any disturbances can travel down it and return from the far end. Such a set-up provides us with a convenient reference for understanding what goes on in an air column of normal length. The microphone pressure signal measured at the "mouthpiece" end of this long duct proves to be independent of frequency, having a magnitude that is equal to the product of the capillary driver's source strength and the wave impedance of the duct. For a duct having a *strictly uniform* cross-sectional area A, the wave impedance is the ratio of the pressure to the volume flow injected into the duct. Its value is:

$$\text{wave impedance} = \left(\frac{1}{A}\right)\sqrt{Bd}$$

Here d is the density of air and B is its bulk modulus, a measure of the springiness that we feel when a small volume of air is compressed. (Compare this formula for wave impedance with those given in section 17.1 for a piano string and for a soundboard.) If the cross section of the duct varies somewhat in the region next to the input end, the wave impedance will have a value that is somewhat different from the one given here, and this value will depend on the excitation frequency used in measuring it.

Let us now consider what takes place when we measure the pressure response of a piece of cylindrical tubing of more normal size—e.g., about the length of a trumpet. The flow disturbance produced by the source gives rise, as before, to a pressure wave that travels down the length of the pipe. This pressure wave loses amplitude as it goes because of viscous friction and the transfer of heat from the wave to the walls of the pipe. At the far end, where the pipe opens into the room, there is a strong discontinuity in wave impedance, since the room can be imagined to be a second duct of enormously large cross-sectional area, which therefore has a very small wave impedance. Just as we found that a mechanical displacement sent down a piano string is almost totally reflected at the point where it joins the high-impedance bridge and soundboard, so also we find here that the acoustic pressure pulse is almost totally reflected at the junction of the pipe and the room, where the wave impedance suddenly becomes very much lower. In both cases the return pulse is inverted: an upward impulse on the string returns as a downward one, and a high-pressure pulse in the pipe is reflected as a momentary rarefaction. The wave that is reflected back up the pipe toward the excitatory and measurement end combines with newly injected waves to produce what is called a standing wave.

If the round-trip time that the wave takes to go from the mouthpiece or excitation end to the open end is suitable, the waves traveling in the duct reinforce one another, and in due course a large pressure disturbance is set up in the pipe. All this is simply another way of saying that if we excite the pipe at one of its characteristic frequencies, the corresponding vibrational shape builds up in the duct, after a more or less complicated transient takes place. At certain other frequencies, the returned pressure wave arrives out of

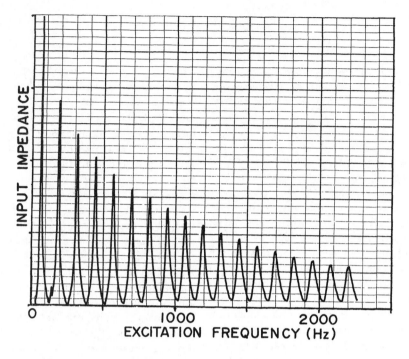

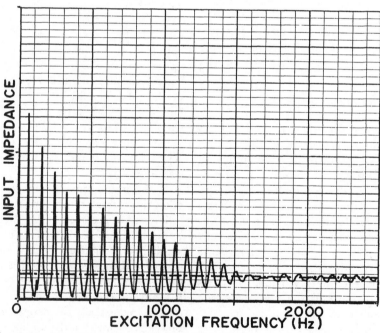

Fig. 20.4.   Input Impedance Curves for a Piece of Cylindrical Trumpet Tubing. *Top,* tubing alone; *bottom,* tubing with normal bell attached.

step with the excitation, and the overall response of the air column is at a minimum. The top part of figure 20.4 shows the resonance response curve produced when one measures the properties of a cylindrical piece of trumpet tubing about 140 cm long. The curve shows dozens of peaks lying at regularly spaced frequencies that are *odd* multiples of about 63 Hz. Since the frictional losses and thermal dissipation taking place at the pipe walls increase with frequency, these resonance peaks become less and less tall at higher frequencies. Because of the wave-impedance discontinuity at the open end, the sound that escapes into the room is nearly inaudible under the conditions of this experiment.

Just as we find that the pressure response at the driving end of a *very long* pipe is proportional to what is defined as the wave impedance of the pipe, so also is it convenient to talk about the response of a duct of *finite length* in terms of what is called its *input impedance*. The measure of input impedance is larger or smaller than the duct's wave impedance, depending on the relationship of the excitation frequency to the natural frequencies of the duct. The peaks we observe in our resonance curve lie at the natural frequencies associated with that duct if the air within it is set ringing by slapping it closed abruptly at the "mouthpiece" end with the palm of one's hand.

A real brass instrument is provided with a flaring expansion to the air column at its open end, which means we should consider the simpler acoustic consequences of adding an actual trumpet bell to the piece of tubing that we have been studying. The lower part of figure 20.4 shows the input impedance curve measured for such a combination. Compari-

son of this curve with the one just above it for the pipe alone shows us immediately that this new air column has its resonance peaks shifted toward lower frequencies, as befits a duct in which sounds will take a longer time to make a round trip. The peaks are also less tall, which is in accord with the greater amount of dissipation which takes place at the pipe walls. We also notice that above about 1500 Hz the input impedance peaks and dips have almost disappeared. We shall postpone an examination of the reasons for this till sections 20.4 and 20.5, and look briefly at the frequency relations between the resonance peaks, since it is these which will enter into any possible regimes of oscillation.

Using the instrument whose resonance curve is shown in the lower part of figure 20.4, a player attempts to sound a tone based on the 60-Hz first-mode resonance. He will find this note extremely difficult and wobbly, because almost all of its upper harmonics fall near dips in the resonance curve, and therefore subject the lip-valve to a great deal of disruptive influence. However, the player will find it possible to sound a reasonably stable tone near 165 Hz, where peaks 2, 4, 6, and 8 are quite harmonically related and so join without trouble to form a well-defined regime of oscillation. The musician will discover several more such tones that he can play, but none of them will give him the free-blowing, stable, and ringing tone that he has come to expect from a truly fine brass instrument.

Our rudimentary trumpet and its resonance curves show that while it is helpful to have resonance peaks corresponding to all of the lower harmonics of each of the desired tones, this alone is not sufficient to give us a good instrument. In the next section we will learn of the important role played by the mouthpiece itself in contributing to the proper behavior of a brass instrument, and then apply our knowledge to a study of the properties of various notes throughout its musical range.

20.4. The Influence of the Mouthpiece on the Heights of Resonance Peaks; Some Playing Properties of a Trumpet

I have studied a wide variety of air columns of different shapes chosen to meet in varying degree Bouasse's requirement that their natural frequencies must be suitably related if they are to join with the player's lip-valve to set up stable regimes of oscillation. The more resonances that are present to cooperate and the more accurately these are aligned, the easier it is to play the notes. Such cooperatively tuned air columns must however meet one additional requirement before they are ready to play properly as brass instruments: they must include some cousin to a normal mouthpiece having a cup cavity and a constricted back bore. The reason for this additional requirement is implied by the air-column physics that we have already studied.

Let us turn our attention back to the lower part of figure 20.4, which shows the input impedance curve of a piece of tubing to which a trumpet bell is attached. We have already noticed that the resonance peaks almost disappear when the excitation frequency is above 1500 Hz, leaving a trace that fluctuates slightly above and below the horizontal dashed line that is drawn across the chart. If we were to distribute many small wisps of cotton along the pipe and in the bell, so

as to increase the damping of our oscillatory system, we would find that all the resonance peaks become less tall and all the dips less deep. As more damping is added, the peaks and dips of the curve would gradually merge (at all frequencies) with the horizontal dashed line, a line which is precisely what we would have obtained from a wave-impedance measurement of an infinitely long piece of tubing. These auxiliary experiments with cotton tell us how to interpret the disappearance of resonances above 1500 Hz: high-frequency sound sent down toward the bell is transmitted almost totally into the room—very little of the sound returns to set up a standing wave with its resulting resonance peaks and dips.

A close examination of the heights of the resonance peaks and the depths of the dips shows that the corresponding impedances have a curious relationship with the value of the wave impedance (which is represented on our chart by the horizontal reference line). Let us introduce the relationship by means of a few examples. Peak 1 turns out here to represent an input impedance that is about 7.5 times as large as the wave impedance, while the input impedance measured at the dip next to this peak has a value about $(1/7.5)$th that of the wave impedance. Anywhere along the chart we find similarly that adjacent peaks and dips differ from the wave impedance by very nearly the same numerical factor, which can be called Q_0. To summarize:

(impedance at peak) = (wave impedance) × Q_0
(impedance at dip) = (wave impedance)/Q_0

We have already had indications that the heights of the resonance peaks (and therefore Q_0) depend on the amplitude of the return wave arriving at the input end relative to the one sent out by the source. As a matter of fact, we can calculate Q_0 very easily in terms of the fractional reduction wave amplitude produced by a single round trip in the air column:

$$Q_0 = \left(\frac{1 + F}{1 - F}\right)$$

For example, if in some duct the return wave has an amplitude of 85 percent of the original one, then $Q_0 = 1.85/0.15 = 12.33$. You may wish to verify that for our pipe-plus-bell the round-trip reduction is 76.5 percent. Notice that Q_0 takes account of all forms of attenuation, whether the dissipation takes place at the pipe walls or at the bell end, where sound leaks out into the room.

We are now ready to consider the mouthpiece as the lead-in part of an elongated air column. If we excite and measure the response of a duct consisting of a trumpet mouthpiece connected to an extremely long piece of tubing, we do not expect the wave impedance to remain constant, because of the variation of cross section found at the driving end of the composite duct (refer back to the remarks subsequent to the formula given for wave impedance in sec. 20.3). As a matter of fact, measurement of this sort using trumpet parts shows that, at very low frequencies, the wave impedance starts out with a value equal to that of the pipe alone. It then rises in the neighborhood of 850 Hz to a value almost five times larger. Above 850 Hz it decreases steadily, falling below the simple pipe value in the region above about 3500 Hz.

This broad peaking-up of the wave impedance near 850 Hz turns out to be connected with the fact that the mouthpiece, taken by itself, has its first natural frequency near 875 Hz. This resonant influence of the mouthpiece shows that it retains some vestige of its own identity when it is merged with the rest of the extended duct. The other resonances of the mouthpiece do *not* show up recognizably in the wave impedance curve. The mouthpiece's own lowest frequency will henceforth be called its *popping frequency* (F_p) because even in the absence of laboratory equipment it can conveniently be measured by listening to the lowest impulsively excited sound produced by taking the mouthpiece cup and slapping it closed against the palm of the hand.

Figure 20.5 shows the resonance curve for a piece of trumpet tubing about 72 cm long, with and without a normal mouthpiece. The values of Q_0 are roughly the same in the two examples (since the wall and radiation losses are closely similar), so that it is easy to compare the two curves. Mode 1 in both cases has about the same peak input impedance, because the wave impedances are alike here at low frequencies. On the other hand, peaks 4 and 5 are about five times taller for the composite tube than for the plain one, because these peaks lie in the region near 850 Hz where the wave impedance is particularly altered. Notice also that the impedances in the dips also show a fivefold increase when the mouthpiece is present, thus confirming that the effect has been properly associated with the variation of wave impedance.

The presence of the mouthpiece cup cavity and its associated back-bore constriction produce the same large increase in the heights of impedance peaks in the resonance curve of a complete trumpet, and we now have an explanation of the musical superiority of the conventional construction over air columns which achieve suitable frequency relationships

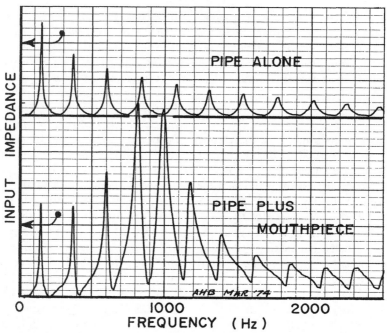

Fig. 20.5.   Input Impedance Curves for a Piece of Cylindrical Trumpet Tubing. *Top,* tubing alone; *bottom,* tubing with mouthpiece attached at input end.

without making use of a normal mouthpiece. The player's lips form a rather massive vibrator, which does not respond very well to the bidding of an air column unless the pressure fluctuations due to a given flow are made very large; i.e., the input impedances of the resonances must be magnified by whatever means are available and the conventional mouthpiece can be arranged to do this job very well.

Figure 20.6 shows the measured input impedance curve for a first-quality modern B♭ trumpet, along with diagrammatic indications of how the resonance peaks are related to the production of the written notes C_4 and G_4. The regime of oscillation for C_4 is based on the second of the input impedance maxima of the air column acting in consort with the 4th,

6th, and 8th peaks in the curve. When the tone is sounded at the pianissimo level, the flow variation produced at the player's lips is very nearly sinusoidal, so that only the second mode of the pipe is appreciably concerned with maintaining oscillation. In other words, we are back at Helmholtz's version of oscillation theory, and the playing frequency closely matches that of the second peak. As the loudness level increases, the progressively more abrupt motion of the lip-valve generates stronger harmonics, which then actively reinforce themselves and each other by interacting more vigorously with the other peaks mentioned above. An amateur musician finds this note wobbly when he plays softly, because the not-very-tall peak that sustains the fundamental component of his tone is not able to com-

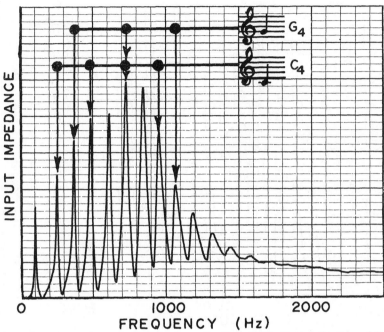

Fig. 20.6. Resonance Curve of a B♭ Trumpet. Regimes of oscillation for C₄ and G₄ are indicated.

mand much steadiness in the vibrations of his untrained lips. As he plays louder, however, the higher resonances become influential in the regime of oscillation, thereby stabilizing the tone.

When the player sounds the note G_4, the input impedance maxima that collaborate to form the regime of oscillation are peaks number 3, 6, and to some extent 9. The dominant member of this regime is of course peak number 3, which contributes primarily to the fundamental component of the tone. Since this peak is considerably taller than peak 2, we can readily understand why G_4 is a much more stable note when played pianissimo than is C_4. As one plays somewhat louder, the very tall 6th peak enters the regime, providing a great deal of energy at the frequency of the second harmonic.

Since G_4 has two tall peaks which dominate its regime, it proves to be one of the strongest and easiest notes to play on the trumpet.

In figure 20.7 we show once more the response curve for our trumpet; this time the regimes of oscillation are indicated for the written notes G_5, C_6, and high E_6. These regimes show us why notes become increasingly hard to play as we go up the scale. G_5 is quite easy to play at the pianissimo level, because it is maintained by the action of the tall 6th impedance peak. There is no increase in the ease of playing of this note during a crescendo, however, because the 2nd harmonic, as it grows by heterodyne action at the lips, is not itself regenerated by the minute contribution from peak 12. We might very well describe the production of G_5 as a solo per-

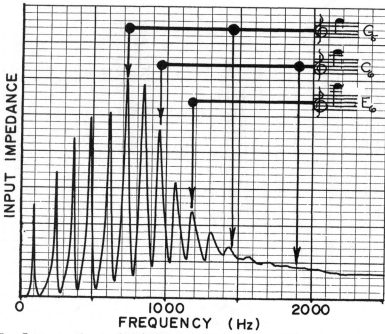

Fig. 20.7. Resonance Curve of a B♭ Trumpet. Regimes of oscillation for G₅, C₆, and E₆ are indicated.

formance by peak 6 at all dynamic levels. The same remark applies to C₆ and E₆ above G₅. Both of these notes are somewhat difficult to play (quite aside from any problems the player might have in getting adequate tension in his lips) because each has only a single active peak that is not very tall. It takes an athletic trumpeter to play the highest notes, where his lips must operate almost solely under the influence of the oscillatory Bernoulli force, almost exactly as the vocal cords function. At these frequencies the air column has changed from a resonator into a sort of megaphone which spews out every part of the sound into the room without returning any of it to breed the next generation, so to speak. (On the baroque trumpet the design of the bell and mouthpiece is such that the resonance

peaks that help sustain the upper notes are tall and therefore active to somewhat higher frequencies than is the case for the modern instrument.)

We close this section with a brief examination of the notes which are available to the air column of a normal brass instrument when the trombone slide or piston valves are not employed. On a trumpet having none of its pistons depressed, modes 2, 3, 4, . . . cooperate with one or more of the higher modes to give us the following sequence of notes:

$$C_4, G_4, C_5, E_5, G_5, (B_5\flat), C_6, D_6, E_6, \ldots$$

(These are the notes the player sees on his music. On the commonest B♭ trumpet, the C₄ shown above sounds a pitch of B♭, since all its notes sound a whole step lower than their written value. Trumpets are built in a variety of other sizes.) This sequence is familiar because the lowest half dozen tones are the ones used in playing bugle and hunting calls.

Notice in the above open-horn sequence that the frequency ratio (and hence the musical interval) between any pair of notes in the sequence is in exact agreement with one or another of the special relationships that lie at the root of formal music. We can say this more succinctly by noting that the repetition rates' belonging to these tones are the second and higher members of a harmonic series whose fundamental lies at C_3. (The trumpet's pedal note C_3 is peculiar in that resonance peak 1 is located at too low a frequency to cooperate. This tone is sustained totally by the contributions that peaks 2, 3, 4, etc., make to the 2nd, 3rd, 4th, etc., harmonics of the tone.)

The basic shape of a trumpet is dictated by the need to provide a set of harmonically related air-column resonances that can be used in various combinations to set up oscillatory regimes. The physical requirements for successful oscillation run parallel with those that point the way toward musically useful pitch relationships. This parallelism is not surprising, since in both cases we are dealing with the ways in which various frequency components are combined and separated by heterodyne action in a nonlinear system.

20.5. Musically Useful Shapes: *The Flaring and Conical Families of Brasses*

The earlier sections of this chapter have sketched out a pretty clear picture of how the positions and heights of the various input impedance peaks must be arranged in a musically useful air column. Now we should look at the interplay between the desired input impedance requirements and the horn shapes that are useful for producing these input impedances. The horn shape also governs the way in which the sound pressure spectrum measured in the mouthpiece is modified to produce the sound that is heard in the concert hall. Finally, we would like to have some idea of the way in which small corrections to the air-column shape can be worked out in a systematic way to improve an already fairly good instrument. For all of these reasons we should turn our attention to the ways in which waves travel in a duct of varying cross section.

The acoustical study of waves in what is generally referred to as a duct or a horn goes back to the eighteenth century. The Swiss physicist Daniel Bernoulli (whom we met earlier as the discoverer of a relation between pressure and steady flow in a duct), the Swiss mathematician Leonhard Euler, and the French mathematician Joseph Louis Lagrange were the first to discuss the equations for waves in horns during the decade following 1760, although the theory did not have much application until the 1920s.[6]

Let us list here some of the properties of waves in a horn that can be deduced from what we already know.[7] It should, for example, be fairly obvious that as a wave travels into the enlarging portion of any horn its pressure amplitude will decrease systematically, simply because the acoustic disturbance is being spread over an ever-wider front. Furthermore, we can suspect that in a duct that starts out with a gradual taper and then flares out abruptly (as is the case in the bell of a trumpet, a trombone, or a French horn), waves traveling toward the large end might well find themselves reflected at some point where the increasing flare causes an excessively rapid change in the wave impedance. This phenomenon, which is of paramount importance in the behavior of musical horns, is a gentler version of the reflection that happens at the end of a tube opening into a large room. (If a pipe opens through a large disc attached flush to its end, we could consider the abrupt transition from the cylindrical pipe to the flat disc as being an extremely rapidly flaring bell!)

The above deductions are given confirmation and quantative meaning by a mathematical study of the wave equation and measurements of many sorts of ducts. Moreover, it should be easy to understand that sounds propagate with different speeds as they travel through different parts of a horn: wherever the duct walls curve outward to produce the familiar flaring shape of a trumpet, the speed is greater than the 345 m/sec expected in the open air; on the other hand, in any part of the horn where the walls are straight-sided, as in the cylindrical part of a trumpet or in the simplest of conical bells, the velocity of sound is exactly the same as it is in free air.

When a disturbance produced at the small end of a horn reaches a trumpetlike bell whose flare is rapidly increasing toward the open end, we find that most of its musically important frequency components are trapped within the flare some distance back from the bell end; these trapped components are reflected back to help produce the standing wave. Only a small fraction of the original and continuing disturbance can penetrate the acoustical barrier posed by what we might call the acoustically forbidden region near the open end, a region where nearly everything that enters is strongly reflected by the rapidly changing wave impedance. Low-frequency sounds are turned back in the smaller, less flaring part of the bell, while those having high frequency penetrate to regions of greater flare. As a result, the lowest-numbered modes of a flaring horn have higher frequencies than the same modes of a cylindrical pipe of equal length (in which waves can run clear to the end before reflection), whereas the highest modes in flaring and cylindrical air columns tend to have roughly the same frequencies. If you refer back to figure 20.4, you can see an illustration of the different ways in which low- and high-frequency sounds leak out through a trumpet bell. In this figure, the peaks for the low frequencies are tall because only a small amount of sound can leak out into the room through the thick barrier created by the bell flare; at high frequencies this barrier is thinner, so the high-frequency excitations have to penetrate only a short way to lose some of their energy into the room. Above 1500 Hz, the barrier has disappeared, and waves simply run out of the horn with negligible reflection.

The solid lines in figure 20.8 show the first three characteristic shapes of the pressure distribution in a flaring horn that is similar to those used in musical instruments. These mode shapes remind us of sinusoids that are progressively stretched-out in the parts nearest the open end (as is to be expected from the increasing wave velocity in this region). Notice that these patterns all lose their sinusoidal shape and become strongly attenuated in the rapidly flaring part of the bell. In order to help you visualize what

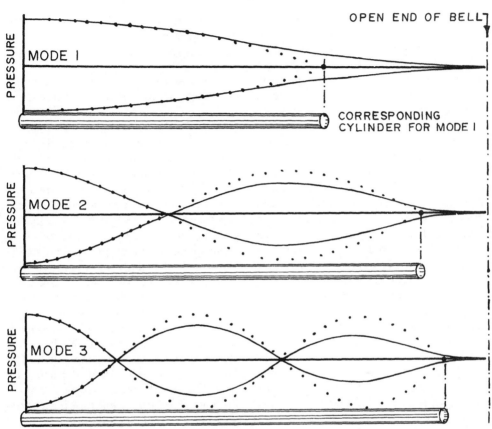

Fig. 20.8.   First Three Characteristic Shapes of the Pressure Distribution in a Flaring Horn

is going on, dotted lines are drawn to indicate the nature of the standing wave patterns that would be found for each of these modes in a cylindrical pipe whose length is chosen to give an equal frequency for this mode. Notice that the horn may be said (in a purely metaphorical sense) to behave like a short pipe at low frequencies and like a long pipe at high frequencies.[8] It is important to notice that all successive modes have an odd number of half humps in their vibrational

shapes, so that the nth mode has $(2n - 1)$ half humps. The half humps near the mouthpiece end look fairly sinusoidal, whereas the one nearest the bell has a considerably different shape as a result of the reflection behavior in this region.

I am often asked what the mathematical description is of the sort of air column that is useful in a trumpet, a trombone, or a French horn. There is in fact no simple answer to this question, because there are many combinations of bell flare,

Fundamentals of Musical Acoustics

408

mouthpipe taper, and mouthpiece proportion that can produce a fine instrument. It is a waste of time to look for the ideal shape for any one of these individual segments of an instrument, since each one must be fitted to the others. Very few of the acoustical properties of a complete instrument can be associated with any one segment alone. For research purposes, however, it is useful to have available an easily specified and mathematically tractable idealized air column. Erik Jansson (now of the Speech Transmission Laboratory in Stockholm) and I have found that a certain family of what are called Bessel horns, which were first studied in the 1760s, serves this purpose admirably.[9] Their usefulness to us is greatly enhanced by the fact that their shapes correspond closely enough to what has proved musically serviceable to permit quite passable instruments to be made from them.

Figure 20.9 shows a few Bessel-horn shapes, along with an indication of how their dimensions are specified. For a Bessel horn, the diameter D at any point is defined in terms of the distance y from the large open end:

$$D = B/(y + y_0)^m$$

where B and y_0 are chosen to give proper diameters at the small and large ends, and m is the "flare parameter" which dominates the acoustical behavior of the air column. Notice that the nonflared cylindrical pipe is itself a member of the Bessel-horn family; in such a pipe, m = 0. To the extent that brass instruments are of the Bessel form, we can say that the value of m differs from one instrument to another, depending on its mouthpiece and mouthpipe design and on the length of cylindrical tubing which is included in the complete instrument. Over a period extending from the present on back to at least 1600, the bell parts of trumpets and trombones have been made in shapes that correspond closely to the shapes of Bessel horns having values of m lying between the limits of 0.5 and 0.65 (the vibrational shapes shown in figure 20.8 are those belonging to a Bessel horn with m = 0.5). French-horn bells tend to

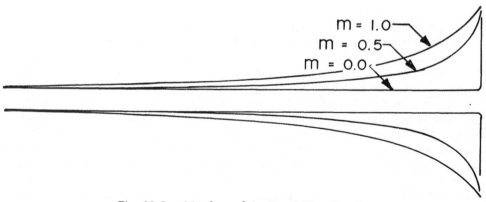

m = 1.0
m = 0.5
m = 0.0

Fig. 20.9.   Members of the Bessel Horn Family

have a value of m that is somewhat larger, in the range from 0.7 to 0.9. It is interesting that the bell shapes which have evolved by the tradition of practical experience combined with eye-pleasing artistry are notably similar in their acoustical description.[10]

A rather simple formula for the characteristic frequencies of a Bessel horn that is closed at the small end can be given in terms of its overall length L, its flare parameter m, and the wave velocity v of sound out-of-doors. For the nth mode of oscillation, the frequency f_n is:

$$f_n = \left[\frac{v}{4(L + y_0)} \right] \left[(2n - 1) + 2/\pi \sqrt{m(m + 1)} \right]$$

For horns similar to those used in trumpets and trombones (for which y_0 is no more than 2 or 3 cm) the formula gives frequencies that differ by only a fraction of one percent from those found by exact calculation. Above m = 0.8, the formula becomes equally accurate if the numerical factor is changed from 0.637 to 0.707, whence we notice that for m = 1, the successive resonances become exact whole-number multiples of the first-mode frequency $f_1 = (v/2L)$, and so form a harmonic series. We have noticed already that for m = 0 the frequencies are the odd-numbered multiples of the first-mode frequency $f_1 = (v/4L)$. For intermediate values of m the resonances are not arranged in harmonic relationships, and so would fail to set up very many useful regimes of oscillation. This limitation does not make it impossible to use Bessel horns having intermediate values of m as parts of real musical air columns, in which account must be taken of the presence of cylindrical tubing, of the mouthpipe, and of the mouthpiece. Such accounting is perfectly possible and is in fact the convenient way to proceed in designing an instrument.

Digression on the Effect of Bends and Loops in the Tubing of Brass Instruments.

The more or less sharp bends that are made in the tubing of brass instruments to fold them enough for easy portability have an acoustical effect of their own. Even a pipe of uniform cross section acts somewhat like a flaring duct if it is given a curved shape. Just as for horns with flare, the speed of sound is increased within the bend, and the wave impedance is reduced (i.e., the duct acts as if it is a little oversize). This latter effect differs from that in flaring ducts. Moreover, at the junction of curved and straight pipe segments one can have several kinds of wave reflections. For all these reasons instruments with many sharp bends act quite differently from their straighter cousins. The resonances can be shifted quite enough to be noticed in playing steady tones, and the beginnings of notes can be affected even more.[11]

So far we have confined our attention to air columns of the sort used in trumpets, trombones, and French horns, all of which start out with a very slight taper near the mouthpiece and have a rapidly flaring bell at the other end. Let us now find the connection between these instruments and the other major family of brasses, which have a more or less conical shape throughout their length.

In 1965 Robert Pyle, then at the Harvard Acoustics Laboratory, recognized a

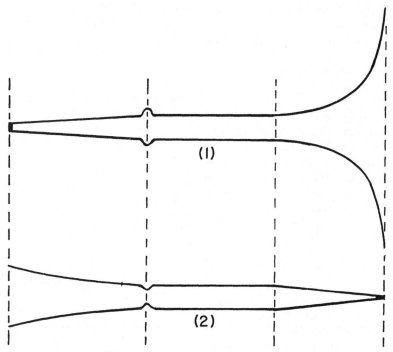

Fig. 20.10.   A Horn and Its Dual

remarkable property of waves in horns. Consider a pair of horns such that the product A_1A_2 of their cross-sectional areas is a constant from one end to the other, as is illustrated for a somewhat peculiar special case in figure 20.10. Notice that if one horn has an enlargement of its cross section at some spot, the other horn must have a corresponding narrowing of its cross section at the same place for the product of their cross sections to remain constant. If the small ends of both these horns are closed off, the two air columns turn out to have identical natural frequencies! The simplest musical implication of this is the following: if we can somehow find a useful horn shape, then its mate (or *dual,* as it is technically called) can easily be calculated, making it

also available for musical application. (In recent years, electrical engineers have found uses for signal transmission lines which are dual to one another.)

We have already noticed that the Bessel horn having a flare parameter $m = 1$ can be considered to be a candidate for musical use, since its characteristic frequencies form a harmonic series. It is easy to show mathematically that the dual of such a horn is the ordinary straight-sided cone, so that it too is a candidate for serious musical consideration. A mathematician would say that the cone is a Bessel horn with flare parameter $m = -1$.

It must be emphasized that even though horns that are dual to one another have the same characteristic frequencies, they do not necessarily have the same standing wave patterns, radiation behavior, or variation of wave impedance with frequency. We note in particular that because a cone has straight-sided nonflaring walls, the speed of the pressure waves remains constant as the waves run toward the large end, rather than increasing as it does in the case of flaring horns. For the same reason, in a simple cone there is no acoustically forbidden region in the large part of the horn and all the reflection takes place at the open end. As a result, the conical instruments begin to leak sound at lower frequencies than do their flaring cousins having the same bell diameter, and this leakage deprives conical instruments of their upper resonances.

Looking in at the small end of the horn, we find that the wave impedance of a conical duct rises very rapidly from zero at low frequencies to a high-frequency value equal to that of a cylindrical pipe having the same inlet diameter. The rapidly varying wave impedance at the small end combines with the reflected wave behavior (which by itself is almost exactly like that of a parallel-walled pipe) to give resonance peak frequencies that are members of a complete harmonic series, as is to be expected of the dual to a horn in which $m = 1$.

Another consequence of the low wave impedance at low frequencies (caused by the conical entryway to the horn) is that the resonance peaks in this neighborhood are even less tall than they are for the flaring horn. To help boost these peaks, the musical cone is provided not only with a conventional mouthpiece, but with a mouthpipe which generally has a smaller taper than that of the main run of the air column.

The required presence of a cavity-plus-constriction mouthpiece on both flaring- and conical-type brasses spoils the strict duality between their shapes. To get the needed cooperative effects between resonances in the fluegel horn, the alto, and the baritone, their makers include in the mid-section of the horn some cylindrical or mildly tapered tubing, and they give the bell end a slight outward flare as well. In other words, the basic mouthpiece design that is shared by the two families (which is forced by the need to get sufficiently tall resonance peaks) leads to a considerable similarity in other elements of their design; all of these design elements are dictated by the need for the resonance peaks to be properly located for setting up useful regimes of oscillation.

We have already noticed a peculiarity in the flaring-horn family of real instruments: the first resonance peak of these instruments is not properly placed to join with other peaks in the pedal-note oscillation. It only proves possible to get good cooperation among the rest of the resonances when the desirable location of the first resonance peak is sacrificed. A conical instrument, on the other hand, normally has its first-mode resonance peak very close to the desired pedal-note frequency, so that this note is easily produced. This is the reason why the lower brass instruments tend to be members of the conical horn family. It is interesting to note that cornets and tubas do not fit neatly into one or the other of the two families of brass instruments. One could say that some members of their tribe are found settled in each of the two musical territories, between which there is no clear line of demarcation.

20.6. The Selection of Valve Slides to Give a Complete Scale

Most of us have an intuitive idea of how to fill in the gaps in the scale of what the brass player calls the open horn; it is only necessary to lengthen the instrument a little bit to get a set of notes whose playing frequencies are a semitone lower, a little more for a set a tone lower, and so forth. This is of course exactly what the brass player does. Plausible as this scheme may appear, there is a catch to it. No matter how you do it, the addition of tubing into the middle of a horn makes its average taper less than before; crudely speaking we can say that the average flare parameter is reduced. This means that the addition of a piece of tubing to a horn will make a bigger percentage change in the frequencies of its lower modes than it will for the higher ones.

Brass-instrument makers have for many years based their valve length calculations on a rule of thumb whose origin lies in a misconceived analogy between brass instruments and a doubly open cylindrical pipe. In such an oversimplification, no account is taken of the change of flare produced by adding tubing or of effects due to the mouthpiece. One simply calculates tube lengths in the same way that one works out the positions of frets on a guitar. Let us compare the predictions of the hornmaker's rule with what actually happens.

A typical design for the valves of a brass instrument is the following. The first valve is arranged to add enough tubing to lower G_4 (the regime based on peaks 3, 6, and 9) by exactly two semitones to F_4. The second valve is similarly arranged to lower G_4 by one semitone (to $F_4\sharp$), and the third valve tubing is ar-

ranged so that when it is used in conjunction with the already determined length added by the first valve, the resulting lowering of exactly five semitones produces D_4. The rule of thumb leads one to choose tubing extensions that are 181, 88, and 314 mm long if we consider the trumpet to have a nominal length of 1840 mm. When these extension tubes are used in different combinations to provide other notes in the scale, various tuning errors will arise. For example, calculating the change produced by simultaneously using the three lengths of valve tubing given by the rule of thumb tells us that the trumpet is 30 mm too short for the $F_3\sharp$ note (33 cents sharp). The top part of figure 20.11 shows the tuning errors expected over the main part of a trumpet scale when all calculations are made on the basis of the instrument-makers' rule. The circled notes are the ones that are made exact by adjustment of the instrument's main tuning slide and by the three valve slides. Notice that the "theoretical" errors range from 20 cents flat to 33 cents sharp.

The lower part of figure 20.11 shows the measured tuning errors on an instrument whose original excellent design I have modified in small ways to provide the best possible cooperations between the modes that participate in its various regimes of oscillation. The pitch measurements were made at a mezzo-forte playing level, so that the upper partials in the tone "talked" to the upper resonances enough to exert considerable influence in stabilizing the oscillation and in equalizing the tuning.

Notice that over the main playing range from $B_3\flat$ up to E_5, this trumpet has a much more even scale than the one calculated by traditional means. While

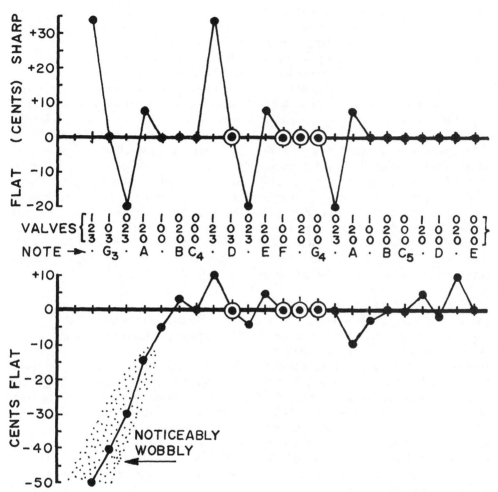

Fig. 20.11. Traditionally Calculated Valve Tuning Errors Contrasted with Those Measured on a Good Trumpet

the fluctuations above and below equal temperament on this instrument are somewhat smaller than on most trumpets that are in daily use, the main trend is quite typical: reasonably smooth tuning is found in the main part of the scale, while below C_4 the notes run progressively flat, as the elongated tube used for these notes (whose regimes involve peaks 2, 4, 6, . . .) exaggerates the downward frequency shift of resonance peak 2, and thus weakens its cooperation with the upper peaks. These notes play even flatter when sounded more and more softly, as the upper resonances lose their stabilizing influence.

When a carefully aligned instrument of the sort just described is played at a mezzo-forte dynamic level, a shift of 5 cents above or below the optimum playing frequency produces a clearly defined change in tone color, stability of pitch, and "feel" at the player's lips. Meaningful pitch measurements can therefore be made on such an instrument to an accuracy that is unimaginable on a mediocre one.

We can now understand why a careful player must continually use his finger-operated tuning slides in the course of music-making. To play strictly in tune with his fellows, he must be able to play a dozen cents above and below the equal-temperament pitch; this amount is more than twice the distance he can "lip" a note without suffering a significant loss of tone.

For reasons we met at the end of section 20.5, the bottom two resonances of a conical-type brass instrument do not tend to be as flat as they are among the flared instruments. Thus, conical instruments react to their valves more nearly according to the traditional expectation than does the trumpet we have been discussing. As a practical consequence, the bottom notes of conical instruments tend to be better tuned than they are on flaring-horn instruments, while the middle notes are less satisfactory.

One might well wonder what happens to all of the varied cooperations of a brass instrument when any of the pistons are depressed. Interestingly enough, nothing radically new takes place. The bell, the mouthpipe, and the mouthpiece design dominate the overall pattern or "envelope" of the resonance curve (the pattern of peaks getting taller and taller as one goes from low frequencies to about 850 Hz and then falling away and disappearing at high frequencies). As we have already noticed, the frequency ratios between the various modes (which ultimately determine the effectiveness of any cooperations) are not drastically altered when reasonable amounts of tubing are inserted. To be sure, the instrument works best with a particular set of proportions, but players are not unduly disturbed by the addition of enough tubing to increase the overall length of the instrument by the 40 percent or so that is required for the valves described above. However, the problem becomes serious in the cases of the French horn, the bass trombone, and certain tubas, where the addition of tubing by means of valves can in one way or another double the instrument's overall length.

20.7. Further Properties of the Mouthpiece; Adjustment Techniques

We have already learned of the crucial role played by the mouthpiece in getting the input impedance peaks to be sufficiently tall, and you may also have noticed (from fig. 20.5) that joining a mouthpiece to the end of a cylindrical tube has a considerably greater effect on the upper resonance frequencies than on the lower ones. It is time for us to study these effects in a more detailed manner in order to see how a mouthpiece can be adjusted to fit a particular instrument.

A very convenient laboratory method for studying the effect of a mouthpiece on the resonances of a cylindrical pipe is to determine experimentally for each vibrational mode the length of purely cylindrical tubing that has the same resonance frequency as does the composite pipe-plus-mouthpiece.[12] Subtraction of the shorter of these lengths of cylindrical tubing from the longer one found in the two parts of each experiment allows us to deduce a somewhat metaphorical quantity—the *mouthpiece equivalent length* L_e (there is a different mouthpiece equivalent length for each frequency at which the measurement is made). A long series of such comparisons is carried out by exciting several modes of each of several tube lengths attached to the mouthpiece; such a series allows us to determine the variation of L_e over the whole range of musically relevant frequencies. Figure 20.12 shows experimentally measured values of L_e which I have obtained for three different trumpet mouthpiece configurations.

It has been known by some acousticians and some instrument makers for about a century that the use of any sort of cavity (regardless of its shape) at the closed end of a cylindrical tube gives at low frequencies a value of L_e equal to the length of a piece of pipe whose volume is equal to the total volume of the cavity. The left side of figure 20.12 illustrates the truth of this observation very well. The two mouthpieces having a volume of

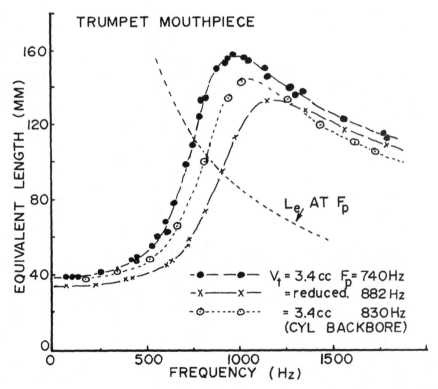

Fig. 20.12.   Variation of Equivalent Length with Frequency for Three Trumpet Mouthpieces

3.4 cubic centimeters (whose curves are marked by black dots and open circles) both show a 40-mm L_e; reducing the total volume of the cup of one of these mouthpieces by partially filling it in with wax lowers the value to about 34 mm (the curve for the mouthpiece with reduced volume is marked by x's).

A much less widely known but still long-recognized property of bottle-shaped cavities that are attached to a cylindrical pipe is the following: at the mouthpiece's own popping frequency, L_e is the length of a pipe whose own first-mode (popping) frequency matches that of the mouthpiece. The dashed line curving downward toward the left in figure 20.12 shows the trend of L_e's that go with various popping frequencies. This line intersects each of the L_e curves at the popping frequency belonging to that mouthpiece. At frequencies above the popping frequency, the L_e continues to rise, until it reaches a maximum which, for mouthpieces having a cup and a back bore, is always about 40 percent larger than the value it has at the popping frequency. The frequency at which this maximum is found is about 30 percent above the popping frequency. At yet higher frequencies we notice that all mouthpieces that might be used on an instrument have pretty much the same variation of L_e.

The important features of mouthpiece acoustics can be summarized as follows:

1. For a cylindrical pipe, the equivalent length L_e of a mouthpiece at low frequencies is equal to the length of cylindrical tube whose volume matches the *total* volume of the mouthpiece, regardless of its shape.

2. At the mouthpiece popping frequency F_p, L_e is the length of cylindrical tube (closed at one end) whose first-mode frequency equals F_p, that is, $L_e = v/4F_p$. This result is also in-dependent of the internal shape of the mouthpiece.

3. To a very great extent, the total volume and the popping frequency determine the variation of L_e by "anchoring" it at two points along the frequency scale. Subtle differences in the value of L_e at other frequencies are caused by variations in the proportions of mouthpiece cup and back bore.

4. The overall trend of L_e with frequency is a steady increase nearly to the top of the instrument's playing range. If two mouthpieces have the same volume, the one having lower popping frequency will show a greater total change in effective length as one goes up in frequency.

Our measurement of the equivalent lengths associated with a trumpet mouthpiece at different frequencies was only a laboratory convenience, and cannot be put simple-mindedly to use in predicting the resonance frequencies of trumpets. The remarks made earlier about the complications associated with the use of valved extensions to the air column apply with particular force to the variable length contribution associated with the mouthpiece. Your appreciation of this fact will perhaps be made more vivid when you learn that measurements of L_e made with a normally tapered mouthpipe interposed between the cylindrical tubing and the mouthpiece give rather different results. Under these more realistic conditions, L_e at low frequencies has only about half the value shown in figure 20.12; it then rises along a slightly wavy curve, through very nearly the original L_e found at the popping frequency, and continues to rise on up to a slightly reduced maximum at 1100 Hz, after which it joins the original curve. The overall sloping trend is thereby made less steep than before, and the slope continues to lower frequencies.

Let us now consider the simplest aspects of the way in which one actually goes about adjusting a good mouthpiece to make it play properly with a particular trumpet which is known to be of good quality. One warms up the instrument by playing over the entire mid-range, at the same time making sure that the various tuning slides are properly set. One next plays crescendos and diminuendos between pianissimo and mezzo-forte on the trumpet's written note G_4, where modes 3 and 6 of the open horn dominate the regime of oscillation (see fig. 20.6). At several dynamic levels one floats the pitch up and down to seek out the fullest, clearest, and steadiest tone, without regard to the correctness of its tuning. It is helpful to concentrate your attention on the second-harmonic component of the tone, because it is often heard most clearly and steadily when the pitch setting associated with steadiest tone is attained. When one plays softly, peak 3 is the only influential member of the regime, so that the playing frequency and best-oscillation conditions are predominantly controlled by the frequency of this resonance. Playing more loudly brings in the influence of mode 6, which acts on the second harmonic of the tone. If this peak is placed too high in frequency relative to peak 3, the pitch will rise a little when you have found the most favorable playing condition. Conversely, if the playing pitch falls during a crescendo, the upper resonance is on the low side of its correct position.

Suppose that our trumpet is one that runs flat during a crescendo at its written note G_4 (fundamental frequency near 350 Hz on a B♭ trumpet). We would then want to change the mouthpiece in such a way as to raise the frequency of peak 6

(near 700 Hz) without moving peak 3. Since changes in resonance frequency are correlated at least qualitatively with changes in the mouthpiece equivalent length L_e, we deduce the need for reducing L_e near 700 Hz, leaving it untouched near 350 Hz. Inspection of figure 20.12 suggests that we seek a way to raise the popping frequency (to make the correction near 700 Hz) without making much change in the total volume (which controls L_e near 350 Hz). Reducing the volume of the cup will raise the popping frequency, but at the expense of a decreased total volume; we wish to preserve the total volume for many reasons having to do with getting a correct wave impedance. Our other option is to enlarge the narrowest part of the back bore by a *small* amount. This can significantly raise F_p with only a minuscule change in total mouthpiece volume.

At this stage, however, one does not cut anything; it is essential to do some additional diminuendo-crescendo experiments (at least at C_4 and C_5) to discover whether they also have implications for mouthpiece adjustment that are consistent with those determined at G_4. If all the symptoms are consistent in indicating that it is appropriate to raise F_p, then the back-bore constriction is enlarged by no more than about 0.05 mm, after which the whole procedure is repeated. It is essential to stop making changes somewhat short of complete correction. To make "just one more little scrape" beyond this point is an easy route to a ruined mouthpiece. It is good tactics to leave a little metal, because careful playing of the improved instrument will undoubtedly expose discrepancies at a subtler level than those manifested earlier. Correction of these elsewhere in the instrument may very well lead to a situation where the back-bore enlargement is already sufficient. It goes without saying that if the instrument is one that runs consistently sharp during a crescendo, we are faced with the more difficult problem of lowering F_p, which requires one to lacquer or electroplate the interior of the back bore. This change is a serious one, however, because it can easily lead to excessive damping of the resonances unless the back-bore profile is carefully modified.

An instrument whose resonances are carefully adjusted under the guidance of laboratory measurement and player's experiments along the lines just described is much admired by musicians. They find it easy to make friends with, and different performers tend to play it at very much the same pitch. This is because of the rewards it gives when the player finds its frequencies of maximum cooperation.

Brass players have built up an enormous lore about the influence of mouthpiece cup depth and back-bore shape on the tone and response of their instruments. Much that is mysterious in their observations becomes clear when it is recognized that easy blowing, clear speech, and good tuning all are dominated by the relationship of the total mouthpiece volume and the popping frequency. If these are not suited to the instrument, one musical effect must then be bought at the expense of another. A favorite lecture demonstration of mine is to ask a trumpeter to play a few scales on his own instrument, using each of three mouthpieces that I provide (which he is not permitted to examine beforehand). Even when the audience consists mainly of brass players, they agree that the sounds produced using the three mouthpieces are very similar. The player also

agrees that while he has small preferences among the mouthpieces, they all feel very much alike to him. Everyone is astounded to discover afterwards that only one of the mouthpieces is a high-quality commercial model. The others have the same outward appearance, but one is provided with a cylindrical rather than tapered back bore (whose diameter is nearly 6 mm), while the other has a short tapered back bore with an unusually deep and almost conical cup. The acoustical features that these mouthpieces have in common are total volume and popping frequency, accurately matched to well within one percent. As a result they behave very similarly on any reasonably good instrument whether they are precisely adjusted to it or not.

20.8. The Internal and External Sound Spectra of a Trumpet

In this section we will concern ourselves with the internal sound pressure recipe generated by a regime of oscillation, as measured in a brass-instrument mouthpiece, and then we will consider how this internally measured spectrum is related to the external spectrum, which is what we actually hear.

When one plays pianissimo on any of the lower notes of a brass instrument, the internally measured sound has an almost purely sinusoidal waveform that shows only traces of the higher harmonics. As one plays more vigorously, the sound spectrum develops, harmonic by harmonic, the lower partials growing first. Any tones that are generated by an oscillatory regime involving several resonance peaks develop their higher partials rather quickly, and the internal sound fills out at a lower dynamic level than is the case for notes that rely upon only one or two air-column resonances. We also find that, as a rule, any particular partial generated is strong if the resonance peak associated with it in the regime is tall and well aligned, and weaker if the peak is less tall or is displaced from perfect frequency matching. At present we will look at qualitative relationships among the playing level, the heights and loca-

tions of the resonance peaks, and the internally generated sound spectrum of wind-instrument regimes of oscillation, reserving a consideration of the more quantitative aspects of these for chapter 21.

As part of a continuing study by Edward Tarr and myself of the relationship between modern and baroque trumpets, a series of measurements was made with the help of Charles Schlueter, who plays prin-

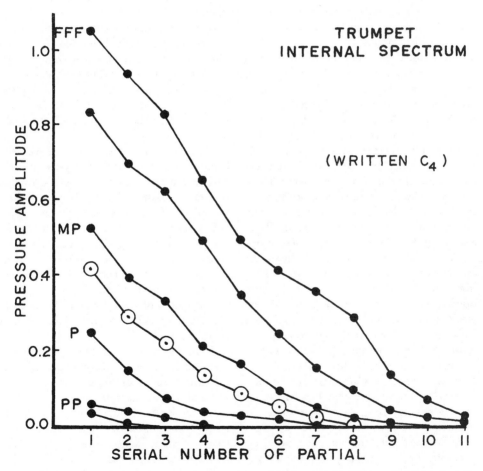

Fig. 20.13.   Internally Measured Pressure Spectra of a Trumpet for Various Dynamic Levels

cipal trumpet in the Minneapolis Symphony (when the experiments were done in 1970, he was a member of the Cleveland Orchestra). Among other things, Schlueter played a series of crescendos and diminuendos on various notes of one of my instruments (the one we have already met in this chapter). This was equipped with a probe microphone to detect sounds inside the mouthpiece cup, and also with an external microphone mounted on a lightweight "spider" attached to the bell, so that it was held about 5 cm away from the end of the bell. Signals from the two microphones were fed to a tape recorder so that they could be studied at leisure. An example of the curves made from these tapes is shown in figure 20.13, which displays the relative amplitudes of the internally measured partials belonging to the written note C_4 (see fig. 20.6 for the air-column resonances that participate in the generation of this tone). The uppermost of the curves connects black dots that indicate the strengths of the first eleven partials produced when the trumpet is played fortissimo. The lower families of curves indicate similarly the strengths of the partials at lower dynamic levels. We can see clearly here that as one plays more softly, the partials having higher frequency become weak more quickly than do the lower ones. At the weakest pianissimo that can be sustained by a player, the internal tone contains almost nothing beyond its fundamental component. I should like to emphasize that data of this sort are extremely stable. Several C_4 tones were taped, some starting *mp* and swelling to *fff* and some diminishing from *mf* to *ppp,* and the tapes were analyzed and the spectra plotted on a graph. At any given playing level the analyzed sounds were essentially the same

for all the samples. For example, the open-circled data points in figure 20.13 refer to a tone which I myself played and recorded in the course of setting up, testing, and calibrating my equipment several days before Schlueter came in for the more formal experiments. Since I am primarily a player of woodwinds rather than brasses, the agreement of this curve with the others shows that the behavior we are studying is determined chiefly by the trumpet and its mouthpiece, provided the player is able to recognize a suitably cooperative relationship between his lips and the air column. Note that the spectra described here have been plotted to include only the first eleven harmonic components of the tone. The components at higher frequencies are very much weaker, but cannot be totally ignored since, taken together, they have a small effect on the overall tone color.

Up until now in this section we have been discussing the strengths of the various harmonic components of a tone as they are measured inside the mouthpiece by means of a special microphone. What one hears in the concert hall is of course a very different thing. The spectrum generated inside the mouthpiece is transformed into the spectrum found in the concert hall by the selective nature of the transmission of sound from the mouthpiece out through the bell flare into the room.

It is not easy to obtain a meaningful measure of the external sound spectrum of a trumpet or other brass instrument. As we learned in section 12.2, a trumpet bell tends to concentrate the high-frequency components of its sound into a narrow beam, while spreading the low frequencies more or less equally in all directions.[13] Because of this, when one works in an anechoic chamber, placing the microphone some distance away along the bell axis will lead to an overestimation of the strengths of the partials whose frequencies are above about 1000 Hz. In similar tests with the microphone placed off to one side of the bell, on the other hand, the data will show a deficiency in the high-frequency spectrum.

Our ears appear to do best in gaining an impression of musical tone color when they operate on signals picked up from all directions in a reverberant room, with the signals integrated over a time whose duration is about that of the precedence effect—30 or 40 milliseconds (see sec. 12.2). Because of this, we should provide ourselves with composite sound spectra calculated by combining the analyzed data from each one of many microphones placed in a reverberant room, with people moving around within the room to "stir up" the various room modes (see chap. 11).

The radiation behavior of flaring horns is such that a microphone placed just in front of a bell (about one bell radius away) receives a sound signal that is in reasonably good agreement with what one expects from the complicated room-averaging procedures described in the preceding paragraph.[14] It is for this reason that the microphone was mounted by means of a spider just beyond the end of

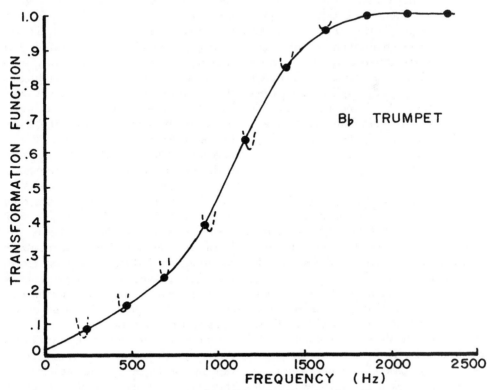

Fig. 20.14. Spectrum Transformation Function for a Trumpet

the bell in the experiments with Schlueter.

As we have learned earlier, the qualitative nature of the transformation of the spectrum from inside the mouthpiece to that heard in the concert hall is reminiscent of the treble-boost control of a hi-fi amplifier, because the higher components of the internally generated tone are preferentially radiated. Figure 20.14 shows the general trend of the *spectrum transformation function* T relating the externally measured pressure amplitudes of the various partials to the amplitudes of the same partials as measured within the mouthpiece. The dots along this curve show the value of the transformation function at the various harmonics of the tone whose internal spectrum was presented in figure 20.13. One can get the shape of the external sound pressure spectrum from the internal spectrum simply by multiplying the internally measured pressure component amplitudes p_n (int) by the value T_n of the transformation function corresponding to their frequencies. This relationship can be written out as a formula:

$$p_n \text{ (ext)} = T_n \times p_n \text{ (int)}$$

Figure 20.15 shows the result of this sort of calculation, which converts the spectra shown in figure 20.13 into the corresponding spectra for the same dynamic levels as they are measured just outside the trumpet bell.

Returning to figure 20.14, you should notice the small, U-shaped, dotted curves superimposed on the solid curve. These are intended to show that the overall behavior of a trumpet is complicated by the fact that the ratio of external to internal sound pressure is at a *minimum* at frequencies lying close to those generated within

the instrument. Because of this, if one lips a note up or down in pitch, the external strength of each of its partials generally *rises* relative to the internally measured pressure amplitudes. Notice that the minima in T do not fall precisely at harmonics of the playing frequency, nor do their positions correspond exactly with the internally measured resonance frequencies. They lie above or below, depending on whether we examine resonances lying above or below the mouthpiece popping frequency.

Let us examine the tonal consequences of having dips in the transformation function at frequencies that roughly correspond to the peaks of the input impedance curve. As the player lips a given tone above and below the frequency giving maximum cooperation within the regime of oscillation, we expect the strengths of the various internally measured partials to rise or fall depending on their positions relative to the various resonance peaks. We also expect the higher partials to be somewhat stronger relative to the lower members of the collection making up the tone when the regime is under its most cooperative conditions. In brief, the various internally generated partials tend to become stronger as their frequencies are matched up with those of the horn resonances. The presence of dips in the transformation function means on the other hand that, in simplest terms, the effect of changed playing pitch on the measured external spectrum is somewhat offset by the opposite behavior of the transformation function.

Our ears treat these things somewhat differently: they take into account the nature of the entire spectral envelope (as they do in recognizing the vowels in speech). They also pick up the special

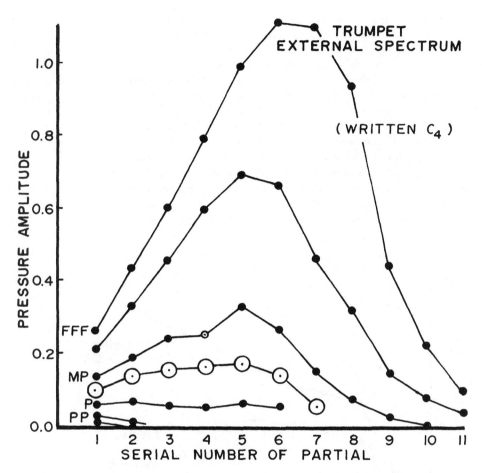

Fig. 20.15.   External Spectra of a Trumpet Obtained by Use of the Transformation Function

status of the well-aligned notes simply because, whatever spectrum changes may be taking place, the well-aligned notes show a singular and well-marked behavior relative to notes played slightly higher or lower in pitch.

There is a further clue that the player's ears are provided with as he seeks the best playing pitch. The vibrations of the player's lips are subject to small, random fluctuations, just as the vocal cords are.

Lining up the air-column resonances will produce an added smoothness in the tone for the reasons discussed in section 19.5 in connection with the soprano's subtle kind of formant tuning. Also (and much more significantly), the tone is made smoother because the amount of random fluctuation in the lip-valve action is greatly reduced when a solidly organized regime of oscillation is set up. This is one reason why a well-played instrument is

described as having a "clear" tone: its individual notes are steady because their
partials are made up of narrowly clustered
sinusoidal groups that clearly display the
basic musical relationships.

Before we leave the subject of brass-instrument sound spectra, a little attention
should be given to the loudnesses of the
various partials as they present themselves
to our ears. Figure 20.16 shows the general nature of the loudness spectrum of
the partials, each one being calculated by
itself from the data in figure 20.15 with
the help of the curves for perceived

loudness given in figure 13.4. Notice
how much the sound-pressure spectra and
the loudness spectra differ (especially
above 2000 Hz where the sensitivity of
the ear becomes particularly great), and
also how much change there is in the
overall shape of the loudness spectrum
with changes in the player's dynamic
level.

We have little difficulty in telling
whether a trumpet is loudly or softly
played, regardless of its distance from our
ears. (This is also true of a radio or a
record player.) The spectrum itself

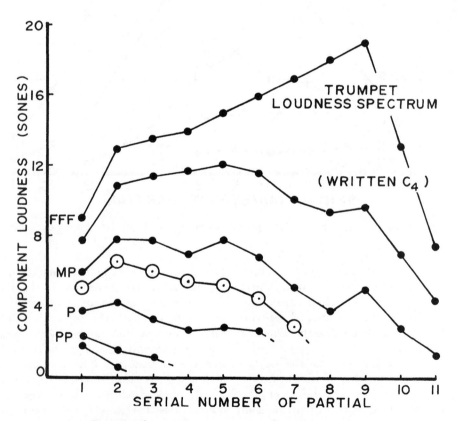

Fig. 20.16. Loudness Spectrum of a Trumpet Tone

changes with playing level in a fashion that is characteristic not only of brass instruments as a group, but also of the individual instrument and the accuracy of its alignments. It is no wonder that a musician and someone using a sound level meter so often differ in their usage of the words "loudness" and "intensity"; they are actually talking about quite different things.

20.9. The Problem of Clean Attack

So far we have explored the acoustical requirements that must be met by a brass instrument if it is to play steady tones one by one. I have also implied that in general an instrument that speaks with stability and clarity will also have a good tone, in the musician's sense, and that it can be built to play accurately in tune. There is one more attribute that is required of a musical instrument if it is to be considered of first quality: it must *start* its tones cleanly and promptly and be forgiving of small inaccuracies in the player's lip tension as he shifts rapidly from one note to the next.

The acoustical properties of an air column that contribute to a clean attack for every note may be looked at in two parts. To begin with, anything that makes for a "happy" collaboration during the time a note is sustained will in general contribute to a prompt build-up of an oscillation when the tone is started. For the woodwind player, this is very nearly the complete story. The brass player must also deal with the fact that it takes a long time for acoustical "messages" to travel from mouthpiece to bell and back, informing the lips of the collaborative job they must do with the air column.[15]

Let us see what happens to the initial part of the acoustical disturbance set up by the player's lips as he attempts to start a tone. This disturbance travels down the bore with a speed that depends on the rate of flare of the air column, and then in the flaring part of the bell some of this wave is reflected back toward the mouthpiece. The reflected wave, upon returning to the mouthpiece, "tells" the lips how and when they must reopen to admit the next puff of air in the sequence of puffs that sustain the tone after everything has settled down. Until the first reflections begin to come back, the lips are on their own. The air column has not yet expressed its preference for one or another of the frequencies with which it is able to collaborate. Assuming the player has buzzed his lips accurately for the desired note, the air column is happy to begin collaboration as soon as there has been time for the initial sound to make at least one complete round trip of the air column. Several more round trips are required before the regime of oscillation has set itself up completely. In a fast running passage, there is barely time for one regime of oscillation to be set up before it must give way to the next. Trouble can be caused by a small change in cross section, a sharp bend, or an ill-chosen change in the taper (of the sort that is particularly common in tuba construction). Such discontinuities return a premature echo of significant size to the mouthpiece, an echo that is not even a replica of the original disturbance. Such ill-timed, ill-shaped return echoes can upset the best-trained of lips, and, having spoiled the steadiness of their initial vibration, will ruin the attack. Such irregularities are of course a complete disaster for the less skilled player, even if he can maintain a good sound once it is started. Curiously enough, it is possible to build an instrument that is unwilling to start well even though it gives a strong, clear, sustained note. Various discontinuities may deliberately be introduced to offset one another, or to counteract other faults of the air column. This kind of patchwork can lead to a well-tuned instrument that has good tone and stability, even though it will be treacherous during the attack of its various notes. Every musician has met such instruments, as well as those that attack cleanly but lack other virtues that are needed for the satisfying production of music.

The second item contributing to clean attack on brass-instrument notes can be understood in terms of the speed with which disturbances travel in an air column. There are two different sorts of speed that must be dealt with in these circumstances: (1) the *wave velocity*, which is the speed with which any particular frequency of sinusoid travels (the wave velocity determines the air-column resonance frequencies; see sec. 20.5), and (2) the *group velocity*, which is a measure of the speed with which abrupt disturbances travel down an air column. The group velocity depends on the frequency components that predominate in the disturbance, and, once again, it depends on the rate of flare of the horn. The group velocity for sounds in a straight-sided air column is independent of frequency and is equal to the open-air speed of sound.

The actual values of the group velocity and the wave velocity most closely related to it are not at all the same in most horn-like air columns. The round-trip time for the initiating disturbance of a brass-instrument tone is calculated from the group velocity rather than the wave velocity. In other words, the instrument maker has the very interesting technical problem of getting a whole set of wave velocities to come out right if he wants good *steady* sounds, while at the same time achieving a correct set of group velocities if he wants these tones to *start* cleanly!

20.10. Examples, Experiments, and Questions

1. Tying two layers of a handkerchief over the bell of a trumpet has very little effect on the heights of the first three or four input impedance peaks, but by peak 7 they are reduced to about 80 percent of their normal heights, and the resonances are obliterated above peak 10. Why is it that at pianissimo levels the player of low notes will hardly feel the addition or removal of the cloth, but at forte levels he notices a big difference? Regimes above the written note G_5 are somewhat influenced by the additional damping when the instrument is played pianissimo, and these regimes are very strongly affected in loud playing.

Musicians have no trouble recognizing the effects of heavily damped resonances, regardless of their degree of alignment. Players are so prone to describe the resulting feel as "stuffy" that we will formally define *stuffiness* as the perceptual correlate of high damping (small Q_0) in a wind instrument.

2. Thin-walled brass tubing in many sizes suitable for brass-instrument experimentation is commonly available in hobby shops. In the U.S. the sizes run in 1/32-inch (0.794-mm) increments. A

good approximation to the tubing used in trumpets has a 7/16-inch inside diameter. You might wish to figure out and then test which combinations of resonances in the lower part of figure 20.5 are properly related for setting up regimes of oscillation.

Insert a trumpet mouthpiece into the end of a piece of this sort of tubing that is long enough to extend about 15 cm beyond the end of the mouthpiece shank. Such a composite air column will have its first and second mode resonances near 440 Hz and 880 Hz. Perhaps you can explain for yourself how the variation of mouthpiece L_e combines with the 15-cm tube to give this approximately harmonic frequency relationship. Playing near A_4 will allow you to feel out the cooperation between the two almost-aligned modes. Why should you put tape on the mouthpiece shank to prevent a dead air space in the region between its outside diameter and the inside of the tube wall?

3. A piece of 20-mm tubing about 86 cm long (so that its input impedance maxima lie close to 100, 300, 500, 700, . . . Hz) will show an interesting set of mild collaborations between its resonances and your lips. Start at the fairly well-defined 300-Hz tone $(D_4 + 37¢)$ produced by your lips in conjunction with the 300-Hz second mode, the 900-Hz 5th mode, and the 1500-Hz 8th mode, and gradually slacken your lip tension. The pitch will drop fairly steadily until it "hangs up" slightly near 250 Hz $(B_3 + 21¢)$, as pipe mode 3 interacts with the 500-Hz second harmonic of your tone. A similar hanging up, or at least recognizable alteration in the tone production, comes near 233 Hz $(A_3\sharp)$ where the 3rd harmonic partial talks to the pipe's 4th mode (at 700 Hz). Perhaps you

can work out for yourself the ancestry of events that may call attention to themselves near 225 Hz $(A_3 + 39¢)$, 175 Hz $(F_3 + 4¢)$, 166 Hz $(E_3 + 13¢)$, and 150 Hz $(D_3 + 37¢)$. Why would the presence of any sort of mouthpiece totally rearrange the frequencies at which such effects are observed?

4. The lower curve of figure 20.17 shows the input impedance curve measured on a French horn without the insertion of its player's hand in the bell. The upper curve shows that the player's hand greatly increases the number of resonances (how so?) which can be adjusted to aid the various regimes of oscillation in the normal playing range; notice that the hand in the bell also raises the upper limit of this range. A skilled player is constantly trimming-up the resonances note by note with his hand as he plays.

As the hand progressively closes off the bell end, the various resonances move downward in frequency in a way similar to that described for the pipe in section 19.7, example 2. If a player tries to hold his playing pitch steady while gradually closing the bell, the tone becomes progressively weaker and more wobbly as the combination of the rising tension of the lips and the falling pipe resonance frequencies makes for ever weaker collaboration. Finally the playing pitch jumps upwards (roughly a semitone in many parts of the playing range) to the next higher set of resonances, which are able to seize control of the regime because they agree satisfactorily with the preferred vibration frequency of the more tightly set lips. This upward jump to the next higher set of resonances whose frequencies have been lowered by the hand is the physical basis of the ancient technique of "hand-stopping," which is used as a

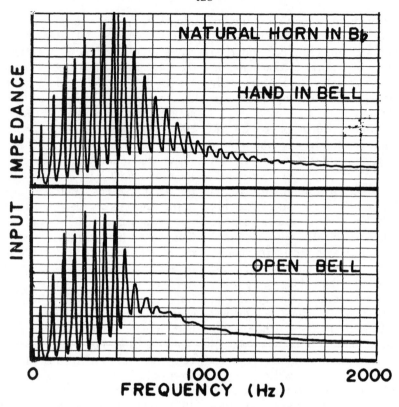

Fig. 20.17.   The Effect of the Player's Hand on the Resonance Curve of a French Horn

means of acquiring extra notes on a valveless horn.

5. You may wish to experiment with the effect of dropping a small wooden or plastic object (such as a kitchen match) into various parts of a trumpet air column. The resonance frequencies of the instrument will be shifted upward or downward (depending on the position of the object relative to the standing wave humps of the modes). An object of this size lying anywhere in the middle three-quarters of a trumpet will make changes that will range up to about 0.3 percent (4.4 cents). On a properly made instrument these alterations will be reflected clearly in its playing properties. Some notes may be improved and some

spoiled. There will also be changes in the way in which notes start, and in their stuffiness or clarity. Perhaps you can work out the reasons for these changes. I once helped a manufacturer of excellent French horns, who was refining the mouthpipe design for a new horn, to discover needed alterations that were only one-fifth of the amount mentioned above.

Notes

1. Excellent accounts of the development and playing properties of various brass instruments are to be found in Philip Bate, *The Trumpet and Trombone: An Outline of their History, Development and Construction* (London: Benn; New York: Norton,

1966), and Robin Gregory, *The Horn: A Guide to the Modern Instrument* (London: Faber and Faber, 1961).

2. Hermann Helmholtz, *On the Sensations of Tone,* trans. Alexander Ellis from 4th German ed. of 1877, with material added by translator (reprint ed., New York: Dover, 1954) pp. 388–94.

3. Daniel W. Martin, "Lip Vibrations in a Cornet Mouthpiece," *J. Acoust. Soc. Am.* 13 (1942): 305–8.

4. H. Bouasse, *Instruments à Vent.* 2 vols. (Paris: Librairie Delagrave, 1929 and 1930), I:115–16, I:312–14, II:47. An elementary account of these cooperative effects is to be found in Arthur H. Benade, *Horns, Strings and Harmony* (Garden City: Doubleday Anchor Books, 1960), pp. 151–70. See also A. H. Benade and D. J. Gans, "Sound Production in Wind Instruments," *Annals of the N.Y. Academy of Sciences* 155 (1968): 247–63. Since that time progress has been very rapid.

5. Diagrams of these various excitation devices, as I use them, are shown in Arthur H. Benade, "The Physics of Brasses," *Scientific American,* July 1973, pp. 24–35. See also Josef Merhaut, "Method of Measuring the Acoustical Impedance" (abstract), *J. Acoust. Soc. Am.* 45 (1969): 331; John W. Coltman, "Sounding Mechanism of the Flute and Organ Pipe," *J. Acoust. Soc. Am.* 44 (1968): 983–92; and John Backus, "Input impedance curves for the reed woodwind instruments," *J. Acoust. Soc. Am.* 56 (1974): 1266–79.

6. Edward Eisner, "Complete Solutions of the 'Webster' Horn Equation," *J. Acoust. Soc. Am.* 41 (1967): 1126–46. This paper is an excellent source of technical and historical information back to the 1760s.

7. Philip M. Morse, *Vibration and Sound,* 2d ed. (New York: McGraw-Hill, 1948), gives a good discussion of horn acoustics, although certain limitations are incorrectly laid down upon the validity of the theory. The acoustics of horn shapes of a musically useful sort are very thoroughly discussed in E. V. Jansson and A. H. Benade, "On Plane and Spherical Waves in Horns with Non-Uniform Flare: I, Theory; II, Prediction and Measurements," *Acustica* 31 (1974): 79–98, 185–202.

8. An excellent discussion of these matters can be found in Robert W. Pyle, Jr., "Effective length of horns," *J. Acoust. Soc. Am.* 57 (1975): 1309–17.

9. Jansson and Benade, "On Plane and Spherical Waves."

10. For descriptions on some early trumpets upon which I base this remark, see Eric Halfpenny, "William Bull and the English Baroque Trumpet," *Galpin Soc. J.* 15 (1962): 18–24; Eric Halfpenny, "Two Oxford Trumpets," *Galpin Soc. J.* 16 (1963), 49–62; and Joseph Wheeler, "Further Notes on the Classic Trumpet," *Galpin Soc. J.* 18 (1965), 14–22. E. G. Richardson, in his book *The Acoustics of Orchestral Instruments* (London: Edward Arnold, 1929), is the probable source for the mistaken belief that brass instrument bells are of exponential form. He also promulgated some peculiar notions about the flow of air in the mouthpieces of brass instruments.

11. Cornelis J. Nederveen, *Acoustical Aspects of Woodwind Instruments* (Amsterdam: Frits Knuf, 1969). Two papers by W. Rostafinski, "On Propagation of Long Waves in Curved Ducts," *J. Acoust. Soc. Am.* 52 (1972): 1411–20, and "Transmission of wave energy in curved ducts" (letter), *J. Acoust. Soc. Am.* 56 (1974): 1005, are significant, though they are difficult to read and are marred by several important errors. See also G. S. Brindley, "Speed of Sound in Bent Tubes and the Design of Wind Instruments," *Nature* 246 (21/28 December 1973): 479–80.

12. Earle L. Kent, U.S. Patent 2,987,950, filed 24 April 1958, granted 13 June 1961, and W. T. Cardwell, Jr., "Working Theory of Trumpet Air-Column Design" (abstract), *J. Acoust. Soc. Am.* 40 (1966): 1252.

13. Jürgen Meyer and Klaus Wogram, "Die Richtcharakteristiken von Trompete, Posaune und Tuba," *Das Musikinstrument* 19 (1970): 171–80.

14. I am indebted to Dr. Earle L. Kent, formerly Director of Research, C. G. Conn Ltd., who in 1970 sent me some very careful measurements which he made in 1963 of the sound field at various distances in front of a cornet bell. The combination of his data and the later work that Jansson and I carried out leads to this simplification.

15. A. H. Benade, "Effect of dispersion and scattering on the startup of brass instrument tones" (abstract), *J. Acoust. Soc. Am.* 45 (1969): 296–97.

21
The Woodwinds: I

Woodwind musical instruments, like the brasses, have a flow-control device (the reed-valve) the function of which is to alter the rate at which air enters the mouthpiece from the player's lungs. Woodwinds, again like brasses, also make use of an air column whose natural frequencies must be properly arranged to set up regimes of oscillation in conjunction with the reed-valve. The woodwinds achieve a complete scale by placing along the air column a set of tone holes that can be opened to give different sets of natural frequencies.[1]

The lowest note of a woodwind instrument uses a regime of oscillation based on the complete air column's first vibrational mode acting in conjunction with modes 2, 3, 4, etc. Successively higher notes of the low-register chromatic scale are produced by opening holes one by one along the tube, beginning with the one farthest from the mouthpiece. This successive opening of holes shortens the effective length of the air column, which of course raises the frequencies of its modes. The idea of an effective length is as useful to a discussion of woodwinds as it was for the brasses, since the standing pressure waves within a woodwind are very reminiscent of those that exist within a flaring, trumpetlike horn: these standing pressure waves are roughly sinusoidal near the woodwind mouthpiece, and in the region where holes are open they show the same rapid tailing-off and attenuation that we have learned to associate in brass instruments with the "acoustically forbidden" rapidly flaring part of the bell.

The low register of a woodwind has all its notes based on mode-1 vibrations of the air column. The highest note in the low register is reached when mode 1 of the shortened tube has the same frequency as does mode 2 of the complete tube. The player continues up the chromatic scale by reclosing all the holes and then again opening holes in succession while shifting his manner of playing to one that produces a tone based on mode 2 and its higher collaborators; this sequence is known as the second playing register of the instrument. The tuning of these second-register notes will of course be correct only if the frequency ratio (and therefore the musical interval) between the first and second characteristic modes is the same for the complete horn as for one that is shortened by opening a few holes. Preserving a constant frequency ratio between the vibrational modes as the holes are opened is essential in all woodwinds and provides a limitation on the types of air column (often referred to as the bore) that are musically useful. We need not worry about this limitation, however, because it is automatically satisfied when we select air-column shapes that are also able to set up useful regimes of oscillation. For the reed woodwinds, these limitations permit us to confine our attention to air columns whose shapes are based on the cylindrical pipe (e.g., clarinets) and on the straight-sided cone (e.g., saxophones, oboes, English horns, and bassoons).[2] Since the flow-control device of a flute is not of the pressure-controlled type, we will postpone all discussion of this instrument until chapter 22.

21.1. Resonance Curves and the Characteristic Shapes of Woodwind Vibrational Modes; The Tone-Hole Cutoff Frequency

Let us consider the standing waves that exist in an air column that is stopped at one end and provided with a sequence of tone holes at the other; the upper few holes of this sequence are closed and the lower holes are open, as indicated in the uppermost part of figure 21.1 Initially we need not commit ourselves to any particular shape of air column, since at the present moment we are concerned only with those aspects which are common to all stopped air columns that are provided with tone holes.

Whether the basic air column is cylindrical, conical, or of any reasonably continuous form (such as that sketched), the pressure standing wave patterns belonging to the lowest few natural frequencies of the air column are always of the gen-

eral sort sketched in the second, third, and fourth lines of figure 21.1. (Figure 21.2 shows, for purposes of comparison, the standing wave patterns for the lowest two modes of vibration of air in an ideal cylinder and an ideal cone. Notice the similarity of these to the patterns worked out in figure 21.1 for an air column of more general shape.) In figure 21.1, we can see that at the closed end (marked X in the diagram) the pressure wave has the largest possible amplitude. The point M marks the ending of the closed tone holes and the beginning of the open tone holes. (We will call any sequence of open tone holes a *tone-hole lattice*.) At the point M where the lattice of open tone holes begins, the standing-wave pattern has a reversal of curvature, and it trails off in ever-weakening fashion down the lower part of the bore which, as a result, has only a very small influence on the nature of the vibration. This trailing-off part of the standing wave corresponds exactly to the strongly attenuated part of the waves in a trumpet.[3]

The length XN in figure 21.1 is that length of our air column which, when stopped at one end and sawed off to produce an ideally open end at the other, will resound in unison with the actual air column that is provided with open tone holes. The distance MN is what some people call the open-end correction associated with the open-holes lattice (compare with the dotted sinusoids shown in fig. 20.8).

Notice that here, as in the case of the brass instruments, the standing wave consists of an odd number (1, 3, 5, etc.) of half humps, depending on the serial number of the vibrational mode. Notice that so far we are speaking about a perfectly general air column, which means

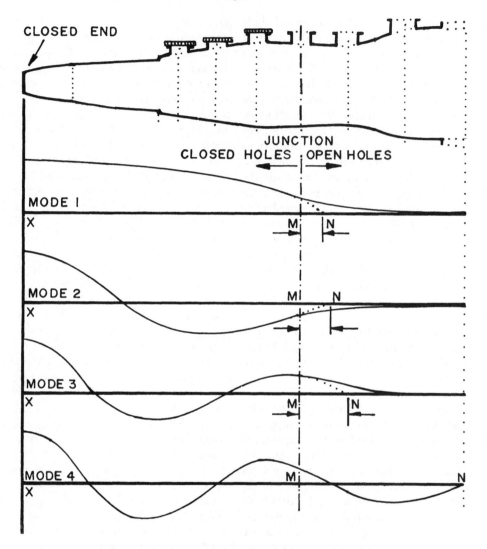

Fig. 21.1. Standing Wave Patterns Typical of a Woodwind Air Column

that these half humps are *not* necessarily of equal length in various parts of the bore (see the lower part of fig. 21.2, and also fig. 20.8).

In figure 21.1, a closer look at the standing wave diagrams for the first three modes shows that the tone-hole length correction (the distance MN) increases in magnitude as one goes from mode 1 to modes 2 and 3. This tells us that an air column provided with open tone holes "looks" longer when it is asked to vibrate

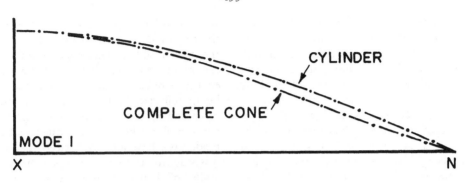

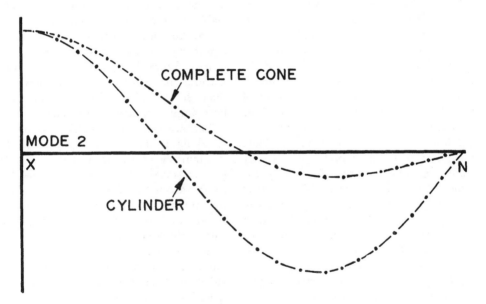

Fig. 21.2. Lowest Two Standing Wave Patterns for a Cylinder and a Cone

in a high-frequency mode than it does when it is vibrating in a lower-frequency mode. On woodwinds, this phenomenon by itself accounts for a flattening of any upper resonance frequency relative to the lowest one. This flattening (which can amount to an appreciable fraction of a semitone) may need to be offset by alterations in the bore profile when the instrument is adjusted to play properly.

We turn our attention now to the bottom line of figure 21.1, where the standing-wave pattern of the fourth vibrational mode is displayed. Here there is no particular change in the shape of the wave at the point M where the open tone holes begin. The wave is distributed throughout the whole air column, and has a pressure node at the bottom end of the bore, almost exactly as though there were no open tone holes present! It is a characteristic property of any duct provided with a sequence of open tone holes that at low frequencies the sound waves are not able to travel down along the lattice, and as a result they are reflected at the place where the lattice meets the more ordinary air column. This ability of a set of open tone holes to lop off an air column by providing a strong reflection at a predetermined length is what we have been discussing in connection with modes 1, 2, and 3. However, at frequencies above a certain critical value determined by the sizes of the holes and their spacing, the open-hole system becomes able to transmit waves to the lower end of the air column, where they may be reflected back, just as they would be in an ordinary pipe having the same open-end diameter. The critical frequency above which sound waves can run through a lattice is technically known as the *open-holes lattice cutoff frequency*, for which we will use the symbol f_c. For the purposes of illustration, the diagrams of figure 21.1 were drawn to correspond to a lattice whose cutoff frequency lies between natural frequencies of the third and fourth modes of vibration, so that the active air column terminates near the top open hole for modes 1, 2, and 3, but extends to the bottom of the instrument for mode 4.

Let us digress for a moment to see how sound may be expected to leak out of a woodwind into the room. In the lowest one or two modes of vibration, the pres-sure disturbance penetrates so little into the tone-hole lattice that only the first of the holes is able to emit much sound into the room. As a result, very little wave energy is radiated into the room, the rest being reflected back toward the mouthpiece end so as to produce a strong resonance peak at the natural frequency of the mode. We have already noticed that successively higher frequency modes have the "tails" of their pressure wave patterns extending farther and farther into the open-hole region, so that an increasing number of tone holes are able to contribute appreciably to the acoustic excitation of the room. Air-column modes that exist above cutoff, such as the one shown at the bottom of figure 21.1, have standing wave patterns that extend all the way down the duct, so that all of the open tone holes have ample opportunity to radiate.

We are now in a position to understand figure 21.3. The top part of this diagram shows the measured input impedance curve of a piece of clarinetlike tubing about 61 cm long, as you can verify from the fact that the resonances fall at odd multiples of 140 Hz. The lower part of the figure shows the input impedance measured on this same piece of tubing when another piece of tubing provided with a long row of uniformly spaced tone holes is added to it. (Note the similarity of these two curves to those appearing in fig. 20.17.) We recognize clearly that, as the excitation frequency rises, more and more of the sound leaks out of the tone holes; this reduces the reflected wave amplitudes, thus reducing the heights of the resonance peaks and raising the dips. Above the cutoff frequency the tone holes radiate so effectively that Q_0 for the higher (complete-

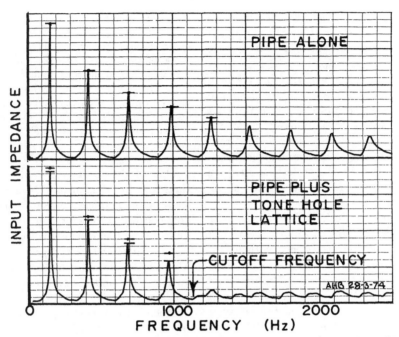

Fig. 21.3. Impedance Curves for a Piece of Cylindrical Clarinet Tubing. *Top,* tubing alone; *bottom,* tubing extended by section having equally spaced tone holes.

bore) modes is very close to unity, and thus the measured input impedance wiggles only a little above and below the wave impedance itself for that size of tubing.

We should by now have enough knowledge of wind-instrument acoustics to recognize that both the production of sound within a woodwind and the way in which it is transmitted out to our ears will be strongly influenced by the presence of the tone-holes cutoff frequency. We will learn in due course that specifying the cutoff frequency for a woodwind is tantamount to describing almost the whole of its musical personality (this statement assumes the proper tuning of playing pitches, and the correct alignment of resonances for good oscillation).

21.2. The Flow-Control and Elastic Properties of Reeds

In chapter 20 we leapt directly from a quick examination of the flow-control properties needed to maintain oscillation in a water trumpet to a study of the collaborations that take place between the player's lip-valve and the air-column resonances. It is not easy to measure (or describe) what is going on at the brass player's lips. The reed-valve of a single-reed woodwind is amenable to closer examination, and this examination will help us to understand a great deal about what goes on in the playing of all sorts of woodwinds.

In 1830, the German physicist Wilhelm Weber described experiments on the action of organ reeds that led him to a correct theory for the effect of a compliant structure (the reed, or, for that matter, the brass player's lips) on the input impedance of a column of air. The effect of the reed in providing a yielding closure to an air column is quite separate from its function as a valve. Bouasse devotes a very large part of *Instruments à Vent* to a description and extension of Weber's work on organ reeds, as well as his own application of it to the cane reeds of orchestral woodwinds.[4]

While many workers have studied the behavior of reeds since the time of Bouasse, his results were neither improved upon nor extended until 1963, when John Backus of the University of Southern California described a series of very careful experiments on the behavior of clarinet reeds. More recently the Dutch engineer Cornelis Nederveen has repeated and extended Backus's work. Nederveen's studies on woodwinds are detailed in his excellent little book, *Acoustical Aspects of Woodwind Instruments.*[5]

We can summarize in three statements the overall influence of the reed elasticity on the natural frequencies of an air column:

1. The resonance frequencies of an air column terminated by a reed are always lowered by the reed's presence, and they are never higher than the natural frequency with which the reed cane itself would vibrate if plucked like a tuning fork. (Note: this natural frequency is *not* the one obtained by blowing on an oboe or bassoon reed or on a clarinet mouthpiece; in all these cases there is present inside the reed cavity a miniature air column that has significant influence.)

2. Changes in the reed's natural frequency (produced for example by changes in the way in which it is pressed onto its mouthpiece by

the player) produce small but parallel changes in the air-column modes that lie far below the reed's natural frequency. These changes become progressively larger for higher modes that lie nearer to the reed frequency.

3. The reed damping produced by the player's lips serves among other things to reduce the magnitude of the changes described in statements 1 and 2, although they are still musically important.

One of the most important contributions made by Backus and Nederveen has to do with the measurement of the actual flow-control characteristics of various kinds of reed as they are acted on jointly by two different kinds of pressure: (1) the pressure P maintained by the player in his own mouth, and (2) the pressure p that exists within the mouthpiece of the instrument (the pressure p is ordinarily of an oscillatory nature).

The lower part of figure 21.4 shows schematically the way in which a steady pressure difference $(P - p)$ acts to close the aperture between a clarinetlike reed and the tip of its mouthpiece. A long tube filled with fiber glass is attached to the mouthpiece, so as to provide a duct through which the air can escape without returning any acoustical signals that might accidentally set the reed into vibration as part of an oscillatory regime.

The upper part of figure 21.4 shows a pair of curves relating the rate of airflow through the reed aperture to the pressure difference $(P - p)$ across it. The upper curve, labeled "loose embouchure," corresponds to what is observed when the laboratory replacement for the player's lower lip and teeth presses gently on the reed so that it is not held very close to the *facing,* which is the gently curved part of the mouthpiece onto which the reed rolls as it closes off the aperture. The curve marked

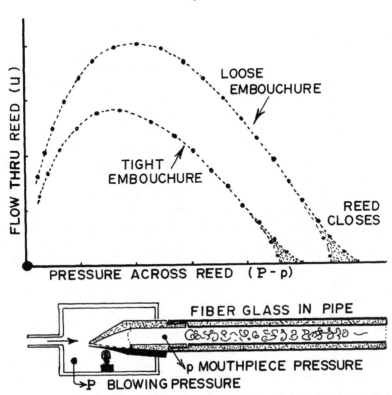

Fig. 21.4. Flow-Control Characteristics of a Clarinetlike Reed and Mouthpiece

"tight embouchure" shows similarly the flow behavior expected when the player presses harder on the reed to hold it more nearly closed. (Note that the pressure p within the mouthpiece will always be very small under the conditions of the present, non-oscillatory experiment, so that for now we can neglect its influence.)

If we follow either one of the curves shown in the upper half of figure 21.4 upward from zero blowing pressure (P = 0), we will notice first that the flow through the aperture rises with increasing pressure in a way that anyone would expect for air pouring through a small hole. As P rises further, however, it begins to push the reed progressively more closed so that, after the initial increase, the flow rate through the aperture decreases until eventually the reed is blown completely closed. It is not surprising that, for any given blowing pressure P, the flow rate is less when a tight embouchure is used than when the embouchure is more relaxed. We also notice that tightening the embouchure reduces the blowing pressure required to close the reed completely.

When the reed is very nearly closed, the air flowing past it into the mouthpiece tip has a particularly high velocity, which means that there is a Bernoulli force acting there trying to help close the reed (see sec. 19.2, statement 4). The magnitude of this extra closing force depends critically on the inside shape of the mouthpiece tip—the region known to clarinetists as the *baffle*. The shaded region at the right-hand end of each flow curve in figure 21.4 shows how different baffle profiles can alter the way in which the reed closes off the airflow. When the Bernoulli effect is made large, a lower blowing pressure P is required to close off the reed. In 1969 my co-worker Walter Worman showed that in the simplest case the Bernoulli force is about 3.5 percent of the maximum total force acting on the reed due to pressures P and p.[6] However, we find that small changes in the Bernoulli effect above and below this value can have dramatic influence on the musical behavior of reed instruments. For example, the saxophone loudness changes described in section 13.7 were produced by deliberate alterations in the shape of the last 2 mm of the mouthpiece baffle.

Let us now investigate the manner in which a reed finds it possible to keep an air column in oscillation. Suppose we remove the tube filled with fiber glass from our experimental apparatus, and replace it by a musical instrument air column, such as that from a clarinet or saxophone. Suppose further that our compressed-air supply is adjusted to maintain some steady pressure P in the iron mouth cavity that surrounds the mouthpiece. Choosing P in this manner locates us at some point on the flow-versus-pressure curve, and we can determine what happens to the flow if we somehow impose a small oscillatory variation of pressure *within* the mouthpiece. If P has a fairly high value, locating us on the falling part of the curve, then a momentary increase

of p will reduce the quantity (P − p) and thus increase the flow through the reed. To say this another way, an increase of pressure within the mouthpiece has the effect of pushing the reed aperture wider open, so as to permit more air to flow in. We can therefore conclude that on the downhill side of the flow-versus-blowing-pressure curve an increase of mouthpiece pressure produces an increase of airflow. This is precisely the relationship required for the maintenance of oscillation (see sec. 20.1 on the water-trumpet valve). Notice that on the rising side of the curves of figure 21.4, before the pressure P giving maximum flow is reached, the relation between the mouthpiece pressure p and the airflow is exactly backwards from what is needed to sustain an oscillation.

Whenever the flow-control curve we have been studying is steeply sloping, a small change in mouthpiece internal pressure will produce a large change in the flow; on the other hand, in the less steeply sloping region near the maximum of the curve, a small change in p produces almost no change in flow, which means that under these conditions the reed-valve does not respond sensitively to the influence of an air column.

The important features of a reed-valve flow-control system can be summarized in a continuation of our set of numbered statements:

4. A reed-valve can sustain oscillation in an air column only when the player's embouchure tension and blowing pressure set the "operating point" of the reed somewhere on the downward-sloping part of the flow-versus-blowing-pressure curve.

5. The steeply sloping portions of this curve correspond to operating conditions in which the flow is sensitively controlled by

acoustic pressure variations p within the mouthpiece.

6. The presence of the Bernoulli effect at the reed tip results in an increase in the steepness of the flow-control curve in the region where the reed is about to be blown shut.

7. Partly because of the Bernoulli effect at the reed tip, increasing either blowing pressure or embouchure tension will generally move the operating point toward a region of greater steepness in the curve (there are important exceptions to this remark, however).

8. The shapes of the pressure-control curves for various embouchure tensions are such that, in order to produce a specified steepness of the curve at the operating point (i.e., to maintain a given air column in oscillation), the player can trade off blowing pressure for embouchure tension in many combinations.

9. The fact that the flow-control characteristic curve is not straight (or, equivalently, the fact that the slope varies from point to point along the curve) is an indication that heterodyne effects can take place. It is this nonlinear feature of the flow-control behavior that leads to the existence of regimes of oscillation, in which oscillation is maintained by excitations taking place simultaneously at several frequencies.

10. Due to resonance phenomena, the flow-control sensitivity of the reed itself becomes large in the frequency region just below its own natural frequency. If the reed is insufficiently damped (e.g., by the player's lips), high-pitched squeaks may take place at the frequency of the reed even though the air column itself may be above cutoff and so lack a resonance peak in this region.

The double reeds used on oboes and bassoons act in a fashion very similar to what has been outlined here for the flow-control properties of a clarinetlike reed. However, the fact that the two halves of a double reed run close to one another for a considerable distance near their tips means that peculiarities arising from the presence of Bernoulli forces become particularly important in understanding the detailed properties of double reeds.

21.3. Woodwind Regimes of Oscillation; Worman's Results

For various reasons, scientists tend to begin their studies of woodwind-instrument acoustics with an examination of the ways in which the reed collaborates with resonances of a cylindrical air column; in other words, they begin by looking at the prototypical clarinet. In this book, however, there are advantages in starting our explorations with a single-reed instrument having a conical air-column shape, since the acoustics of such an instrument can be related more directly to what we learned about brass instruments in chapter 20. The saxophone is the most familiar example of such an instrument, but some experiments done on another woodwind, the Hungarian tarogato, will give an even clearer initial picture of the behavior of single-reed conical instruments.

One can think of the tarogato as being a wooden B♭ soprano saxophone except that the tone is clearer, with generally more stable regimes of oscillation. Ernest Varosi, a member of Cleveland's large Hungarian community, served his apprenticeship as an instrument maker and repairman in Budapest under Janos Stowasser (1865–1923), whose tarogatos are much admired. Varosi tells me that one of the five Stowasser brothers invented the instrument late in the nineteenth century

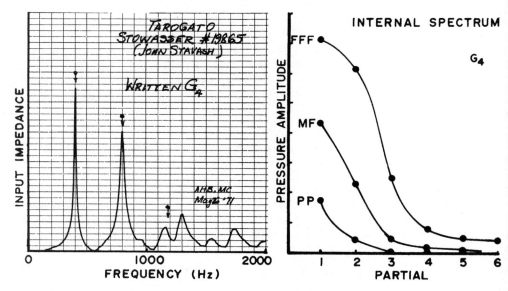

Fig. 21.5. Input Impedance Curve and Internal Spectra for G_4 on a Tarogato

as a reaction to the then-new saxophone, whose metal body and large tone holes offended him. It is certainly true that the tarogato has very much the shape and key mechanism that one might expect from the hands of a thoroughly competent maker of German-style woodwinds, although it incorporates several ingenious acoustical innovations that I have seen nowhere else.

The left side of figure 21.5 shows the measured input impedance curve for the air column of a tarogato when the fingers are placed to play the written low-register note G_4, a note for which the tone holes on the lower half of the instrument are open and those on the top half are closed. The first thing we should notice about the resonance curve is that the cutoff frequency for the open-hole sequence is somewhere near 1000 Hz. Below this frequency we find two tall resonance peaks (corresponding to modes 1 and 2), whereas above cutoff there are only small, random-appearing squiggles associated with the heavily damped resonances of the complete air column (compare with the lower part of figure 21.3).

When one plays the tarogato's low-register G_4, the fundamental component of the tone is fed by the first resonance peak, while the second harmonic is fed by peak number 2. Little downward-pointing arrows on the diagram show the frequencies of the first three harmonics of this tone; it is easy to see that the regime of oscillation is dominated by the first two resonances, whose frequencies are in an accurate 2-to-1 relationship.

On the right-hand side of figure 21.5 is a diagram for the same tarogato note G_4 showing the amplitudes, at various dynamic levels, of the first six harmonics of the internal pressure spectrum measured inside the mouthpiece by means of a probe microphone. At the pianissimo level, only the fundamental component has appreciable strength, a small amount of second harmonic being almost its only accompaniment. When the tarogato is played more loudly, so as to double the amplitude of the fundamental component, we find that the second harmonic has grown about fourfold, and the third harmonic has evolved to an easily observed magnitude. Notice that at this mezzo-forte playing level the envelope of the internal sound spectrum is very similar in shape to that of the air-column input impedance curve itself. The two tall resonance peaks below cutoff give rise to two strong components in the tone. Above cutoff, the small impedance of the air column means only a small production of higher harmonics in the tone, and most of what is present arises by heterodyne action at the reed between the main components of the tone. At fortissimo playing levels, the spectrum envelope again has a shape reminiscent of the resonance curve envelope, except that the strength of the second harmonic has begun to "catch up" with that of the fundamental. Furthermore, the heterodyne-produced harmonics that lie well above the cutoff frequency all have attained roughly equal amplitudes. Study of the reed motion under such very loud playing conditions shows that the air from the player's lungs is shut off for a considerable fraction of each cycle of the playing frequency; only a brief puff of air is admitted at the peak of each oscillatory swing of the pressure p within the mouthpiece.

In 1971, Walter Worman completed a very detailed study of the way in which regimes of oscillation set themselves up in wind instruments.[7] Although he gave most of his attention to clarinetlike systems played at low and medium amplitude, his results give us a mathematical basis for the unification of the earlier work by Weber and Helmholtz with a quantitative understanding of Bouasse's observation of intermode cooperations as they take place in all kinds of instruments. He found that it is possible to calculate the sound spectrum produced within the mouthpiece of an instrument. This calculation is done in terms of the measured input impedance curve of the air column, the flow-control properties of the reed, and the blowing pressure. If we combine our exploration in this chapter of the playing behavior of the note G_4 on a tarogato and our knowledge of the behavior of brass instruments, we will have a good background for understanding the implications of the work in which Worman and I have collaborated and of the more recent developments based on them. Once again it is convenient to make a set of numbered statements:

1. At low-to-medium levels, with a pressure-controlled reed-valve (with negligible Bernoulli forces present at the reed tip), the strength of the second harmonic of the internally measured pressure spectrum is proportional to the square of the amplitude of the fundamental component. The third harmonic component has an amplitude proportional to the cube of the fundamental pressure amplitude, and so on. That is, the amplitude p_n of the nth harmonic component of a tone is related to the amplitude p_1 of the fundamental component by the formula:

$$p_n = p_1^n \times (\text{a constant})$$

The above relationship means, for example, that starting from pianissimo playing levels there are virtually no harmonics present in the tone beyond the fundamental; then, for every doubling in the amplitude of the fundamental component, harmonic 2 increases from its initial tiny value by a factor of $2^2 = 4$; similarly, harmonic 3 will grow by a factor of $2^3 = 8$ for each doubling of the fundamental component. (We have already noticed an example of this behavior in connection with the tarogato.)

Another way to state the mathematical relationship between the partials of the internally measured pressure spectrum is to say that, for every decibel change in the sound pressure level (SPL) of the fundamental component, the SPLs of partials 2, 3, 4, etc., change by 2, 3, 4, etc., decibels. The three parts of figure 21.6 make use of this decibel relationship to display the accuracy (and limitations) of statement 1. Figure 21.6-A shows the variation (expressed in decibels) of the strengths of the harmonic components in the C_4 trumpet crescendo described in chapter 20. The sloping dotted lines show the trends predicted for partials 1, 2, 3, and 4 by Worman's theory. Notice how closely the experimental points follow the theoretical lines at playing levels below the line marked "change of feel." Above this playing level the theory breaks down, and all the partials grow, decibel for decibel, in a manner that parallels the growth of the fundamental component. Figure 21.6-B shows in similar fashion the trends of variation observed for the odd-numbered partials in the note C_4 played on a fine clarinet using an excellent reed. Once more we observe good agreement with statement 1 below a certain level at which the player notices a change of feel. Figure 21.6-C shows the radically different behavior observed within an oboe reed cavity. We will re-

turn to a discussion of this diagram at the end of this section.

The departures of the observed trend of pressures from that predicted by statement 1 prepare us to understand the next one of our numbered statements:

2. The simple relationship described in statement 1 between the partials of a tone is only observed when the motion of the reed-valve parts themselves is of small enough amplitude that the variable, pulsating airflow through them is never entirely shut off. Once the blowing pressure is raised to the point where the reed is blown entirely closed for a portion of each cycle of its oscillation, the player notices a change of feel, the listener notices a change of tone, and the higher partials tend to grow in a way that parallels the growth of the fundamental.

In figure 21.5 we noticed that the strengths of the partials were related to the heights of the corresponding air-column resonances. This observation introduces us to the third member of our set of statements:

3. In an instrument that uses a pressure-controlled reed, the amplitude of each sound-pressure component within the mouthpiece is proportional to the height of the air-column input impedance curve measured at the frequency of the component.

Let us continue our study of woodwind tone production with the help of figure 21.7. On the left we find the input impedance curve measured for the air column used in the playing of the written note D_4 on the tarogato, and on the right is the internal sound-pressure spectrum measured when this note is played at various dynamic levels. To begin with, we notice from the resonance curve that the cutoff frequency for this new set of open tone holes (a set which begins far-

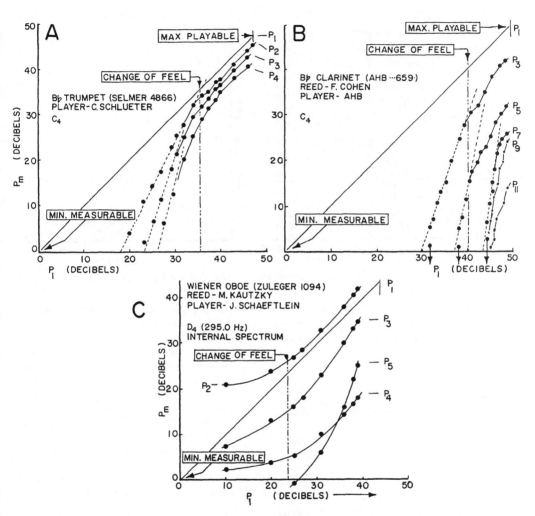

Fig. 21.6.   Relation between the Amplitudes of the Higher Partials and Their Fundamental. A, trumpet; B, clarinet; C, oboe.

ther down the air column) is near 1000 Hz, just as it was for G_4. Because we are dealing now with an effectively longer air column having lower resonance frequencies, there is "room" for three modes below cutoff rather than two. The first two of these are tall, and they are in ac-

curately harmonic frequency relationship, while the peak for mode 3 is found at a somewhat lower frequency than a truly harmonic relationship would require. This shift downward is a consequence of the enlarged length correction produced near cutoff. The tallness of the mode-3

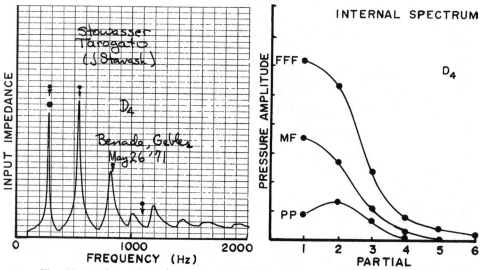

Fig. 21.7.   Input Impedance Curve and Internal Spectra for D₄ on a Tarogato

peak is also reduced for a related reason, which is the increased leakage from the set of open tone holes. Notice also that peak 2 is taller than peak 1.

Digression on Conditions Leading to a Reduced Height of the First Resonance Peak in a Woodwind.

Normally we expect the first-mode resonance peak of a woodwind to be the tallest, since the damping caused by the escape of sound energy into the room and by its absorption by the pipe walls acts least strongly on this mode. There are two ways in which the first peak can have its tallness reduced. (1) Reduction of the tallness of the first-mode resonance peak is a characteristic feature of long, conical woodwind air columns in which the missing part of the cone at the apex is relatively short compared to the length of the body of the instrument. Progressively shortening the cone by cutting segments off its large-diameter end leads toward a shortened air column that does not have this property. (2) The influence of friction in the flow of air in and out of a small hole in the upper part of an air column can also reduce the tallness of all the resonance

peaks; if the friction effect is combined with that of flow inertia in the hole, the first peak is influenced the most.

Figure 21.5 shows that when the tarogato plays G₄ the cone has been shortened enough for cause (1) not to apply. The air column used in playing D₄ on the other hand, is sufficiently long that the first peak is reduced through cause (1) to a height that is roughly equal to that of peak 2, as indicated by a small dot over peak 1 in the diagram. The further reduction in tallness of this peak comes about in our present example from the presence of a slight leak through one of the pads closing off a tone hole near the top of the air column.

When one plays D₄ loudly on this tarogato (which has a slightly leaky pad), an internal sound spectrum is produced that differs very little in its nature from that belonging to G₄ (compare the top curves on the right-hand sides of figures 21.5 and 21.7). If one then plays D₄ at a mezzo-forte level, the first partial will drop to about 55 percent of its amplitude at loud playing, and partial 2 will have an amplitude that is 50 percent of its original value. A calculation of the sort described in statement 1 would lead us to expect partial 2 to be down to 30 percent, since $(0.55)^2 = 0.30$; such a change from prediction suggests that some new phenomenon is calling itself to our attention. Continuing the diminuendo to the pianissimo level leads us to a spectrum in which the fundamental component has fallen to an amplitude *less* than that of partial 2, as shown by the lowest curve on the right-hand side of figure 21.7. Careful listening to the sound of a D_4 diminuendo and analysis of its spectrum as the tone dies all the way to nothing reveals that the second harmonic disappears very slowly, whereas the first partial (along with the third one) falls away entirely to zero. In other words, the *pitch* of the tone "sneaks" up an octave just before the sound disappears! The tendency of the low notes of conical instruments to change octaves in this way during a diminuendo is a familiar and troublesome one, particularly for saxophonists.

The explanations of the octave "sneak" and of the anomalous behavior of the sound spectrum just before it takes place can easily be understood: as the player reduces his blowing pressure, the reed's operating point moves upward and toward the left along a curve (resembling the curves shown in fig. 21.4) into a region where the slope is less steep. This slowly reduces the pressure sensitivity of the reed in its function as a valve, and allows the amplitude of oscillation to fall. Harmonic generation by the reed nonlinearity becomes less, thus weakening the cooperative hold of the various resonances on the regime of oscillation, until the tall second peak *acting by itself* at its own frequency is able to take over from a progressively enfeebled cooperative regime using harmonics of the mode-1 frequency. When the tarogato we have been discussing has its leak repaired, it is able to play a stable diminuendo on D_4 all the way to complete silence. However, the lower notes, down to B_3b, give increasing evidence of instability. Let us use these remarks as the background for three more statements about oscillation theory:

4. The pressure amplitude measured within the mouthpiece for any given component of a tone is somewhat increased if the height of the air-column resonance curve at the frequency of this component is related to the steepness of the reed's flow-control curve in a way that would permit this oscillation component to sustain itself if it could be studied in the absence of the other resonances (i.e., in the sense of Helmholtz's theory).

5. Spectrum components lying near the reed's own natural frequency will be enhanced very similarly, this time because the resonantly increased steepness of the control curve itself may permit the reed to sustain oscillations in the absence of an air-column resonance.

6. Alterations of pressure amplitude of the sort referred to in statement 4 are not particularly large at ordinary playing levels in the low register, because the interlocking nature of the regime of oscillation distributes any oscillatory contributions by this component across the entire spectrum. The alterations can however lead to profound changes near the threshold of playing and also in the second register where the reed resonance effect may be called upon as a means for setting up a regime of oscillation in the absence of air-column peaks at harmonics of the playing frequency.

Before we consider some of the ways in which certain instruments depart from the behavior described so far, we should broaden our understanding of the musical implications of this behavior.

Anything that works against the maintenance of oscillation (such as the reduction of the heights of air-column resonance peaks by frictional or radiation damping, or the misalignment of these resonances so that they fail to set up strongly cooperative oscillatory regimes) requires the player to operate the reed on the more steeply falling portion of its flow-control curve. In order to produce this increased steepness, the musician is required to exert more effort in his playing, so as to provide a combination of increased blowing pressure and greater embouchure tension (see fig. 21.4 and the numbered statements in sec. 21.2). This explains why instruments having either heavily damped or grossly misaligned resonances are usually described as "hard-blowing," and why the player is likely to find them physically tiring to play.

It is a common observation that a really fine instrument with accurately aligned resonances can be played comfortably with a reed that is considerably stiffer than can be used on a less well-aligned instrument, even if the heights of the various resonance peaks are the same in both cases. When several air-column modes "gang up" on a reed as members of an oscillatory regime, they can satisfactorily push a much stiffer reed open and closed at the blowing pressure and embouchure tension preferred by a particular player.

It is a matter of a musician's taste whether he chooses to make use of a stiff reed and an open facing on the mouthpiece or the opposite extreme—a soft reed and a close facing (an *open facing* is one that curves considerably away from the reed so as to produce a large aperture at the tip in the absence of embouchure tension). In the first case he can play a large part of his total dynamic range in such a way that the reed tip never completely closes the aperture at its end, so that there is a considerable change in tone color as he changes the vigor of his blowing (see statements 1 and 2 above). In the other extreme style, the reed aperture goes shut for a considerable portion of each cycle of its oscillation during normal playing. Here the shape of the internal sound pressure spectrum envelope changes relatively little as the dynamic level is altered, since everything takes place in the region to the right of the vertical line marked "change of feel" in figure 21.6-B. An extreme form of the German style of symphonic clarinet playing belongs to the first of these categories, while the French prefer the second. Most players today make an intermediate choice in which they cover the entire range of musical possibility, and the reed tip closes at each swing only when one is playing above a mezzo-forte level. Figure 21.6-B was made using a clarinet in which the reed, the mouthpiece facing, and the instrument make an excellent combination for this sort of performance, although many players and listeners prefer the instrument when small changes are made to the mouthpiece to increase *minutely* the amount of Bernoulli force that is exerted on the reed tip.

The higher notes of a trumpet, the bottom half-octave of the range of a bassoon, and all of the notes of an oboe fail to show an unfolding of the spectrum during a crescendo of the sort implied by statements 1 and 2 in this section. These peculiarities are themselves understandable on the basis of what we have learned so far. The higher notes of the trumpet are produced by the cooperation of only one air-column resonance with the player's lip-valve. Generally speaking this resonance peak is not very tall, and so cannot dominate the lips of the player in the way in which an air column normally dominates a clarinet reed (a brass-player's lips are massive when compared to a reed, or in view of the forces within the mouthpiece that help to control the lips). As a result, the player arranges things in a manner which sustains the oscillation by increasingly large amounts of the oscillatory Bernoulli force (see sec. 19.2). The resulting oscillatory regime is no longer of the completely pressure-controlled sort that we have been assuming, since the Bernoulli force depends on the flow velocity itself.

The low notes of a bassoon are played using a very nearly complete conical air column, so that the first and sometimes even the second resonance peaks are less tall than the higher-numbered ones. Only when the player blows quite hard, so that his reed slaps shut during part of each vibrational cycle, can the *cooperative* efforts of modes 1, 2, 3, etc., set up a low-register regime of oscillation strong enough to overcome the influence of the single tallest peak (see the explanation of the tarogato note D_4 earlier in this section). In the bassoon the "change of feel" takes place only a little above the threshold of pianissimo playing.

Figure 21.6-C shows the internally measured sound spectrum curves of a note on the Vienna oboe. The drastically different behavior seen here is associated with a very large amount of Bernoulli force exerted at the reed tip over an appreciable fraction of the cycle. The mathematical physics of oscillatory regimes

dominated by a Bernoulli-type reed-control force has hardly been studied. It is possible to show, however, that this sort of influence on a pressure-controlled reed has several consequences for the player beyond those implied already. The reed tends to *snap* shut at the end of its swing rather than closing smoothly, as would be expected in the absence of Bernoulli forces. This means that a relatively low blowing pressure will take one into the loud-playing part of the playing range, in which the reed remains closed over an appreciable fraction of each cycle. This results in considerable production of high harmonics even at the pianissimo level. In particular, the Bernoulli force tends to make a great increase in the second harmonic component of any tone that may be produced. (This effect is clearly shown by the relation between the saxophone spectra discussed in sec. 13.7.) In figure 21.6-C you will notice that at ordinary and loud playing levels, the amplitude of the second component p_2 is 2 or 3 dB greater than the fundamental component p_1. At the pianissimo playing levels this excess is exaggerated, despite the fact that on a Vienna oboe the first and second resonance peaks of the air column used to play D_4 are equally tall. A diminuendo on this oboe will therefore not produce the octave "sneaking" we observed for this note on the tarogato (produced by the tarogato's tall second peak).

21.4. Acoustical Properties of a Set of Closed or Open Tone Holes

It has been pointed out earlier that the acoustical behavior of a woodwind is very strongly influenced by the design of its system of tone holes. The existence of a cutoff frequency associated with the set of open holes has been our first example of their influence. Another important influence is the effect of the row of closed tone holes that lies along the upper part of a woodwind air column. We will begin our study of tone-hole properties with an account of the action of these closed holes.[8]

A. *The Closed Tone Holes.* Figure 21.8 shows how we can look at a lattice of tone holes as being made up of a sequence of T-shaped sections, each consisting of a piece of the main bore having radius a (i.e., diameter 2a) and length 2s.

Each of these segments is provided at its center with a side branch, which is made by drilling a hole of diameter 2b through the pipe wall, whose thickness is t. Notice that the length 2s of each segment is also equal to the spacing between successive tone holes. In a real woodwind the tube diameter 2a is not generally the same as we go from one part of the instrument to another, nor do the tone-hole sizes or spacings form a uniform progression. This need not concern us for the moment; it will be sufficient for us to think first about the properties of a duct

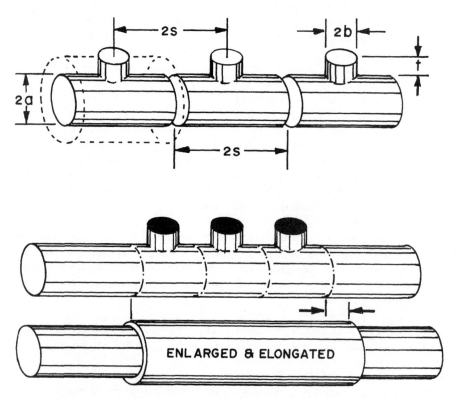

Fig. 21.8. *Top,* representation of woodwind tone holes on their air column as a series of T-shaped sections; *bottom,* closed tone holes effectively enlarge and lengthen the air column.

made up of a set of identical segments, and then about a long row of segments whose properties vary in a smooth progression from one end to the other. Eventually we will learn how to deal with the very irregular hole diameters and spacings that are found on real woodwinds.

When all of the tone holes are closed at their outer ends, which converts the air column into a duct provided with a series of small cavities, the compressibility of the air in each T-shaped segment is slightly increased because of the increased volume provided by the tone-hole cavity. The fact that the air in the cavity is restrained from moving back and forth along the duct means that this additional air does not in addition change the net inertia of the moving air. Taken together, these two remarks imply for us that the values of both the wave velocity and the wave impedance of the modified duct are smaller than the corresponding values for the original smooth-walled duct (see sec. 17.1). We met a cousin to these remarks in section 20.5 when we looked at the effect of sharp bends in a duct.

For practical purposes, we can translate the effect of the closed tone holes into a simpler shape in the manner sketched in the lower parts of figure 21.8. A pipe provided with closed tone holes can be replaced acoustically by a pipe whose length and cross-sectional area have both been enlarged by a numerical factor which we shall call E_c:

$$E_c = \left[1 + \frac{1}{2}\left(\frac{b}{a}\right)^2\left(\frac{t}{2s}\right)\right]$$

For most woodwinds, the change implied by this formula ranges from 2 to 5 percent. From our study of brass instruments we already know that uncompensated changes of this magnitude can have serious consequences.

B. The Open-Hole Lattice Cutoff Frequency.[9] Let us return now to the first and most important property of a lattice of *open* tone holes: their influence on the cutoff frequency. When these holes are proportioned in the manner normally found on clarinets, oboes, and bassoons, the cutoff frequency f_c is given quite accurately by the following simplified formula:

$$f_c = 0.110(b/a)v\sqrt{1/st_e}$$

Here v is the speed of sound (345 m/sec) in free space, and t_e is the length of a cylindrical plug of air whose inertia is identical with that of the air which flows in and out through an actual tone hole drilled through a wall of thickness t. We find that t_e is greater than t, because there is always a small amount of moving air immediately beyond the inner and outer ends of the hole. The relation between t and t_e for various kinds of tone holes is complicated, but for present purposes we can use the sum of the physical wall thickness and 3/4 of the tone-hole diameter 2b; that is, $t_e \cong (t + 1.5b)$.[10]

We can see from the formula that enlarging the ratio (b/a) of tone-hole size to bore size will raise the cutoff frequency, while an increase in effective thickness t_e or interhole spacing 2s will lower it. If the lattice is irregular, theory shows that: (1) if the first and second open-hole segments of the lattice (taken by themselves) have widely different cutoff frequencies, the observed value of f_c for the composite system has an intermediate value for its cutoff frequency; and (2) at the lower frequencies, the properties of the first segment still dominate the implications of

f_c. Considerations of this kind show that it is technically possible to take care of the irregularities arising in the spacing or proportions of the first two open holes. The effect of an anomalously large spacing (whole-tone instead of half-tone), for example, can be hidden almost entirely by the use of an enlarged first tone hole. Similarly, if the second hole should be anomalously small, its effect on f_c, etc., can be compensated by reducing its own t_e, or by increasing the size of the first hole, and so on. We can realize from these observations that one has considerable latitude in the design of a woodwind since one can trade an alteration of hole size for a change in wall thickness and still preserve some desired cutoff frequency and its acoustical relatives.

C. The Open-Holes Length Correction.[11] Now that we have an expression for the cutoff frequency, we are in a position to set down a pair of simplified but very instructive formulas that allow us to think about the length correction associated with the junction of an open tone holes lattice with the upper body of a woodwind. This length correction, for which we will use the symbol C, is the distance between the points marked M and N in figure 21.1. As we have already learned in section 21.1, C increases somewhat with frequency up to f_c, above which it loses any sensible meaning, since the air column simply extends itself all the way to the lower end of the instrument.

For frequencies well below cutoff, the length correction C varies only slowly. At very low frequencies it is accurately given in terms of the tone-hole dimensions and spacing by the formula:

$$C_{low} = s\left(\sqrt{1 + 2(t_e/s)(a/b)^2} - 1\right)$$

For ordinary woodwind tone-hole lattices, we find that C_{low} has values running between about 1.5s and 4s, which is a way of saying that the effective length (the distance XN of fig. 21.1) extends down into the open-hole lattice a distance varying from somewhat less than the interhole spacing 2s to about twice this spacing.

We find that the length correction C grows slowly at first (far below cutoff) and then more rapidly (just below cutoff). On most woodwinds, C increases on the order of 12% or less at three-quarters of the cutoff frequency.

Inspection of both formulas for C shows that making the interhole spacing larger will increase the magnitude of the correction, as will an increase in the effective wall thickness t_e. We also notice that decreasing the hole size relative to that of the bore increases the magnitude of C, and so flattens the played note.

Our simplified formula for the open-hole length correction C has useful accuracy for serous woodwind design as long as there are at least two open holes in the lattice, and as long as the hole diameters do not differ by more than fifty percent. In the formula, one uses the radius b of the uppermost of these holes, and the radius a of the bore at the position of this hole. One also takes s to be one-half the interhole spacing of the top two open holes, and evaluates the equivalent wall thickness t_e at the position of the top hole.

If more exact results are needed or if the lattice is very irregular, meaningful calculations can be carried out, but they become extremely tedious and fairly subtle. A detailed discussion of the mathematical design of woodwind tone holes regardless of the irregularity of their proportions is to be found in Nederveen's book. He limits himself to frequencies such that f/f_c is negligibly small, so that cutoff phenomena are ignored.

Let us interrupt our description of standing waves in a pipe with tone holes to notice some of the practical implications of what we have learned so far. We can now glimpse the reasons why closing a tone hole at some distance down the bore following a series of open holes has very little effect on the tuning of the first natural mode of vibration. At low frequencies the main standing wave does not "visit" the region in which we have introduced an anomaly, and so is not perturbed by it. The higher-frequency modes (that still lie below cutoff) are progressively more influenced by such a closure, and the effect on them is *always* to lower the natural frequency. On the other hand, above cutoff the influence of a distant closed hole in the lower bore can be considerable, because the strength of the standing wave here is large. One can obtain either a raising or a lowering of the frequency, depending on the complexities of the situation. This is a phenomenon which is sometimes baffling, particularly to players of baroque instruments.

D. Irregular Lattices and Fork-Fingerings. In our discussion of air columns provided with a complete set of open tone holes, we found the open holes length correction C to be associated with a sequence of open holes; this sequence is dominated by the dimensions of the highest open hole in the series, and by the spacing between this hole and the next one. At first sight, this simplification of what is otherwise an exceedingly complicated problem appears to be valid only as long as the series of holes has a reasonably smooth progression of sizes and spacings. However, closer examination of the physics shows (in agreement with practice) that the lattice of holes need not be physically regular in its dimensions as long as sufficient *acoustical* regularity can be obtained for the system. Under these conditions the general conclusions remain valid. Because fork-fingering introduces a geometrical irregularity into the lattice of open holes while preserving a certain amount of acoustical regularity in the system, this is a good time to consider the effects of this useful technique.

A *fork-fingering* is one in which the regularity of the open-hole lattice is interrupted by closing one or more of its holes. A typical fork-fingering occurs when one attempts to flatten a note a semitone by closing the second hole down in what had originally been a series of open holes. Such a situation is diagrammed in the middle part of figure 21.9. The figure shows both the original, normally fingered note with its complete set of open tone holes, and the lattice modified by closing either one or two extra tone holes. It is at once apparent that the spacing between the first two open holes is drastically increased by the fork-fingering shown in the middle part of figure 21.9. It is a fact long familiar to musicians that closing yet another hole (in this case the one marked Q) will produce very little change in the tuning of the fork-fingered note, even though it supplies the instrument with two (rather than one) of the new lattice segments having extended interhole spacing. This observation drawn from experience serves as a beautiful example of the self-regularizing powers of lattice acoustics, and so helps us to understand the theory.

In the preceding part of this section we set down a pair of formulas for C to which we should return our attention. It

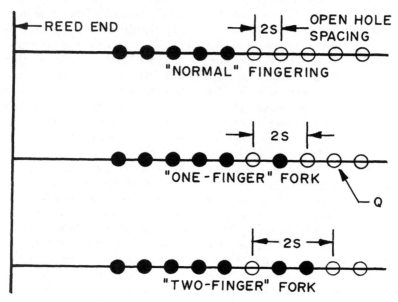

Fig. 21.9. Normal and Fork-Fingerings

is at once obvious that an increase of interhole spacing 2s produced by fork-fingering will increase C (and so flatten the note) simply because s multiplies everything else in the formula. However, C does not increase quite in simple proportion to s; the diluting effect of the factor (1/s) under the square root sign somewhat lessens the change in C, while the concomitant lowering of the cutoff frequency f_c also works on C to make it slightly larger at mid-frequencies. In any event, we find that closing the hole always increases C *somewhat* and so flattens the note. Furthermore, we can deduce that when one plays in the instrument's second register instead of the first (so that the playing frequency is increased), the amount of flattening caused by the fork-fingering increases, in general accord with experience.

If we look more closely at the problem of fork-fingering, it turns out that, if the cutoff frequency f_c is about four times the playing frequency, there is a mathematical possibility of arranging holes to give a perfect semitone fork. However, upon further calculation we find that such a state of affairs can be attained in the smaller (treble-clef) woodwinds only when the pipe walls are very thin and the tone holes very small. For example, on an ordinary thin-walled flute of 19-mm diameter, the tone holes would be only 3 mm in diameter! Mathematics and experiment agree that the frictional loss of energy in such small holes gives hopelessly large damping, making such an instrument all but unplayable. For bass instruments, however, it turns out that the required tone-hole proportions are perfectly practicable, and indeed simple fork-fingerings of this sort were standard practice for the baroque bassoonist. On smaller woodwinds having tone holes of practicable size, many low-register semitones may be fork-fingered by closing two adjacent holes down the bore instead of only one (as shown in the lowest part of figure 21.9). On the other hand, the simpler kind of fork-fingering will work in many cases in the second register because of the nearness of f_c to the playing frequency.

The knowledgeable musician may have noticed certain apparent discrepancies between his experience and the assertions about fork-fingerings that were made in the preceding paragraphs. In particular he will be aware of inconsistencies in the fork-fingering behavior of flutes, oboes, and clarinets, which might (at first examination) be expected to behave similarly to each other. Most of these apparent discrepancies arise as a result of the differences in the cooperative effects that occur in the various instruments between the first and second vibrational modes of the air column when one is playing in the low register; this means that we should not expect to predict the intonation behavior of a fork-fingered note from the length corrections for the first and second modes considered separately.

As preparation for a discussion of register holes in the next section, we turn our attention now to standing waves in air columns that are provided with but a single tone hole. Consider first the case of a single tone hole drilled through the wall of a conical air column three-quarters of the distance from the apex of the cone to

its large open end. The size of the hole and the wall thickness are such that when the hole is open, the first-mode frequency of the air column is increased by 25 percent above the value obtained with the unpierced bore (cutting the cone off bodily at three-quarters length would raise the frequency by 33 percent).

The top part of figure 21.10 shows the air column and its single tone hole in diagrammatic fashion. The second part of the figure shows the first-mode standing waves for the air column when the hole is opened, and again when it is closed. The most salient feature of the open-hole standing wave is the presence of a "kink" located at the position of the hole (marked M). It is worth pointing out that the portion of the standing wave lying to the left of M is exactly the same as one belonging to the complete, unperforated cone if it were to be shortened enough to raise its natural frequency by 25 percent. The point marked N on the diagram shows where this shortened cone would have its open end, and the dotted line indicates the manner in which the standing wave would continue beyond M in this cone. If we like, we can call the distance MN the length correction belonging to the tone hole and the lower bore, in a manner analogous to the way in which C was defined for a lattice of many open tone holes. Methods for calculating such a length correction have been known to acousticians for well over a century. They underlie the tone-hole design procedures worked out by Nederveen.

The bottom part of figure 21.10 shows the first- and second-mode standing pressure waves for our cone with its open tone hole. Once again we notice the break or kink in the curve that occurs at the location of the hole; one finds, however, that

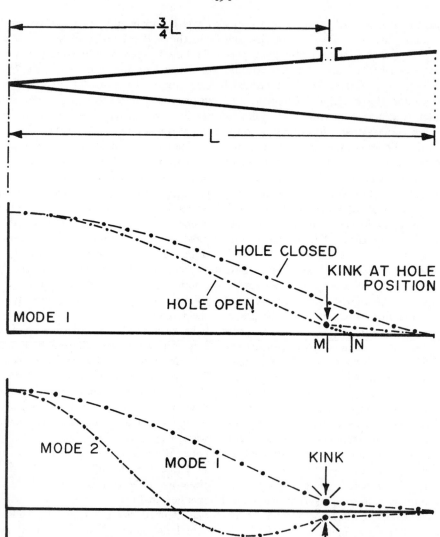

Fig. 21.10. Standing Wave Patterns for a Conical Tube Having One Open Hole near Its Lower End

the second mode's length correction (analogous to the distance MN in the middle diagram) is larger than the first-mode correction. This increase makes the overall equivalent length of the cone 1.42 percent longer when it is vibrating in its second mode than when the oscillation takes place in the first mode. Let us say this in another way: we learned in chapter 20 that the ratio between the frequencies of the second and first vibrational modes of an ideal complete cone is exactly 2-to-1 (i.e., musically speaking there is an octave interval between them). When a single hole is drilled in a cone as shown in figure 21.10, the musical interval between the frequencies of the second and first modes of the altered air column is reduced to one that is 24 cents narrower than an octave. Once again the analogy is apparent between the qualitative behavior of a tube provided with one tone hole and that of one supplied with a whole series of them. There is however no cutoff frequency to be recognized in the one-hole case.

21.5. The Higher Registers of Woodwinds; The Function of Register Holes and Cross-Fingerings

When one plays at a mezzo-forte level on any reed woodwind, the production of low-register notes is normally favored over tones in the second and higher registers, if only because several air-column resonances are able to collaborate in setting up a regime of oscillation. On the clarinet and in those parts of a cone-woodwind scale where the air column is relatively short, the low register is additionally favored even at pianissimo playing levels because the first resonance peak

is the tallest. We have already noted, however, the problem faced by players who wish to play the bottom notes of a conical instrument softly, since these notes may want to make an octave transition to a regime dominated by the tall second peak. The above observations suggest some of the acoustical changes a player must make whenever he wishes to sound notes in the second register of his instrument. These required changes can be summed up in generalized form in two statements.[12]

1. For a register change in pianissimo playing, some means of selective damping must be provided that reduces the tallness of the air column's first-mode resonance peak to something less than the height of the second resonance peak.

For playing at louder dynamic levels, the above requirement is not sufficient, since two or three weakened resonance peaks may join together to produce a low-register regime that is favored over a second-register regime involving only the tall second-mode peak, or the second-mode peak plus the peak belonging to mode 4 (if mode 4 has not been obliterated by lying above f_c).

2. For a register change at greater dynamic levels, it is necessary to shift the frequency of the first resonance peak in such a way as to destroy the possibility of its joining a regime of oscillation supported in part by some of the other air-column resonances.

The player can accomplish these needed acoustical changes in a number of ways: he may open a specially proportioned *register hole* in the upper part of the air column, or he may use various combinations of open and closed tone holes to produce the desired changes by means of what is called *cross-fingering*.

The proper placement of a register hole designed to influence mode 1 without changing mode 2 is not particularly hard to find for either a cylindrical pipe or a cone. Examination of figure 21.2, which shows the first- and second-mode standing pressure waves for a cylindrical pipe, might suggest to us that a hole located one-third of the way from the reed end of a clarinet will have no influence whatever on mode 2, since this is a nodal point, and at such a point there is no pressure variation to drive air in and out through the aperture. However, mode 1 is affected by a hole at this point, which is the effect we are looking for.

Let us look at the behavior of a clarinet which I provided with an interchangeable pair of specially designed register holes, one of which is arranged to meet only the pianissimo playing requirements, while the other meets only the requirements for loud playing. These register holes were designed to apply particularly to the low-register note A_3 and its second-register counterpart E_5 a twelfth higher. Both holes are located the required one-third distance from the reed end, and only one is used at a time.

Let us first consider the register hole designed to be used exclusively for soft playing. This hole is supplied with a wad of porous material, so that the oscillatory flow of air through the hole is controlled primarily by the friction of its passage through the porous material rather than by the inertia of the air in the opening. This causes a considerable increase in the damping of mode 1, so that the height of its resonance peak is reduced, but with only a tiny change (5 or 10 cents) in the natural frequency of the mode. A porous aperture of this sort is what an engineer would call a *resistive* aperture. When the

resistive register hole is opened on my experimental clarinet, the tallness of peak 1 is reduced to about one-third of its original value, and peaks 3 and 4 are also made somewhat less tall, whereas peaks 2 and 5 are left unchanged (because the hole lies at a pressure node for each of these modes).

If one plays the low-register note A_3 loudly without opening a register hole, harmonics 1, 3, 5, and 7 of the tone are supported in a regime of oscillation dominated by the first four resonance peaks. When the resistive register hole (designed for soft playing) is opened while the instrument is playing loudly, the note becomes a little harder-blowing for the player and the tone color is altered somewhat, but there is no change in playing pitch. If one then plays a diminuendo, the influence of the higher resonances disappears as the higher partials of the note diminish (see statements 1 and 2 in sec. 21.3) until a point is reached where the tall second peak takes over, whereupon the pitch rises by the interval of a twelfth to the clarinet's second-register note. If one starts the note softly, one unambiguously gets either the high- or the low-register note depending on whether the hole is open or closed.

The other register hole on my special clarinet can be called a *reactive* register hole, i.e., an aperture in which the flow depends mainly on the inertia of the air moving through it (as is the case also for tone holes used to produce notes of the scale). When the reactive register hole is used, the first-mode standing wave is modified in a manner reminiscent of that shown in figure 21.10, giving it a higher frequency, whereas mode 2 is not changed at all because the opening is at a nodal point for this mode. There is a small and unavoidable loss in the height of peak 1 due to friction in the hole, but it is possible to keep peak 1 considerably taller than peak 2, so that the instrument will still play pianissimo in the low register (though the frequency of the low-register note is raised because of the open hole).

When the clarinet is being played softly in its low register, opening the reactive register hole (designed for loud playing) shifts the pitch of the tone from A_3 up to the neighborhood of $C_4\sharp$ as the oscillation follows the frequency of the altered first resonance. An attempt to make a crescendo from a soft beginning with the reactive register hole open will either cause the reed to choke up as the higher harmonics of the tone $C_4\sharp$ discover that they have to cope with dips rather than peaks in the resonance curves, or cause the instrument to make a "break" across

into the undisturbed second-register mode of oscillation. However, a loudly played note will always start in the high register when the reactive hole is open.

The register holes described above are extremes that would be useless on a real musical instrument. For a register hole to be practical, it must of course serve for playing at all dynamic levels; this means that it must be proportioned so as to exert suitable amounts of both resistive and reactive influence. In other words, the first resonance peak must be made less tall than the second one, and also its frequency must be shifted so that it cannot collaborate with the other peaks in forming a regime of oscillation.

On the conical instruments the choice of the register hole's position and its optimum proportions is simple. Figure 21.11 shows us that the correct position for the hole is exactly at the midpoint be-

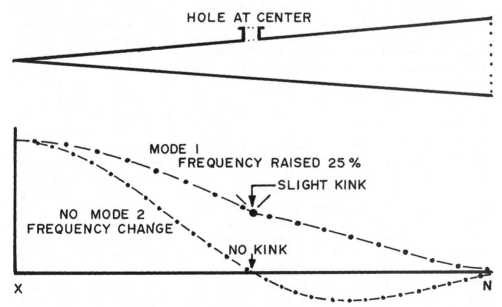

Fig. 21.11. Standing Wave Patterns for a Conical Tube Having One Open Hole at Its Midpoint

tween the apex of the cone (marked X) and its effective open end at N (see also figs. 21.1 and 21.2). The resistive properties of the register hole will take care of themselves, provided the thickness t of material through which the hole is drilled is made as small as possible (one cannot improve on the 1/2-mm thickness that is customary on oboes; the same thickness would be ideal for the other woodwinds, large and small). The reactive (inertia-related) properties of the hole must be chosen to raise the mode-1 frequency by very nearly 25 percent, so that its second harmonic lies at the dip between peaks 2 and 3. Notice in figure 21.11 how slight a change the register hole produces in the shape of the mode-1 standing wave when its frequency is raised by the requisite amount.

A rather simple formula relates optimum register hole placement, size, and wall thickness for cones. If the length of the complete cone for the note of interest is L, then the size of the hole and the thickness of the wall through which it is drilled must have proportions that are related to the local radius of the cone and to its length by the following formula:

$$(b/a)^2(L/t_e) = 3.253$$

This formula is easy to use, since t_e (i.e., $t + 1.5b$) is already chosen for us by the resistive part of the design.

A closely related formula applies for cylindrical pipes. If the register hole of the clarinet (which is basically cylindrical) is to work properly, it must be located one-third of the way down the tube from the reed end, as we have already seen. The clarinet's register hole must move the mode-1 resonance upward by 20 percent in order that its second and third har-

monics nicely straddle peak 2. An error either way slightly spoils the effectiveness of the hole. Once again t_e should be very small, so that the resistive part of the register hole's duties can be properly taken care of. The other proportions are calculated from the formula:

$$(b/a)^2(L/t_e) = 0.7570$$

This expression is almost identical with the one for conical instruments, except for a numerical factor that calls for a considerably smaller hole size than would be appropriate for a conical tube whose diameter (at the register hole) is the same.

The second register of every woodwind encompasses a dozen semitones or more, so we are faced with the apparent need for an equally large number of register holes. As a practical matter, the oboe (whose empirically developed register holes almost always satisfy our acoustical requirements to perfection) gets along very well with three register holes. The saxophone is generally supplied with two and the clarinet with one; register-hole design can be a problem in both these instruments.

One occasionally sees a saxophone on which the register holes are proportioned in approximate agreement with the prescription outlined above, and I have installed such on other instruments. (Even with a well-proportioned saxophone register hole, it may be necessary to compromise the resistive requirement by enlarging both t_e and b.) However, it is far more common to find saxophone register holes consisting of a tube whose length can be 10 or even 15 millimeters, and of equally unsuitable diameter. The instrument tends at best to ignore these holes. Such register holes also cause serious tuning problems which are an irregular version of those which we shall meet next in connection with the clarinet.

The ordinary-sized clarinet almost never has more than one register hole, and to make matters worse, this hole is forced to serve as a tone hole as well. Its length and its diameter are both too big for it to function as a good register hole and too small for it to work as a good tone hole. The hole is typically proportioned so that the right-hand side of our formula comes out close to 1.28 instead of the desired value of 0.757. It would take us too far afield to consider here the reasons why clarinetists have chosen to do without additional register holes and the reasons why their choice is at all possible acoustically. We should, however, learn some of the consequences of having a misplaced register hole on any instrument— that is, a hole which is not placed exactly halfway between the apex and the effective open end of a conical woodwind, or exactly one-third of the way down from the reed end of a clarinet. Because misplaced holes have almost no practical implication for oboes, and need have very little for saxophones and bassoons (whose many register holes have various degrees of appropriateness), we shall devote most of our attention to the clarinet, where the problem is particularly serious.

We can easily deduce from figures 21.10 and 21.11 that opening a hole anywhere along an air column will raise the frequencies of all the modes except those which happen to have a pressure node at the position of the hole. This tells us that if the register hole is misplaced, mode 2 will have its frequency raised somewhat (along with the desired raising of the mode-1 frequency). We can also see that this upward change in the mode-2 frequency grows as the register hole is displaced farther away from the nodal position *on either side* of the node.

For musical convenience, it is appropriate to give the pitch shift S (expressed in cents) produced when one fingers a second-register clarinet note whose second-mode resonance frequency is supposed to be r times as great as that of the note for which the register hole is ideally designed and located.

$$S = (132/r)(r - 1)^2(b/a)^2(L/t_e) \text{ cents}$$

This formula is a simplified but accurate summary of computer calculations which were first done for me in 1958 by James Gibson and greatly refined and extended by Robert Steiglitz in 1964. It can be applied without modification to a cylindrical pipe having a row of open tone holes at its lower end, although the presence of a bell or an over-soft reed can alter the behavior somewhat.

Let us see how this formula can be applied to a typical clarinet whose register hole is located to work ideally for the transition between the low-register A_3 and the second-register E_5. For such a clarinet, opening and closing the register hole has no effect whatever on the frequency of mode 2 belonging to the A_3/E_5 fingering. A musical fifth higher, at the fingering intended to produce the second-register note B_5, opening the register hole will, on a clarinet with normal register-hole proportions, pull the second mode sharp by about 28 cents (since $r = 3/2$ for the interval of a fifth). A minor third ($r = 6/5$) above the perfectly proportioned fingering we find the note G_5. Here the second resonance is shifted upward by only about 6 cents. The bottom note of the second register is B_4, an interval of a fourth *below* the reference E_5, making $r = 3/4$. According to our formula, the register hole would pull mode 2 up by 14 cents for this fingering. The presence of an open register hole means that it is impossible to build a clarinet shaped in such a way as to give good low-register cooperations and at the same time play both registers accurately in tune (except for the note A_3!). In chapter 22 we will look into some of the practical implications of this remark.

There is yet another way of destroying a regime of oscillation based on the first resonance peak of an air column, so as to force the instrument to play in its second register. We have the option, known as *cross-fingering*, of closing certain combinations of lower tone holes to produce an air column terminated by a lattice having a low cutoff frequency that suitably rearranges the resonances. The technique of cross-fingering was used by baroque oboists to play above $B_5\flat$, and it remained a part of the classical oboist's routine technique well into the nineteenth century. Players of today's Vienna oboe enjoy several advantages over their colleagues elsewhere because their instruments are particularly well-suited to the use of cross-fingerings. Exactly similar fingerings were used by players of the baroque flute and the recorder, while the bassoonist has never given up the routine use of such fingerings for notes above $E_4\flat$.

A particularly clear-cut example of the acoustical manner in which cross-fingerings work is provided by the way in which the player of the present-day Vienna oboe prefers to play the second-register note B_5. The upper half of figure

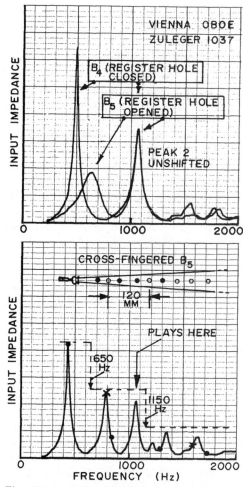

Fig. 21.12. Register Change on a Vienna Oboe. *Top*, using conventional register hole; *bottom*, using a cross-fingering.

21.12 compares the input impedance curves for the low-register and second-register fingerings when the player makes use of the normal register hole which is available to him as an alternate fingering for this note. The lower part of the figure shows what the input impedance curve looks like when the player fingers the note in the preferred manner—a cross-fingering that leaves open the middle-finger tone hole on each hand. This fingering may be thought of as producing an air column having two different open-hole lattices. The upper lattice belongs to the cross-fingering itself, and it has a very large (about 120-mm) interhole spacing, so as to give a cutoff frequency in the neighborhood of 650 Hz. The lattice at the lower end of the instrument is the one belonging to the more closely spaced sequence of tone holes left open below the fingers when one closes the middle-finger holes to play D_4. The cutoff frequency for this second lattice is in the neighborhood of 1150 Hz. The stepped line drawn over the resonance curve in this figure serves to call your attention clearly to the two cutoff frequencies. Mode 1 of this complex air column has a frequency that lies below the 650-Hz cutoff, so that the standing wave is restricted very much to the same short region of upper cone that is normally used in playing the low-register note B_4. Resonance peaks 2 and 3 have frequencies which show that the corresponding air-column modes lie between the two cutoff frequencies. The standing waves for these two modes have 3 and 5 half humps respectively, and the primary, quasi-sinusoidal portion of their shape extends down to the region below the player's fingers in a manner reminiscent of mode 4 sketched at the bottom of figure 21.1. These two resonance peaks are less tall than peak 1 because there is a certain small escape of sound from the two holes of the long lattice; however, there is still sufficient wave amplitude reflected back from the closely spaced lattice at the bottom end to assure reasonably strong resonances. The small resonances beyond 1150 Hz are the characteristic squiggles that an air column provided with many tone holes produces when it is excited above cutoff.

Let us now examine the possibilities for the reed to set up a regime of oscillation with this sort of air column. The solid black dots located at peak 1 and at whole-number multiples of its frequency show that the air column actively works against the production of harmonics 2, 3, and 4 of a low-register note based on peak 1. Because of its large Bernoulli-force sensitivity, an oboe reed cannot normally be played at low enough levels for peak 1 to be able to function independently of what goes on at higher frequencies, so a low-register regime is impossible for this air column. The points marked X on the resonance curve show similarly that resonance peak 2 is also unable to find a collaborative helper at high frequencies that can set up a successful oscillatory regime.

The third resonance peak is the one that produces the desired B_5 tone. At first glance this seems mysterious, because this peak is no taller than peak 2, and yet on a properly arranged instrument the note leaps forth solidly and with stability at any dynamic level the player may choose for it. The explanation lies in the reed. When the reed is correctly made, one of its attributes is a natural frequency for the cane itself that can comfortably be varied by the subtle motions of the player's lips and blowing pressure over a range extending upward from about 1500 Hz. Our B_5 is played in such a manner that the reed is tuned to match the second harmonic component of the tone to become a part of the regime of oscillation. In other words, this second-harmonic component enters the regime via the sensitivity of the reed, enhanced by its properly chosen resonance frequency, rather than via an air-column resonance peak located to cooperate in the familiar way (see statement 10 in sec. 21.2). The cross-fingering is a good way to play B_5 and C_5 because it makes use of nearly the whole air column instead of only the top third of it. Because a much larger volume of vibrating air is able to exert its influence on the reed, the tone and response are stabilized at all playing levels.

It is worth remarking here that the second-register notes of most woodwinds are given much of their stability and fullness of tone by the proper adjustment of the reed's natural frequency to match the second harmonic of the tone being played. This is a practical possibility over the musical scale because even a wide-ranging alteration by the player of the reed resonance frequency produces relatively small changes in the frequencies of the air-column resonances themselves (see statements 2 and 3 in sec. 21.2).

21.6. Examples, Experiments, and Questions

1. If you finger the low-register clarinet note E_4 and then open the highest tone hole on the instrument, an air column will be produced having a strong first-resonance peak that is not harmonically related to anything else. Playing the low-register note using this fingering (its pitch will be a little above A_4) will give you a feeling for the peculiar behavior of a reed which oscillates under the helpful influence of only one air-column resonance. There is relatively little of the second and third harmonic components in the vibration recipe. If you play a crescendo, the tone hole will begin to hiss from the turbulent oscillatory flow of air through it, and, as the attempted crescendo continues, the reed will choke up and shut off the flow of air. See if you can figure out why this choking-up takes place, given the information that as the turbulent damping grows, the air-column resonance peak rapidly becomes less and less tall.

2. Suppose you are playing mezzo forte a low-register note on some woodwind, and you find that "shading" the first or second open tone hole with your finger makes the note sound steadier and fuller, while also making it feel easier to play. From the way in which the open-holes length correction varies with tone-hole size and with frequency, see if you can understand why it is correct to deduce that mode 2 for this air column was originally too high in frequency relative to mode 1, and that shading the hole brings it into a better relationship within the regime of oscillation.

3. Consider a typical clarinet which, in the hands of an inexperienced player, sounds its low-register notes accurately in tune only when it is blown at a forte level, and runs sharp during a diminuendo. Taking into account the changing influence of the second resonance peak on the regime of oscillation for a low-register note during the playing of a diminuendo, figure out whether it is the first or the second peak that is mislocated relative to the correct tuning.

4. In section 21.4, part A, a formula is given for the effective enlargement and elongation E_c of a tube produced by a sequence of closed tone holes. You will find it worthwhile to make rough estimates of E_c at various points along the bore of a clarinet, oboe, saxophone, flute,

or bassoon. It may be helpful to recognize that the algebraic combination $(1/2)$ $(b/a)^2(t/2s)$ corresponds to half the ratio of the tone-hole volume $(\pi b^2 t)$ to the volume (πa^2) $(2s)$ of its segment of the main air column.

5. As an adjunct to the other special register holes which I have made for an experimental clarinet, there is one whose reactive properties are such that the mode-1 resonance frequency is raised 50 percent above its normal value. Why does this hole make the low register of the clarinet sound very much like a saxophone? Does this sort of register hole favor playing in the second register at any particular dynamic level? What sort of musical properties would a saxophone show if it were provided with reactive register holes that raise the first-mode frequency by 50 percent over the whole low-register scale?

6. While playing in the second register of an ordinary clarinet, observe the drop of a few cents in pitch which takes place when the register hole is momentarily closed (see sec. 21.5). With a little practice you may be able to learn how to keep any of these second-register tones playing mezzo forte even with the register hole closed. (Many clarinetists practice doing this as a way to develop embouchure control.) What adjustments to the reed acoustics do you think must be made for the second register to be so maintained? Note: the second-register tone C_6 has its fundamental component supported by the upper one of only two air-column resonances that exist below the tone-hole cutoff; the note G_5 similarly rests upon the middle one of three resonances whose frequency ratios are very nearly in the sequence 1:3:5.

7. Notes above the ordinary woodwind second register are usually played by various types of cross-fingerings. However, certain of the upper notes of a clarinet (i.e., $C_6{}^\sharp$ through F_6) are played with the help of the third vibrational mode of the air column, whose frequency is nominally five-thirds that of the second register (a major sixth above). Verify that this is so. Figures 21.1 and 21.2 will help you to figure out where a pair of register holes should be placed to facilitate the production of these notes.

8. The topmost finger hole of almost every oboe from the baroque era on is located almost precisely at the midpoint of the long cone used to play D_4 and D_5. A register-hole action is produced when the player rolls his finger a little bit off this hole. Due to its placement, completely closing or fully opening this hole once the second-register D_5 tone is established produces no change in pitch. On the baroque oboe, the C_4 key near the bottom of the instrument is used to produce the second-register note $C_5{}^\sharp$ with the help of this same top tone hole, this time opened fully. The semitone sharpening from the expected C_5 is due to the top hole's acting as a large and displaced register hole.

Notes

1. The history and nature of woodwind instruments is authoritatively described in Anthony Baines, *Woodwind Instruments and their History*, rev. ed. (New York: Norton, 1963); Philip Bate, *The Oboe: An Outline of its History, Development and Construction* (London: Ernest Benn, 1956); Philip Bate, *The Flute: A Study of its History, Development and Construction* (London: Ernest Benn; New York: Norton, 1969); and F. Geoffrey Rendall, *The Clarinet: Some Notes upon its History and Construction*, 3rd ed. rev. and added to by Philip Bate (London: Er-

nest Benn; New York: Norton, 1971). See also Oskar Kroll, *The Clarinet*, rev. Diethard Riehm, trans. Hilda Morris, ed. Anthony Baines (New York: Taplinger, 1968). Rendall's book views the clarinet from the vantage point of the Boehm instrument, whereas Kroll's book takes its viewpoint from today's non-Boehm instruments.

2. A. H. Benade, "On Woodwind Instrument Bores," *J. Acoust. Soc. Am.* 31 (1959): 137–46.

3. The theory underlying most of the discussion on tone holes in this chapter is to be found in A. H. Benade, "On the Mathematical Theory of Woodwind Finger Holes," *J. Acoust. Soc. Am.* 32 (1960): 1591–608.

4. See, for example, H. Bouasse, *Instruments à Vent*, 2 vols. (Paris: Librairie Delagrave, 1929 and 1930), I:68–79.

5. John Backus, "Small Vibration Theory of the Clarinet," *J. Acoust. Soc. Am.* 35 (1963): 305–13, and Cornelis J. Nederveen, *Acoustical Aspects of Woodwind Instruments* (Amsterdam: Frits Knuf, 1969), pp. 28–37.

6. Walter E. Worman, "Self-Sustained Nonlinear Oscillations of Medium Amplitude in Clarinet-like Systems" (Ph.D. dissertation, Case Western Reserve University; Cleveland, Ohio, 1971), Appendix A.

7. Worman, "Self-Sustained Nonlinear Oscillations."

8. Benade, "Mathematical Theory of Woodwind Finger Holes," sections II and IV. See also Nederveen, *Acoustical Aspects of Woodwind Instruments*, pp. 54–60.

9. Benade, "Mathematical Theory of Woodwind Finger Holes," sections III and V.

10. For the corrections needed at the inside and outside ends of a tone hole drilled through a cylindrical tube, see A. H. Benade and J. Murday, "Measured End Corrections for Woodwind Toneholes" (abstract), *J. Acoust. Soc. Am.* 41 (1967): 1609.

11. Benade, "Mathematical Theory of Woodwind Finger Holes," section V. See also Nederveen, *Acoustical Aspects of Woodwind Instruments*, pp. 45–53, where the holes are dealt with one by one rather than as parts of a lattice.

12. A. H. Benade, "Register Hole Design for Cone Woodwinds" (abstract), *J. Acoust. Soc. Am.* 54 (1973): 310.

22
The Woodwinds: II

In chapter 21 we built up a fairly detailed picture of the ways in which a reed and an air column can collaborate to produce the various notes of a woodwind instrument. In this chapter we will look into the ways air columns must be modified from prototypical cylinders and cones to give them the actual shapes that can collaborate with a reed to produce stable regimes of oscillation. We will also examine the relationships between the internal spectrum (whose properties we have studied in some detail) and the external spectrum of the sounds we hear in the concert hall. We will consider next the similarities and differences between instruments of the flute family and those of the reed woodwind tribe, closing with a brief examination of the manner in which the playing behavior of all woodwinds (and brasses, for that matter) is influenced by the material from which they are constructed.

22.1. The Reed Cavity and Neck Proportions in Conical Instruments

As we have already learned, the reed of any woodwind has two roles to play: it serves as a pressure-controlled valve between the player's lungs and the air column, and it also functions as an elastic boundary to the air column at its blowing end. In section 20.7 we learned that at low frequencies the so-called equivalent length of a trumpet mouthpiece mounted on a piece of cylindrical pipe is equal to the length of this pipe which has the same total volume as the mouthpiece. While the reasons for this relationship are easily understood by acousticians thinking about the properties of a hard-walled cavity, such as a trumpet mouthpiece, it is not at all obvious that the same idea should be applicable to the cavity contained between the two flexible halves of an oboe or bassoon reed. It is hardly more obvious that it should be appropriate for the description of a clarinet or saxophone mouthpiece, which has after all an elastic reed as one of its boundaries.

We have already learned that Weber showed how the yielding air-column termination provided by a reed acts to lower the natural frequencies of the air column, and it will not surprise us that Helmholtz, as usual, added to our understanding: he showed that the flow-control action of the reed produces an additional reduction of playing frequency below the corresponding natural frequency of the air

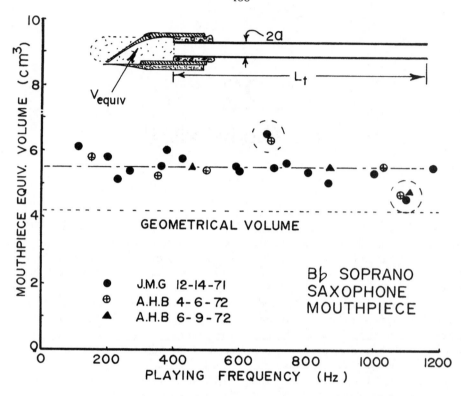

Fig. 22.1. The Equivalent Volume of a Soprano Saxophone Mouthpiece at Various Frequencies

column. In the light of these facts, we can hope to represent a reed and its mouthpiece cavity in terms of an "equivalent" hard-walled cavity whose shape is chosen to make its acoustical effect on the natural frequencies of an air column identical with the composite effect of the actual reed-plus-cavity on the playing frequencies of the air column. It turns out that this can be done, as long as we deal only with frequencies well below the reed's own natural frequency.

Figure 22.1 shows the results of a series of measurements which James Gebler and I carried out as a part of a broad investigation of mouthpiece acoustics.[1] We measured the playing frequencies produced by a soprano saxophone mouthpiece and reed attached to various lengths of metal tubing. By comparing the lengths of tubing for each tone with the calculated lengths of simple tubes (closed at one end) having a natural frequency matching the played one, we were able to calculate the "equivalent" volume of the mouthpiece *under playing conditions* for a wide range of frequencies. Over most of the experimental frequency range, data were obtained using the second or even third modes of a long tube, interlaced with measurements using the first mode of a short pipe. The following three numbered statements summarize the results of such observations on woodwind reed systems:

1. The measured equivalent volume for a single-reed mouthpiece under constant playing conditions is quite constant over a considerable fraction of an instrument's playing range (as long as we remain well below the natural frequency of the reed itself).

2. The equivalent volume measured under playing conditions is considerably larger than the geometrical volume of the hard-walled mouthpiece cavity itself.

3. Double reeds of the sort used in oboes and bassoons show exactly similar behavior (if the measurement excludes the reed tube or bocal). In all cases softening or thinning the cane walls of the reed cavity enlarges its equivalent volume.

Closely related experiments carried out by Nederveen and by Backus show that the equivalent volume determined by resonance frequency measurements using laboratory excitation devices is somewhat smaller than the value we got under playing conditions.[2] However, there is no real discrepancy between their results and ours, since they measured under circumstances where the reed effect studied by Weber is the only one present, whereas we sought figures for the contributions due to the oscillatory effect discovered by Helmholtz as well as the contributions due directly to the elasticity of the reed, as studied by Weber. In any event, by many experiments similar to the ones described above, Gebler and I confirmed in the laboratory what is implied by customary methods of instrument construction: we can in fact think of the cavity within an active reed as being equivalent to a fixed volume whose size is controllable to

some extent by the player as he makes changes in blowing pressure and embouchure tension. I wish to make it explicit that these remarks apply only to the frequency region below the natural frequency of the reed cane itself. In the immediate neighborhood of the reed resonance the idea of an equivalent volume fails, and we have to use a more elaborate representation.

Let us look now at another, more complicated, example of the reed cavity studies which we carried out. An oboe reed mounted on its little brass tube (called a *staple*) may be thought of as a tiny woodwind in its own right, with a playing frequency that is extremely sensitive to the forces exerted on the reed by the player's embouchure and by his blowing pressure. (This tone is *not* the familiar rattling "crow" that is used by oboists to test their reeds.) If a player first uses the reed to sound a specified note on his instrument and then plays with the same embouchure and blowing pressure on the reed alone, the resulting frequency F_{rs} of the reed-plus-staple turns out to be well defined upon test and retest. On certain types of instrument, the player's customary embouchure shifts progressively as he goes along the musical scale; for example, on the conservatory-system oboe that is almost universally used today, the bottom four or five notes (from D_4 on down to B_3b) call for a progressively slackened embouchure and so also a falling F_{rs}. Individual notes in the scale of an instrument sometimes also call for specially chosen values of F_{rs} as the player seeks out an adjustment that best serves to compensate for discrepancies in the air-column and tone-hole design.

The oboe used in Vienna today provides us with a particularly clear picture of what requirements must be met by an oboe reed and its staple (or, for that matter, by the bassoon reed and bocal, or by the saxophone reed, mouthpiece, and neck). The fact that F_{rs} for Vienna oboes is very nearly constant over the main playing range makes analysis of its behavior particularly straightforward. Surprisingly enough, we also find this simple behavior for the reed-plus-staple frequency belonging to various notes in the scale of a baroque oboe.

Figure 22.2 shows the results of measurements on the two kinds of oboe. The diagram gives the playing frequencies F_{rs} of the reed and staple alone that are produced when the player has first set his embouchure by normal playing of the notes whose frequencies appear on the horizontal axis. We see in the lower part of the figure that there is a smooth progression of black dots belonging to the Paulhahn baroque oboe played by Jürg Schaeftlein, who uses the instrument in performances of the Vienna Concentus Musicus. Notice that these points closely follow a horizontal dashed line whose meaning we will learn later in this section. In the upper part of the figure, we find a set of open circles, again running along a fairly horizontal line. These data points too were deduced from notes played by Schaeftlein, this time on the instrument he uses in his position as principal oboist of the Vienna Symphony. Note that these open circles lie very close indeed to a second horizontal dashed line.

We see also a few black triangles, all lying slightly above the higher of the two dashed lines. These correspond to sounds produced by Schaeftlein playing on my own Vienna oboe. The circles with crosses

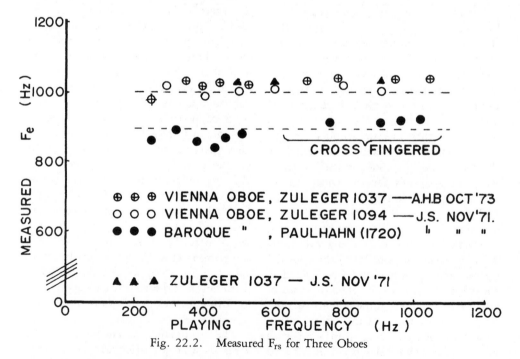

Fig. 22.2. Measured F_{rs} for Three Oboes

represent measurements which I myself made two years later on the same instrument. Notice that my crossed circles and Schaeftlein's black triangles are mutually consistent and systematically lie above the dashed line. Let us add to our numbered collection of observations by summarizing a part of the information contained in figure 22.2:

4. On these three oboes, there is a well-established embouchure that is used over the entire playing range. The reed and staple taken together are well-characterized by their sounding frequency F_{rs}.

5. The constancy of F_{rs} shows that the equivalent volume contained within the reed cavity under playing conditions is constant, since it is this volume which joins with the properties of the fixed miniature air column provided by the staple to determine F_{rs}.

6. For the baroque oboe the reed on its long staple plays at a considerably lower frequency than does its more modern descendant. (The modern Vienna oboe reed cane itself has very nearly the same proportions as those which best suit the baroque instrument.)

Digression on Experimental Techniques Used in Musical Acoustics.
Schaeftlein and I made many observations while trading our instruments back and forth, with both of us playing alternately. Analysis of the tape-recorded data permits a check on the relative influence of the player on the acoustical behavior of a good instrument. It also permits the expert performer to criticize or comment upon the way in which I play individual notes on his instrument. Just as in the case of my experiments with Schlueter on the trumpet, we find that the expert player chooses for artistic reasons to play his instrument in a manner that agrees closely with the far less fluent adjustments made by a scientist who, though he may have only a serious amateur player's fluency on an instrument, has taken pains to become thoroughly

acquainted with its musical behavior, and has sought out means for recognizing clearly the acoustical conditions for setting up the strongest possible cooperations within each oscillatory regime. If this parallelism of behavior did not exist between two very differently motivated players, each having his own area of expertise, we would not be justified in drawing scientific conclusions from these experiments on the behavior of wind instruments.

Let us now see why the playing frequency F_{rs} of the reed and its staple is constant for so many notes on the instrument, despite the fact that the player can easily vary this frequency by 50 percent or so by simple changes in lip pressure.

In chapter 21 we generally acted as though the air column of a conical instrument were a straightsided cone complete all the way to its apex. On an oboe this assumption seems hardly to be justified, since the distance from reed socket to apex (about 160 mm on a conservatory oboe if we make a crude average of the taper of the not-quite-conical bore) is roughly half the length of the complete cone needed to play C_5 at the top end of the low-register scale, and one-fourth of the length of the cone needed for C_4 at the lower end of this scale. We find similar discrepancies between actual air-column lengths used in the bassoon and saxophone and the cone lengths one would expect to use on the basis of simple air-column acoustics. What then is the resolution to the conflict? If the total air column is to have properly placed resonances for setting up good regimes of oscillation, it must have at least the overall behavior of a conical air column. The reed cavity plus the constricted passageway through the staple (or the reed plus bocal in the bassoon, or the mouthpiece plus neck in the saxophone) must therefore be arranged to imitate the acoustical properties of the missing part of the cone.

In chapter 20 we met the idea that at low frequencies the mouthpiece as seen by its trumpet appears simply as a cavity whose shape has no significance. So also we find in the present connection that a reed and its staple must have an equivalent total volume equal to that of the missing part of the cone. Let us add this observation to our collection of numbered statements:

7. For a conical woodwind instrument to work properly, the equivalent volume of the reed cavity added to the mechanical volume of its staple (or bocal or neck) must closely match the volume of the missing part of the cone.

We can continue our search for a useful imitation of the missing part of the cone by trying the effect of matching F_{rs} for the reed system to the first-mode natural frequency of the cone apex itself. In the general frequency neighborhood of F_{rs} the oboe will then "see" an object at its upper end whose acoustical behavior is quite similar to that of the missing apical cone. In particular, there will be a pressure node in the neighborhood of the junction of the main bore with the reed staple, lying a little inside the staple at frequencies somewhat above F_{rs} and moving down below the junction at oboe playing frequencies below F_{rs}—behavior that is identical with that found in an ideal cone. In section 20.5 we met a formula for the natural frequencies of a Bessel horn of given length L and flare parameter m. Applying this to our piece of missing cone whose length we shall call x_0 (and whose flare parameter m is zero), we find it possible to calculate the value

of F_{rs} needed for a reed and staple that is to suit an oboe having a given x_0. Let us describe and explain the simple formula for this calculation in our next two numbered statements.

8. The correct playing frequency F_{rs} of an oboe reed on its staple (or the analogous frequency for a bassoon reed on its bocal, or a saxophone reed on its mouthpiece and neck) can be calculated from a knowledge of the length x_0 of the missing part of the cone, by means of the formula:

$$F_{rs} = v/2x_0$$

Here v is the wave velocity of sound (347 m/sec is a good value to use for the warm, damp air at the upper end of a woodwind).

9. For most instruments, the actual air column is not quite conical in its physical shape, since account must be taken of both the closed and the open tone holes. However, many instruments behave like nearly perfect cones, and it is often possible to calculate the value of x_0 belonging to this "behavioral" cone for use in the formula given above.

Let us turn our attention back now to figure 22.2, noticing in particular the pair of horizontal dashed lines referred to earlier. The lower one of these shows the value of F_{rs} calculated from measurements of the Paulhahn baroque oboe that were supplied to me along with those of many other instruments by Paul Hailperin (who not only makes fine baroque oboes but also plays one along with Schaeftlein in the Vienna Concentus Musicus). Notice how well the calculated value of F_{rs} agrees with the values measured with the help of an expert performer.

The upper dashed line in figure 22.2 was similarly calculated from mechanical measurements which James Gebler made of the bore and tone holes of Schaeftlein's Vienna oboe (serial number 1094). The calculated F_{rs} indicated by this line matches quite well with the open circles representing the reed playing frequencies produced by Schaeftlein himself on this oboe. Notice that the frequencies shown by triangular points all lie above the dashed line. The points were measured from reed sounds produced when Schaeftlein set his embouchure by playing on my Vienna oboe (serial number 1037). The fact that these reed frequencies are indeed determined by the oboe itself and not simply by the caprice of the player or his reeds is shown by the fact that not only at the time, but also two years later, I got an entirely consistent set of values for the played F_{rs} on my instrument, as shown by the crossed circles. These frequency measurements on my oboe imply that its air column differs somewhat from that of Schaeftlein's instrument. Comparison of the dimensions of the two shows that the calculated values of x_0 differ from one another in such a way as to explain the different measured values for F_{rs}.

One more property of the reed cavity itself is of great practical importance to everyone who deals with woodwinds:

10. On a conical air column with only a small missing apical part, an alteration of the reed cavity effective volume which changes the mode-1 resonance frequency by a small percentage will produce four times as much change in the mode-2 frequency, and nine times as much in the mode-3. Thus a reduction in the reed cavity volume produces a widening of the resonance frequency ratios, while an increase in the cavity volume narrows these ratios. On less complete cones, the effect on the frequency ratios is less.

We are now in a good position to understand why it is that oboists and bassoonists must be so careful to get the right combination of reed dimensions and cane stiffness. Not only must these variables suit the average requirements of the instrument throughout its playing range, they must also be such that the player's own embouchure control is sufficient to allow the final trimming-up of the resonances as he goes from note to note. For all this to become possible one must simultaneously meet two requirements: (1) a low-frequency requirement on the total equivalent volume of the reed cavity and the constricted tube (e.g., the staple, bocal, or neck) associated with it, and (2) a higher-frequency requirement that the joint playing frequency F_{rs} of these two objects be properly related to the proportions of the air column. At a considerably more subtle level, small changes in the shape of the reed cavity and of the connecting tube can be expected to improve the accuracy with which the reed and its tube succeed in their job of imitating the missing apical part of the air column at all acoustically relevant frequencies.

I have carried out experiments on oboes constructed at various times in the eighteenth, nineteenth, and twentieth centuries, as well as on old and new bassoons, English horns, and saxophones. Gebler and I have also constructed an experimental saxophone. All these experiments confirm that the principles outlined so far in this section can be used not only to help us understand the construction of certain instruments, but also as an efficient guide in devising suitable reeds, bocals, and mouthpieces for instruments whose original parts are missing or damaged. It is important to realize that when these methods are used for reconstruction purposes, they are applicable only on instruments that were properly proportioned in the first place. A badly built instrument appears to call for a discordant variety of reed and staple proportions, or a wildly varying style of blowing as the player struggles from one note to the next in its scale.

Saxophone players would lead much easier lives if the mouthpiece cavities used on their instruments were fitted as meticulously to their instruments as are the double reeds used by their colleagues. Mouthpieces with long narrow cavities or with dual cavities are particular troublemakers; such mouthpieces require considerable acrobatics from any player who hopes to play in tune, and they prevent him from enjoying a responsive instrument. The useful attributes of such mouthpieces can often be attained by other means without spoiling the instrument's tuning, stability, or response.

22.2. Reed Cavity Acoustics for Cylindrical Instruments

In section 22.1 we learned that each conical woodwind can be made to play properly with its own carefully adjusted reed cavity when this cavity is connected to the air column via a suitably proportioned constriction (variously known as the oboe reed staple, the bassoon bocal, or the saxophone neck). Clarinetlike instruments, being basically cylindrical, have a vastly simpler situation: there is no need to adapt the mouthpiece to its air column by means of a constricted neck, and even further simplification comes from the fact that changing the equivalent volume of the mouthpiece cavity by reaming it out or filling it in with wax alters each pipe mode by almost equal percentages, so that the ratios between the resonance frequencies are very little changed.

Experiments similar to those described in connection with figure 22.1 demonstrate that a typical clarinet mouthpiece and reed combination, when measured below about 700 Hz, shows an equivalent volume of 13.25 cm^3. It is rare to find a workable mouthpiece and reed which together have an equivalent volume that differs by more than 3 percent from this value. The length L_e of cylindrical tube to which this mouthpiece is equivalent depends of course on the diameter of the tube. For example, on a tube having a 15-mm diameter, L_e for our mouthpiece turns out to be close to 75 mm. Enlarging the diameter of the tube by only 0.2 mm reduces L_e by 2.1 mm, while a smaller size tube has a proportionally enlarged value for L_e.

As we continue our experiments to higher frequencies, the effects of the mouthpiece-cavity shape and the progressive approach to the reed's own natural frequency cause L_e to grow slowly at first and then more quickly. At 930 Hz, L_e has grown by 3.6 mm above its value at 310 Hz, which means that the second resonance peak of the air column that cooperates in playing the written note F_4 is lowered in frequency by about 22 cents relative to mode 1. This is enough to weaken noticeably the cooperations in the low-register regime of oscillation if suitable corrections are not made by changing other parts of the air column. We find similarly that resonance peak 3 of the air column used to play the low-register note C_4 is pulled down by the mouthpiece by about 37 cents from its properly collaborative 1175-Hz position, because of an 8-mm growth in L_e at this frequency. Note: this third peak for the C_4 fingering is also used to play the top-register note E_6 (see sec. 21.6, question 7). About half of the stretching of L_e at high frequencies comes from the reed itself, as its own natural frequency is approached. (The natural frequency of the reed can be varied at the discretion of the player from a little below 2000 Hz on up to about twice that as he shifts his embouchure. In normal playing of the low and second registers this frequency tends to stay at the lower end of this range, and it is sometimes set at or near a harmonic of the note being played; see sec. 21.2, statement 10.)

For many practical purposes in the low and second registers, a clarinetist or instrument maker can think of the mouthpiece simply as a small length of tubing. If he wishes to substitute a small-volume mouthpiece for a larger one, it is simply a matter of pairing it with a suitably longer barrel joint between the mouthpiece and the rest of the instrument in order to keep the instrument in tune with itself. This is a far simpler procedure than one would meet on the saxophone, for instance, in which a smaller mouthpiece cavity would have to be teamed with a differently designed neck having a slightly larger volume and a shape such that the new neck and mouthpiece still play at the same F_{rs}, as is required by the instrument. In the somewhat brutal world of practical music, however, the instrumentalist cannot carry a different neck for each mouthpiece cavity setting. If he reduces the mouthpiece cavity volume in an effort to raise his instrument's pitch, he should also pull the neck out a little bit. The two complementary adjustments will usually permit the saxophonist to do a reasonably satisfactory job of tuning his instrument to the required pitch, retaining at the same time a useful degree of cooperation among the modes.

Wherever it is necessary to worry about the high-frequency aspects of clarinet mouthpiece behavior, as when one strives for best tone and response in the upper part of the second register and in the top register, it is not sufficient to trade mouthpiece volume for barrel-joint length. The two are not quite interchangeable. However, it is sometimes possible to arrange small changes in the size and taper of the barrel-joint bore that will successfully adapt the instrument to a different mouthpiece. These changes are much subtler than those referred to in the preceding paragraph on the saxophone neck, although both sorts of adjustment can be made with the help of principles which are discussed in the next section.

22.3. Adjustment of Natural Frequencies by Means of Small Changes of Air-Column Shape

Throughout chapters 19, 20, and 21 we have met situations in which the natural frequencies were to be adjusted by making changes in the shape of the air column itself. Aside from some brief explanations of how this may be done in the adjustment of brass instrument mouthpieces and in the proportioning of reed cavities and neck constrictions of conical woodwinds, we have not so far given much of a hint as to what actually must be done.

Back in chapter 9 we had an introduction to the basic physics of the problem when we examined the ways in which one might scrape away or add to the thickness of a plate in order to modify selectively the frequencies of its modes of vibration. At that time we learned that knowledge of the standing-wave patterns on the plate was an essential guide to the adjustment problem, and we also noted that a change made near a vibrational node produces smaller effects than does a change made in the middle of some hump. We found as well that it was necessary to keep track not only of changes in frequency produced by altering the amount of moving mass in a system, but also of changes associated with modifications of its stiffness coefficients. This double concern is necessary because a local increase of mass in a vibrating system always lowers its frequencies, whereas an increase in stiffness always raises them.

In an air column we have a similar need to keep track of two aspects of the vibration: the variations in pressure and those in flow. It is by now a familiar idea to us that there are points of maximum pressure variation at various places along a vibrating air column; in between these points of maximum pressure amplitude there are pressure nodes where there is maximum longitudinal flow of air (see sec. 6.6, example 3, on the identical behavior of water in a channel). If we contract the diameter of an air column at a point of large pressure amplitude and continue to send the same flow of air into this segment of the air column, the airflow will be opposed by a larger rise in the local acoustic pressure than would be present without the constriction. In other words, the reduction in cross section will produce a local increase in the springiness coefficient of the air within it. On the general grounds that increasing the springiness of a system raises its frequencies, we can recognize that such a contraction will produce an increase in the vibration frequency of the mode in question. If on the other hand the contraction is applied at the location of a pressure node, it goes almost without saying that it will cause no alteration in the natural frequency.

Let us now look at the consequences of contracting the air column at a point where there is a large oscillatory flow. As air enters the narrow channel it requires an increased pressure difference to speed it up, meaning that a given pre-existing driving pressure difference across a segment of air in the channel will produce slightly less flow if the channel is constricted somewhat; we could produce the same effect by locally increasing the density of the air (and thus its inertia), whence we deduce that constrictions at a point of large oscillatory flow lower the natural frequency of vibration. Notice that if the constriction is located at a velocity node, it will have no effect on the inertia properties of the enclosed air and so cannot change the vibrational frequency.

The interlacing of pressure nodes and velocity nodes allows us to deduce the following general principle, which was first enunciated a century ago by Lord Rayleigh:

1. A localized enlargement of the cross section of an air column (a) lowers the natural frequency of any mode having a large pressure amplitude (and therefore small flow) at the position of the enlargement, and (b) raises the natural frequency of any mode having a pressure node (and therefore large flow) at the position of the enlargement.

It is possible to calculate curves giving the effect of a small, localized enlargement or contraction on the frequencies of each vibrational mode of an air column. We will call such curves *perturbation weight function curves,* or *W curves* for short. The mathematical techniques for working out such curves and for putting them to use are a highly developed part of mathematical physics. These techniques are known collectively as *perturbation*

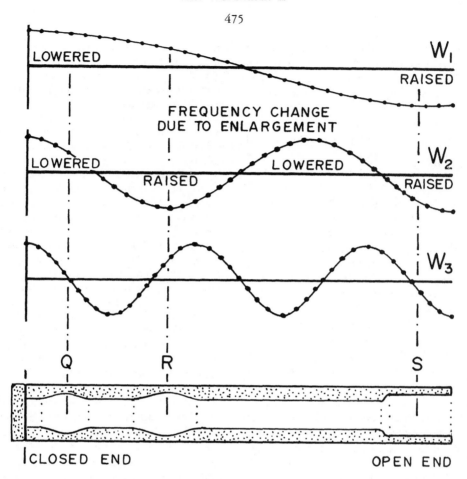

LOWERED

RAISED

W₁

FREQUENCY CHANGE
DUE TO ENLARGEMENT

LOWERED

RAISED

LOWERED

RAISED

W₂

W₃

Q

R

S

CLOSED END

OPEN END

Fig. 22.3.   The Use of Perturbation Weight Functions for a Clarinetlike Air Column

theory because they are all based on the idea of taking the exact analysis of some simplified or familiar system and then working out the changes or perturbations produced in its behavior by various small changes in its structure.[3]

The top three lines of figure 22.3 show the perturbation weight functions W_1, W_2, and W_3 calculated for the first three modes of oscillation of air within a cylindrical pipe that is closed at the left-hand end. At the bottom of the figure is a pic-

ture of a slightly modified pipe whose properties we can estimate with the help of these curves. Any point along the air column where a given weight function curve is drawn above its axis is a point where enlarging the bore lowers the mode frequency. Conversely, a raised natural frequency results if the pipe is enlarged at a point where the weight function curve lies below the axis. For example, the top curve (W_1 for mode 1) shows that an enlargement located anywhere in the left-hand (closed-end) half of the pipe lowers the mode-1 natural frequency, while enlargement of any place in the right-hand (open-end) half of the tube raises it. Enlargement of the pipe at the point marked R, located about one-third of the way along the pipe from the closed end, lowers the first-mode frequency, raises that of mode 2, and makes only a slight decrease in the frequency of mode 3. It is to be emphasized that the W curves are not the same as the standing wave patterns (the W curves have more humps), so that a point where the perturbation has zero influence is to be construed as lying neither at a pressure node nor at a velocity node, but rather at some intermediate point.

Let us turn our attention now to the effect of a bulging enlargement located at a point Q fairly near to the closed end of the pipe. Mode 1 is lowered considerably, mode 2 is lowered only somewhat, while mode 3 is hardly altered at all, since the leftward and rightward halves of our perturbation straddle a zero of the W_3 curve, and so act oppositely on this mode's standing wave. Similar examination of the enlargement located at the point S near the open end shows that it raises the frequency of mode 1 considerably, raising mode 2 somewhat as well, while leaving mode 3 almost unchanged.

We are now in a position to extend our collection of statements about the effect of pipe size on perturbations.

2. In any air column, the natural frequency of a given mode can be raised or lowered by a given perturbation, depending on where it is applied. In a cylindrical air column, the maximum percentage change in the frequency (up or down) is equal to the percentage change in the total air volume that is produced by the perturbation, whether it is an enlargement or a contraction. Conical instruments are more sensitive to the effect of small perturbations.

3. The maximum frequency changes described in statement 2 come about when the perturbation extends over a very short segment of the air column located at the center of an upward or downward hump of the weight function. An example of such a perturbation is the short cavity produced when two sections of a woodwind are pulled apart slightly at the joint between them. A compact perturbation can have very irregular consequences over the playing scale of an instrument.

4. A more broadly distributed perturbation acts on the lower modes very much more than on the higher ones, whose weight functions W may oscillate appreciably across the span of the perturbation and so tend to average out. The action of wide and narrow perturbations applied at various points along a weight function is in exact analogy to the excitory effect of narrow or broad hammers acting at various points on a string.

A. Perturbations of the Clarinet Air Column. Let us apply our new knowledge of the effect of enlargements and constrictions to an examination of the effect of the tapered enlargement and bell that is found at the lower end of every normal clarinet. Let us first consider the air column produced by closing all the holes. Here we find that the lower quarter of the air column has been given a tapering enlargement that opens out eventually into the bell. We will temporarily ignore the complications of the mouthpiece and closed tone holes in the upper part of the bore, treating it as an ideal (nontapered) cylindrical pipe. If you make some sketches analogous to those in figure 22.3, it should not be difficult for you to deduce that the tapered perturbation at the lower end of the pipe raises mode 1, raises mode 2 slightly, and has almost no effect on mode 3. The consequences of these changes for the playing of the clarinet's bottom note are the following: the frequency ratio between resonance peaks 1 and 2 is less than the 3-to-1 value belonging to a straight pipe (the discrepancy typically amounts to 30 or 40 cents); peak 3 lies a roughly similar amount below the otherwise expected ratio of five times the frequency of mode 1. Because the perturbation spoils the whole-number relationship among the resonance frequencies, only very poor cooperation is possible in the low-register regime of oscillation, and the pitch of notes in the low register will depend strongly on the loudness with which they are played (see sec. 21.6, example 3).

Suppose that we now open one or two tone holes at the lower end of our clarinet, so that the standing waves reach down only a little way into the tapered part of the tube. There is thus only a small enlargement in the lowest fraction of the tube that is "visited" by the various weight functions. We find now that mode 1 is raised slightly because of the short perturbation at its lower end. Mode 2 is raised by a nearly equal amount, because the perturbation extends appreciably only over the last half hump of W_2. Mode 3 is raised in this case, but only slightly. The musical consequences for this note are as follows: since the frequency of peak 2 is raised nearly as much as that of peak 1, the frequency ratio between them is left very nearly in the 3-to-1 ratio preferred for good tone production (the discrepancy may be as small as 10 or 15 cents on a clarinet that has a good low register).

For our third example we will consider a fingering such as that used to play the low-register note C_4, where enough tone holes are left open for the lower part of the active air column not to reach down

into the expanded part of the instrument. Here there is no perturbation, so that the cooperations can be essentially perfect. While many clarinets have a frequency ratio between modes 1 and 2 that is 20 or 30 cents narrower than the value desired for best cooperation, it is perfectly possible to achieve an instrument in which the error in cooperation is no more than 5 cents for this part of the scale. Such instruments can be recognized instantly and are much admired by good players.

The design of the upper end of a clarinet calls for some rather subtle maneuvering, which is made very difficult by the use of only a single register hole. The instrument maker is presented with a dilemma—either he aligns the peaks to get a, good clear low-register note, or he leaves them unaligned (too close together) in order to get an accurate twelfth between notes in the low and second registers. Because the cooperative effects have not in the past been well understood and because tuning is very important to the musician, instruments are normally built to sacrifice low-register tone. However, everyone complains about the problem. An instrument in which an intermediate compromise is made usually proves very satisfactory in the hands of a good player, who generally notices the virtues of the unfamiliar arrangement rather than the problems caused by it. He is not likely to be particularly aware of the tuning changes, since he has already learned to make pitch corrections of an equal magnitude routinely elsewhere in the scale. He does not have to learn new habits of pitch correction: rather he adapts his old ones to the new circumstances.

The preceding paragraphs help us understand why it is that the bottom end of a clarinet is flared and the slight enlargement at the top end is smaller than what one might use to compensate for open tone-hole effects, closed-hole perturbations, and mouthpiece corrections. The most important function of the clarinet's conventional shape is to correct the tuning errors caused by the misplaced single register hole, which pulls mode 2 upward in frequency at both ends of the second-register scale. This shape has evolved through the past two centuries to give a fairly accurate played twelfth between the registers, but it does this at the expense of pitch stability, promptness of speech, and clarity of tone in the low register. Once again, I should emphasize that it is possible to make a musically successful compromise that is approved by practical musicians, although it is an unhappy business to temporize thus with a problem that could be done away with almost completely if the instrument were to be supplied with two properly proportioned register holes.

B. Perturbations of a Conical Air Column: The Bassoon. The perturbation weight function curves calculated for a conical air column have a rather different appearance from the sinusoidal W curves shown in figure 22.3 for the clarinet's cylindrical air column. However, a quick inspection of figure 22.4 indicates that we can deal with the perturbations of a conical instrument bore in exactly the same way we did in cylindrical air columns. At the top of this figure we see a schematic diagram of a bassoon air column. Immediately below this are the W_1 and W_2 curves drawn in approximately correct proportion for the fingering which produces the low-register note F_3. Notice that these curves are mostly crowded up into the bocal, where they retain only a qualitative significance. Because the first open tone holes must always occur at a point above

the "bottom" end of a standing wave, the weight function curves are shown to extend into the region of open tone holes. However, be warned that the curves lose their validity in this region; perturbations at this end must instead be dealt with using the theory of open tone holes.

Immediately below the weight function curves for F_3 in figure 22.4 we find those for C_3, which extend farther down the instrument. The bottom part of the figure is devoted to the weight function curves W_1 and W_2 as they apply to the first two modes used in playing the low-register note F_2.

The way in which one uses the W curves as a guide in adjusting a woodwind can easily be illustrated with the help of a simplified description of some of the things I did while improving a certain bassoon. Playing experiments and laboratory measurements agreed in showing that, under this instrument's playing conditions, the air column used to play F_3 was such as to make the frequency of resonance peak 2 more than double the peak-1 frequency, thus spoiling not only the tone and response of this note but also its tuning. In the middle of the low-register scale at the note C_3, the opposite error was observed: the frequency ratio between air-column modes 1 and 2 was less than two. Lower down in the scale, at F_2, the overall effect of the original air column was to provide an excellent alignment of peaks 1 and 2. This note played beautifully, so much so that it stood out among the rest of the notes of the low-register scale.

Since the upper part of the air column is common to all of the notes while the lower part affects only the lower ones, it was necessary to start the correction process at F_3 and work progressively down.

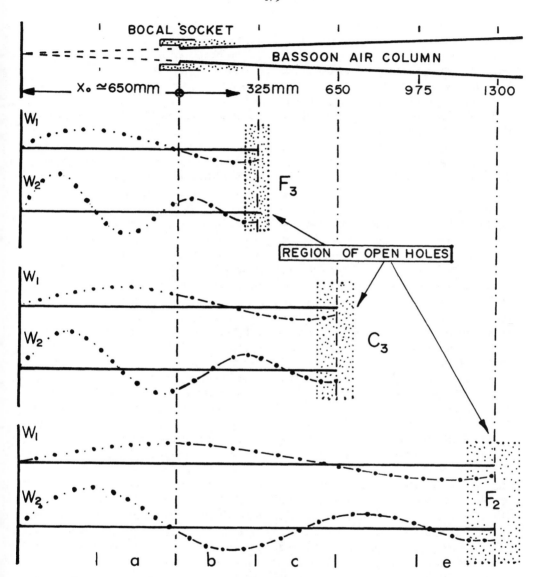

Fig. 22.4. The Use of Conical-Instrument W Curves for the Alignment of Various Notes on the Bassoon

For convenience in explaining the adjustments, various parts of the bassoon air column are given labels in figure 22.4: region (a), region (b), etc. A glance at the W_1 and W_2 curves for F_3 shows that sandpapering or reaming in the middle of region (b), which is near the top end of the bassoon's tenor joint, will raise the frequency of resonance peak 1 and slightly lower that belonging to peak 2. The alternation of reaming and testing soon led to a successful correction of the mode alignment errors of F_3. Inspection of the W curves for the note C_3 shows that the enlargement just described in region (b) had almost no effect on the resonances of this note, and in fact no change was noted in its playing properties after the first reaming. However, the originally beautiful F_2 was spoiled because enlargement of region (b) lowers mode 1 and raises mode 2 away from their original and desirable 2-to-1 frequency ratio. The correction of this new error was postponed, however, until C_3 was taken care of.

The air column for C_3 could not be trimmed up by working in region (b), because of its previous commitment to the correction of F_3. However, lacquering the bore along the upper two-thirds of region (c) to reduce its diameter lowered the frequency of peak 1 and raised that of peak 2. This process was carried on step by step until playing experiments showed that the intermode cooperation in the C_3 regime of oscillation was maximized. It was also confirmed that the adjustment of F_3 done earlier was not disturbed. Checking the F_2 fingering now showed (in agreement with the predictions of the W curves for this note) that reduction of bore diameter in region (c) somewhat off-

set the damage done to F_2 by our earlier reaming in region (b).

The next step in the alignment procedure was to correct the remaining wideness error in the frequency ratio between peaks 1 and 2 of the note F_2 by a slight reaming in region (d). The lower part of the bassoon air column was aligned in very similar fashion by correcting the behavior at C_2, and finally the bell segment of the instrument was adjusted during the testing of the bottom note, A_1#.

As a practical matter one must, when adjusting the cooperations in an instrument, keep running track of the pitches of the various notes of the instrument's low-register scale as well as of the quality of the regimes that produce them. It is also necessary (but not quite so important initially) to keep tabs on the behavior of the second and higher playing registers. The planning of the whole adjustment procedure requires a thorough understanding of the instrument and of the implications of various changes throughout the scale. Careful preliminary planning is essential if there is to be any hope of success in a game that is very similar to a diagramless crossword puzzle in three dimensions. One of the things that makes it possible to win such a game is the fact that air-column perturbations have their predominant influence on the lowest mode, whereas perturbations in the proportions of tone holes are most active at high frequencies. One makes sure the tone holes are plausible, corrects the bore, and then trims up the hole sizes. It may be worthwhile to go through the whole process again if the quality of the instrument and the skill of its player warrant the extra effort.

22.4. The Radiation of Sound from a Woodwind; Some Problems Faced by Recording Engineers

So far in chapters 21 and 22 we have confined our attention to the ways in which sounds are produced and controlled within the air column of a woodwind, and only at the beginning of chapter 21 was any mention made of the way internally generated sound makes its way out into the surrounding air. Let us recapitulate briefly what we have already learned about the sound-production process, and then consider the spectrum transformation function which relates the sound pressure spectrum measured within the reed cavity of a woodwind to the external spectrum that we obtain by a suitable averaging process within the listening room (see fig. 20.14 for the analogous transformation function for brass instruments).

Two of the things we learned in chapter 21 are (1) the strengths of various partials measured within the mouthpiece cavity tend to match the heights of the corresponding resonance peaks (see statement 3 in sec. 21.3) and (2) because of the leakage of high-frequency sound through the open tone holes, the tallness of the resonance peaks near (or especially above) cutoff are reduced from the heights they would have on a simple pipe without open tone holes. Taken together, these pieces of information imply that the existence of a cutoff frequency leads to an internal spectrum having progressively weaker upper partials, with only a small amount of sound production taking place above f_c (chiefly by heterodyne action).

The spectrum measured *outside* an in-

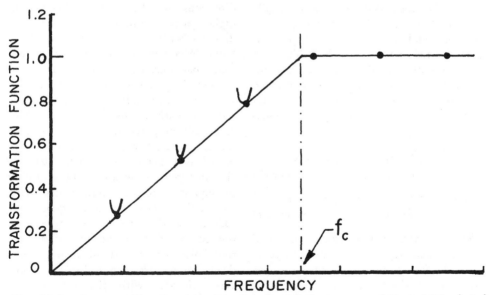

Fig. 22.5. Spectrum Transformation Function for All Components of Conical Woodwind Tones and Odd-Numbered Components of Clarinet Tones

strument does not show this weakening in the strengths of the upper partials to any great extent, because the instrument's greater efficiency for high-frequency radiation will "treble-boost" the weakened internal sounds as they make their way out of the instrument. Figure 22.5 shows the calculated variation of the spectrum transformation function T as it applies to all of the harmonics of a tone produced by a conical instrument that is provided at its open end with a very long sequence of open holes, all arranged to give the same cutoff frequency. The diagram also applies to the odd-numbered partials produced by a cylindrical (clarinet-type) instrument. Notice the peculiarly simple shape of the T curve: it is a sloping, straight line from zero frequency to cutoff, and a horizontal line thereafter. The effect of this transformation function can be summarized in two equations that show the relationship of the internally measured pressure amplitudes p_1, p_2, p_3, . . . and the amplitudes of the same partials measured externally.[4] The two equations apply to all the partials of conical instruments and to the odd-numbered ones of a clarinet (the change in behavior at f_c explains the necessity for two equations):

$$p_n(\text{external}) = np_n(\text{internal}) \times K$$
(for components below cutoff)

$$p_n(\text{external}) = (f_c/f_1)Kp_n(\text{internal})$$
(for components above cutoff)

Here K is a small numerical constant of no particular significance to us at present, f_c is the cutoff frequency, and f_1 is the frequency of the fundamental component of the tone being played. The above could be restated in hi-fi terms by saying that the filtering action of a set of open tone holes starts out with a treble boost at the rate of 6 dB/octave up to f_c, above which the transmission is flat.

The even-numbered partials of a clarinet tone are radiated much more strongly than are the odd-numbered ones. It is only a slight oversimplification to borrow the second one of the above formulas (which applies to odd-numbered components above cutoff) and use it for all the even partials of a clarinet tone, whether they are above or below cutoff. Just as in the case of the trumpet, the transformation function for woodwinds has narrow dips located at the resonance frequencies of the air column (see sec. 20.8). The anomalous behavior of the even partials of a clarinet is associated with the fact that these fall between the resonance peaks.

We learned earlier that the lower-frequency partials of brass instruments spread around the bell uniformly in all directions in the room, whereas the higher partials form a progressively more directed beam out along the axis of the horn. Woodwinds show a similar but somewhat more complicated behavior. It is possible to show mathematically and verify experimentally that an air column provided with a long row of open tone holes (all proportioned to give roughly the same cutoff-frequency) radiates each one of the below-cutoff partials equally in all directions, as measured by a distant microphone. Sound components lying only a little above cutoff are radiated in such a way that the signal produced by the combined contributions of all the tone holes is sent predominantly out and down along a sort of conical surface whose axis coincides with that of the instrument, while the partials whose frequencies are high (e.g., more than 50 percent greater than f_c) leave the tone holes and combine to form a fairly narrow beam that is aligned with the axis of the instrument, so that they appear to come directly from its bell.

It is easy to see from such details that a single distant microphone used in an anechoic chamber can give quite a misleading impression of the external spectrum of a woodwind, even more so than is the case with the brass instruments. The problem is compounded for woodwinds by the fact that a microphone placed only a meter or two away from the instrument may totally miss some one or another of the partials, or else pick up a grossly exaggerated amount of it (in either an anechoic chamber or a normal room). Small motions of the microphone or the player can completely rearrange the amplitude relationships among the partials. While it is best to use a studio-sized room for spectrum measurements and to make numerous independent measurements for eventual averaging, there is a microphone placement available that can give a reasonable imitation of the external spectrum for certain kinds of tones from a woodwind. Placing a tiny microphone within a few millimeters of the highest open tone hole of a normally fingered note will give a plausible spectrum, but the method fails for fork-fingered or cross-fingered notes. It is also useless of course for the recording of musical passages, because each note requires its own microphone placement.

The thoughtful reader will by now be asking himself whether the cutoff frequency is as musically important to the perceived sound of woodwinds as it is to an understanding of the behavior of these instruments. For instance, will changing the cutoff frequency of a tone-hole lattice produce an audible change in the emitted

sound? Stated another way, since a reduction of f_c will result in a reduction in the amplitudes of the internally generated partials, might not this reduction be exactly offset in the room by the increased efficiency with which these partials are radiated? Some of the answers to such questions will be given in the next section, but it is appropriate here to deal at least briefly with the subject.

In 1969, John Patterson, who is professor of bassoon and saxophone at the Louisiana State University School of Music, spent some months in Cleveland as a visitor in my laboratory; among the many experiments we carried out was one in which we recorded musical passages by means of a probe microphone carefully inserted into the bassoon reed cavity in such a manner as not to disturb its normal functioning. Such recordings are of course representative of the internal spectra produced by the instrument. When they are played back through an ordinary sound system one hears curiously muted tones that sound vaguely woodwindlike, but are not (to many listener's ears) recognizable as originating from a bassoon. However, when this recording is transmitted to a loudspeaker via an electronic filter arranged to simulate the transformation function, the result is at once recognizable as a bassoon sound. Experiments of this sort done with other conical instruments confirm the following conclusions:

1. Our ears process the low-register sounds coming to them from all directions in a room in such a way as to reconstruct the internal spectrum of a woodwind as it is modified by the spectrum transformation function. This is true despite the fact that no single sample of the direct or reverberant sound coming to the

listener's ears has a spectrum of exactly this nature.

2. The importance of the cutoff frequency in controlling the perceived sound also extends into the second register of a woodwind (unless the notes are cross-fingered), despite the fact that often only the first partial of the tone is directly supported by a strong resonance peak.

3. When internally recorded tones are passed through an electronic imitation of the transformation function, the result is a good imitation of normal sounds as long as the filter's cutoff frequency is approximately equal to that of the original instrument's tone holes. The instrument remains reasonably recognizable even in parts of its scale where the tone holes have a somewhat different cutoff frequency from that set on the filter.

4. The cross-fingered notes of the second and third registers are controlled by their own pair of cutoff frequencies, which parallel the normal ones since they are determined by new combinations of the same tone holes.

Clarinet experiments similar to the bassoon ones using a probe microphone are not so easy to carry out or interpret. The odd-numbered partials give no trouble, since they can all have their strengths compensated by a single electronic filter which will take care of all notes, just as in the case of the conical instruments. The even-numbered partials of the clarinet tone cannot be given such simple treatment, though, since they can only be compensated properly by means of special filter settings for these partials in each individual note.

Many of us who have the opportunity to listen closely to musicians in a variety of settings (in large and small concert halls, in the laboratory, or in our living rooms) are struck by the similarity of the sounds we hear them make in person in these varied surroundings, and struck even more by how different from this the recorded music produced by these same artists can be, even when it is recorded in the same concert hall in which we have heard them perform in person. Many a student has struggled to exhaustion to produce the tone which he hears in recordings by an admired performer, and an avid record listener may find himself disappointed when he goes to hear a favorite artist in person. There are two aspects of these discrepancies between live and recorded performances that are worth our comment here.

Microphone placement for musical recording is a difficult art. If the microphone is distant from the player in a large hall, the listener will be bothered by too much reverberant sound which his processor cannot cope with via the precedence effect; on the other hand, close microphone placement picks up predominantly those components of the direct sound that happen to be radiated in the direction of the microphone, so that the overall tone is altered because the listener is deprived of reverberant cues that let him deduce the complete spectrum. This sort of close miking may give the listener the sense of being "right there," but in many musical contexts it robs the performance of the wholeness conceived by a composer who originally planned his music for performance in a concert hall.

Superimposed on the tonal differences produced by microphone placement is the tendency for the engineer to "equalize" the recording by manipulation of various tone controls before transferring the music to its final form. It is of course impossible for him to deal accurately with the complexity of the radiation process, so he simply does the best he can. All too often the equalization is done by a man who listens to very little live music, and who may have altered his hearing by many hours of listening to monitor loudspeakers (or, worse, headphones) at sound levels that make anyone not inured to them cringe in pain. These are some of the reasons why so many records sold today have excessive treble and bass, to the annoyance of many performers and those listeners who are familiar with music played "live."

22.5. Characterization of a Woodwind by Its Cutoff Frequency

We have had many occasions to notice the important role played by the open holes cutoff frequency in determining the behavior of a woodwind instrument as it generates one note or another. We have also just learned of the important role it plays in the way we perceive woodwind

sounds in the concert hall. As it turns out, we can go so far as to use the cutoff frequency as a number that implies a great deal about the entire musical personality of the instrument, a number which can be followed through the course of the past two centuries of woodwind development. Let us see how this brought itself to my attention and then investigate some of its implications.[5]

In 1971, Michel Chotteau completed a project in my laboratory which called for the design and construction of a special clarinet in which the tone-hole cutoff frequency for each fingering was placed at exactly six times the corresponding low-register playing frequency.[6] To put it another way, Chotteau's clarinet was arranged to provide each tone in the low-register chromatic scale with three resonance peaks to collaborate with the reed. Figure 22.6 shows in condensed form the resonance curves that he measured on his

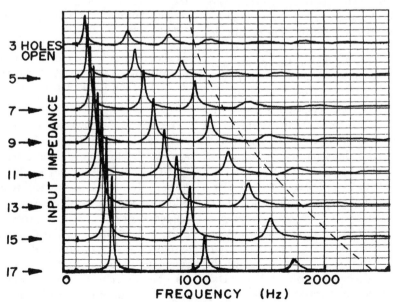

Fig. 22.6.   Resonance Curves for Various Notes on Chotteau's Clarinet

instrument. The top line shows the input impedance curve obtained when only three holes are opened at the bottom end of the instrument. The other curves belong to configurations having 5, 7, 9, . . . 17 holes open. In every case there are three well-marked peaks displayed below the cutoff frequency, the design value of which is indicated by a dashed line cutting downward and across the right-hand part of the diagram. Chotteau took pains to arrange the specified cutoff frequency and a carefully tuned chromatic scale on an air column whose peaks were quite accurate in their harmonic relationships. I helped him make the final adjustment (using a small scraper and a bottle of lacquer) in the alignment of the peaks for best cooperation with the reed for all notes in the low register.

This experimental instrument makes musically satisfying sounds that have great clarity, but we noticed at once something curious about it: the tone color at the lower end of its low-register scale is unusually dark (as a musician would describe it), and at the top end it is unusually bright. In the middle of the scale (near C_4) the sound is very similar to that of a clarinet of normal construction. While writing a description of his work, Chotteau commented that, despite the considerable irregularity in the *geometrical* proportions of the tone holes of a normal clarinet, the observed cutoff frequency for notes over the entire scale of most clarinets is roughly constant, lying near 1500 Hz. In other words, the *acoustical* proportions of the ordinary tone-hole layout are very uniform along the scale. On Chotteau's experimental clarinet, only the region near C_4 has a cutoff frequency that matches that for normal clarinets. This fact accounts in a general way for the sim-

ilarity of the sounds from the two instruments at this part of the scale. The observation that the bright tone was associated with the high-f_c end of Chotteau's scale and the dark tone with low f_c eventually gave me a hint as to the relationship between tone-hole design and overall tone color.

In recent years I have measured the cutoff frequencies of clarinets, oboes, and bassoons constructed over a considerable range of history, using only instruments in good condition which were or are now played by leading musicians, and which were made by some of the best craftsmen of their time. Three major conclusions can be drawn from these measurements:

1. On most of the standard woodwinds, the cutoff frequency remains roughly the same as tone holes are progressively opened to finger the notes of the low-register scale.

2. It proves possible to correlate the tone-color adjectives used by musicians to describe the overall tone of an instrument (dark or bright, for instance) with the value of its average cutoff frequency.

3. Trends in f_c on a given instrument run parallel to trends in the described tone color; furthermore, anomalies of certain notes on a given instrument can be related directly to local anomalies in f_c.

Figure 22.7 shows the cutoff frequencies measured for various oboes, plotted against the low-register note names that specify the various tone-hole arrangements. Number 2 in this family of curves is drawn with a heavy line to serve as a reference for the eye. This curve, which is quite typical of all modern conservatory-system oboes, was obtained from an instrument used in the Cleveland Orchestra. Notice how flat this curve is (i.e., how constant the cutoff frequently is) over the whole scale, except for the jog

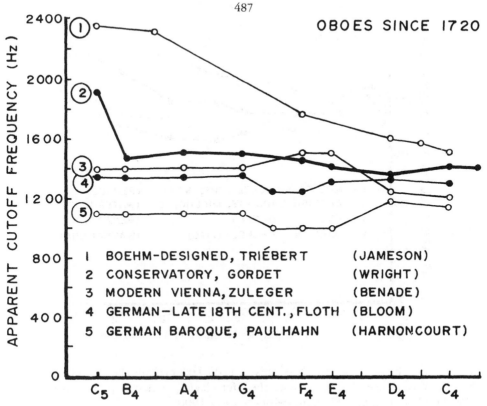

Fig. 22.7.   Cutoff Frequencies Measured for Various Oboes

upward to the 1900-Hz value found for C$_5$ at the top end of the low-register scale.

Curve 5 at the bottom of the figure shows similarly the range of cutoff frequencies for the baroque oboe that we met earlier in section 22.1. The instrument was made in 1720 and is quite typical of several instruments of its era that I have measured. We notice that the f$_c$ is close to 1100 Hz almost all the way across the scale, and that there is a slight dip in the neighborhood of F$_4$# through E$_4$. I will not discuss the other curves except to remark that the top one (number 1) was obtained from a beautifully constructed oboe whose acoustical design was worked out by the developer of today's flute, Theobald Boehm, in collaboration with the instrument's builder, Frederic Triébert, who developed the conservatory-system oboe which is almost universally used today. Notice the exceedingly high cutoff frequencies measured for this instrument, which was never considered musically successful chiefly because of an exceedingly bright tone that borders on harshness. It is otherwise a masterpiece of tuning and of workmanship, such as one might expect from its originators.

Let us turn our attention now to figure 22.8, which shows the variation of f$_c$ for a selection of bassoons. Curve 4, which is again shown by a heavy line, is typical of a first-quality Heckel bassoon. This particular instrument is one normally used

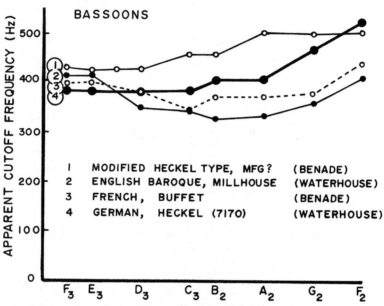

Fig. 22.8.   Cutoff Frequencies Measured for Various Bassoons

by the well-known British bassoonist William Waterhouse. Curve 1 shows the behavior of a modified Heckel-type instrument which has a relatively high cutoff frequency. It has a pleasant and full sound, although musicians typically remark that the sound is "somewhat too open."

Figure 22.9 shows the variation of cutoff frequency across the low-register scales of several clarinets. For reference purposes, the curves for both A and B♭ Boehm-system clarinets are drawn with heavy lines. One can see clearly the close correlation between the darker tone color and lowered f_c of the A clarinet relative to its B♭ brother. Clarinet number 4, a C clarinet from the time of Beethoven, is particularly interesting in this connection since it has a lower cutoff frequency than any of the other instruments. Cutoff frequencies on today's Boehm-system C clarinet normally lie in the region of

1700 Hz, making the instrument bright for playing orchestral parts written in the early 1800s.

I have taken a pair of brand new B♭ clarinets (part of a gift made in support of my research activities by Vito Pascucci and the Leblanc Corporation) and carefully reworked them so that one has its f_c raised by about 3 percent while the other has its f_c lowered an equal amount. Both instruments are well tuned and have excellent response. Players of classical music are very much attracted by the low-f_c instrument, while they consider the other clarinet to have been ruined; serious jazz clarinetists are equally positive in holding the opposite opinion! Both instruments have been borrowed from time to time for public performance. We have here a beautiful example of the way in which good musicians select their instruments to fit their musical requirements.

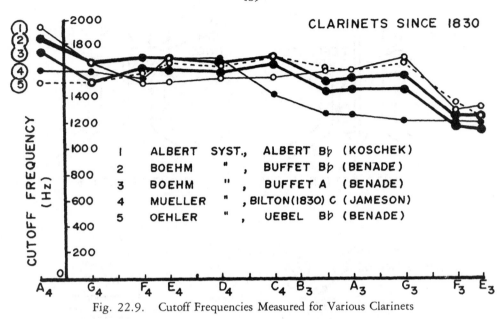

Fig. 22.9. Cutoff Frequencies Measured for Various Clarinets

22.6. The Flute Family of Instruments

The flow-control mechanism that is used to maintain the oscillation of flutes, recorders, and organ flue-pipes is of an entirely different sort from the one used by the reed woodwinds and brasses. In all of the instruments of the flute tribe, one directs a small jet of air *across* an opening located at one end of the instrument, rather than blowing directly *into* the mouthpiece through a reed. Even people who do not play the flute are likely to have had personal experience with this sort of sound production, since almost everyone has at some time made hooting sounds by blowing across the mouth of a bottle.

A. Helmholtz's View of Flow-Controlled Oscillation. The following is an adaptation (in terms of blowing across a bottle top) of Helmholtz's explanation of how flute-type oscillations are maintained.[7] A stream of air is directed across the opening of a bottle by the player. If he has chosen a proper angle and blowing pressure, an oscillatory flow of air will be set in motion in the neck of the bottle. As shown in the top of figure 22.10, when the oscillating air in the neck is flowing inward, the stream of air from the player's mouth is deflected so that a part of it also flows into the bottle. During the later phase of the oscillation, when the air in the neck is moving outwards, the stream of air from the player is also deflected out and away from the neck. The excitory flow of air is thus steered alternately into and out of the neck of the bottle by the acoustic flow variations of the oscillation. The player's air is directed into and out of the bottle exactly in step with the governing oscillatory flow, so that we are assured that an oscillation will be maintained.

This picture of the way in which a jet of air is steered in and out of the blowing end of a flute or organ pipe is, as we shall

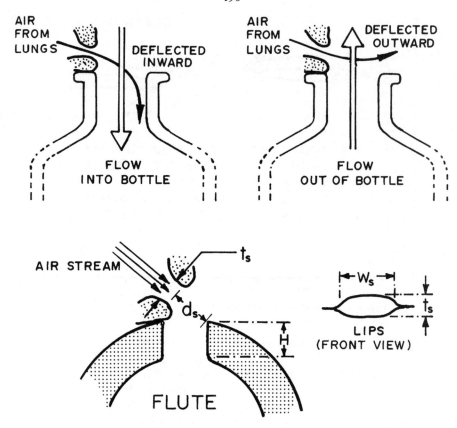

Fig. 22.10. Flow-Control Action for Air Blowing Across a Bottle or a Flute Embouchure Hole

see, somewhat simplifed, but it provides us with a good introduction to the notion of a *flow-controlled valve*, which may be contrasted with the pressure-controlled valves we have studied so far.

B. *Implications of Putting a Flute Head Joint onto a Clarinet.* A favorite lecture demonstration of mine, the purpose of which is to display the varying behavior of an air column when it is coupled first to one and then to the other of the two types of air controller, makes use of a special flute head joint made to fit on a clarinet as a replacement for its normal mouthpiece and barrel joint. When the instrument is played with this special head joint in place, the listeners are astonished to hear the characteristic sounds of a flute. Closer attention to what is going on shows that the low-register notes of this flute make up a well-tuned scale that is pitched an octave above the low-register clarinet sounds belonging to the · same fingerings. When the instrument is played as a flute the second-register notes are an octave above the low-register notes, while in its clarinet aspect the second register plays a twelfth above its low register. The high-register notes of this flute will not play, which is not hard to understand since they would lie above the tone hole cutoff frequency, and so are obliterated by the lack of whatever resonances are making the system work.

The acoustical implications of using a single cylindrical air column to produce both clarinet and flute sounds can be clarified if we imagine the experiments to be carried out with the help of a pipe whose length is such as to give resonance peaks at 100, 300, 500, 700, . . . Hz. When this pipe is coupled with a reed, the low-register regime of oscillation runs at the frequency of the first (100-Hz) peak with the help of the higher resonance peaks. The second register is dominated by the second peak, and so runs at 300 Hz, a musical twelfth higher in pitch.

When this pipe is played as a flute, the low-register tone is an octave higher in pitch than the clarinet tone. In other words, it has a fundamental frequency of 200 Hz, exactly halfway between the first and second resonance peaks of the air column. The flute's second register plays at 400 Hz, halfway between resonance peaks 2 and 3 of the pipe. Inspection of the resonance curve of a cylindrical pipe shows us that the *dips* in this curve lie at frequencies that are exactly halfway between the frequencies of the peaks. This observation introduces us to the first of a set of statements on the oscillation physics of the flute family.

1. A flow-controlled valve system collaborates with an air column at frequencies at which the air column has *minimum* input im-pedance, i.e., at the *dips* of our measured response curves. This is in contrast with the pressure-controlled valve, which works at the input impedance maxima, i.e., at the peaks.

2. The frequencies of minimum input impedance of an air column are identifiable as the characteristic frequencies belonging to this air column when the mouthpiece end is open to the air. It is therefore permissible to talk about these resonance dips in exactly the same way that we have heretofore talked about resonance peaks. (Recall that the impedance at a dip is the wave impedance divided by Q_0, whereas one multiplies by Q_0 to get the heights of the peaks.)

3. Regimes of oscillation are set up when an air column collaborates with a flow-controlled valve (we will sometimes refer to the latter as an *air reed*). The joint influence of various air resonance dips on these regimes shows much but not all of the behavior familiar to us from the reed woodwinds.

C. The Player's Control of the Air Reed. While in its barest essentials Helmholtz's model of an air reed is correct, it fails to take into account the inertia of the player's airstream; this inertia makes the airstream's deflections lag considerably behind the aerodynamic forces that are exerted on it by the oscillatory flow in and out of the flute's *embouchure hole* (which is the part of a flute that is analogous to the neck of the bottle). It also neglects the much subtler influence that one part of the stream exerts on its neighboring parts. Very careful measurements reported in 1968 by John Coltman on the sounding mechanism of the flute have formed the basis for further measurements and calculations presented in 1974 by the Australian physicist Neville Fletcher.[8] These reports, which greatly clarify and extend the meaning of much that was known earlier, give us much useful information on tone production by air-reed devices that form part of a musical instrument.

Digression on Flute Tones and the Edge Tones Produced by Free Air Jets.

Until recently there has been a tendency (evident in the literature) to confuse the sounds produced by blowing a narrow air jet against a sharp edge when the edge forms part of a flute or an organ pipe (air-reed behavior) with those produced when the system is run in isolation (edge-tone behavior). In the latter case a type of repetitive eddying called vortex shedding takes place on alternate sides of the air jet, and a sound is produced if a sharp edge is used to separate the two sets of vortices. Vortex phenomena have only a secondary influence on flute-type sound production; moreover, at ordinary musical blowing pressures the edge-tone frequencies are so high as to be nearly inaudible. Bouasse was one of several acousticians who performed definitive experiments to show the distinction between the two types of sound production.

The lower part of figure 22.10 shows in cross section the way in which a flute player places his lips next to the embouchure hole to direct a stream of air across it and down against its far side. The symbol t_s will denote the thickness of the excitory airstream, w_s its width, and d_s the distance it travels across the embouchure hole to the opposite side. The letter H denotes the height of what is called the *riser* or the *chimney* of the embouchure hole; this dimension is of course strictly analogous to the thickness t of pipe wall through which an ordinary tone hole is drilled.

Depending on whether the blowing pressure in the player's mouth is large or small, the airstream (and any transverse disturbances which may be set up in it) travels the distance d_s in a shorter or longer time. It should be fairly obvious that there must be a suitable relationship between this *transit time* and the timing of the inward and outward parts of the oscillatory flow that deflects the stream. Let us elaborate on this idea in some additional numbered statements:

4. Everything in the flow-control mechanism of a flute depends on the relation between the transit time (the time it takes disturbances in the stream to travel a distance d_s from the player's lips to the far side of the embouchure hole) and the repetition time (the period of oscillation) of each of the sound components present in the tone.

5. The type of oscillatory support most like that depicted in figure 22.10 takes place most strongly if the transit time has a duration equal to half the time of oscillation of a given partial. Oscillations can also be maintained by this sort of influence when the transit time is shorter or longer than this value by less than about 50 percent. This simplest type of excitation is used in every playing register to sustain the fundamental component of the flute tone.

6. Certain relations between transit time and the repetition time of the higher partials of the tone allow the higher partials to enter actively into the regime of oscillation.

7. Certain other partials have repetition times whose relation to the transit time causes the air reed to work against the maintenance of oscillation.

The flute player has great flexibility in tone production because there is a *range* of transit times that will suit the maintenance of each note of the scale. Furthermore, he has many optional ways in which he can attain the desired transit time, because he is free to trade off a larger or smaller stream distance d_s against a smaller or larger flow velocity. He can control the thickness t_s and the width w_s of the airstream by altering the spacing between his lips as well as the angle at which he blows. All of these things permit the skilled player to elicit musically useful sounds from practically any sort of flute, whether it is properly made or not; on a well-made instrument, they give him an enormous (but seldom fully exploited) range of tonal possibilities. We learned for example in chapter 5 that the odd-numbered partials of the flute tone can be smoothly weakened while the even ones grow to the point of producing an imperceptible transition from the low to the second playing register. This can be done at any playing level above pianissimo. Another example of the control of the variables shows up in certain recorders that are *voiced* (i.e., given values of d_s, t_s, and w_s) in such a way as to weaken partials 2 and 4 greatly, while leaving the odd-numbered ones, 1, 3, and particularly 5, strongly present in the low-register tone. Flute players also have this as an option.

D. Suitable Shapes for a Flute-Type Air Column. We already have a preliminary idea about the air-column shapes that will give whole-number frequency ratios between their resonance dips: since a cylindrical pipe has its peaks arranged in a 1, 3, 5 . . . frequency relationship, it is

not surprising to find that the same pipe is able to play as a flute on the dips located at the interlaced frequencies 2, 4, 6, etc. Further inquiry into the properties of air columns shows that *any* straight-sided air column, cylindrical or conical, will have its input impedance dips arranged in the desired way (although in a cone the peaks are no longer symmetrically placed between the dips). The top part of figure 22.11 shows the three prototype flute possibilities: a cone that grows, a cylinder of constant diameter, and a cone whose diameter shrinks as we go away from the blowing end.

For reasons that will become apparent in part E of this section, good cooperation among the members of each low-register regime of oscillation requires that the head-joint end of any flute be contracted relative to the main trend of its body. This shrinking of the head joint (the need for which was discovered late in the seventeenth century) is illustrated in the lower part of figure 22.11.

The standing-wave patterns for the various modes in these three air columns are very similar to one another, so that it will suffice for us to look at only one. Figure 22.12 shows the basic structure of a cylindrical flute, together with the

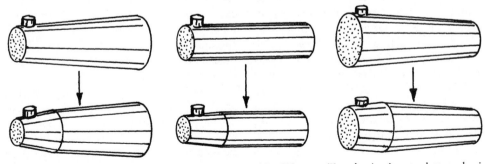

Fig. 22.11. Suitable Shapes for a Flute-Type Air Column. *Top,* basic shapes; *bottom,* basic shapes modified by required contraction at blowing end.

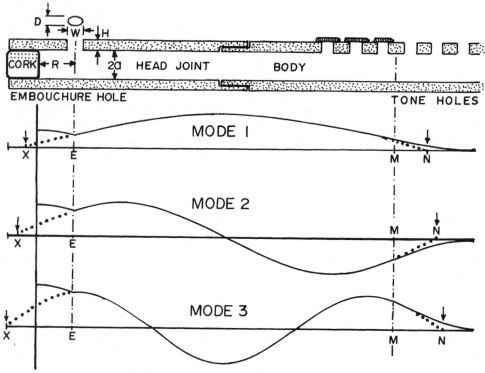

Fig. 22.12.   First Three Pressure Standing Wave Patterns for a Flute

standing pressure-wave patterns belonging to its three lowest modes. At the right-hand end of the flute, where the tone holes are open, the standing waves have a character that is identical with that seen in the lower part of a reed woodwind. The behavior in the neighborhood of the embouchure hole, however, is quite different. There is a kink or break in the pattern at the embouchure hole position E, of the sort that we have seen before in connection with a single register hole or tone hole. To the left of this kink, the pressure amplitude rises to a local maximum at the position of the head-joint cork. The main tendency of the left end of each mode's standing wave is to

head toward a pressure node (whose position is marked X in the diagram for each mode). We shall speak of the distance from E to X as the embouchure hole length correction C_{emb}, and think of it in exactly the same way as we did the open holes lattice correction C that represents the analogous distance MN at the right-hand end of each standing wave (see fig. 21.1).

As indicated by the changing position of X in the different parts of figure 22.12, the magnitude of the embouchure hole correction C_{emb} varies with frequency. While the diagram only shows it growing, different relationships between the cork-to-embouchure hole distance R and the embouchure-hole dimensions (width W, breadth D, and riser height H) can make C_{emb} either grow or shrink. In 1965 James French and I published an article on flute head-joint acoustics.[9] We showed among other things that, no matter how it varies at high frequencies, C_{emb} always starts out with a low-frequency value given by the formula:

$$C_{emb} = (4a^2/DW)H_e$$

Here a is the radius of the air column, while H_e is the effective height of the chimney as it is increased by the nearness of the player's lips (see also the explanation in sec. 21.4, part B, of the analogous quantity t_e that applies to tone holes). The most important function of the head-joint cork is to provide, in conjunction with the player's lip position, a suitably varying value for C_{emb}; this serves to clean up the last subtle details of the air column perturbations that are needed for good alignment of the modes. On most flutes C_{emb} is in the neighborhood of 50 mm.

E. Perturbation Curves for the Flute and the Need for a Reduced Head-Joint Diameter. Inspection of a flute's perturbation curves can show us why a flute needs to have the diameter of its air column shrunken slightly in the neighborhood of the embouchure hole, and can illustrate some of the tricks that are available to any instrument maker. Figure 22.13 shows the first- and second-mode perturbation curves for the notes D_4, G_4, B_4, and $C_5\sharp$. Sketched at the top of the figure is an air column that is similar to those used before the development in 1847 of the familiar cylindrical Boehm flute; this air-column shape is based in particular on an extremely successful flute that I designed

and built in 1973, which combines the modern Boehm mechanism with a tone-hole size giving a cutoff frequency (and resultant tone color) characteristic of the older flutes. Most of the examination of the nature of (and reasons for) the various jogs and irregularities will be postponed to the final section of this chapter.

Notice in figure 22.13 that the right-hand ends of all the W curves (near the tone holes) look very much like those for the reed woodwinds, whereas at the blowing end the effect of a perturbation on flutes is the opposite of that produced on other instruments. In particular, the contraction which has been noticed at the top end of every flute has the effect of widening the frequency ratio between mode 1 and mode 2 beyond the 2-to-1 value that goes with the simplest flute tubes. On a good flute we find that the perturbation of the measured mode-2 resonance frequency puts it 25 to 35 cents more than an octave above the measured first-mode frequency. On such a flute, this widening must be arranged to be uniform over the whole low-register scale.

The need for a contraction in the head joint of a flute may seem a little paradoxical to those of you who have come to understand the benefits conferred by accurate harmonicity in the resonances of a wind-instrument air column. Let us see what the explanation is for the apparent exception in flutes. John Coltman has shown that when a stream of air is used to excite the oscillation of an air-column mode, the presence of the stream lowers the natural frequency *of the mode itself* when the system is gently blown, and raises it under hard-blowing conditions. This alteration explains why the sounding pitch of a whistle can vary (by as much as a semitone) when one tries to play a cre-

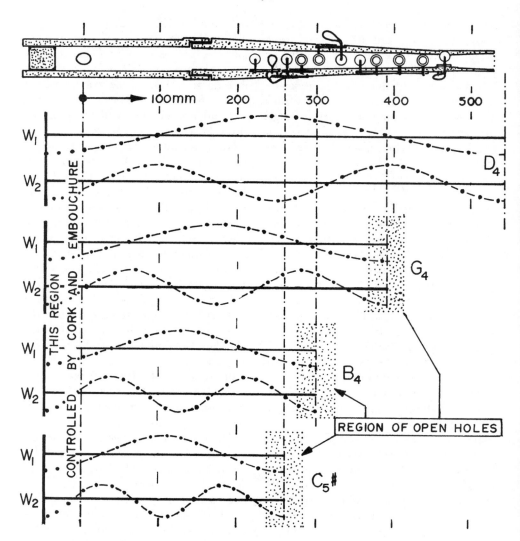

Fig. 22.13. The Use of W Curves for the Alignment of Various Notes of Any Flute

scendo or diminuendo. It also explains in part why the playing frequency of a flute seldom matches the *unblown* resonance frequency as normally measured in the laboratory. In 1967 Walter Worman and I succeeded in measuring the resonance curves of various air columns while an air reed was acting on them to produce a tone.[10] Our observations of the behavior of the resonance that supports the fundamental component of the tone agree exactly with those of Coltman (although we did not obtain the detailed numerical information that he was able to get). We obtained an additional important piece of information: the air-column mode that lies near the second harmonic of the tone being sounded does *not* have its frequency shifted by the excitatory airstream. The musical significance of this result is that at pianissimo playing levels in the low register, the second air-column mode has little influence on the regime of oscillation, so that there is no limitation on its placement relative to the frequency of the first mode. As one plays harder, the oscillatory regime picks up the influence of the second-harmonic component of the tone as it "talks" to the second air-column resonance. At the same time, the first-mode frequency is rising under the influence of the harder blowing. If the unblown second air-column resonance is not placed (by suitable perturbations of the air column) at a frequency that is more than twice that of the unblown first-mode resonance, it will lie too low for good cooperation when the instrument is played loudly, since it does not move up as the blowing is strengthened.

It is possible to arrange flute-type instruments to play particularly well at any desired wind pressure (even with fixed arrangements of the airstream, as in a recorder); this can be done simply by perturbing the air-column shape to locate the second resonance exactly an octave above the shifted first resonance produced at the specified blowing pressure. But the problem is to find a relationship that will work well at all dynamic levels. This can be accomplished by carefully shrinking the top of the head joint (and sometimes also perturbing other parts of the instrument). The resulting widening of the octave relationship counterbalances the narrowing of the octave that happens in loud playing, as the low register moves up in pitch relative to the second register. Sensitive playing experiments based on this phenomenon can be used to guide the adjustment of flute-type instruments for good musical usefulness. The adjustments themselves are of course carried out in a manner reminiscent of that described earlier for the bassoon. There is clear evidence that many of the leading makers of flutes and recorders in the past knew a good deal about such techniques (though of course not in scientific terms). Curiously enough, the makers of artist-quality flutes today (with one or two individual exceptions) show very little knowledge of such methods, as is evidenced by the variable quality of the instruments many of them produce.

F. Limitations on the Highest Playable Note of a Flute. In the course of adjusting any flute for best playing in its lowest two registers, one observes that a difference of a tenth of a millimeter in the position of the cork relative to the embouchure hole has a recognizable influence on the playing behavior of the instrument. To a practiced ear, the change in response and clarity can sometimes be heard across the room. One notices also that some flutes become very difficult indeed to play in the higher register if their head-joint corks are adjusted to make them play best in the lower two registers. This is invariably associated with an unusually large cork distance. For example, on baroque flutes, which have a cylindrical head and a tapered bore, the typical cork-to-embouchure distance is about 25

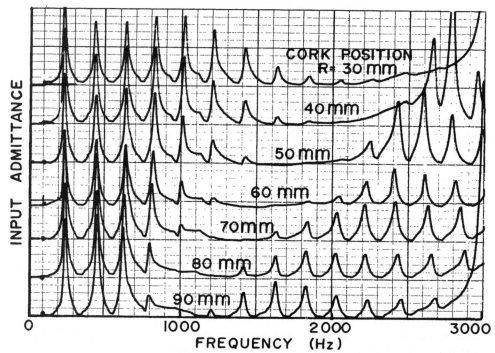

Fig. 22.14.   Influence of Cork Position on the Input Admittance Curves of a Flute

mm as against the 17 mm that is typical of the Boehm design. On such a baroque flute one can hardly force notes above G_6. Furthermore, notes that can be played near this top note become very stuffy, as though the resonances were heavily damped. Let us seek the acoustical reason for the difficulty with high notes.[11] We should recall that the flute's flow-control mechanism favors oscillation at frequencies near the impedance dips as measured at the embouchure hole. Acoustical engineers sometimes find it convenient in their work to speak of the input *admittance* of an air column rather than the input impedance.[12] Since the admittance is defined simply as the reciprocal of the impedance, a dip in the impedance curve corresponds exactly with an admittance

peak, and vice versa. As a result we can say that flutes run themselves with the help of the admittance peaks of an air column, whereas clarinets, etc., run on the impedance peaks.

The top resonance curve shown in figure 22.14 shows the input admittance measured at what might be called the embouchure hole of a T-shaped piece of copper tubing having a cork-to-hole distance R of 30 mm. Notice that the peaks start out with a 2, 4, 6 sequence of frequency ratios of the sort we expect for a cylindrical tube. There also seems to be some kind of cutoff frequency near 2000 Hz despite the fact that there are no tone holes! It is this phenomenon that we will need to study more closely.

The second, third, etc., curves in figure 22.14 show the effect of increasing the cork-to-hole distance R, with the length of the main tube being adjusted in each case to keep the first-mode resonance frequency the same. When we look at all the curves together, it is plain that there is a sort of 'dead' spot in each one of them where there are no resonances at all, even though there are strongly marked peaks on both sides of it at higher and lower frequencies.

You may by now have formed the correct suspicion about the reason the top notes of a flute are so sensitive to the position of the cork. If R is increased, the dead spot in the resonance curve moves to lower frequencies, and so kills off the top notes of the instrument. On either side of this dead spot, the admittance peaks are less tall than normal, and so make the instrument difficult to play. The head joint of a baroque flute can be made to play at notes above C_7, using resonances above the dead spot, even though this spot kills off the possibility of playing in the region just above G_6. It is possible to follow trends of this sort by moving the cork on any flute.

If we refer back to figure 22.12, we can see the acoustical origin of the dead spot. We have already noticed that the left-hand node of each standing wave lies beyond the cork position. As we go to higher and higher modes, the position of the embochure hole itself lies ever closer to the first pressure maximum of the standing wave. The dead region we have been talking about is located in a frequency region which puts the embouchure hole near a pressure maximum of the standing wave. Mode 3 in figure 22.12 is drawn to illustrate this state of affairs.

22.7. The Effect of Wall Material on the Playing Properties of Wind Instruments

The question of whether or not the playing properties of a wind instrument are influenced by the material from which it is made has been the subject of curiously bitter controversy for at least 150 years. We at once recognize the influence of dimensional changes that may be forced on an instrument maker when, for example, he makes a wooden rather than a silver flute, or those inadvertent ones which come about from the different ways in which a bore reamer cuts wood and plastic. At a subtler level, many kinds of things can lead to questions concerning the influence of materials: when identical woodwind air columns are made using wall materials of different porosity or rigidity, the resulting sounding pitch of the instrument may vary by as much as twenty cents; thin-walled instruments on which one can feel vibrations are often improved (but sometimes spoiled) by putting layers of adhesive tape on the outer surface at an empirically chosen spot; repairmen and players alike are aware of the quite noticeable changes in the playing properties of an instrument when pads of differing material are installed for use in covering the tone holes, or when the bore is oiled.

Theory also poses questions, some of which are not hard to answer. For instance, it has been known for many decades that the walls of a perfectly round pipe cannot vibrate enough to radiate audible sounds into the room. When such a pipe is slightly out-of-round (elliptical), it can be excited much more strongly by internal pressure variations, but even so it cannot radiate sound into the room with sufficient amplitude to be heard in the presence of the other sources of excitation. Because of this, changes in the material or the thickness of the walls cannot detectably alter the sound of an instrument insofar as it depends on radiation by the walls.[13]

The vibration of wind-instrument walls can sometimes influence the playing behavior significantly for a different reason. Just as vibrations of the piano soundboard can alter the natural frequencies of the string modes, so also wall vibrations can alter the frequencies of the air column. The air column "looks" oversize at points of large wall vibration if the natural frequency of the wall lies above that of the air mode which drives it, and undersize when this frequency relationship is reversed. I have seen instruments (thin-walled metal flutes in particular) whose behavior seems perfectly insane unless the complex influence of wall vibrations on regimes of oscillation throughout the scale is suitably damped out.

In wind instruments, the vibrational damping provided at the walls by air friction, oscillatory temperature effects, porosity, etc., far outweighs the damping produced by the escape of sound through the tone holes into the room. Because the player and his reed are in the business of maintaining an oscillation in the air column, it is clear that the major portion of his physical effort is devoted to the feeding of acoustic energy directly to the walls of his instrument. Since different materials provide varying amounts of damping, it is logical to wonder about the magnitude of this effect.

Since 1958 I have made several studies of the possible differences in damping that can be made by using copper, silver, brass, nickel silver, or various kinds of wood as the air-column wall material. If the walls are thick enough not to vibrate and if they are smooth and nonporous, experiment and theory agree that switching materials will make changes in the damping that are generally less than the two-percent change that most musicians are able to detect.

Turbulence in the vibrating air is another phenomenon that can be influenced by the nature of the wall material, though the relation is indirect, since it comes from the ability of the material to take and keep a sharp edge. The presence of sharp edges brings about airstream turbulence at blowing pressures lower than those that would elicit it in the absence of such edges. As one plays louder than mezzo forte on a flute, oboe, or clarinet, the sound level becomes high enough for new phenomena to appear. At mezzo forte, the oscillatory flow through the first one or two open tone holes is no longer of the simple, smooth-flowing type found in soft-playing, but neither is it quite of the fully developed turbulent type that causes the rushing and roaring noises from a strong wind. Two undesirable things happen in the tone holes when turbulence starts: (a) the damping rises greatly, even before the tone holes begin to hiss in a manner that is familiar to many players, and (b) the nature of the flow through the holes is such as to make them act as though their sizes had been changed, thus spoiling the careful voicing adjustments of the instrument. From this point it is only a short path to the realization that rounding the corners of the tone holes and of any other projections or angles in the air column (e.g., at the junctions of its various parts) will postpone and regularize the onset of turbulence and so make the instrument play well over an extended dynamic range, provided that these corner roundings are carried out in a way that preserves the acoustical alignment of the instrument. In 1972 John Cuddeback worked with me to measure the damping of a clarinet air column over a wide range of excitations, before and after its corners were carefully rounded. The results confirmed these conclusions and resolved certain discrepancies in some earlier experiments.[14]

The connection between sharp edges on the corners of an instrument and the material from which it is made is not difficult to find: instruments normally come out with their corners sharper when plastic or metal is used than when wood is the material of choice. It is the instinctive tendency of a skilled craftsman to show his competence by producing crisp clean edges for all his tone holes and joints, and the degree of sharpness of these corners depends very much on the nature of the materials with which he works and the sort of tools he uses. I have found historical and contemporary examples of instruments made by the best workmen in which the corners were deliberately rounded, as well as those (much more common today) which are left with sharp corners. In every case players prefer the ones with rounded corners. In the normal course of traditional instrument-making, rounded corners are most often produced on wooden instruments. A number of metal and plastic instruments which I have reworked have prompted musicians to remark in public that they play just like good wooden ones; players have also remarked that instruments I have worked on have good "personalities" which are independent of the materials from which they are made. One must of course be sure that the mouthpiece, the air column, and the tone holes are properly adjusted to one another, since mere postponement of turbulent damping does not by itself give an attractive instrument.

It is interesting to consider the history of woodwind-making in the light of the turbulence phenomena. In the old days when undercutting of tone holes was prevalent, the general sharpness of corners in all handmade woodwinds was slight enough that turbulence effects were usually not very noticeable. By the mid-nineteenth century, woodwinds were beginning to be made with accurate jigs for drilling precisely sized holes in their exact position along the instrument. Corners became sharp and neat as harder materials came into use and also as an indication of fine workmanship—all of which provided the perfect conditions for nurturing turbulence troubles! Instrument makers found that the more "scientific" they became in their mechanical methods, the more unsatisfactory the older designs became and the more sensitive the instruments became to the material from which they were made. Essentially all of today's mass-produced woodwinds would benefit from a careful rounding of tone-hole corners. Our growing understanding of these things suggests simple solutions to many problems that have heretofore seemed to require an alteration in the tone-hole design and the key mechanism. (Note: the embouchure hole of a flute cannot be tinkered with in simple application of these suggestions.)

22.8. Examples, Experiments, and Questions

1. On a bassoonlike instrument played mezzo forte with a certain embouchure pressure on the reed, the first three resonance peaks lie at 100, 198, and 291 Hz,

and they work together to produce a tone whose fundamental frequency is a little below 100 Hz. A *very slight* increase in the player's lip pressure reduces the reed cavity volume enough to raise the resonance frequencies to 101, 205, and 320 Hz. While the change is being made, it is found that the playing pitch jumps abruptly by nearly a semitone, so that the fundamental frequency now lies near 104 Hz. See section 22.1, statement 10, for the reason why the percentage change in frequency is so much larger for the higher modes than for the lowest mode. This abrupt jump in pitch is a phenomenon that is familiar to players of many baroque instruments and certain of today's bassoons. Can you figure out the reason for it? How would you alter the air-column shape to prevent this behavior.

2. Reaming to make a slight enlargement in the top end of a clarinet barrel joint and the bottom end of the mouthpiece causes, as its most significant result, a rise in the pitch of the note E_6, which is played with dominant support by mode 3 of the air column used in playing C_4. See if you can figure out where this enlargement falls on the perturbation curves shown in figure 22.3. Hint: mode 2 is left almost unchanged, while mode 1 is slightly lowered, so this reaming may help somewhat in the playing of the low-register note.

3. The curves giving the cutoff frequencies for various notes in the scale of oboes, bassoons, and clarinets (see figs. 22.7, 22.8, and 22.9) can be used for estimating the number of cooperating peaks that are available to support each note in the low-register scale. For instance, on a conical instrument having f_c at 1300 Hz, the note G_4 (392 Hz) is played with the help of three resonance peaks; the third

peak lies below cutoff near 1176 Hz, whereas a fourth peak, near 1570 Hz, cannot exist. On a tarogato, f_c is very nearly constant over its scale. What does this imply about the "feel" and tone of the instrument when it plays C_5 and C_6? (Recall that the tarogato is a transposing instrument pitched in B♭.)

4. The responsible recording engineer at a classical music recording session will try to keep a reasonable distance between the player and the microphone. If he places the microphone above the head of a clarinetist or oboist, the direct sound will be very deficient in the downward-aimed higher partials, which are only recorded by way of reflections off the floor and scattering by nearby musicians. The resulting sound is typically judged to be a little dull. If the microphone is placed out in front or a little to the side, about waist-high for the player, a stronger share of the medium-frequency partials just near f_c will be recorded directly, and the partials well above cutoff will also be reflected strongly into the microphone. The resulting sound will be much more realistic, but a little on the bright side. Why is it impossible to equalize a recording made in either of these ways to match what one would hear in a live concert?

5. On a flute, lengthening the cork-to-embouchure-hole distance R, raising the chimney height H, reducing the hole size WD, and covering more of the hole with the lips are interchangeable ways of increasing C_{emb} for the lower few modes. Notice that changes in any of these can be offset by changes in the others, to permit reconciling the many requirements that must be met. One effect of an increase in C_{emb} is to slide all the perturbation (W) curves to the left in figure 22.13. Verify that this change lowers the ratio between

the frequencies of modes 1 and 2 in all parts of the scale. This effect is the basis of the final trimming-up of a good flute.

6. On the flute shown in figure 22.13, the cylindrical head joint was given a slightly larger diameter than the top end of the main cone. Perhaps you can figure out why the difference in the mode tuning caused by this slight oversize joins with the cavity deliberately left in the joint in offsetting the ratio-narrowing produced by a low cutoff frequency near C_5. Why must the bottom end of such a flute flare out in the region below the tone holes?

7. Our recognition of the importance of turbulence in the air columns of loudly played instruments puts us in a good position to understand why "poor venting" and fork-fingerings have traditionally been a bugbear to the instrument maker. Not only must he try to preserve the intermode cooperations in order to get a good solid mezzo-piano tone, he must also cope with the fact that the tendency toward turbulent dissipation rises in direct proportion to the magnitude of the open holes length correction C. Increasing the hole size will partially accomplish the desired effect, but thinning the wall by counterboring to get f_c right (as one might also propose) can easily make the turbulence worse. Holes that are ill-vented (in the traditional sense) need to have their sizes chosen and their corners rounded with particular skill if they are not to be troublesome. This is almost a lost art today, and most of the possessors of it do not seem to be consciously aware of what they are doing—they seem simply to be following a magnificent instinct.

Notes

1. A. H. Benade and J. M. Gebler, "Reed Cavity and Neck Proportions in Conical Woodwinds" (abstract), *J. Acoust. Soc. Am.* 55 (1974): 458.

2. Cornelis J. Nederveen, *Acoustical Aspects of Woodwind Instruments* (Amsterdam: Frits Knuf, 1969), pp. 34–41. John Backus, "Small Vibration Theory of the Clarinet," *J. Acoust. Soc. Am.* 35 (1963): 305–13.

3. E. V. Jansson and A. H. Benade, "On Plane and Spherical Waves in Horns with Non-Uniform Flare: I, Theory," *Acustica* 31 (1974): 79–98; see section 9. See also A. H. Benade, "On the Mathematical Theory of Woodwind Finger Holes," *J. Acoust. Soc. Am.* 32 (1960): 1591–608, section IV-B. Another very useful approach is described in P. Mermelstein, "Determination of the Vocal-Tract Shape from Measured Formant Frequencies," *J. Acoust. Soc. Am.* 41 (1967): 1283–94. Also see M. R. Schroeder, "Determination of the Geometry of the Human Vocal Tract by Acoustic Measurements," *J. Acoust. Soc. Am.* 41 (1967): 1002–1010.

4. The mathematical physics underlying this section and the next one is worked out in part VII of Benade, "Mathematical Theory of Woodwind Finger Holes."

5. A. H. Benade, "Characterization of Woodwinds by Tone-Hole Cutoff Frequency" (abstract), *J. Acoust. Soc. Am.* 54 (1973): 310.

6. Michel Chotteau, "The Isospectrum Clarinet System" (master's thesis, Case Western Reserve University; Cleveland, Ohio, 1971).

7. Hermann Helmholtz, *On the Sensations of Tone,* trans. Alexander Ellis from 4th German ed. of 1877, with material added by translator (reprint ed., New York: Dover, 1954), p. 92.

8. The basis for our current understanding of flow-controlled oscillations is contained in L. Cremer and H. Ising, "Die selbsterregten Schwingungen von Orgelpfeifen," *Acustica* 19 (1968): 143–53; John W. Coltman, "Sounding Mechanism of the Flute and Organ Pipe," *J. Acoust. Soc. Am.* 44 (1968): 983–92; and N. H. Fletcher, "Nonlinear interactions in organ flue pipes," *J.*

Acoust. Soc. Am. 56 (1974): 645–52. H. Bouasse, *Instruments à Vent,* 2 vols. (Paris: Librairie Delagrave, 1929 and 1930), also gives a great deal of worthwhile attention to the excitation mechanisms of flutes and flue organ pipes. Much of the other literature on this subject is riddled with errors. Use the bibliographies of Cremer and Ising, of Coltman, and of Fletcher as your guide to trustworthy material.

9. A. H. Benade and J. W. French, "Analysis of the Flute Head Joint," *J. Acoust. Soc. Am.* 37 (1965): 679–91. The mathematical physics in this paper proves to be essentially correct. However, the reasons given for the reduced head-joint diameter are incorrect. The next part of this chapter deals with this question. See also John W. Coltman, "Mouth resonance effects in the flute," *J. Acoust. Soc. Am.* 54 (1973): 417–20.

10. A. H. Benade and W. E. Worman, "Search-Tone Measurements in Blown Wind Instruments" (abstract), *J. Acoust. Soc. Am.* 42 (1967): 1217.

11. A. H. Benade, "Flute Headjoint Cork Position and Damping of Higher Modes" (abstract), *J. Acoust. Soc. Am.* 54 (1973): 310.

12. One of the attractive features of the impedance-measuring devices devised by Merhaut and by Coltman (see the digression in sec. 20.3) is that they require only a simple interchange of connections to adapt them for admittance measurements, which then allow us to see clearly what is going on in the air-column frequencies that are important to flutes.

13. John Backus, "Effect of Wall Material on the Steady-State Tone Quality of Woodwind Instruments," *J. Acoust. Soc. Am.* 36 (1964): 1881–87, and John Backus and T. C. Hundley, "Wall Vibrations in Flue Organ Pipes and Their Effect on Tone," *J. Acoust. Soc. Am.* 39 (1966): 936–45. The reader will find it interesting to figure out why the interpretations placed by the authors on these carefully executed experiments are at variance with my own conclusions.

14. A. H. Benade and John K. Cuddeback, "Quasi-Turbulent Damping at Wind Instrument Joints and Tone Holes" (abstract), *J. Acoust. Soc. Am.* 55 (1974): 457. Earlier indications of the phenomenon are to be found in Coltman, "Sounding Mechanism of the Flute."

23

The Oscillations of a Bowed String

Bowed string instruments such as the violin, viola, cello, and bass viol are like the wind instruments in their ability to produce steady tones. The wind player uses a control device to convert the steady air supply from his lungs into the longitudinal oscillations of his instrument's air column; in place of the wind player's air supply, the violinist uses a bow that he pulls steadily across a string. The periodically varying frictional force between the string and the bow maintains the transverse oscillations of the string. The nature of the interaction between bow hair and string can be compared to that between reed and air column, since the end result of both systems is the setting-up of regimes of oscillation. Cooperation among the various string resonances is mediated in familiar fashion by the production of heterodyne components that transfer oscillatory energy generated at the frequencies of some pair of sinusoidal components to oscillations taking place at other frequencies in the total vibration recipe.

23.1. The Excitation Mechanism of a Bowed String

Let us begin our investigation of the bowed-string excitation mechanism by looking, as is our usual custom, at the behavior of a simple mechanical device. The top part of figure 23.1 shows a mass M mounted between a pair of springs S to form an oscillatory system having its own characteristic natural frequency. The presence of some cotton stuffed into the springs provides the frictional damping D that is an inevitable part of any real oscillatory system. This damped spring-and-mass system represents any one of the characteristic vibrational modes of the violin string in which we are interested (compare this with figure 22.10, which uses a bottle within which air oscillates to represent any mode of a flute). The oscillating mass in figure 23.1 rests on a moving motor-driven belt B; the belt runs steadily toward the right with velocity V, which represents the speed at which a musician might drive his bow across the strings of his instrument. The oscillating block M represents the string, and the belt B represents the bow hair; the friction between them is the focus of our attention at this time.

If the block shown in figure 23.1 is oscillating horizontally with a varying velocity v while the belt is moving steadily, the velocity of the block *relative to the belt* will be less during the time that the block is itself moving in the direction of belt movement (to the right in the figure)

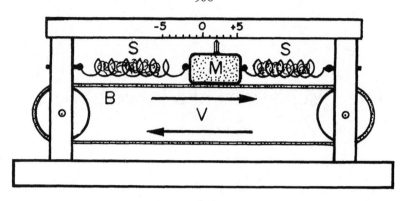

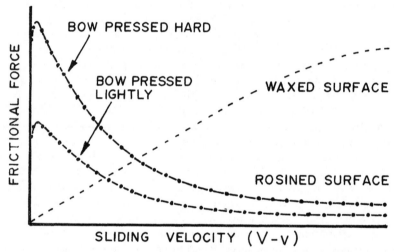

Fig. 23.1.   Spring-Mass System on a Moving Belt for the Measurement of Frictional Force between Sliding Surfaces. The velocity V of the moving belt B represents the velocity of a violin bow; the velocity v of the mass M corresponds to the velocity of the string's own motion at the bowing point.

than it is during the half of the oscillation in which the block moves in the opposite direction (leftward in the figure). Some friction always exists between the belt and the block; in the system shown in figure 23.1 this friction is at all times directed toward the right. During the block's rightward travel (when the sliding velocity is smaller than V), the frictional force is exerted in a direction that is helpful for the maintenance of oscillation,

whereas the frictional force tends to kill off the oscillation during the return half of the cycle (when the sliding velocity is large). Sustained oscillation is of course only possible if the helpful frictional force has an overall contribution that is larger than the negative effect of the force during the return.

The lower part of figure 23.1 shows curves that relate the block's frictional sliding force to the belt speed V, assuming that enough cotton is packed into the springs to prevent any oscillation ($v = 0$). The upper member of the beaded curves (labeled "bow pressed hard") shows the behavior of the sliding force for a block pressing firmly against the moving belt, which is analogous to a player exerting considerable pressure on the string with his bow. The other beaded curve (marked "bow pressed lightly") shows the very similar variation of sliding friction produced when the rosined surfaces are not pressed so firmly together. These curves slope downward from left to right, which tells us that the frictional force is largest when the sliding velocity ($V - v$) is smallest; this is exactly the condition required for the maintenance of oscillation. Notice that the interpretation of the bow-friction curves in figure 23.1 is exactly analogous to the interpretation of the flow-control curves for woodwind reeds shown in figure 21.4.

The lightly dotted curve that rises from left to right in figure 23.1 shows how the sliding friction would vary if the belt or violin bow were to be treated with wax or grease instead of with rosin. Such a treatment will not permit the maintenance of oscillation, since under these conditions the frictional force is largest rather than smallest when the sliding velocity is high. The slight leveling-off of the dotted curve at the right-hand side of the diagram calls our attention to the fact that when the sliding speed is very large the wax begins to melt, which reduces the friction.

The important features of the bowed-string excitation mechanism are outlined below in numbered statements, many of which are closely analogous to those given for reeds in section 21.2.

1. The sliding-friction behavior of a bow acting on a string can only sustain oscillations when the surface treatment (i.e., rosin) is such as to give a downward slope to the force-versus-bowing-speed curve. (See the analogous statement for woodwind reeds in sec. 21.2.)

2. The steeply sloping portions of this curve correspond to operating conditions in which the excitatory force is sensitively controlled by oscillatory variations in the string velocity v at the bowing point.

3. The shapes of the excitatory friction curves are such that the player can move the operating point for the oscillation toward a region of greater steepness either by pressing harder or by bowing more slowly.

4. The fact that the excitatory-friction characteristic curve is not straight (i.e., the slope varies from point to point along it) is an indication that heterodyne effects can occur, giving rise to regimes in which oscillation is maintained by excitations taking place at several frequencies simultaneously. The bowing conditions which increase the steepness of the curve also increase its curvature.

23.2 The Resonance Curves and Regimes of Oscillation of a Bowed String

In the case of wind instruments, we found it convenient to study the response of an air column to an excitation produced by pumping a constant-amplitude sinusoidal flow of air in and out of the mouthpiece, measuring the resulting pressure variations inside the mouthpiece by means of a tiny microphone. A response curve measured in this way has peaks at certain frequencies, and these peaks represent frequencies at which the air column can exert maximum influence on the reed, thereby setting up a regime of oscillation. In figure 20.3 we saw one of the ways to measure the response curve for a reed-instrument air column.

To help our understanding of violin-

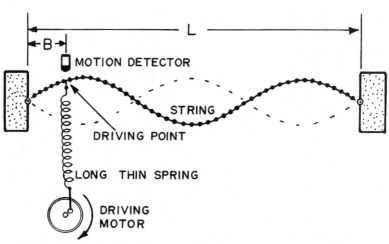

Fig. 23.2. Excitation Mechanism for the Study of the Velocity Response of a String at the Bowing Point

family instruments, we can similarly imagine measuring the response of a string to an excitatory force applied at the spot where a bow will eventually be placed, making use of a (slightly impractical) machine of the sort sketched in figure 23.2. Here a long, thin spring connects the rotating crank to the driving point on the string. This spring plays a role analogous to that of the capillary tube shown in figure 20.3, transmitting excitation from the crank to the string while at the same time leaving the string able to respond without any direct constraint coming from the position of the crank pin. The oscillatory response of the string to its sinusoidal force excitation can be measured by means of some sort of motion detector placed near the string at the driving point. A pickup similar to those used on electric guitars is particularly suitable for this purpose, since it responds to the velocity v with which the string vibrates (see also experiment 5 in sec. 7.4). A response curve plotted with the help of such a machine contains infor-

mation on the frequencies at which an applied sinusoidal force gives the maximum oscillatory velocity; the peaks on the response curve tell which frequencies best communicate with the bow friction in setting up regimes of oscillation.

We already know that the string will respond strongly to the driving force at the frequency of each one of its characteristic modes. The frequencies of these modes are of course in very nearly harmonic relationship. We also have met and repeatedly applied the idea that an excitation applied near the middle of a vibratory hump will produce much more of a response than will a driving force applied near a node (see secs. 7.3 and 10.7). All these ideas are apparent in figure 23.3. The uppermost resonance curve shown here is what one calculates for a hypothetical string in which the damping of all the modes is the same. The length of the string is L, and it is driven (and measured) at a distance $B = L/16$ from one end. Notice that the resonance peaks corresponding to modes 1 through 8 are

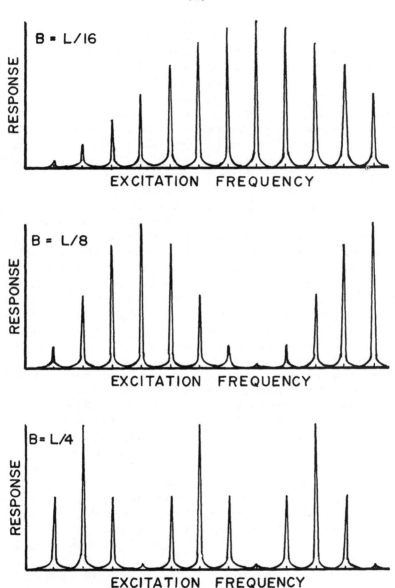

Fig. 23.3. Bowing-Point Resonance Response Curves for a Hypothetical String All of Whose Modes Have Equal Damping

progressively taller as the excitation point finds itself lying ever closer to the middle of a hump of the corresponding standing wave. The higher modes beyond mode 8 are more and more weakly excited, until at mode 16 there is essentially no response, because the driving point lies at a node for that oscillation.

The middle diagram of figure 23.3 shows how our hypothetical string would respond if it were excited at a point one-eighth of the way from one end, so that the distance $B = L/8$. Here we see that modes 4 and 12 have particularly tall peaks, since the driver acts on them at mid-hump, whereas modes 8, 16, etc., are hardly excited at all, because the driving force is applied at a node for each of them. The bottom diagram of figure 23.3 shows in exactly similar fashion the driving-point resonance curve expected when $B = L/4$.

If the bowed string behaves like reed instruments (which, as the dynamic level increases, progress from using a single resonance to using many), then we would expect from these curves that a lightly pressed bow, moving quickly over the string at a distance $B = L/16$ from the end, would preferentially excite mode 8 (since this mode has the tallest peak in the top curve of figure 23.3). Increasing the bow pressure might be expected to set up cooperative regimes involving two resonance peaks (e.g., 6 and 12, or 5 and 10), and then three peaks (e.g., 4, 8, and 12), etc., leading ultimately to a fully developed oscillation in which all the peaks collaborate to give a strongly controlled regime whose fundamental frequency is equal to that of the mode-1 resonance, in exact analogy to the low-register regime of a woodwind instrument.

Actual experimentation on a violin shows that none of these theoretically based expectations are borne out in practice, nor are the analogous expectations based on bowing points at $B = L/8$ or $L/4$. It turns out that the resolution of our difficulty lies in correcting the assumption that the damping of all the string modes is the same. It is extremely difficult to make a direct measurement of the string's resonance curve, because the narrowness of the resonance peaks and the associated long duration of any transient behavior would require the complete measurement to be spread over an hour or so, during which time tiny temperature and humidity changes could easily destroy the validity of the experiment. It proves possible, however, to *calculate* the needed resonance curve on the basis of measurements of the characteristic frequencies and ringing times of the various string modes when the string is plucked or struck. Painstaking measurements made in 1967 by Walter Reinicke at Lothar Cremer's laboratory at the Technical University in Berlin, West Germany, provide us with an example of this sort of information.[1] His measurements show that the half-amplitude time for the decay of mode 1 of the A-string on a particular violin is about 0.5 seconds, about five times longer than the decay times for modes 2 and 3, and about fourteen times longer than the decay times of modes 4 through 10. The damping rises very rapidly for the higher modes beyond mode 10. Since the heights of the resonance-curve peaks are closely related to the decay times of the corresponding string modes, the heights of the response peaks for any modes that are heavily damped will be reduced.

Figure 23.4 shows the response curve calculated (using Reinicke's data) for a real violin string driven at a point located at $B = L/8$. Notice that (in contrast to the corresponding curve in figure 23.3) resonance peak 1 is the tallest. The next two or three peaks are also quite tall, so that light bowing can be expected to give a tone whose fundamental component has a frequency of 440 Hz, in agreement with

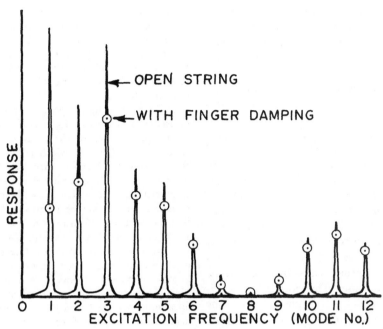

OPEN STRING

WITH FINGER DAMPING

RESPONSE

EXCITATION FREQUENCY (MODE No.)

Fig. 23.4. Bowing-Point Resonance Response Curve Based on Measured Dampings of the Various Modes of a Violin A-String

the mode-1 natural frequency. Pressing harder on the bow simply adds cooperative contributions from the other string modes, and the system plays in a regime of oscillation dominated by half a dozen peaks. This behavior is in accord with experiments one can carry out on the open (i.e., full-length) A-string of an actual violin. When the string is shortened by pressing it against the fingerboard with the tip of a finger, the string-mode frequencies will of course be raised because of the shortened string, but at the same time the damping of the modes will be increased by frictional effects at the fingertip. The small open circles drawn part way up each resonance peak in figure 23.4 show the height of each peak when a typical amount of finger damping is added to everything else. Notice that

when one bows at $B = L/8$ using finger damping, peak 3 (rather than peak 1) is the tallest, which explains why the lightest possible bowing now produces a sound whose fundamental frequency is $3 \times 440 = 1320$ Hz (at a pitch of E_6, a twelfth above A_4). Heavier bowing causes the pitch to drop down to the normal A_4 as the main, low-register regime takes over.

The above example will be recognized as a type of what violinists call a *harmonic*. Harmonics are almost exact counterparts of second- and third-register tones on a woodwind, in that the normal, low-register regime of oscillation involving all of the modes is somehow disrupted so as to favor regimes based on peaks 2, 4, 6, etc. (an octave higher), or on peaks 3, 6, 9, etc. (giving a tone whose pitch is a twelfth higher). When a violinist wishes to play an octave harmonic, he fingers the string very lightly at its midpoint, which has the selective effect of damping the odd-numbered modes; this lowers the corresponding resonance peaks without altering the heights of the even-numbered ones. As long as the bow is lightly wielded, it is only necessary to lower the tallnesses of peaks 1, 3, 5, etc., below those of peaks 2, 4, 6, etc., in order to permit the second-register tone to come forth. With heavier bowing, the pitch drops back to the normal position. Notice that there is a complete parallelism between this behavior and what we met in woodwinds in connection with the pianissimo-type (resistive) register hole. The violin player ordinarily lacks a cognate to the fortissimo-type (reactive) register hole, which functions by displacing the frequencies of certain modes rather than by increasing their damping.

23.3 The Effect of Inharmonicity and Damping on the Setting-Up of Regimes

In the course of our earlier studies of wind instruments, we learned of the advantages that come with the proper alignment of air-column resonances into a harmonic relationship. We also came to recognize that a given resonance can participate to some extent in a regime of oscillation even when it is not perfectly aligned, provided that some harmonic of the generated tone lies reasonably well up on the resonance peak. Let us formulate this remark with some care and outline its implications in a set of three numbered statements:

1. In any multi-resonance oscillating system, a given resonance peak can take part in the regime only if its own natural frequency differs from that of the nearest harmonic of the tone by an amount that is less than the half-amplitude bandwidth $W_{1/2}$ of the peak (see sec. 10.3).

2. Increasing the damping of a given mode of oscillation has two effects on the nature of the resonance curve: (a) the height of the peak is reduced, and (b) the width is increased by the same factor. These in turn have two opposing effects on the ability of the resonance to participate in a regime of oscillation: (1) a reduction in the height of the peak means that the influence of this resonance is reduced, and (2) for a given small amount of detuning, an increase of the width means that the peak is given additional influence over the regime.

3. In wind instruments it has been unambiguously verified that for reasonably small misalignments the benefits of increased resonance width usually offset the disadvantages of reduced peak height. This means that if a peak cannot be aligned quite perfectly, it is worthwhile to make sure that there is enough damping to give reasonable overlap of the peak with the closest sound component. A similar behavior appears to manifest itself among the bowed strings.

Let us see what implications these statements have for the violin family of instruments. John Schelleng, a retired Bell Laboratories engineer whose skillful experimentation and imaginative use of mathematics have made him a recognized leader in violin physics research, has measured the coefficients for stiffness-produced inharmonicity for many kinds of violin and cello strings (see sec. 16.5).[2] Using his data for a typical unfingered violin A-string, we can work out the amount by which the frequencies of successive string modes are raised by stiffness effects (this assumes the string to be mounted on a solid metal frame rather than on an actual violin, where resonances of the front plate and of the bridge can alter the inharmonicity; see sec. 16.5 once again). These upward shifts of frequency away from harmonicity are tabulated below for modes 1, 4, 8, and 12, along with the resonance widths calculated from data obtained by Reinicke for such a string:

mode no.	1	4	8	12	
freq. shift	0	+1.5	+13.0	+44.0	Hz
res. width	0.3	1.0	2.6	6.2	Hz

We can see at once that the upper resonances of a rigidly mounted violin string are not at all well aligned: above mode 4 the various harmonics of a 440-Hz tone lie considerably more than the half-ampli-

We already know that the measurements made by Reinicke show that the string is more heavily damped when it is in its normal surroundings than when clamped on a rigid frame. The numbered statements earlier in this section should then lead us to expect the string mounted on a violin to be more forgiving of any inharmonicities that may be present. We also recall that the inharmonicity itself will be altered when the string is mounted on a violin. In the following tabulation you will find the frequency shifts that I have measured for an A-string on a violin of good quality; also listed are the resonance widths appropriate for a string so mounted (once again calculated from Reinicke's data):

mode number	1	2	3	4	5	6	7	8	
frequency shift	0	+1.0	+2.0	−1.0	+1.0	+5.0	+2.0	+8.0	Hz
resonance width	0.8	3.7	4.3	11.0	10.6	11.0	10.9	11.0	Hz

tude bandwidth $W_{1/2}$ away from the resonances which might contribute to their support. In other words, we are led to expect that only the first few resonances participate directly in the regime of oscillation, and any higher partials that may be present in the tone arise only as the result of heterodyne action via the lower components. That is, the upper partials are produced in very much the same way as are those partials of a woodwind tone that lie above the tone-hole lattice cutoff frequency. The essential correctness of these deductions relating string inharmonicity to the nature of the spectrum has been verified by Schelleng.

Let us now turn our attention to the behavior of strings mounted on a violin.

This tabulation shows that the resonance frequencies of a violin string in its normal environment are considerably closer to being harmonic than they are when the string is mounted on a rigid frame. We also notice that the resonance widths are sufficiently broad (even for the open string) that the peaks all find it easy to join in a regime of oscillation according to the requirements outlined in the numbered statements given at the beginning of this section.[3]

On the violin that I measured, a mezzo-forte bowed A_4 sounds at a pitch that is about 5 cents higher than A-440 when the string is tuned in such a way as to place its plucked first-mode frequency at 440 Hz. Let us examine some of the reasons why the bowed playing pitch of the tone does not exactly match the pitch of its plucked first-mode frequency taken alone. The pressure of the bow upon the string and the sideways drag that it also exerts raise the average string tension somewhat (and so also its natural frequencies). However, the effect is very small, particularly when the bow is applied in normal fashion near the bridge end of the string. We must therefore look elsewhere for further contributions to the observed difference in pitch, and to do this it will help if we find out something of the behavior of the various modes of a plucked string.

When an unbowed string is plucked or otherwise vigorously excited, a measurement of mode 1 shows that the initial, large-amplitude vibration takes place at a frequency of oscillation that is noticeably higher than what is observed later on as the vibration dies away. The explanation of this phenomenon at first appears simple: the large-amplitude vibration requires a slight stretching of the string to permit the existence of the vibrational hump. This stretching produces an increased average tension in the string, and the frequency-raising effect of the increased tension is only partially offset by the contrary influence exerted by the thinning of the string that is another consequence of the stretching. As the vigorous initial vibration dies away, the frequency shift due to the tension change dies away even more rapidly (the frequency shift falls by a factor of four in the time the amplitude falls by a factor of two), so that we quickly arrive at the steady frequency that is characteristic of the small-amplitude vibration of the string's first mode. It was this small-

amplitude frequency that I set to 440 Hz for the experiments described above.

The frequency behavior of the higher modes of a plucked string shows a much more complicated pattern. The initial frequency changes observed for higher modes during the decay are of the sort displayed by mode 1, but they do not show a clear-cut pattern of decay; changing the vigor of the plucking as well as the plucking point can produce changes in the nature of the frequency fluctuations. These peculiar fluctuations in the vibration frequencies of decaying string modes have been noticed by many people during the past century, and the explanation for them was provided in 1939 by my colleague Robert Shankland and his student John Coltman (whose recent work on the flute we have already met). Shankland and Coltman studied the departure from harmonicity of the natural frequencies of a vibrating wire.[4] In their experiments, any one of the modes of the wire could be run as a self-sustaining oscillator by making use of an ingenious electrically controlled driving mechanism. They recognized that the presence of a standing wave on a wire produces variations in the average string tension along its length and that these variations act to perturb the mode frequencies (much as do perturbations produced in wind instruments by small changes in the diameter of the air column). A small extension of their calculations shows that the variation in tension along a plucked violin string produced by the mode-1 vibration strongly influences the frequency shift of the higher string modes. Depending on the plucking point and the rate of decay of the various modes, the overall effect of the tension variation is to narrow the frequency ratios between the modes to an extent that quadruples for every doubling of the vibratory amplitude of the predominantly influential first mode.

We can now return to the difference between the playing frequency of a bowed string and the frequency of its first mode measured at low amplitude. When a violin string is bowed in a way that maintains a fairly large-amplitude oscillation, the resonance peak for mode 1 may shift upward in frequency by a dozen cents due to the vibratory increase in tension. The higher modes are not shifted upward so much, however, because of the nonuniformity of this added tension along the string. Since the playing frequency is determined jointly by all of the resonance peaks that participate in the regime of oscillation, the 5-cent pitch rise associated with bowing is less than the 12-cent shift belonging to the string's first mode.

Our study so far of the bowed string has made heavy use of the regime-of-oscillation point of view which grew out of Bouasse's observation that harmonically related air-column resonances can cooperate with the reed in producing a sustained tone. As we have seen, this approach to the study of musical tone-producers proves to be an immensely powerful tool for the qualitative understanding of what goes on in a musical instrument on a steady-state basis, and it serves also as a convenient guide for the adjustment of instruments to make them play well. However, when one tries to make accurate calculations of the vibration recipe produced by a given air column and a given reed, my co-workers and I find that the mathematical difficulties become almost insuperable in many cases of practical interest. Our formulation also cannot

be used to predict how a tone évolves at its beginning. The quantitative limitations of the regime-of-oscillation calculations are particularly oppressive when an attempt is made to apply them to the violin family of instruments, where one has to deal with a high degree of nonlinearity in the bow-friction characteristics and with a very large number of narrowly resonant string modes. During the past two or three years Robert Schumacher of Carnegie Mellon University at Pittsburgh has gone on from our analysis of the intermode cooperative effects to devise a mathematical formalism that promises calculation of many hitherto inaccessible features.[5] The British mathematician Michael McIntyre, of Cambridge University, is also working along these lines. We can look forward to much progress as these newer techniques are refined and their uses become more widely understood.

23.4. A Description of the Bowing Mechanism; Helmholtz and Raman

Hermann von Helmholtz in 1860 presented the first clear account of how a violin string responds to bowing, providing us with a mathematical description that has served as the basis of practically all the work that has followed.[6] Helmholtz's whole approach to the problem is quite different from the one we have used so far in this chapter, and we should give it our careful attention since it is particularly illuminating in those parts of the subject for which the cooperating resonances formulation is least effective.

As an introduction to Helmholtz's description of the bowing mechanism, let us consider what happens when someone causes a piece of chalk to screech across a blackboard. Examination of the line drawn during such a screech shows that it is made up of a series of fine dots or dashes. If the piece of chalk is long and it is held lightly at one end while the other end hops along the blackboard, one can easily observe the chalk alternately sticking to the board (making a mark) and then leaping forward to where it recatches during the return trip of its more or less sinusoidal oscillation. This sort of oscillation can arise whenever the frictional force between two bodies is less when they are in relative motion than it is when they are stationary.

The bowing of a violin string works in very similar fashion to the screeching of chalk. When the bow is placed on the string and drawn to one side, the string sticks to the bow, which pulls it aside until the elastic restoring force produced by the string tension becomes large enough to break the string loose from the bow. It now swings back in much the same way it would after slipping off the plectrum of a harpsichord jack; there is, however, a small amount of damping produced by the rapid (and therefore low-friction) sliding of the string against the steadily moving bow hair. At the end of its backward swing the string will come to rest and then recommence its motion in the direction of the bow velocity. At this time it is once again caught by the large sticking friction of the bow and carried forward to begin a new cycle of the oscillation, just as the chalk alternately caught on the board and broke free of it.

Helmholtz studied the motion of the bowed string at the bowing point and at other points along it by observing an illuminated speck of starch attached to an otherwise blackened string, using what

he called a vibration microscope (this device is an optical cousin of today's oscilloscope). The top part of figure 23.5 shows the sort of vibratory pattern that one normally sees at the bowing point of a string. The longer, more gently sloping part of the oscilloscope trace shows the steady upward motion of the string as it is carried along by the bow. The duration of this part of the cycle is known as the *sticking time*. When the string reaches the upper limit of its travel, it breaks away from the bow and runs downward quickly to the opposite extreme of its motion, where it is recaught by the bow for a steady upward trip. The time during which the string is sliding quickly back against the motion of the bow is called the *flyback time*. Helmholtz was able to show that the theory of undamped vibrating strings agrees quite well with experiment in predicting that the ratio of the flyback time to the total repetition time will be equal to the ratio of the bowing point distance B to the total string length L. For example, in figure 23.5 the diagram is drawn to show a flyback time that lasts one-quarter of the time for a complete cycle of oscillation, which means that we are dealing with a string that is bowed one-quarter of the way along the string from the bridge.

On the assumption of zero damping of the string, Helmholtz was able to show that the vibration recipe observed at the bowing point (corresponding to the motion we have been discussing) is the same as the recipe for the amplitudes of the modes of a plucked string (which we met in section 7.2). He also pointed out that the expected effects of large bow-hair width on a stiff string would be similar to those of a broad plectrum exciting it (see secs. 8.1, 8.4, and 8.5). In particular, he

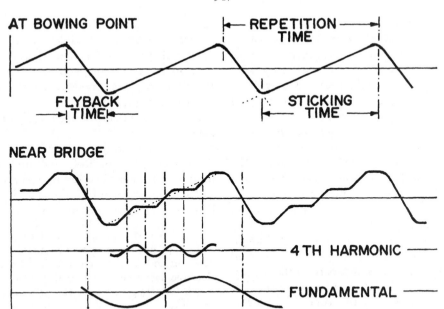

Fig. 23.5.   Simplified Representation of String Motion at Two Points on a Bowed String

noted that any frequency component having a node at the bowing point is expected to be missing unless the bow has appreciable width. If B = L/4, as in our present example, we are led to expect that harmonic partials 4, 8, 12, etc., will be very nearly missing from the vibration recipe. Helmholtz also described observations of the unsteady oscillations produced by bowing a badly made violin: the steady sawtooth motion is replaced by a spluttery one in which extra kinks appear randomly from time to time.

We must not forget that what we hear is not the vibration recipe at the bowing point but rather the excitation transmitted to the violin and thence to the room by means of forces exerted by the end of the string where it passes over the bridge. As a first step in working out the driving

forces at the bridge, we should turn our attention to the lower part of figure 23.5; this shows the motion of the string, driven as before at B = L/4, but now observed with the vibration microscope focused on a point near the end of the string (either bridge or nut end will do). Here we still see the basically sawtooth waveform, but superposed on it are small steplike wiggles (*crumples* is the name given to them in the English translation of Helmholtz's book). It turns out that 4 crumples are visible on a steadily maintained waveform if one bows at L/4, 7 crumples if one bows at L/7, and so on. You can perhaps deduce from the diagram that these crumples are themselves made up of precisely those harmonic partials that were missing from the recipe or too weak to detect easily at the bowing point. Helmholtz recognized the existence of a problem here. The essential invisibility of these extra components at the bowing point is not in itself surprising since one does not expect to see evidence of their presence at a place where they all have nodes. However, how the bow has managed to excite them by means of forces exerted at the bowing point is not instantly apparent. Helmholtz expressed a suspicion that the phenomenon had something to do with damping of the string modes; as we shall see, his suspicion proved correct.

During the period from 1909 through 1921, the Indian physicist C. V. Raman published a series of papers on the properties of bowed strings, along with the first half of a book on the same subject. Raman's scientific reputation today rests chiefly on his later work in optics (which earned him the Nobel Prize in 1930), but his careful experiments and thorough analysis of the properties of bowed strings underlie or anticipate most of the more recent work in the field. In 1969 Raman sent me a copy of his out-of-print book, *On the Mechanical Theory of the Vibrations of Bowed Strings* (published in 1918).[7] The book includes (among many other things) a large number of photographs showing the motions of a bowed string, excited and observed at many different points along it. These photographs and Raman's analysis of the string motions confirm and greatly extend Helmholtz's work, taking into account the presence of string damping. Raman assumed, however, that all modes are equally damped, as we did for the sake of simplicity in our discussion of the hypothetical string shown in figure 23.3. He also assumed a pure form of stick-slip friction which ignores the way the frictional force varies with the sliding velocity, as sketched in figure 23.1. Nevertheless, Raman was able to account quite well not only for oscillations of the type which we might describe as involving all of the string modes equally in the oscillatory regime, but also for those in which only a selected set of these participate.

Before we continue our examination of the consequences of the stick-slip bowing-point motion discussed by Helmholtz and Raman, we should summarize its salient features as we have met them so far:

1. In normal operation the string of a violin-type instrument remains "stuck" to the bow hair and travels along with it for a considerable fraction of each vibratory cycle, after which the string flies back abruptly to begin the next cycle, which takes place at very nearly the first-mode frequency of the string. (The physics of this sort of oscillation is very reminiscent of that of a reed instrument in which the aperture snaps open for a fraction of each cycle.)

2. The string motion at the bowing point has a simple appearance: the ratio of flyback time to repetition time is, to a good approximation, equal to the ratio of bowing-point distance to string length.

3. As a consequence of statement 2, the vibration recipe observed at the bowing point shows very little oscillation at the frequencies of modes that have nodes at or near the bowing point.

4. The components which are apparently missing at the bowing point are easily detected when the motion of the string is studied at points other than the bowing point. The origin of these components will be discussed later in this section.

Let us turn our attention now to some of the practical consequences of the Helmholtz-Raman approach to bowed strings and its later developments. If one wishes to play more loudly, for instance, it is clear that any given point on the string must make a wider excursion to each side of center in the course of each oscillation. Since the number of these back-and-forth trips per second is fixed by the playing frequency, we are led to conclude that the point must move with greater velocity to cover a larger round-trip distance in the time of each oscillation. Because the bow and the string are moving together during one part of each cycle and because the string cannot move faster than the bow, it is obvious that loud playing demands fast bow motion. These observations lead to two additions to our numbered statements:

5. Since the amplitude of oscillation of a bowed string is directly determined by the velocity of the bow, loud playing calls for a faster bow velocity V. The firmness with which the bow is pressed on the string does not affect the amplitude of the oscillation as long as the bow pressure is within a certain range of suitability.

6. The amplitude of motion at the bowing point itself is smaller than the amplitude of the motion measured at the string's midpoint. As a result we realize that the bow velocity required to produce a given oscillation amplitude is less when the bowing point B is near the bridge than it is when B is a larger fraction of the total string length.

The next question that concerns us is what limitations on bow pressure arise from the necessity for the bow to control the string vibrations adequately. Besides elucidating the general behavior of bowed strings, Helmholtz observed the effect of applying what a musician would call low bow pressure. Raman extended these studies and clarified the manner in which the velocity and position of the bow affect the minimum pressure that is required for proper tone generation. He also observed that the required bow pressure is altered when the played note contains frequencies that match some of the resonances of the violin itself. In 1937, the physicist Frederick Saunders of Harvard University published an account of further work on the relationship of minimum bow pressure to the body resonances.[8] He is also credited with the first recognition of an upper limit to the usable force, though one can find a brief section devoted to this subject in the middle of Raman's book.

In 1973 John Schelleng published an article, "The bowed string and the player." The account he gives in it of his own work and that of others on the relationship of the bow to its strings provides the background for my discussion here of the bowing-pressure requirements.[9] Let us begin our examination of this question by noticing that the minimum pressure is that which is just sufficient to carry the string along with the bow. In other words, the bow must be able to synchronize all the string modes into a motion of the desired sawtooth type (i.e., to set up a fully developed regime of oscillation). Obviously, if some of the string modes are somewhat inharmonic or if their damping is high, more bow pressure will be required. On the other hand, the bow pressure must be small enough to allow the string to break loose cleanly at the end of its sawtooth swinging motion in order to make a good flyback.

We have already learned that a large bowing velocity is needed to produce a large-amplitude oscillation of the string. The bow supplies the frictional force necessary to produce these large deflections, and this force is proportional to the downward pressure exerted by the bow against the strings (compare the two force curves in fig. 23.1). We conclude, therefore, that the minimum required bow pressure that the player must exert increases and decreases in proportion to the speed with which he propels the bow. The complete relationship of the minimum bowing pressure to all of the properties of the string, to the bowing point, and to the nature of the frictional force can be summarized with the help of the formula:

slightly less than a fourfold increase, the reason being that the bowing point at L/4 is getting rather close to the point of maximum excitation for the string. Even when the influence of additional peaks is taken into account, the above conclusions remain valid and can be stated briefly as follows: [10]

7. The minimum bowing pressure required to maintain oscillation of the normal

$$P_{minimum} = \left(\frac{V}{K_{stick} - K_{slip}} \right) \times \left(\frac{1}{\text{the aggregate tallness of the string resonance peaks}} \right) \times \left(\frac{L}{B} \right)^2 .$$

Here K_{stick} and K_{slip} are the coefficients that determine the size of the frictional forces produced by the bowing pressure P under sticking and slipping conditions, and V is the velocity of the bow itself. Since increasing the damping makes the resonance peaks less tall, such a change leads to a higher value for P_{min}. Detuning a peak so that the string harmonic does not lie directly on top of it will also raise P_{min}.

Because mode 1 has the largest amplitude at the bowing point, the aggregate tallness of the resonance peaks is effectively dominated by the behavior of peak 1 (even though it is not generally the tallest peak). If we take the simplified view that only peak 1 is to be taken into account and if we assume the bowing point to be fairly near one end of the string, it is not hard to verify with the help of figure 23.3 that for every doubling of the bowing-point distance B, there is a fourfold decrease in the minimum required bow pressure. That is, in going from B = L/16 to B = L/8, we notice that peak 1 has risen fourfold in height. A comparison of the peak-1 heights for B = L/8 and B = L/4 shows

(i.e., simplest) Helmholtz-Raman type is proportional to the velocity V with which the bow is moved across the strings.

8. The minimum bowing pressure required to maintain normal oscillation on a string is large when one bows near the bridge, and falls to a quarter of its value for every doubling of the distance B from bridge to bowing point.

The final item in our investigation of the bowing properties of strings is the limitation placed on the maximum bow pressure. If the pressure is too high between the moving bow and its string, the string simply pulls to one side, scraping and stuttering against the bow hair without ever going into oscillation. The following more or less describes what goes on when heavy bowing pressure is employed. When the string sticks to the bow and is carried forward with it, an impulse is sent along the string toward its fixed end. This impulse is reflected at the fixed end and comes back in inverted form to the bowing point. If the bow pressure is not excessive, the impulse succeeds in breaking the string free in a manner that is quite reminiscent of the way in which the reflected pulse from a piano hammer blow returns to throw the hammer off the string (see sec. 17.4). Schelleng shows that the maximum bow pressure that permits the string to break loose properly is proportional to the bow velocity and inversely proportional to the distance B between bridge and bowing point. This is interesting in itself, but its practical implications are better displayed if we consider the way in which the ratio P_{max}/P_{min} depends on the bowing conditions:

$$P_{max}/P_{min} = 2(B/L) \times \begin{bmatrix} \text{aggregate tallness} \\ \text{of the string} \\ \text{resonance peaks} \end{bmatrix}$$

This tells us, for example, that the nearer the bow is to the bridge, the narrower is the range within which the player must maintain the pressure it exerts, a fact well known to string players. Notice also that an instrument having heavily damped string resonances (so that the peaks are less tall) is one that is less forgiving of chance variations in the bowing pressure. One cannot, however, leap from this observation to a statement that a musician would automatically prefer to play on lightly damped strings—there must always be enough damping to permit proper cooperation among the string modes, as outlined in section 23.3.

23.5. The Bridge Driving Force Spectrum

In our study of wind instruments we found it necessary to distinguish between the sound spectrum produced inside the mouthpiece (as a result of the cooperation between reed and air column) and the spectrum of sounds transmitted out into the room by way of the bell and/or the tone holes. The problem for stringed instruments is very similar, though it is somewhat more complicated: we must go from the bowing-point spectrum to the vibration recipe of the forces exerted by the string on the bridge before we can usefully consider how these forces drive the wooden parts of the instrument to make them act as a sound source in the concert hall.

In chapter 7 we learned how to estimate the amplitudes of the string modes themselves when they are excited by plucking or striking. In section 23.4 of this chapter we learned that these same rules apply very nearly unchanged to the recipe produced by the bowed excitation of a string *when it is observed at the bowing point*. We must now learn how to translate the recipe for the amplitudes of the various modes of a string into the driving force recipe which these modes give rise to at the bridge. The sideways force exerted by a string on its anchorage at any instant during its vibration depends not only on the tension under which the string is kept, but also on the angle to which the string end is momentarily deflected. Figure 23.6 shows the vibrational shapes of the first four modes of a uniform string, drawn in such a way that at the left-hand end all of these modes cause the string to be tilted to the same angle. In other words, the amplitudes of these particular vibrations have been chosen in such a way as to make them all exert the same amount of driving force on the left-hand string anchorage. You can verify from the diagram that mode 2, because of its shorter and more abruptly rounded humps, can run at half the amplitude of mode 1 and still exert the same driving force on the anchorage. Similarly, modes 3 and 4 are three and four times as ef-

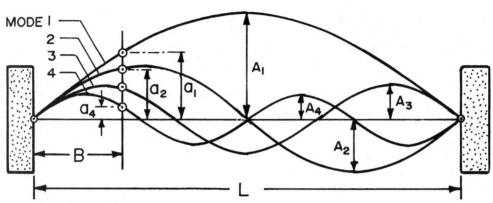

Fig. 23.6. Relationship between the Displacement at the Bowing Point and the Amplitude of Various Modes of a String

ficacious as mode 1 in driving the anchorage, which accounts for their proportionately smaller amplitudes in the diagram. Let us distill the content of these observations into a single statement:

1. In order to estimate the magnitude of the driving force F_n exerted on the bridge by the nth vibrational mode of a string, one must multiply the amplitude A_n of the mode by its serial number n and by the tension T of the string, according to the formula:

$$F_n = nTA_n \times \text{(a numerical constant)}$$

The numerical constant in all cases turns out to be (π/L), where L is the vibrating length of the string.

Look now at the vertical line at the point B along the string in figure 23.6. Notice that the amplitude of motion observed at B associated with each mode is considerably less than the amplitude of the mode itself. This calls to our attention the fact that one must convert the bowing-point amplitudes a_1, a_2, etc., into the corresponding mode amplitudes A_1, A_2, etc., before making use of the formula given in statement 1. When we do this as a strictly mathematical prob-

lem, considering the strings to be ideally flexible and completely undamped (in accordance with Helmholtz's simplified description of the motion), we obtain the following rather simple result:

$$F_n = (1/n)A_1 \times \text{(a numerical constant)}$$

In other words, this simplified calculation implies that the driving force components fall away as $1/n$ in a way reminiscent of the vibration recipe of a struck string. This almost-true formula applies to all modes except those that happen to have nodes precisely at the bowing point, and the formula is entirely independent of the bowing position! Clearly we have oversimplified something in the mathematics leading to the formula, since every string player knows that his tone can be altered by changes in bowing point and bowing pressure. We have looked at the behavior of enough oscillatory regimes to know that the bowing-point oscillation is itself altered when the bowing point is changed, and these alterations cannot be compensated by changes in the bridge driving behavior of the sort we have been discussing. If we look again at the two parts of figure 23.5, we will find that hints are available as to the source of the trouble: the upper figure shows slightly rounded corners which already signal the departure of the real bowing-point motion from a simplistic pattern made up of straight line segments joined together.

John Schelleng, Lothar Cremer, and Cremer's co-worker Hans Lazarus have studied the way in which the rounding-off of these corners (which represents incipient slipping at the point of release and the beginnings of sticking at the end of the flyback time) depends on bow pressure, damping, inharmonicity, etc.[11] They also have studied the small wiggling motions that arise because the string undergoes a sort of twisting and rolling oscillation about its own axis under the influence of the bow. All of these give rise to departures from the straight line segment motion used to calculate the formula given above. To summarize, we can say that at the minimum-force end of the useful range of bowing pressures, the higher partials in the bridge force recipe are weaker than those given in our formula, whereas heavy bowing makes these partials stronger.

Helmholtz's own observation of the crumples shown in the lower part of figure 23.5 and Raman's later study of them show that these early workers were well aware of the very thing that most clearly shows the limitations of their pioneering efforts to describe the behavior of bowed strings. Because of the central position of the crumples in our recognition of the shortcomings of the simplest version of the Helmholtz-Raman theory, let us give some attention to the way in which the unexpected vibration components these crumples represent may be excited.

Those of you who have assimilated the ideas presented earlier in this book about the production of heterodyne components by the action of a nonlinear system will not find it impossible to imagine that the strongly generated pairs of components in the motion of a bowed string, such as the second and sixth, the first and fifth, or the third and seventh components, might each act with the nonlinearity of the bow friction to generate a contribution to the fourth harmonic vibration of a string bowed at $L/4$. Similarly, we might expect a double-frequency heterodyne component arising from component 2, and so on. We have already met examples of this sort of behavior among the wind instruments. For instance, the pedal tone of a trumpet contains a fundamental component that is almost totally derived by heterodyne action from the upper partials of the tone, there being no resonance peak at the fundamental frequency. The even-numbered partials making up the internal spectrum of the clarinet tone are similarly strengthened by heterodyne action far above the levels one would expect from direct cooperation of the reed with the resonance-curve minima that are found at these frequencies. The question still remains how the bow can communicate this extra vibrational excitation to string modes that nominally display no motion at the driving point.

It is at this point that we come to understand the shrewdness of Helmholtz's suspicion that string damping must have something to do with the phenomenon of the excitation of vibration components that have a node at the bowing point. In section 20.3 we learned that the resonance peaks and dips measured at one end of an air column could be understood in terms of the relationship between a wave sent down the air column by the excitation mechanism and the reflected wave that comes back from the far end. We learned there that the reason the resonance dip does not fall all the way to zero is that the reflected wave is reduced in amplitude because of the damping it has suffered, and so cannot totally cancel the initiating wave on its return. It is perfectly correct to look at what goes on at the driving point on a string in exactly the same way (although account must be taken of the waves on both sides by adding their impedances). In other words, the so-called node is not a point of true rest in a driven system that suffers damping. The resonance curves shown in figures 23.3 and 23.4 do not, as a result, fall all the way to zero at the positions of the dips, any more than do the resonance curves of wind instruments. There is a small motion even at what we might call a nodal driving point, so that a bow or other driving mechanism can in fact provide some excitation to the corresponding modes.

Figure 23.6 shows us that even a very small excursion produced at or near a node (e.g., at or near B = L/4) can be associated with a reasonably large vibrational amplitude for the mode in question, which results in a considerable contribution at this frequency to the bridge driving force spectrum. The physics of this behavior is exactly the same as that underlying the unusually large transmission of the even-numbered harmonic components out of a clarinet (see sec. 22.4). Recall that these components are produced at frequencies for which the air-column resonance curve is not tall, showing that the pressure standing waves corresponding to these even numbered modes have an approximate node within the mouthpiece.

23.6. Examples, Experiments, and Questions

1. A vivid way to demonstrate the importance of cooperative effects among the various modes of a bowed string is to disrupt the harmonic relationships of their frequencies. A small strip of masking tape can be rolled tightly around a violin A-string at a point about three-eighths of the way from either end of the string. The added load will lower the frequencies of the various modes in an amount determined by the position of the paper relative to the nodes. If the load has a mass of one percent of the string mass, the calculated frequency shifts are as follows:

mode number	frequency shift
1	−3.8 Hz
2	−2.2 Hz
3	−0.6 Hz
4	−4.4 Hz
5	−0.6 Hz
6	−2.2 Hz

The negative signs here indicate a lowering of the mode frequency. When these shifts are added to those tabulated in section 23.3, we find that the resulting inharmonicity is enough to prevent the playing of a normal tone, although various raucous screeches are sometimes possible. You might find it worthwhile to experiment with different loadings and points of application. It will be possible for you to figure out the regimes of oscillation that sustain some of the resulting sounds.

2. When a string is working well with its bow, the two are caught together over a considerable fraction of each cycle of the oscillation. In figure 23.5 the sticking

time is shown to be three-quarters of the repetition time for a bowing point $B = L/4$. You should estimate the sticking times associated with more normal points of bow application. See if you can put together the information contained in the friction curve shown in figure 23.1 with what you have learned about the sticking time to deduce the reason why a bow seems to skate across the strings when oscillation conditions are unfavorable, and why it seems to require a considerable push to move it along when it takes hold to generate a proper tone. You can study the phenomenon very easily as follows. First, bow good vigorous strokes on an open string of a cello or a violin to establish the feel of the bow in your hand. Next, while continuing to bow vigorously, close your eyes and have a friend periodically press a large rubber sponge or wadded up sweater against the string and fingerboard, so as to provide enough damping to kill the oscillation. Whenever the damping is applied the bow will appear to slip abruptly ahead in its travel. String players generally recognize that putting a heavy mute onto the bridge of an instrument not only changes the sound, but also makes quite an alteration in the feel of the bow in the player's hand. Investigate this change by simple playing experiments, keeping in mind that a massive object attached to the bridge will not only alter the inharmonicity of the strings but also reduce their damping.

3. It is possible to learn a great deal about the motion of a violin bridge by attaching various objects to it in various ways, or by touching it. To begin with, verify by plucking the open strings one by one that their vibrational decay times are little influenced by any sort of pinching or sideways pressure on the bridge that you can exert with your fingers (as long as you do not touch the strings themselves). Notice at the same time that the tone color of the various twanging sounds from the plucked strings is also very little changed by such finger pressure. These preliminary experiments tell us that the wave impedance of the bridge and violin body is high enough that the additional effect of the finger pressure is fairly small.

Now take a steel or brass rod some 10 cm long and 1 cm in diameter (the size of a fountain pen) and press its end firmly against the bridge in various directions. For example, press straight down on the bridge at right angles to the violin's top surface at the E-string end of the bridge, at the G-string end, and in the middle. The tone color of both plucked and bowed sounds will be altered in various ways depending on the point of contact. You should also try pressing on either end of the bridge, the rod being held parallel to the top surface of the instrument and at right angles to the strings. Repeat the experiment with the rod held more or less parallel to the strings, pressing from the tailpiece side for convenience. The relative magnitudes of the resulting tonal changes indicate the amount of bridge motion that occurs in the various directions assumed by the rod. It is possible to estimate the amplitudes of these various components of the vibration by pressing the bar *very lightly* against the bridge so that it buzzes. If you are scientifically inclined, you may also be able to estimate the acceleration of the vibrating bridge in terms of the mass of the rod and the magnitude of the force with which it must be pressed in order to *just barely* stop the buzzing.

Notes

1. Walter Reinicke, "Übertragungseigenschaften des Streichinstrumentenstegs," *Catgut Acoust. Soc. Newsletter* 19 (May 1973): 26–34. (See note 7 below for two other sources for some of the data shown in this article.) The Catgut Acoustical Society was founded in the early 60s by a group of people (centered around Frederick Saunders of Harvard) interested in research on bowed-string acoustics. In recent years its membership has expanded to several hundred, including musicians and scientists all over the world. The Newsletter has come to be the leading source of technical and semi-technical information on the stringed instruments. It is published from the society headquarters at 112 Essex Avenue, Montclair, N.J. 07042.

2. John C. Schelleng, "The bowed string and the player," *J. Acoust. Soc. Am.* 53 (1973): 26–41, see especially part III. See also John C. Schelleng, "The Physics of the Bowed String," *Scientific American*, January 1974, pp. 87–95.

3. Very recently it has become possible to make useful measurements of the resonance curves of violin strings. The response peaks show all kinds of asymmetry, splitting, and displacement as a result of the various influences that act on the string. See Maurice Hancock, "The Mechanical Impedances of Violin Strings," *Catgut Acoust. Soc. Newsletter* 23 (May 1975): 17–26. An earlier brief preliminary report appeared in the *Catgut Acoust. Soc. Newsletter* 22 (November 1974): 25.

4. R. S. Shankland and J. W. Coltman, "The Departure of the Overtones of a Vibrating Wire from a True Harmonic Series," *J. Acoust. Soc. Am.* 10 (1939): 161–66.

5. R. T. Schumacher, C. J. Amick, and C. B. Croke, "The bowed string: an integral equation formulation" (abstract), *J. Acoust. Soc. Am.* 56 supplement (1974): S26. A more extended account of this work (including some application to wind instruments) has been submitted for publication in the same journal. The title is "Self-sustained musical oscillators: an integral equation approach."

6. Hermann Helmholtz, *On the Sensations of Tone*, trans. Alexander Ellis from 4th German ed. of 1877, with material added by translator (reprint ed., New York: Dover, 1954), pp. 80–88, 384–87; and A. B. Wood, *A Textbook of Sound*, 3rd rev. ed. (1955; reprint ed., London: Bell, 1960), pp. 101–3. See also Schelleng, "The bowed string and the player," and Schelleng, "The Physics of the Bowed String."

7. C. V. Raman, *On the Mechanical Theory of the Vibrations of Bowed Strings*, Bulletin no. 15, The Indian Association for the Cultivation of Science (Calcutta, Indian Association for the Cultivation of Science, 1918). Raman also provided me with a listing of his published acoustical papers; this list is reproduced in *Catgut Acoust. Soc. Newsletter* 13 (May 1970): 6–7.

8. F. A. Saunders, "The Mechanical Action of Violins," *J. Acoust. Soc. Am.* 9 (1937): 81–98.

9. Schelleng, "The bowed string and the player," and Schelleng, "The Physics of the Bowed String." See also L. Cremer, "Der Einfluss des 'Bogendrucks' auf die selbsterregten Schwingungen der gestrichenen Saite," *Acustica* 30 (1974): 119–36. There is an earlier version of this article in English: "The Influence of 'Bow Pressure' on the Movement of a Bowed String: I and II," *Catgut Acoust. Soc. Newsletter* 18 (November 1972): 13–19, and 19 (May 1973): 21–25. Reinicke's string damping data (which form the basis for the example in the present chapter) are summarized in figure 7 of Cremer's *Acustica* article, and in figure 3 of part I of Cremer's *Catgut Acoust. Soc. Newsletter* article.

10. The arrangement and tallness of the peaks is strongly influenced by the resonances of the violin bridge and body, so that the minimum bow pressure satisfying our requirements is not at all constant as we go from note to note in the scale. See figures 7.6 and 7.9 in Alexander Wood, *The Physics of Music*, 6th ed., rev. J. M. Bowsher (New York: Dover, 1961), p. 103.

11. See the references in note 9 above, and also Hans Lazarus, "Dynamical Theory of String Excitation by Bowing" (abstract), *J. Acoust. Soc. Am.* 48 (1970): 74.

24
Instruments of the Violin Family

In chapter 23 we learned how the strings and the bow of a violin can work together to maintain a stable oscillation. We also considered the relationships that hold between the vibration amplitude of a string mode, observed at the bowing point, and the corresponding amplitude of the driving force component which is exerted on the bridge. In the present chapter we will follow the consequences of these excitatory forces through the resulting vibrations of the violin body and thence out into the room.

24.1. The Body and the Bridge of Instruments of the Violin Family

It is customary to think about instruments of the violin family as being made up of three reasonably distinct parts: (1) the sound-generating portion of the instrument, consisting of the bow and the strings working cooperatively; (2) the body, whose resonances strongly influence the way the sound is radiated into the room; and (3) the bridge, which mediates between the oscillating strings and the body. Having devoted chapter 23 to a discussion of the bow and strings, we should now acquaint ourselves with some

of the acoustical properties of the body and the bridge.

Figure 24.1 shows top and side views of a violin, along with the names of various parts of the structure that will be of particular interest to us. Each of the violin-family instruments consists of carefully arched *top* and *back plates* joined at their perimeters by thin strips of wood called the *ribs*. These combine to form an eggshell-like box whose shape is remarkably well adapted to support the direct pull of four strings as well as a rather significant downbearing force that is exerted on the bridge. On a violin the total tension of the strings is around 25 kg (55 lbs); the strings' downbearing amounts to about 8 kg (18 lbs).

While outwardly the violin body looks quite symmetrical, its inner structure reveals some departure from symmetry. The foot of the bridge on the side carrying the treble strings is supported by a *soundpost* that is lightly wedged between the top and back plates; its placement serves not only to give mechanical strength but also to couple the vibrations of one plate directly to the other. Under the bridge foot on the bass side a long strip of wood known as the *bass bar* is glued onto the inner surface of the top plate, running

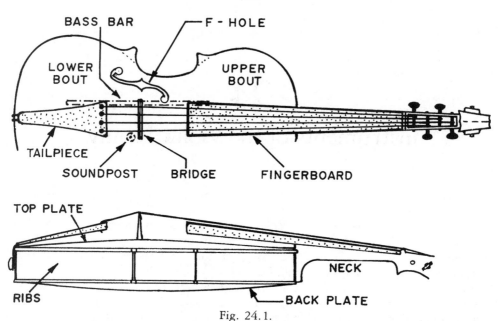

Fig. 24.1.

more or less parallel to the direction of the strings. This reinforcement serves structurally as a means for distributing the downbearing force from the bridge over the surface of the top plate. In the simplest of acoustic terms, the bass bar also serves to couple the bridge vibrations effectively to both rounded portions of the top plate: these two areas are otherwise somewhat isolated from one another by the nipped-in waist section which contains two cutouts of graceful shape known as the *f-holes*. The f-holes not only influence the vibration properties of the top plate in a direct way, they also serve as a passageway through which the enclosed air can communicate its oscillations to the room as part of the total radiation process.

My brief description so far of the structure and function of the various parts of the violin body makes it seem as though these parts somehow maintain their acoustical identity when the instrument is played. Nothing could be farther from the truth. The similarity of the wave impedances of the various wooden parts guarantees that these parts all act as a single vibrating system whose overall behavior cannot be determined by a naïve adding-up of the characteristic vibration properties of the separate parts (see the second digression in sec. 17.1).

A. *The Bridge as a Coupling Lever between Strings and Body.* Despite the general warnings of the preceding paragraph, it is possible for us to introduce ourselves to the gross features of the coupling between bridge and body by making use of the fact that at frequencies well below the first-mode resonance of the bridge (as measured with its feet standing on a rigid support), it is correct to treat the bridge as a rigid object that can act as a simple lever. This means that for violins the validity of our simplified viewpoint is restricted to frequencies well below 3000 Hz ($F_7\sharp$), while for the cello the corresponding resonance frequency is near 1000 Hz (B_5), exactly in proportion to its lower musical pitch range.[1]

To the extent that it is permissible to treat the bridge as a simple lever, we see from figure 24.2 that the soundpost (which is placed very nearly under the treble foot) acts as a fulcrum about which the bridge can rock, so that it can exert a twisting force on the part of the front plate that lies between the f-holes. Notice that each of the string notches on a rocking bridge moves along an obliquely curving path. If it is permissible as well to treat the bass bar as rigid (a much riskier undertaking), the bridge also appears to exert up-and-down forces on the plate sections lying at its two ends. Whatever validity the simple lever and brace functions attributed to the bridge, soundpost, and bass bar have is limited to their action at low frequencies. The overall musical behavior of a violin depends on much more, however. The determination of the exact placement of a soundpost, for example, is one of the challenges to a good instrument maker— a misplaced soundpost can ruin the tone of the finest instrument.

The bowed string has two very different ways of exerting a driving force on the bridge. The most obvious one comes about directly from the side-to-side oscillation of the string in a direction parallel to the motion of the bow. We discussed the recipe for this sort of driving force earlier with the help of figure 23.6. This excitatory force, which we shall refer to as *direct excitation* of the bridge, is parallel to the surface of the top plate; a leverlike action of the bridge is required to convert it into a force at right angles to the plate surface that can effectively drive the body of the instrument.

The second means whereby the string vibrations are able to drive the top plate is somewhat more subtle. As we have already noticed, the tension of the string goes through two cycles of variation during every cycle of the vibration, reaching maxima when the string moves to its extreme positions on either side of the rest position. The fact that a fiddle string has a great deal of downbearing means that

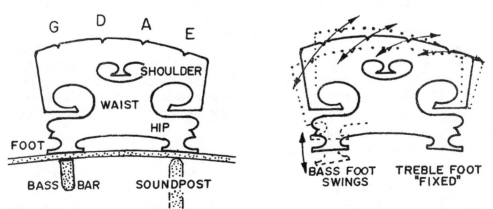

Fig. 24.2. *Left*, violin bridge, bass bar, and soundpost; *right*, predominant motion of the bridge.

oscillatory changes in string tension give rise to corresponding changes in the downward force exerted by the string on the bridge, a force which is ultimately applied to the top plate. Notice that the frequency of this *indirect excitation,* as we shall call it, takes place at twice the vibration frequency of the string. This means, for example, that mode 1 of a violin A-string produces direct action on the bridge at 440 Hz, whereas this mode acts by the indirect process to excite the bridge at 880 Hz. Similarly, mode 2 acting by itself produces direct and indirect driving force excitations at 880 and 1760 Hz. For the sake of brevity we will refer to the two kinds of driving force as F_n^{dir} and F_n^{ind}.

Let us now compare the driving-force recipes that are produced at the bridge by the direct and indirect excitation processes. To begin with, we almost instinctively recognize that the direct driving force F_n^{dir} produced by the corresponding string mode acting alone has an amplitude that is proportional to the vibrating amplitude A_n of that mode, so that F_n^{dir} doubles with every doubling of A_n, and so on. We also take it for granted that when several modes are in action, the force spectrum can be found by simply listing the actions of the several modes acting independently.

The indirect excitation process behaves quite differently. Here we find that if a *single string mode is excited to an ampli-*

simo playing conditions the indirect excitation process is negligible in comparison with direct excitation, whereas at mezzo-forte and higher levels the sound emitted via the indirect process can equal or even exceed the direct contribution.

The change in the sound spectrum arising from the relations between the two kinds of driving force is even more elaborate than is suggested by the discussion so far. When a number of string modes are excited (as in normal playing), the nonlinearity of the relation between A_n and F_n^{ind} results in a great deal of heterodyne action among the various frequency components. In particular, then, for a bowed string whose frequency components are arranged in the harmonic series 100, 200, 300, 400, . . . Hz, indirect excitation takes place at 100 Hz by way of heterodyne action *between all pairs of adjacent partials* (e.g., $500 - 400 = 100$ Hz; $400 - 300 = 100$ Hz; etc.). Similarly, an indirect excitation at 200 Hz takes place because of heterodyne contributions between *alternate* partials (such as $400 - 200 = 200$ Hz, $500 - 300 = 200$ Hz), as well as the double-frequency heterodyne action ($100 + 100 = 200$ Hz) that was our introduction to this type of excitation. I have calculated that the simplest Helmholtz-type vibrational amplitude spectrum (that makes F_n^{dir} scale as $[A_1/n]$; see sec. 23.5 following statement 1) gives rise to an indirect-excitation spectrum whose components have the following sizes:

component number	1	2	3	4	5
indirect driving force F_n^{ind}	1.00	1.25	1.11	0.98	0.87

tude A_n, the corresponding indirect bridge-force amplitude F_n^{ind} is proportional to the square of A_n, so that F_n^{ind} grows fourfold for every doubling of A_n. This tells us right away that under pianis-

These figures indicate that the overall spectrum of the force that drives the bridge is not drastically altered when one plays loudly enough to make the indirect type of bridge excitation important. Nevertheless, the efficiency of the transfer of oscillatory energy from string to fiddle increases significantly under fortissimo conditions as the indirect processes come into action.

B. *The Air Resonance of a Fiddle Body.* In 1937 Frederick Saunders devised an ingenious and straightforward means for studying the sound output of a stringed instrument: one simply plays a chromatic scale on the instrument at a forte level in a room of reasonable size and for each note writes down the readings of a sound level meter.[2] The reverberant properties of the room, the moving-around of the player and his helper (if one is present to record the data), and the effects of any vibrato all conspire to give a good average of the statistical properties of the room and of the radiation behavior of the instrument. What Saunders called *loudness curves* are obtained by plotting the sound level readings against the note names of the corresponding tones. Such curves show certain stable features that are characteristic of good instruments of each category. Even though each reading on the sound level meter indicates the aggregate effect of all the partials of the tone being played, it will show a certain increase if one of these partials happens to be unusually strong. This is the main reason that loudness curves of this type and some of their more recent descendants prove valuable in the study of stringed instruments.

One of the first things we can see in a violin loudness curve is evidence for a strong peak in the sound output whenever a partial of the played tone matches a well-defined frequency that is found in the neighborhood of 290 Hz. This peak, which is known as the *main air resonance*

of the instrument, is a consequence of the resonant excitation of the lowest characteristic mode of vibration of the air within the violin body. In the introductory remarks about the excitation mechanism of a flute, we learned of the way the slug of air in the neck of a bottle can bounce sinusoidally on the springiness provided by the air within the bottle (see sec. 22.6). The air within a violin body acts in exactly similar fashion as a spring upon which the mass of air in the f-holes can oscillate. The natural frequency of such a bottle-shaped air resonator will be lowered if the volume of enclosed air is increased, and it will be raised if the area of the f-holes is increased. If the walls of our cavity are elastically yielding, the natural frequency of its air resonance will be lowered (see sec. 22.7). The thin walls of violin-family instruments make this effect particularly pronounced. However, the soundpost and strings contribute significantly to the re-stiffening of the body, as is shown by the following simplified figures for a violin air-resonance frequency, which are based on measurements by Carleen Hutchins:[3]

without soundpost or
   strings . . . . .227 Hz
with soundpost, without
   strings . . . . .282 Hz
normal conditions . . . . .290 Hz
rigid-walled cavity of
   same proportions . . . . .350 Hz

Let us see how the bridge can excite this air resonance of the fiddle body, and how the excitation is then communicated to the air. To begin with, we see that the rocking of the bridge on its soundpost at low frequency alternately contracts and expands the volume of air contained within the body, so that air is alternately exhaled and inhaled by the f-holes in a manner exactly reminiscent of the breathing behavior produced when a plastic squeeze bottle is pressed periodically between the fingers. This indicates that the f-holes themselves are able to function as a simple acoustic source of the kind defined in section 11.2 However, not every transfer of air through the f-holes will give rise to a sound. It is fairly obvious that denting the violin body by the local pressure of a bridge foot gives rise to a flow of room air into the region of the dent, i.e., into the volume vacated by the inward motion of the plate. This flow of room air into the dent takes place at the same time that other air is expelled into

the room through the f-holes from within the cavity. From the point of view of the room, then, there is no *net* flow of air into or out of the region immediately surrounding the violin as a whole (and so no production of sound), as long as these two flows compensate each other exactly. This equality of flow is what one observes at low frequencies of excitation, so that at low frequencies a fiddle body provided with f-holes is almost totally unable to radiate sound into the air! As the bridge excitation frequency rises toward the air-cavity resonance frequency, the oscillatory flow in and out of the f-holes becomes progressively more vigorous and so overcomes the cancellation produced by the

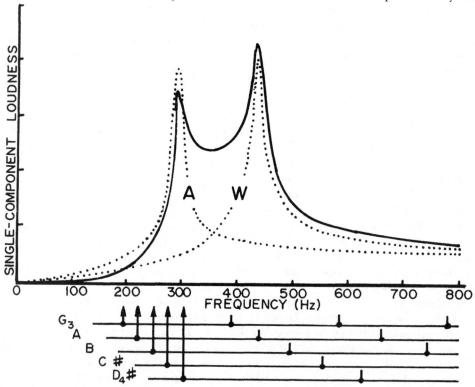

Fig. 24.3. Influence of Violin Air and Wood Resonances on the Loudness of a Single Component as a Function of Frequency

oppositely moving body walls. Above resonance, the motion of the enclosed air reverses in its relation to the driving force exerted by the walls (see sec. 10.1, statements 4 and 7), so that now the maximum outward flow coincides in time with the outward motion of the walls and the two contributors to the radiation act in concert.

The dotted curve marked A in figure 24.3 shows the influence of the first air resonance of a violin body on the perceived loudness of the sinusoid one would hear if a constant-amplitude sinusoidal driving force were applied to the bridge (we are assuming that nothing else is going on). At the bottom of the figure a set of lines is drawn which are labeled with the note names of a whole-tone scale beginning at the bottom note of the violin's playing range (G_3). Each line has marked on it dots at the frequencies of the various harmonic components of the corresponding note, so that you can understand how the loudnesses of these components are affected by the resonance peak.

C. The Main Wood Resonance and Its Connection with the Air Resonance. The next item of information one can extract from a study of the Saunders loudness curves is evidence for the existence of a strong sound output peak for string excitations taking place in the neighborhood of 440 Hz. This peak, which is usually referred to as the *main wood resonance,* has been traced to a vibrational mode of the wooden body itself. The upper part of figure 24.4 shows the part of this vibration which is observable on the top plate of a violin. The back plate has a similar but somewhat more symmetrical and much weaker motion. Notice that this mode is particularly easy to excite by means of the bridge and bass bar since

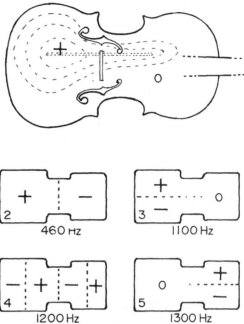

Fig. 24.4. *Upper,* coupling between first air mode and main wood resonance of a violin; *lower,* schematic diagrams of the air pressure distributions of the next four air modes within the violin body.

these act in the region of maximum top-plate excursion. This type of oscillation is sometimes called a "breathing mode," since the body as a whole expands and contracts its total volume. Such a mode (acting by itself) can function as a very effective source of excitation for sound in the room. The dotted curve marked W in figure 24.3 shows how the loudness perceived by a listener in a room would vary if this main wood-resonance mode were to act in the absence of any other property of the violin body. You will recognize that the air resonance whose radiation consequences are illustrated by curve A in figure 24.3 is excited by the same oscillatory breathing action of the cavity walls that gives rise to curve W, except that we earlier imagined the walls to be driven inexorably, with constant amplitude, by some mechanical device.

The solid curve in figure 24.3 shows how the air and wood resonances combine their influences in controlling the sound of a real violin. It is based on a calculation reported in 1962 by John Schelleng and confirmed by various experimental studies.[4] This overall curve has an interpretation that is very similar to that for the vocal-tract curves of chapter 19 (see figs. 19.5 and 19.6). A listener does not of course perceive enormous changes in the loudness of the complete tone when the strength of a single partial is altered. However, he will have no trouble in hearing a clearly marked change in tone color as a note with changing pitch slides some partial through the resonance peak (see sec. 19.5). We should notice in passing that for violin notes between G_3 and A_4, the fundamental component and/or its second harmonic always has its loudness considerably enhanced by the joint effect of the main air and wood resonances. Similar remarks can be made about the lower notes of the other members of the bowed string family of instruments.

D. *The Influence of Other Air Resonances.* In part B of this section we learned that because the walls of the violin are yielding, the first air-mode resonance is lowered quite significantly. We can recognize that this yielding of the walls is simply the response of the main wood-resonance mode to the pressure variations of the enclosed air, the excitation taking place well below the natural frequency of the walls. In a series of experiments carried on since 1972, Erik Jansson in Stockholm has found that this coupling behavior of the air and wood modes works both ways: he and Harry Sundin have shown that on a violin the second mode of air vibration can have a significant effect on the frequency of what we have been calling the main wood resonance.[5] Let us see how this comes about and at the same time make the acquaintance of some of the other air-cavity modes.

The lower half of figure 24.4 shows diagrammatically the acoustic pressure distributions and nodal lines for air modes 2 through 5. The dashed lines indicate nodes and the regions marked 0 are places where very little oscillatory pressure variation is detectable. Mode 2, whose natural frequency lies in the neighborhood of 460 Hz, is a simple sloshing of air back and forth between the ends of the cavity; this mode closely resembles the first air mode of a pipe that is closed at both ends in having a pressure maximum at each end and a node at or near the middle. Comparison of the top-plate vibration pattern shown in the upper part of figure 24.4 with the pressure pattern for air mode 2 shows that the large excursion of the lower half of the plate (on the tailpiece side of the f-holes) strongly drives the lower half-hump of the air-mode standing wave—an internal excitation that is not canceled by the weaker vibrations of the upper half of the plate which act on the oppositely varying air pressure in this region.

Jansson has shown that the mutual influence of air mode 2 and the main wood resonance is so strong that the peak marked W in figure 24.3 is generally split into two peaks that can have quite a deep notch between them. The exact behavior of the sound output in the neighborhood of what we have been calling the main wood resonance thus turns out to be a complicated version of the behavior we first noticed in the kettledrum; it is not correct to consider air and mechanical properties independently—the two peaks have frequencies that are determined jointly by the air and by the walls, and one should not in general assume that the predominant motion is to be found in either of the two subsystems. The fact that air mode 2 has a nodal line running across the waist of the instrument tells us that very little air will be driven in and out of the f-holes by this type of air motion. The radiated sound associated with both parts of the split W-curve peak is thus produced almost entirely by the wall vibrations acting directly on the outside air.

The higher-frequency air modes will be excited to a greater or lesser extent by the various higher modes of the violin body, although their influence on these higher wood resonances is not expected to be very large. However, we can look for contributions to the radiated sound at the frequencies of those air modes having pressure maxima near the positions of the f-holes.

24.2. High-Frequency Radiation Properties of Bowed String Instruments

We have just completed a close examination of two prominent peaks which are found at the low-frequency end of every violin-family instrument's range. At higher frequencies we still find many peaks and dips, but these do not in general show very much similarity as we go from one violin to another, for example, or from one cello to another. The overall trend of the transmission behavior is very similar for all stringed instruments, however, and we can gain a fairly good understanding of the reasons for this trend.

Before we begin to list the various acoustical properties of the body which help to control this trend, we should remind ourselves that, to a reasonably good approximation, the magnitude of the driving force F_n^{dir} exerted on the bridge by each component of the played tone is roughly constant. For instance, we learned in section 23.5 that in the theory of Helmholtz the direct-excitation F_n's decrease as $(1/n)$ for increasing mode number n. Furthermore, in section 24.1 we learned that the indirect excitation arising from oscillatory variations in the string downbearing has a set of driving-force components F_n^{ind} that decrease only gradually as we shift our attention to the higher-numbered modes. Since the two forms of bridge excitation give us roughly equal driving forces at all frequencies, in our attempts to understand the sound output of an instrument we need consider only the varying ability of the body to convert a driving force into sound in the room.

We learned in sections 11.2 and 12.4-C that the radiating power of a loudspeaker or other sound source in a room rises steadily as we go to higher frequencies until the dimensions of the source become comparable with the hump dimensions (half wavelengths) of the room modes. At higher frequencies the excitation becomes progressively less effective, for reasons that we first met in connection with the excitation of strings by a broad plectra and hammers (see secs. 8.1 and 8.2). For a violin-sized object we would expect this dimensional limitation on its ability to radiate to begin advertising itself with a gradual leveling-off of the sound output above the 1000 Hz.

As the excitation frequency applied to the body by the strings rises, it excites the plates into increasingly complicated vibration modes, each one having more nodal lines than the one before.[6] This is a way of saying that the vibrating surface divides itself up ever more finely into vibrating segments each of which acts oppositely on the room from its neighbors. A glance at the plate and drumhead vibrational shapes illustrated in chapter 9 will confirm this. A violin driven at the bridge in the frequency region between 1500 and 2000 Hz shows vibration patterns having two or three dozen humps distributed over the entire body surface. An engineer who forgets that the violin is not a loudspeaker might criticize it for being an extremely inefficient radiator of sound at these frequencies, since these vibrational humps (which may be only 2 or 3 cm across) have a span that is very much shorter than the 8-to-12-cm widths of the room-mode humps in this range of frequencies. The presence of many small humps gives us a second reason to expect a falling-off in the high-frequency sound output of a violin, this time with a limitation that becomes significant above about 2000 Hz.

Studies of the energy lost within the wood itself show that the damping produced by both cross-grain and along-the-grain frictional losses rises sharply at frequencies above about 3500 Hz.[7] Above this frequency, then, an ever-increasing share of the string excitation is diverted away from its tortuous path to the room, spending its effort instead on frictional heating within the structure of the instrument. This gives us yet another reason to expect a reduction in the strengths of the high-frequency partials of a violin tone.

When all three of the high-frequency limitations described above are taken into account, we would expect the partials of a violin tone that lie above about 2000 Hz to be very much attenuated. Even when we take into account the increasing sensitivity of the ear for high-frequency sounds, we should expect an extension of the curve shown in figure 24.3 to fall to very small values indeed above about 3000 Hz. Let us see what actually happens.

Figure 24.5 shows the loudnesses of the various partials as a function of frequency (I have calculated these loudnesses on the basis of measurements made by many different experimenters). Below 500 Hz (about C_5) the curve is simply a replotting of the information contained in figure 24.3. It is at higher frequencies that we notice something surprising: while this high-frequency region contains many sharp peaks and dips (whose positions vary from instrument to instrument), the output averaged over the peaks always shows a *rising* trend that extends past our expected 2000-Hz limitation and continues up to about 3000 Hz before the strengths of the higher partials begin to be strongly attenuated! We are forced to recognize that something in the complete vibratory system is able to do much more than merely counteract the attenuating effects listed earlier.

We do not have to go far to discover the explanation for this modified behavior. In section 24.1, part A, I pointed out that it is proper to treat the bridge as a simple lever only at frequencies well below the 3000-Hz first-mode resonance of the bridge itself. It is not difficult to show mathematically that as the frequency of the string driving force on the bridge rises toward the bridge's own

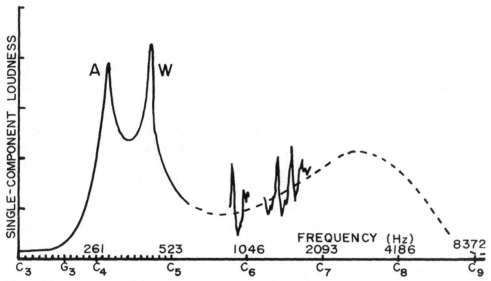

Fig. 24.5. Summary of All Influences on the Loudness of a Single Component as a Function of Frequency

resonance frequency (as measured with the feet clamped), the effective lever ratio of the bridge grows so as to magnify the force available at the bridge feet to drive the top plate. Walter Reinicke has measured not only the resonance frequencies of violin and cello bridges, but also the actual transformation ratio between the string and foot forces.[8] Reinicke's figures for the resonantly peaked driving efficacy of the bridge account for the increased strengths of the string partials shown around 3000 Hz in figure 24.5. Reinicke was also able to use data on the properties of the bridge to explain the variations he observed in the damping of the A-string modes that we made use of in section 23.3. The measured dampings of the string modes correlate with the ability of the bridge to steal the vibratory energy of the string by passing it along to the violin body and thence to the air.

24.3. Characteristic Features of the Violin, Viola, and Cello; A Recent Development: *The New Family of Large and Small True Violins*

In the preceding two sections of this chapter we have learned of three stable features of the acoustical behavior of the body of a typical bowed string instrument which underlie its predominant tonal characteristics. Two of these features are resonance peaks: (1) the strong resonance associated with the lowest mode of oscillation of the air enclosed within the body of the instrument and (2) the equally strong resonance associated with the simplest of the vibrations of the body's wooden parts. These resonances exert their influence on the lower notes of the instrument by altering the strengths of the first and second partials of the tone. The third stable feature is a broadly rising amplitude of the higher partials up to a frequency that can be predicted from a knowledge of the first-mode resonance of the bridge itself (as measured with its feet clamped). In the following paragraphs we will look at how these features are related to the tunings and sizes of the violin, viola, and cello.[9]

The violin has its four strings tuned in fifths to the notes G_3, D_4, A_4, and E_5, and on a good instrument the air resonance lies near 290 Hz, within a semitone of the fundamental frequency of the D-string. Similarly, the so-called main wood resonance (which is in fact the joint consequence of a body resonance and mode 2 of the air within it) is located around 440 Hz, within a semitone of the A-string tuning. On a violin the strengths of the low A_3 and its two neighbors are enhanced greatly by the fact that the second partials of these tones sit more or less on top of the main wood resonance. All these things taken together explain why a Saunders loudness curve typically shows maxima for the notes near A_3, D_4, and A_4. One also frequently gets strong notes in the general regions of C_5 and C_6. In the neighborhood of 3000 Hz the peaks and dips follow a trend having a broad maximum that is controlled by the resonant force-transformation properties of the bridge.

Because violas are built in more widely varying dimensions, we find less uniformity among different instruments. However, the following figures are reasonably representative. The strings are tuned a fifth below those of a violin, at C_3, G_3, D_4, and A_4. The first-mode air resonance is often around 230 Hz (near $B_3\flat$), being somewhat lower on large instruments and higher on small ones. Already we can see why the lowest notes on a viola tend to be somewhat weak and dull: the air peak lies about ten semitones above the bottom C_3, so the fundamental components of the lowest few notes are very weakly radiated. The viola's main wood resonance is likely to be around 350 Hz (near F_4), so that the two resonances are related by approximately a musical fifth, as they were in the case of the violin. (Having made this remark, I must hasten to warn my readers not to make too much of its direct musical significance. The tolerances of the locations of these resonances are easily sufficient to permit this interval to range on good instruments from as little as a fourth to as much as a sixth—the particular relationship is not important in itself.) The musical characteristics of the lower viola notes from $E_3\flat$ on up are reminiscent of the notes of a violin going up from G_3. The resemblance can be traced to the similar placement of the resonances relative to these notes on the two instruments. Because of the differences in proportion between violins and violas, the mode-2 air resonance of a viola is somewhat higher in relation to the wood resonance than it is for a violin. As a result, in the Saunders loudness curves of a viola one can see evidence for the separate identities of these resonances. Data are unfortunately not available on the resonance frequencies of the viola bridge, but there is evidence to suggest that the spectrum has its high-frequency maximum in the general region of 2000 Hz. In brief, the string tunings and playing range of a viola are transposed a fifth below those of the violin, and the high-frequency behavior seems also to be transposed downward by this amount. However, the crucially important lower two resonances are *not* transposed down a fifth, and this change in the overall relationships gives the viola a musical character distinctly different from that of the violin. It is not a closely related larger brother of the violin in the way that a B♭ tenor saxophone is the lower-pitched brother of the E♭ alto.

The cello has its strings tuned an octave below those of a viola (a twelfth below those of the violin) at C_2, G_2, D_3, and A_3. The main air resonance is found to lie in the neighborhood of 125 Hz (between B_2 and C_3). This is even higher in relation to the bottom-string tuning than is the case for the viola. While the actual sharpness and tallness of the air-resonance peak of a cello are roughly the same as on the smaller instruments and while the peak's presence is clearly audible, its visibility on a Saunders loudness curve is considerably less, for reasons that we will consider shortly. The main wood resonance of a cello lies near 175 Hz (about F_3), which places it therefore somewhat more than halfway in pitch between the upper two strings of the instrument. Notice that so far the properties of the cello and viola appear to be quite consistent with one another, since the corresponding resonances, as well as the string tunings, are an octave apart on the two instruments. In fact their behavior is quite different, one reason being connected with the peculiar behavior of the cello's air response. The other distinction comes about because the tall bridge of a cello leads to an extremely strong response of the body to string excitations having a frequency near the main wood resonance. This response can sometimes detune the string's own mode-1 frequency sufficiently to disrupt the formation of a normal regime of oscillation; in its stead, various more complicated types of vibration may take place that are collectively known to musicians as wolf notes.

Because a cello bridge has legs proportionately much longer than those of a violin bridge, its first-mode vibrational shape has a rather different appearance. Nevertheless, Reinicke finds, as before, a large increase in the ability of the string to drive the body at the bridge's third mode (near 2000 Hz), and there is a deep notch in the transmission ability at an intermediate frequency a little above 1500 Hz. Both the notch and the second maximum lie within the musically important range of a cello spectrum, whereas the analogous features of a violin bridge transmission curve lie at about 5000 and 6000 Hz, too high to be of much significance.

Let us turn now to an examination of the cello's behavior when it is played near the main air resonance. As expected, the air resonance has clearly audible effects. To pick it out, one does not listen for loudness changes (since loudness is a property of all the harmonic partials taken together); instead one listens for changes in tone color and for the special smoothness of tone that is associated with sounds whose components are placed on transmission resonances. The main air resonance, which is easy enough to hear that with a little practice one can notice it under the rapidly changing conditions of musical performance, shows up on a Saunders loudness curve as a peak of surprisingly modest dimensions. This points out the danger of too much reliance on readings from a sound level meter, which can register only the combined sound-pressure contributions from *all* the harmonics of the played tone. This means that it may overlook a change in the amplitude of some partial of particular interest, such as the main air resonance, and allow it to be partially masked by the welter of other components. An example of how the sound level meter can shortchange the strength of a resonance occurs when some higher partial of the tone falls into a dip in the radiation curve at the same time that the fundamental component is placed on a peak. The two effects manage to offset each other in the meter reading even though they give rise to an easily recognized auditory sensation. Let us look at an example of such behavior, since there is reason to suspect that a typical cello shows a weakening of the radiated second harmonic of the tone whose fundamental is reinforced by the first air resonance.

The dimensions of a cello body are such as to give its second air mode a frequency that is very nearly an octave above the frequency of its first air mode (rather than a wide fifth above, as on a violin). As a result both of these modes will be strongly excited when a note is played at the main air-resonance frequency, since they match the first and second vibrational components of that note. A glance at figure 24.4 will remind us, though, that the second air mode will not radiate much even though it may be strongly excited, because the f-holes lie in the nodal region of the second mode of vibration. This means that we should not expect this resonance to enhance the second harmonic component of the sound. However, two acoustical consequences can be expected from the excitation of air mode 2. First, we find that the cello's top plate is made to "feel" more than normally rigid to the bridge feet when the air mode is strongly excited, thus reducing the transmission of vibratory energy from the string to the body. Second, the frictional losses and other losses of energy incurred by the nonradiative sloshing of the

second-mode air oscillation will absorb some of the excitation from the string, once again reducing the sound output from the instrument. Both of these phenomena will show a broadly tuned effect: air mode 2 need not lie exactly an octave above the mode-1 frequency for the reduced second partial of the string tone to offset the resonant increase in the strength of the fundamental component significantly, thus producing only a small peak in the sound level meter reading for this note.

Bowed instruments of the violin family were perfected during the seventeenth and eighteenth centuries, giving us the violin, the viola, and the cello. The lowest member of the bowed string tribe today, the bass viol, is a descendant of the acoustically different family of viols, which otherwise exists today only in antiquarian surroundings. Contrary to the almost universal practice of wind-instrument makers since the Renaissance and of the early makers of the viols, the early violin makers were not successful in developing a complete set of instruments having overlapping playing ranges spaced apart in fifths or fourths (e.g., soprano, alto, tenor, and bass). The violin and viola have this relationship, but there is a member of the family missing between viola and cello, and another between cello and bass viol. From time to time over the centuries efforts have been made to fill these gaps, but until recently the resulting instruments proved to have shortcomings that prevented their acceptance for serious musical purposes.

In 1958, during a series of intensive experiments carried on by Carleen Hutchins and Frederick Saunders on the effects of moving violin and viola resonances up and down in frequency, the composer Henry Brant and the cellist Sterling Hunkins proposed the development of eight instruments in a series of tunings and sizes to cover the entire musical range, all of these to have their main air and wood resonances placed close to the frequencies of the two middle strings, as they are on the conventional violin. This suggestion was timely both from scientific and musical points of view, because an attack on the design problems connected with such a project promised to reveal a great many things about the acoustics of conventional instruments.

In the years since 1958, Hutchins has herself worked indefatigably and has enlisted the cooperation and aid of many others to bring this "new family of fiddles" into existence. The musical and scientific rewards of these efforts have proven to be at least as great as was originally hoped.[10] The family has two instruments that are above the violin in pitch: the treble, with strings tuned an octave above the violin, and the soprano, with tunings a fifth higher than the violin. The alto, which is the viola member of the new family, has a length of about 82 cm (in place of the 70 cm typical of a viola). This added length is required because an ordinary viola is physically too small to have its resonances placed in the desired manner. Some people play the alto vertically on a peg, cello-fashion, while others place it under the chin as is done with a conventional viola. Next comes the tenor, which is somewhat smaller than an ordinary cello (107 cm rather than 124 cm in body length), with its strings tuned a fifth above the cello. This instrument fills the tuning gap that is normally left between viola and cello. Below the tenor comes the baritone, which has the same string tunings as a

cello but a larger body. Finally there are a small and a large bass (these now being true violins), with their strings tuned in fourths, at A_1, D_2, G_2, C_3 and E_1, A_1, D_2, G_2.

John Schelleng worked out the scaling rules that determine the proportions of the new family. We can summarize here some of the main requirements that his scaling design had to meet to ensure the musical usefulness of the instruments.

1. String lengths had to be scaled to fit human proportions: a half-length string for the treble would be too small for the playing of a chromatic scale, and a bass string length of 3.6 meters (twice the height of a man) would clearly be beyond the abilities of the most athletic bassist.

2. Once string and body lengths are chosen to fit the needs of the player, one has only the thickness (and to some extent the arching) of the plates available for adjustment to get the wood resonances in the desired positions. It turns out that the plates of the smallest instruments must be an astonishing 5 mm thick. On the large bass the astonishment has an opposite cause—the plates are so thin that one feels he could punch holes in them by a vigorous tap with a pencil.

3. The frequency of the main air resonance (i.e., air mode 1) depends chiefly on the volume of the body cavity and on the area of the f-holes. Since the plate sizes and also the f-hole dimensions are chosen to satisfy the requirements listed earlier, the chief recourse here is to adjust the depths of the ribs. Even this does not suffice in the treble violin since an over-shallow body not only looks peculiar, it also lacks sufficient strength to withstand twisting forces. For this reason, the ribs are fairly deep, but they have extra vent holes to bring the air-resonance frequency up to the

desired value near $2 \times 290 = 580$ Hz. The problem is also difficult at the bass end of the scale: one cannot build too deep a body or the player will not be able to put his bow arm around it. However, the yielding of the thin walls of the body makes it possible to get the resonance down to the desired frequency. Another possible problem is that if the violins of the new family were all to be built with rigid walls, the large instruments would have exceedingly narrow air resonance peaks of unacceptable tallness. Fortunately, the motion of the progressively thinner walls provides enough extra damping to keep the peaks within limits of tallness and breadth that give good acoustical results.

4. Once the body proportions of each member of the family are set, corresponding string sizes must be assigned. As we learned in our study of pianos and harpsichords, it is important to get a proper relationship between the wave impedances of the strings and of the body (as mediated by the bridge). This means that the thicknesses of the strings on each instrument must be chosen along with their tensions to meet simultaneously the needs for correct vibrational frequency and for a suitable string-to-body wave impedance ratio.

Two sets of the new violin family of instruments have been built. They have excited a tremendous amount of interest and enthusiasm wherever they have been demonstrated. Their tonal homogeneity poses a challenge to composers who are used to the distinctly different sounds of the violin, viola, and cello; for instance, care must be taken in part-writing to prevent the various musical voices from running together into a full but somewhat bland overall sound. The new instruments cannot normally be used as replacements for the conventional ones, because of their different tone and power, but for certain purposes they have begun to make their way into standard usage. For example, the fullness and power of the alto violin will tear up a string quartet if it is substituted for the viola, but the alto can serve beautifully on occasion as the solo voice in a viola concerto where it must compete with the entire orchestra. The superior power and tonal fullness of the bass members of the family as compared with the conventional bass viol have also aroused considerable enthusiasm on the part of players and conductors.

The success of Carleen Hutchins and her co-workers in building a consort of true violins in accordance with John Schelleng's scaling procedures is impressive. Their instruments' musical usefulness is a tribute to the combination of scientific understanding and craftsmanship of a high order that went into the making of them. Once the first set of new instruments was in existence, it was natural to want to find a way to cross-check the acoustical relationships against their perceptual analogs. In the spring of 1964 it seemed to me worthwhile to compare the tone of various members of the Hutchins family of instruments with the tone of a good conventional violin that had been tape-recorded and played back at altered speed in order to transpose its sounds to the pitch ranges of the various new instruments. The violinist Edith Roberts and I made a preliminary tape of this sort which was promising enough to warrant our carrying out a more careful experiment in 1968.[11]

In such an experiment there are several musical and technical implications to the required alternation of recordings and playbacks made at two-thirds and one-half speed. The tempo is drastically altered along with the pitch change, as is the rate of vibrato. For instance, to make an acceptable imitation of the tenor instrument (which plays an octave down), it is necessary to play at a very fast tempo (approximately double) so that the music will come out at a reasonable pace on playback. Recording and playing back at differing speeds brings about alterations in the frequency response and internal noise properties of the equipment, and these must be carefully compensated.

The recording was done in the living-room/music-room area of my home, a region that is large enough to guarantee that hundreds of room resonances will be excited by any one of the violin partials. The final tape put together from our recordings has a very pleasant sound but, far more interesting, it is easy to recognize that the tonal characteristics of the various new instruments are present in the transposed sound of the ordinary violin. A particular example of this is the presence of an almost unpleasant squawkiness in the tones of both the treble violin and its transposed counterpart. Hutchins and I verified that increasing the damping of the air resonance of the treble violin by stuffing a certain amount of cotton into its f-holes would eliminate the difficulty. This shows that an air resonance whose tallness and sharpness contribute to what we like very much in the tone of a violin is not suitable for "best" sound when a high-pitched instrument is built.

24.4. The Adjustment of Violin Plates and the Required Properties of Their Material

The making of instruments of the violin family has always been among the most demanding of arts. There are so many variables involved and so much time elapses between the carving of a plate and its assembly into an instrument ready for testing that the maker can hardly learn from experience unless he is possessed of a perfect memory, remarkable intuition, a fine ear, and endless patience. Many craftsmen can make a respectable instrument, but it is given to very few in any generation to create a superb one, and these special individuals are not always able to pass on their knowledge.

Because she is a skillful instrument maker in the conventional sense as well as an expert in musical acoustics, Carleen Hutchins has been able to add greatly to our fund of teachable knowledge on how to adjust the various parts of an instrument in the course of construction. Her success in this activity and that of her collaborators have encouraged increasing numbers of instrument makers to learn and to make use of acoustical testing as a guide in their work.[12] We cannot detail here many of the ways in which acoustical science provides information to the maker, but it is worthwhile to outline some of the complexities of the problem as well as some of the ways in which these complexities can be exploited or circumvented.

The vibrational properties of any part of a violin, viola, or cello depend not only on the easily measured size, thickness, and arching of the wood, but also on the elasticity, density, and internal damping—properties which change from sample to sample, and even from day to day as the temperature and humidity change.[13] From the earliest days instrument makers have intuitively recognized that the less-tangible properties of the wood affect the vibrational properties of the isolated plate as well as those of the finished instrument. Because of this, an extensive lore has grown up on how to listen for certain sounds called *tap tones* that can be heard when the plate is held in certain ways and tapped at particular spots. Such tests are of course informal explorations of the characteristic modes of the plate—not merely their natural frequencies of oscillation but also the nature of their vibrational shapes. Hutchins and others have systematized the exploration of tap tones with the aid of laboratory apparatus that can extricate one sinusoidal component at a time from the complete collection that we perceive as the tap tone. It is much easier to tell someone what spectral components are to be sought in making a viola plate than it is to teach him by repeated example exactly what sort of woody, ringing sound he is supposed to listen for. This in turn makes it easier to explain where to scrape and carve in order to arrange the various sound components into a desired relationship.

Another approach that has proved immensely fruitful is to mount the plate on a well-standardized system of supports (clamps or rubber bands) and then to excite it at a carefully chosen point by a magnetic drive coil. The resulting vibrations are detected either by a pickup located somewhere on the plate or by means of a microphone placed a short distance away. Response curves plotted in this way contain a great deal of useful information about the vibrational properties of the plate, especially when the peaks and dips observed in one experimental arrangement are correlated with those in another (see the tin-tray experiments in sec. 10.7). Once a craftsman has taken the time to become familiar with two or three major features of the response curve of properly carved plates, he can then carefully work over each new plate until its vibration signature, as evidenced by these characteristic features, is of the proper sort. It is of course very helpful for any instrument maker working in this way to have a fairly good idea of the vibrational shapes of the various plate modes, so that perturbation techniques of the sort outlined in section 9.4 can guide his efforts.

The positions of plate resonances are not at all easy to deduce on the basis of response curves made with a microphone. When the microphone is placed only a short distance away from the plate (1 to 50 cm), it responds in a very complicated way to the sound output of all parts of the plate and displays certain consequences of the local flow of air across the nodal lines and also around the edges of the plate. A vibrational mode of the plate may manifest its presence in the response curve by a paired dip and peak, by a simple peak or an unsymmetrical peak, or even by a dip. One also finds extra peaks and dips in the microphone response curve that have no counterparts in the modal frequencies of the plate. Despite these complexities, measurements using carefully placed microphones have proved immensely useful in practice. Techniques based on sound-pressure averages made in a reverberant room are also available. These tend to give plate resonance data in much more direct form than similar averages gathered from microphones placed at large distances from the plate in an anechoic chamber.

It is not difficult in principle to discover the characteristic shapes of the various plate modes. One has merely to drive the plate at the proper frequency and then map out the vibrating surface, either with an optical or magnetic probe, or by means of a small microphone held so that the distance between the vibrating surface and the microphone diaphragm is *much* less than the microphone diameter (the distance must be very short, otherwise the microphone signal consists of a surprisingly equal mixture of disturbances coming from all parts of the plate). A quicker but much more elaborate way to obtain the vibration pattern of a plate mode is to use photographically recorded laser holograms, following a technique first applied by Karl Stetson.

In practice, working out the characteristic shapes of the free-plate modes is almost as difficult (and treacherous) as is the determination of the characteristic frequencies themselves. Much of the difficulty, in fact, lies in finding these plate-mode frequencies (as discussed in an earlier paragraph). If one does not drive at a plate resonance, there will be significant excitation of at least two adjacent modes, so that the plate is moving in a complicated way having a peculiar set of nodal lines and hump regions that are in reality the result of superposing two characteristic shapes. Such shapes are easily misinterpreted. In certain cases, two or more of the natural frequencies may lie so close together that it is impossible to separate their contributions. Under these conditions considerable ingenuity is required to extricate the true patterns of the individual modes. Here the non-holographic methods often show an advantage.

The vibrational properties of a wood plate are very much dependent on the fact that the cross-grain stiffness is only about ten percent of the stiffness along the grain (see the digression on wood plates in sec. 9.2). If one wanted to simulate the vibrational behavior of a wooden violin plate in metal or plastic, it would be necessary to cut it so that the ratio of length to width would be close to unity, instead of the customary ratio of about three-to-one. Let us understand the implications of this remark with the help of figure 24.6, which shows in schematic form the first five mode shapes of the top or back plate of a violin. Mode 1 is the twisting mode that we first met in figure 9.3. In the violin the frequencies of top and back free plate mode 1 are not similar, mostly because of the action of the f-holes in the top plate. Two versions of mode 2 appear. Though rather dissimilar in appearance, they have very nearly the same frequency—about 50 percent higher than that of mode 1. The theory of vibrating plates agrees with experiment in predicting both versions of the mode-shape; theory also predicts its frequency relative to mode 1, but only for plates that are functionally square. Modes 3 and 4 have vibrational shapes that are very reminiscent of the motion of a free disc vibrating with three nodal lines crossing its diameter. In one of these two modes we find a nodal line running parallel to the grain, while in the other the corresponding nodal line is at right angles to the grain. Different pieces of wood may reverse the order of these two

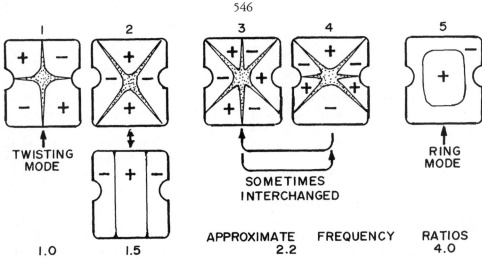

Fig. 24.6. Relation between Free Plate Modes of a Violin and Those of an Approximately Square Metal Plate

vibrational patterns, as indicated in the figure, or further work on a given plate, such as thinning, may result in reversal. Theory and experiment agree in placing the frequencies of these two modes at somewhat more than double the mode-1 frequency. The frequency spacing between modes 3 and 4 can vary from 10 percent to nearly 50 percent. The reversibility of the order of these two modes and the near equality of their frequencies constitute a direct proof that the plate is very nearly "square" in its acoustical properties, since on a perfectly square or perfectly circular plate they would have identical frequencies. Modes 3 and 4 are particularly difficult to separate in holographic experiments—one or the other may be overlooked or obscured.

String-instrument makers find that it is especially important to obtain the correct vibrational shape for mode 5, which is often called the ring mode. The inner parts of the plate move in one direction while the outer parts move in the other. It has a frequency about 4 times that of

mode 1. When the vibrational shape is that sketched for mode 5, the arching of the violin plate adds great stiffness to the vibrating system, and this stiffness raises the frequency. If the plate were flat, the mode having this shape would be recognizable by mathematicians as forming a pair with the upper version of mode 2. (The stiffness due to arching has relatively little influence on the lower modes we have sketched since these are primarily of a twisting character.)

Every string player knows of instruments that play well in dry weather, and others that perform best when the humidity is high. The reason is simple to find once we realize that the two stiffnesses of wood (measured along and across the grain) change differently with changes in humidity. This means that an instrument can only be in its optimum vibratory condition with a single sort of weather. The maker is left with the choice of tuning the two plates of a string instrument relative to each other under identical conditions or finishing each on a different day in the hope of building an instrument that performs at least acceptably under all conditions.

Recent developments in the science and engineering of artificial materials have encouraged serious work on the possibility of making musical instrument bodies out of suitably designed composite materials. Carleen Hutchins, Donald Thompson of the C. F. Martin Company, and Daniel Haines of the University of South Carolina have recently demonstrated guitars (1974) and violins (1975) whose top plates are made in the form of a sandwich.[14] The inner core is a kind of paper over which are laid long strands of carefully aligned carbon fibers held together by epoxy cement. The desired ratio between the stiffnesses along and across the grain is achieved through the enormous tensile strength of these fibers combined with the flexibility of the epoxy. The relative thicknesses of the paper and the outer coverings are adjusted to provide the desired density and also the variation of internal damping with frequency of the sort that is needed for a successful imitation of wood. Holograms of the vibrations of the carbon-epoxy violin plate show essentially no difference from those for a wooden violin plate of good quality. The assembled violin plays very well and has excited the serious consideration of a manufacturer interested in dependable production on a commercial basis.

24.5. Musical Properties of Bowed String Instruments

Certain special properties of the sound from bowed string instruments set these instruments apart from other members of the orchestra. Each member of this family has a pair of strong air and wood resonances that influence the radiated sounds of its lower notes. Moreover, one finds in the total radiated sound of each member of the family a large number of higher-frequency peaks and dips fluctuating about a broadly humped maximum whose frequency is determined largely by the resonance properties of the bridge (see fig. 24.5). If we stop our considerations here, we are led to think of the string sound as being determined in a manner almost strictly analogous to the transmission of the human voice: a more or less autonomous source has its oscillations transmitted to the room by way of a filter that has a number of transmission peaks. In other words, the air and main wood resonance peaks appear to be simple analogs of the first two voice formant peaks (see figs. 19.5 and 19.6).

However, when radiation behavior is considered, we recognize that the analogy sketched above is a gross oversimplification. Voice sounds are emitted by a small aperture that functions as a simple source to radiate almost equally in all directions. By contrast, the complicated vibrational shapes of the violin body cause it to send into the room an exceedingly complex pattern which, for example, is different for every direction in which the sound can go in an anechoic chamber.[15]

On an average basis, the violin radiates its low-frequency partials equally in all directions; its higher components are radiated in a progressively tighter beam in a direction perpendicular to the plates (this behavior is reminiscent of the progressively increasing directionality of sound components emitted by a trumpet or a woodwind; see secs. 20.8 and 22.4). However, superposed on this average behavior are the elaborate directional patterns of the separate partials mentioned above. It is this complicated radiation pattern for each partial of a violin tone (a pattern that changes drastically for any change in frequency) that distinguishes the violin family from other instruments.

Because of the integrative abilities of our hearing mechanism, we are able to collect all of these radiative complexities as they come to us via multiple reflections in the room. The vibrato (taking place at the rate of about half a dozen cycles per second) plays a particularly interesting role among the bowed string instruments. It supplies a sort of timing cue for the relationships among all the partials, whose strengths fluctuate more or less randomly in amplitude but concurrently (at least at the source) in time. There are many implications to be drawn from the fact that the 30-to-50 millisecond "collecting time" of the hearing mechanism associated with the precedence effect (see secs. 12.2 and 12.4) is comparable with the 80-millisecond time it takes for the vibrato to sweep the component frequencies from maximum to minimum or back. One's thinking can also be stimulated by the fact that each of the first half-dozen harmonic partials of a tone lies within its own critical bandwidth for the ear (see sec. 13.5) and so has its fluctuations processed for loudness, etc., more or less as an individual, whereas the higher partials are spaced closely enough relative to the critical bandwidth (which is approximately one-third of an octave) for overlapping collections of them to be processed together. This aggregate processing on the one hand tends to average out the radiation and room fluctuations; on the other hand, it can lead to a harshness of tone if these higher partials are too strong relative to the lower half-dozen.

The difference between the ways in which we aurally process the loudnesses of low- and high-frequency phenomena helps to explain why we had to pay such close attention to the details of the low-frequency end of the curve in figure 24.5, whereas we looked only at the general trend of the high-frequency part of the curve. We also gain some insight into the reasons why a violin (or any other instrument) must be provided with a means for ensuring a reasonably small acoustic output at high frequencies.

The fact that our hearing mechanisms can winnow out the common elements provided by the body resonances of a violin or cello while at the same time permitting us to enjoy the fluctuating variety of the unprocessed sound provides us with a unity in the midst of diversity that is extremely difficult to imitate.[16] We can readily understand the limited success of attempts at electronic synthesis of bowed string sounds, even when the vibrations of an actual bowed string are picked up electrically and run through a fixed set of filters on their way to a high-fidelity loudspeaker.[17] No matter how elaborately the peaks and dips of the filter transmission curve are matched to the radiation of a violin in a given direction, our ears have no difficulty recognizing the artificiality of the sound. The successive versions of the sound that reach us from different parts of the room all share the same common origin—the filter and loudspeaker. One would require at least several filter sets separately radiating into the room to simulate the diversity of the sound reaching us from a normal instrument.[18] This gives us a hint why even such simple sounds as those produced by tapping a board with a stick or snapping a rubber band stretched across a cigar box are so difficult to synthesize by conventional means. It is not so much the particular frequency components or the damping of the modes that gives us such a clear impression of the woodiness or the twang in these sounds, but rather the fact that they are radiated in a way that is characteristic of vibrating plates.

There is one more feature of string tone that has a very large influence on its musical behavior. There is an inherent unsteadiness to the bowed string tone that has been noticed from the earliest days. On a bad instrument the unsteadiness of the oscillatory regime becomes a splutter or scrape (whose dynamical implications were pointed out by Helmholtz in his first paper), whereas on the best instruments we find this unsteadiness becoming a sort of warmth and richness.

While I was still an undergraduate I noticed that one does not hear clear-cut beats between mistuned violin tones of the sort that painfully advertise slight errors between two wind instrument sounds. It was not difficult for me to recognize at that time that the weakness of the beats implied unsteadinesses in the sticking and slipping of the rosined bow on the string. In 1963 and later, correspondence with John Schelleng raised the question again. Examination of published photographs showing string motion at the bowing point confirmed that there are small fluctuations in the oscillation. Rough measurements of the separated fundamental and second-harmonic components of a violin tone showed the variations to be essentially random and spread over a frequency range of somewhat less than one percent. Lothar Cremer and others have more recently made careful

measurements of the periodicity of the overall sound (rather than of the individual components), getting a spread somewhat greater than one percent (about 20 cents), as would be expected from the combined influence of all the partials.[19]

The fact that each partial of a string tone is spread over a bandwidth of about 20 cents means that there is a diffuseness to the string tone which has enormous implications for the musician. On the one hand it allows larger tuning errors to be made in ensemble playing before the discrepancies become unacceptable, and on the other it permits the composer to write a wide variety of chords having many degrees of consonance and dissonance. We have here an elaboration of phenomena we met in connection with the multiple stringing of pianos (see sec. 17.3). The diffuse string sound explains to a large degree the greater versatility of the string quartet as compared with a wind ensemble. The skilled wind group can produce on demand chords of oily smoothness or dissonances of astonishing harshness, neither of which are attainable to the same degree by stringed instruments. But the tendency of the wind ensemble sound to push consonance and dissonance toward their extremes means that the subtleties of the middle ground must inevitably be neglected, and this is just the region where the string ensemble is unsurpassed.

24.6. Examples, Experiments, and Questions

1. A good preliminary to other violin-family experiments is to find the first-mode air resonance and main wood resonance of a violin. To locate the air reso-

nance, bow the G-string and slide your finger up and down the fingerboard to produce a tone whose pitch varies above and below D_4. As the fundamental component of the tone sweeps past the air-resonance frequency there will be a distinct change in tone quality and a certain increase in loudness. A few traversals of the resonance will help you to pinpoint its position. Comparison of the tone played at the resonance with notes on a piano will allow you to estimate its pitch (estimations to about 25 cents are easily made). Verify that you have actually found the air resonance by making sure that your resonance falls in frequency when one of the f-holes is partly closed off by a finger, and that it weakens and disappears as more and more tufts of cotton are tucked into the f-hole apertures.

Continue now by bowing in the neighborhood of A_4 on the D-string to find the main wood resonance lying near 440 Hz. Verify that tinkering with the f-holes does not make changes in the frequency and strength of this resonance. Having found the main wood resonance, you can try to excite it by playing an octave lower (near A_3). The second harmonic component of this tone should make the main wood resonance ring out, helped somewhat by indirect excitation produced by the fundamental component.

2. Experiments with a metal rod similar to the one described in section 23.6 can usefully be carried out on the plate of a violin. (Note: it is advisable to protect the finish of the violin by covering the end of the rod with a disc of vinyl electrical tape or masking tape.) You may be able to detect the slight lowering of the main wood resonance frequency produced by pressing the end of the rod gently but firmly against the top plate next to the bridge foot under the G-string. Why would you not expect much change from pressing next to the other foot of the bridge?

3. It is possible to get a very good idea of the influence of yielding walls on the frequency of an air resonance with the help of an empty plastic squeeze bottle of the sort commonly used to hold white household glue. When a 4-oz (near 100 cm^3) bottle of this sort is held gently at its edges and blown across like a flute, a tone can be coaxed from it whose pitch lies close to F_4 (near 350 Hz). When the tone is sounding, the flat sides of the plastic bottle will be vibrating vigorously. If one sticks more and more lumps of modeling clay onto the sides to increase their inertia, the walls become progressively less able to move in and out in response to the internal air-pressure variations, thus making the bottle act more and more like a hard-walled container. The sound produced by blowing on the bottle will rise progressively in pitch to the neighborhood of C_5 (near 520 Hz). Exactly the same rise in pitch is produced by gluing stiffening braces onto the bottle, although the physics of the situation is somewhat altered (see sec. 22.7).

4. Many interesting acoustical games can be played with half- and three-quarter-size violins, violas, and cellos. For example, the air resonance of a three-quarter-size violin can often be brought down to near 290 Hz, typical of a full-size instrument, by covering one f-hole almost completely by a strip of vinyl tape. This change will greatly improve the tone of the lower notes, even though the wood resonance is still too high.

You might find it interesting to use one of these undersized instruments to approximate one or another of the Hutchins family of violins. First move its air-resonance frequency downward once again, this time to a frequency two-thirds that of the main wood resonance (i.e., a fifth down from it in pitch) and then tune the strings in fifths (as usual), choosing the pitch of these fifths so that the middle two strings will lie violin-fashion near the two resonances.

5. If you have a cheap violin to experiment with, much can be learned about the acoustical properties of the bridge and body by attaching lumps of modeling clay at various places on the plates or on the bridge, by slipping paper clips onto different parts of the bridge, or by carving away here and there on an expendable bridge. For example, the first-mode resonance of a violin bridge can be lowered by cutting away wood in the horizontal part where the hips run out to join the legs (see fig. 24.2). Thinning the legs themselves will have the same effect on a cello bridge. What would you expect to change in the overall spectrum of an instrument when such alterations are made to the bridge?

6. Notice from figure 24.2 that the rocking leverage exerted on the bridge of a violin by the side-to-side motion of the bowed strings is somewhat greater for the G-string than it is for the E-string. Does the difference in thickness (and hence in wave impedance) between these strings tend to offset or increase the resulting variation in the driving ability these strings possess (see sec. 17.1 and 17.5)? Because the indirect excitation process depends on an oscillatory variation in the downbearing force exerted by the strings on the bridge, you will be able to deduce from figure 24.2 that the E-string should produce relatively little indirect excita-

tion of the violin body, while the lower strings become progressively more able to exploit this possibility. The fact that the indirect excitation process drains appreciable energy from the strings only when they have a large vibrational amplitude means that the string modes have a heavier damping (and so a greater bandwidth) when bowed vigorously, which is exactly the condition under which the large-amplitude inharmonicities discussed by Shankland and Coltman become most important. You should try to work out some of the musical implications of these remarks, and also to devise various playing experiments to display them.

7. Some years ago I was sent a pair of violas for resonance testing and for musical comparison. One of these was a good quality mass-produced instrument of conventional design. Its mate was similar in all respects except that its bass bar was cut away so as to reduce greatly the stiffness in its mid-portion, directly under the bridge foot. Examine figures 24.1, 24.3, and 24.4, and try to work out some of the acoustical consequences of this alteration. Your considerations should include some of the following matters: changes (if any) in the first air mode and main wood resonance frequencies, changes in the heights of the corresponding loudness peaks, changes in the damping of the string modes, and thence changes in the bowing feel. Can you figure out why sound level meter readings were very similar for the two instruments, although the modified one sounded rather "boomy"? What would you predict for the relative durability of the two instruments?

8. Harking back to the discussion of the individual flavors of different musical key signatures in section 16.4, what mu-

sical values would you expect for the keys of D, A, and G as played on a violin (even if open, unstopped strings are not used), compared both with each other and with other keys such as Bb or E major?

Musical pitch has fluctuated up and down considerably in the past three centuries. What does this imply about the key-flavor ideas that a violin-playing musician might hold in any given era? Since Bach's day, for example, the pitch has risen nearly a semitone. The Vienna Concentus Musicus, which specializes in baroque music, plays close to A-420. I have measured the main air and wood resonances of the unmodified Stainer violin used by Alice Harnoncourt as soloist with this group, and found that their frequencies are entirely similar to those measured on modern instruments and on most older ones. Most of these older violins were modified in the nineteenth century to give them more power and brilliance by stiffening the bass bar and using a taller bridge to produce more downbearing. Speculate on the acoustical implications of these modifications and on their musical correlates.

Notes

1. Walter Reinicke, "Übertragungseigenschaften des Streichinstrumentenstegs," *Catgut Acoust. Soc. Newsletter* 19 (May 1973): 26–34. Notice in Reinicke's figures 7 and 16 that the vibrational shapes for modes 1 and 2 for cello bridges are quite different from those belonging to violin bridges.

2. F. A. Saunders, "The Mechanical Action of Violins," *J. Acoust. Soc. Am.* 9 (1937): 81–98. See also F. A. Saunders, "Recent Work on Violins," *J. Acoust. Soc. Am.* 25 (1953): 491–98.

3. See, for example, Carleen M. Hutchins, "A Note on the Function of the Soundpost," *Catgut Acoust. Soc. Newsletter* 21 (May 1974): 27–28. Hutchins is one of the founders of the Catgut

Acoustical Society. She is a skilled and tireless experimenter and is a highly regarded maker of violins, violas, and cellos. She also has a most remarkable ability to stimulate others to think deeply and to experiment.

4. John C. Schelleng, "The Violin as a Circuit," *J. Acoust. Soc. Am.* 35 (1963): 326–38.

5. E. Jansson, "Recent Studies of Wall and Air Resonances in the Violin," Royal Institute of Technology (KTH), Stockholm, Speech Transmission Laboratory, *Quarterly Progress and Status Report*, 15 January 1973, pp. 34–39; E. V. Jansson, "An Investigation of Acoustical Properties of the Air Cavity of the Violin," Royal Institute of Technology (KTH), Stockholm, Speech Transmission Laboratory, *Quarterly Progress and Status Report*, 15 April 1973, pp. 1–12; and Erik Jansson and Harry Sundin, "A Pilot Study on Coupling between Top Plate and Air Volume Vibrations," *Catcut Acoust. Soc. Newsletter* 21 (May 1974): 11–15.

6. There are many beautiful pictures of vibrational shapes and a very thorough discussion of them in E. Jansson, N.-E. Molin, and H. Sundin, "Resonances of a Violin Body Studied by Hologram Interferometry and Acoustical Methods," *Physica Scripta* 2 (1970): 243–56. See also W. Reinicke and L. Cremer, "Application of Holographic Interferometry to Vibrations of the Bodies of String Instruments," *J. Acoust. Soc. Am.* 48 (1970): 988–92.

7. A fair amount of information about the behavior of wood can be found in the papers listed in reference 14 below.

8. Reinicke, "Übertragungseigenschaften des Streichinstrumentenstegs."

9. C. M. Hutchins, "The Physics of Violins," *Scientific American*, November 1962, pp. 78–93.

10. Carleen Maley Hutchins, "Founding a Family of Fiddles," *Physics Today*, February 1967, pp. 23–37.

11. Arthur Benade and Edith Roberts, "Tape Recorder Transposition of Standard Violin to Simulate the Highest Seven Members of C. M. Hutchins' Family of True Violins," *Catgut Acoust. Soc. Newsletter* 13 (May 1970): 8–10.

12. There is a large literature on this subject which may be discovered via the references in the following three reports: Carleen M. Hutchins and

Francis L. Fielding, "Acoustical Measurement of Violins," *Physics Today*, July 1968, pp. 34–40; Carleen M. Hutchins, "Instrumentation and Methods for Violin Testing," *J. Audio Eng. Soc.* 21 (1973): 563–70; and Carleen M. Hutchins, "Progress Report on a Method of Checking Eigenmodes of Free Violin Plates during Instrument Construction," *Catgut Acoust. Soc. Newsletter* 19 (May 1973): 17–20.

13. An enormous amount of scientific study has been devoted to the acoustical properties of wood during the past half century. Despite this, it is only recently that a coherent picture is beginning to emerge. Inadequate recognition of the influence of vibrational mode shapes on the measured elasticity and damping has often compounded the problem of reconciling partial measurements from various experiments. See H. Meinel, "Regarding the Sound Quality of Violins and a Scientific Basis for Violin Construction," *J. Acoust. Soc. Am.* 29 (1957): 817–22; Schelleng, "The Violin as a Circuit," part VIII; John C. Schelleng, "Acoustical Effects of Violin Varnish," *J. Acoust. Soc. Am.* 44 (1968): 1175–83; Yoshimasa Sakurai and Eugen J. Skudrzyk, "Acoustic Properties of Wood" (abstract), *J. Acoust. Soc. Am.* 46 (1969): 124; and N. Ghelmeziu and I. P. Beldie, "On the Characteristics of Resonance Spruce Wood," *Catgut Acoust. Soc. Newsletter* 17 (May 1972): 10–16. See also the papers listed in note 14.

14. Daniel W. Haines, Nagyoung Chang, and Donald A. Thompson, "Can spruce be replaced?— a guitar with a graphite-epoxy top plate" (abstract), *J. Acoust. Soc. Am.* 55 supplement (1974): S49, and Daniel W. Haines and Nagyoung Chang, "Violin with a graphite-epoxy top plate" (abstract), *J. Acoust. Soc. Am.* 57 supplement 1 (1975): S21. The following short paper gives an excellent summary of the acoustical properties of any material that can serve usefully as a violin top plate: Daniel W. Haines and Nagyoung Chang, "Application of Graphite Composites in Musical Instruments," *Catgut Acoust. Soc. Newsletter* 23 (May 1975): 13–15.

15. Jürgen Meyer, "Directivity of the Bowed String Instruments and Its Effect on Orchestral Sound in Concert Halls," *J. Acoust. Soc. Am.* 51 (1972): 1994–2009. The excitation mechanism used in these experiments has a high mechanical impedance, which causes the instrument to vibrate with mode shapes having very nearly a node at the driving point. For this reason, details of Meyer's results do not quite correspond to the bowed-string case, even though the overall trends at high frequencies are directly applicable. See also Ion Paul Beldie, "Vibration and Sound Radiation of the Violin at Low Frequencies," *Catgut Acoust. Soc. Newsletter* 22 (November 1974): 13–14. The presence of string resonances makes the interpretation of these data complicated.

16. Paul C. Boomsliter and Warren Creel, "Research Potentials in Auditory Characteristics of Violin Tone," *J. Acoust. Soc. Am.* 51 (1972): 1984–93.

17. M. V. Mathews and J. Kohut, "Electronic simulation of violin resonances," *J. Acoust. Soc. Am.* 53 (1973): 1620–26. This is an interesting and useful paper, despite the fact that it was apparently impossible to match the spectrum envelope of the electronic instrument to that of the real violin used as a reference.

18. W. S. Gorrill, "Viola with Electronically Simulated Body Resonances" (abstract), *J. Acoust. Soc. Am.* 52 (1972): 147, and W. S. Gorrill, "Viola Tone Quality Study Using an Instrument with Synthesized Normal Modes" (abstract), *J. Acoust. Soc. Am.* 54 (1973): 311. Gorrill's instrument is a very successful variant of the electronic instrument devised by Mathews and his co-workers; Gorrill uses a small loudspeaker mounted in the body of a viola. Filtered signals to this speaker are further modified by the resonances and radiation properties of the body itself and of the loudspeaker, thus restoring the multi-source nature of the audible sound.

19. L Cremer, "Der Einfluss des 'Bogendrucks' auf die selbsterregten Schwingungen der gestrichenen Saite," *Acustica* 30 (1974): 119–36, fig. 23, and Lothar Cremer, "The Influence of 'Bow Pressure' on the Movement of a Bowed String: II," *Catgut Acoust. Soc. Newsletter* 19 (May 1973): 21–25, fig. 14. See also Irwin Pollack, "Detection and Relative Discrimination of Auditory 'Jitter,'" *J. Acoust. Soc. Am.* 43 (1968): 308–15. This is the first of a series of papers having considerable musical implication.

25

Half-Valved Octaves, Burrs, Multiphonics, and Wolf Notes

Wind instruments and members of the violin family are able to make certain peculiar sounds in addition to the tones they normally produce. Many composers have begun to call for some of these sounds as an integral part of their music, so that performers are increasingly expected to produce them on demand and under good control. These nonstandard methods of sound production are of particular interest to us because they cast a great deal of light on the way we perceive complex collections of partials and on the way oscillations can maintain themselves even in the absence of ordinary regimes involving cooperation among harmonically related resonances. The discussion of these matters will illustrate for us, one final time, that interweaving of perception processes and the physics of vibration which we have found to be of such great importance to the activities of musicians.

25.1. The Playing of Half-Valved Octaves on Brass Instruments

Most of us have heard the half-strangled sounds that a jazz trumpet player will occasionally insert for effect between his more ordinary tones; he achieves such sounds by the simple expedient of pressing one or more of the valve pistons only part way down. When this technique is used, one finds a few tones of startling clarity mixed in among the rather choked sounds. These clear tones are exactly an octave above the pitch of the tone produced when the valve is fully up or fully down. Curiously enough, the player's embouchure does not have to make any marked adjustment as he half-depresses the valve, even when the upper tone of the sound he gets lies above the limits of his normal playing range!

The *half-valved* condition that produces these octave sounds disrupts the normal oscillatory regimes of the air column by presenting the player's lip reed with a duct having a side branch in it, as sketched in the upper part of figure 25.1. The valve serves its usual function of adding a loop of tubing to the main air column, but the loop communicates only through constricted, half-opened apertures, while at the same time the direct path through the open horn is not completely closed off.

Because the half-valved octave sound is most easily demonstrated on instruments having lower pitch than the trumpet, I

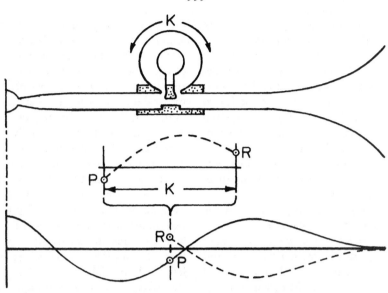

Fig. 25.1. Air Column for a Half-Valved Note and Standing Wave Pattern for the Fundamental Component of the Generated (but unheard) Sound

shall present my entire discussion in terms of the B♭ baritone horn, with the understanding that the tuba and French horn behave equally well and that the various higher brasses also show the phenomenon but with less convenience. Let us begin by listing the harmonically related series of tones which are produced by a baritone horn when no valves are pressed:

Peak number and note name:

1	2	3	4	5	6	7	8	9	10
C_2	C_3	G_3	C_4	E_4	G_4	x	C_5	D_5	E_5

Notice that the sixth member of this collection (G_4) lies an interval of a minor third (three semitones) above the fifth tone (E_4). If one plays E_4 on the open horn and then fully operates the third valve on the instrument, the sound does not change in pitch, since tone 6 on the lengthened horn matches tone 5 played on the shorter one. If on the other hand one plays E_4 on the open horn and *slowly* depresses the valve, a narrowly defined intermediate position of the valve is reached at which the listener hears the tone raise itself by an exact octave. This octave change happens without an appreciable alteration of feel at the player's embouchure. By the way, the player himself may or may not perceive the octave shift.

Before we look into the air-column acoustics and the perception processes that are associated with this phenomenon, let us list other places in the scale where it occurs. Half pressing the (two-semitone) first valve while playing C_5 will produce an octave transition to C_6, and the same valve action will also produce an octave rise from D_5 to D_6. Instruments such as the baritone or tuba are provided with an extra valve that lowers the basic pitch of the instrument by five semitones; this fourth valve will similarly give an octave transition up from G_3 to G_4. In every case the phenomenon takes place when the musical interval associated with the valve exactly matches the interval between the note being played and the next one higher in the open-horn series of tones. Since an interval of a semitone has a frequency reatio of 16/15, a French-horn player will be able to produce a stratospheric octave to the fifteenth note in his series by making use of his (one-semitone) second valve.

Let us now see what is going on in the air column when a half-valved octave is played. To begin with, we should recall that every standing wave pattern within any brass instrument includes an odd number (e.g., 1, 3, or 5) of half humps. Every time we go from one air-column mode to one having the next higher serial number, two more half humps are fitted into the standing wave. The solid curve in the lower part of figure 25.1 shows the mode-3 standing wave (having five half humps) which would provide the basis for playing G_3 on the unvalved baritone horn. When a valve is normally operated to add extra tubing whose length K is precisely two half humps long at this frequency, we can have a mode-4 standing wave that starts out exactly as before at the mouthpiece and joins the dashed curve at P; this standing wave continues through the valve tube length K and re-joins the main air column at R, and from there the dashed curve continues out to the bell with a reversal of sign as compared with the solid curve belonging to the open horn. At the playing frequency belonging to this pair of modes, any disturbance that reaches the bell via the valve tubing tends to be cancelled by a disturbance of opposite sign that reaches it directly through the leaking valve. If

the valve is depressed exactly the right amount, these two disturbances cancel exactly, so that the fundamental component of the tone no longer reaches the listener's ears.[1] You may find it possible to extend my discussion to verify that under these same conditions none of the odd-numbered partials of the internally generated tone can find their way out, whereas the even partials proceed unhindered almost exactly as though the valve were in one of its more normal positions. This of course explains why the perceived pitch of the externally heard tone is raised an octave: whenever one steals partials 1, 3, 5, . . . from a complete harmonic series, one is left with partials 2, 4, 6, . . . which themselves form a complete harmonic series having twice the fundamental frequency of the original tone.

Let us now look at what sort of oscillatory regime governs the player's lips under the special half-valve conditions we have been studying. The air-column input impedance curve for a half-valved horn has a very messy pattern of resonance peaks and dips. The details of this mess vary from instrument to instrument and from valve to valve. In the midst of all this complexity, however, we always find that there is a resonance peak at the position of the fundamental frequency of the played note. This peak is enormously tall on some instruments, less tall on others. (The existence and frequency of the fundamental peak are independent of the location of the valve along the air column, however.) At the second harmonic of the playing frequency, there is an ordinary-looking resonance peak, and there is often a tall one at the third harmonic. In other words, when the horn is used to play a half-valved octave, the performer's lips are receiving instructions very much of the familiar sort, which explains why they feel quite normal under our special conditions. They are as a matter of fact vibrating in such a way as to generate a fairly normal internal spectrum in the original octave. This unchanged behavior of the player's lips is the reason why he may fail to hear the octave shift. The buzzing of his lips and the sound transmitted to his auditory mechanism via the bones of his head all imply the normal (lower) pitch for his tone. His ears receive only the even harmonics from the room, but this may not be enough to overcome the sense impressions from his buzzing lips and bony structure, in which case what arrives from the room air will produce a change merely in tone color rather than in pitch.

25.2. Brass-Instrument Burrs

While no brass player likes to make a burble at the start of a tone, he may at times wish to have a slight *burr* at the beginning, or as a special effect he may want it to continue all the way through a tone's duration. We will look briefly at the nature of such sounds, in part because of their inherent interest and in part because of the insight they will give us into the way woodwind multiphonics and violin-family wolf tones are produced and perceived.

In section 20.9 we learned that a brass player who wishes to produce a clean beginning for a note must set his lips vibrating correctly, with no help from the air-column resonances until the initial sound has had time to be reflected from the bell region of the instrument and to return with proper instructions for the flow-control process. It is useful to ask

ourselves what happens during the first few round trips if a slight tremor of the player's lips makes them shift their buzzing frequency from one that agrees with some resonance peak of his instrument to one more nearly in agreement with the neighboring peak on either side. In the simplest of all worlds (ignoring any difficulties produced by stray reflections from discontinuities in the air column) we might imagine that two tones of alternating pitch would chase one another up and down the horn taking turns instructing the lips in what they want done. While the actual sound may begin in this manner, the two types of oscillation are in fact mixed together very quickly (in the time of only two or three round trips) to produce a somewhat different sort of composite. This mixing together takes place in part because of the difference between the ordinary wave velocity of sound in the horn and the group velocity for impulsive disturbances within it (see sec. 20.9), and in part because of the marked preference of the player's lips for sustaining one or the other sort of tone depending on their tension. The mixed sound is heard as a short burble during which the tone alternates at a rate determined by the round-trip time in the horn (about 44/sec for a French horn in F), after which the sound settles down into a normal oscillatory regime.

In 1968 I had occasion to study the start-up behavior of brass instruments,[2] and I found that with only a little practice it was possible to select a lip tension and starting technique that permitted me to play whole lungfuls of steady burrs at various pitches on French horns or other brasses. It is surprisingly easy to maintain such sounds and it is not difficult to analyze their acoustical nature.

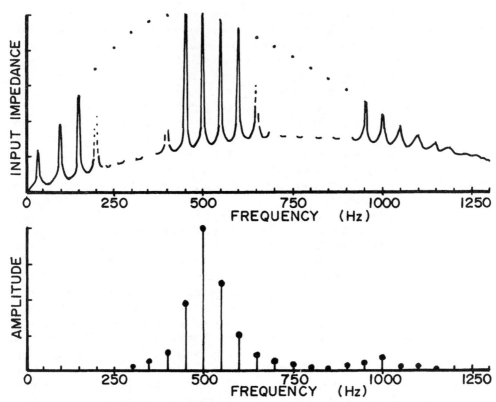

Fig. 25.2. Simplified French-Horn Resonance Curve and the Internal Spectrum of a Sustained Burr

Figure 25.2 shows the kind of behavior that one observes in a steady burring sound. The upper part of this figure shows the simplified outlines of the resonance curve for a French horn drawn as though its pitch were 35 cents above G_1, which makes its resonances fall at multiples of 50 Hz. The lower part of the figure shows the amplitudes of the various partials making up the internal spectrum that I measured for a burring sound that is based on resonance peak 10, which lies at 500 Hz in our simplified version of the instrument.

One sees at once that the sound is not an ordinary tone at all. Instead of a 500-Hz fundamental component plus a second harmonic at 1000 Hz we find a group of partials spaced at 50-Hz intervals in the neighborhood of 500 Hz, and similarly a few weak satellites around 1000 Hz. Our ordinary ideas on how a regime of oscillation sustains itself via harmonically related peaks do not apply in this case, but it is nevertheless clear that each partial of the new tone is sustained by a strong resonance peak at its own frequency. The details of just how oscillations of this type are maintained have not yet been fully worked out, but there are indications that heterodyne frequencies of the type $(2P - Q) = R$ play an important role. For example, subtracting the 550-Hz component frequency (supported by peak 11) from twice the 500-Hz component (supported by peak 10) produces a heterodyne component that talks to peak 9 at 450 Hz. (Higher-order heterodynes of this sort abound in the normal regimes as well, but we have had no need before this to take them into account since they produce no new component frequencies.) The influence of such heterodynes cannot extend more than a few resonances away from the 500-Hz "center" of the oscillation, because the player's lip valve cannot respond well as a flow controller at frequencies that are far from the one to which it is "tuned."

To the listener, the sustained burr that we have been discussing sounds very much as though the player had played a normal tone broken up into a rapid sequence of short bursts produced by what is known as flutter tonguing. Curiously, a burr whose strongest component has a frequency of 500 Hz is heard as having a pitch that closely matches that of a normal tone whose fundamental frequency is 500 Hz, although very few components of the burr sound are harmonically related. The burr still matches the 500-Hz tone even when the components near 1000 Hz are removed by an electrical filter, leaving us with a complex sound with *no* components arranged in the harmonic series whose pitch it matches. Examination of such a signal on the oscilloscope shows an acoustical disturbance that exactly matches the listener's description of the sound as a rapidly pulsating tone, and a physicist would deduce from this that a short "wave packet" of 500-Hz sound must be shut-

tling back and forth in the horn in a self-sustained cousin to the flutter echo we met in section 12.4, part A.

25.3. Reed Woodwind Multiphonics

In the early 1960s, a music-loving engineer wrote to me to ask how the jazz saxophonist John Coltrane produced certain multiple-sounding tones on his instrument. My initial guess was that perhaps Coltrane was singing as well as playing, since the dual control of the airflow by reed and larynx can give rise to complicated heterodyne components (see sec. 25.5, part 2), or that he was producing similar acoustic effects by some type of flutter tonguing or by getting his soft palate to oscillate rapidly in his throat's airstream. Some months later my correspondent reported that Coltrane denied using techniques of this sort (although he knew of them), but would not divulge the methods he actually used. Similar questions arose again from time to time in the years that followed, particularly after the publication of Bruno Bartolozzi's little book, *New Sounds for Woodwind*.[3] One does not have to listen to very many of these sounds (which have come to be called *multiphonics*) to realize that their components are not usually in any obviously harmonic relationship. One or two preliminary experiments led me to a picture of what was going on that will serve as a convenient introduction to the somewhat more complicated behavior typical of the hundreds of such multiphonic sounds that are now known to be producible on all of the woodwinds.

Figure 25.3 shows the resonance curve belonging to a certain fingering on a hypothetical woodwind. Particularly appar-

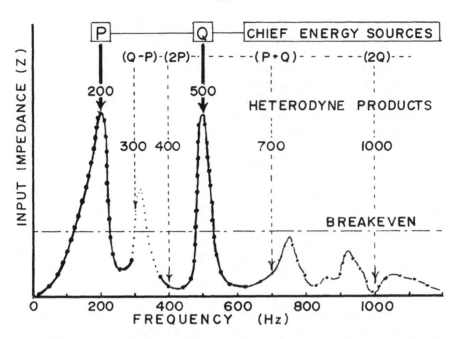

Fig. 25.3. Hypothetical Woodwind Resonance Curve Showing the Production of a Simple Multiphonic Sound

ent are two equally tall peaks located at 200 and 500 Hz, either one of which is enough taller than the "break-even" line drawn across the figure that it could act alone to sustain oscillation at its own frequency. If we blow on such an instrument, we would expect the internal spectrum to contain not only the directly produced components at 200 and 500 Hz (labeled P and Q), but also heterodyne components arising from the nonlinear valving action of the reed. The simplest of these heterodynes would be found at $(500 + 200) = 700$ Hz, $(500 - 200) = 300$ Hz, etc. If all the parts of the resonance curve that are distant from the tall peaks lie below the break-even line, the heterodyne components serve as an oscillatory drag upon the system and work

against the production of sound, in a manner that is put to good use by the register-hole systems normally used in woodwinds. Suppose however there is a small peak such as the one near 300 Hz, shown as a dotted line in figure 25.3. This small peak could aid in the maintenance of oscillation in the following manner: there is direct production of oscillatory energy at 200 and at 500 Hz, and the 300-Hz heterodyne descendant of these two frequencies is able to add to the maintenance of oscillation because it lies near a small peak which itself could maintain oscillation near 300 Hz. This behavior is a close cousin to that observed in the regimes of oscillation supporting tones having harmonically related partials.

Looking more closely, we can see that the peak near 300 Hz would "vote" in the regime in favor of a value for $(Q - P)$ having a slightly higher frequency, which could be arranged by having component P run slightly below 200 Hz, and/or by having Q run a little bit on the high-frequency side of its 500-Hz peak. I realized several years ago that it would on the face of it be plausible for the system to choose the latter alternative because raising Q above 500 Hz, not only moves the $(Q - P)$ component closer to the top of its peak, but also slides both the 700-Hz $(P + Q)$ and the 1000-Hz $(2Q)$ components in a direction that puts them more nearly on top of their own small resonance peaks. However, I believed then that every self-sustained steady oscillation of necessity *had* to be of a repetitive type, and therefore built up of harmonically related components, so that these adjustments were not totally free. In our present example I would have assumed, for instance, that the basic repetition frequency is close to 20 Hz, so that the components would be as follows:

$$P = 200 \text{ Hz (10th harmonic)}$$
$$Q = 520 \text{ Hz (26th harmonic)}$$
$$Q - P = 320 \text{ Hz (16th harmonic)}$$
$$Q + P = 720 \text{ Hz (36th harmonic)}$$
$$2P = 400 \text{ Hz (20th harmonic)}$$
$$2Q = 1040 \text{ Hz (52nd harmonic)}$$

Notice that a frequency arrangement of this sort would gain considerable support from the air-column resonance peaks lying a little above 300, 700, and 1000 Hz, with only a small loss of cooperation from the fact that component Q now lies somewhat too high for the peak at 500 Hz.

In 1972 James Gebler and I studied one or two clarinet multiphonics that ap-peared to confirm the viewpoint taken above, and my knowledge of human pitch perception was not sufficiently great to make me suspect that something was wrong. We could clearly make out several tones in each sound, something that today I would not expect for a collection of harmonically related partials, since such collections normally join together to give the sensation of a single tone.

More recent work has shown that steady oscillations of the multiphonic type are not always made up of har-monically related components of the sort described above. It is only necessary to have a number of resonance peaks match-ing some of the components in the tone, without any constraints on their frequen-cies beyond the simple arithmetical rela-tions that govern all heterodyne pro-cesses. Let us look at some examples.[4]

The top part of figure 25.4 shows the resonance curve belonging to fingerings used in the production of one of several clarinet multiphonics that I have studied in cooperation with Larry Livingston, a member of the music faculty of Northern Illinois University in Dekalb. (Livingston has compiled a dictionary of about 150 multiphonic sounds for clarinet, along with their musical properties, and it is the serial number from his catalog that appears on the resonance curves shown in figures 25.4 and 25.5. In figure 25.4 the components of the sound which contrib-ute most directly to the maintenance of oscillation are given names (P, Q, R, etc.) and their frequencies are indicated in relation to the positions of the resonance peaks.

The lower part of figure 25.4 shows how the first twelve measured frequency components of the internal spectrum are related to one another by elaborately in-

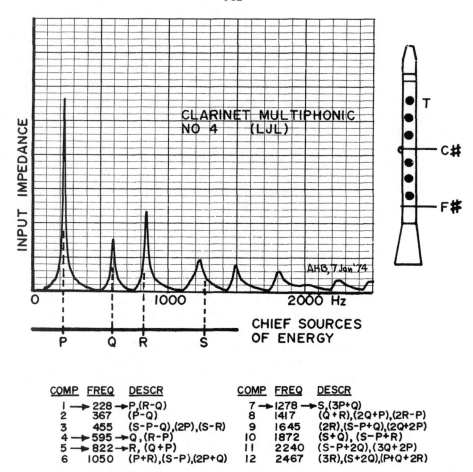

COMP	FREQ	DESCR		COMP	FREQ	DESCR
1 →	228 →	P,(R-Q)		7 →	1278 →	S,(3P+Q)
2	367	(P-Q)		8	1417	(Q+R),(2Q+P),(2R-P)
3	455	(S-P-Q),(2P),(S-R)		9	1645	(2R),(S-P+Q),(2Q+2P)
4 →	595 →	Q,(R-P)		10	1872	(S+Q), (S-P+R)
5 →	822 →	R, (Q+P)		11	2240	(S-P+2Q),(3Q+2P)
6	1050	(P+R),(S-P),(2P+Q)		12	2467	(3R),(S+2Q),(P+Q+2R)

Fig. 25.4. Measured Resonance Curve and Spectral Components for a Clarinet Multiphonic

terlocking heterodyne arithmetic. The components that are the main contributors to the oscillation are emphasized by arrows pointing to them. I should like to emphasize that one *never* finds a frequency component that fails to show a heterodyne relationship with all the other partials in the sound, and also that these relationships are mathematically exact. Component 7 is listed as having a frequency of 1278 Hz, while the heterodyne $(3P + Q)$ that is identified with it comes out at 1279 Hz; this fact is sim-

ply a consequence of my having rounded off the exact frequencies for simplicity in the tabulation. In the laboratory, there is agreement among the frequencies to within 0.1 Hz, which was the accuracy of measurement.

Figure 25.5 shows another example of a clarinet multiphonic, while figure 25.6 provides an illustration of exactly similar behavior observed for an oboe. The internal spectrum from which the data shown in the lower part of figure 25.6 were extracted was made with the cooperation of

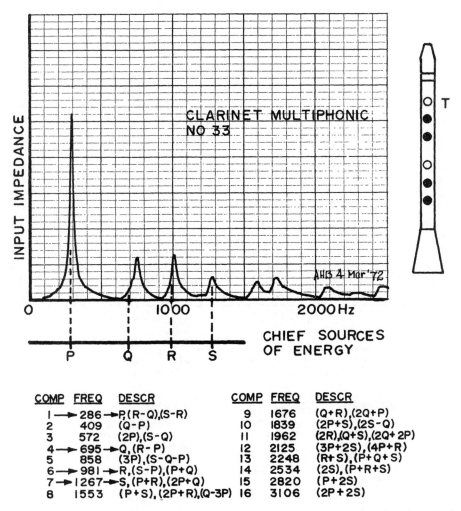

Fig. 25.5. Measured Resonance Curve and Spectral Components for Another Clarinet Multiphonic

the oboist Wilma Zonn of the University of Illinois. A set of data in which the external rather than the internal spectrum was recorded by means of a single microphone in an anechoic chamber had been given to me earlier by Zonn and James Beauchamp, who is a member of both the school of engineering and the school of music at the University of Illinois.

I find that with a little practice it is not difficult to unravel the spectrum of a woodwind multiphonic, even when it contains 25 to 30 important components. One first makes a list of the heterodyne components that one would expect to arise from pairings of the strongest three or four components, these presumably being the ones that are most influential in

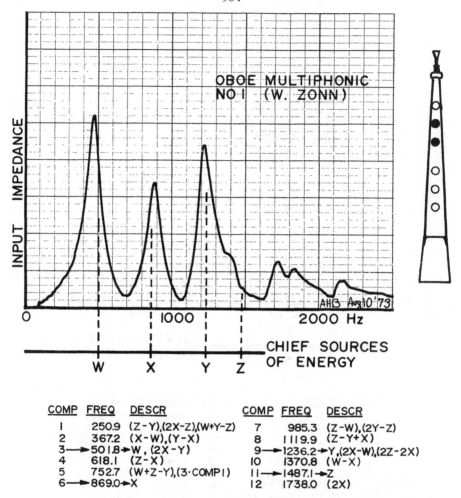

COMP	FREQ	DESCR	COMP	FREQ	DESCR
1	250.9	(Z−Y),(2X−Z),(W+Y−Z)	7	985.3	(Z−W),(2Y−Z)
2	367.2	(X−W),(Y−X)	8	1119.9	(Z−Y+X)
3→	501.8→	W, (2X−Y)	9→	1236.2→	Y,(2X−W),(2Z−2X)
4	618.1	(Z−X)	10	1370.8	(W−X)
5	752.7	(W+Z−Y),(3·COMP1)	11→	1487.1→	Z
6→	869.0→	X	12	1738.0	(2X)

Fig. 25.6. Measured Resonance Curve and Spectral Components for an Oboe Multiphonic

telling the reed how to oscillate. Such a computation makes it easy to recognize many of the weaker components in the measured spectrum, after which it is possible to check everything by making sure that all of the remaining components in the recorded spectrum match the pattern established so far. It is important to recognize that calculations of this sort can be carried out even in the absence of a mea-

sured resonance curve, although it is always advisable to obtain one for final confirmation of the analysis.

A brief account of my analysis of the oboe multiphonic will show how clear-cut the interpretation can be, and also will illustrate the need for considerable caution in the use of spectrum analysis based on data from a single-microphone recording in an anechoic room. Beauchamp's original tape from which I made a preliminary version of the table shown in the lower half of figure 25.6 contained indications of all the components *except for the one near 500 Hz.* I did not at that time have on hand a resonance curve for the air column, so that there was nothing initially visible that would suggest any need for a 500-Hz component. However, it took only a few minutes of arithmetic to show that there were many ways in which the components would combine to produce something near 500 Hz. For example, components 5 and 1, 6 and 2, 10 and 6, and 11 and 7 all differ by 501.8 Hz. There were also relations between the amplitudes of the components that appeared to be consistent only with the presence of a strong component near 500 Hz. More sensitive analysis of the tape recording disclosed no trace of this component, although a number of other, small-amplitude components were unearthed which joined the rest in calling for a major contributor near 500 Hz. At this stage I measured the resonance curves for several oboes and found always that peak 1 was tall and was located very close to 500 Hz, in exact agreement with the implications of my arithmetic. The conclusion was almost inescapable that the microphone, by an exceedingly improbable quirk, had been placed at a point toward which the instrument radiated none of the 500-Hz component!

My own playing of this multiphonic in an ordinary (slightly reverberant) laboratory room gave a recorded signal whose components included one near 500 Hz, while the rest followed the same pattern as the original tape. Later on I had the opportunity of recording the internal and external spectra of this sound played by Wilma Zonn herself, and of verifying ex-

perimentally that her recollection of the original microphone position was very close to a spot where there is in fact a sharp null in the 500-Hz radiation pattern. A displacement of only two or three centimeters in the position of the microphone relative to the instrument proved sufficient to restore the missing component to an easily detectable amplitude. Of course, in an ordinary room the presence of reflections almost totally eliminates the possibility of trouble of this sort.

Let us now summarize the physics involved in the production of woodwind multiphonics:

1. A multiphonic oscillation is made up of a collection of components whose frequencies are connected to one another by an elaborate set of heterodyne relationships. The ordinary tones of woodwind instruments also fit this description, but the frequency components in normal tones are limited to those belonging to a single harmonic series.

2. A multiphonic oscillation is maintained by cooperations set up between several of the components and several of the taller peaks in the air-column resonance curve. Because neither the components nor the peaks need be in harmonic relationship, oscillation is not as easily maintained for multiphonics as it is for normal tones. The chief reason for the difficulty lies in the profusion of heterodyne components found in the inter-peak regions of the resonance curve.

3. The player must make rather subtle adjustments of his embouchure and blowing pressure in playing multiphonics. On the pianissimo side, the instrument may lapse into producing an essentially pure tone based on the tallest resonance peak, and on the loud-playing side the reed may simply choke up and snap closed if too many of the generated components lie at dips in the resonance curve.

4. Because of the great importance of heterodyne effects, multiphonics are most easily

played using reed and mouthpiece combinations that have a highly nonlinear flow-control characteristic and that include a great deal of sensitivity to Bernoulli forces at the reed tip. Such reed and mouthpiece combinations give bright or harsh-sounding normal tones.

5. The internally measured spectrum can change drastically when the player makes small changes in the size of the reed cavity (this is particularly true among the conical instruments). The reason for this is that cavity changes shift the frequency relationships among the air-column resonance peaks, and so upset the often subtle interplay between them and the generated components. The relationship between the internal and the external spectrum of a multiphonic sound is not of the simple sort we find for more normal woodwind tones.

Let us turn our attention now to the way our hearing mechanism tends to perceive the multiphonic sounds whose production we have been discussing.[5] Someone listening to the clarinet multiphonic described in figure 25.4 will always pick out what he calls a tone having a pitch about 40 cents below the clarinetist's written C_4. Examination of the spectrum of the multiphonic shows us that our listener has seized upon components 1 and 3, which are the first two harmonics of a 228-Hz musical tone. Not until we get to components 11 and 12 do we find any that are even approximately members of this same set of harmonics. Another easily picked out tone in the complex is assigned a pitch about 20 cents below B_5b. This one is associated with components 5, 9, and 12, which constitute the first three harmonics of 822 Hz. Beyond this our ears have difficulty: different people will make different *groupings* of the remaining partials and assign each of these a more or less well-defined pitch. For example, par-

tials 4, 7, 10, and 12 are in approximately harmonic relationship, which leads some listeners to hear them as a single but slightly ill-defined tone whose pitch is close to the clarinet's written F_5 (whose fundamental is at 622 Hz).

In the sound of the clarinet multiphonic shown in figure 25.5 our ears find a great deal of recognizable pattern: that is, they can pick out several clearly marked sets of harmonics or quasi harmonics. For instance, components 1, 3, and 5 are the first three exact harmonics of 286 Hz, which would generally be heard about halfway between the clarinetist's $D_4\sharp$ and E_4. However, some people feel that this pitch assignment is not quite clear-cut, and also that it is on the sharp side. The reason for this is to be found in the fact that components 9, 11, 13, 14, 15, and 16 constitute the sixth through the eleventh harmonics of a tone based on 281 Hz, which can be "melted down" with the 286-Hz components to give something of different pitch. Most listeners also perceive a tone whose pitch is close to G_5 because of their grouping of components 4, 12, and 15 as approximate harmonics 1, 3, and 4 of a tone whose fundamental frequency is close to 700 Hz. They also tend to pick out a tone just below $C_6\sharp$ associated with components 6 and 11, which are in an exact two-to-one frequency relationship. In similar fashion harmonic components 7 and 14 usually join to produce a perceived tone whose pitch is about 30 cents above the clarinetist's F_6. It is interesting to notice that our listeners have managed to use some of the upper partials in more than one way as members of the various perceived tones. We should also notice that components 2, 8, and 10 do not become members of any tonal grouping, but rather tend to be heard separately if at all.

You may wish to try to verify for yourself that listeners to the oboe multiphonic will generally hear (among other things) a strongly marked tone that they will identify as being 20 cents above B_3, another one a little below $D_5\sharp$, and another one almost equally far below A_5. The original tape recording I was given of this sound (with component 3 missing) does not sound very different from the tone heard "live" or from a tape recording made in an ordinary room. The reason for this should be fairly clear to us at this point in our studies of musical acoustics: the 500-Hz component is merely one of several partials that are associated by our ears into the B_3 tone. Its presence or absence can therefore lead to changes in tone color, but does not alter the nature of the groupings which we have perceptually imposed on the components.

Our collection of numbered statements on multiphonics can now be extended by adding a few statements on the way in which multiphonics are perceived:

6. When we hear the conglomerate of partials making up a multiphonic sound, our hearing mechanism tends to pick from the collection sets of harmonically related or almost harmonically related components. Each of these sets is then heard as a tone of a more or less normal sort, having a pitch that is related in the normal way to the fundamental frequency of the set.

7. Our auditory habit of lumping a harmonically related set of partials into something that is perceived as a single tone explains why musicians give the name *multiphonic* to the sound we have been discussing. Each multiphonic, because it has sounds in it that are not harmonically related to each other, is perceived as being made up of a number of tones. The ordinary sound of a woodwind, being made up of a single set of

harmonic partials, is perceived as a single tone.

8. A single, relatively strong component in the spectrum of a multiphonic sound is sometimes perceived as a separate tone in its own right if none of the other components present are even approximately related to it as harmonics. Apart from this special case, the strengths of the various partials as they come to our ears play a relatively small role in determining the way in which we group them into tones.

25.4. The Wolf Note on Violin-Family Instruments

Players of bowed string instruments, particularly cellists, are troubled by spots in the playing range of their instruments in which it is more or less impossible to produce a steady tone of good quality. A bowed note may suddenly leap upward an octave or give a rough, pulsating sound whose pitch is close to that of the desired note but which contains strong hints of the octave, as though it were thinking of jumping into what a woodwind player would call the second register. It is this latter, pulsating sound that is commonly known as a *wolf note*. String players and craftsmen have given a lot of attention to the wolf note because of the practical importance of suppressing or weakening it, or at least moving it to a place where notes ordinarily used in playing do not provoke it into action. The wolf note has also received a fair amount of scientific attention, with Raman and Schelleng being the major contributors to our present knowledge of its behavior.

Let us begin our examination of the wolf-note phenomenon with a brief description of the conditions under which it occurs and of the effect of changes in bowing pressure on its behavior. The wolf is usually encountered at places in the scale where the first-mode frequency of the bowed string is in the general neighborhood of some strong resonance frequency of the body. The so-called main wood resonance frequency (see sec. 24.1) determines the region in which the wolf takes place. If one uses very light bow pressure to play a chromatic scale, the tone is likely to jump up an octave as one gets into the wolf region. Heavier bow pressure gives rise to the characteristic rough sound of the wolf tone; in certain mild cases of the disease, increasing the bowing pressure even more may suppress the wolfing and produce a more or less normal tone.

We have had numerous occasions in this book to recognize that a strong resonance in one part of a two-part system can lead to shifts in the resonance frequencies of the other part, the shift being relatively small if the two parts have widely different wave impedances, as is the case of a string coupled to the body of a cello. We conclude here that under wolf-tone conditions the instrument's wood resonance is able to shift the string's first-mode frequency away from its normal position as the lowest member of a harmonically related set of string resonance frequencies. The octave change arising from the wolf-note displacement of the first-mode frequency produces a change analogous to the loud-playing type of woodwind register change (see sec. 21.5). In section 23.2 we encountered a different kind of octave rise associated with light bowing which is analogous to register changes found for pianissimo playing in woodwinds.

Let us glance briefly at the reason why it is sometimes possible to stabilize the oscillation and prevent a wolf by use of heavy bow pressure. At any sliding speed, increasing the bow pressure makes the bow-plus-string interaction more nonlinear, so that the various heterodyne effects become more pronounced (see fig. 23.1). If we assume, for example, that a dozen of the string resonances are available for participation in a regime of oscillation, heavy bow pressure may make it possible for the upper eleven resonances jointly to control the disruptive influence of the detuned first mode so as to give a slightly shifted playing frequency of the sort that is familiar in the playing regimes of ordinary wind instruments (whose resonances are almost never in perfect alignment).

Raman's studies led him to describe the wolf note as an alternation of a fundamental frequency tone and its octave, this alternation taking place several times a second at what we shall call the *pulsation frequency*. In 1963 Shelleng provided us with a somewhat more illuminating way of describing Raman's observation, a way that allows him to demonstrate that the phenomenon is consistent with the basic stick-slip physics discussed by Helmholtz and Raman (see sec. 23.4).[6] Schelleng points out that the even harmonic components of the string oscillation run fairly steadily during the entire pulsation cycle, whereas the odd harmonics appear to grow and shrink more or less *en bloc* at the pulsation rate. The perceived switching of octaves is easily understandable in these terms, since it coincides exactly with the physical changes that are taking place. At instants when the odd partials are of appreciable amplitude, our ears are presented with the complete harmonic series based on the string modes, and we assign the pitch accordingly. At those moments, on the other hand, when the odd compo-

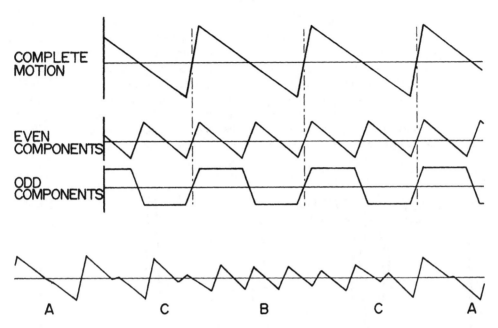

Fig. 25.7. Separation of the Bowing-Point String Motion into Its Even and Odd Harmonic Parts

nents are insignificant, we perceive the even partials in their own right as a tone having its pitch an octave higher.

The top three lines of figure 25.7 illustrate Schelleng's explanation of how the idealized sawtooth motion at the bowing point of a normally operating string (top line) can be separated into the parts contributed by the even-numbered components (second line) and those contributed by the odd-numbered ones (third line). It is clear from a comparison of lines 1 and 2 that abolition of the odd components leaves us with a double-frequency oscillation that is otherwise of normal appearance. The bottom line of figure 25.7 shows the appearance of the bowing-point motion during the course of a wolf tone. At instants (marked A) when the odd components are of normal strength, we find the sawtooth wave belonging to ordi-

nary operation of the string. At other times (marked B) the odd components have disappeared, leaving a sawtooth whose repetition rate is double that of the normal oscillation. In between these two, we have intervals (marked C) during which small amounts of odd harmonics are present, producing a jagged waveform which nevertheless is of the stick-slip type discussed by Helmholtz and Raman.

So far we have provided ourselves with a description of one type of wolf-note motion for a bowed string and have verified that it is consistent with the stick-slip behavior expected of such a system. We have also recognized that the presence of a wood resonance near the wolf-note frequency is required and that it will alter the first-mode vibrational properties of the string (but not those of the higher modes). We will now consider the ways in which the complete dynamical system comes to choose the wolf tone as its preferred type of oscillation.

Schelleng in his discussion of the wolf note points out that the presence of a wood resonance converts the ordinary first-mode string resonance peak (measured at the bowing point) into a *pair* of peaks. The upper part of figure 25.8

shows the nature of the bowing-point resonance curve that is found when this wood resonance lies below the first-mode string frequency. For simplicity, the string is assumed to be tuned to 100 Hz. Notice that this resonance has caused the original 100-Hz first-mode peak to be displaced upward in frequency, while the other peak lies below the natural

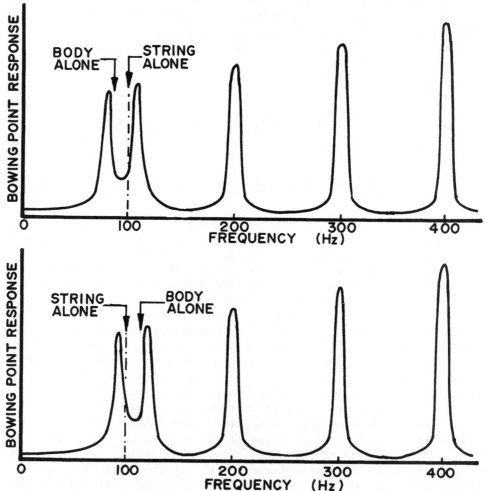

Fig. 25.8. String Resonance Curve Showing Splitting of First-Mode Peak by a Wood Resonance. One or the other of these paired first-mode peaks is the principal contributor to the wolf-note phenomenon.

frequency of the body itself. Notice also that the dip between the pair of peaks is not as deep as the dips that lie between the normally spaced resonances of the string. The lower part of figure 25.8 shows similarly that when the wood resonance lies above that of the isolated string, the string resonance is displaced slightly below its original 100-Hz position, while the newly added peak lies somewhat above the natural frequency of the body itself.[7]

The feature essential for the production of a wolf note on a bowed string is the presence of a strong resonance immediately above or below the ideal position of the lowest string resonance relative to the higher modes. (In woodwinds there is an exactly analogous type of oscillation to which I have given considerable study since it provides a valuable diagnostic tool for the adjustment of flutes and the conical woodwinds.) The presence of the second member of the pair of peaks is not required for the production of the wolf, although it can aggravate the wolf-tone tendency if it is placed symmetrically opposite its mate so that the unmodified (100-Hz) first-mode frequency of the string lies exactly halfway between the two peaks.

The physicist Ian Firth of the University of St. Andrews in Scotland has made a number of experimental studies of the wolf-tone behavior of cellos, some of which he carried out during the summer of 1974 at the Speech Transmission Laboratory in Stockholm.[8] Firth's data confirm the general correctness of Schelleng's analysis and contain a wealth of additional information. Despite certain apparent inconsistencies in the data and in Firth's interpretation of them, his results underlie a considerable portion of my explanations in the remaining part of this section.

Keeping figure 25.8 in mind with its pattern of the first resonance peak slightly misplaced and everything else neatly lined up, we can now make an analysis of the oscillation possibilities; this analysis is very similar to those we carried out in connection with the production of woodwind multiphonics. Notice particularly that the even-numbered resonance peaks of the string tone are all harmonically related and are thereby admirably set up to generate a set of components whose frequencies are even multiples of the string's normal playing frequency. If we confine our attention to these even-numbered peaks by themselves and to the components that they generate directly, it is clear that no matter what sort of non-linearity is present at the contact point between bow and string, all the heterodyne frequencies that are generated among the even-numbered peaks will themselves be members of this same collection of even-numbered harmonics. In other words, these components will be very strongly generated in a stable kind of sub-regime.

Let us now ask what happens to the oscillatory contribution of a first-mode peak that is displaced to run a little sharp, generating a component at 102 Hz. The simplest heterodyne offspring of this component and the strongly maintained even harmonics turn out to be of the following type:

$$102 \pm 200 = 98, 302 \text{ Hz}$$
$$102 \pm 400 = 298, 502 \text{ Hz}$$
$$102 \pm 600 = 498, 702 \text{ Hz}$$
etc.

Notice that each of these heterodyne components lies close to the frequency of one of the odd-numbered resonance peaks and so has a reasonable chance of gaining support from it. Pay particular attention to the 98-Hz heterodyne component; although it lies in the dip between the pair of first-mode resonance peaks, this dip is relatively shallow, so that the component is able to gain considerable oscillatory support in its own right. Because of this help, the component can have an amplitude that is quite comparable to those of its higher-frequency odd-numbered heterodyne brothers, which sit on the shoulders of their respective resonance peaks.

Here is the first place where we can make a direct comparison with experience: in the neighborhood of 100 Hz we have found a pair of components—98 and 102 Hz—of appreciable (but not necessarily equal) amplitude, which can beat together. This is exactly what one observes in a typical wolf tone. Their joint appearance is roughly that of a pulsating fundamental component of the sort recognized by Raman and by Schelleng, although (contrary to a common impression) it is not correct to say that the pair of components at 98 and 102 Hz is equivalent to a single 100-Hz component of fluctuating amplitude except in the unusual case in which the two actual components have precisely equal amplitude.

We can continue our examination of the descendants of the two fundamental components by noticing that pairs of components are found centered about all the odd harmonics of 100 Hz—e.g., 298 and 302 Hz, 498 and 502 Hz, etc. As has been remarked earlier, these pairs will feed themselves from the odd-numbered resonance peaks, and in general one or the other member of the pair will be particularly strongly supported as a result of the small upward and downward frequency displacements of these peaks that are an inevitable consequence of various kinds of string inharmonicity. These paired components will beat at exactly the same 4-Hz rate as does the fundamental pair. This beating rate is in further agreement with the observation of Raman, as reformulated by Schelleng and confirmed by Firth's data, that the paired odd partials all give rise to a pulsation at exactly the same frequency, regardless of the accidents of placement of string tuning and body resonance. The fact that we do not expect the members of each pair to be of equal amplitude is also in accord with experiment. During the course of a wolf-tone pulsation, one does not generally find a total extinction of the odd partials, nor does one find the degree of extinction to be the same for all of them.

When one looks more closely at the details of the vibration spectrum of a wolf tone there are many components present besides the ones that we have listed so far. These other components tend to be somewhat weaker, and their presence does very little to alter the basic behavior that has been outlined—i.e., reasonably strong and steady even partials and synchronously beating odd partials. Let us examine a few examples of these less important additional components, chiefly with an eye to seeing why they play a minor role in the behavior of the string. Here are some of the heterodyne components that are generated by the odd-partial pairs themselves:

$$98 \pm 102 = 4, 200 \text{ Hz}$$
$$298 \pm 302 = 4, 600 \text{ Hz}$$
$$498 \pm 502 = 4, 1000 \text{ Hz}$$
etc.

In every case we find the same low-frequency (4-Hz) component and an exact even-harmonic component that can cooperate with its corresponding peak to aid the net oscillation in a vigorous way. The low-frequency component is low enough to be felt by the player's hands as a pulsation or stuttering of the bow and perhaps of the instrument itself.

When we combine each odd-numbered component with one from another pair, the following frequencies result:

$$98 \pm 298 = 200, 396 \text{ Hz}$$
$$98 \pm 302 = 204, 400 \text{ Hz}$$
$$298 \pm 502 = 204, 800 \text{ Hz}$$
etc.

Once again we find that exact even harmonics are produced by each combination, along with something we have not seen before—a set of weak satellites that are 4 Hz away from the strong even harmonics in the tone. The fact that even the paired, pulsating, odd partials themselves give rise to even-harmonic components in all their dealings serves to stabilize them by binding them ever more closely to the more normal oscillatory behavior of the even partials. Adding weak satellites to these even partials does not make them pulsate very much, since there is little chance for a few weak components of differing frequency to gang up simultaneously on the strong central component and cancel it out.

In the preceding paragraphs we have learned how the displacement of the first-mode peak in the response curve of a bowed string can give rise to the wolf tone: an oscillation is produced in which the even partials run fairly steadily (i.e., with weak satellite components) while the odd partials pulsate strongly, which is a simple way of saying that they are in fact constructed out of two or more components of roughly equal amplitude. Since the first mode's displacement (and splitting into two resonances) depends on the

mutual influence of the string and the cello body, it is clear that the presence or absence of the wolf phenomenon depends on the relationship between the wave impedances of the string and of the body (see secs. 17.1 and 24.3). Schelleng studied this relationship and has provided us not only with the means for predicting whether or not a given instrument will have a wolf but also with the ability to devise changes in the design that can minimize its effects. Schelleng's own experimental observations plus more recent ones by many other people confirm the correctness of his analysis.

25.5. Examples, Experiments, and Questions

1. Half-valved octaves can be played on a double French horn or on the bass trombone by use of the Bb-F thumb lever, with acoustical relationships identical with those described for the Bb octave of the baritone horn. Certain additional half-valved octave notes become available when you exploit the possibility of using the other valves to change the tube lengths of the two branched parts of the air column. You may find a number of octave possibilities that appear on the Bb side of a French horn when the extra-length valve crooks are transferred from the F side of the instrument. Why is it not possible on any brass instrument to half-depress valves 1 and 2 together to produce the same octave that is generated by the use of the third valve acting alone? Why, on the other hand, will the use of the French horn's third valve work just as well as the second valve to produce the octave of tone 15 of an open horn, whereas the first valve will not produce the desired effect? Hint: how many half

humps in the valve loop are required to produce a reversal of the standing wave in the bell region?

2. Brass players, in particular those who perform on the French horn, sometimes sing into their instruments while they play them, so that the airflow is controlled both by the larynx and by the lip reed. Under these conditions the resultant spectrum contains not only the two harmonic series belonging to the played and sung notes, but also the heterodyne components that arise from various pairings of these partials. Suppose a trombone player sounding G_3 on his instrument (using a regime based on peaks 3, 6, 9, . . .) is asked to sing a fourth lower (at D_3) and then a fourth higher (at C_4). Compare the frequencies of the newly born heterodynes with those of the various resonances of the instrument to see which combination will tend to feel more secure at the player's lips. Attempt to work out the ways in which a musically trained listener's ears might group the various partials coming to them from the instrument, and deduce how he might describe the resulting "horn chords."

3. Brass instruments, particularly French horns, often "talk" to one another, so that the sound radiated by one of them enters the bell of its neighbor and thence joins in at the player's lips to influence the regime of oscillation.[9] Consider the exchanges between three horn players sounding the notes of a major or a minor triad. With the help of some sketched resonance curves and heterodyne frequency computations, see if you can work out the reasons why each player feels very secure and safe in his share of the enterprise as long as everyone else is playing his part correctly. As a matter of fact it is rather difficult for any one of

them to play out of tune with the rest, since the horns very much "want" to pull together into a beat-free relationship. On the other hand, if one member of the group accidentally misses a note and arrives at something a tone or semitone away, he may very well succeed in disrupting his colleagues' playing if they are not skilled enough to hold fast.

4. A clarinet multiphonic played with all tone holes closed except for the B♮ cross key for the right hand has a strong resonance at about 230 Hz, another peak near 580 Hz, and one near 720 Hz. These three peaks manage among themselves to generate considerable oscillatory energy at the following frequencies: P = 214 Hz, Q = 575 Hz, R = 697 Hz, and S = 764 Hz. I have found 29 components up to 1822 Hz (2R + 2P). You would find it worthwhile to tabulate enough possible heterodyne components to verify that a listener tends to hear the multiphonic as being made up of four reasonably well-established *tones* having P, Q, R, and S as their fundamental frequencies. Note: this direct association of the perceived tones with the primary sources of excitation is not a common occurrence among the multiphonics.

5. One of the favorite methods used by cellists to prevent a troublesome wolf note is to add a small mass to one of the strings in the region between bridge and tailpiece. If the mass is of the correct magnitude and is properly located, it can be given a natural frequency of transverse vibration that is in the same general region as that of the troublemaking body resonance.[10] When such a mass is in place, the double peaks shown near 100 Hz in the two parts of figure 25.8 become three peaks (!) of somewhat reduced height and having slightly less deep dips

between them (particularly if the added mass is a piece of rubber or if other means of vibrational damping are provided). Attempt to deduce locations for the three peaks that would tend to restore normal, wolf-free operation to the bowed string. Notice in particular that there can be more than one way of arranging the natural frequency of the suppressor to serve the desired purpose.

6. Look back at the experiments suggested in part 1 of section 23.6, and repeat them with an ear out for sounds that can be interpreted with the help of your newly gained understanding of multiphonics and wolf notes. A number of additional experiments may suggest themselves to you, and it may even be possible for you to devise string-players' cousins to the woodwind multiphonics for possible use in music.

Notes

1. The problem of a branched tube without constrictions at the junctions is dealt with in George Walter Stewart and Robert Bruce Lindsay, *Acoustics* (New York: Van Nostrand, 1930), pp. 90–93, and G. W. Stewart, "The Theory of the Herschel-Quincke Tube," *J. Acoust. Soc. Am.* 17 (1945): 107–8.

2. A. H. Benade, "Effect of dispersion and scattering on the startup of brass instrument tones" (abstract), *J. Acoust. Soc. Am.* 45 (1969): 296–97.

3. Bruno Bartolozzi, *New Sounds for Woodwind,* trans. and ed. Reginald Smith Brindle (London: Oxford, 1967).

4. A. H. Benade, "Mechanism of multiphonic tone production in woodwinds" (abstract), *J. Acoust. Soc. Am.* 55 (1974): S49.

5. A. H. Benade and L. J. Livingston, "Identification of the separate tones heard in a woodwind multiphonic sound as grouped subsets of its spectral components" (abstract), *J. Acoust. Soc. Am.* 55 (1974): S49.

6. John C. Schelleng, "The Violin as a Circuit," *J. Acoust. Soc. Am.* 35 (1963): 326–38; see especially section VI.

7. Maurice Hancock, "The Mechanical Impedances of Violin Strings, II," *Catgut Acoust. Soc. Newsletter* 23 (May 1975): 17–26.

8. Ian M. Firth and J. Michael Buchanan, "The wolf in the cello," *J. Acoust. Soc. Am.* 53 (1973): 457–63, and I. M. Firth, "The wolf tone in the cello: Acoustic and holographic studies," Royal Institute of Technology (KTH), Stockholm, Speech Transmission Laboratory, *Quarterly Progress and Status Report,* 15 January 1975, pp. 42–56.

9. This phenomenon has been called to my attention by several horn players. The first to do so, in 1961, was Christopher Leuba, then of the Chicago Symphony.

10. J. C. Schelleng, "Adjusting the Wolftone Suppressor," *Am. String Teacher,* Winter 1967, p. 9.

Index

Index